The Art of the Hoop: 1860 - 1869

Fashion, Sewing, and Clothing Care Advice

Compiled from Original Sources

Deb Salisbury

Elephant's Breath & London Smoke:
Historical Color Names, Definitions and Uses in Fashion, Fabric and Art

Fabric à la Romantic Regency:
A Glossary of Fabrics from Original Sources 1795 – 1836

Victorian Bathing and Bathing Suits:
The Culture of the Two-Piece Bathing Dress from 1837 – 1901

The Art of Fashion: 1850 - 1859
Fashion, Sewing, and Clothes Care Advice

The Art of the Mantua-Maker: 1870 - 1879
Fashion, Sewing, and Clothes Care Advice

The Mantua-Maker Historical Sewing Patterns
Abbott, Texas

The Art of the Hoop: 1860 - 1869
Sewing, Dress, and Clothing Care Advice

Copyright © 2019 by Deb Salisbury

The Mantua-Maker Historical Sewing Patterns
100 PR 232
Abbott, TX 76621
deb@mantua-maker.com
https://www.Mantua-Maker.com

Cover illustration is from *Peterson's Magazine*, January 1865

I'd like to dedicate this book to my mom, Dona Salisbury, and to Karen B., who inspired me to work on the decade of the 1860s.

Le Follet, Journal du Grand Monde, July 1865

Table of Contents

Introduction 1
1860 3
    Shopping Woes 26
    New Fabrics 26
1861 27
    Dress for Out-Door Work 54
    Mourning Attire 54
1862 55
    Dressmaking Advice 81
    Science of Dress-Cutting 81
1863 84
    Sins Against Good Taste 121
    All Things Scottish 121
1864 122
    How to Dress the Best at the Least Expense 157
    Young Lady's Manual 160
    How to Make a Dress 161
1865 165
    On the Subject of Dress 204
1866 205
    Hints on Dress 232
    The Economies of Dress 233
1867 234
    Making the Short Walking Dress 272
    Mr. Worth's Influence 272
    Traveling Dress 273
1868 274
    Hints About Dress-Making 331
    Servants' Dress 333
    The Grecian Bend 334
1869 335
    Manner of Making Dresses 366
    The Grecian Bend 367
Clothing and Fabric – Cleaning, Repair, and Care 368
1860 368
1861 370
1862 372
1863 375
1864 375
1865 379
1866 380
1867 383
1868 385
1869 388
Bibliography 393
About the Author 394

Arthur's Home Magazine, August 1860

Peterson's Magazine, February 1869

INTRODUCTION

The great desire of a fashionable woman of the present day, is to possess a costume which is like nothing ever seen before.
Peterson's Magazine, April 1865

The art of the hoop was an everchanging ideal. During the 1860s the shape of the crinoline shifted from a simple cage-hoop to panniers, with styles updating almost monthly. Ladies of means seemed desperate to stay *a la mode,* and even middle-class women tried to keep up.

The rules of the toilette can therefore be reduced to one word – fitness. Fitness of form, of color, of proportion; fitness to time, place, condition and occupation, and whatever offends against this delicate intellectual perception, whether sanctioned by custom or not, must be considered as a crime against good taste and a truly artistic conception of the beautiful.

Extremes meet, and an era of remarkable development in one respect is sure to be followed by an era quite as remarkable in an exactly opposite direction. Just now we are in the midst an age of gilt and show, which will be succeeded by a season the sternest, severest simplicity. Indeed, it is only in this that the followers of fashion can be confined to a charmed circle. The masses love show and color; they do not appreciate fine effects or the grand accessory of details.
Frank Leslie's Monthly, December 1860

Taste and Neatness in Dress. – Nature has wisely given woman a love of neatness and generally an excellent taste in dress. To look like a "fright" is the dread of all the sex. A few touches in the way of ornament; a graceful, stylish fit; neat collars and laces; how these transform a lady! Not to know how to dress is to be only half as agreeable and pretty as you might be. Taste and knowledge, too, supply the place of money. There is more truth than is usually supposed in the old saying, "As well be out of the world as out of the fashion."
Peterson's Magazine, November 1862

Fashion magazines were studied and dissected, scoured for details on how each effect was created, how seams were manipulated, and where hems fell. They learned why changes were made, when they went out of date, and how to recreate the styles they liked. And, of course, the American civil war intruded.

One of the advantages, which American ladies have over European ones, is, that the magazines here are so cheap as to be within the reach of everybody, and thus, with the aid of the patterns given in the magazines, every woman, by the exercise of a little ingenuity, can dress elegantly for a comparatively small sum. It is taste rather, than money, that makes a costume elegant. Indeed, it is often really vulgar to dress expensively: as vulgar, in its way, as to wear diamonds at breakfast. Style is everything.

We repeat, it has been an error, heretofore, on the part of American ladies to dress too extravagantly. It has now come to be considered, we hope, both more patriotic and in better taste, to dress more simply. It shall be our effort, by furnishing the earliest patterns, to enable ladies to be elegantly dressed, and yet economically also. And the present number is an earnest of this.
Peterson's Magazine, October 1864

But the 1860s were difficult for dressmakers, since fashions changed so rapidly. Styles cycled between the ages, from Louis XV. to Marie Antoinette, and even tried forays into high-waisted Empire dresses.

The demands of fashion are so numerous, that it is almost impossible to supply them, and so old styles have to be renewed, but nearly always with some slight modification.
Peterson's Magazine, March 1864

There seems to be a great deal of searching into former times now in reference to fashion, hunting up old fashions, and copying *toilettes* from historical pictures. Our age is accused, and not without truth, of possessing no originality; it can neither invent nor create – it can but imitate or copy. Now, after many hesitations, we seem to have decidedly come back to the fashions worn in the reign of Louis XV. and the

earlier part of that of Louis XVI. There are modifications, of course, and exact chronology is not always attended to; but one may safely say, that the style of dress most copied in our time, is that of the before-mentioned period. How many models are called by the name of the most graceful woman of her age, Marie Antoinette? The most fashionable coiffure, dress, fichu, mantle, and slipper bear her name. We are, however, far from the scant, unbecoming dress of the First Empire. Skirts are gored, it is true, but they are ample and flowing. Crinolines, far from being left off, have merely changed their shape; they are plain in front, but puffed out on either side, so as to remind one strongly of the hoops or paniers of the last century. These paniers will not be adopted as yet; we think the tournure will be more generally worn. These skirts are made of puffed hair-cloth, with a few steels at the bottom; they are ungraceful whatever way worn. But Fashion declares them necessary in some degree, to support the heavy sashed now so much worn; as yet but few of our most fashionable belles have adopted them.
Godey's Lady's Book, June 1868

Trains lengthened or disappeared into "short" dresses, trim exploded or vanished altogether. Fashion's idea of simplicity astounds me.

One dress, which was particularly admired for its simplicity, was made of white silk, and trimmed with seven flounces about four or five inches broad, and edged with groseille-colored silk.
Arthur's Home Magazine, February 1861

In Evening Costume the dress must train at least half a yard behind, and the skirt must be very fully trimmed. This surplus of ornament denotes that plain skirts will ere long reappear. Exaggeration in fashion is the sure forerunner of simplicity.
Peterson's Magazine, August 1862

Dresses were made for every event of the day, and woe to the lady who wasn't prepared.

The London season brings with it not one only, but many requirements in the way of fashions. It demands costumes for the morning, costume for the concert, costumes for the promenade, costumes for the carriage, costumes for the dinner, costumes for the evening, costumes for the ball, leaving out of the question all the varieties of these demands, and a great many more for different occasions.
The What-Not, March 1864

After the dress was made and worn, it must be maintained. Clothing care was interesting, if often odd, or even dangerous. Don't try most of their efforts at home!

To Take the Stains out of Black Cloth. – Boil a large handful of fig-leaves in two quarts of water until reduced to a pint; squeeze the leaves quite dry, and put the liquor into a bottle for use. The article should be rubbed with a sponge dipped in the liquor. The word "poison" should be written on the bottle, to prevent accident.
Peterson's Magazine, September 1862

This book compiles sewing and fashion advice given in books and magazines during the 1860s, given in the words of writers of that time. Each entry shows the name and date of the periodical quoted. It has three sections:
1) Sewing tips and fashion advice
2) Fabric cleaning and care.
3) Bibliography of magazines and books I found useful.

I've included over 960 black and white period engravings to help show the details of their work.

It is a general rule, applicable to both sexes, that persons are the best dressed when you cannot remember how they were dressed. Avoid everything out of the way, uncommon, or grotesque.
How to Do It, 1864

But Tyranny in Fashion exists no longer; a lady can dress herself according to her own individual taste; she can choose her colors to suit her complexion and the shade of her hair; her dress can be cut in accordance with the style of her figure, and provided her toilet is selected with taste, she will be found fashionable.
Peterson's Magazine, November 1863

1860

EVENING DRESS.

Robes. – For full toilet, the brocades enlivened with small figures embroidered in gold, silver, or silk, distributed a few inches apart throughout, is lie cream of the cream. The very low *décolleté* cut is giving place to half-length flowing sleeves, and not exposing the arms entirely, which – though ever so long the fashion – were only appropriate for *demoiselles* and ladies under a certain age. Skirt ornaments are confined to ruffles, embroidery, flounces, and passementerie, in rows round the skirt, from one to two-thirds up the skirt from the bottom; and the sleeves, of pagoda cut, are trimmed to harmonize with the trimming of the skirt. Pointed bodies have superseded *basques,* and high bodies are preferred for all occasions but the ballroom or private dancing sociables. Neither are bonnets or dresses so elaborately trimmed as they were last year.

Arthur's Home Magazine, January 1860

The Redingote Magicienne. – This style of dress is at present very fashionable in Paris. The material is black silk. The body is high, and ornamented with a cape or pelerine, trimmed round with a narrow puffing of silk. The sleeves, which are shaped to the elbow, are demi-wide, and are finished at the lower edge by a turned-up cuff, bordered with a small quilling, like that on the cape. The skirt and body are both made open in front, and the redingote is fastened from the lower edge of the skirt to the throat by a row of buttons. On each side of the skirt that is a pocket covered by a small flap, trimmed with a quilling, and fastened in the centre by a button. This flap is fixed to the dress by a narrow band of plain silk.

Among the prettiest dresses recently made, there is a dress of plain black silk which has just been completed. The skirt is trimmed with two deep flounces, each edged with two narrow gauffered frills. The corsage, high and buttoned up the front, is ornamented with a berthe pointed before and behind, and trimmed with two very narrow gauffered frills. The sleeves are wide pagodas, cut on the bias; they are finished at the lower edge with a double gauffered frill, and at the shoulder there is a gauffered trimming in the form of an epaulet.

Figure 1. – Ball Costume.

We have selected from among the most choice modes a Ball Costume that, by its novelty, will elicit the admiration of the gayer portions of our lady readers during the present season of festivity. This costume may be made of any light textures or of taffeta. The corsage is cut straight across the shoulders, and is formed by reversed plaits graduated to fashion the shape, being very narrow at the waist, from which they widen until lost in the drapery of the skirt. The sleeves, similarly plaited, are cut square below, and are open entirely to the shoulders, allowing a *very* short lace under-sleeve or hand above to be seen. The points of the openings are adorned by neat clusters of the foliage and flower of the purple-streaked and pink convolvulus. The upper skirt is festooned in four sweeps of drapery, the front one being the highest, while the back – in one large curve – almost seems to form a train. The several places where it is looped up are marked by flowers, to match the sleeves, but in larger clusters. When the dress is made of taffeta, a cable cord can be twined on the top of the dress, so as to form circular loops – one in the front face of each plait – in the centre of which loop may be placed a drop tassel, now so much in favor; and if preferred, the flowers may give place to ties of cord, with tasseled ends, at each point instead; a heavier girdle of the same, in this case, should be twice very loosely brought round the waist and carelessly tied, with long ends.

Under-sleeves to match this costume may be easily fashioned by adopting the full flowing form, slashing it up to the elbow, and placing at the point of separation very small bunches of flowers, or ribbon ties to correspond. Round the corners, and let the border have a transparent run through.

Harper's New Monthly Magazine, January 1860

ZOUAVE JACKET FOR A LADY.

There is quite a rage in Paris to obtain a pattern of this jacket. As will be seen, it is without sleeves, and should be made of blue cloth, and decorated with gold braid, or with velvet embroidered gold, if to be worn at evening parties.

No. 1. One Front.
No. 2. Half the Back.

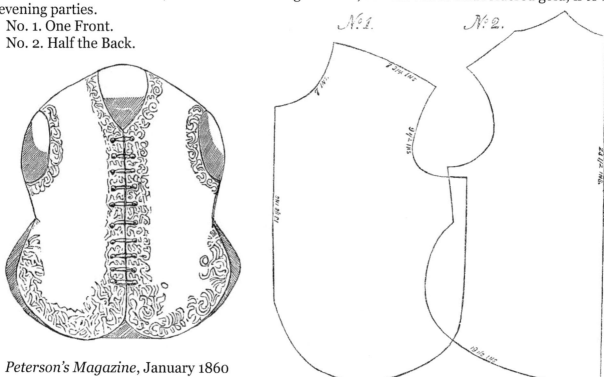

Peterson's Magazine, January 1860

Of dresses, or robes, the latest style is the "*princess*," not cut across at the waist, but double-breasted in form at the breast, with lapels cut at an angle downward, *à la militaire*. The right skirt has the corner clipped off from 9 inches back of top edge on the bottom of the skirt, and 9 inches up the front edge from the bottom of the skirt, in a straight line. The edges, even across the bottom also, are bound with a black velvet band, *(lissere)* striped with four lines of gold. The material of the dress is a lustrous black *taffetas*. The sleeves are cut a quarter longer than the arm, in *demi-gigot* shape, and a velvet band, like that which edges the dress, starts from under the velvet binding of the neck, and extends over the shoulder and down over the top of the sleeve to the correct length of the sleeve at the wrist, the sleeve being gathered to it in order to shorten the sleeve to its proper length. The end of the sleeve, which nearly fits at the wrist, is bound with an edging of the gold-striped velvet band. The front is closed with holes and buttons of velvet and gold. Some of our belles, who have just returned home from Paris, brought with them samples of this robe, to the real admiration of Fifth Avenue and Murray Hill. It is stated that only two dress-makers in New York know how to make the *robe princess*. It is indeed a novelty.

Bodies are cut with pointed waists, two points before and one behind, and a piece of lead is fitted to each point, and is inserted between the lining and outside to keep the point down. Full dress skirts are generally plain because the choice silks and brocades are woven with small figures of velvet, and offering much better flow. In fact, trimmings on the skirts would spoil the harmony and disguise the beauty. Of plain silks for full dress, *blondes* and laces are the favorite trimmings, in puffs and flounces.

It is the style to plait the tops of the skirts (in walking dresses) to a waistband; but don't make the plaits too large, for it has a bad effect on heavy goods; the skirt is plaited quite full behind, moderately at the sides, and nearly plain at front. The crinoline should be formed of hair cloth, full behind, moderately so at the sides, and nearly plain before. The size of the crinoline has been reduced about one-fourth, and it maintains the pyramidal form instead of the cage or barrel ones. Hoops and steel surroundings are losing favor.

LADY ON THE LEFT. The *dress* is called, by the ladies in Paris (where it was invented), a *"Redingote Magicienne."* The body and skirt are not disconnected by a cut across at the waist, but it is formed to fit at the waist on the back, by three large box-plaits; and at the sides, by taking out two large darts, one under each arm, and one between that and the front edge; the front edge is then shaped to the form of the figure. As this *genre* of cut and make is so similar to the robe called the *"Princess"* – the most select evening dress in Paris – and just becoming the rage with our *haut ton,* we invite the reader's careful perusal of our description. –

The *Redingote* is surmounted with a collar formed in *demi-pelerine,* enlivened with a little ruche edging of the same goods as the robe, being black *taffetas;* the knot under the collar is of *taffeta ribbon,* and the collar and manchettes (undersleeves) are of fine linen, piquée; that is, a goods similar to fine white *marseilles.*

The sleeve is cut with an elbow, half large, terminated with a deep cuff, open on the under side, edged like the collar. The front – all the way up – is trimmed with buttons and holes, by which it is closed, and there is a row of back-stitching two inches back of each edge, and five inches above the bottom of the skirt.

On each side of the skirt – fifteen inches below the arm-hole – is a diagonal pocket, covered with a little scalloped lid, closed up the centre with a hole and button, and bordered with a ruche, like that on the cuffs and collar.

It is difficult to design a more modest dress than this, and yet there is none more attractive and *récherché* for *demi-toilette.* Gloves of russet kid.

Toilette de Promenade. – The lady on the right, clad in a walking or carriage dress, wears a blue crape bonnet.

Robe of imperial blue velvet, ornamented with black lace. A round waist of the body is trimmed with four lace *choux,* each one formed of four infinitesimal widths of lace.

The front of skirt is ornamented with 8 *choux,* enlarging progressively towards the bottom.

The *ceinture,* cut from imperial velvet, forms a point at front and on the back, with the view to render the appearance of the waist very long. It is *agraffed* at the left side with a knot *écharpe* – meaning square ends – of long *coquet,* falling in two lappets, all bordered with a row of stitching and edged with narrow black lace.

Sleeves oval, and short in front, the ends gently rounded, and the sleeve falling straight behind. On each one is a band which parts at the top of the shoulder, at the arm-hole, and descends to the bottom between two little widths of lace. A *chou* trims the top of the cut in front. A white ruche trims the under edge of the opening of the sleeve, and a black lace trims the outer edge.

Collar of white lace. Under-sleeves of white *tulle,* with a little black lace trimming to relieve the cuffs.

The tight sleeve is gaining favor. The next greatest favorite in cut is the one represented by the colored plate on the figure with a blue dress [*on the right*]. It is of the *pagode* genre. Buttons are regarded as the favorite trimming of dresses, this winter; High bodies, even for full dress, are also fashionable, and they are trimmed with a row of buttons and holes up the front of the bust, and then two rows, starting two inches apart at the waist in front, and diverging to the shoulder point and back to the waist behind, two inches apart. The sleeves are also, more or less, trimmed with velvet buttons. These buttons are an inch in diameter, a little convex, and the dress-maker distributes them according to caprice. Passementerie is also a fashionable edging this winter for all garments and for all occasions. All overdresses are cut very long, being something within six inches of the carpet. Even those *sorts des bal et de l'opera,* are of white cashmere, with a hood, and extend behind to near the bottom of the dress. Double skirts are losing favor and narrow flounces are gaining.

Arthur's Home Magazine, February 1860

Dresses are made quite high; the most in favor will be those with round waists and *ceintures* with broad floating ends; some ladies still prefer the pointed body, but in this case the points should be short, and the dresses lace up the back.

A Paris paper describes a [ball] dress recently made for a Russian Princess, which must be very beautiful. The underslip was of white satin, over this was a skirt of tulle bouillonne, which was covered with a shower of golden stars; the corsage of the same.

Fig. I. – Dress of light blue Silk; skirt trimmed with twelve narrow flounces. Corsage draped with folds meeting in the middle of the body, and round the waist. Sleeves trimmed to correspond with the skirt. Sleeves, collar, and cap of Brussels *applique*.

Fig. II. – Dress of black Satin, trimmed with a fawn-colored satin plaided with black. The satin trimming is put on in scallops, around the bottom of the skirt are eight ruffles of the light satin, *en tablier*, and finished at the ends with black velvet bows. Body and sleeves trimmed to correspond with the skirt.

The fashionable Parisian morning dresses, usually called *peignoirs*, rarely present much novelty, as far as regards form; but the materials of which they are composed, and the trimmings which ornament them, admit of great variety, in accordance with the taste of the wearer. One, in a style very fashionable in Paris, is composed of white cashmere. It is open in front, and worn over a skirt of white muslin, trimmed with a tablier just filling up the opening between the two sides of the dress. The skirt is lined with mauve-colored silk, and is bordered with a fluted quilling of ribbon the same color as the lining. The corsage is high and close, and has a small collar; a plaiting of ribbon passes up the centre of the corsage, and trims the edge of the collar. The sleeves are rather wide, and are slit up their whole length in the inner part of the arm. They are lined with mauve silk, and edged round with a plaiting of ribbon. Long under-sleeves of white muslin, closed at the wrist and finished by turned-up cuffs. A bow of ribbon with long ends is fixed on each shoulder, and round the waist is a ribbon ceinture, fastened in a bow with long ends flowing over the front of the dress.

Fig. III. – The Compeigne. – The corsage of this wraps over and fastens on the left side. The skirt is very wide at the lower part, and is trimmed with a band of velvet, edged with gold. Square pocket-holes, trimmed with velvet and gold. Long sleeves, set in full at the armholes, and trimmed down the outside of the arm with bands of gold. The cuffs are trimmed in corresponding style, and fastened with buttons of velvet and gold. Round the throat a narrow ruff of quilled tulle, and cuffs of the same. Of course any colored braid may be substituted for the gold braid.

Peterson's Magazine, February 1860

Pointed waists are still in vogue for full dress; and for *demi-toilette,* the front of the body terminates in two plain points – long and sharp – and the back in three points, as follows: – the seamless back terminates at the waist in a diamond form, and each side-body is pointed; and then the side-body and back are closed down to the upper point of the diamond, leaving the lower point and the point of each side separate.

The front of bodies for promenade wear are cut in the best form, with very long points, but the buttons with which it is closed in front extend from the chin to the most hollow part of the waist only.

Figure 1. – Home or Promenade Dress.

The costume illustrated on the previous page is singularly useful, as well as elegant, since, wrought by a slight change in the accessory pieces, it is equally adapted for a promenade dress or a *demi-toilette* for home. The style, moreover, is calculated for almost any material, and looks well both in plain and figured fabrics.

Our illustration is taken from one of those beautiful *mousseline de laine* fabrics which are such universal favorites this season. It has broad stripe of a purplish crimson, with a wave similar to that of watered silk, alternated with stripes of green, in which are sprays of roses in natural colors, with leaves *feuille à mort*. The stripes are perpendicular, not *à la bayadere*.

As an in-door toilet, it is worn as represented in the illustration. The Corsage *à la Pompadour*, the waist having the slightest approach to a peak. The skirt is set on in minute plaits. The sleeves are narrow at the top, rapidly widening toward the bottom, funnel-wise; they then fall open in broad folds. They are lined with taffeta, creased so as to resemble quilting. The under-sleeve and neck-piece are of medallion lace. The Fichu is striped with very narrow velvet ribbon, a medallion design being wrought into each compartment. The under-sleeves are en suite, the medallions occupying the lower *bouillonnée*.

Harper's New Monthly Magazine, February 1860

First Toilet. – Robe of *taffetas tourterelle,* clear; skirt ornamented on each seam with a narrow ribbon *tuyanté pensée,* and one row of *taffetas pensée* buttons. Body plain, trimmed like the skirt; sleeves, very large, with imitation cuff, as shown on the top side of left arm, with buttons and ribbon edging on the imitation cuff and ribbon end of sleeve. Sleeve-lining of white sarsenet. *Ceinture* with knot and long ends, of the same stuff as the robe, edged in keeping; cravat-knot, instead of a brooch, edged like the ceinture (waist-ribbon). Sleeves and collar of muslin, embroidered with application.

Lady on the right – Robe of Havana *taffetas;* deep flounce *à l'Anglaise,* surmounted either by five puffs (*bouillonnes*), or five narrow flounces. This robe is equally fashionable, of black silk. End of sleeve trimmed with one deep flounce and two puffs or little flounces; shoulder-knot, a double bow and ends. Plain body, with long ceinture.

The most beautiful carriage dress of the season is a red *taffetas* robe, in the style of Louis XV., with the lower half of the skirt trimmed with four pinked and scolloped flounces in front, and six behind, leaving a space at each side to give the front the appearance of an apron, and at the end of each flounce up the side, a knot of black velvet ribbon, with which each flounce is headed. Plain body and black velvet waist ribbon, with knot and long lappet ends. Over this is worn a mantilla of the same goods as the dress, with square front ends, and round over the back, all trimmed with three rows of pinked flounces, like the skirt of the dress, with bindings also of black velvet, and the top edge and hood of the mantilla edged with velvet ribbon.

The present fashion of skirt is quite full behind, moderately so at the sides, and nearly plain at front. The skirt is plaited to a waistband, in large box-plaits behind, smaller ones at the sides, and small, shallow plaits at front. For evening wear, the skirt is nearly as full as it was last fall, and about as long; but for morning wear, it is much shorter.

Velvet buttons and passementerie trim morning dresses, and silk buttons encircled with black lace, and black lace, trim dinner dresses.

TOILETTE DE VILLE.

The robe is intended for wear on almost all occasions; but it is eminently adapted for wear at home on reception mornings. The material is known as *moire Française gris tourterelle*; it is trimmed with buttons of green silk and *plissé* of *taffetas pensée*, with a border of green silk.

High body and square at the waist, encircled with a *ceinture* to match the dress, closed with two steel agraffes.

Sleeves plain and bias, without a seam in front, and the seam behind stops at the elbow, from whence it is buttoned to the wrist by a row of green silk buttons. The wristband is of white lace, which turns back over the end of sleeve.

Skirt formed in large box-plaits at the waist, much the fullest behind. The bottom is faced with a narrow band of velvet, which represents a binding on the bottom of only a fourth inch wide, to protect the edge and give substance to it.

Little green cravat encircles the neck under the collar and brooch. Collar of lace, lace-edged kerchief, bright russet kid gloves.

Arthur's Home Magazine, March 1860

Fig. V. – New Style of High Body, called the "Sheaf." Dress of black silk, with Pompadour bouquets in rich colors over it. The body is ornamented with for darts of green velvet, two on each side of the row of green buttons which fastens it up the front. Belt of green velvet. Sleeve nearly tight, with a jockey.

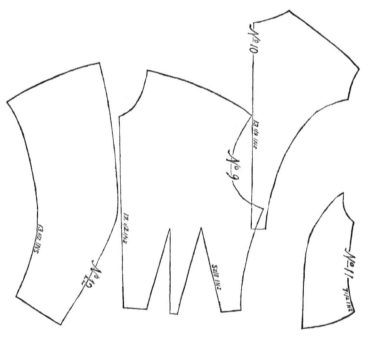

NEW STYLE OF HIGH BODY.

In the front of the number we give, under this title, a full length engraving of a figure, with an entirely new style of high body, just out in Paris, which is round at the waist, and has straight sleeves with elbow. The ornaments consist of four velvet tabs on the front: two on the left on the plaits of the waist, and two on the right; also of three similar tabs placed on in the middle of the bottom of the back, and one on each of the side seams. These tabs are narrow at the bottom, and lance-shaped at the top. Above, we give diagrams by which to cut it out.

No. 9. One Front of Body.
No. 10. Half of Back.
No 11. One Side Body.
No. 12. Sleeve.

Fig. I. – Carriage Dress of Pearl-colored Silk, crocheted with black. This dress is made *a la imperatrice*, that is with the body and skirt cut in one piece, like a large basque. The skirt is, of course, very much gored to fit the figure at the waist. The dress is trimmed down the front with large bows of ribbon, finished with crocheted ornaments of the color of the dress. The sleeves are very large, made with revers, and trimmed with bows of ribbon like the dress. Bonnet of white chip, trimmed with black lace and pink roses.

Fig. II. – Walking Dress of Green Silk. – The skirt is trimmed with a pyramid of ruffles reaching half up the skirt on each seam. The body is quite plain, and confined at the waist with a belt. Sleeves large, and trimmed with a pyramid of ruffles on the outside of the arm. Bonnet of white crape, embroidered in spots with lilac floss silk, and ornamented with a wreath of lilac flowers on the top.

A new way of setting in skirts at the waist, is to make four large flat plaits – one under each arm, and two behind.

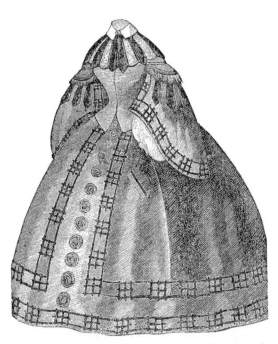

NEW STYLE DRESS.

This is a new style of dress, just now very fashionable in Paris. The material is chesnut brown silk – a color which is now taking the lead in fashion. It is made with a single skirt, trimmed with black velvet round the bottom, with a second trimming of the same turning in the centre of the front, and ascending to the waist, leaving a space sufficiently wide for a row of black velvet macaroon buttons, which are surrounded with rows of black lace. The body is made with the waistcoat in front, and the point behind; the upper part being ornamented in a new style – namely, with pieces of pointed velvet narrowing upward toward the throat, having fullings between each, of the silk of the dress. The sleeves are of the bell-shape, having similar pieces of pointed velvet, at the top of which is placed a small epaulette of the silk, bordered with fringe. This epaulette is not placed at the shoulder, but a little way down the arm, which it does not encircle, being merely on the outer part of the sleeves, the bottoms of which are trimmed to match the skirt.

Peterson's Magazine, March 1860

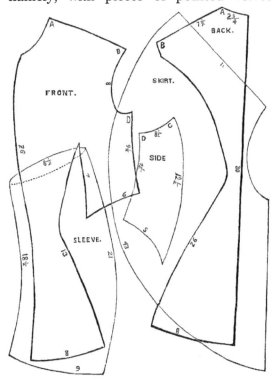

It may not be amiss to remark, that all the best *couturieres* have decided that a skirt should not be trimmed with an even number of flounces; and when the weaver makes them even, they generally use one of them for trimming *a fichu, epaulette,* or dividing the body by a surplus *berthe*.

Morning Toilet. – Lady on the left. – Robe in the *redingote* style of cut, made of lilac, green or gray *taffetas*, with little *rayures* of a darker shade, ornamented with *chiné* bouquets, either in keeping with the stripes, or of a subdued shade to blend. This silk is very fashionable.

The high body is cut with a lapel and square waist. The cut at front is faithfully illustrated by the picture; the edging being of velvet or black *taffetas* ribbon, and the large buttons are of the same material, slightly convex in form. The sleeve is headed with a jockey, cut bias, and trimmed with two rows of buttons. The turn-back cuff is vandyked, edged and buttoned, as represented. The cut of the sleeve is a *demi-gigot,* or half full. The skirt is very full behind, and plaited in double box-plaits to a waistband. It is regarded as the best taste to separate entirely the body from the skirt. The ceinture harmonises in color with the dress.

Lace *chemisette* and wristbands, the former trimmed with stripes of black velvet and jet buttons, or with ribbon inserted and fancy buttons.

Lady on the Right. – *Costume for a young lady. – Robe* of white muslin, in thread *rayures broches,* ornamented by the weaver with gooseberries, in blue, green, or purple. The body is low – *décolleté* – round waist and ribbon *ceinture*. Sleeves large and puffed, descending to mid-arm, with a wristband large enough to relieve the passage of the arm; at the bottom is a relieved flounce, forming a cuff. Over the body is worn a high-neck *fichu,* forming a *canezou*, retained at the waist behind, and front of the ceinture, and trimmed on each side with a scolloped flounce; the flounce is laid in box-plaits in the seam; it is four inches deep on the shoulders, and diminished to a point at the waist. The front is closed with buttons, covered with the same, or to match the figure in the robe. At the neck is worn a diminutive standing collar of lace, or a *ruche*. The bottom of the skirt is trimmed with three graduated flounces. The flounces are gathered to the skirt, and both edges are scolloped or pinked. Kid gloves and lace-boots.

The *Marie Antoinette* is an organdy robe of double skirt, the upper one having a deep border in chintz flowers and imitation lace, most elaborate and rich. The lower skirt has three chintz flounces, extending one-third up the skirt, to meet the upper jupe. The *pagode* sleeve is open to the *bouillon* below the arm-hole, and edged with ribbon; thus differing from the stuffs of last year, when all the trimmings of the body and sleeve were woven to correspond in colors with those of the skirt. The ground is enlivened with little flowers, distributed throughout, except on the flounces, rather sparsely, in natural colors.

These flounces, being designed by the weaver, are not, like all other flounces, to be cut bias.

The organdies in nine flounces, with striped edges, in all lively colors, are very appropriate for demoiselles, for the little ruffle flowers extend all the way up the skirt, leaving a space between each skirt. They are all the same width, and not graduated as they were last year. The short sleeve is formed of two *bouillons,* with flounce end. Low bodies, and a knot of ribbon, or of the same goods, trims the front of the *berthe*. A *canezou* or *fichu* may be appropriately worn with this dress.

Organdies, Grenadines and Bareges are also worn in patterns *a tablier,* with tunic. That is to say, they are apron-fronted in figure, as the tunic is separated at the waist, and diverges downward to two-thirds the length of skirt, where its corners are rounded, leaving the front of the skirt in an apron form. This style of cut is called "*a tablier.*"

Taffetas is a French name for the most lustrous silks of first quality, distinguishing them from those not the richest, such as *poult de soie*. All plain silks of first quality are therefore called, by the weaver, *taffetas*. The desirable shade of this blue *taffetas* is called *chine*. It is a China blue of yellow nuance, like the ether which occasionally panoplies the "Celestial Empire."

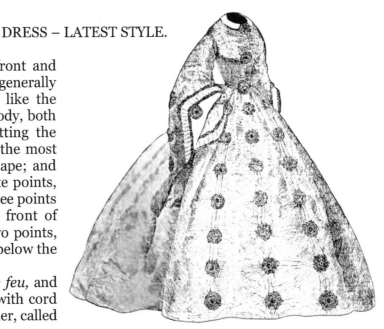

DRESS – LATEST STYLE.

Waists for balls are still cut pointed in front and behind, while for morning wear they are generally square, with large ceinture of flowing ends, like the figures with the last number. A new style of body, both for evening and promenade, is made by cutting the back without seam, forming the point below the most hollow point in the waist, into a diamond shape; and then the points of the side body form separate points, rounding the form of the bottom of back in three points – the centre one diamond-shape – and the front of body being in the vest form, terminates in two points, as the buttons closing the front do not extend below the hollow of waist.

The small tight basque, called the *coin de feu,* and the loose basque, trimmed up the front edge with cord loops and small velvet buttons set close together, called the Zouave jacket, is in vogue.

The long black cloth *basque* or *casaque,* extending to within a few inches of the bottom of the dress, single-breasted, flowing, and loose, is still a favorite with *demoiselles,* but cannot be worn with becomingness by portly ladies. The style of cut for all mantillas is long. Waists of dresses are not so long as they were last year. The half-tight sleeve, with lace cuff to turn up over end, is gaining favor. Plain skirts are gaining favor. There is nothing new in *coiffures.* Simplicity is the rule.

Arthur's Home Magazine, April 1860

For traveling dresses, walking dresses, or other dresses made of heavy material like pique or Marseilles, those without seams at the waist are getting more in favor. These robes must have a seam in front, from the manner in which they are cut, so must necessarily be trimmed down the front with buttons, bows of ribbon or rosettes.

Tight sleeves will not be so popular as the warm weather advances, and the *extremely* large ones will be generally used except for traveling dresses. ... Some courageous ladies lately made their appearance at the Tuileries without hoops, but the change was almost too violent. If the hoops could be reasonably reduced in size, the appearance of the ladies would be improved, and their health would not suffer, as it will most certainly do, when hoops are entirely abolished.

Peterson's Magazine, April 1860

Figure 2. – Home Dress.

The Home Toilet is adapted for almost any material. In the illustration it is represented as composed of a silvery-hued taffeta. The corsage and skirt are cut in one piece. At the side back-seams broad plaits are sewed under to adjust it to the figure. An expert *modiste* is required to fit this style, on account of the great bias in which it is cut. The sleeves are finished by a ruche of the same material, or a ribbon to match, and with under-sleeves.

It is reported that the Empress Eugénie has discarded hoops. It remains to be seen whether her example will be followed in this country. On sanitary grounds we should regret their disuse, though we should be quite willing to see their amplitude diminished.

Harper's New Monthly Magazine, April 1860

Lady on the Left. – Robe of green figured *taffetas*. Skirt ornamented with nine flounces, edged with narrow green ribbon. Plain, high body. Waist with a ceinture of the stuff of the dress, with long flowing ends and double-bow, edged like the flounces. Sleeves large, trimmed with three flounces at the end, and two at the top. Collar and under-sleeves of embroidered muslin.

This dress duplicates the *robe Marie Antoinette* in the Spring organdies and barges, with the difference, that in place of the upper flounce in this, they are woven to be made in double skirt. It will be perceived that the effect is the same in each, because of the increased weight and substance of *taffetas* over the thin tissues.

Lady on the Right.—Robe of bright lilac *moire*. Skirt trimmed with bands of the same goods in one shade darker, or with velvet; there being four bands which terminate in knots, and three bands alternating which extend the whole length of the skirt. The *pagoda* sleeves are trimmed in keeping, and a band passes over each shoulder from the point in front to a point at the waist behind; the point of the back at the waist being cut in the diamond shape, as there is no seam up the centre of the back. The skirt is cut in the gored form, and pyramidal, except that the greatest length and fullness is behind. This is a plain, rich dress, serving both the purposes of promenade and evening wear.

Arthur's Home Magazine, May 1860

FLOUNCED LAWN DRESS.
Fig. IV. – Lawn Dress with eleven flounces.

The Robe Imperatrice, or Polonaise, as it is now sometimes called, and of which we gave a plate earlier in the season, is very popular with our fashionable dress-makers. The body and skirt of this dress are cut in one piece, like a very deep basque. For those who may like a quieter style, bodies with sharp points behind and in front are being made. Although, as a general thing, all skirts are put on in *very large*, hollow plaits; still some few of the new dresses have the skirts gathered on around the point, quite in the old style.

Gored skirts are almost entirely worn. This kind of skirt is very graceful, as it throws the fullness to the back, and prevents the great bunches on the hips, which a very full skirt necessarily has. A gored skirt is usually four and a half to five yards wide at the bottom, and about three yards at the top. The new hoop skirts are made in a bell shape to suit dresses cut in this style.

Peterson's Magazine, May 1860

Pure white kid gloves is again the fashion for full toilet, and *tarlatane* is a favorite material for an evening party *robe*. The cut, for a party *dansant,* is a square neck, quite high on the shoulders and behind, and not low at the front of the neck. It can scarcely be termed *décolleté,* though the sleeve is barely a round flounce extending six inches below the arm-hole; underneath is one very large puff or balloon of tulle, drawn close to the arm, four or five inches above the elbow. The neck is made with a plaiting at the top one and a-half inches wide, below which is a cherry ribbon separating it from a wider plaiting below; and below this still, a plaiting like the top one is repeated. There is a plaiting also at the ends of the short sleeves. These plaitings are headed and divided by cherry-colored ribbon, and the bottom and ends of sleeves are trimmed with an inch wide fall of lace. The waist is square, with a narrow waist-ribbon bound with cherry ribbon; and towards the left side of the *ceinture* is a large double-bow knot, with long, wide, diagonal-ended lappets, edged with cherry ribbon, and diagonally striped with infinitesimal black velvet ribbon. The skirt is plain one-third below the waist, and the remainder is divided into five flounces, headed and edged with a cherry ribbon and row of very narrow black lace. The goods is white *tarlatane,* sprinkled over with black peas.

LADY ON THE LEFT.

Toilet for the Country. – Dress and *casaque* of white marseilles, braided with red and white *soutache.* The buttons on the *casaque* are of mother-of-pearl, put on with rings and oilets. The body of the *casaque* fits closely, with high neck, surmounted with a small ruche collar.

The fitting sleeve terminates in a *Louis XV.* cuff. On each side of the skirt is a pocket under a scolloped flap. Drab kid gloves, and *satin français* laced boots.

This costume – only a shorter *casaque* – was received with great favor by our demoiselles, year before last; since which it has maintained vogue, and with the increase of its length the ornamentation has become more and more elaborate.

LADY ON THE RIGHT.

Dinner Dress. –Robe of triple *taffetas, broche* with little bouquets *à la Pompadour.*

The high body is closed with little silk buttons. The cuts formed by taking out the pinches on the stomach are covered with darts of green silk, and three darts trim the back in harmony with the front.

The silk waist-ribbon is closed at front by a steel clasp, or *agrafe.*

The close-fitting sleeve is ornamented on the under side with a row of buttons reaching from the elbow to the turn-back wristband.

The jockeys to the sleeves are trimmed with ribbon like that which trims the body.

The plain skirt is edged at the bottom with a narrow velvet ribbon.

Collar of embroidered muslin edged with lace. *Manchettes* in keeping. Gloves of straw-colored kid.

ROBE,

Of plain silk, with trimmings volants of the same material, presenting a plain but at the same time elegant appearance.

As the Rosa Bonheur costume is coming into vogue, and increasing in favor for wear on rural recreations, we will here describe it: –

Short French basque to fit the form of the body, and close with a row of buttons up the front. Rosa Bonheur wears a short, loose velvet basque, over a vest cut like that for gentlemen's wear; but the close basque, without vest, rolling on the chest to disclose a finely plaited breast of a *chemisette,* is preferred by our ladies. The skirt of the dress reaches to about the middle row of the trimmings of skirt, fig. 1 on picture plate. Skirt and basque entirely plain edges, and the lower skirt buttons or buckles to straps on the under side of the basque at the waist, to prevent the necessity for wearing the dress too close for vigorous exercise.

Grecian trousers, cut remarkably full, and fulled to a band at the ankle. If boots are worn, the legs should be very [l]arge, and from eight to ten inches long, to admit the very full bottoms of the trousers; but many ladies prefer lace-boots, high enough to cover the band to which the bottom of the trouser is gathered.

Light mixed cashmerette, *drap d'été,* or cassimere, are the goods preferred; and boots are the best near on trouting excursions, through pastures, meadows, and along the rippling brooks, whose waters kiss the bending willows and overhanging alders.

This costume is entirely classical, being composed of a Rosa Bonheur *hat,* a **French** *basque,* Styrian *skirt,* Grecian *trousers,* gauntlet *gloves,* and Suwarrow *boots.*

Arthur's Home Magazine, June 1860

THE SARATOGA.

This is a new and very beautiful dress, particularly appropriate for summer. The body is low, square, cut on the straight, and buttoning in front; the waist round; the sleeves composed of a puffing cut on the straight, falling over a bell-shape sleeve cut on the bias; at the edge of the bell, as well as round the body, is a chicory ruche. Under the bell sleeve is a double frill of tulle forming a puff. The flounce of the skirt, on the bias, is gathered under a chicory ruche. The *empress* waistband fastens at the side, falling something like a scarf. It is made of silk, and composed of two loops and two long ends, bordered by a narrow quilled frill. The whole dress is very stylish.

We give the diagram, on the next page, by which to cut out the body of the dress.

No. 1. Front of the Body.
No. 2. Back.
No. 3. Side-piece of Back.
No. 4. Little Short Sleeve, on which the puff No. 5, and the frill No. 6 are sewed.

Peterson's Magazine, June 1860

The *demi-gigot,* or half-full sleeve, is quite in vogue, with lace cuffs; but large enough at the wrist to admit the hand easily.

Pointed waists for full dress, and square waists with *ceinture* and brooch for dinner and *demi-toilette.* Skirts for full dress are either flounced, or trimmed in horizontal rows of puffs in threes, being nine rows of puffs on a skirt. Fine white tarletane, with puffs of *blonde,* is very fresh, enlivening and attractive for a ball robe. The body is always trimmed in keeping with the skirt, only the rows of trimmings are not so deep. The pagoda sleeve is still in wear. For ball dress, the body is square, not very low, and the sleeve is like a full half-circular cap over a puff of blonde.

SUMMER WALKING DRESS.

In the above illustration we give the design for a Robe, whose rich trimming and material adapts it for either a promenade or visiting dress. It is of violet-colored "poult de soie." The skirt is ornamented with three stripes of Rusche "a la vielle," interwoven with the same material as the dress. The stripes are arranged at corresponding distance from the waist. The sleeves hang in folds their entire length, with two puffs of Rusche beneath a broad reverse of velvet. The girdle is of the same material as the dress, trimmed with velvet.

Arthur's Home Magazine, July 1860

CARRIAGE TOILETTE.

This is a very elegant carriage toilette. The robe, of plain poult de soie, has the skirt and corsage in one, à la Princesse; and perfectly plain except broad bretelles of the same silk, cut bias, wide on the shoulder, very narrow at the waist, and continued, gradually increasing in width, down the sides of the robe, leaving the front en tablier. It is trimmed with a row of rich guipure lace; and macaroons of the same silk, with frills of guipure, are set, at intervals, up the front, graduated in size from the hem to the waist, and from thence to the throat reversed. The sleeve is open, deep at the back, and cut up the front, the fore part closing over the other, and the lace trimming carried round it and up to the shoulder. Shawl of Chantilly lace; bonnet of white crape and colored silk, with white feathers tipped with the same color.

Dresses continue to be made in the "Princess" style, corsage and skirt in one, the latter gored to the waist. But this is suitable only for rich and heavy silks, which are still worn, although in a great measure replaced by lighter and more seasonable fabrics. In all light materials, a number of flounces are invariably seen; and although we observe as few as three and as many as fifteen, yet seven and nine seem to be in the majority. The organdies and some of the bareges have also four narrow flounces on the lower skirt, with an upper one forming a deep flounce over them – and this may, perhaps, be considered the most popular of trimmings. The robe pieces always comprise suitable trimming for the corsage. Organdies have, very generally, pagoda sleeves with three or more frills edged with Valenciennes. Such materials as do not pass under the hands of the laundress have puffings and other trimmings of a more façonné description.

GIRDLE.

The greatest novelty is in the girdle or band, which is made with two points in front, one down and one up. When the band is made thus, bows and long streamers of ribbon, like those of a sash, are added. It is remarkable also, that the colored sashes worn with white and light dresses will also have this pointed belt, which is called the Medicis. The ribbon used for the streamers is very wide; never less than No. 80; and sometimes taffetas is used, split down the length, which gives a sash nine inches wide. (The ordinary narrow silk is eighteen inches.) We give an illustration of this sash, which forms so very pretty and dressy a finish to a simple muslin dress. It will be observed that the ends are handsomely fringed.

We mentioned, last month, that there was a probability of aprons being much more worn than they have of late been by ladies. We are glad of it; since they are both convenient and ornamental appendages to the toilette; and we proceed to describe some of the many novel modes of trimming them, by which it will be perceived that they have shared in the general progress of taste and elegance in dress.

We have before us nearly a dozen different designs for aprons. The material, in all cases, is black silk, glacé, *poult de soie*, or watered silk. Like every other article of dress at present, they are elaborately ornamented, principally with silk cord and macaroon trimmings; but fringe, tassels and passementerie are also employed.

The first apron of which we give an illustration is made of black silk, trimmed with black satin ribbon and colored silk, purple, green, blue, or, in short, any color that will look well with the robe with which it may probably be worn. As will be seen in the engraving, this colored silk forms the pockets, and a band of eight inches or so along the bottom. The colored silk should be honeycombed; but if this be thought too troublesome, the Wheeler and Wilson Sewing Machine has made quilting as easy to execute as it is ornamental when done.

The shape of the pockets is very pretty, something like the sabretache of a cavalry officer. They have a top falling over, trimmed round with cord, and finished with bows of cord and silk tassels. The cords are continued up each side of the apron to the band, which materially strengthens pockets. These are trimmed with a ruche of quilled ribbon, and a row of the some forms a heading to the colored silk border.

The other apron we have selected for illustration has rounded corners; and is trimmed with a flounce of fluted pinked silk, gradually narrowed towards the waist. A ruche of narrow quilled ribbon forms a heading. There are no pockets; but side trimmings of passementerie with tassels at the ends, and knots of cord at the top, are placed at each side, for ornaments; and it would be no difficult matter to put in pockets, as in a dress, and make the openings between the two rows of buttons forming the passementerie.

Another of a simpler character is in plain black glacé silk, with no ornament round the edge, but merely thick cord ornaments on each side, where pockets should be, but extending from the belt nearly to the hem. Four cords, each seven-eighths of a yard long and ending with a tassel, are wanted; two on each side, set on at three inches apart. Each pair makes a series of oval medallions, crossing here and there; and where they cross, one of the pretty macaroon trimmings is placed by way of ornament.

Others have a border of velvet ribbon down the sides, and along the bottom; with a narrow black lace on the inner edge, as well as on the outer; with rosettes, graduated in size, placed at intervals up each side.

Braided pockets, trimmed with deep fringe, afford another variety; and the apron itself may also be braided. Another style has the edge cut like shells, each flounced with pinked silk, so that one wraps over another, with a medallion rosette at. the termination of each; and two other rosettes with ends of ribbon, placed to ornament the pockets.

All these are made either with cord and tassels, for girdle, or the Medicis sash; which latter is the most elegant.

Frank Leslie's Monthly, July 1860

THE ROSETTA.

This is a very fashionable dress, just out in Paris. The sleeve, it will be seen, is cut so as to form a very wide pagoda at bottom. There is no plait at top, and the pattern is all of one piece, which makes both the sleeve and the revers. About the straight part of the stuff several plaits are made so as to raise that part the distance required to meet the seam in front of the sleeve, which is hollowed out at the bend, to give it the appearance of a wide sleeve with an elbow. The inner side of this sleeve should round off at bottom, and be wider than the outer part, so as to leave visible the ruche put inside.

This sleeve is ornamented with a plain revers formed out of the same pattern, which is folded back in front, above the seam at the bend of the arm. This revers, beginning in front of the sleeve-hole, covers the seam, the beginning of the plaits, and joins the bottom of the sleeve at the corresponding mark, a star. This revers is bordered by a narrow lace gathered very full, and has three buttons on in encircled by two rows of narrow lace also very full; a fourth button similarly surrounded seems to fasten the beginning of the revers at the bottom of the sleeve behind.

The body of this dress has no seam at the waist; a side-piece is put in front to join the letters A and B. The back of this body is composed of three parts: the first, that forming the middle, meets a side-piece at the letters C and D; this first side-piece meets a second at the letters E and F. When these seams are made, the front and back of the body are complete, and are joined by the seam under the arm. When the seams of the body are sewed, the stuff that remains free at the bottom, behind, and in front, is laid in the plaits round the waist.

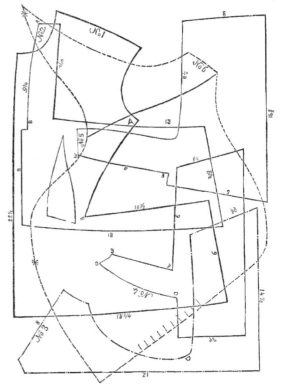

The seams of the skirt should be made and cut sloping off toward the waist. The bottom of the skirt must be at least five yards round.

No. 1. Front of Body.
No. 2. Side-piece of Front.
No. 3. Middle of Back.
No. 4. First Side-piece of Back.
No. 5. Second Side-piece of Back.
No. 6. Pattern forming the Sleeve and its Revers.

Dresses for the promenade have the skirts very wide at the bottom, slightly gored toward the waist, and are considered very stylish without flounces, but the lighter materials, such as *taffetas*, thin *glaces*, and all of that class, will have flounces still, and even a second skirt to meet the flounces.

Fig. III. – Dress for the Sea-Shore of very light gray Barege Anglaise. – The skirt is trimmed with twelve ruffles, put on with but little fullness, and bound with black velvet. The upper ruffle is also headed with black velvet. The body is plain, with a black velvet belt; and the very large sleeves are simply bound with black velvet.

Peterson's Magazine, July 1860

Flounced robes, with the flounces edged with a bias, are extremely delicate and fascinating. Six flounces form the tour of the skirt, continuing up the front in the shape of an apron. The round-cornered tunic, edged with a large *bouillonné*, is regarded as quite *récherché*. When the body is *décolleté* – in case of a ball dress, for example – the *plissé* or plaiting, as the head of the body, is open *en cœur*; but when the body is high, it is completed by a *fichu pelerine* in stuff similar, with plaiting and flounce at the edge.

Casaques of black silk, cut nearly as long as the dress, and with flowing sleeves, are still the favored over-dresses for young ladies; they are lined with white silk, which, at the ends of the sleeves, is formed in a *plissé* a couple of inches deep.

The evening robes of tulle and tarlatan are cut with pointed bodies, *demi-décolleté*, one or two *bouillons* forming the short sleeve, and the skirt covered with *bouillons*, diminishing in size as they ascend, and either all white, or alternating with rose, blue, and orange.

Arthur's Home Magazine, August 1860

ZOUAVE JACKET.

We give this month a picture and diagram of a new style of *Zouave* Jacket. The pattern consists of four pieces, the front, back, side-body, and sleeve; we have given a different style of sleeve to that in the costume; it is fulled at the top, instead of being plain, and may be lengthened as much as required; some ladies are wearing them the length of the pattern only; the sleeves of the *chemisette* should always be the very full bishop. The jacket may either be ornamented by *arabesques*, or braided round in any design, such as the Grecian border, &c. The front of *chemisette* is cut on the bias, so as to sit full over the top of the skirt. This jacket will be very much worn this autumn, made in cashmere, and braided with a contrasting color.

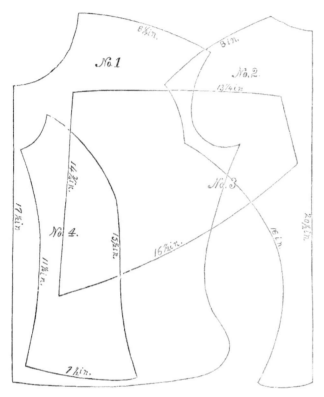

Peterson's Magazine, August 1860

In dresses for out-door wear – and no one thinks of being in-doors now, if it can be helped – gray is still the prevailing hue. Nothing so delicate and charming was ever before in vogue. It is really refreshing to the eyes, these hot days, to look at the soft-tinted toilettes. One great advantage of the universal color besides its delicacy, is that it harmonizes with every bright hue. We saw lately a dress and mantle of the quiet tint, the latter bound, and the dress trimmed with Solferino silk, cut cross-wise.

Frank Leslie's Monthly, August 1860

DRESS FOR YOUNG LADY.

The material is thin Swiss muslin, formed with a double skirt, each having a broad hem. The body is high, with an insertion band trimmed with lace. Over this is worn an upper body of white taffeta, with a small shoulder piece, and cut square across in front and back. This body is quadrilled by narrow black velvets, which cross each other at intervals of about an inch. They commence at the edge, under a small bow, and extend the full length of the waist, terminating at the bottom in loops and ends, which fall over the skirt in the form of lappets. The short puffed sleeves are gathered into a narrow band, and ornamented with bows and ends of black velvet.

Arthur's Home Magazine, September 1860

At A. T. Stewart's are wonderful bargains in the way of embroidered vests, to be worn with Zouave jackets. Our readers in distant parts of the States may be glad to learn that these vests are extremely long in front, so as to bag or fall over the skirt of the dress. They have long muslin sleeves with embroidered fronts, cuffs and collars. Some are as low as four dollars, and from that up to fifteen or twenty. Nothing can be more elegant than this vest with a Zouave jacket of black cloth, heavily braided. A broad ribbon-sash, with long floating ends, is imperative with this costume, whilst with ordinary dresses belts and gold buckles only are in vogue.

At present, the Zouave jackets are made of the same material as the dress – piqué, brillante, or whatever they may be; but as the cool weather returns, black cloth will be the favorite material; with black silk braid for morning wear and gold for evening.

WALKING COSTUME.

This is a walking costume, consisting of a dress and long casaque, the latter as near an approach as is at present attempted towards the pelisse which, at no distant period, promises to be universal. The engraving is of a dress of plain Havana colored poult-de-soie, the skirt trimmed all round with three flounces of the same, cut bias, each headed with a ruching of taffetas ribbon. The flounces are about five inches deep, and set on with an interval of about an inch and a half between. The same trimming is continued, *en tablier*, up the front. The skirt of the casaque, although gored, is still somewhat full in the waist – in this respect differing from the ordinary basquine. It is put on in large box plaits, like the fashionable dresses. It is trimmed along the edge, and up the sides, with a flouncing like that on the robe, which is diminished in width as it reaches the waist. The corsage perfectly plain and tight, with a small reverse collar round the throat. It is closed with silk buttons up the front, and ornamented with bows of ribbon, edged with lace. The sleeve, a moderate pagoda in form, is trimmed with three flounces on the outer side; but they cease within two inches on each side of the arm seam, and the ruching of ribbon is carried along the edge of this plain part, up the sides, to finish the frills, and as a garniture to the top of the upper frill. Under it is worn a plain embroidered muslin sleeve. An Albanito hat, with long plume, completes the costume.

For the pleasant hops given at the Pavilion and other hotels during the season no dress is so pretty or suitable for young ladies as white muslin; and the present style of trimming and ornamenting with gold enables the wearer to make the dress as rich and handsome as she may desire.

Frank Leslie's Monthly, September 1860

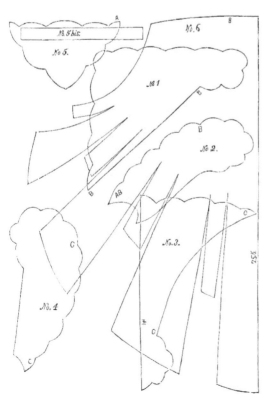

LOW SPENCER BODY.

We give, this month, the pattern for a new style of low spencer body for a young lady; and also a pattern of a new sleeve which is worn with it.

An engraving of the body and sleeve is given in the front of the number, and a diagram, by which to cut them out, are given on the next page, which see.

No. 1. Front of Spencer Body.

No. 2. Side-piece of Front; the vandykes should lap over on the front No. 1. These two patterns join at the corresponding letters.

No. 3. Back of Spencer Body.

No. 4. Side-piece of Back.

No. 5. Jockey, figuring the sleeve of the spencer body, to be added to the band, No. 5 *bis* forming the shoulder-piece.

No. 6. Sleeve puffed at bottom.

Nearly all the new silk dresses are being made without a seam of the waist, trimmed down the front by rosettes of lace or *passementerie*. Some silk dresses are made open to the waist with lappels turned back: the sleeves are tight, with large puffings at the top, and deep cuffs turned back. Other dresses have the bodies plain, fastened by buttons, and trimmed all down the front by a series of bows or gimp ornaments; sleeves wide, lined with white, and bordered just inside by a small white ruche; in some instances the sleeves are slashed and the bodies pointed. Even where the skirt is set on to the body, it is almost invariably gored, in order to have but little fullness at top. Flounces are only worn around the lower part of the skirt.

Sleeves are still of the wide pagoda form, the *pagoda*, *Isabeau*, and *Mandarin* all being synonymous, and varying only in the degree of width given to them.

Peterson's Magazine, September 1860

PROMENADE COSTUME AND CARRIAGE DRESS.

Lady on the Left.

Robe of *taffetas pansée* silk, trimmed with a ruffle edged puffing of white *taffeta*, disposed in form of a tunic, and continuing across the back to simulate a *pèlerine* in a pointed form, extending to the waist. The end of the sleeve fringed, above which – several inches – is a band of ruffle-edged puffing. The *ceinture*, or waist ribbon of the same, is closed with a steel or silver clasp. The front the robe is garnished with a row of buttons covered with the same, and diminishing in size toward the waist.

Collar and undersleeves of application. Straw-colored kid gloves. Lace boots of *satin français*.

This costume is appropriate wear for a young wife to an opera or concert *matinèe* or *soirèe*, and would be appropriate for a young lady at an evening opera, with a simple head-dress of white lace and blue ribbon, enlivened with a few flowers to heighten or tone the complexion.

Lady on the Right – Robe of *taffetas* – plain skirt for *promenade*.

Winged mantle of black *taffetas* or velvet, but the former is the most fashionable. This mantle is often cut with sleeves – either pointed or square – which reach to the bottom of the mantle. The trimming is formed of biases cut from silk striped with black and *pensée*. It is cut with a yoke, covered with a pelerine, and edged in with the rest.

BRETELLES.

Waists, Sleeves, and Skirts. – The Venetian corsage for home dress is very popular. It is made of white muslin to fit the body, and divided lengthwise in front by five black velvet ribbons, to which it is gathered. There is a black velvet ribbon at the top round the neck, edged with a narrow band of scolloped black lace. There is no collar worn with this body. A velvet epaulette, in the form of a half moon, is widest at the top of the shoulder, below which are two puffs in the sleeve; from the lower puff the sleeve is divided lengthwise by six velvet ribbons, to which the sleeve is gathered. The wristband is trimmed round with a velvet ribbon and a knot on the top of the wrist. There is a waist-ribbon of black velvet two inches wide, tied in a double bow knot at front with flowing ends. This body is pretty with a skirt of rose *taffetas*, or with any skirt of carmine *nuance*.

The sleeve in highest favor for morning dresses is cut full at the armhole, and tapering all the way to the wrist, and formed into eight graduated puffs, terminating in a fitting wristband, closing with a hook and eye. A sleeve of this kind for a dinner-dress, to be more dressy, is ornamented with a knot of ribbon like that which trims the rest of the dress between each puff on the top of the arm. The sleeve of graduated puffs is destined to have quite a run.

The Art of the Hoop: 1860 - 1869

The *pagode* sleeve, and the full, flowing, pointed sleeve, both with one or two puffs near the armhole, are in favor, as is also the tight-fitting sleeve with one or two large puffs near the top, and fitting at the wrist, over which is turned a deep lace cuff.

Square bodies are worn for promenade and carriage dresses, with *ceinture* and ornamental brooch. Pointed waists for all *décolleté* bodies. Vest-pointed waists in front, and three points on the back with a diamond centre, is still in favor.

Short sleeves for *décolleté* dresses are formed of one or two puffs and a flounce.

Arthur's Home Magazine, October 1860

FRONT OF LADY'S WAISTBAND.

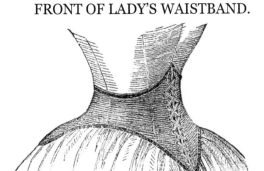

FRONT OF LADY'S WAISTBAND.

BACK OF LADY'S WAISTBAND.

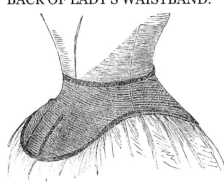

LADY'S WAISTBAND.

This new and pretty affair is intended especially for those ladies to whom the short round waist is unbecoming, or for those who object to an untrimmed body. It is laced up front; the under-point, and the little jacket-piece at the back, falling over the skirt; the remainder of the band trims the full, short-waisted body, over which it its worn – the points coming up the front and back forming a pretty outline. The half is cut in four pieces, as shown in the above engraving, from A to B, C to D, E to F. The dotted lines, in our next engraving (see next page) form the pleats behind, and the two pieces, A A and B B, should be joined together.

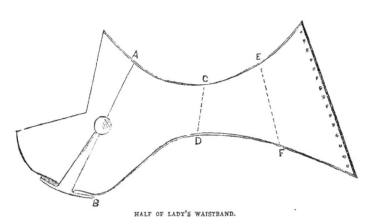

HALF OF LADY'S WAISTBAND.

HALF OF LADY'S WAISTBAND.

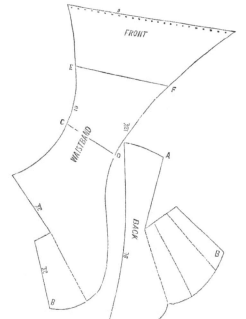

DIAGRAM OF LADY'S WAISTBAND.

All skirts should be slightly gored (one breadth on each side is just enough to set them out well), and sloped two or two and a half inches at the bottom, from the front to the back, to prevent so much slope at the top. In mounting a skirt on the body, the fullness should be arranged in five or six small pleats on each side of the front, and in three or four box pleats behind. Sleeves of almost every shape are worn; a few of the tight ones, and some half tight.

NEW STYLE FALL DRESS.

One of the prettiest dresses, which has lately appeared in Paris, is given above. It is of mauve silk, trimmed with pansy silk; the body high, buttoned in front; waist round, with band closed by a clasp in the Byzantine style. The lower part of the body consists of a corselet of the same silk formed by four rows of drawings, by which the silk is fastened in very small plaits. The top is decorated by a band of pansy silk an inch wide, pinked at the edges on each side, and drawn in the middle so as to form a full ruche. On the next page, we give diagrams, by which to cut out this new style of body.

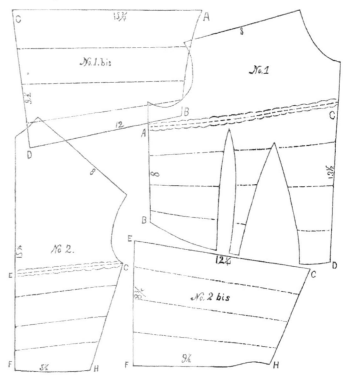

No. 1. Front of Body; the top, made of mauve silk, is plain; the lower part is composed of the lining on which the drawn corselet that cover it is fitted, as represented in the pattern.

No. 1 *bis*. Pattern of the Front of the Body to be placed on No. 1 at the corresponding letters.

No. 2. Back of the same Body with the plain top of silk, and the lower part terminated by the lining and covered by the corselet.

No. 2 *bis*. Back of the Corselet to be applied according to the letters.

DIAGRAM FOR NEW STYLE FALL DRESS.
Peterson's Magazine, October 1860

The colored cloth Zouaves have facings and trimmings of silk of another color, in some instances, which gives them a very showy and handsome appearance; but for general use we do not think any will obtain so much popularity as the black cloth Zouave, braided with silk braid of the same color. Our readers will remember that a proper Zouave has an ornamental figure embroidered or braided twice on the centre of the back, once between the shoulders, once the lower edge; also on the fronts and on the fore part of each sleeve.

The muslin and lace Zouave vests always have the fronts very long, so that they bag somewhat over the sash or belt. There will be found at Stewart's an extensive assortment of these with delicate embroidery running up each plait, and cuffs and collars to correspond.

Frank Leslie's Monthly, October 1860

Lady on the Left.
Evening Toilet. – Robe of *taffetas rayé* white and green, or light green with stripes several shades darker. Skirt sewed to the body in large double box plaits from the hips across the back, and a band of *taffetas* as dark as the stripes forms a trimming eight inches wide at the bottom, and turned up the front to the waist where it is but three inches wide, leaving the space in front of the apron shape; the band is edged on the inside with a narrow band of black lace. The body is plain, with a

revers similar to the band on the skirt, extending out well on the shoulders, and square behind, edged with narrow lace. Sleeves large and plaits behind in harmony with those in the skirt. Open jockeys and band trimming for the sleeves like that on the skirt. The knots up the front are also edged with lace.

Collar and sleeves of application. Straw-colored kid gloves.

Lady on the Right – Visiting Dress. Dress china gray *taffetas*, ornamented with bands and biases (*lisérées*) – edged with pink ribbon flounces – the upper one a third of length of above the bottom, edged like the trimmings on the body with either pink or rose ribbon. Sleeves full at the arm-hole, and tapering to the wrist, formed into seven or eight bias puffs, closing a hook and eye at the wrist. Collar of application and russet-colored kid gloves, with lace boots *satin français*.

Arthur's Home Magazine, November 1860

ZOUAVE VEST AND JACKET.

Pattern of Zouave vest and jacket, the directions for enlarging which are given elsewhere.

DIRECTIONS FOR ENLARGING OF PATTERN OF ZOUAVE JACKET AND VEST

Take one or more sheets of paper of convenient size, fold or rule them into squares of one and a quarter inches each, corresponding to diagram (the squares of which are a quarter of an inch only), mark with a pencil lines on the paper from square to square, as in diagram, and cut out with scissors. This, if done with care, will take about one hour, and the operator will be in possession of perfect-fitting, full-sized patterns.

N B. This is a simple and accurate system of obtaining correct patterns; but, as it is as yet untried by our readers, we shall esteem it a favor if those who attempt the task will inform us by letter of the results of their trial, whether it good or bad. Any practical suggestion calculated to this system will be thankfully received.

Zouave jackets will be as fashionable as ever, and a little more. Some are made with inner vests, buttoning to the throat; others have vests of embroidered muslin or fine linen, with large full sleeves. We suspect that these will be the most worn, especially in the house. This is the one garment on which gold is not, except to a very limited extent; silk braid having almost entirely superseded it. Our readers will not forget that a Zouave is not a Zouave unless it is braided; it may be a pretty jacket ornamented in any other way, but a Zouave it is not. The braided design should have an ornament between the shoulders, at the centre of the back seam along the outer edge, on the fronts and on the sleeves.

The present month presents rather a realization of our previous anticipations than any special novelty of its own. In the article of dress we find the same amplitude of skirt that has been popular for so long a period, without any flounces except for evening dress. The corsages of all but evening dresses are, in like manner, invariably round, and worn with a belt or sash and a double buckle. The sashes are extremely wide, reaching about three-quarters of the depth of the dress, and richly embroidered at the ends. Some are so ornamented by hand, others have magnificent designs brocaded on them, …

For evening dress, white and the most brilliant colors are the favorites. Orange, corn, lemon, cerise, Solferino, Magenta, Fleur de Pêche, are all the rage; pale, pink or blue being comparatively neglected. These tints may be softened down by the judicious admixture of black or white lace, which always looks elegant, whether it be worn in wide or narrow flounces, tunics, or any other form. If flounces, they should entirely cover the skirt; and the bertha and handkerchief – a very important part of the toilet – must correspond.

The corsages of *robes décolletées* are plain, and are worn with a bertha if of silk, but full when a transparent material is employed; and in the latter case the waist is at least as often round as pointed.

Frank Leslie's Monthly, November 1860

Fig. I. – Evening Dress of white Tulle, spotted in black, trimmed with five flounces; each flounce is trimmed with a narrow crimson velvet, and edged with narrow black lace. The body is made without a point, and has a broad, wide sash of white silk striped with black velvet, and edged with crimson velvet. The body is square in the neck, *a la Raphael*, and is trimmed with puffings of tulle and velvet. Fan-shaped short sleeve over large puffs of tulle. Head-dress of crimson velvet and gold braid.

Fig. II. – Dinner Dress of Mauve-colored Silk. – The skirt is much narrow at the top than at the bottom, and is trimmed with five quillings of silk put on very full; each quilling is pinked at the edges, and decreases in width as they approach the waist. Body plain, with a point. Pagoda sleeve, trimmed to correspond with the skirt.

Several of the newest silk dresses are trimmed with flounces, and a pretty variety is obtained when the flounces are of two different colors. For example, flounces composed of the same silk as the dress, are often places alternately with others of a tint harmonizing with them, of them may be formed of two different shades of the same color. We have seen a dress trimmed with lilac and violet flounces, and another with flounces in two tints of green. Sometimes the flounces are disposed in separate sets, or series, and with them are intermingled narrow pinked ruches. A bias row of silk of the darker shade is also placed on the edge of the skirt. The corsages of these dresses are high, and the sleeves either long or demi-long. The trimming one the corsages and sleeves should corresponds with that on the skirt.

For dress trimmings, gimps in all the fancy styles are very much used. Fringes are not at all worn.

Sleeves of every variety will be worn, either very large and flowing, or tight to the arm, or partially close with a cuff. When buttons are worn on the dress, the tight sleeve is slit up to a certain height, and buttoned behind the arm with large buttons like those on the front of the body. These buttons are continued down the front of the skirt in the cassock or Empress dresses, which are quite plain in front, and laid in wide plaits behind and at the sides.

Peterson's Magazine, November 1860

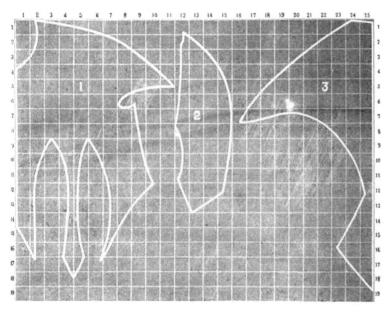

EPAULETTE WAIST.

This is a very novel and pretty waist pattern, with points extending from the shoulders and forming a polka to the corsage.

No. 1 – Front.
No. 2 – Sidepiece.
No. 3 – Back.

Gored dresses have as yet only found a very small degree of favor; the effort to introduce them has been made with an amount of perseverance worthy of a more successful result; but as yet the attempt may be considered a failure. As a wrapper, with plaits in the back and puffed demi leg-of-mutton sleeves, the style has a look of novelty and refreshing simplicity which commends it to notice and favor; but for full dress purposes it finds no favor in any eyes.

A new style of skirt is said to be meeting with great favor in Paris. It supports the dress without springs of any kind, relying for this purpose simply on the harmonious and skilful disposition of the plaited muslin of which it is composed. The Multiplied Skirt, or *Jupon Multiple*, as it is called, supports a series of volants, tapered and grouped like a fan, which are moved at will by means of metallic eyelets.

The only novelty about this skirt is the fan-like grouping. Muslin skirts with a multiplicity of volants have been worn by both French and American ladies for a long time, to effectually disguise and give the requisite circumference to a small hoop; but they are too costly and too much trouble to be worn generally or to take the place of hooped skirts.

The following are descriptions of the toilettes illustrated on pp 563-7, and of the Prince's partners:

The first dress, which is only partially seen, consisted of rich green velvet, with wide tulle sleeves, trimmed with lace and ribbon ruching. The necklace consisted of large pearls, and the head-dress of diamonds and pearls and superb white ostrich feathers.

The second figure represents the elegant costume of Mrs. Gould Hoyt – one of the Prince's partners. The robe was of pink glacé silk, with a tulle over-skirt, ornamented with medallions of exquisite Honiton lace. Head-dress of flowers.

The third dress was much admired for its simple elegance. It consisted of very rich white rep silk, with berthé of point lace and wreath of gold leaves and berries.

The fourth was a charming toilette of white tulle, with several rows of narrow ribbon ruching round the skirt, and elegant black Chantilly lace flounces, headed with ribbon ruching and flowers. Splendid diamond necklace and headdress of diamonds and flowers.

The fifth dress was pure white, of the thinnest, most transparent tulle, ornamented with point lace and Magenta roses. A scarf of broad white ribbon, striped and brocaded with Magenta, was worn over the right shoulder and crossed under the left arm. Pearl necklace with diamond pendant; headdress of diamonds and Magenta roses.

The sixth dress was one of the most costly and exquisitely beautiful of those present. It consisted of deep elegant flounces of *point appliqué* over very transparent tulle, looped up at intervals with lovely bouquets of flowers; the ornaments were superb, and heightened the splendid beauty of the fair wearer. A diamond crescent glittered on the white forehead, and large, magnificent emeralds formed the pendant to a costly necklace of pearls.

The seventh figure represents a robe of dark magnificent green velvet, ornamented with superb flounces and bertha of point lace. The necklace was diamonds and pearls, and the head-dress a sort of turban composed of velvet flowers and ostrich feathers.

The eighth illustration gives a correct idea of the superb costume of Mrs. John Day of this city. It was of rich black velvet, with a little pointed antique vest of magnificent point lace, with lace talma to match. The head-dress was ostrich feathers with diamond ornaments.

Frank Leslie's Monthly, December 1860

Dresses for the house have the skirts long, extremely wide at the bottom, this width being reduced at the top by the breadths being gored; the fullness is set into the waist in large, hollow plaits; this refers equally to silks, poplins, mohairs, and all the more substantial materials. For silk dresses, narrow flounces are fashionable, either trimmed with narrow black lace or the edges pinked. Deep fullings of silk divided into puffings by straps of narrow black velvet, is also a very stylish trimming. Fluting is also very much employed on the skirts, sleeves, and bodies of dresses. The extent to which it is used is quite remarkable, and its variety in width, in application, endless. This fluting is made by putting on a trimming of silk or velvet in deep box plaits, which are caught at the bottom of and fastened by a stitch. This gives the fluted appearance to the trimming.

Bodies of dresses are made high and generally close to the throat, though those made slightly open in the front are becoming more popular; these last have pieces like the lappels of a coat turned back: sometimes these lappels or *revers* are of the same material of the dress, and sometimes of velvet.

Peterson's Magazine, December 1860

Shopping Woes

Although, in the city, we are still suffering from the broiling heat of an almost summer sun, yet the windows of the stores in Broadway give clear evidence that we may expect the approach of winter at any moment whatever. Every dry goods house displays a rich and magnificent stock of new silks, velours de Paris, popelines, &c.; and our eyes ache with gazing at the gem-like brilliancy of many of the materials.

No wonder we see so many ladies bewildered with the variety of designs and colors displayed before their eyes, until they lose the power of selection, and rush out of the store to regain their senses and eyesight in the fresh air. These women bent on spending a morning shopping afford, very frequently, a curious study to the spectator, whilst their conduct excites ideas in the minds of the clerks who wait upon them the reverse of what they would desire, if they gave any thought to the matter.

When, for instance, a lady goes into the silk department of an establishment, and signifies that she "wants a dress," but has no idea whether it is for morning or evening toilette – whether she can afford to give one dollar a yard for it, or five dollars, it is a fair presumption that she comes, not intending to purchase at all, but simply to get rid of a little of the idle time which hangs so heavily on her hands; and this suspicion is frequently confirmed by her leaving the store without making any purchase, after occupying the clerk for an hour or two, merely remarking that "she guesses she will look somewhere else before she decides;" a guess which she speedily converts into a certainty by strolling into the next and the next dry goods' store, until she has fairly worn out herself, and every one with whom she has trifled away time.

The same annoying want of decision and good feeling is practised to a great extent towards milliners, whose choicest goods are frequently dragged on and off the head until their beauty and freshness have departed; whilst the thoughtless visitors will perhaps finish with the remark, "Well, what would you charge for making me up a hat like this of my own materials?" although they must be perfectly aware such things are never done by the house.

There is a want of right feeling in this proceeding which cannot fail to be very irritating to those honored by the "custom" of such ladies; and although there is, undoubtedly, cause to complain at times of the indolent indifference of clerks – and this is especially the case where young women are employed – still, as a rule, it is far more the fault of visitors themselves, if they meet with inattention in their shopping excursions. Certainly, when a purchase is really intended, a lady must know something of the style she requires, and the price she is willing to pay; and it must be needless to take up a clerk's time in showing brocades and moiré antiques, when a simple poult de soie is the only thing within her means.

Frank Leslie's Monthly, October 1860

New Fabrics

At A. T. Stewart's we find a fine assortment of what are called vesting silks – silks of that rich and thick texture that is appropriated generally for gentlemen's vests. The ground is for the most part black – a rich reps silk, over which golden stars are scattered profusely, whilst a delicate vine-leaf, in Magenta, petunia, or any other color, is brocaded on it at in intervals. It is hard to imagine anything much more elegant for an elderly lady, whilst the same design, with a white ground, would be equally handsome and suitable for a young one.

The cable cord silk – so called because an imitation of the world-renowned bits of cable cord are woven in – is a perfect novelty. The evening dresses are very superb colored velvet designs being wrought in white silk and white velvet on colored silks.

Printed de laines and cashmeres are in great variety; small chintz designs being the favorites. They will make charming home dresses, especially for young ladies.

The cashmeres adapted only for dressing-gowns, in shawl patterns, are very brilliant, and will doubtless be popular with many, although not to be compared in elegance with such a dressing-gown as we have described in our notice of the styles for the month. Such a robe, even if made of any color less delicate than white, would still be far more elegant and *comme il faut* than those gorgeous shawl patterns, which combine every hue under the sun; still, they look rich and handsome enough always to command a certain popularity.

Frank Leslie's Monthly, October 1860

1861

EVENING, OR PARTY DRESS.

A robe of thin material, color to suit, flounced. Pointed waist, trimmed with Grecian folds. Our fashion artist shows, in this figure, a compression of waist, not only destructive of beauty in form, but also destructive of health. All attempts to improve that most wonderfully symmetrical of all forms, the human, result in a loss of both health and beauty. Waist compressions are among the worst of these attempts.

DINNER DRESS,

Of plain silk, with a broad bias fold of striped silk, ground color, same as dress, on the bottom, and a second narrow fold above. Wide sleeves, with narrow trimmings, same as skirt. Full, plain undersleeves, and collar to match. The style is neat and elegant.

Arthur's Home Magazine, January 1861

Simple and elegant dress of green crape, over green silk; the bouffantes of the skirt, corsage, and sleeves caught up by ruches of white crape. Chatalaine of Cape Jessamine blossoms, without foliage; cluster of the same on the left of the skirt, drooping wreath to correspond, mixed with foliage.

Our Fashion-plate naturally leads to a few more items on the subject of evening dress.

First, as to the width and shape of the skirt: "Ill-made crinoline, worn under ridiculous or wretched toilets, had inspired some ladies who have a strong dislike to anything ugly or common, with a desire to diminish the fulness of dresses and return to the Greek or Roman tunics, but the change was soon found to be altogether impracticable;" is the fiat of the *Moniteur,* to which admirable counsellor we are also indebted for the following valuable suggestion as to the arrangement of the amplitude of evening dress draperies, on which their peculiar elegance so entirely depends: –

"To secure all possible gracefulness in ball dresses, the plaits at top are made wide and then doubled again, and without cutting the stuff to a point; but three points of gores are added at the bottom of the under skirt, one between the widths at each side, and one behind. These points make the lower part of the skirt spread well, and form a train. The front of the skirt is always made shorter to give freedom to the feet."

Again, as to the sleeve: the bell-shaped puff is quite as much in favor as ever; it is always becoming to freshness and youth. Where the arm needs more concealment, a puff and flounce, or two wide flounces may be worn, falling nearly as low as the elbow.

"An ornament on the sleeves of a very pretty nacarat velvet dress made by Mme. Bernard, one of our first rate dressmakers, should be noted. The ornament was formed by a broad gold band, and the body, which was high, was fastened by gold buttons. The skirt, quite plain and long behind, *was eleven yards round*.

"Another dress by the same maker was made of light peach-bloom velvet, with a plain skirt, a low body, short sleeves formed of large *beret* of velvet, arranged so as to leave at intervals, hollows, in which was seen a large puff of white satin. The body has draperies arranged contrariwise, reproducing the ornaments of the sleeves, that is to say, in the intervals left by the waved plaits of the velvet white satin puffings were visible. This new fashion, which it requires the pencil rather than the pen to represent intelligibly, is most happily effective."

In a splendid ball given in Paris, one of Gagelin's Pompadour costumes, worn by a youthful bride of remarkable beauty, attracted much notice. This costume consisted of a skirt of green silk looped up in two places on each side by white and pink chicories forming ribbon. The front of this skirt, which was in the apron style, was white satin decorated with white and red roses. The body had a white and pink bertha, rounded behind, and beginning in front from the point of the body. The sleeves were white thulle. The headdress consisted of a white and pink chicory on one side, accompanied by roses on the other, and two large white marabout feathers.

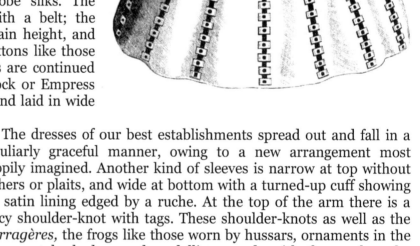

WALKING DRESS FOR A YOUNG LADY.

Made of steel colored poplin; trimmed with Magenta-colored velvet and buttons. The velvet is crossed at intervals by squares of the poplin, having a button in the centre, which makes a very stylish trimming.

Plain dresses continue to be made of thick tissues such as druggets, terry velvets, and poplins.

Ottoman velours is perhaps the favorite material for street dresses, and offers a sensible, suitable resistance, for once, to the mud and mire which last year fringed the rich floating flounces of costly robe silks. The corsage is almost invariably round, with a belt; the sleeves are often plain, slit up to a certain height, and buttoned behind the arm with large buttons like those on the front of the body. These buttons are continued down the front of the skirt in the cassock or Empress dresses, which are quite plain in front, and laid in wide plaits behind and at the sides.

The dresses of our best establishments spread out and fall in a peculiarly graceful manner, owing to a new arrangement most happily imagined. Another kind of sleeves is narrow at top without gathers or plaits, and wide at bottom with a turned-up cuff showing the satin lining edged by a ruche. At the top of the arm there is a fancy shoulder-knot with tags. These shoulder-knots as well as the *fourragères,* the frogs like those worn by hussars, ornaments in the guipure style, badges and medallions made with the crochet, the fichus and berthas of the same kind mixed with jet, are all worn more or less on rich plain goods.

Godey's Lady's Book, January 1861

Figures 1 and 2. – Visiting Costume and Girl's Dress.

We illustrate a dress designed for a Dinner or Visiting Toilet. While it may be made of any chosen material or colors, it is specially suited for plain fabrics of a single color. The corsage is high, with a somewhat rounded waist, and having *revers* or lappets; it is open one half its depth. The sleeves are funnel-shaped, cut open, the outside portions at the bottom being turned up and held in place by a tasseled cord, brought through, lacing the slashing of the upper sleeve. Under the opening made by the slashing a piece of the same is placed. The corsage is similarly laced and adorned with a rosette *passementerie*. The skirt is set on in wide plaits. For in-door wear, open lace under-sleeves are worn; but for out-doors closed under-sleeves, as in the illustration, are preferred. The coiffure is of pearl netting.

Harper's New Monthly Magazine, January 1861

PLATE I. – *Promenade* Dress.—Robe of droguet and manteau of brown cloth, trimmed with a guimpe torsade, closing it up the centre, and forming scroll at each side; it also edges the pelerine. Bonnet of velvet and satin.

Walking Dress. – Pelisse of black taffetas, ornamented by soutache and buttons. The sleeves are with revert, ornamented with bands of velvet and soutache as the body and skirt; bonnet of dark blue satin.

Dinner Dress. – Robe of green taffetas, corsage Gabrielle, trimmed with black guipure and ribbon, half-long sleeves, with revers. Ceinture of velvet, with nœud and long ends; two rows of guipure, headed by ribbon ornaments, the skirt guimpe, and sleeves of embroidered muslin, with small ruche round the throat. Coiffure of hair, with flowers intermixed with the back hair.

Ball dresses will be of tulle lamé, some of bouillonnes of tulle, or with several skirts ornamented with dentelle d'or, plats of gold and spangles, the guimpes prepared for them are particularly splendid, the rich dentelles d'or grelots, wheat, plats of gold and silver, gold guipure, spotted tulle, etc., formerly gold and silver were only used for splendid attire, but of late years they have both been commonly used on ball dresses; it is but rarely a toilette is seen without some gold, even on dress caps the velvet flowers have the centres of gold and often the foliage.

Guimpes are much used to ornament dresses and manteaux of velvet, and plain materials are seldom without them; it is no longer a simple little trimming, but forms a parure of itself, rivalling lace; it is made in pines and plaques of every colour, violet and black, marron and black, groseille and black and of pyramidal form, placed on the front of the skirts on black velvet; these plaques of violet and black are put on en tablier seven, five, etc., gradually diminishing to the top of the body for manteaux and all out-door costumes, even if lace is used, it is headed by guimpe. Pelerines entirely made of guimpe with deep fringes, or in Oriental designs, are preferred for manteaux of velvet.

PLATE II. – *Evening Dress.* – Robe of taffetas, with low body. The skirt is ornamented in the tunic style, with three frills, edged with pink fluted ribbon, the half-long sleeves to correspond. Fichu of tulle, trimmed with lace and ribbon, guimpe and sleeves of lace. Coiffure à l'Eugenie, ornamented with ribbon.

Child's Dress. – Frock of striped droguet, trimmed with velvet and guimpe ornaments. Sleeves with revers, and under ones of cambric muslin.

Carriage Dress. – Robe of taffetas, the body and skirt without division at the waist, buttoning from top to bottom. A single flounce, with heading at the bottom of the skirt, and similar ones terminating the bell sleeves. Chicorée forms jockey. Bonnet of velvet and satin, with flowers.

The fashion is tolerably decided as to the make of bodies, all are high, many of the Gabrielle form without having the waist defined in front and without ceinture, but rather different from last year's; the present style suits all figures and all toilettes, forming long casaque, increasing by gores to the bottom, from under the arm it is in large plaits as other dresses, the body high, exactly the same behind, plain and round at the waist, elbow sleeves with revers; the sleeves for dress toilettes are open and wide; for demi-toilette two styles prevail, those with elbow having jockeys, and revers open behind.

A Robe Imperatrice of violet taffetas, a gros grains had the bottom of the skirt trimmed with a wide band of violet velvet, edged by a small one of black pluche, and about the middle of the skirt a deep plissé of violet velvet also edged with black pluche, the corsage was without trimming, but buttoned as well as the skirt the whole length; the sleeves with revers of velvet fluted with a narrow black pluche.

PLATE III – *Evening Dress.* – Robe of moire, low body, with pelerine, berthe of white lace, crossing In front,, with rounded ends tying behind. The skirt is ornamented by several rows of ribbon ruches.

Carriage Dress. – Robe of taffetas, with pelisse to match. The skirt is covered by flounces edged with puffings of ribbon, and a row of black velvet above. A trimming composed of black velvet, edged at each side with flutings of ribbon, borders the pelisse, and ornaments the body and sleeves. Bonnet of satin and black lace.

Ball Dress. – Robe of white taffetas, with alternate flounces of white lace and taffetas pinked, put on in festons, with nœuds at the points; the berthe to correspond. Coiffure of hair in bandeaux, terminating in ringlets, with bunch of crysanthemums.

PLATE IV. – *Dinner Dress* – Robe of Magenta taffetas, trimmed with guimpe of the same colour. The bodice is made open, to show a lace habit shirt. The skirt is trimmed with narrow flounces, edged with guimpe, and placed in festoons round the bottom. Coiffure of flowers and velvet.

Evening Dress. – Robe of pink silk, made with a wide frill and puffings of silk to form a stomacher on the bodice, which is ornamented with flowers at the breast and on the sleeves. The skirt is trimmed to match.

Demi-Toilette. – Robe of lavender taffetas, trimmed on the bodice, which is made square over a muslin habit-shirt, and down the front with violet velvet, edged with a ruche. The sleeves are full, and drawn down into a ruche at the seam, and trimmed with the same. The coiffure of violet ribbon.

The London and Paris Ladies' Magazine of Fashion, January 1861

Dresses continue to be made long and full; there is said to be a tendency to have the skirts rather less voluminous, but we certainly have not yet seen any signs of such a change.

Bodies are still made high for walking and morning calls; for evening toilet low, with short, full sleeves.

Bertha and fichus, with long ends, are still worn, and are likely to be, for they are most becoming ornaments.

As for sleeves, they are extremely various; but the plain ones, and those with puffs, are only admissible for half dress.

The Art of the Hoop: 1860 - 1869

DRESS FOR EVENING PARTY.

Robe of pink gaze de Chambèry, with five goffered flounces, which are placed round the dress in such a manner as that the ends of three of them are brought up on one side of the skirt, where they terminate graduatingly, as shown our illustration. These three pieces of flouncing finish with a large simple bow without ends. The corsage is round, with a plaited front, the sleeves (of tulle) having three rows of narrow goffering descending from the base of the shoulder. To the back of the waist is attached a bow, from which depend two streamers of silk ribbon of the same color of the dress.

[*At the opera*] The dress worn by another of our leaders of fashion was composed of white tulle with two skirt, the lower one trimmed with ruches of bouillonné, and the upper one looped up on one side, and trimmed with a deep flounce of black lace. One dress, which was particularly admired for its simplicity, was made of white silk, and trimmed with seven flounces about four or five inches broad, and edged with groseille-colored silk.

ZOUAVE JACKET.

The engraving gives the detail of this garment, which has become quite a favorite. It is especially suited to persons of a slender figure. The trimming of the one we give is composed of heavy braidings on the outside, and is suited particularly for persons who desire effect. A plainer style of trimming is, we think, more appropriate.

Arthur's Home Magazine, February 1861

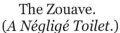

The Zouave.
(*A Négligé Toilet.*)

We vary our report for this month, and give an indoor costume instead of the pardessus to which we have hitherto confined our illustration. The season for the latter has so far advanced that no further novelties are desirable. Instead, therefore, of them, we present this graceful undress for home wear.

We need only explain that the ornamental design is wrought in gold braid upon a black cloth ground. This embroidery is much improved by a bright green silk cord, or braid, accompanying the gold, as the harmonizing effect of this color relieves the garnish crudity of the metal. The sleeves are also cross-laced with cording to match, completed by tassels.

Velvets, instead of cloth, make extremely beautiful and becoming articles of this description, and any favorite color may be employed.

We have just opened a pretty design for a dress of plain silk; the skirt full, the breadths gored without overlapping, and trimmed at the bottom by five narrow flounces, *fluted,* not plaited or gathered on, the upper part only being attached to the dress with a small heading. Between each flounce there is a space of about half an inch; the dress is of black silk, the flounces and headings being bound with white silk. The corsage is plain, and ornamented by a row of buttons, quite large, black with white centres. The sleeves are demi-wide at the lower part, and finished by turned-up cuffs or revers. These are cut with large scallops, and bordered by a narrow fluted frill of black silk edged with white. A similar frill extends up the back seam to the shoulder. The ceinture, or broad sash, is of black ribbon edged with white, the bow quite on one side.

The Promenade Dress.

Coat of black silk, having at the bottom a ruffle of purple silk, over which falls a rich lace. The bishop sleeves and small cape are trimmed to correspond.

The Zouave suite for little boy is made of poplin, braided.

One deep flounce or *plissé* of the same silk as the dress is also worn. If a *plissé*, it should be about ten inches wide, and the same distance from the bottom of the dress. If a flounce, it is about fourteen inches deep, headed by one row of wide black velvet ribbon, and several widths of narrow. A wide velvet is placed above the hem of the flounce, which is an inch deep, and corresponding rows of smaller ones.

Another skirt – the dress being violet silk – has three narrow flounces or ruffles around the bottom of the skirt, beaded by a *bouillonné* of the same. The corsage is low, and made high for ordinary wear by a small round pelerine, coming just on the shoulder, buttoned up in front, trimmed with a puff (*bouillonné*) and two frills. The sleeves are demi-wide, puff at the top; at the bottom the same trimming that is on the pelerine. Black velvet waist ribbon, bow, and long ends.

In some of the gored dresses – we mean where each separate breadth of a plain skirt is gored – one edge of each breadth is trimmed and made to lap over the next. It is a pretty style for some materials. Skirts gored in this way insure a good slope, and are generally becoming; but few people like to waste the material, and prevent all future repairs by turnings upside-down, where economy is a consideration, as we are glad to suppose it is with most of our readers.

Shirts having plastrons or a plain piece set on the front, variously ornamented, or side trimmings of lace, ruches, or passementerie, are frequently seen; also plain skirts, with *pateés* of passementerie, mixed with jet or tassels, and most elegant of all, flat bows of guipure lace, are perhaps the favorite style of the larger part of the community the present season. The trimming on corsage, sleeve, and skirt should always correspond.

Godey's Lady's Book, February 1861

PLATE I. – *Dinner Dress.* – Robe of taffetas, the body is high with a trimming of pinked frills forming plastron of a square form on the body and descending en tablier down the skirt, sleeves with cuffs and epaulets.

Morning Dress. – Robe of droguet, the body is full, fastening down the body and skirt with small buttons and ceinture of wide ribbon with large nœud at the side, half-long sleeves with deep culls, edged by a plisse of ribbon, coiffure of hair and ribbon.

Child's Dress. – Frock of pink popeline, the skirt is ornamented by two biais up the sides, edged by two rows of narrow black velvet and buttons in the centre. Zouave jacket and chemisette of white muslin with sleeves.

Chere Amie, – The toilettes for outdoor use continue much the same, for neglige various fancy articles of cloth, silk for demi-toilette, and velvet for richer style of dress. Light colours are not worn at all in morning toilette, the form Imperatrice cut bias and the body without separation from the front breadth is the style most generally adopted, scarcely any other is used except for very rich materials, and even for these when the body is required to be high; the dress is trimmed in front with buttons matching the colours prevailing in the material.

A very splendid new material rivals velvet this season in Paris for full dress, it is black lampas with bouquets Pompadour embroidered in the material, others of light colours checked in another shade with stars of gold or silver thread.

PLATE II. – *Carriage Dress.* – Robe of satin and manteau of cloth trimmed with black velvet and ornamented with tassels. Bonnet of white satin with coral coloured flowers.

Ball Dress. – Robe of tulle with treple skirt, the two under ones ornamented with bouquets of flowers put on at intervals, the upper skirt plain, looped up at the side by a chatelaine and nœud with ends of white satin; the body with berthe in folds, and edged with lace, short bouillon sleeves with flowers as on the skirt, and similar ones in the hair with nœud of black velvet at the back.

Evening Dress. – Robe of pink satin. Opera cloak of green velvet trimmed with ermine. Coiffure of hair with flowers.

Ball dresses are still made with double skirts. A robe of white satin was covered by three skirts of tulle; at the bottom of each was a ruche of white taffetas pinked and placed a little above the hem; these three skirts were gradually raised on the left side, supported by a chatelaine of poppies, corsage drapé, short bouffantes sleeves with double square sleeves entirely open and floating. Another toilette was of pink tarlatane; on the skirt were fourteen Pompadour flounces fluted, pointed body with berthe of tarlatane trimmed with frills, bouffante sleeves, at the point of the body in front a nœud Duchesse of tarlatane trimmed with a plissé of pink ribbon. Most are with tunic skirts this winter, and when the tunic is of tulle it is termed Voile. Tarlatane has rather lost favour. Tulle is the most fashionable, with gauze satinée, plain or spotted with gold; for young ladies, however, tarlatane is used with pinked flounces, or trimmed with narrow velvet or ruches; the flounces are to the knee, and a Voile of tulle is on the skirt attached by nœuds and flowers, sometimes the tunic is the same trimmed with a narrow flounce or a bouillonne.

PLATE III. – *Morning Dress* – Robe of French moire, the body and skirt in one, and ornamented by black velvet, which descends from the shoulders to the waist, from which it gradually widens and is continued round the bottom of the skirt, a row of buttons from top to bottom, bell sleeves with velvet cuffs. Coiffure of hair and velvet ribbon.

Walking Dress. – Manteau of black moire with pelerine, ornamented by a deep band of velvet, a second forms a collar. Bonnet of satin ornamented with black lace and velvet, roses at the side.

Carriage Dress. – Pelisse of satin, opened in front and trimmed with a bouillon edged by narrower ones, the body is open to the waist with a plissé at the edge, the sleeves in bouillons with plissés between and cuffs. Straw hat turned up with velvet and long feather.

The London and Paris Ladies' Magazine of Fashion, February 1861

All dresses for full toilet are made with wide, open sleeves. Closed sleeves are only admitted for half dress or négligé. Flounces are still worn as trimming for skirts; they are too graceful a variety to be ever entirely set aside.

PROMENADE DRESS – HOME COSTUME.

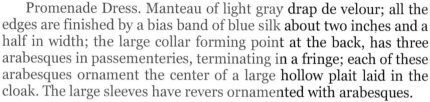

Promenade Dress. Manteau of light gray drap de velour; all the edges are finished by a bias band of blue silk about two inches and a half in width; the large collar forming point at the back, has three arabesques in passementeries, terminating in a fringe; each of these arabesques ornament the center of a large hollow plait laid in the cloak. The large sleeves have revers ornamented with arabesques.

Home Costume. Dress of green silk; at the bottom of skirt a flounce about ten inches in depth set on with a narrow heading; a small space is left, then three narrow flounces; another space, then a flounce about eight inches deep; another space, and then two narrow flounces; the flounces all edged with an extremely narrow black velvet. Plain high body, closing with small black velvet buttons; ceinture of black velvet buckling in the front. The wide sleeves are open to the shoulder, and are covered by narrow flounces; they are held together by straps of narrow velvet place at the edge of each flounce. Bouillon sleeves of Brussels net; cap of the same; the narrow bouillon forming border, looped with velvet, at the back, lappets edged with velvet; at the left side a rosette of white ribbon, from which fall long ends edged with narrow velvet.

The short oriental jackets, to which the name of Zouaves has been given, continue in high favor. They are very pretty garments for home négligé. We also see a good number of casaques, bordered with stripes of quilted silk, of a contrasting color, and having pockets in front. These casaques are neither more or less than a revival of the bodies with long lappets, which were in fashion some time ago, except that they have on all the seams a colored welt, always of the same tint as the silk at the edges.

DINNER DRESS,

Of green silk, trimmed with quilled ribbon. The front breadth is gored; sleeve cut loose, with gauntlet cuff.

For ordinary evening parties, where there is no dancing, dresses are often made half low, square across, in what is called the Raphael style. This is not a novelty; but as every possible form has already been worn at some time or other, nothing can be absolutely new.

Flowers for balls are worn in round garlands, sometimes with trailing branches; nothing can be more graceful.

Arthur's Home Magazine, March 1861

Cotton Balmoral petticoats, in the same neat, light colors that have distinguished those in wool, silk and wool, etc. the past winter, will be found a most serviceable article for spring wear, or for travelling through the season. They are much lighter, and of course cooler than those our readers are generally familiar with. They are also suitable as an underskirt for equestrians.

Barège Anglais is still expected to be the popular fabric for street dress in the summer heats, both in and out of mourning – large importations have been made. At Benson's we find some entirely new designs in black and purple, gray and white, white and lilac, etc., distinguished by the dotted, striped, and *chiné* grounds, and a set figure *printed* upon the material; as, for instance, a mauve pansy without leaves, on a black ground.

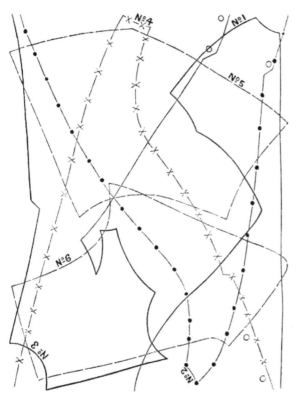

IMPERIAL BASQUINE FOR A LADY.

This garment, for winter, is made of stout cloth or velvet; for summer, thin cloth or silk. When made of cloth it has a pretty binding or narrow velvet turned over the edge; when silk, it is trimmed with guipure and has velvet buttons.

The skirt of the side-piece of the back laps over on the skirt of the back, so as to form a plait like that seen in men's coats. At regular intervals, large buttons like the trimming fasten the two skirts together. The sides remain open, but require a trimming similar to that of the back.

In front, the skirt laps over on the side-piece and offers the same repetition of trimming as the skirt of the back.

No. 1. Back. Half a yard in length and width to be added to the pattern.

No. 2. Side-piece of back. Add 10 inches in length and 12 in breadth.

No. 3. Front. Add 17 inches in length, 23 inches in width. It is fastened by large buttons.

No. 4. Side-piece of front. Add 8 inches in length, and 26 inches in width.

No. 5. Under side of sleeve.

No. 6. Upper side of sleeve. It is to be trimmed like the skirt.

Puffed sleeves, whether in a straight graduation from the shoulder to the wrist, or two above the elbow terminating in a tight sleeve below, will be worn for the plainer materials, early silks, etc.; the black velvet point, or bodice-girdle as it might be described, is suitable for the same materials. It is a very favorite style, nearly superseding the broad scarf-girdles.

Godey's Lady's Book, March 1861

Figure 1. – Carriage Dress.

The Carriage Dress, illustrated on the preceding page, is decidedly novel, as well as serviceable, being well adapted not only for the carriage, but for a home-toilet, upon occasions when full dress is not required. The only ornament of the buttons and the cording of the side-frill at the top of the skirt. The dress from which our illustration is copied is of fillemot-colored silk; the style may be produced in almost any kind material.

Harper's New Monthly Magazine, March 1861

EVENING DRESS.

This dress, of which we give an illustration, is remarkable for its elegance of style, united with the most perfect simplicity.

Very little trimming is worn on the bodies of high dresses; the *ceinture Suissesse* is again coming into fashion for both morning and evening dresses.

Arthur's Home Magazine, April 1861

For walking dresses, plain silks or small stripes are much in vogue; the skirts are much trimmed up the front with fan-shaped ornaments of silk edged with lace, *pattés* of velvet and lace, etc. etc.; *bouillonnés* and ruches are much in favor; also, small flounces at the bottom of the skirt; many are sewed on in waves. We notice a very *récherché* dress of wine-colored silk with five small flounces at the bottom of the skirt, then a row of bows placed *à volonté,* then five more small flounces; the body is plain, with a point; sleeves loose, and trimmed with flounces and bows to match the skirt.

We have seen some black silk dresses with *bouillonnés* of apple green or violet silk, edged with a ruche of black guipure, inserted between every breadth of the skirt, which had a charming effect. Some dresses are made with the skirt perfectly plain in front, the plaits commencing about two inches on either side of the centre.

The Zouave jacket, with Greek vest, or full embroidered muslin shirt falling about two inches over the skirt still continues a favorite both for ladies and children, and is made of both thick and thin materials.

Godey's Lady's Book, April 1861

Figures 2 and 3. – Morning Negligee.

The Morning Negligee, in the above illustration is adapted for any fabric. We present it composed of two materials: the one of black taffeta, braid ornamenting; the other of white merino, with embroidered needle-work.

Harper's New Monthly Magazine, April 1861

The skirts are invariably full, and the custom recently introduced, of cutting gores from the top of the breadths, to render the skirt less ample at the waist than at the lower part, is now very generally followed for silk dresses. The richest and most beautiful silks which have yet appeared are figured with bouquets of flowers, and some having a black ground, ornamented with flowers of various tints, have been much admired.

SPRING FASHIONS

Home Costume. – Dress of green poplin, the skirt long and full, without any ornament. *Zouave* jacket, bordered entirely round by *Arabesques* in gold; it closes at the top with gold buttons and loops of gold cord. Wide sleeves, open at the back of the arm, and trimmed the same as the jacket; gold buttons and cord at the opening, so that the sleeves may be closed at pleasure.

Home or Visiting Costume. – Robe *Chinois* of blue silk, with open tunic of the same. The skirt is trimmed *à la robe*, with dark claret velvet, the upper edge cut in festoons, and corded with amber silk. The point of each festoon is finished by an amber button. The tunic is trimmed to correspond, the points of the velvet all meeting at the waist, under a silver clasp. The plain, high body, is sewn on to the tunic; it has a *plastron* of velvet to correspond with trimming of the skirt; tight-shaped sleeves, with velvet jockeys and cuffs.

Some of the richest evening dresses are composed of satin or silk, trimmed either with flounces of lace, or having a tunic of splendid lace over the skirt. A dress of cerulean blue silk has just been trimmed with a flounce of Alençon lace, surmounted by a quilling of silk, edged with a narrow row of the same lace. Beneath the flounce, and quite on the edge of the dress, there is a light ruche of silk, pinked.

Dresses for the *promenade* are all made high, the waists round, with either the *suissesse ceinture* of black velvet, or the narrow *ceinture* with clasp or buckle. Tight sleeves are decidedly becoming fashionable; they have always *epaulettes* or puffings and deep pointed cuffs. The wide open sleeve, as well as that of a more moderate size, with *rever* turned back, are still in favor.

Arthur's Home Magazine, May 1861

The Art of the Hoop: 1860 - 1869

Fig. 4 – Rich purple silk, with plain round waist with velvet belt. The skirt is made three-quarters of a yard longer than usual, and is drawn up at intervals to the proper length, forming puffs, with pointed pieces of purple velvet put on to cover the seams. This is one of the newest trimmings, and ivory stylish. The sleeves are done in the same manner. Black straw hat, with peacock plumes.

THE CHEVRON ORGANDY DRESS.

We saw a few seven and five flounced robes, but the novelty of the season is the Chevron dress, of which we give a cut in the front of the Book (page 387). This dress has diagonal stripes of *rose de chiné,* about an inch and a half in width, meeting in the centre of the breadth, and between these stripes are bouquets of roses with their foliage, which has a charming effect. We have had this design in silk, but this is the first appearance of diagonal stripes on muslin.

Godey's Lady's Book, May 1861

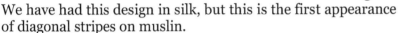

The prevailing favourite colours are grey, mignonette, periwinkle, Persian lilac, a new print of soft lilac tint, pale green, and porcelaine blue, etc.

PLATE I. – *Public Promenade Dress*. – Robe of checked taffetas, with tight high body, ornamented down the front with nœuds of taffetas, edged by black lace. Pagoda sleeves with plisses and nœuds to correspond. Bonnet of mauve crape with white feathers.

Carriage Dress. – Robe of moire, with jacket-body closing up the front with buttons, and edged all round by a ruche of taffetas, the large open sleeve to correspond. Bonnet of white satin and crape with carnations.

Morning Dress. – Robe of poil de chevre; the body is open, with revers trimmed with a fluting of ribbon, two rows of the same ornament the skirt as tunic. Mousquetaire sleeves, with cuffs similarly finished, round cap of tulle, with trimmings of lace and red ribbon.

The robe Imperatrice is preferred to all others for demi toilette or negligé, which is regulated by the material. Thus mohairs, thick taffetas, broché materials, if made with high body are mostly of the Imperatrice form, which name is given to the dresses that are not separated from the front breadth of the skirt; the sleeves worn with this body are of the Mousquetaire form with revers – the *nervures* of the body and front breadth are often ornamented with guimps or niches of taffetas, similar to the material of the dress. When this style of dress is objected to the body is made high, round at the waist, or with very small point; the round body is however mostly used. With this the ceinture Medici of velvet is very fashionable just now, as well as the ribbon scarf one, very wide with fringe. There is also a kind made of urise [cerise?] or green velvet to wear with low bodies of tarlatane. The point is deeper than that of the Medici ceinture, and has points also under the arms.

PLATE II. – *Carriage Dress*. – Robe of taffetas, broché ornamented by bands of black velvet; the body is plain, with small buttons up the front, ceinture of velvet with long ends; the sleeves are open to the armhole. Bonnet of mauve taffetas, with feathers at the side.

Walking Dress. – Robe of gros grain of the Imperatrice form the skirt hanging in deep flutes; scarf of deep blue taffetas, embroidered with velvet. Bonnet of white crin, trimmed with flutings of ribbon and flowers.

Evening Dress. – Robe of pink satin, the skirt is ornamented by three rows of tulle fluted, and black lace; low body, with berthe similar to the trimmings on the skirt. Short bouillon sleeves, with white tulle, one under. Coiffure of hair in ringlets, with feathers at the side.

We again see the dresses with flounces, particularly for summer materials what could be substituted for them on bareges, muslins, or organdy; even some taffetas are with flounces. One of black had very narrow flounces piped with violet taffetas. Some are put on in the apron style, each band encircling the dress with about eight flounces. Others have trimmings made of thick ruches of the same material as the dress edged by white taffetas.

PLATE III. – *Dinner Dress*. – Robe of grey taffetas; the body has a berthe formed of ribbon plissé and black lace, the sleeves to correspond, and deep flounce of black lace on the skirt, with plissé of ribbon above and below it.

Promenade Dress. – Robe of taffetas, closing up the centre with buttons, a trimming of mauve, fluted taffetas forms bretelles on the body, and descend each side of the skirt.

PLATE IV. – *Carriage Dress*. – Robe of moire, with ornaments of guimp up the skirt and body, and also on the bell sleeve, which is finished with a fringe. Bonnet of crape and taffetas, with feathers.

Walking Dress. – Pelisse of taffetas, open from the waist, and trimmed all round with a plissé; a deep flounce on the under skirt with heading, and edged at the bottom with a plissé. Bonnet of straw, with soft crown of coloured silk and ruches.

The London and Paris Ladies' Magazine of Fashion, May 1861

DINNER COSTUME FOR HOME.

High dress of pearl gray silk, the skirt having narrow flounces arranged in festoons; in the front of the skirt, the flounces are of pearl gray silk, bound with mauve silk; on each side of these is a smaller festoon of mauve silk flounces; again, a large festoon of the gray flounces, and so on, entirely round the skirt, the whole headed by a small mauve rouleau. The plain, high body has a trimming à la bèrthe, composed of three frills, those crossing the back and front of gray silk, edged with mauve, those on the shoulders of mauve silk. The sleeves are tight, with two bouffants at the top, one gray, the other mauve; deep pointed cuff, of rich lace, with a double ruffle falling over the hand.

Arthur's Home Magazine, June 1861

Quilting dresses in all colors, with pardessus to match, are the most *distingué* walking-dress for the country or seaside this season.

Surplice dresses with revers, or the dresses crossing in front and fastening at the side are much worn. Ribbons seem to be the favorite trimming. They are goffered and placed at the bottom of the skirt, either sloping or in lozenges, sometimes of two colors in alternate portions about a quarter of a yard in length. Some of the charming spring dresses are bordered by five rows of narrow satin ribbon, plaited, others are ornamented with a front trimming consisting of bows of ribbon of the same color as the dress, passing one above, another from the edge to the point in the centre of the corsage. A bow of the same ribbon is fixed at the top of the corsage in front.

LATEST FASHIONS.

Fig. 1. – Dress of Mozambique, gray ground, with Magenta flowers. The dress is gored; body and skirt in one piece; the skirt bound with Magenta silk, and Magenta ribbon bows up the front of the dress.

Fig. 2. – Dress of gray summer poplin. Skirt plain; the body has lapels trimmed with blue silk, and a linen collar turned over on this lapel. The sleeves have a blue gauntlet cuff. Sash of gray poplin, bound with blue silk. Blue chenille net, trimmed with ribbons.

For young ladies, most of the dresses are made low in the neck, in order to wear the very becoming spencers now so much in vogue. These are of muslin, embroidered, or else puffed, the puffs running lengthwise or crosswise as taste may dictate, or else puffed only to form a yoke. The one in our plate is intersected lengthwise with velvet, which gives it more style; ribbons or black lace can be substituted, or the spencer can be sprinkled with small bows of ribbon or velvet. The sleeves can be long or short, but most of them are puffed to the wrist. Black and white lace spencers are also much worn, and are very pretty for evening, particularly so when worn with a Spanish corsage of black velvet or some bright-tinted silk.

Fig. 1. – Zouave jacket and vest for dotted muslin, trimmed with a ruche of the same, through which is passed a braid, or narrow velvet ribbon of some bright color; bow of the same shade. This is an extremely simple and serviceable pattern, easily done up as the ribbon is only caught on; and as the jacket will be almost universal the present season (together with the white spencer and black velvet point), we consider the present design very serviceable.

Zouave jackets are worn both for morning and full dress; for the former they are made of the same material as the skirt, or else of white *piqué*, braided or embroidered. We have seen some very pretty ones with a narrow vine running all round them, and large bunches at each corner in front, smaller ones being placed at the neck where the jacket is fastened, also in the middle of the neck behind, and just above the hem or scallop at the back, directly in the centre. Colored braids are much used on the *piqué,* and the effect is good. Some of the shirts have a frill down the front plaited like a shirt frill and decorated with velvet. ... The evening Zouaves are made of mull muslin, embroidered, with shirts to match, or figured blonde lace trimmed with ruching or narrow blonde edge; the skirt is also of lace. This last style of Zouave is quite new, particularly light and graceful, and at the same time stylish.

Godey's Lady's Book, June 1861

PLATE I. – *Public Promenade Dress.* – Robe of moire with body and skirt without division at the waist, the skirt hangs in deep flutes, and is ornamented at the bottom with plisses headed by ruches and bouillons between the body high with berthe pelerine, sleeves in bouillons. Bonnet of paille de riz with soft crown of the azuline colour and white feather.

Evening Dress. – Robe of lilac gauze, the skirt ornamented by ruches, the body open en cœur with folds and ruches, very large sleeves of white tulle over shorter ones, coiffure of hair in bandeaux and ringlets with flowers.

Carriage Dress. – Robe of fancy silk, with high body closing down the centre with large fancy buttons. Pelisse of black silk, with pelerine trimmed with a rich fringe and guimpe heading, large sleeves, edged with a plisse of ribbon. Bonnet of Leghorn straw with flowers.

Dresses continue to be made very full and very bouffantes, the style being similar to that in favour during the winter, the materials being merely lighter in colour and less heavy in texture; flounces, ruches, plissés, of every kind. Plain dresses are not much worn, even for young ladies; some kind of trimming is preferred, more especially on the skirt. Many of the summer dresses will be with open bodies, particularly muslins, either white or coloured, inside of them. A little embroidered chemisette trimmed with Valenciennes, the sleeves of various forms, some with revers with a deep hem, trimmed with Valenciennes lace.

The make of sleeves is much the same, and they are a good deal ornamented. Ceintures with points and very long nœuds are much worn still; it is doubtful that they will be generally used this summer, but they may be made of silk the colour of the dress. They are prettier of velvet on dark dresses, and in light colours on white tarlatane or organdy, as white dress with ceinture pointed before and behind, of taffetas, white pink or sea green. Guimpes also afford numerous methods of ornamenting silk bodies and confections, which this year will have guipures, fringes, ruches, or pelerine, even on the casaques, which, of a loose form, seems the favourite style for walking costume.

The Art of the Hoop: 1860 - 1869

PLATE III. – *Dinner Dress.* – Robe of green taffetas, the corsage of the square form with stole of velvet descending the sides of the skirt and puffings of ribbon, rosaces of lace down the centre of the skirt, the sleeves mosquetaire, the cuffs to correspond with trimming of the skirt, guimpe of lace with ruche round the throat and bouillon sleeves.

Walking Dress. – Robe of taffetas, closing the whole length with small buttons, band and buckle at the waist, the sleeves are full with pinked ruches length ways, and cuffs edged with ruches.

Evening Dress. – Robe of white taffetas, the body is pointed with berthe of lace and mauve ribbon edged with black velvet, the skirt is ornamented by a mauve ribbon edged with black velvet, and fluting of white ribbon put on in deep Vandykes with large nœuds of white satin ribbon between coiffure à l'Eugenie, with ribbon in puffings across the head terminating in nœuds.

PLATE IV. –*Carriage Dress.* – Robe of taffetas, with high body, trimmed en tablier with pinked frills terminated at each side by a chicoree continued up the body, a deep flounce round the bottom of the skirt. Bonnet of crape and lace, and scarf of muslin with frill headed by a bouillon.

Promenade Dress.—Robe and pelisse of taffetas, the pelisse is open in front and rounded off, trimmed with a wide plissé which also edges the large open sleeve and revers of the body.

The London and Paris Ladies' Magazine of Fashion, June 1861

ZOUAVE SHIRT.

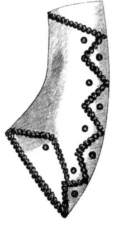

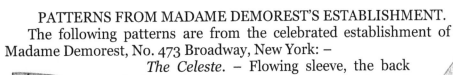

PATTERNS FROM MADAME DEMOREST'S ESTABLISHMENT.

The following patterns are from the celebrated establishment of Madame Demorest, No. 473 Broadway, New York: –

The Celeste. – Flowing sleeve, the back laid over the front in points, and trimmed with braid and buttons. ↖

Zuleika Sleeve. – An elegant sleeve, in the style of the Arab hood Decorations tassels and buttons. →

Lelie Sleeve. – Flowing sleeve, with revers and straps, bound with velvet, and ornamented with buttons. ←

Godey's Lady's Book, July 1861

Summer Fashions. – The lady's dress is gored, and with button trimming from the throat down. Loose sleeves.

Morning Robe. – The style of this garment is chaste as well as elegant. A portion of the front breadth is white, crossed with embroidery. Linen collar and sleeves, finished with narrow ruffle.

Arthur's Home Magazine, July 1861

We illustrate two styles for Home toilet, the elegance and simplicity of which will commend them to favor. The fullness of detail in the illustrations precludes the necessity of verbal description.

Figure 1. – Home Toilet.

Figure 2. – Home Toilet.

Harper's New Monthly Magazine, July 1861

At length the light robes belonging to the season have made their appearance: the most popular are *barege,* garnished with flounces. For *negligée* and the country, *piqués* and mixed fabrics are in favour. For dress, silk-grenadines, *taffetas,* and French *moire* quadrilled with satin of divers colours, such as pale-yellow, blue, green, rose, &c., the grounds preferred being white or pearl grey.

The Ladies' Companion, July 1861

PLATE I. – *Promenade Dress* – Redingote of taffetas, ornamented up the front by bands of velvet en tablier, which are continued on the body; mousquetaire sleeves, with cuffs and epaulets, edged with velvet. Bonnet of paille Beige, with field flowers.

Young Lady's Dress. – Robe of alpaga, closing with small buttons; manteau of taffetas, edged with quilted band. Turban hat, with white feather.

The Art of the Hoop: 1860 - 1869

Skirts continue to be worn full and long; the bodies are pointed, or round at the waist, according to taste.

PLATE IV. – *Promenade Dress*. – Robe taffetas with square body, trimmed with a ruche. The skirt has a flounce festonné, and headed by two ruches in deep scollops, and upper skirt festonné; small mantelet of the same, with frill, the upper part covered with ruches. Leghorn hat, with feather.

Morning Dress. – Robe of mohair, with corsage open in front and edged by a band of taffetas; full sleeves, crossed by bands, and a wider band round the bottom of the skirt. Small round cap, with flowers.

Walking Dress. – Robe of poil de chevre; the body is covered by a small pelerine, edged by a black lace ruche, full sleeves with deep cuffs. The skirt is trimmed with two rows of plisse at the bottom. Bonnet of crin, with flowers.

Muslin bodies will be much worn, with silk or grenadine dresses, or even jaconet. They recall the former fashion of spencers, with a little modification. Some are made of organdy, the sleeves closing with a ruche of Valenciennes, and the same round the throat. A low body is worn under either, of the colour of the skirt, or all white, which is most usual, the skirt only being coloured. Guimpes of embroidered muslin or jaconet are worn with the little Zouave jacket. The long Medicis ceinture, with points before and behind, with long revers of silk fringe, complete a youthful toilette.
The London and Paris Ladies' Magazine of Fashion, July 1861

SUMMER COSTUME.

The jacket and skirt are of white *piqué*, trimmed with two rows of very narrow colored braid. As the jacket is only intended for morning wear, it is much longer than the ordinary Zouave; with it is worn a shirt with plaited linen bosom, and fancy silk neck-tie. Tuscan braid hat, trimmed black velvet and straw.

THE NANNETTE.
Organdy dress, with white muslin fichu. White straw hat, trimmed with black velvet and game plumes.

THE NINA.
White muslin dress, with plaited waist; finished at the throat with a lace muff. Spanish corsage of fancy colored silk, trimmed with quilled ribbon and buttons.
Godey's Lady's Book, August 1861

Surplice dresses, and dresses crossing in front and fastening at the side, are much worn.

Dresses for young ladies are generally made low, in order to wear with them, the very pretty spencers of white muslin just now in fashion. They are either embroidered or puffed; the puffs running lengthwise or horizontally, according to taste. Some are puffed only, to form a yoke, when the style allows of it. Black ribbon velvet intersected longitudinally has a very pretty effect; lace or ribbon may be introduced instead, so as to vary the toilet when desired: the puffings may be sprinkled with little bows. Most of the sleeves are puffed to the wrist; but they may be made either long or short.

The Ladies' Companion, August 1861

FASHIONS FOR SEPTEMBER.

Fig. 1. – Dress of colored muslin; the skirt long and full, has at the hem a plaiting of *mauve* ribbon, which constitutes its only ornament. The low body, in the *Agnes Sorrel* style, has the waist round, with *ceinture écharpe* of broad *mauve* ribbon, the ends falling nearly to the bottom of the dress: a plaiting of ribbon finishes the top of the body, and is continued down the centre of front to the waist. The full bishop sleeve is three-quarter length, and terminated by a lace ruffle; it is gathered at the seam in the front of the arm, the seam being covered by a plaiting of ribbon.

Fig. 2. – Plain high dress, of lilac *moire antique*, the skirt without ornament. *Paletot* of rich black silk, the form half tight; the edges are corded with white silk, and at each side is a *montant*, also corded with white. The *montant* is ornamented by three triangular pieces of silk, enclosed by a white cord, and having a *arabesque* in each, worked in white; on the fronts, just below the collar, are *arabesques* to correspond. The wide, loose sleeves, are slightly shaped at the elbow, have pointed *epaulettes* and *revers* at the bottom; these are edged with white, and have *arabesques* the same as on the skirt.

Fig. 3. – Dress of *organdi*, the design *pompadour*, with blue stripes between, arranged in points. The body is high, the waist round; the dress is ornamented up the front by *pompoms* of the same material as the dress. Small bishop sleeve, the bottom not set into a band, but left plain.

Arthur's Home Magazine, September 1861

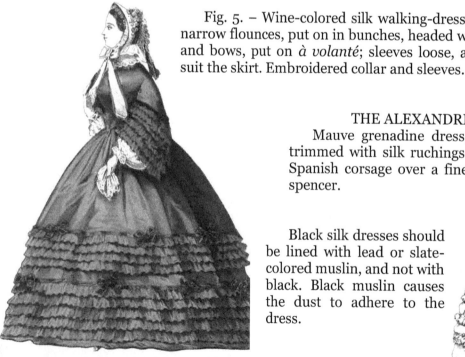

Fig. 5. – Wine-colored silk walking-dress, trimmed with narrow flounces, put on in bunches, headed with black velvet and bows, put on *à volanté*; sleeves loose, and trimmed to suit the skirt. Embroidered collar and sleeves.

THE ALEXANDRINE.
Mauve grenadine dress, trimmed with silk ruchings. Spanish corsage over a fine spencer.

Black silk dresses should be lined with lead or slate-colored muslin, and not with black. Black muslin causes the dust to adhere to the dress.

The Art of the Hoop: 1860 - 1869

THE MATHILDE.

Made of dark blue silk, with three bias folds, edged with a ribbon ruffle. The pockets are trimmed to match.

Godey's Lady's Book, September 1861

Figures 1 and 2. – Dinner Toilet and Promenade Costume.

The Dinner Toilet is made of mauve taffeta. The Corsage is half-high, round waist, *revers* front, with a frill of Valenciennes lace. Madonna fichu, closed in front by small gold buttons. The Valenciennes is continued from the waist, waved down the front of the skirt; a *passementerie* of black rosettes is placed at each folding of the lace. The sleeves, which are laid in plaits, are banded in four divisions; with frills of lace, *en suite,* forming cuffs. As every lady of taste consults that style of coiffure which is individually most becoming to her countenance, we do not think it necessary to specify any special mode.

Promenade Costume. – The material is a gray foulard; plain close body, cut in one with skirt. The cape and bottom of skirt are trimmed with a reversed plaiting. The dress has buttons down the entire front. The sleeves are made to fall open, handkerchief style, from a small puff at the top of each. The under-sleeves have two flounces.

Harper's New Monthly Magazine, September 1861

The reign of flounces continues, but we see a crowd of other garnitures. Here a deep flounce, with a plaited heading; there several flounces, surmounted by, or over, a *bouillonné*. A very popular style of ornament is a coloured band of plain silk, of a brilliant contrast with the sadeh [?] of the material; another, not nearly so general, is made by setting on a deep *biais* fulled as high as the knee, and divided at intervals by *ruches,* buttons, or bands of silk or velvet.

Barege dresses are frequently made with five or seven narrow flounces. White muslin robes are in great vogue for elegant dress at the watering places, where they give many *soirées dansantes*; in which case nothing so well replaces a veritable *robe de bal.* They are garnished with embroidered flounces, or with goffred *volants de Pompadour,* or *bouillonnés;* in short, caprice is the order of the day, and everything pretty and graceful is the fashion. Dresses of *barège,* silk *grenadin,* and *tarlatane* are also much employed on the same occasions. Corsages are made both high and low, according to the material, and the purpose of the dress. Wide sleeves and those with elbows and *revers* are preferred. I spoke in my last letter of the revival of muslin shawls and mantelets – these are always fresh and convenient, especially for the toilet *de campagne.* Black shawls of embroidered cachemere and garnished with lace are very much worn, but so are a great many other shawls of silk *grenadin,* with satin borders and embroidered in the corners. Grey paletots and *burnous* have a constant vogue, and the same may be said of the black silk *pardessus.*

The Ladies' Companion, September 1861

NEW STYLE JACKETS.

We give three of the newest forms: –

The loose jacket in Fig. 1 is made of various materials; for instance, cloth, cashmere, and cashmerette. The trimming is narrow beaded velvet, in which are inserted small squared of moire. The jacket is lined with silk.

Fig. 2. – (*Zouave Jacket.*) – The same materials as those used for the loose jacket depicted in Fig. 1 may be employed for this. The most elegant are, however, made of glacé or velvet. The embroidery is in a rich and light pattern.

Fig. 3. – This jacket fits closely to the figure, and is made of cloth, ornamented with trimmings, in the military style.

For the cooler weather that we are now having, these garments are well suited, and they are of such simple forms, that they may readily be made at home, the trimming adapted to the wearer's taste.

Corsages are made either high or low, according to the style of costume for which the dress is required, and the material of which it is composed. Wide sleeves, and those shaped to the elbow with revers, are in general favor.

Arthur's Home Magazine, October 1861

Fig. 1. – Morning costume. Robe of rich gray taffetas broche in small bouquets, or tiny fruit, of a violet or cerise color. The skirt is gored in front, and fastened with knots of ribbon the same shade as the figure in the silk. Over this is worn a casaque of the same material, trimmed with a border of quilled ribbon, and having wide open sleeves, which display the elegant undersleeves of mull, drawn on the front of the arm with narrow ribbon to match the trimming of the dress. Full chemisette of mull muslin, and a silk net which confines the hair in a loose knot, complete a most elegant morning toilet.

An elegant dress intended for dinner costume has just been made of silver gray silk, figured with a Pompadour pattern of various hues, cerulean blue being the predominating color. The lower part of the skirt is ornamented with a trimming in blue and rose-color, the two intertwined so as to form a chain pattern. The corsage is low, and with it is worn a fichu of thulle puffs. A sash of the same silk as the dress is fastened in a bow with long ends, the trimming on the ends corresponding with that on the skirt.

A Bishop sleeve. Sufficiently wide to show the present style of undersleeve. A side cap, with pendent ends, is laid on the upper part of the sleeve, and a plain band connects under the points and confines it slightly, and forms a puff.

← Simple close sleeve.

→ Pretty close sleeve, for a dress sleeve open in front; the puff of Swiss muslin has a worked inserting the whole length, which shirs the sleeve to shape it to the arm. The wristlet is composed of alternate puffs and insertings.

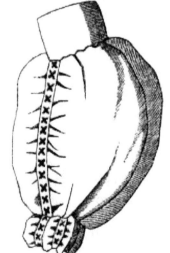

The style of dress known as the "Gabrielle" will still be popular this fall for street or house dresses, for the mixed woollen stuffs especially. It is more generally known as the "gored dress." The *Imperatrice* is a decided improvement on the original Gabrielle; it is more graceful and more easily worn by all figures. In front it is formed like a long casaque, widening considerably at the bottom. At the seam, under the arm, there are wide plaits, like other dresses, and the back is flat and rounded at the waist; the sleeves are with elbows and turned back cuffs.

A favorite style for trimming these dresses is a bound band of velvet placed two or three inches above the edge of the skirt, and not quite meeting in front, where the ends are pointed and either turned back …

or held plainly in their place by fancy button.

In a rich dark material we have seen a flounce of guipure lace, set on with slight fulness in the same way, but continued up the front on each side of the waist quite plain, so as to appear like the trimmings of a tunic skirt. From the waist the lace, which has been narrowed to shape to the front, is carried up the corsage, and descends from each shoulder to the centre of the waist at the back, where the two ends are crossed over the other after the fashion of lappets. A trimming passementerie heads the lace. A row of lace button extends down the front of the dress.

Skirts are worn as ample and full as ever, and are generally gored to throw them out at the bottom. Stiff muslin petticoats, with flounces, or one deep flounce at the bottom, are very suitable for wearing with evening-dresses, as they set the dresses out in a more graceful manner than does a very large crinoline. A moderate-sized steel petticoat, and a muslin one – with, of course, a plain one over it – make a muslin dress look very nicely. We are told that the Empress usually wears one of these muslin petticoats, with a series of narrow flounces to the waist. Of course, this style would not suit every one, on account of the difficulty and expense of washing, etc.

Godey's Lady's Book, October 1861

PLATE I. – *Promenade Dress.* – Robe of taffetas, with plain high body, ornamented with buttons; embroidered shawl, trimmed with black lace; Leghorn bonnet, with trimmings of black velvet and feathers.

Walking Dress. – Paletot of black taffetas, buttoning the whole length, and ornamented round the bottom by a band of mauve silk and black velvet: small bell sleeves with cuffs, and pelerine with similar trimming. Hat bound with mauve velvet and white feather.

Carriage Dress. – Paletot of light gray drap, ornamented up the front by lozenge shaped trimmings and buttons; the pagoda sleeve similarly trimmed; bonnet of green crape, ornamented by flowers.

PLATE II. – *Dinner Dress.* – Robe of white barege; the body is open, with revers of ribbon trimmed with lace, and crossing a little at the waist with round ceinture; the skirt has two rows of taffetas up each side, with bouillons between; full sleeve with wristband and cuffs. Coiffure of hair, intermixed with flowers.

Walking Dress. – Paletot of black silk, with pipings of white, and small white buttons; revers collar of velvet; mousquitaire sleeves with cuffs of velvet; straw hat, with velvet bow and feather.

Evening Dress. – Robe of blue figured mousseline de soie, looped up at the side by a bunch of roses and wheatears; the body is low, with draperie of tulle, and bunch of flowers on the shoulders; under skirt of blue silk quilted with flowers on every point. Coiffure of hair, with flowers as on dress.

During the last month the dresses have still continued of barege, mousseline de soie or grenadine, some with a single flounce, a thick ruche of pinked taffetas placed as heading, others with tucks and braid, or ruches of taffetas on the dress. Narrow black velvet is also again in use, put on in several rows, and gauffered flounces are again in favour. Flounces put on in festoons are much approved, and have a pretty effect. The dresses of thin materials are all made with low bodies, over which are worn fancy fichus of tulle or muslin, some with long ends, others ending under the arms; the sleeves full at the top, bouffantes, with open wristband. Dresses of other materials are preferred, with the elbow sleeve and revers. The point at the waist is again replacing the waistband. The long ceintures are made very wide, and fringed frequently, with the ends embroidered; they are worn on white dresses, in every colour, but dark colours are much approved. The Medici ceintures, pointed before and behind, are with the ends embroidered. For silk dresses, ceintures are almost indispensable; they complete the toilette, and render it more elegant. The ceinture dragonne is new; it is of taffetas or ribbon; it has two small ends behind, with fancy buttons, two buttons in jewellery, as rich as wished; in front it forms corselet, fastening at the side, with two ends trimmed with lace or narrow fluted ribbon. This ceinture is made of two colours, black and violet, cerise and white, mauve and white, etc., according to the colours of the dress and toilette.

Barege dresses are very pretty, ornamented by black and white or red braid; it borders the flounces or plisses, but the colour of the barege must be selected, that the trimming accords. A white barege with small blacks, having five narrow flounces with headings, had three rows of black braid on the flounce and confining the heading. The single deep flounces are often headed by several narrower ones. On dresses of grey materials, small black silk flounces are worn, and plain bands are very numerous. Wide plisses of the same material as the dress, or of contrasting colour, with embroidered heading. Three or five rows of bouillonnes, five or seven rows of black velvet in bands, not wider than the little finger, is a style much in vogue for simple toilettes, whether in fancy materials or jean. On simple toilettes wide plisses are used, sometimes a quarter of a yard wide, with double heading, edged with taffetas. All plain skirts are bordered with velvet.

PLATE III. – *Dinner Dress.* – Robe of blue Louise taffetas; the body is high, the sleeves open, both ornamented, as well as the bottom of the skirt, with large rosaces of velvet, encircled with black lace and nœuds of black ribbon. Coiffure of hair, with nœuds of ribbon.

Child's Dress. – Frock of rose coloured taffetas, with low body and revers bretelles; the skirt is with alternate narrow flounces of rose colour, and black taffetas chemisette and long sleeves of muslin. Hat with wreath of flowers.

Morning Dress – Robe of ecru taffetas ; the body is high and pointed, fastening with small buttons; sleeves à la mousquitaire, with cuffs and nœud on the shoulders, ornamented by a plat of mauve; the skirt has a row of the same plat round the bottom, and two biais on each side, terminating with point and edged by a mauve plat. Coiffure of mauve ribbon and black lace.

Negligé dresses, as Orleans, etc., are with narrow flounces bordered. The morning toilettes for the seaside are often of alpaca or foulard, either light or dark, grey, nankin, marron. In alpaca, violet is a favourite colour. These morning toilettes are generally plain, or trimmed with ribbon, checked violet and white, black and white, groseille and black, according to the colour. Some are ornamented by nœuds or pompons, all black, the corsage with waistcoat and veste of the same material as the body. Taffetas dresses are sometimes made with a single deep flounce, on which are placed thick ruches of black lace; there are five rows of ruches. This is a pretty style also for dresses of silk gauze, foulard or tarlatane. It is observed that the skirt trimmed with ruches is much less effective than when they are placed on a flounce, which is made fuller than the upper part of the skirt, which to be fashionable must be flat, and biaises at the top, increasing in the bell form at the bottom. That is absolute just now in the world of fashion. All dresses must be of this style, training a little behind.

PLATE IV. – *Little Girl's Dress.* – Frock of barege, with square body and chemisette; pardessus of gray cloth, with band of velvet round the bottom and on the sleeves. Hat of crinoline, with feather.

Walking Dress. – Robe of foulard, with high body and large open sleeves, white ones in bouillons under. Bonnet of white crin, trimmed with lace and flowers.

Evening Dress. – Robe of tarlatane, with flounce put on in deep festons and large rosaces in each scollop, a band of ribbon heading the flounce; pointed body, with berthe of lace and ribbon. Coiffure a l'Eugenie, with diadem wreath of flowers.

The London and Paris Ladies' Magazine of Fashion, October 1861

GARIBALDI SHIRT.

Conspicuous among the Parisian novelties of the season, and to all appearances destined to produce a change amounting to revolution in ladies' costume, is the Garibaldi shirt (of which we give an engraving), which can be had in printed flannel, merino, muslin de laine, printed cambric, foulard, or pique. In shape and pattern it is made in the same way as a gentleman's shirt, with plaits, in front, extending just below the waist, full sleeve, small collar, and cuffs to turn down, corresponding with the collar, all being of one material; the ends are left so as to go underneath the dress skirt, and are long enough to allow of the shirt hanging over in bag fashion all round, producing an easy and graceful effect. It is the prettiest and most elegant garment that a lady can put on for morning, breakfast, or demi-toilet, and is already said to be in great demand in London and Paris.

The extreme comfort, as well as the tasteful appearance of the jacket for morning costume, continues to keep it as a favorite fashion not soon to be displaced. Its form may undergo changes and modifications, but the article itself has become a sort of standard in every wardrobe. One of the prettiest of the fashions now in preparation is a small jacket made of fine black cloth, ornamented with a pattern in steel beads.

Arthur's Home Magazine, November 1861

The Mathilde Jacket. – This pretty jacket is very much in vogue for matinee costume for young married ladies, and also for *demoiselles*, It consists of fine light blue or green cashmere, bordered with black velvet, upon which are embroidered scallops and dots in white silk. On the front of the sleeve, the velvet extends up on the arm, forming the half of a pyramidal block. A side seam gives shape to the front, and there are also seams in the back which fit it to the waist, where the skirt is laid in a hollow plait. This jacket is very pretty in Solferino or Magenta cashmere, with a simple border of black velvet.

Godey's Lady's Book, November 1861

Figures 3 and 4. – Evening Costume and Walking-Dress. The Evening Costume and Walking-Dress are of silk, of any favorite color. In the Illustration the full costume is of the new *azurline blue*, with a quilling of the same *en tunique*; the heading being falls of Valenciennes.

Harper's New Monthly Magazine, November 1861

Many dresses, when of thick materials, are made without trimming, but skirts of thin texture, even soies d'été, are never made without some ornament, a plissé, a narrow flounce, or a ruche. The high bodies are frequently ornamented with a little ruche of tarlatane, gauffered instead of collar. It is a matter of little importance, but is simple, and, in good taste, suitable for young persons. The same style is applied to muslin sleeves.

Some of the dresses of mixed materials have ornaments of plush, and the effect is very good. One of marron silk had three bands of plush of the same colour. A black one with Arabic designs of violet plush, the body and sleeve similarly ornamented. A pelerine of plush should be placed on the body. The pelerines of guipure worn over high bodies are frequently in festons; this style was introduced some time since, and is now very generally adopted; it forms a pretty addition to a dress.

PLATE I. – *Walking Dress*. – Robe of foulard and pardessus of black taffetas, ornamented by bands of blue, edged by black lace and rosaces of black lace.

Morning Dress. – Robe of maïs taffetas with deep flounce, headed by four narrow ones, the alternate flounce being of a darker shade; open body, with revers, lappel, and collar, trimmed with frill of darker tint. Mousquetaire sleeves, with revere cuffs.

Promenade Dress. – Robe and pardessus of mauve taffetas, the skirt of dress ornamented by a velvet train, rising in foliage; the same, smaller, is placed in festons on the pardessus, rising up each side of the front, which buttons from the waist. Mousquetaire sleeves, with cuffs trimmed with black lace, as are the little pockets of the skirt.

PLATE II. – *Evening Dress*. – Robe of black lace, forming tunic. Opera cloak of blue cachemire, trimmed with velvet, and lined with white silk wodded [sic? wadded]. Coiffure a l'Eugenie.

Evening Dress. – Robe of white taffetas, with single deep flounce, headed by narrow ones of black lace and taffetas en feston, with bunch of red roses at each point; the corsage is pointed at the waist, with berthe trimmed with black lace. Coiffure of hair in ringlets, and wreath of roses across the forehead.

Morning Dress. – Robe of pearl grey taffetas, the skirt ornamented by two bands of velvet. Zouave jacket, with velvet band round the bottom of the basque and sleeves. The hair is in curls, and ribbon ruche coiffure.

For young ladies a charming style for an evening toilette is a robe of white tarlatane, with three fluted flounces on the bottom of the skirt the body full en gerbe, with ceinture Aragonaise of blue taffetas, edged by a white blond and black lace, with very wide ends. This style is graceful; short sleeves with bouillons and small frills, terminating with a bouffant of tarlatane.

PLATE III. – *Promenade Dress*. – Robe of taffetas, with single deep flounce, headed by a band of velvet, with fluting of taffetas on each side; the body is high, buttoning to the throat, with bretelles of velvet, Mousquetaire sleeves, trimmed with velvet, and flutings as the skirt. Leghorn hat, with trimmings and feathers of cerise velvet.

Carriage Dress. – Robe of pearl grey barege; the skirt is almost covered by flounces put on almost plain, and edged with marron velvet. The body is high and pointed, closing with marron velvet. Bell sleeve, with jockeys trimmed to match the skirt. Bonnet of crin, with black feather.

Walking Dress. – Pardessus of black taffetas, fitting to the waist; pelerine marked by plisses of ribbon. Large sleeves, with fall of rich black lace. Bonnet of azuline taffetas and black lace, with bunch of flowers on the top drooping a little to the side.

PLATE IV. – *Dinner Dress*. – Robe of moire, the skirt ornamented by velvet in a Vandyke and dice pattern. The body is high, with velvet waistband, pointed before and behind; the sleeves are in full plaits, the body plain. Coiffure of hair, with plats which encircle the back of the head, and flowers on the front.

Young Lady's Morning Dress. – Robe of mohair. The skirt has a single fluted flounce at the bottom, headed by a band of velvet, edged with white nœuds up the centre of the skirt. Jacket open, en cœur at the throat, with revere; the whole trimmed with a narrow fluting and velvet.

Carriage Dress. – Pardessus of taffetas in full plaits at the back, fitting to the figure in front, ornamented by a plissé and buttons up the front; the sleeves are full, confined by plissés of ribbon, put on lengthways. Bonnet of straw, trimmed with velvet and flowers.

The London and Paris Ladies' Magazine of Fashion, November 1861

We have before said that the gored dresses, known as *Gabrielle* and *Imperatrice*, will be much worn. Many define the seams with a thick cord, or piping in the same, or a contrasted color; others by flat velvet ribbons, or ruches of velvet plaits; others, again, by double silk ruches pinked at the edges, like those worn on the bonnets the past fall. Again, the velvet or ruching is placed *en bretelle* on the shoulders, and sweeps down *en tablier* on the skirt, ...

Flounces are used only on plain silks and evening dresses, and these are usually set on in groups, in waves, or points, or diagonally, with puffs between. We have seen a very striking style, in brown *Havané* silk, five or six flounces, of five inches in width, each flounce trimmed by a black satin cord at the edge of the hem; the sleeves were made in the same way; on each side of the front breadth, and on the forearm of the sleeve, a band of plain silk, edged on each side with hem and cord, is placed over the flounces, from the waist to the hem, and from the shoulder to the edge of the sleeve. On the skirt it is eight inches wide, on the sleeves five; at moderate distances apart on this plain space, bows of rich ribbon, with ends, are placed. The effect is very good.

THE PARIS SKIRT.

For the winter season we introduce, as a substitute for the Balmorals, black silk skirts, quilted with white, gold-color, or crimson silk. This work is to be done by a machine, or otherwise it would be exceedingly expensive and tedious. They can be wadded or not, as the person may desire, but when worn over hoops they are seldom wadded. Any design can be put on them, and they are far handsomer and more *distingué* than the striped woollen skirt of former seasons. If a very rich skirt is desired, narrow bands of crimson velvet can be stitched on to form a pattern.

Fig. 10 is termed the Rifle Corps jacket, and fits tightly to the figure, but allows ample space for a full and pretty lace sleeve.

Godey's Lady's Book, December 1861

For ball dress white *tulle* and white muslin are at present favourite materials. They are frequently ornamented with pinked silk trimming, of a bright colour, placed over or on flounces of the material. One very pretty robe is trimmed with a deep flounce of the material, edged and headed by a narrow frill of pink silk. The *bertha* is formed by rows of pink cut silk, with *entre-deux* of the same fabric as the dress. The waist is round, with a waistband, finished with long ends and bows behind.

The Ladies' Companion, December 1861

PLATE I. – *Evening Dress.* – Robe of pink taffetas, with four flounces, headed by bouillons. The corsage is square, with berthe of white lace and bouillons.

Walking Dress. – Robe of moire, with waistcoat body and Zouave jacket. Pardessus of cloth, ornamented with black velvet.

Dinner Dress. – Robe of mauve taffetas. The skirt is ornamented to the knee with narrow frills placed transversally, and headed by a plissé. The body is high, ornamented with buttons and bands, edged by a plissé, and ceinture with long ends to match.

Chere Amie, – Two distinct styles are at this moment acknowledged by the fashionable world in the composition of dresses. The skirt may be overcharged with trimmings, or it may be without any. A dress prepared for a lady in high station, though made of so thin a material as Chambery gauze, was without trimming; the underskirt of white taffetas was covered by another of tarlatane. Dresses of thick materials, as velvet, gros grains, or other thick taffetas, may also be made without ornament on the skirts; the bodies have more, and the sleeves guimpes, lace, nœuds, or ruches.

The other style, which is more generally adopted than this, but not more elegant, is to load the dress with ornaments. A single flounce, not very deep, is sometimes surmounted by a Grecian design in ruches, or a deep flounce en biais, trimmed with a narrow guipure and bands of velvet, also edged with guipure, rising at intervals up to the knee, attached by a large velvet button at the top, the body of the dress with waistcoat, closing with large buttons. A robe of the colour termed Havane was pinked at the bottom in rather large Vandykes, falling on a very narrow flounce plisse of the same colour, or black, the Vandykes festonnes with twisted silk, either black or the same colour.

PLATE II. – *Evening Dress.* – Robe of white gauze, looped up at the side by a bouquet of white roses and black velvet in three bands, extending to the bottom of the under skirt, which is of pink taffetas, ornamented at the bottom by alternate bouillons and pinked flounces. The body is with berthe formed of velvet and bouillons. Short sleeves, with frill.

Dinner Dress. – Robe of green moire, with high body. Sleeves and under skirt of spotted muslin. The body of the dress is open, en cœur, to the waist, with lappels edited by a plissé of ribbon, and continued down the revers of the open skirt.

Child's Dress. – Frock of white popeline; full body, of a square form, with bands across of blue velvet, and revers edged with velvet. The front of the skirt is en tablier, with frills edged with velvet; and a deep one forms tunic, continued round the back of the skirt.

PLATE III. – Dress composed of mauve glacé, train skirt, with deep bouillonné of the same, partially covered with a flounce of real black Maltese lace, headed by a small bouillonné of the glacé, and insertion of the same lace.

Bodice pointed waist, with berthe of alternate bouillonné of the glacé; frills of black lace, with white tulle puffs, showing a little from the sleeve.

Dress of black glacé, with deep flounce across the front width, headed by a double plaiting of black glace, bound with gold coloured ditto. Side trimming Vandyked, bordered with gold glacé, and plaiting of black ditto, caught back with rosettes of the two glacés. Bottom of skirt finished with Vandykes, and trimming to suit. Square bodice, trimmed to correspond.

Mantle slightly shaped to figure, made of rich black corded silk, with crochet trimming on back and sleeves.

PLATE IV. – *Walking Dress.* – Robe of moire, with narrow frill of black taffetas, with heading. Pardessus of black velvet, trimmed with Astracan fur, and loose sleeves, edged by the same. Bonnet of black velvet, trimmed with black and mauve ribbon.

Carriage Dress. – Robe of popeline. The body is high, with waistband and buckle, and plissés of ribbon up the front on each side, with row of buttons in the centre. The sleeves of moderate width, with cuffs in Vandykes, edged by plissés of ribbon, and button in each point. The skirt is ornamented by plissés of ribbon, put on in deep Vandykes, and circlets of plissés in the Vandykes. Burnous of cachemire, lined with silk. Bonnet of crin, with wreath of velvet flowers.

Evening Dress. – Robe of gauze Chambery, with double skirt, trimmed with guimpe. Square body, similarly trimmed, and opera cloak of white satin, lined with blue plush.

The London and Paris Ladies' Magazine of Fashion, December 1861

Dress for Out-Door Work

At a farmers' club-meeting held at Ghent, N.Y., the ladies of the neighborhood participated in the meeting, and one of them – Miss Powell – read a very sensible original paper with the above title.

Miss Powell alludes to the decline of healthy constitutions among American women, a well-known and much to be lamented fact; and though we attribute it as much to inherited delicacy, arising from the wear and tear of nerve and brain which every American parent undergoes, doubtless it may be greatly obviated by out of door exercise, as Miss Powell suggests. We have only to look to ourselves to see that we are oftentimes hindered in this by unsuitable clothing. Embroidered skirts, open wrappers, and dressing slippers are not particularly suited to a morning walk or work in the garden. The case is still worse in the afternoon; a heavy ottoman velvet or a nice silk in winter, and the delicate organdy and *barège* robes of summer are not improved by trailing along wet gravel walks or sloppy pavements; so we stay at home to take care of our "good clothes," instead of going out to take care of ourselves.

Every city woman should have a walking-dress, every country lady a working-dress as well. The walking-dress should be of a stuff stout enough for all pedestrian accidents, clearing the ground as to length, with a neat dark petticoat, and kid or kid-dressed walking-boots; these strengthen and support the ankle, and keep the stocking free from dust; in short, such a costume as a thrifty Philadelphia housekeeper wears to market. The slow, full-dress saunter in a dress that has to be carried with both hands, is of little use; it is the brisk, unimpeded walk that sets the blood coursing through the veins and brings the flush of health to the cheek.

For out of door *work* Miss Powell says: "I would suggest that the waist should be cut so as to give entire freedom to every muscle; the skirt for a woman of ordinary height twenty-five or twenty-six inches in length, with plain or Turkish trowsers of the same material. Every woman acknowledges the benefit of such a modification in dress, and in the actress, skater, and gymnast society respects and approves it. We commend it for all industrial pursuits, for in-door and out of door work."

A design of a dress for working in the garden, not unlike the above, appeared some time ago in the Lady's Book, the material to be of shepherd's plaid, or any woollen and cotton stuffs; made with plenty of pockets, and in every way convenient and comfortable. As for hoops, they are an impossibility, and a trailing skirt would soon prove its own torment to the wearer.

One of the gentlemen present suggested "that the Empress Eugenie be memorialized to adopt a style of dress which should embody all the physiological benefits and advantages" desired, thinking that "whatever she might adopt would soon become a popular and fashionable dress." We doubt whether the dainty little lady could be brought to forego the graceful and becoming, which has very little part or lot in a really useful working garb. The lilies of the field are allowed to wear gay clothing, for "they toil not, neither do they spin;" but we, of every-day, industrial life, must be content with more serviceable garments.

Godey's Lady's Book, November 1861

Mourning Attire

In mourning, the distinguishing feature is a mixture of clear white with black; mauve and royal purple continue to be mingled with black also. We describe two handsome toilets in half mourning. The first, a robe of black silk trimmed with *froncés* (close *bouillonneé*) of the same, fixed at equal distances by quillings of narrow black velvet ribbon. The corsage is high, buttoned up the front, and not pointed in front of the waist. The trimming which forms the epaulette, as well as that on the ends of the sleeves, consists of *froncés* similar to those on the skirt. Collar of lace, Undersleeves of thulle, trimmed with lace.

A dress for half mourning is made of light gray silk, trimmed at bottom with three flounces of about a hand's breadth, surmounted by very small flounces of a dark gray. This dress, all the plaits of which are turned backwards, spreads handsomely in the fan shape, and presents a decided train. All the flounces are cut in festoons. The body is plain, and fastens in front with dark gray buttons. Larger buttons are put down the front of the skirt. The sleeves, wide and gathered, have a jockey formed of one deep and one narrow flounce, and end in a loose band drawn slantingly and trimmed with two of the same frills.

Godey's Lady's Book, August 1861

1862

Fig. I. – Evening Dress of Pink Tulle. – The bottom of the skirt is trimmed with four flounces edged with narrow white blonde. Above the flounces is a narrow gathered frill. The upper part of the skirt is puffed lengthwise, and separated by narrow gathered frills. White tulle undersleeves, below the short pink cap. The berthe corresponds with the skirt.

Fig. I. – Ball-Dress of White Tarletane. – The bottom of the skirt is trimmed with ruffles of tarletane, pinked; above these are five puffings, and surmounting all is a rich black lace flounce, gathered on one side by a bow of tarletane. Body and sleeves trimmed to correspond with the skirt.

A white muslin dress may be described as follows: The skirt is trimmed with narrow frills reaching from the edge to about the height of the knees, and disposed in a diagonal or slanting direction. Above them descends a flounce four or five inches broad. This flounce has a heading, through the center of which passes puffing with a running of mauve-color ribbon. The corsage is low, and over it is a fichu trimmed with ruches. The sleeves are demi-long and in puffs.

BRAIDED MORNING DRESS.

Braided Morning Dress. – This dress is made of slate-colored cashmere, braided in black. A kind of vest is made by a puffing of white muslin or cashmere, and the Zouave jacket is like the skirt, and braided in black.

The skirts of all the new dresses are long, expanding very much at the lower part, and gradually narrowing from the edge to the waist. Dresses braided, as in *Fig. V.*, are very fashionable. Sometimes the braiding extends only up the skirt of the dress, and on the body and sleeves, but it is usually around the bottom of the skirt. One of the prettiest for house wear which we have seen, was composed of beautiful shade of purple cashmere, and braided in around the bottom or the skirt and up the front. The Zouave Jacket was also braided to correspond.

Dresses for the house and for walking, are still made in the Polonaise or Imperatrice style, that is, without any joining at the waist.

Fashion has made white almost uniform for evening dresses. Some dresses of silk and tarletane are made with bows of the same material, which sometimes sustain the upper flounce; at others, are thrown carelessly at intervals over the whole. Ribbon bows and flowers are also used. An evening dress of white tarletane, just completed for a young lady, is trimmed with fluted flounces at the lower part of the skirt. The corsage is full, and the fullness is drawn to a point in the center of the waist. A ceinture or waistband of blue silk has the ends edged with white blonde and black lace.

Whilst dresses continue to be worn long, and to require the skirt to be raised up in promenading, the jupon, or petticoat, will always be an object of some importance in costume. However pretty the petticoats of former seasons may have been, those of the present year are even more so. They are now made in almost color and material, and are ornamented with trimmings the most varied. Some consisting of cashmere, taffety, or reps are richly embroidered; others are braided or trimmed with velvet to about the height of the knees. Many, composed of black or violet silk, are trimmed with several rows of plaited ribbon; and some few are ornamented with five narrow flounces alternately of black and violet, black and blue, or black and groseille-color silk. These flounces are placed very close together at the lower part of the jupon, and are frequently edged with a piping. The trimming just mentioned, besides its elegant appearance when the skirt of the dress is held up, has also the advantage of supporting and expanding the edge of the dress when allowed to fall completely over the petticoat. The same kind of trimming, but more plain in style, is employed for jupons of alpaca, Orleans, or any other woolen materials. Several of those composed of woolen textures figured with stripes have a broad row of black velvet placed just above the hem. A beautiful and serviceable petticoat can be made of gray flannel, and braided with wide black worsted braid in a Greek border.

Peterson's Magazine, January 1862

Fig. I. – House Dress Of Pearl-colored Silk, Figured With Magenta. – The skirt is trimmed with two ruffles, one of pearl-colored silk without figures, and one of Magenta silk, pinked. Above the ruffles are eleven ruches of pearl and Magenta silk. The body is high and plain, and the sleeves are trimmed to correspond with the skirt. A broad sash of Magenta silk, pinked, finishes this beautiful dress. Head-dress of white lace, black velvet and bunches of cherries.

Fig. II. – House Dress Of French Gray Silk. – The skirt is trimmed with two ruffles, the lower one quite deep, and above each ruffle is a ruche of green silk. Body high and plain. Sleeves rather close. Head-dress of green ribbon.

There is still no change in the make of dresses. The corsages of those destined for out-door costume are high, and may be either pointed or straight at the waist; this depending on the taste of the wearer.

In sleeves the variety of form is very great. Some are slit up the whole length of the arm, and edged with plaitings or bands, or with any trimming corresponding with that on the rest of the dress. In others the slit extends only a few inches in length, and the sleeves are rounded at the ends; the same trimming which passes round the edge is placed over the seam. Sleeves full at the arm-hole, close at the wrist, and with cuffs retain their wonted favor; and we may enumerate the following as among the most popular forms: 1st. Sleeves demi-wide and with revers, but without fullness at the arm-hole. 2nd. Wide flowing sleeves, not very long, set in with large plaits fixed by bows of ribbon or lace. 3rd. Sleeves of narrow width, shaped to the elbow, and with revers. 4th. Lastly may be mentioned sleeves demi-wide, without revers, and finished at the ends with as plisse or any trimming in harmony with that employed for the skirt of the dress.

The Garibaldi Shirt of white muslin ... is a beautiful addition to these dresses on a slender figure. As basques are out of style, one of the most economical articles of dress of which we know is the Garibaldi shirt. These shirts need no jacket over them, and one shirt will answer to wear with two or three old dress skirts, after the bodies are no long fit for use. They can be made of either velvet, silk, merino, cashmere, or flannel. Grey or dark blue flannel is a favorite material; and we have seen one of bright scarlet on quite a young lady, which looked charmingly with a black silk skirt. These shirts are much improved by braiding.

LADY'S PETTICOAT BODY OR JACKET.

In giving a pattern of this description, it is impossible to suit everybody's figure, but we have made the diagrams suitable for a middling-sized person. Any slight alteration may very easily be made in the size of the waist without changing the cut of the pattern, which may be made either larger or smaller according to the dimensions required. When the jacket is required very much larger, each piece should be cut larger than the diagrams, taking care, however, to preserve the exact proportions. The most durable and suitable material for petticoat bodies is twilled calico, which should be rather fine; longcloth is sometimes used, but it does not wear so well. The seams, with the exception of the two under the arms, should be stitched on the right side, the top and bottom of the jacket corded, as well as the arm-holes and the bottom of the sleeves. The insertion and work which form the trimming should not be put on until the cording is completed, and, to make the insertion round the neck shapeable, a piece of narrow soft braid should be run in on the upper edge where the work is joined to it, so that it may easily be drawn in to the size required.

A false hem should also be put on inside the hem on the left side, in which six button-holes should be made. This will be found a more tidy method than making the button-holes in the jacket itself, the buttons being quite hidden, as will be seen in our illustration. We must not omit to say that turnings must be allowed for, in cutting out this jacket. We give above engravings of the front and back of this jacket; and on the next page diagrams by which to cut the paper pattern: the reader understanding that the paper patterns will have to be enlarged to the sizes marked on the diagrams.

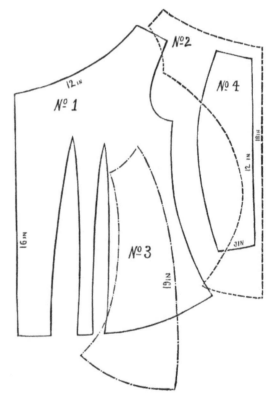

No. 1. Front.
No. 2. Half of Back.
No. 3. Side-piece.
No. 4. Sleeve.

As new subscribers may not know how to cut an enlarged pattern from these diagrams, we will give the directions. First – to enlarge No. 1.

Take a piece of newspaper, or brown paper, whichever is most convenient, making sure to have it large enough. Draw a straight line up it, sixteen inches long; then draw the curve, at top, for the shoulder, twelve inches long; and finish, back to where you began, in the same proportions. Do the backs, sleeves, and sidepiece in the same way.

Peterson's Magazine, January 1862

A good many dresses have capes or pelerines. In one of plain green silk, the collar, rounded and bordered with a green frill, is continued in a graceful lapel, cut at the edge and bordered with the same small frill and a row of Valenciennes.

Zouave Jackets in all their varieties continue to be worn. Some are very richly ornamented with colored braid, of these we noticed a very original one with bright red braid, jet beads, and a fringe of jet and red tassels. With these are worn those chemisettes of embroidered cashmere which divided favor with muslin ones during the past summer, and will altogether replace them now.

Balmoral Petticoats are universally worn, particularly in wet or muddy weather when it is necessary to loop up the dress. They are made of a variety of materials: some of the prettiest consisting of gray flannel, braided with red or black braid, or having a band of black velvet around the bottom. A very beautiful one has a rich pattern in gold braid on a black silk or alpaca.

Peterson's Magazine, February 1862

Fig. I. – Walking Dress of Stone-colored Watered Silk. – There is a quilling of black ribbon down the front of the dress and around the bottom. Large black silk buttons also ornament the front. The body is made open a short way down the front, with lappels also trimmed with black ribbon, turned back. A plaited chemisette and worked collar are worn with this dress. Sleeves shaped to the arm and trimmed to match the rest of the dress.

Fig. II. – House Dress of Lilac Delaine. – The skirt as well as the Zouave Jacket are braided in black, and a white cashmere vest is worn under the jacket, with a cashmere collar. Cape of guipure lace, trimmed with bows of lilac ribbon.

The costumes of the season are remarkable for their fullness. Dresses present a great variety of trimming on the skirts. The *bodies* of those intended for dishabille are still made plain, buttoned, and generally round at the waist, with a buckled band. Those for more elegant toilet are pointed before and behind, with the top of the body cut rather low either in the heart-shape straight across. But few very low bodies are now seen. For family parties, high bodies with short and very small sleeves are worn.

Dresses are now worn open in front, with revers, under which a lace chemisette is required. They are made so that they can be closed at pleasure. Our first figure in the fashion plate is represented with a dress of this description.

THE MARIANA.

Fig. X. – The Mariana or Polonaise Dress of Green Silk, with one rather wide ruffle at the bottom. The front is ornamented with ruches of silk, and another ruche which extends down the back to the waist, passes over the shoulders down the front on each side of the *en tablier* trimming, and above the flounce. Pagoda sleeves open far up the arm, and trimmed to correspond with the skirt.

Flounces are seldom put to the bottom of the skirt, and are placed together, or in rows with spaces between, according to the fancy of the wearer. Many are placed in twos or threes, and each set headed by a ruche or band of color. They are seldom put straight round the skirt, but in vandykes or scollops. The flounces are not hemmed; they are either bound or pinked. Many dresses are trimmed *en tunique*; and it is expected that this style, being a becoming one, as it gives height and grace to the figure, will long remain in fashion. The bodies of dresses are made either round or with two points; if the latter, the points in front open.

THE LUCIA.

Fig. XI. – Lucia Dress of French Gray Silk. – There is a quilling of black silk extending from the shoulders down the sides of the front, and around the bottom of the dress. The front of the dress and sleeves are cut out in the shape seen in the engraving and bound with black silk.

Light or dark colored Alpacas and plain Foulards are becoming very fashionable. Nankeen, gray, and brown are preferred. A chesnut-color, which we have seen in alpaca, and a violet-colored foulard were extremely beautiful. Braiding in narrow black braid is becoming very fashionable for these dresses.

GARABALDI SHIRT.

Garibaldi Shirt of White Muslin, embroidered with red working cotton. This shirt is to be worn under a Zouave jacket.

The Garabaldi Shirt of white muslin, like *Fig. VIII*, is a beautiful addition to these dresses on a slender figure. As basques are out of style, one of the most economical articles of dress of which we know is the Garabaldi shirt. These shirts need no jacket over them, and one shirt will answer to wear with two or three old dress skirts, after the bodies are no longer fit for use. They can be made of either velvet, silk, merino, cashmere, or flannel. Gray or dark blue flannel is a favorite material; and we have seen one of bright scarlet on quite a young lady, which looked charmingly with a black silk skirt. These skirts are much improved by braiding.

THE MADELINE WRAPPER.

This comfortable and elegant wrapper can be made of either silk, delaine, or any other material which is most convenient. The trimming is composed of silk, quilted with white in diamonds. The silk should be of a contrasting color with the dress, such as a crimson or blue trimming on a dress of gray. For mourning, a black delaine, with a trimming of black silk quilted in white, is very beautiful. The wrapper should be confined at the waist by a cord and tassel.

Cut out the wrapper by the diagram, which is exactly one-half of the wrapper. D D, the front, is cut the straight way of the material; C C represents the seam at the back, and is the only seam in the wrapper, except the shoulder seam, which is made by joining A A and B B; this forms the shoulder and makes also the armhole.

The wrapper should be lined. The trimming is to be shaped as seen in the design and then quilted, fitting it to the wrapper and finishing at the top with a large silk cord. Bind the bottom with worsted braid. The pocket pieces, cuffs for sleeves, and the collar are finished in the same manner.

One of the dresses which we have seen was for a young married lady, consisting of a muslin dress having four flounces, each trimmed with two narrow black velvets; the body was open and had a row of black lace laid flat round the top, a similar row passing over the shoulders,

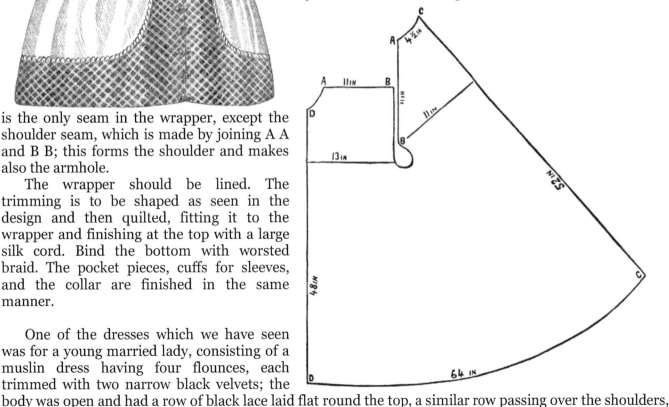

and wide sleeves with the same lace round the wristbands. The long muslin sash was ornamented with two rows of narrow velvet and a row of lace.

Long sleeves have no particular form, but are varied according to the taste or fancy of the wearer and maker. They are, however, wide or half-wide, rather than narrow, and end in a cuff in harmony with the rest of the trimming. Some are slit up in front and trimmed all down the seam. Others are puffed and slashed; while others again have puffs at top and end in a very wide velvet wristband.

The Russian, Swiss, and Medici Waistbands are worn more than ever. Some are plain, some stitched in colored silk, others embroidered with silk braid, etc. The long sashes tied at the side, and generally black, are also embroidered with a design to match the dress they accompany. These sashes, edged with a fluting or a row of lace, with braces and pocket trimmings to match, are in great vogue, and especially when adopted to muslin chemisettes, are extremely pretty for very young ladies.

The ladies of Paris have introduced an easy and graceful mode of *raising the skirt of the dress* in outdoor walking costume. A ceinture, usually of black velvet, is worn round the waist, and to it are attached loops of the same material. These loops are so long as to descend to a little more than midway down the dress, and through them the edge of the skirt is drawn so as to raise up the whole of the lower part of the skirt in festoons. By this means the edge of the dress is secured from contact with the ground. This ceinture has been named the *Ceinture Louis Quinze*.

Laces of all kinds are very much used for trimming bonnets, shawls, mantles, dresses, etc.

Peterson's Magazine, March 1862

Fig. I. – House Dress of Dove-colored Silk. – The skirt is trimmed with five flounces, the alternate ones being of a darker shade than the others. Above the flounces is a ruche of the two shades of silk. The body is high and plain with a point in front. The cording of the dress and buttons are of the darker shade of silk. The sleeves are large and full, and trimmed around the points which are open with a ruche. Head-dress of lace and pink ribbon.

Fig. II. – Dinner Dress of a White Organdie Striped with Green. – The skirt is plain, and around the waist is a broad green sash. The cape is trimmed with a ruche of green ribbon. The sleeves are very thin, plain white muslin. Head-dress of green ribbon.

There have been but few new goods imported this season, economy being the order of the day. Old dresses are "made to look like new" as nearly as possible. Skirts worn out at the bottom are renewed or lengthened by a bias band, plaiting or ruffle, or silk of black or some color contrasting with the dress. In this way two old dresses often make one stylish new one. Then antiquated bodies, or worn out bodies, are discarded, and jaunty Zouave jackets with white shirt bodies and sleeves, or Garibaldi shirts, take their place. As the season advances, pique or Marseilles will take the place of silk or flannel for these articles.

Dresses for evening wear are generally made with low-necked bodies, with points before and at the back, with a fullness extending from the shoulders to the of the body. But bodies partially open, either square or the heart shape, are the most popular.

We have been asked to describe a dress suitable for a young lady. We give below one which is not very expensive, and can be modified according to the taste or purse of the wearer. We must promise that the combination of black and white is not at all confined to mourning, but, on the contrary, is one of the most fashionable of costumes. The dress of which we speak was composed of white tarlatane; the skirt ornamented with six narrow flounces at the bottom, each flounce trimmed with a row of tiny black velvet. The flounces were headed by a broad plaiting of tarlatane, trimmed at the top and bottom with black velvet. The low body was gathered, and cut square on the shoulders, also trimmed round with a plaiting, and finished off round the neck with a blonde tucker, having a narrow velvet run in it. A head-dress, composed of black velvet and bunches of rose-buds, completed this simple but elegant toilet.

PATTERN FOR BALL DRESS.

Should any of our readers feel inclined to make one of these dresses themselves, we would hint that tarlatane can not be too little or too lightly handled, and therefore the flounces should be as quickly trimmed and put on as possible. To accomplish this, the flounces should be hemmed and the velvet put on at the same time, by turning the tarlatane once on the right side, and running the velvet on over the raw edge. In this manner the material need not be much tumbled.

IN-DOOR DRESS.

A very pretty dress may be arranged in the following way: A black silk skirt, either plain or trimmed, may be accompanied with a full body of white muslin, having bands of black velvet over the shoulder, crossed with the same in front in the form of a stomacher, and having a bow at the waist of the white muslin, wide, and with long ends crossed with black velvet at the bottom.

MORNING DRESS.

Fig. IV. – Morning dress for the country of buff pique trimmed with black velvet.

BRACES AND WAISTBAND.

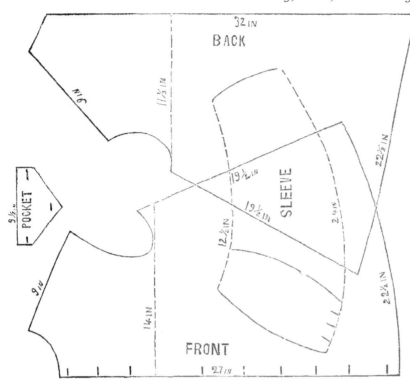

LADY'S WALKING SACK.

These sacks are all the rage this spring. We give, here, a diagram of one, and below a diagram by which to cut it out. These sacks are not only pretty and fashionable, but economical also: and they are destined, therefore, to come into universal use.

Peterson's Magazine, April 1862

Fig. I. – Walking Dress of Grayish Blue Silk. – The skirt is trimmed with seven bands of black velvet. The body is high and plain; the sleeves are loose, but somewhat shaped to the arm, and trimmed with four bands of black velvet. Bonnet of white silk, trimmed inside and out with pansies.

Fig. II. – House Dress of Nankeen-colored Foulard. – The skirt has a narrow bias band around the bottom edged with white. The pointed belt is braided and edged with white. Over the low body is worn a high white body of Jaconet, plaited down the front. The collar and cuffs of this body are made of foulard, braided. Head-dress composed of blue velvet bows.

There is but little that is new as yet in the make of dresses. Many bodies, particularly those in silk and more expensive materials, are made with a point, both at the back and in front. For quite young ladies, the round waist is much worn, with either a belt, sash, or one of those pointed *ceintures* known as the *Medici* ceinture. One of the most beautiful of these latter is made of black velvet, having a point both at the back in in front, and with two long black velvet tabs, about a quarter of a yard in width, depending down each side, widening toward the ends, which are rounded. The waistband, as well as the tabs, are braded with very narrow white silk braid.

The Skirts of Dresses are still gored so as to be quite wide at the bottom, but narrow at the waist.

For Walking Dresses the skirts are made quite plain, or with only a little trimming up the sides or front; but silks are usually ruffled, except they be of very good quality, when they are made plain.

Bodies of Dresses are usually made high, buttoning down the front; but, as the season advances, low bodies and capes, or Raphael bodies (that is, bodies cut square in the neck), will be worn.

Many of the newest walking dresses have sleeves shaped to the elbow; they are slit up to a short distance at the styled lower part, and the ends are rounded. But sleeves are made in all styles, according to the fancy of the wearer.

WALKING DRESS.

Fig. III. – Walking Dress suitable for the country. This dress is composed of one of the black and white silk and wool materials which are now so popular and are found so useful. The body is made *a la Parodi*, that is, with a slight fullness at the waist, back and front, but plain on the shoulders. The deep cape, collar, sleeves, and front and bottom of the dress are trimmed with a plaiting of ribbon.

The Garibaldi Shirt is gaining in favor, having been sufficiently well supported to carry it through the formidable opposition with which it was at first encountered. The Emperor of the French, on first seeing the Empress in one of these articles, expressed the most forcible disapproval; but this being in a clear white material might, as we imagine, make the objections all the stronger. These Garibaldi shirts are now made in colored flannels and other wool manufactures, and they have the merit of being warm and comfortable, and inexpensive, leaving to the limbs all that freedom of motion which is essential to health. Stripes of white and some gay color are now the most fashionable, but scarlet, and Solferino, and violet are also much worn. Almost every lady has in her wardrobe one or more silk dresses, of which the skirts have survived the bodies, and these are extremely suitable for wearing with those Garibaldi shirts, making a stylish morning toilet, and at the same time, preventing the necessity of purchasing new dresses. Dark-colored silks are also made up in the same way, with the fronts, cuffs, and collars stitched in white by machinery, and in these the skirt and the body are some times alike, and sometimes different. Thus, a black skirt may have a violet shirt, a brown one a black, or the reverse. For the young ladies of a family between the ages or eight and twelve, these loose bodies are extremely suitable; for instance a black or a French blue merino skirt, bordered with five or six inches of scarlet, and worn with a Garibaldi body of the same scarlet, has a very good effect; or the black may have the same accompaniments in the blue, with equal propriety of taste. For a young lady under eight years of age, a brown Brussels cord, having a band of French blue silk turned up from the bottom, and a narrow velvet of a little darker color laid on the silk half an inch from its upper edge, makes a very pretty dress, with a large circular cape trimmed to match. This Garibaldi shirt is also made in black and white stripes of different widths, all of which have a very striking effect.

Peterson's Magazine, May 1862

Fig. I. – Out-door Dress of Buff Pique, or Marseilles, for the country. It is trimmed with five rows of black velvet ribbons, and with black velvet buttons. The straw hat is trimmed with latticed work of black velvet around the brim, and with buff and black feathers.

Fig. II. – House Dress of Pearl-colored Grenadine. – The skirt is trimmed with flounces. Above the lower four is a quilling of mauve ribbon; then there are three more flounces with another quilling of ribbon above them. The body is low in the neck, with short sleeves, and over it worn a white body, embroidered and trimmed with quillings of mauve ribbon. The sash is also trimmed to correspond with the body.

Dresses still continue to have the skirts gored, thus diminishing the fullness around the waist, though they are not made quite as narrow at the top as heretofore. Trimmings of various descriptions are again coming into favor: one favorite style being very narrow fluted flounces of the same silk as the dress, placed two and two together: another style is a fluted flounce about six or seven inches deep, set on with narrow heading. A very striking trimming for a dress of light gray silk is formed by rows of ribbon, the four colors of the rainbow; they should be either eight or twelve in number, and the widths should graduate. Narrow *ruches*, waved or formed into Greek borders, is a favorite trimming, these should be the color of the dress. Ribbon or velvet, contrasting in color to the dress, and arranged in the Greek or Ionic border, will be likewise worn.

Bodies of dresses, when high, are closed with small buttons. Many of the new dresses are opened part of the way down the front of the body in a heart-shape, or square, *a la Raphael*; whilst others, of very thin material, are made low in the neck, and can either be worn with a cape, or a white over-body. Over some of the high bodies are worn what is called the Spanish jacket, which somewhat resembles the Zouave jacket, but fits the figure more closely, and is much shorter.

Another style of high body will have a small jacket at the back only, similar to a habit. A favorite style of trimming high bodies will be *Arabesque* designs in braid, very narrow velvet, or silk gimp: with this style a kind of fringe should ornament the sleeves and round the waist.

Sleeves are large, even when shaped at the elbow; puffed sleeves will be worn, but very few tight to the arm.

THE PRINCESS ALICE.

Fig. III. – House Dress of Black Silk. – The skirt is braided around the bottom and up the front in a Greek border put on in white braid; on each side of this braiding there is a black lace insertion over white silk. The ornaments down the front of the dress are of black lace, edged with white lace. A pointed *Marie de Medici* waist, which, as well as the small Zouave jacket, is also braided in white. An under-body of white plaited muslin has a small ruffle around the neck. A dress of this kind braided in purple, or green, is very beautiful.

MEDICI GIRDLE OF BLACK VELVET AND LACE.

The Medici Ceintures appear to be now, with many persons, an indispensable article of dress.

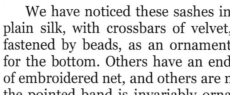

They are made in a variety of ways, and are trimmed in so many different styles that it would be impossible to describe all we have seen. The ceintures are all made with pointed bands round the waist and have two ends falling down the skirt on each side of the point. Small trimmed pockets are generally inserted in the ends, or a trimming to imitate them is substituted.

We have noticed these sashes in plain silk, with crossbars of velvet, fastened by beads, as an ornament for the bottom. Others have an end of embroidered net, and others are merely trimmed with ruches; but the pointed band is invariably ornamented to correspond with the two ends.

THE EUGENIE.

Fig. IV. – House Dress of Pearl-colored Silk. – The skirt is trimmed with rows of narrow black lace. A *Medici ceinture* has long ends, edged with black lace, and is embroidered in pearl-colored silk. In the upper parts of the ends are small pockets, also embroidered.

Peterson's Magazine, June 1862

The Art of the Hoop: 1860 - 1869

THE IMPERIAL JACKET

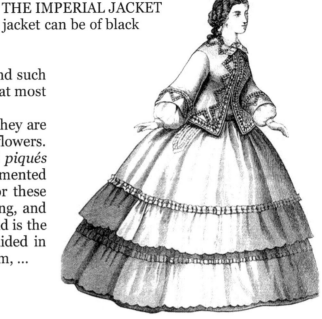

Violet silk skirt, with ruches of a darker shade. The jacket can be of black silk, trimmed with violet or of the same as the skirt.

Gored skirts are much worn, especially for *piqué* and such materials, and the skirts are very full and training, as that most decidedly gives grace to the figure.

For the seaside, quilting dresses are very suitable; they are either plain white, striped, or sprinkled over with field flowers. Buff, mauve, white, and various shades of tea-colored *piqués* are also much liked. Zouave jackets, very highly ornamented with red, white, or black braid, are generally made for these dresses. We have seen a great deal of the black braiding, and pronounce it decidedly the most *distingué*. Mohair braid is the most suitable for the purpose. The skirts are also braided in various styles, some *en tablier*, others just above the hem, ...

ZOUAVE VEST.
Made of scarlet cloth of velvet, braided with black.

ZOUAVE JACKET.
Made of black silk or cloth, braided with red.

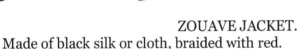

Wilmine Jacket – consists of five parts, front, side shape, back and side shape, and sleeve. Each seam is laid over from the waist to the edge, and braided the same as the rest of the jacket. Sleeve plain, and rounded up at the back, and braided the same as the body. These jackets are made in white piqué, braided with black; and nankeen, braided with white or blue. Cerise and green are sometimes used, but do not form so good a contrast.

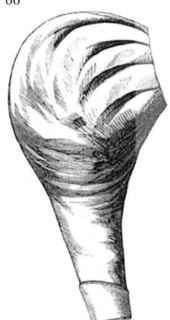

PLAIN GIGOT SLEEVE.

The gigot, or "leg of mutton," sleeve, which used to be such a favorite with our grandmothers, has now come into fashion again, and is a style which is more used for morning wear than any other. It is very simple in its construction, being cut in one piece, with a very decided slope at the top, and, when pleated in to the armhole, very much resembling the shape of a leg of mutton. It is made to fit tightly to the wrist, being fastened by means of buttons and loops, or hooks and eyes, over which a pointed white linen cuff should be worn. We have illustrated a plain gigot sleeve as being the easiest to make, but they are also worn trimmed in a variety of ways, and are much more elaborate in their construction.

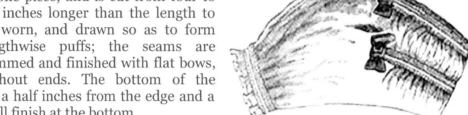

Annie Sleeve. – This sleeve is all in one piece, and is cut from four to six inches longer than the length to be worn, and drawn so as to form lengthwise puffs; the seams are trimmed and finished with flat bows, without ends. The bottom of the sleeve is bound about two and a half inches from the edge and a quilling set on which forms a full finish at the bottom.

Godey's Lady's Book, July 1862

Fig. I. – Evening Dress of White Barege, trimmed with two rows of black guipure lace. Bournouse of white barege trimmed like the dress.

Fig. II. – Evening Dress of Pink Grenadine. – The skirt is trimmed with puffings of grenadine, lengthwise of the skirt, edged with narrow white blonde. Sleeve reaching to a little below the elbow, made quite wide. The body is pointed both back and front, and has a square trimming of puffed grenadine.

Dresses composed of silk of two different colors are becoming more and more fashionable. A very pretty dress in this style has just been completed. The robe itself is of silver-gray silk, and the skirt is edged with three graduated rows of plaiting of violet silk. The corsage is trimmed in corresponding style, and the long ends of the ceinture are edged with violet-color plaiting. The fashion of employing two colors of the same material has extended to ball and evening dresses; for instance, a dress of white tarletane may be trimmed with flounces and ruches of pink tarletane.

Dresses are worn very long behind, and are much gored; and evening dresses, of light material, are arranged in this manner. As the mode appears to lessen the width of the skirt at the top, it is absolutely necessary that the material be well gored, to give sufficient width to the bottom. These gored training skirts are exceedingly becoming to the figure, and in a drawing-room nothing is more elegant. It is a pity that this fashion cannot be confined exclusively to in-door toilets, and not adopted (as it too generally is) for walking. What can be more disagreeable than to see a lady's rich silk skirt sweeping the streets as she walks? It is extravagant, inelegant, and exceedingly dirty. However, if ladies will be in the fashion, and wear trained skirts in the streets, in dirty weather, they may keep them in order by wearing them looped up over a pretty petticoat. The latter garments are being worn more elaborate, and of richer material, than ever; and it will soon be necessary to have the petticoat made as handsome as the dress – the fashion of looping up the dresses necessitating an elegant under-skirt.

LOUIS XV. ROBE DE CHAMBRE.

We give in the front of this number, an engraving of a new style of *robe de chamber*, called the Louis Fifteenth. We also give here diagrams by which to cut it out.

No. 1. Front.
No. 2. Side-Piece.
No. 3. Sleeve.
No. 4. Back.
No. 5. Half the Plait in middle of Back.
No. 5. *bis*. Plait at the side of Back.

We have given the upper part of the garment only, no paper being long and wide enough to give so ample garment quite complete. But it will be easy, on examining the pattern, to understand that, with the exception of the middle of front, all the seams are very divergent in order to obtain the fullness and train behind. In making up this *robe de chambre*, be careful to observe that the pattern No. 4 serves as lining to the back, that the waist cord or girdle is fastened at the place marked with a circle on the side-piece, which is afterward covered by the plaits falling over it, and produced by the patterns Nos. 5 and 5 *bis*. These plaits, three in number, begin at the neck, are folded under and fastened on the back, which forms a lining, and from the waist they are confounded with the skirt. Nothing can be more stylish than this *robe de chambre*.

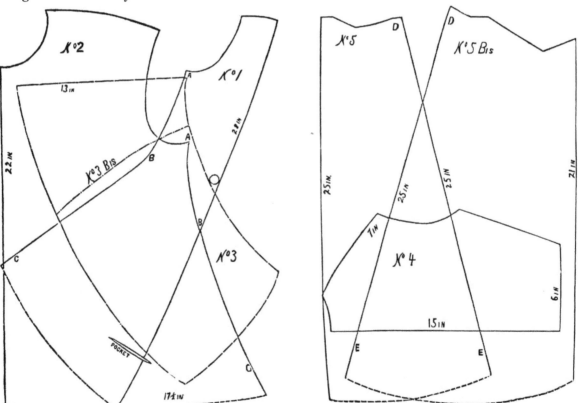

We have remarked some charming Petticoats, made of bright-colored French merinos, and trimmed with velvet and elaborate braiding designs; and we have even seen them embroidered. Two little fluted flounces, placed quite at the bottom, form a pretty finish, and are besides, useful in assisting to keep out the bottom of the dress.

White petticoats, made with two little fluted frills at the bottom, are exceedingly comfortable wear for muslin dresses, and are much more *distingue* than the *open* embroidery, which of late has become so very general. The thick satin-stitch, or raised embroidery, is always in good taste, and it is now much used for under skirts. Tabliers of this rich and handsome embroidery are frequently inserted in the front of the petticoat; so that if a morning dress, open down the front, be worn with it, the effect is very good.

THE CLEOPATRA.

Fig. III. – Dinner Dress of Gray Silk, Figured, trimmed with plain gray silk edged with black lace.

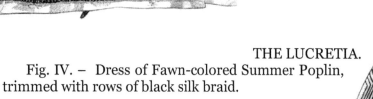

THE LUCRETIA.

Fig. IV. – Dress of Fawn-colored Summer Poplin, trimmed with rows of black silk braid.

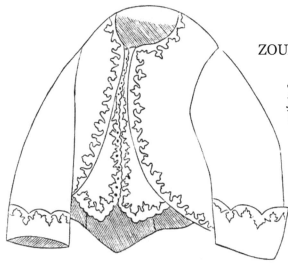

ZOUAVE JACKET AND VEST, BRAIDED.

In the front of the number is a pattern for a lady's Zouave Jacket and Vest, furnished by J. B. Obersteller & Co. The jacket may be in velvet, cloth, or cashmere. The vest should be in cashmere of a corresponding color to the jacket.

Our ladies will continue this season to wear Zouave jackets of muslin or nansook lined with colored silk. We have seen some very pretty specimens of these very charming plaited chemisettes to be worn under them. Plaits are much employed now in all linen articles, such as petticoats, night-jackets, etc.

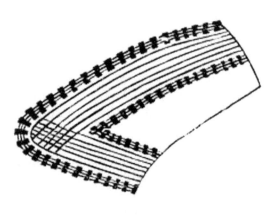

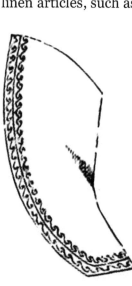

THE GRECIAN SLEEVE.

MATILDA SLEEVE.

CRESCENT SLEEVE.
Peterson's Magazine, July 1862

PUFFED SLEEVE.

THE ALBERTINA DRESS.

Watering-place dress, made of Satin de Mai. White ground, with linked rings of porcelain blue. Four flounces are on the skirt, and the front is made *en tablier*, with the flounces extending to the waist; the edges of the flounces are concealed by a puffing. Fancy lace fichu.

Many of the thin skirts are laid in single plaits round the waist, and the skirts faced about three fingers deep with crinoline instead of being lined. In Paris they are sewing straw in the facings of dresses to make them stand out.
Godey's Lady's Book, August 1862

Fig. I. – Evening Dress of White Book-Muslin. – The skirt is made with one deep flounce, edged top and bottom with a narrow Valenciennes lace, and has a blue ribbon run in the flounce just above and below the lace. The body is made low and plain. The berthe is round at the back, passes over the shoulders, crosses in front, passes under the arms, and is tied behind with two long ends. Full puffed sleeves.

Fig. II. – House Dress of Black Silk, made in the Polonaise, or, as it is sometimes called, the Gabrielle style – that is, with no seam at the waist. The dress is trimmed down the front with buttons inserted in a small lace rosette, and round the bottom with a ruffle put on in flutes and surmounted by three rows of black velvet, edged on each side with black lace. The sleeves are lined with white silk, cut open on the inside of the arm, and confined at the wrist with a black velvet band edged with lace.

The "Ceinture Florian" is an elegant novelty, which gives effect to a simply trimmed dress. It is made of taffety of a color harmonizing with that of the robe, covered with black guipure, Chantilly, or blonde. Sometimes it is merely edged with lace or rows of velvet. The ceinture is pinned at the back of the body so as to form a point or fichu. The ends are then passed over the shoulders, crossed on the bosom, and linked one in the other at the back of the waist, very much like the berthe in first figure of our fashion plate.

In Evening Costume the dress must train at least half a yard behind, and the skirt must be very fully trimmed. This surplus of ornament denotes that plain skirts will ere long reappear. Exaggeration in fashion is the sure forerunner of simplicity. Many ladies, as if anticipating the impending change, are wearing skirts very slightly trimmed, but extremely full, set in large box-plaits at the waist, the only trimming being a narrow quilling at the bottom of the skirt just above the hem.

One of the prettiest Evening Dresses which we have seen was made of white tarletane, entirely covered with flounces of moderate width. Each flounce was bordered by a narrow black velvet. The body, cut low and straight across in front, was surmounted by a muslin chemisette drawn with a narrow velvet. The wide waistband was tarletane bordered with velvet.

CARACO ESPAGNOL.

Our full sized pattern this month is that of the *Caraco Espagnol*, of which we give above a back and front view. The side-piece is cut with the front, to avoid a seam under the arm; the pattern therefore consists of three pieces only, the front, back, and sleeve. The hole, cut near the edge of front, shows the place where a small tab may be stitched on underneath, by which the jacket may be pinned to the dress, to hold it in its position, if required. The sleeve is slightly shaped at the elbow, the small notch out in the back of the sleeve showing how far it is to be left open. This style of *Caraco* will be much worn for morning and promenade dresses. Some ladies may prefer the tight-fitting dress body, trimmed to represent the *Caraco*, in which case this pattern may be placed on the body, and the form marked by a tacking thread. This *Caraco* may be depended on as a correct and graceful pattern, and one suited to any material.

No. 1. The Front.
No. 2. The Back.
No. 3. The Sleeve.

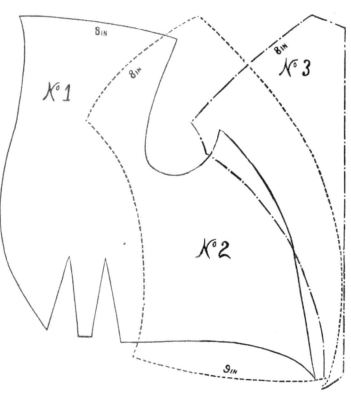

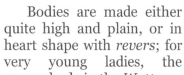

Bodies are made either quite high and plain, or in heart shape with *revers*; for very young ladies, the square body in the *Watteau* style is very becoming.

Sleeves are worn large, those of the *Isabel* and pagoda form being preferred; these may be slightly shaped at elbow.

THE TULIP SLEEVE.
Peterson's Magazine, August 1862

Most of the fashionable Petticoats are being made with flounces, which assist to throw the dress out at the bottom, and are particularly suitable for wearing muslin or thin dresses. There is a very nice material now being manufactured, and which seems to be in great favor for ladies' summer petticoats, consisting of a striped fabric, with a mixture of cotton in it, and which is very cool, comfortable wear. We have seen it in pink and white, blue and white, mauve and white, and brown and white; and some petticoats made of this material are braided, or ornamented with velvet, or made with little flounces. They are very economical, as they save much washing, and are particularly suitable for traveling, when much luggage is objected to.

WALKING DRESS.

Fig. III. – Dress of Pearl-colored Barege. – The flounce is trimmed with two narrow ruffles, between which are run five rows of braid of a shade deeper than the dress. The body, sleeves, and sash are trimmed to correspond with the skirt.

The distinctive characteristics of the dresses of the present season are of enormous amplitude and length in the skirts, the back breadths being made to trail at least a quarter of a yard on the ground. Everything looks best when in its proper place, and no thing certainly is more elegant than a train dress in a drawing-room. A long flowing robe will impart a certain grace and dignity even to the wearer in whom those qualities are wanting. This fact was fully understood by our grandmothers, and they turned it to the best account. But the most enthusiastic admirer of long dresses will readily admit that nothing is more unpleasing and more out of place than a train in the street. All the grace and elegance of flowing dresses vanish when they are seen sweeping the dust and dragging through the mud.

The proverb says, "Fools set the fashion, and wise people follow it;" but in respect to trains worn in out-door walking dress, the folly or wisdom of the wearer are questions which admit of little doubt. Certain it is that few ladies are sufficiently philosophical to view with indifference the injury which a beautiful dress must sustain when exposed to the outrage of every clumsy foot that passes. The only remedy for all the difficulties involved in the important question of long dresses is, that for walking costume, skirts should be made so as just to clear the ground, and that trains should be reserved exclusively for the drawing-room. There at least a beautiful trimming may escape destruction, a rich and delicate silk may retain unsullied freshness.

WALKING DRESS.

Fig. IV. – Dress of Nankeen-colored Pique. – It is trimmed with black velvet buttons and rows of black velvet. There is a deep Casaque, like the dress, and trimmed to correspond.

Narrow Flounces are worn on some of the thinner silks; narrow plaitings and quillings of ribbon are both also fashionable; Greek designs, in ribbon or velvet, contrasting in color to the dress, are very elegant, and will be in great favor.

Braiding is still much in vogue, and we see, for the present season, a great number of dresses with a jacket of the same, made of white pekin, or of nankeen, either plain, flowered, or striped, but in all cases ornamented with braiding. One of the patterns in vogue, both in light tissues and silks, presents small designs inclosed between stripes forming squares.

Peterson's Magazine, August 1862

Flounces are still fashionable, and are made rather closer. Some of the dresses are trimmed to give them the appearance of a jacket, others are made with a square jockey at the back, others are cut diagonally, the fastening beginning on one shoulder and ending at the waist on the opposite side. Pockets are sewed on the inside of the dress, and the ornamented opening is all that is seen.

VESTE OR CHEMISE RUSSE.

This veste can be made of Nansouk or of white or colored cashmere. It is ornamented with chain stitch or braiding. Patterns of it can be furnished by our Fashion editress.

The chemise, or vests Russe, of which we give an illustration on page 225, will take the place of Garibaldi shirts, which will only be worn by children. The veste Russe will be made of both thick and thin materials, and very heavily braided.

Figaro and Zouave jackets, made of sprigged muslin, lined with colored silk, and trimmed with ribbon ruches, are much worn.

Violetta Sleeve. – The body of this sleeve is gathered on to a plain piece at the top, and the second part is about four inches shorter than the first, and narrower; it is gathered and joined in with the same seam as the under. The top of the sleeve is a puff, the upper edge laid in box-plaits, and fastened with buttons.

Godey's Lady's Book, September 1862

Fig. I. – Carriage Dress of Purple Silk. – The skirt is trimmed with two fluted ruffles, headed by a band of silk braided with black. The body is very close, and is covered by a Spanish jacket of the same material as the dress, and together with the sleeves is also heavily braided with black. The pointed belt corresponds with the jacket.

Fig. II. – Riding habit of Blue Cashmere. – The skirt is three-eighths longer than an ordinary dress skirt. The body is made with a Hungarian basque. The sleeves are close to the wrist, but slashed about the middle of the arm, showing a white under-sleeve.

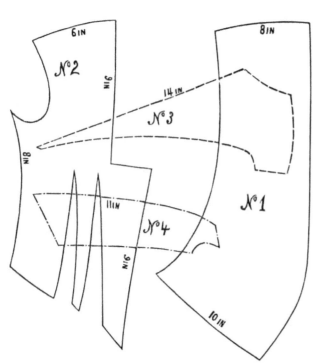

MARQUISE DRESS BODY.

Our pattern, this month, is that of a dress body in the *Marquise* style, three-quarters high at the back and square in the front; this style is suitable for a dinner dress, where quite an evening dress is not required: the neck may be finished by a *ruche* of ribbon or lace. We give diagrams for the front, back, side-body, and sleeve.

A pretty new article of the toilet consist of a broad band of white guipure lined with blue ribbon, which encircles the throat, and is then crossed in front; and after passing under the arms, the ends are linked together at the back of the waist. This is called the "Ceinture Diane," and it may be worn with any dress, or it may be made either of black or white guipure, and lined with any color. It has a very pretty effect.

Braiding is still in high favor. It is used on cloaks, dresses, and flounces. Light designs are best suited for this purpose, and those of the fret kind seem to be preferred. In some cases nothing more is done than putting numerous rows of braid one above the other as small velvets used to be formerly. A great many dresses and jackets made of white or buff quilting are braided with black.
Peterson's Magazine, September 1862

HOME-DRESS.

Made of slate-colored alpaca, trimmed in diamond form with black velvet ribbon. Black and slate-colored belt. Linen collar and cuffs, worked with black.

A very pretty travelling-dress was made of smoke-colored cashmere, the entire suit braided in a narrow Greek border, which is a showy pattern, yet easily and rapidly accomplished. Plain high bodies are now generally closed up in the front and fastened with metal buttons, very small but very costly. The jacket waists only are worn open or turned back *en revers*. Sleeves are generally moderate in size and loose at the wrist, but shaped at the elbow, and in thick materials approach something to the regular coat sleeve, but are generally more becoming.

Lady Franklin Sleeve. – This is a simple, yet very stylish sleeve, and can be appropriately made in any of the gray materials trimmed with black. It is rather full at the top, half long, and demi-flowing. The under-side is laid over the front, as will be seen in the engraving, and forms a loose side cap, with a descending point. The trimming is a flat border of silk, stitched on both edges with white.
Godey's Lady's Book, October 1862

Several dresses have been made this season with round pelerines in the form of capes. A very elegant dress with one of these cape pelerines has been trimmed in a very novel style with narrow black lace edging set on flat and in a foliage design. The edge and front of the skirt, the pelerine and ends of the sleeves, were all ornamented in this style; the effect on the green silk is indescribably rich and beautiful. Another dress of violet-colored Irish poplin has been ornamented in a similar style, but with black silk braid instead of black edging.

Fig. I. – House Dress of Azuline-blue Silk. – Around the bottom is a fluting of black ribbon. The body and sleeves are trimmed to correspond with the skirt.

Fig. II. – House Dress of Gray Silk, spotted with Black. – A heavy black velvet cording passes down the two breadths on each side, as well as around the bottom. The sleeves are also corded with black velvet, and, like the body, are trimmed with narrow black velvet bows, with a steel buckle in the center of each bow.

The skirts of dresses are still worn long, are very wide, and are sometimes made to train a little behind.

Pique dresses, in buff or white, are being made with short cut-away jackets, little waistcoats, and plain braided skirts. For out-door wear this costume is completed by a scarf, braided to correspond, or by a short paletot.

Nearly all dress sleeves this season are made with a seam at the elbow, and a turned-back cuff, projecting an inch or two beyond the seam of the sleeve at the bottom. Black lace and lace rosettes are very much used as a sleeve trimming for silk and grenadine dresses, and silk ruches are much in favor for the purpose.

THE ILLINOIS.

In the front of the number, we give a full length engraving of a new style of walking-dress, which is destined to be very fashionable this fall. It is called The Illinois. We also give, here, a diagram by which to cut it out.

No. 1. Front.
No. 2. Side-Piece.
No. 3. Back.
No. 4. Sleeve.

The sleeve (of which we give half only) has the leg of mutton shape at top and is gathered under the shoulder-piece. At the mark B, several gathers are made. The bottom of this sleeve is cut from six to seven inches longer than the arm, and this excess of length is drawn in small gathers in the interval of the pinkings.

The dress is made of black silk, and is trimmed with violet velvet and narrow black guipure lace. The body, high and plain, has bands of the same on the shoulders, the front, and the back. These tabs are trimmed with a narrow lace and fastened down at the ends by a rather large velvet button. The sleeve, almost tight at the shoulder and wide at the elbow, terminates in a *cornet* at the wrist. A shoulder-piece, of velvet, comes down the side of the arm in a point; it is bordered with guipure and fastened by a large velvet button. The end of the sleeve is cut in points, and these are interlaced with the points of a velvet wristband turned the opposite way. The velvet points reach up on the silk, and those of silk come down on the velvet. These points are bordered with a narrow black guipure, and each of them is fastened down by a velvet button. The silk skirt is cut in points at the bottom, as shown in the engraving, and as we have explained for the sleeve. A band of violet velvet is cut out in the contrary sense, and the points interlace, bordered with guipure and fastened down by buttons at each point. The bottom of this velvet band is cut in vandykes as seen in the plate. Below this band are three narrow flounces of black silk, fluted and bordered with guipure. A silk sash round the waist, with long ends hanging down, each of which is trimmed with velvet to match the rest of the dress.

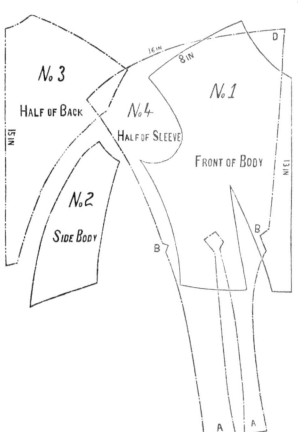

Self-colored *mousseline-de-laine*, such as lavender, gray, drab, or azuline blue, is being much worn for ladies' and children's dresses. This material is now dyed in such beautiful shades, so pure and bright, that, for morning dresses, it has become very popular. It is nice cool wear, and is inexpensive.

The prettiest and most suitable way of making these dresses is with a plain or *slightly* full body (according to the figure), the new bishop sleeve, closed at the wrist, trimmed with rows of silk ruches, and a pleating of silk ribbon, one and a half to two inches wide, *placed quite at the bottom of the skirt, below the braid*. A pointed silk band in front, and two ends of pinked silk worn behind, give a pretty finish to the dress.

The garment we saw made in this style was of a pretty warm shade of fawn or gray, with the quilling rushes [sic: *ruches*], sash, and buttons down the front of the body in silk matching *exactly* the shade of the dress.

THE INDIANA.

Fig. III. – The Indiana, a dress of the new bright fawn-colored silk. It is trimmed around the bottom with three ruffles of the silk; and above the ruffles are six rows of dark brown braid. The sleeves, sash, and berthe body correspond with the trimming on the skirt.

THE VERMONT.

Fig. V. – The Vermont. – Dress of dark blue silk. The skirt is trimmed with a series of ruffles put on in half-scallops. The scarf mantilla of the same silk is trimmed to correspond with the skirt.

A new dress of pale green glace silk has just been made with nine tiny flounces at the bottom of the skirt, put on in three series. Each of the flounces was braided in a small Greek pattern, in narrow black silk braid; and between every series of flounces a larger Greek design in broader braid was arranged. This skirt is new and extremely stylish. The sleeves were cut with a seam down the back, and were open to the elbow. Two rows of braided frilling were carried round the sleeve and up the opening; and the third row was continued quite to the top of the sleeve, where it was put in the armhole. Two long ends of silk, also braided, were worn behind, secured to a braided band, made slightly pointed in front, like the Medici ceintures.

THE KENTUCKY.

Fig. VI. – The Kentucky. – A dress of gray silk, trimmed with narrow black velvet, put on in diamond shape. Body and sleeves are finished to match the skirt.

Peterson's Magazine, October 1862

Swiss muslin dresses are also much worn in the country, and are prettily trimmed with a deep flounce, mounted in plaits, between which a ribbon is run (any bright colour looks well), the body should be made with plaits, fixed down with braces, formed of a small plaited-frill; also having a ribbon between the plaits. The neck is finished with a similar plaiting and ribbon, as are the top and bottom of the sleeves, which these trimmings confine in a wide puff.

The Ladies' Companion, October 1862

Waistbands are more fashionable and costly than ever. Some are made in one piece, with three points back and front, richly braided or embroidered. Others are made to lace up the back and front, the points trimmed with tassels and bordered with tiny gilt or steel buttons, placed just along the cording, and about one inch apart. For mourning they are made of dead silk, and trimmed with *crêpe* and jet beads. Some of these waistbands or corsages are pointed only in front, and are merely a band at the back, where they fasten with a bow and long ends.

THE CLARENDA.

Fancy Zouave, braided with black, and trimmed with black lace. White silk vest. Organdie skirt.

We have seen some very rich ones made of velvet and silk, embroidered with silk, jet, steel or gold, with long, flowing ends, one-quarter of a yard wide, with a network in diamond form inserted in the ends, which are heavily fringed.

Godey's Lady's Book, November 1862

Walking dresses are still worn simply trimmed with a ruching on the hem of the skirt, or a single flounce set on in hollow plaits. For full toilet I have seen a very elegant silk dress trimmed at the bottom of the skirt with a puffing of blue silk, bordered by a black lace *ruche*.

The Ladies' Companion, November 1862

Evening Dresses, if of a thin material, are frequently made with two skirts, the upper one rounding off from the front and trimmed with a ruffle of the same material as the dress, or a narrow lace ruffle.

THE MARIANA.

Fig. III. – The Mariana. – A dress of maize-colored foulard silk, braided with a narrow brown braid. The deep circular cape, the sleeves, sash, Medici waist, and the close-fitting jacket, known sometimes as the Figaro, and sometimes as the Senorita, are all braided to correspond with the skirt.

Taste and Neatness in Dress. – Nature has wisely given woman a love of neatness and generally an excellent taste in dress. To look like a "fright" is the dread of all the sex. A few touches in the way of ornament; a graceful, stylish fit; neat collars and laces; how these transform a lady! Not to know how to dress is to be only half as agreeable and pretty as you might be. Taste and knowledge, too, supply the place of money. There is more truth than is usually supposed in the old saying, "As well be out of the world as out of the fashion."

Trimming is still universal for skirts of dresses, though there is but little on the skirt. One narrow flounce, a few rows of braid or velvet, a braided pattern, or a narrow quilling of ribbon seems indispensable. Sometimes there is a narrow flounce with a design in braiding above it, or two flounces with the braiding between them. Black lace insertion is frequently put on silk dresses of richer description, not only on the sleeves and body but around the skirt.

Most bodies are made with small points at the back and in front, and the bodies are not much trimmed, except they are braided.

The Oriental Vests and the Senorita Vests, at present so extremely fashionable, are at once becoming and convenient. They are simply jackets, varying little from those designated last year the "Zouave" and the "Figaro." In like manner, the "Saute-en-Barque," this year so popular, is merely the paletot of velvet or silk which has been worn with slight modifications during the last two years.

The Art of the Hoop: 1860 - 1869

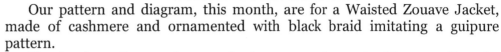

WAISTED ZOUAVE JACKET.

Our pattern and diagram, this month, are for a Waisted Zouave Jacket, made of cashmere and ornamented with black braid imitating a guipure pattern.

The lapels, collar, pockets, and edges, are trimmed with a small ruche alternately black lace and ribbon the color of the garment. It makes a very beautiful garment.

DIAGRAM NO. 1.

No. 1. Front, with narrow lapel on the same piece.
No. 2. Back.
No. 3. Side-Piece of Back.
No. 3. *bis*. Side-Piece of back joining the breasts in front.

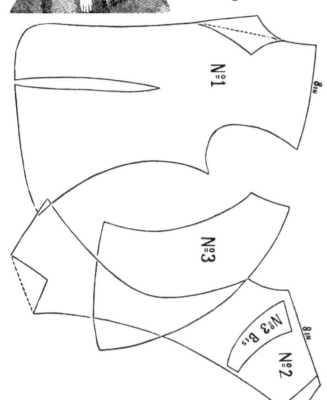

DIAGRAM NO. 2.

No. 4. Front of Sleeve.
No. 4. *bis*. Cuff.
No. 5. Back of Sleeve.

This is destined to be one of the most fashionable articles for this fall and for the coming winter. It can be made, with the assistance of these diagrams, without the aid of a mantua-maker. On former occasions we have described, at length, how to enlarge the diagrams from our engravings and cut patterns from them in paper, so that it is unnecessary to repeat the process now.

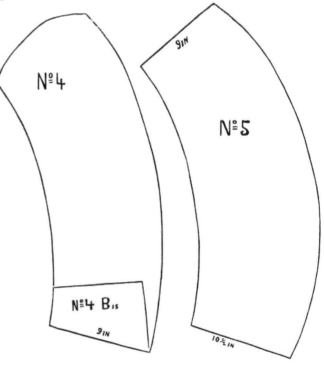

Peterson's Magazine, November 1862

Many of the dresses were made with points both back and front, still the prevailing style adopted for house or walking-dresses is the short waist, or Zouave, which is still regarded with favor. These stylish little jackets are made in a great variety of ways. Some of them scarcely reach to the waist, while others are made with a slight spring which is out straight across the hips, and deepens to a point in front. Others round off from the front, and just touch the waist behind. Another style has a narrow fitting basque, a rolling cellar, and vest fastened with small gilt buttons. One of the prettiest of the high bodies is trimmed to imitate a short jacket, and with excellent effect. A narrow quilled ruffle, surmounted by three rows of narrow velvet, describes the precise shape of a Zouave vest upon the body, and passes round behind, where it is prettily finished by a sash of the material, trimmed with quilling and velvet to match. These jackets, like the Garibaldi shirts, are always made of single and striking colors, trimmed in contrast. Mixed materials, used for this purpose, would show a most unfortunate judgment and want of taste.

BRAIDED JACKET.

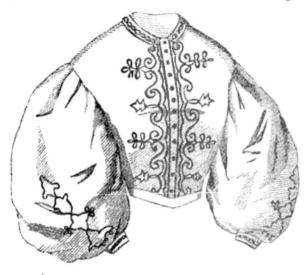

Fig. VIII. – White Marseilles Vest, braided with black, to wear under a Zouave or Senorita jacket.

White is no longer confined to thin materials or evening dresses. White alpaca, embroidered in colors, is made up by Madame D. [*Demorest*] for jackets, morning-robes, and children's dresses and coats. It is much admired for its clearness and beauty of texture, which renders it very becoming to the complexion.

Godey's Lady's Book, December 1862

Walking dresses are still worn simply trimmed with a ruching on the hem of the skirt, or a single flounce set on in hollow plaits. For full toilet I have seen a very elegant silk dress trimmed at the bottom of the skirt with a puffing of blue silk, bordered by a black lace *ruche*. Body plain, pointed, and ornamented with braces made of blue silk, like that trimming the skirt. Sleeve, almost plain, cut with an elbow, and closed at the wrist with three or four buttons on one side. A puffing follows the seam of the sleeve, and goes round the bottom.

Figaro and Zouave jackets of sprigged muslin, lined with coloured silk, and trimmed with black velvet, or ribbon *ruches*, are very pretty and effective for quite parties and home evening wear.

High dresses are often trimmed to give them the appearance of a jacket, and jockeys are set on at the back; sometimes cut square, and at others diagonally, the fastening beginning at one shoulder and ending at the waist on the opposite side.

I cannot resist sending you the following model for evening dress: A toilet of rich *mauve* silk, with a trimming set on about half a yard up the skirt. This trimming consisted of the dress silk, one quarter of a yard deep, scalloped on each edge, and bound with black velvet. It was then run in large diamonds, and the threads drawn, so that each diamond was puffed, and the running was concealed by pipings of black satin. A fall of rich lace was below this trimming, and the body and sleeves were trimmed to match.

The Ladies' Companion, November 1862

Fig. I. – Walking Dress and long Sacque of Black Silk, trimmed with Vesuvius color.

Fig. II. – Carriage Dress of Green Silk. – This dress is of the *Gabrielle* style – skirt and waist cut in one. There is no fullness at the waist, but the skirt is made wide enough by putting in small gores, which are gathered together under a rosette of silk. A narrow ruffle finishes the bottom of the dress. The sleeve corresponds with the skirt.

For Walking-Dresses, braiding is very much in vogue, and it is sometimes mingled with embroidery in silk, which adds very much to the richness of the garment. Embroidery alone is also very fashionable, but is not nearly so quickly accomplished as braiding, and is much more expensive. For useful wear there is nothing so suitable as a drab, gray, or stone-colored alpaca, or merino, as none of these colors show the dust, and, braided in black, have really a stylish and elegant appearance. With this kind of dress there are two sorts of out-door garments which appear to be equally in favor: one, the *saute-en-basque*, or short paletot, with *revers* – a delicious, coquettish little article – and the other, the short circular cloak, which, although only a revival of a fashion that was much in vogue a few years since, is now very popular. These garments are quickly put on, and have, besides another recommendation, that of being easily made.

Any young lady, industriously inclined, could, at a very trifling cost, arrange for herself a pretty costume, by purchasing a few yards of alpaca, or merino, and some black worsted braid. The skirt should be plain and gored, and ornamented, above the hem and up the front, with a pretty braiding design; or, if this be considered to involve too much labor, the braiding up the front may be disposed with. The body of the dress should, of course, be braided, as also the sleeves.

The new-shaped short circular cloak we recommend for this toilet, as being the easiest to make. This should be braided down the front, round the bottom, and round the neck (those circulars being arranged without collars), in the same design as that which ornaments the dress.

CLOSED SLEEVE FOR WALKING DRESSES.

This style of sleeve is very becoming to thin, slim figures requiring a little more width at the shoulders. It is made with a seam at the back, down which the trimming is laid, which in our illustration is composed of narrow lace and silk ruching. It is closed at the wrist by means of hooks and loops, or buttons and loops, underneath the trimming, and is pleated at the top to the size of the armhole of the dress. In cutting the sleeve out, the pattern should be laid on double material, the straight portion being laid evenly with the straight part of the sleeve, so doing away with the necessity of having two joins.

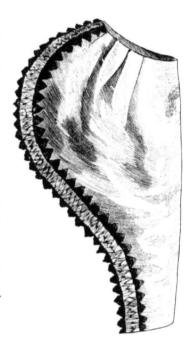

Sleeves, except those intended for walking-dresses, will be mostly made open, and have quite a tendency to increase in width. Those wide ones are usually flowing, and cut in a point, though some of the smaller are rounded, and open on the back of the arm. For full dress toilet, we have slashes of silk, with a mixture of illusion, tulle, or blonde, protruding through openings, the sides of which are held together by bows of ribbon; the effect is very graceful. Evening toilets are all made with short sleeves, and the trimming consists of ruches, blonde, and ribbons to match the flowers in the head-dress.

Bodies are being made with either the short point, or two rather long points similar to a waistcoat; some are perfectly plain, buttoning to the throat, others trimmed to correspond with the skirt.

NEW STYLE BODY.

Fig. III. – Dress of Crimson Merino, with the Yoke. – Medici waist, epaulets, and cuffs of black merino braided in crimson. Gray, blue, or purple, or a pretty shade of green would look equally well for a dress of this kind, with the braiding in corresponding colors, or white. For an evening dress, the material should be thin white muslin, the yoke, etc., of black velvet, braided with white.

The short cut-away jackets appear to be now the prevailing mode for dress bodies, in many materials, both for ladies and children; and the fashion certainly is stylish and becoming. These Spanish jackets reach to the waist behind, fasten about half-way down the front, the bottom portion being very much cut-away, to show the muslin chemisette and pointed band. This chemisette may be allowed to hang slightly full in the front, something like a Garibaldi shirt, or may be drawn tightly up – the latter mode being certainly the more graceful, unless for very thin slim figures. A waistcoat worn with these jackets makes a very charming toilet, and is better suited to stout figures than the chemisettes. Plain pointed dress bodies are now being trimmed to imitate a jacket and waistcoat, the points of the dress forming the waistcoat portion, and the trimming representing the jacket.

BLACK LACE BASQUE.

Fig. IV. – Basque of Black Spotted Lace, trimmed with a very deep fall of lace on the skirt, and with narrower lace on the body and sleeves.

The Spanish Jacket is very fashionable this season, and has almost entirely supplanted the Zouave Jacket. On another page we give a diagram for a Spanish Jacket. This particular one is called the Figaro, and, when braided according to the pattern, (see page 471) makes the most striking of all the various Spanish Jackets that have appeared. The advantage of these Jackets is that they may be worn, like the Zouave, with an old skirt, thus enabling a lady to give greater variety to her costume without being extravagant.

THE FIGARO JACKET.

The Figaro Jacket, one of the most fashionable patterns of the now popular Spanish Jacket, being a novelty in great demand, we give a diagram by which it may be cut out.

The diagram shows the style of braiding to be employed.

No. 1. Front.
No. 2. Side-Piece.
No. 3. Back.
No. 4. Sleeve.

The jacket is made of cloth and braided, of velvet with gold braid, or of silk braided of another color, etc. its effect, when made up, in velvet and gold braid, is very fine.

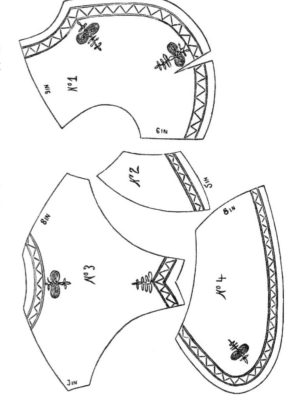

Some of the choicest novelties we give here. First is this very handsome house dress; the sleeves and bodice of which are especially pretty.

For the house, skirts are still made very long, wide at the bottom, but narrower at the top, and nearly all are trimmed – some with bias bands of silk of a contrasting color, richly braided – some with three or four narrow-quilted flounces, ruches, puffings, etc. A novel style of trimming has, however, just been introduced. It consists of crescents, lozenges, and other figures, cut out in silk of a color different from that of the dress, and stitched on at the bottom of the skirt. Yet, for very rich silks, plain skirts are the more distinguished-looking, and some ladies have become so tired of trimmed skirts, that they are wearing plain ones altogether.

Peterson's Magazine, December 1862

Dressmaking Advice
HOME DRESS-MAKING.

Many of our readers have, no doubt, dresses lying by which are almost useless, and which, with a little ingenuity, may be turned to good account. We are speaking of the dresses made with two or three flounces – a fashion which is now obsolete, excepting the cases where lace is used; and deep lace volants are always in good taste.

Many styles have been invented by which dresses somewhat *passe* may be made quite *a la mode*. One of the difficulties to contend with is the narrowness of the skirts of dresses made some few years since, which, at the present time, are scarcely of sufficient width to go over a crinoline. To obviate this difficulty the skirts should have a *tablier* inserted in the front, or *small gores* let in between each *seam*, to the depth of about twenty inches; or bands of silk about four inches wide may, with advantage, be put between every width.

To enable our readers better to understand what we mean, we will describe how to remake a three-flounced dress. Between every width of the silk insert a gore, sixteen inches at the bottom, tapering to a point at the top, and about twenty inches deep. Should the wearer be very tall, allow the gores rather deeper. Ornament these gores with some of the *flouncing*, cut into narrow *frills*, and finish off the point at the top with a rosette of ribbon or ruched silk, or some of the flouncing made into a rosette. This skirt will be found really elegant in its appearance, and sufficiently wide to be comfortable over a *moderate*-sized crinoline.

To remake a two-flounced Dress. – Insert pieces between every width of the skirt, the same as the preceding one, but make use of the deep flounce for the purpose. A width of the flounce should be let in between the seams of the skirt, and the top of the flounce plaited in to form a kind of fan; these plaits being ornamented with a rosette. The shape of the *fan* is very much improved by *slightly sloping* the flounce toward the top, as, by so doing, the material will not have such a bunchy appearance. This skirt, when finished, also has a very good appearance, considering the *old-fashioned* materials of which it is composed.

Before concluding our remarks on contriving to make *new* things out of *old* ones, we will mention another mode of widening plain skirts, such as those of brocaded silk, chine silk, or any material of that description. A straight band of black, or some colored silk to contrast nicely with the dress to be widened, should be let in between every seam; this band is perfectly straight, and looks nicely stitched on with white. Supposing there are but five widths in the skirt, then five bands of silk, each one six inches wide, will increase the width of the skirt nearly a yard. If there are six widths of the material, the band need not be so wide.

We noticed a very pretty gray mohair dress arranged in this manner, with bands of violet silk on the skirt, stitched on with white. This dress was made with a Zouave jacket and waistcoat, bound with lilac silk; and the sleeves (being for morning wear) were closed at the wrist.

Peterson's Magazine, July 1862

Science of Dress-Cutting.

A scientific and accurate method of cutting dresses has now become an indispensable passport to the position of eminence in dress-making; and the art being new so liberally dispensed and so easily and quickly acquired, no one, however humble, need forego the many and great advantages that may be secured by adopting a correct system. A lady or dress-maker having once experienced the superior advantages of fitting by measure, could not be persuaded to return to the old and tedious method of pinning and fitting, even if the art were twenty times more costly to acquire than it really is. By adopting a correct system, the dress-maker is not only advanced to a higher sphere of usefulness, but she is also enabled to give more perfect satisfaction to her customers, and thus not only secure to herself a much easier, but a more profitable business, and her patrons saved from those most annoying delays and uncertainties occasioned by the old method, which costs them so much valuable time and still more valuable patience.

HOW TO CUT A JACKET OR SACK.

Some kind of jacket, or body, loose from the skirt, and which can be worn with a variety of skirts, has been found so useful as to have become an indispensable "institution." In a former number we have given

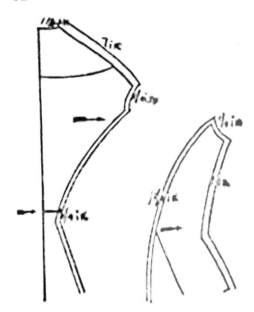

the science of *dress* cutting – that is to say, of cutting a plain waist by the rules of Madame Demorest's model of dress cutting, which will be found easy and infallible, and which has superseded all the old, tedious, and unreliable methods of dress cutting wherever it has been introduced.

ILLUSTRATION OF BACK AND SIDE SHAPE.

We propose now to show by how simple an operation a jacket, that most intricate part of a lady's attire, can be accurately cut and fitted in any style and to any form by the use of Madame Demorest's dress model, and a diagram which we present to our readers.

The extra outside lines indicate the allowance for hem, lap in front, and seams, with a line indicating the shape to cut a low neck.

ILLUSTRATION OF FRONT.

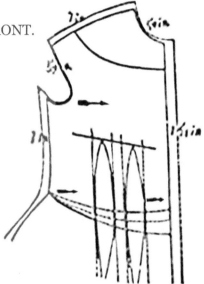

PREPARATORY MEASURES.

And, first of all, it may be useful to say that the changes of fashion never affect the foundation principles upon which accuracy in fitting any sort of dress to the human form is obtained. The length of shoulder or waist, or height in the neck, may be longer or shorter, the shape of the waist may be round, or pointed, or scalloped, or cut in square lappets, the front may be open, or closed, or turned back *en revers*; all this makes not the slightest difference in those first and most important rules, upon the correctness of which success most depends.

Promising thus much, it is taken for granted that, before trying to cut a jacket, the reader has mastered the details given in the science of dress cutting, understanding which, this matter will become perfectly simple and plain to the most ordinary understanding.

To facilitate the operations, however, of those who have not seen the former instructions for cutting a waist, we will premise that the first measures to be taken for the jacket are precisely the same as those for an ordinary waist. Thus: –

"SHOULDER" MEASURE.

Taken by placing the end of the tape at the nape or bone of the neck, and carrying it over the right shoulder, under the arm, and up to the neck, until it meets where it begun. Now mark down the number of inches which this gives you on a slip of paper, say twenty-four. Next –

"LENGTH OF WAIST."

Hold the end of the tape to the same place of the neck again, and measure down for the length of the waist, say fifteen inches.

"BUST" MEASURE.

Place the tape across the fullest part of the bust, drawing it around the form and over the shoulder-blades loosely, so as to give freedom to the chest, and mark down, say thirty-six inches. Last –

"SIZE ROUND THE WAIST."

Take the measure, either tightly or loosely, according as the jacket wants to be fitted closely or not to the figure, and mark down the number of inches, say twenty-three.

Take the measure, either tightly or loosely, according as the jacket wants to be fitted closely or not to the figure, and mark down the number of inches, say twenty-three.

This will give you the following table: –

1. Shoulder measure . . . . . 24 in.
2. Length of waist . . . . 15 "
3. Bust measure . . . . 36 "
4. Size round the waist . . . . 23 "

All the above measures should be taken standing at the back of the person being measured.

Now examine the model, which you have first placed straight and smooth on a sheet of white paper before you, and with a pencil make a dot through the holes in the model on the paper at each number marked twenty-four. These dots will give an accurate outline of the back part of the body.

THE "SPRING," OR JACKET PART.

The outline is now complete for a plain, straight waist, and nothing remains but to obtain the "spring" or skirt part, which forms the distinctive feature of the jacket.

This is done by laying the rule (which accompanies the model) so that the inverse notch will touch the lower point of the side seam, and then draw the spring by the line, as illustrated.

To get the side shape, lay the rule at the centre one of the three dots that mark the back of the arm-hole, half an inch from the centre of the back at the waist, and draw the line in the direction which it will give you, and you will have a perfect side shape.

For the spring at the back, reverse the rule, and place the inside point at the dot at the bottom of the waist, parallel with the line of the side seam, and draw of the spring indicated, which will be plenty long enough for a jacket in the present style. If it requires to be longer for the street or shorter for any fanciful style, the difference is easily made. But, the desirable length determined upon, take the tape measure in the thumb and finger of the left hand, and rest it at the highest point of the neck; then, with the pencil in the right hand, sweep a circle from that point which marked the proper length of the spring. This will give an even length. Should the back or sides require to be deeper, the difference can be easily made, although no strict rule can be given for it, as it is a matter which depends solely upon the caprices of fashion. By cutting out now in the lines marked a perfect back will be obtained, and also side shape, with the exception of a slight deficiency in the latter, which must be supplied in the pattern by piecing in a gore double the size of the one taken out. This gives ample room over the hips.

For the front use the same number – twenty-four. Make a dot on the paper through the holes in the model at each twenty-four, in the same way as before, when, after drawing lines from dot to dot, you will have an outline for the neck, shoulders, arm-size, and under the arm.

Now obtain the front seam; and the easiest way to do it is to double the bust measure (36 inches) and take off the measure of the back, then lay the balance across the bust, and dot, lay the rule by this dot and the dot in front of the neck, and draw the line for the front. To get the length of the waist, for the front lay the back and front evenly together at the side seam, and mark the front by the back, then rest the pencil on this mark with the tape measure held in the thumb and finger of the right band; now carry the tape measure with the left hand to the highest dot in the neck, and hold it firmly at that point till you sweep a line with the pencil from the mark at the side-seam across to the front line of the waist. This will give you the line which is required as the base of the "spring" for the jacket. If the jacket is to be loose, dart seams will not be required; but if it is to "fit" the form, lay the two side-seams together, and half of the waist measure will give the right size across. The balance to be taken up in dart-seams, if desired to fit closely.

Shape the side-seam of the spring by that of the back, allowing one-third less fulness. The length is also obtained in the same way, by sweeping a circle with the tape measure from the highest point of the neck, the line commencing with the starting point given by the proper length of the spring. To make a deeper point in *front*, it is only necessary to hold the tape measure at a lower dot in the neck.

In marking the dart-seams, reverse the rule to form the "spring," as this gives the exact proportion, the "darts" running up to a point above the line of the waist, and *down* to a point below the line.

These directions followed, a woman possessed of some ingenuity and taste can cut different "fancy" styles without the assistance of a dress-maker.

These directions will become very clear and intelligible when the model is examined, which should be procured by every lady who has any desire to cut dresses with accuracy and elegant proportions.

The model of dress-cutting, accompanied with a tape measure and full and accurate instructions, are furnished at $1, and are sent by mail, post free, on receipt of the price.

Godey's Lady's Book, September 1862

1863

Fig. I. – House Dress of Light-colored Silk, trimmed with four flounces. The body is made with sharp points before and behind. Above the upper flounce and on the sleeve is a quilling of purple ribbon. The head-dress is a net with a trimming in front of black lace and scarlet roses.

Fig. II. – Ball Dress of White Silk, trimmed with quilling of white ribbon. The upper dress is of spotted lace, with a broad ribbon of Vesuvius color around the bottom of the lace dress.

Embroidered Muslin Dresses, as well as collars, sleeves, etc., etc., are likely to be very fashionable again, as the Empress of the French and the Queen of England have been lately exerting themselves on behalf of the poor embroideresses, whose means of livelihood have so much decreased since embroidery went out of fashion.

THE GABRIELLE: FRONT AND BACK.

Very small basques, not more than an inch in depth in fact, are now worn; some of these for a superior style of dress are edged with a fall of black lace a quarter of a yard in depth, but they are usually finished with only a heavy cording. One fashionable mode of making high-dress bodies is with a double point in front, a small swallow-tail behind, and straight at the sides; that is to say, with no basque on the hips. The sleeve that best suits this style of body is a demi-closed one, shaped to the elbow, like a large coat-sleeve, the bottom portion being sloped off near the seam in the shape of a V. The sleeve is rather long, and reaches nearly to the wrist. The new under-sleeves, called "*Les Religieuses*," or nun's sleeves, consisting of a broad stitched linen band, large enough for the hand to slip through, and made up on cambric under-sleeves, would assort very nicely with these bodies.

Now that the season for black silk dresses is here, a few hints as to the newest and most fashionable mode of making them will, we hope, prove acceptable to our readers. A black silk skirt looks prettily, ornamented at the bottom with three very tiny plaited flounces, each flounce edged with a row of narrow white blonde. Above these flounces a row of velvet and steel trimming should be run on, the trimming having a slight mixture of white in it, which accords nicely with the blonde. Another mode of making a black silk skirt is with five narrow plaited flounces at the bottom, carrying the flounces up on one side; two rows of black ruching, put on in vandykes, make the skirt still prettier. Another simple but pretty fashion is to have one plaited flounce placed quite at the bottom, with three rows of the tiniest black velvet run on the flounce. This flounce should be brought halfway up the skirt on the *left* side, and finished off with a bow of silk, trimmed with tiny velvet to correspond with the flounce.

Another beautiful dress is of the new brown called leather-color, embroidered in coral pattern, round the skirt with a thick, stiff, black cord. For each spray of coral the silk was pierced, the cord passed through and fastened off on the wrong side, the same as for braiding. The black cord contrasted with the leather-color very well.

The Art of the Hoop: 1860 - 1869

The diagram we give, this month, is that of a high dress-body, called the *Princess Alice*. This very fashionable body is cut with a small jacket with plaits at the back – seams similar to a riding-habit. At the waist line of the back, side-body, and side of front, are pricked lines, showing where a seam may be requisite at this part for most figures. There are four pieces in the pattern, namely, the front, back, side-body, and sleeve; it is very graceful and stylish, and is suited to silk, mohair, etc. The sleeve is shaped at the elbow, and left open at the seam at the back of the arm as far as the notch, the corner being rounded. Any other style of sleeve may be substituted.

No. 1. Front.
No. 2. Back.
No. 3. Side-Piece.
No. 4. Sleeve.

Now that lace forms so prominent a feature in every lady's toilet, we must not forget the new Scarf Sashes of black lace. They form a narrow pointed pelerine at the back, cross over the bosom in front, and tie behind, leaving two very long ends. These scarf sashes are generally composed of a handsome insertion, edged on each side with a narrow lace, put on quite plain, and should be lined with a piece of rather stiff black net to support the scarf, and to keep it in proper order. There is a degree of style and elegance about these scarfs which will render them a favorite addition to the toilet, and, as they can scarcely be worn in imitation lace, they are not likely to become very common.

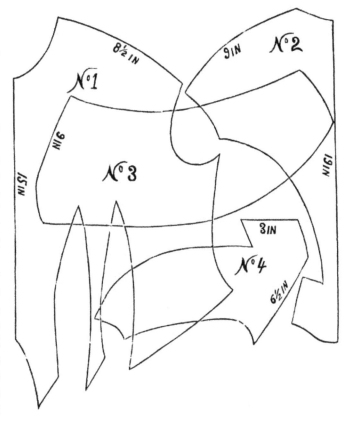

A dress we saw made with one of these new scarfs was of plain white muslin, with a double skirt, the seams of the upper skirt being left open to the height of about eighteen inches, and the corners folded over on the right side, where it was finished off by a large black lace bow made of the same insertion as the scarf sash. The sleeves of the dress were cut with a seam at the elbow, and were ornamented with a lace bow, to correspond with those on the skirt.

Peterson's Magazine, January 1863

Dresses are still worn very full, and long behind. For moires, velvets, or satins the box plaits continue in vogue; for other materials a new style has been adopted – the back of the skirt being arranged in large gathers, and at each side, one triple box plait, the remaining parts of the skirt in small flat plaits.

We have recently seen a walking-dress, which was much ornamented, and had something both novel and bold in its character, and when worn by a tall and elegant woman had a very attractive appearance. The dress was composed of brown taffetas, and the skirt, which was very long, was ornamented with a broad flounce, about a quarter of a yard in depth, on which was placed at equal distances *coquilles* in blue taffetas. These *coquilles* are made with a piece of taffetas a quarter of a yard in depth, and the width of the silk, and are gathered up at one edge quite close, and then attached to the skirt with a steel button. Above this are placed four narrow flounces made of brown taffetas, pinked at the edge, and separated in the centre by a fifth flounce of blue taffetas. These are placed on the dress in undulations, and extend half a yard above the broad flounce.

Our Illustration shows three figures. The principal one, an evening dress, is made of pale blue taffeta, the bottom of the skirt is decorated with five rows of black lace insertion, edged with narrow niches, of taffetas, put on in undulations. The body is low, and is ornamented with a breastplate, on the front, and a *postilion* vest, both of which are made in black lace, surmounted by a ruche.

The second figure shows the corslet ... made of black taffetas and can be worn with a high or low body. It is edged with black lace one and a half inch wide. The upper side is trimmed in addition to the face, with two rows of narrow black velvet ribbon, and ornamented with buttons of black taffetas in the form of stars, sewn on with a black pearl button in the centre. The lower edge is trimmed with three rows of narrow black velvet ribbon. A bow and long ends of taffetas, one quarter of a yard in width, edged with lace and velvet, is placed on the front of the left side.

The third figure is that of a little girl of seven or eight years of age. This little costume can be made in almost any material. The skirt forms in front a pointed waist; it is trimmed with ruches of taffetas and bands of velvet ribbon and oval buttons called olives, the pockets are marked by the same ornaments. The body is a Spanish vest, which is open, and permits to be seen a corsage of white muslin, with the wristbands of the sleeves puffed with a lace ruche. This costume would suit, as an indoor costume, not only young girls, but also women. Our model is in green reps de laine, of a medium shade, the trimming is black.

Dresses with vests will be in great favour during the winter months, the Figaro jacket, of which we gave a full-sized pattern some little time since, being the one now generally adopted. Bodies with two points are very general, as also are those with round waists, with these a sash or belt is worn. Berthes, for high dresses, are coming into fashion, they are put on round the shoulders the same as for a low body.

Another novelty is one called the Mousquetaire dress. It is chiefly distinguished by its military character, being decorated with aiguillettes or shoulder knots and grelots, which are small drop buttons in the form of a bell. It has an elbow-shaped sleeve, and a ceinture with basques or tabs falling all round the waist.

The What-Not, January 1863

For evening and house dress, skirts are made longer than ever, they should form a train at the back, and positively trail on the carpets to be at all fashionable.

Fig. I. – Opera Dress of Blue Silk. – The cloak is made of black cashmere embroidered in gold thread, and trimmed with gold cord and tassels. Head-dress of roses and black lace, and coral comb.

Fig. II. – House Dress – The skirt is of pink silk striped with black. The bottom is trimmed with three rows of black velvet between two narrow ruches. The body is of thin white muslin, puffed lengthwise, with a row of narrow black lace between each puffing. The low peasant's body is of black velvet. Full sleeve, with a deep black velvet cuff, pointed and edged with lace.

In Paris, vestes are extremely popular for wearing with indoor & dresses; they are made of velvet, plush, or cloth, embroidered or braided. Plush vestes have a good effect, and require no trimming, but the velvet ones are generally ornamented with either fur, gimp, or drop buttons. More stylish and expensive vestes are made of white terry velvet, trimmed with a band of marten or

Astrakan fur, but for ordinary wear, they are frequently made of the same material as the skirt. In all cases a chemisette is worn with the veste, and is made either of white muslin, handsomely worked in satin, or of white or colored cashmere.

There is nothing so pretty and so useful as a plain glace silk dress, whether colored or black. This style of silk does not carry its date; and, if not worn out one season, can, by a little alteration in the trimming, be converted the following season into really a very pretty and stylish garment. Not so with silks figured with various patterns, which are very handsome when worn at the time they really are fashionable, and then do not appear again. Of course every one cannot afford to discard a handsome figured silk dress so soon; and it is to those ladies we recommend the plain in preference.

THE EMPRESS.

The Empress Dress of Lilac Silk, trimmed with quillings of the same, and velvet of a much darker shade. The trimming up the front is put on cable fashion. Shawl of white cashmere, braided in black, and trimmed with black lace.

In Paris there is no decided change in the make of the bodice. The *Mousquetaire* dress has many admirers; it is trimmed with drop buttons made of steel. The *Amadis* bodice has a new style of sash, which is cut so as to form small basques all round the waist. There is a decided return to basques for morning dresses of every description, but all that have as yet appeared are very narrow ones, not more than an inch and five-eighths in width; these encircle the waist and terminate in front with two points.

THE JOCKEY.

French Merinos are again in great favor for home dresses, trimmed in a variety of styles. Some are embroidered in silk, others braided, and velvet is frequently used. The bodices of those French merinoes are made tight, and high to the throat, with two points in front and a small basque exactly in the center of the back. This basque, small as it is, is very becoming to a slight figure. The sleeves are made tight as far as the elbow, and then widen out to the cuff. The cuff is pointed and made of velvet, corresponding with the trimming of the dress. French merino has much to recommend it as a material for a house, or, indeed, an out-door winter morning's dress. It is soft, falls in graceful folds, and being made entirely of wool, is warmer than when a mixture of either cotton or silk is introduced in the fabric. With these points in its favor, French merino, like silk velvet, will never be really unfashionable.

THE MARECHELE.

A dress of fawn-colored foulard. The body is made with a basque, and with the skirt is ornamented with foulard in a darker shade, trimmed with large mould buttons covered with silk.

The Black and White Mania that has raged so long, both in London and Paris, extends even to the smallest articles, as that mixture is now very fashionable for aprons. We have seen some very tasteful aprons made of black moire antique, trimmed all round (for the corners were rounded) with a plaited black velvet ribbon, with a white edge; above this was a narrower ribbon of the same description, plaited likewise, carried along the bottom and up the right side. On the left side there was a pocket defined with the narrow black velvet white-edged ribbon. Dull and prosy as all descriptions of the make of fashionable attire must necessarily be, we assure our readers that when made up, these small aprons are exceedingly stylish and tasteful for morning wear.

THE RAPHAEL.

Dress of green rich silk, trimmed with black velvet. The square neck is ornamented with quillings of black lace. Tulle chemisette.

Dresses are generally worn quite high, and closing with small buttons: some, of course, prefer those opening with small *revers,* or the square Raphael style, but they will not be general. Skirts continue to be made long and full, and all plain materials will have trimmings on the bottom either of black velvet arranged in various forms, *ruches,* and even broad flounces with trimmings above them; where the skirts are trimmed, bodies may have a trimming to correspond, or may be left plain. *Moire antiques,* rich figured silks, poplins, etc., have as little ornament as possible.

In sleeves there is very little change as regards the form; wide open styles, shaped at the elbow, continue the most fashionable; the style of trimming must depend on that of the dress.

NAIM CLOAK.

Our diagram, this month, is of a fashionable cloak, called The Naim Cloak in Paris. An engraving of the cloak is given above. It is a paletot pattern and is made short. The material may be either cloth, velvet, or thick silk. The ornaments consist of binding arranged in arabesques.

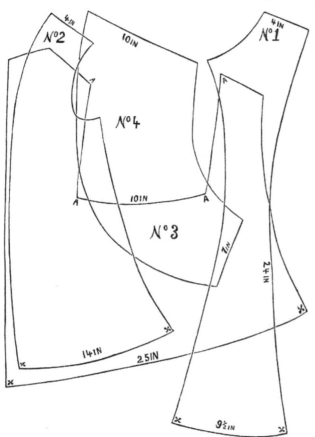

No. 1. Front of Cloak.
No. 2. Side.
No. 3. One Half of Back.
No. 4. Sleeve.

Those who copy this pattern must be careful to lengthen the side 30 C, (12 inches) from the places marked with crosses, following the bias, in order to have sufficient length and fulness. The same must be done with No. 3 back, except that it must be lengthened 45 C (18 inches) from the crosses.

Petticoats now form an important item of the dress. One thing is certain, that ladies will have to wear their dresses looped up out-of-doors, in consequence of the inordinate length of skirt which Fashion has decreed shall hold its sway. Pretty petticoats and well-fitting shoes are, necessarily, imperative: so we have this winter petticoats of every imaginable shade and design, and boots that are faultless in their finish and appearance. White and colored French merino petticoats, braided (for this fashion is carried even to articles of under-clothing), are amongst the novelties for carriage costume. They are exceedingly delicate and elegant, and on that account are scarcely suitable for walking. Quilted silk petticoats are quite taking the place of woolen ones, and black ones are the most fashionable. Eider down, though more expensive than the cotton wadding, being lighter, is used in preference to cotton, but wool is also exceedingly light and warm.

BODICE FOR YOUNG LADY.

Body and Sash of Black Silk for a Lady. – It is trimmed with narrow black guipure lace and rows of black ribbon velvet. It will be still more beautiful if made of black velvet, or if for a young lady, of blue, pink, green, or mauve silk.

Peterson's Magazine, February 1863

Morning dresses of Cashmere, not only of the prevailing colours we have already mentioned, but also of white, trimmed with some one of the prevailing tints, have been much worn in Paris, but up to this time they have been but rarely seen in England.

Ladies purchasing expensive silks should give the preference to the rep silk, this make being the most fashionable. These and the moire antique, are much esteemed for married ladies. The skirts are made very wide, each breadth being slanted towards the top. Those who wear the full complement of crinoline should have these dresses made four inches longer in the back than the front. Some have a thick cord covered with either black or white carried up each seam. The only trimming at the bottom is a row of gimp. This last-mentioned trimming is likely to be again much worn; and even a single row gives firmness to the edge of the skirt. Winseys also continue to be trimmed with the bossed leather, a line being worn up the front of each sleeve and on each plait of the Garibaldi body, when made in that style, as well as round the bottom of the skirt. Narrow bands, sometimes of the real fur, sometimes of the plush fur, are also very fashionable trimmings.

The bodies of dresses being worn much shorter than formerly, has naturally led to the restoration of the dress apron, which is made in various ways. First on the list is one of black velvet, trimmed with two rows of Maltese lace across the bottom, and one up the sides, set on with a slight heading of jet. Others are of black silk, having the Greek pattern in narrow ribbon velvet across the bottom; others are embroidered in coloured silks; others are rounded, the corners having a quilling of ribbon carried all round. We are glad to see the little dress apron restored to favour, as it is not only a protection for the dress, but an actual ornament.

We shall conclude our article with a description of our illustration, which is a dinner-dress for a young lady. The material is a silk of the fashionable green. The braces, with their long flowing ends, are of the silk, trimmed round with a black lace and a white blonde. The chemisette and the puffing of the sleeves are in clear white. Not being a ball-dress, there is no wreath, but simply a cluster of flowers arranged at the back of the hair. A pocket inserted in one of the long ends is both convenient and fashionable. These braces and bands can be made in black silk, and worn with a clear white or any other dress. They are also extremely pretty in Brussels net, embroidered with some elegant pattern, looking remarkably well either with the silk of any colour or a clear white dress.

The What-Not, February 1863

Fig. I. – Dress of Fawn-colored **Silk**, trimmed around the bottom with black velvet. Black **velvet** circular cloak, trimmed with broad lace. Bonnet of white tulle, spotted with black, with a cape and trimming of blue velvet, and a blue feather.

Fig. II. – Riding Habit of Dark **Green** Merino. – The left side of the skirt is finished with large buttons and a band of green silk; this band passes all around the bottom of the skirt. The body is made with a moderately long basque, and is open in front. Sleeves nearly tight, with deep cuff. Black felt hat, with long white floating plume.

Dresses are now made much flatter and narrower on the hips, and are rarely trimmed, except round the bottom of the skirt; and long sleeves grow narrower daily. For the promenade, skirts of dresses, when of rich materials, are generally without trimming, or with as little as possible. Bodies are made high, with the waist slightly pointed, sometimes with two short points; small pointed capes of velvet are being introduced, as are also *berthes* set on the same as on a low body.

THE VELVET JOCKEY.

Fig. IV. – Black Velvet Jockey Body, with long skirt, the back, two points in front, and quite close sleeves.

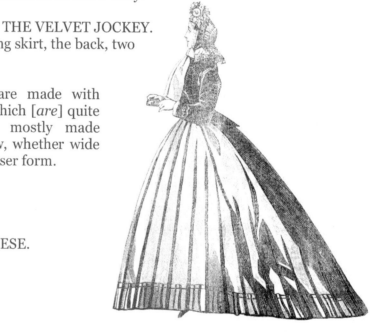

Some dresses are made with *Postillion* jackets, which [*are*] quite plain. Sleeves are mostly made shaped at the elbow, whether wide and open, or of a closer form.

THE MILANESE.

THE FLORINE: BACK AND FRONT

The low bodices are now cut extremely low on the shoulder, but not so much so either at the front or back. The lace tucker should correspond with the lace with which the dress is trimmed, and should be tied in front as well as at the back with black or colored narrow ribbon velvet. Some dress-makers tie the tucker on the shoulders as well, but this is not necessary for its well-fitting. Low bodices as well as high ones are made extremely short at the waist; the short sleeves are flatter and far less puffed out than they were last winter – sometimes they are even made quite flat, and are simply trimmed.

The Art of the Hoop: 1860 - 1869

Fig. III. – The Andalusian. – Dress of violet colored alpaca, trimmed with narrow black lace and velvet. The body is made high, and is trimmed to look like a jacket, shorter a the back than the rest of the body.

THE ANDALUSIAN.

BALMORAL SKIRT.

Fig. VIII. – Balmoral Skirt, trimmed with a wide Greek border and a row of buttons in front. All Balmoral skirts should be placed on a yoke, as in our pattern, as the heavy material is too thick about the waist, for either comfort or elegance, in the present style of gored skirts.

PRINCESS ALICE BODY.

Peterson's Magazine, March 1863

For dinner and evening dresses, the fashion which we gave last month is growing more and more into favour, the long ends being ornamented in various ways. Sometimes these, together with the braces on the body of which they are a part, are in white net, either prettily embroidered, or with a lace at the edge, within which is a quilling of narrow satin ribbon; sometimes they are black net, trimmed in the same way, but with crossings of black velvet half way up; sometimes they are half way of the silk, the remainder being in the black net, crossed as we have said.

The festivities [*for the royal wedding*] which are preparing, not only in the metropolis, but in every town in the kingdom, whether large or small, make us believe that we cannot do better than select a festive dress for all these unusually brilliant occasions. The one which appears in our illustration may be made in two or three different ways without injury to the style. The skirt, ornamented with scallops, is of pale blue silk; but in purchasing care must be taken not to select any of the old-fashioned blues, which now all bear a certain date, but those of the beautiful new dyes which have altogether superseded them. The scallops are formed by laying on successive rows of narrow frills, and gathering them up at regular intervals. A good-faced slight silk is even better for this purpose than an expensive rich one, being more pliant for forming the scallops. The upper skirt may be either blue tarlatan of the same colour or white tulle. The berthe is formed of smaller scallops to match the skirt, being laid on a foundation of stiff net. The clear upper skirt is, before looping up, almost as long as the silk one, being fastened at each place with bunches of flowers, either of white or to match the skirt. A bandeau of pearl beads is carried across the forehead, and clusters of the same flowers as those on the skirt placed towards the back of the head. The necklace and bracelets are also of pearl beads, of which the imitations are now so perfect, that they cannot be distinguished from the real by any ordinary judge, thanks to the Great Exhibition. The scallops should be finished with a narrow blonde edging, which can be bought by the dozen at a very low price. The same dress may be made of tarlatan, the two skirts being of the same material, and the scallops also of the same, but doubled instead of having the blonde edging.

The bodies of dresses are now chiefly made high and plain. In sleeves, one of the newest is cut to fit the arm, having a seam at the elbow as well as the inside, and a short full sleeve divided into three puffings, each fastened with a button. Some have the short sleeve divided into two, each with the same puffings and buttons. On the right-hand side of the skirt is a pocket, the trimming from which being carried up to a point at the waist, gives it the appearance of being suspended.

Another sleeve is made by simply taking a wide breadth of silk, half as long again as the sleeve is intended to be, slightly narrowing it towards the wrist, gathering it up into a band of fifteen inches long, and drawing the fulness at the bottom into a band of twenty inches long, carrying a ruche of pinked silk or a quilling of satin ribbon over each band, and setting in the sleeve with this gathering in up the front.

Another sleeve is made by cutting one as wide as a bishop's at the top, and shaping it down from the elbow, leaving some fulness to gather into a cuff. Up the front half of the sleeve, and close to the seam, is a band of velvet, ornamented with buttons, the same also forming the cuff.

We mention these three sleeves, because we know that ladies often experience some trouble in finding a sleeve to suit their taste.

The What-Not, March 1863

Fig. I. – Evening Dress of White Dotted Lace over White Silk. – The side breadths are lined with pomegranate colored silk. The body is made high at the back, but low and square in front, and is trimmed with a fall of lace. Lace also ornaments the bottom and side breadths of the dress. A narrow pomegranate color ribbon is run through the ruching around the neck, and there is a broad sash of silk of the same color. Head-dress of white lace and pomegranates.

Fig. II. – Carriage Dress of Fawn colored Silk, striped and figured with black. Around the bottom of the dress is a deep ruffle of plain fawn-colored silk, fluted, and surmounted by a row of black guipure lace. The body and skirt is cut in one, and there is a narrow guipure lace, which forms an Andalusian jacket on the body. Large sleeves trimmed to correspond with the body. White tulle hat, ornamented with lace and jonquils.

BREAKFAST DRESS.

Breakfast Dress of Green Silk. – The material is stamped to look like quilling. It is made without a seam at the waist, open in front, and lined with rose-colored silk.

A beautiful style of dress for home wear is the Empress' Veste, which is worn over a white braided foulard bodice, with a colored taffetas skirt. This Empress Veste is generally made either of black velvet or black corded taffetas, embroidered on the seams with black silk and jet.

The style of trimming the skirts of dresses has undergone but little change. The last new body which we saw was made with three points at the back, and four in front. This was particularly pretty.

WALKING DRESS.

Fig. IV. – Carriage Dress of Pearl colored Silk. – There is a narrow ruffle around the bottom of the dress, headed with a ruche of silk. Above this is a deeper flounce cut in deep scallops, and edged and headed with a ruching of silk. The waist is made with points before and behind, trimmed with quite a narrow ruche. A broad sash of silk is tied over these points. The sleeves are trimmed to correspond with the body.

WALKING DRESS.

Fig. V. – House Dress of Fawn colored Silk, Plaided with Black. – The sleeves and bottom of the skirt are trimmed with a fluted ruffle of blue silk. A low Andalusian body of blue silk is worn over the plain, high body of the dress.

Sleeves are usually made quite close to the arm to below the elbow, where they widen out in the funnel shape, or with a wide cuff.

It is very difficult to make under-sleeves to suit the present style of dress sleeves, which are made so narrow that hardly a frill of lace can be seen underneath; this is awkward, as it is impossible to present a dressy appearance in a high dress without showing a considerable portion of the white under-sleeve. For this reason white bodices have been more popular this winter than ever.

SENORITA JACKET.

Low bodices are frequently made of white silk, and over them is worn a high canezou. These canezous are arranged in a thousand different ways; the most simple are made with tucks, and are suitable for young girls; others with alternating rows of Valenciennes insertion and muslin bouillonnes. Some, too, are made with puffings of tulle, with narrow colored velvet ribbon run between, and with a lace collar. The sleeves have a seam to the elbow, and have puffings like the rest of the canezou. It is truly a pretty fashion; all these white bodices have a pleasant effect in a drawing room. White is cheerful and gay-looking, and very becoming; therefore ladies should wear as much of it as is possible in their toilets.

Aprons. – Now that dresses are made with short waists, aprons are very general for home wear. They are made short, and are very fancifully ornamented. Black glace silk and black moire antique are the favorite materials of which these aprons are composed. As we said before, they are short, and are generally rounded at the corners, although some few are made square. Those made of moire antique look well trimmed with three rows of black velvet ribbon, about an inch wide, with a white satin edge. Upon each row steel buttons are sewn. The pockets, which are slanting, are trimmed to correspond. Black glace silk aprons are sometimes ornamented with bands of black velvet, with the Greek design attached in white silk; others with a quilling of black silk all round, headed with a band of jet. All have small pockets in front, and are plaited into a very narrow compass at the waist. Small black velvet aprons are also made, trimmed with bands ornamented with small steel beads; in short, there is an endless variety in these small articles of dress.

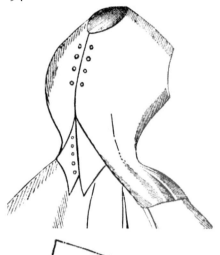

IN-DOOR JACKET.

We give, this month, a pattern for an In-door Jacket: with diagrams by which it may be cut out. The material should be silk velvet, or fancy cloth. This garment buttons in the same manner as the Figaro Jackets. Each side of the front is thrown back a little. From the waist behind, two large plaits are made; then, from the middle seam, one of the two parts composing the middle of the back is laid over ? on the other, as in men's coats. It is trimmed } with small flat buttons at the waist, down the front, and on the sleeves, which may be either closed at bottom, or left open and held together by laces.

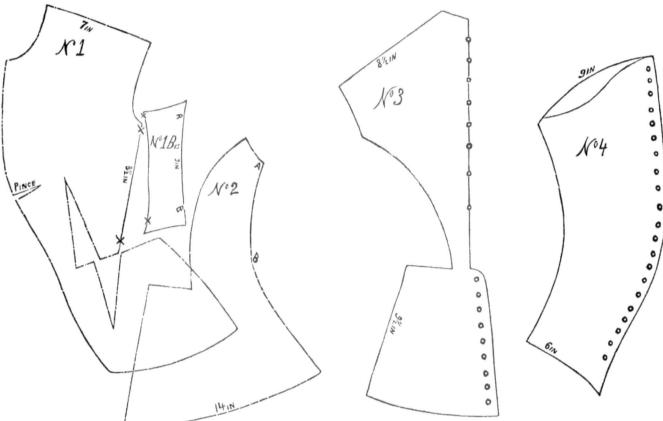

Diagram No. 1.
No. 1. Front.
No. 1. *bis*. Side-Piece or Front, put almost under the arm.
No. 2. Side-Piece of Back.
Peterson's Magazine, April 1863

Diagram No. 2.
No. 3. Middle of Back.
No. 4. Upper and under part of Sleeve.

In dresses, plain silks of those splendid dyes which have now been brought to such high perfection are most in favour. The beautiful colour which has received the name of the Alexandra blue, the magnificent purples and violets, and black, trimmed with any of their many shades, produce excellent effects. We have just seen a good glacé black silk made with a voluminous skirt, and with a ruche of violet round the bottom, merely clearing the edge of the skirt, which looked very elegant. Another of violet silk, with two frills of the same, each three inches wide, quilled at the upper edge, and bordered with black lace. Above these is carried a row of black lace insertion, having a black lace edging on each side, and, in other instances, three rows of narrow ribbon or a narrow niche, form the upper line of trimming.

Another striking style is the following: An Alexandra blue silk dress, with five rows of narrow velvet crossing each other in diamonds round the bottom of the skirt, meeting and crossing each other in the front, and so brought up to the waist in a pyramidal form, ending in two smaller diamonds at the top. The front of the body is crossed to match, commencing with two diamonds, and enlarging upwards to four. The sleeve is a wide bishop, with an epaulette at the top and a small gauntlet cuff at the bottom, both covered with crossings of the velvet.

Before leaving this part of our subject, we may mention that the sleeve which appears to take the lead in general favour is the bishop sleeve, having, as we have said, an epaulette at the top and a turned-up cuff at the bottom; or else three pointed tabs at the top, and the same at the bottom, covered with whatever trimming may have been chosen for the dress.

In our present illustration we give a dress in the simplest style, suitable for any young married lady. The skirt is of either a rich poplin, or one of those small-patterned mixtures of silk and wool which are likely to be much in favour during the present spring. Each breadth is slanted off towards the top. Jackets, which during the last year have been a little on the decline, are now again restored to favour, being at the same time recommended by their comfort and usefulness, and sanctioned by their having been so constantly worn by the Princess Alexandra, as will be seen by reference to numbers of her photographs. This jacket is made of black silk, and trimmed with plush of the same colour as the skirt. The body is of white muslin, formed entirely of folds, and trimmed round the throat with a ruche of narrow lace. Sometimes it is cut square, and finished with a band, having a very narrow black velvet and black lace at either edge. The under white sleeve has a turnover cuff trimmed to match. On one side of the waist a bow is worn, having two long ends made of the material of the skirt, and crossed with velvet, having a deep fringe below, the two bows at the top being arranged to hang down over the ends. The head-dress is simply a netted handkerchief thrown carelessly over the back hair.

The What-Not, April 1863

Morning Dresses still continue to be made in the same form as at the commencement of the winter, but the sleeves are altered. The white under-sleeves, which rather resembled a balloon, upon each hand, which were highly starched, so as to make them stand out more effectively, and which lost their fresh appearance after the first half-hour they had been worn, and assumed a crumpled, untidy look. These, we are happy to say, are at last banished. The sleeve of the dress is now made narrow; it is the same breadth all the way down, but to form it, it is cut with a seam to the elbow. A small ruche is arranged round the edge of the sleeve, and there are buttons as far as the elbow. The sleeves of taffetas dresses for evening wear are also cut in this narrow form, but frequently they are left open as far as the elbow, and the narrow white undersleeves, which are cut in precisely the same manner as the dress sleeve, are trimmed up with broad Valenciennes or Alençon lace, which falls through and imparts a more dressy appearance to the toilet.

Morning Dress of White Pique in Marseilles. – The Spanish jacket and skirt are braided in black. A jaconet Garibaldi skirt is worn under the jacket, and at the back of the waist is tied a black lace sash. Leghorn hat, trimmed with feathers and black lace.

Sleeves are worn rather narrow, and mostly cut like a coat sleeve to the shape of the arm.

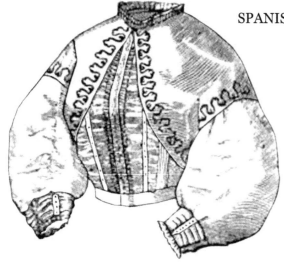

SPANISH JACKET.

A Velvet Zouave Jacket is very frequently worn at this season of the year over a white muslin skirt for evening toilet. The jacket does not reach further than the waistband; and underneath it is worn a satin veste. These Zouave jackets are convenient for wearing with light-colored taffetas skirts, the bodices of which have either lost their freshness, or have become ancient in form. A white lace or muslin veste can be worn instead of a satin one, and the Zouave can be trimmed with a black Maltese insertion, with white ribbon underneath it. This style, although not novel, is a very favorite one. It should be remembered that the sleeves of a velvet Zouave jacket follow the same rule as those of the high bodiced dress; they are made narrow, and if a white under-sleeve should be worn, it should likewise be cut with a seam to the elbow, so that it may set perfectly flat to the arm, and not cause a full or puffed appearance to the Zouave sleeve.

WALKING DRESS.

Fig. III. – Walking Dress of Pearl-Colored Foulard. The skirt is trimmed with two ruffles, above each of which are three rows of velvet. The deep circular cape is trim med to correspond with the skirt.

WALKING DRESS.

Fig. IV. – Walking Dress of Lilac Silk, striped with a darker shade of the same color. The bottom is trimmed with three ruffles, above the upper one is a ruching of plain lilac silk. A scarf mantilla of lilac silk, trimmed with a full narrow ruching of the same on each side, makes this a very stylish walking dress.

Bodies are usually made with small points both at the back and in front; but the postillion body, like that in our plate, is very much worn; and very narrow basques, too narrow almost to be termed such, are becoming fashionable. We will describe the shape of the Postillion Jacket, as, doubtless, there are many of our subscribers who would like to have one. The garment is stylish. The bodice portion is made to fit the figure with two points in front like a dress bodice, and may be arranged to close at the throat or open with revers. A very long basque is attached to the jacket behind, which is sloped off sharply at the hips. The sleeve is usually of the coat shape, with a seam at the elbow, cut rather long, and a lace ruffle is generally the finish to the sleeves at the bottom. We have seen these pretty jackets in velvet, silk, and cloth; and we may here add that they are very useful for wearing with old skirts, the bodices of which are worn out.

Very young ladies still patronize the Garibaldi bodice for evening demi-toilet. A blue or pink grenadine, or foulard, or taffetas dress, with a plain low bodice, and a wide sash, tied with hanging loops at the back, a full loose Garibaldi, made of either figured Brussels net, or of finely embroidered muslin, with a ruche of

Valenciennes lace round the throat, still continues to be a favorite style, and very becoming it proves to tall, slight, youthful figures, but should never be adopted by any others.

HOUSE DRESS.

Fig. V. – House Dress of Fawn-Colored Alpaca. – The skirt is trimmed with a piece of bias silk, opening on one side of the skirt and trimmed with a bow of ribbon. The body is made in the postillion style with a coat skirt at the back. Close coat sleeves, trimmed with silk like the skirt.

Those in velvet are decidedly the most stylish.

A Hint Economical. – Many of our readers are, no doubt, possessors of black silk dresses, which have done good duty and service as dresses. These may be converted into very warm and pretty petticoats, if a little time and patience be expended on them. We will describe the style of petticoats we mean, and then our readers will see the arrangement of the same. These, of course, may be made in *new* material as well as old, or alpaca may be substituted for the silk. The silk should be cut into *narrow* gores, measuring about six inches at the bottom, and sloped off to about two inches at the waist. Between each of the gores a thick piping of colored or white silk should be stitched, and the whole of the petticoat should be lined with eiderdown and good glazed lining. These are amongst the favorite shapes for silk petticoats.

Peterson's Magazine, May 1863

One of the most successful dresses of the season is a dove-colour silk, having three rows of French blue quillings of ribbon round the bottom of the skirt. This is worn with a pardessus of the same, bordered with a quilling to match, the sleeves being trimmed up to the top over the elbow as well as round the bottom. The pardessus is made partially, but loosely, to fit the figure, and is not quite so long as those worn last year.

For a young lady's evening dress the following is one that has not only an elegant appearance, but has all its freshness and purity renewed as often as it comes fresh from the laundry. The material is a spotted muslin, and our illustration shows the upper part of the body, together with the sleeve. This body is completed to the waist by means of a full front, and the fall of lace which borders it hangs from the shoulder over the top of the sleeve.

The skirt of this dress may be completed either by a simple hem or in the following way: Take a ribbon, not less than three inches wide, measure its width at the bottom of the skirt, making the hem the same, so as to give it strength, and lay across at equal distances lengths of a narrow lace insertion, finishing each side with a narrow lace edging, and then thread the ribbon through, merely fastening it at its ends. The colour may be blue, or green, or Magenta. The same insertion which is used for the body should be lined with the same colour ribbon, and the wrist of the sleeve also trimmed with it. The waist bow, which we spoke of last month, with its long ends arranged to correspond with crossings of the insertion over its own width of the ribbon, and the narrow edging all round, makes this very pretty dress complete.

The dear, delightful month of May brings with it the necessity for such a spring toilette as may harmonise with its sweet freshness and the bright tints of its opening verdure. The dress which appears in our illustration is silk of the fashionable blue, and the trimming at the bottom of the skirt is of silk of the same blue, only of a deeper shade, with a quilling of ribbon at each edge. The sleeve is full, but reaching only half way down the arm, having an epaulette at the top, and being also trimmed with a quilling of ribbon. The bow, with its long ends trimmed in the same way, is suspended from the waist by a loop. Sometimes the sleeve is made to reach the wrist, and is worn with a white cuff instead of the full undersleeve. The same dress is also made in the Russia leather colour, with a dark shade of the same at the bottom, and sometimes of light and dark shades of violet, and in all of these, the effect is very pleasing. A more elaborate mode of using the same style is to lay ribbons of the lighter shade upon this dark border, either three rows in Vandykes, or four as a double chain, the ribbon in these cases being not more than an inch wide.

As one of the most convenient fashions of the day is the adoption of the Garibaldi body for morning toilette, we may mention here the little change which has taken place since our last number. These bodies are no longer worn loose and overhanging, but have resolved themselves into simply-plaited bodies, made longer than are required to show, so that the skirt may be tied on over them, the line being covered with a waistband of the same material as the body. We have seen one of blue lama, stitched with white silk, and another of a small-patterned foulard, that looked remarkably well. Varieties have also appeared in Swiss prints, which are at once pretty and useful. These Garibaldi bodies assist an economical toilette very effectually, as they enable a lady to make any sort of skirt do duty for morning wear.

The What-Not, May 1863

Fig. I. – Dinner Dress of very thin White Muslin. The skirt is made with one ruffle, a row of insertion and tucks. The sleeves correspond. Around the waist is a sash of mauve silk, pinked at the edges. Bow and ends of mauve silk at the back of the head.

Fig. II – House Dress of Maize-colored Foulard, trimmed with a band of narrow cherry-colored velvet ribbon. The Spanish jacket is made to correspond with the skirt.

We mentioned in a former number that plain cambrics come with patterns *printed* round the bottom and up the front of the skirts, such as a buff cambric with a black Maltese lace pattern; another buff cambric with a bold braided design in black *printed* upon it, etc., etc. The effect of these printed imitations is so excellent, that at a short distance it is impossible to believe that the lace was not genuine Maltese, and that the design was not in reality braided upon the material.

SPANISH JACKET.

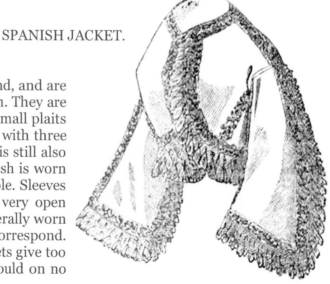

The skirts of dresses are still made very long behind, and are much gored, to throw the fullness nicely to the bottom. They are now arranged behind in large gathers, and plaited in small plaits from the gathers to the front. Bodices are being made with three points behind and two in front; the small tail behind is still also worn, but the round waists are never seen unless a sash is worn tied behind, and then this mode of bodice is admissible. Sleeves are made to fit rather closely to the arm, the long, very open sleeves being now seldom seen. Epaulets are very generally worn at the top, with a turned-back cuff at the bottom to correspond. Unless the figure is tall and slight, we think the epaulets give too much width to the figure, therefore stout persons should on no account wear them.

Basquines are coming in fashion again, though as yet they are so small as hardly to deserve the name.

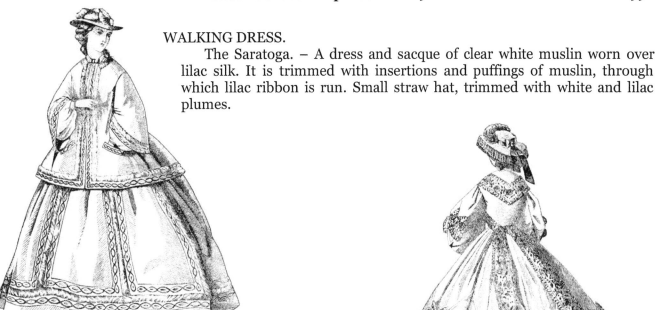

WALKING DRESS.

The Saratoga. – A dress and sacque of clear white muslin worn over lilac silk. It is trimmed with insertions and puffings of muslin, through which lilac ribbon is run. Small straw hat, trimmed with white and lilac plumes.

OUT OF DOOR DRESS.

The Baritz. – A dress of white muslin, made with two skirts. The upper skirt is open part way up at each breadth, and is turned back on each side and confined by bows of black lace. A long, narrow black lace scarf is put on the back in the style of a berthe, crosses in front, passes under the arms, and is tied loosely behind. Straw hat, trimmed with a black plume and black lace.

Dresses are made longer than ever in the skirt. They are generally much trimmed; the invariable plaiting round the bottom; above, either crossway pieces of velvet, hanging buttons, gimp, and floss silk ornaments, ruches, and bows of ribbons are all used for ornamenting the skirts: the trimming frequently reaches as high as the knee. In the street the dress is always raised, and the boots are visible; the most fashionable are those made of Russian leather, with leather or steel heels. These are the great novelties in boots; they are the invention of a noted Parisian boot-maker.

HOUSE DRESS.

The Amazon. – A dress of fawn-colored alpaca, braided around the bottom of the skirt. The body is made plain and high, with a skirt at the back cut in the shape of a leaf. This skirt is ornamented with braid, and the braiding is carried around in the shape of a belt to the front.

Camlets, alpacas, and foulards of one color, as well as figured foulards, are at present the favorite materials for morning dresses. They are usually made high and closely fitting to the figure, with two points in front, and with a small swallow-tail basque at the back. The sleeves are cut either open and very narrow round the bottom, small bell buttons being carried up the seam as far as the elbow, or they are closed at the wrist with a pointed cuff, which is at least a quarter of a yard deep. These gauntleted closed cuffs are very popular for morning wear, being found to be infinitely more convenient and comfortable than the wide hanging sleeves, with the pagoda-shaped white undersleeve, which so speedily lost its freshness, consequently its beauty.

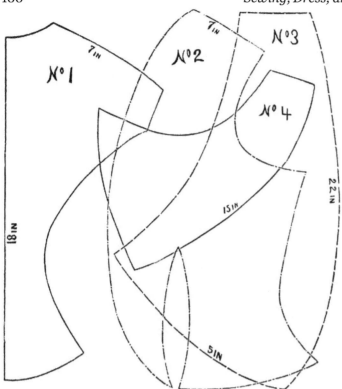

VESTE DANOIS.

The pattern which we give, this month, is that of a new style of vest, called the *Veste Danois,* to be made in black or any rich dark shade of velvet. We have given the pattern complete which consists of four pieces, namely, the front, side-piece, back, and sleeve: it does not close in the front, but forms a graceful curved line from the top of the shoulder seam, to the seam under the arm; there is no seam down the middle of back, and the form of the small jacket is extremely elegant and becoming. The sleeve is of the *gigot* form slightly shaped at the elbow; the fullness at the top is laid in large plaits, and at the wrist, where it fits nearly tight, it has a cuff turned back in the style of *Louis XIII.*: the top of the cuff may be either cut in points or scalloped. This *veste* is trimmed entirely round with rich gimp, the top of the cuffs to correspond; on each of the plaits of the sleeve there should be a gimp ornament. When this *veste* is made in silk the trimming should be velvet *en soutache*. It is intended to be worn either with a waistcoat or over a high dress. This pattern is for a lady of medium size and good figure.

WAIST-BODY: FRONT AND BACK.

Front and Back View of New Style of Swiss Bodies. – These bodies can be made of silk of any color, edged with white or black lace, as may be preferred, or they can be made of black velvet. As will be seen in the engraving, they are worn over thin white muslin bodies.

Peterson's Magazine, June 1863

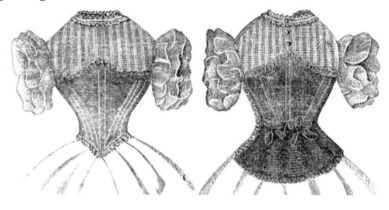

We have for this summer month of June, in expectation of its fervid heat and glowing sunshine, chosen for our illustration, not the dress for the promenade or the ball-room, but one in more constant requisition – namely, an elegant toilette for morning wear. We have selected this because we are aware that there is often more difficulty in choosing a morning than an evening costume. The dress we are now giving may be made in some variety of material. A plain nansook, a small check, or a pea-spotted muslin of mauve or blue, are amongst the prettiest. The skirt is made very wide, with a tablier front composed of rows of tucks and insertion in embroidery, being edged at the bottom and up each side with a narrow border in embroidery. The negligé is of the same material, and trimmed with the same. The fulness at the waist behind is drawn in by means of a slot reaching to the join under the arm, and is tied in the centre of the back with a wide bow, having long, flowing ends made of the muslin, and trimmed at the bottom with the embroidery. The cape may be either round or pointed, and a white muslin necktie edged with narrow lace completes the dress. The cap is simply an oval, left to bag a little for receiving the hair behind, and trimmed in front with a rosette of ribbon, bows, and failings of lace, or a quilling of ribbon at the sides. The sleeves may either be left open or be gathered up into a loose wristband. The advantages of this dress consist in its supplying an elegant costume for the morning, and that in going out it will only be necessary to lay aside the neglige and assume the black silk casaque or paletot, and the dress is at once complete for the promenade. If made of coloured muslin, some ladies will wear the tablier front lined with coloured silk to correspond.

We refer to our last month's illustration of the Fashions for the sake of pointing out some varieties in its application, showing that the style is approved. The broad bordering of silk at the bottom of the skirt is now sometimes covered with figured black net, the colour underneath being white, or mauve, or some other forming a pretty contrast to that of the dress. Again, this border being black on a mauve, or mauve on a black, has patterns of the contrary colour laid on in ruches, sometimes in diamonds, sometimes in serpentine lines. One that we have just seen has a very pretty effect, being in ovals formed by the ruche at regular distances.

The jacket is one of those articles of dress so thoroughly useful and comfortable, that we feel sure it will never again quite disappear from the toilette of any lady, and will be restored in new forms, just in the same way that other parts of dress go through their respective modifications. The latest novelty of this class is the Dagmar Jacket, patterns for which we have received since our last number of this journal. It is made to fit the figure, divides into two points in the front, has very little depth beneath the arms, but deepens again into a sort of jockey jacket behind, being trimmed round from the two points in front with a quilling of ribbon an inch wide. The sleeve is very peculiar, having two puffs let in both on the outer and inner line, with bows of ribbon attached to the points of each, and a quilling round the bottom. If made in velvet, the puffs of the sleeves should be in satin or silk. This Dagmar sleeve is equally suitable for any silk dress.

The What-Not, June 1863

Fig. I. – Evening Dress of thin White Muslin. – Down each breadth of the skirt is a puffing edged on each side with lace, through which a pink ribbon is run. The body is cut low and square, both at the back and in front, with the sleeves, is ornamented like the skirt. Sash of wide pink ribbon.

Fig. II. – Dress of thin White Muslin over an under-dress of delicate blue silk. The skirt sash and berthe are all trimmed with black lace.

White High Bodices for Evening wear are now displayed in great variety, and many of them are very tastefully arranged. The most novel are those which simulate a high and low bodice in one; the top being composed of plain organdy muslin, and the lower part of straps of embroidered muslin insertion, and Valenciennes lace laid on so as to give the appearance of a low bodice; these are generally finished off round the shoulders and throat with Valenciennes lace, and at the waist with a Swiss band in black velvet or taffetas.

Lace tuckers are still composed principally of Valenciennes lace and tulle illusion. As low bodices are now cut so as to require very wide tuckers, puffings of tulle and clusters of small loops of the narrowest ribbon velvet, placed at equal distances, are necessary, as well as the Valenciennes edging. The black velvet, which is introduced into the edging to hold the tucker in, should be tied in front as well as at the back; by doing so the tucker will set more evenly and securely.

There is a very palpable diminution of the amount of trimming upon spring dresses compared with those of last year. Upon the skirt the ornamentation now never reaches higher than from eight to ten inches, and frequently there is only a thick cording (as thick as an upholsterer's cord), made of taffetas or of the same material as the dress, and stuffed with cotton wool. This is sewn at the edge of the dress, either straight round or twisted round at each breadth. It is very strong, and preserves the edge from wearing out as effectively as the plaited mohair braid, which has now become common.

Embroidery and gimp, with jet beads introduced, will decidedly be the fashionable styles of ornamentation for shawls, mantles, and dresses.

EVENING DRESS.

Evening Dress of White Organdie figured with green leaves. The skirt has two ruffles around the bottom, the upper one passing up the right side of the dress in the tunic shape. Short puffed sleeves, and berthe of the same material as the dress. Green grasses and roses in the hair.

Many young ladies still adopt the loose Garibaldi bodice for morning wear for this season of the year. These bodices are very convenient when made in foulard; they are no longer confined with a band round the waist, but are left loose, and the skirt of the dress is placed over them.

SENORITA DRESS.

Dress of Black Silk. – The skirt is plain. The senorita body is made over a vest of violet-colored silk. Sleeves quite close to the arm.

Spanish Jackets. – The very tasteful fashion of wearing Spanish or Zouave jackets over the low bodies of evening dresses is still in great favor. The delicate texture of these jackets has a very lovely appearance over a colored silk, and gives at once elegance and grace to the simplest toilet. They are especially suitable to wear at evening parties and concerts.

WALKING DRESS.

Dress of Mauve colored Silk. – The bottom has a quilling of silk of the same as the dress, edged with narrow black lace. Above this quilling are two rows of trimming of a horse-shoe shape, also edged with black lace. The body is cut with two points in front and a small point at the back.

WALKING DRESS.

Dress of Apple Green Silk, embroidered around skirt with chenille in a feather pattern. The sleeves and the long skirts of the basque, at the back, correspond the skirt.

A great many dresses are made *a l'Empire*, which means quite plain and flat upon the hips; and now a way has been discovered of putting the waist under the arms by means of a wide band. This Roman band is made thick silk; it is very wide, and reaches high upon the bodice in front, and is tied at the back with a large bow. A good share of natural grace is requisite to make this band or sash appear to advantage upon any figure; upon quite young girls from ten to twelve years of age, whose figures are slight, it is the most becoming.

Peterson's Magazine, July 1863

The Art of the Hoop: 1860 - 1869

One of the prettiest styles for a summer dress is the following: A skirt made of some one of those light materials of which there is at present so large a variety, having a flounce of about five inches deep at the bottom, headed with a ruche of silk, and with another ruche of the same silk three inches above. The belt is slightly pointed at the top and bottom, both at the back and front, and at its lower edge is a goffered ribbon, two inches and a-half wide, headed with a ruche; the band being so cut away under the arms, as to be entirely covered with the ruche. At the left side, where the belt fastens, is a bow of the ribbon with long ends. The body is of white muslin, the fronts being formed either of t tasks alone or tucks alternated with a narrow insertion. The bishop sleeve is finished round the wrist with a ruche of the silk.

The same dress may be made in any coloured muslin, substituting three narrow frills at the bottom of the skirt, and making the belt of a silk to harmonise with the most prominent of its colours. In this case the body may be either of white or of its own material.

We commence with describing the dress which appears in our illustration, it being made in tarletane of the new pink, covered with ten flounces, each edged with narrow gimp or black edging. The body is trimmed with a puffing of the tarletane, and two rows of frills, to match those of the skirt, being cut low enough to show the chemisette beneath. The bow is of ribbon to correspond in colour. The hair is dressed with the long Alexandra ringlets, as worn by the Princess of Wales.

The same skirt is also now being made with the ten flounces, bordered with narrow white blonde edging, and a second skirt of white tulle worn over it, exactly of the same length, but finished with a richer and deeper blonde, and looped up at the side with a cluster of flowers as high as the knee. The effect is also extremely pretty when the skirt is made of a slight pink or white taffeta, the flounces being edged with a narrow French hem.

One of the most striking of the dresses now preparing for the fashionable watering places is a plain white cambric muslin, with a handsome border in black braid, worked on just over the hem of the skirt; a body made with three broad box plaits, each covered with a pattern of the black braid; a bishop sleeve, long, but not so wide as they have before been worn, with a turned-up cuff and epaulette, both ornamented with the braid; in front, a bow of the muslin made with long, wide, deeply-braided ends; and, to complete the costume, a large circular cape, almost of the size of a small cloak, made in the cambric muslin, with the border of the braid carried all round above a hem of an inch and a-half in depth. This dress is quite new, and we think well deserves to be recommended, for its air of superior style.

The Geneva body which we mentioned last month appears to be very much approved, and is becoming one of the established modes of the season. We notice one little improvement in it, which we shall here mention to our readers: The line of trimming which gives the apparent form of the jacket-front passing over the plaits which make it fit the shape sometimes appears to cut them in two, especially when the trimming, which is now frequently only one row of quilled ribbon, is rather narrow. To remove this defect, a few inches of the quilling are laid upon the plait, which not only hides the defect, but actually improves the general appearance.

After a long absence, the apron is once again returning into fashion. The one which appears in our illustration is very pretty made in black silk. The frills are pinked, and set on with a beading, being made a little narrower at the ends, where they turn round at the corners of each scallop. Sometimes a slight pattern in black beads is introduced. A macaroon button, covered with black velvet, and set on in the centre of a rosette of narrow black lace, is attached at each corner, and two others, with ends of ribbon placed a little way below the top. This apron should be put on before the belt of the dress, and looks well with one of the pointed or Medici shape.

The Spanish jacket and vest are useful accompaniments for wearing with any skirt; the jacket being rounded off in front so as to show a large portion of the vest beneath, which is made with three points in the centre, open towards the top with a turned-back collar, showing the chemisette beneath, formed of tucks and insertion, and being fastened at the throat with a very narrow necktie. The jacket is made of fine black cloth or silk rep, and the vest of white pique.

The What-Not, July 1863

Fig I. – Evening Dress of White Muslin. – The skirt has a trimming of diagonal puffings of about half a yard in depth. The body is made with a slight fullness, round at the waist, and square on the neck. Sleeves correspond with the body. Head-dress and broad sash of green ribbon.

Fig II. – Evening Dress of Blue Organdy. – The skirt is made without any trimming. Short puffed sleeve of white muslin. Berthe of white lace edged with black, and a broad sash also edged with narrow white and black lace. Head-dress of small white plumes and wheat ears with the body.

The Bodies of Dresses have a tendency to become gradually shorter. Two fashions are now adopted – the round waist and the waist with two small points in front and a jacket tail behind. This is called the *postillon* body, and obtains great success, especially for ladies that are young and of a slender figure. The latest mode of making a *postillon* body is to divide the flap or tail into three equal portions, and of each strip to make a box plait. This is both pretty and novel. With the round waists, bands made with points in front are often worn, with wide flowing ends rounded off at the bottom. Sleeves are decidedly to be *narrow*, like those of men's coats, and nearly as long; they are often slit open a little way at the bottom, and have epaulets, or shoulder ornaments, trimmed in the same style as the skirt, either with velvet, silk bands, or gimp.

WALKING DRESS.

Dress of Gray Foulard Silk. – The bottom of the skirt is cut in waves, and trimmed with perpendicular bands of blue velvet. The body is made with a point at both the front and back, and fastened with blue velvet buttons. The sleeves are trimmed to correspond with the skirt.

WALKING DRESS.

Dress of Fawn-colored Barege. – The skirt is trimmed with three puffings of barege put on loose, and full over bands of green silk, which extends on each side of the puffing. The sleeves are trimmed diagonally to correspond with the skirt. Plain round waist fastened with silk buttons.

The skirts of many dresses are made full, plain, and gored. An extremely thick silk cord, matching the dress in color, is frequently placed above the braid; it is what is called "girdle cord," and is as thick as an ordinary-sized finger. It is rather difficult to sew this cord on without puckering the material, but the difficulty will vanish if the needle is carried in and out, in the same manner as though a piece of Berlin wool work was being worked in a dress frame. The cord is sometimes placed straight round, and sometimes curled at each breadth, but in every case it should be sewn *above* the braid and not at the edge of the dress.

The Bodices of Morning Dresses are made plain with two small points in front; some are cut slightly square at the throat, a becoming and comfortable style to those who cannot wear the high closely-fitting linen collar. The back of the bodice has frequently a small basque in the center; this is formed with three pointed straps of the material; the center one being longer than the two others; these are held together with gimp or lace, and are generally joined on to the bodice with a box plait. They are novel but fantastic-looking, as are the ribbon-sashes which are tied at the back in large bows midway down the skirt; these latter are much worn in Paris by young ladies from twelve to fifteen years of age, the ribbon is carried round the front of the waist in its full width, cutting the bodice in two, and giving the wearer a very ungraceful appearance. Sleeves are decidedly narrow, and are cut to resemble closely a gentleman's coat sleeve, only with short epaulets at the top. Circular cloaks of the same material as the dress, and trimmed to correspond with it, are very fashionable for morning wear.

THE PARDESSUS DANOIS.

Our full-sized pattern, this month, is that of the *Pardessus Danois*. The pattern consists three pieces, namely, the top part of back and front, our paper not allowing us to give the full length, and the sleeve. In giving the full length to the pattern, the *middle* of back must 37 1/4 inches from the top to the bottom; the edge of front must be 30 1/2 inches, and the length of side seam 23 inches. In the sleeve, the seam at the back of the arm is left open at the bottom as far as the notch: this style of sleeve is in great favor, as is also the wide pagoda. This *Pardessus* is generally made in the same material as the dress, the trimming to correspond. The lengths we have given are for a lady of medium height, and they may have to be slightly increased or reduced as required by the height of the wearer.

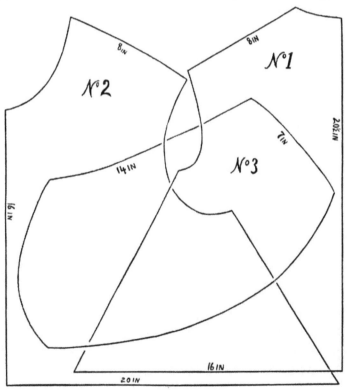

New Petticoat. – In London a new petticoat, christened "The Princess of Wales Petticoat," has lately been introduced, and is found to be an almost perfect invention for wearing under a dress which is made with a train. It is plain in front, like an apron; a flounce, which commences at the sides, is fulled on round the back; and a second flounce, quite at the edge, forms a train and holds out the dress. It is impossible, under thin dresses, to wear anything better than this most excellent contrivance. Many ladies, in Philadelphia and New York, have already adopted it.

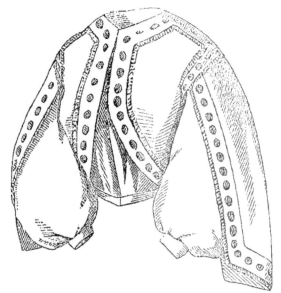

SPANISH JACKET.

Spanish Jacket of White Silk, with black guipure lace put over green.

A great variety of ornamental capes and corslets have made their appearance for wearing over plain low bodices. Small white muslin jackets we have seen braided with narrow colored mohair braid; Spanish belts or bodices, to wear over white Garibaldis, made in black moire antique, the front part being white, with a double row of small round gilt buttons; the black moire sides and box plaits at the back being corded with white; these lace at the sides and are very stylish-looking. Colored silk braces and a broad sash, made all in one piece, and trimmed with black and white blonde, are very general over low bodices; indeed the variety in these ornamental belts braces and sashes is endless; they prove very convenient to those who wish to vary the style of their evening dresses. These corslets and fancy braces are made of net, velvet, and lace, which cross in front, are carried round the waist, and are finished off with ends which form a sash at the back.

Small Aprons are very generally worn, and many we have seen lately were most tastefully arranged. Black moire or poult de soie are the usual materials, but the trimmings are various – rows of velvet with steel buttons; gimp with jet introduced; silk embroidery with jet beads intermingling with the flowers and leaves; narrow black ribbon velvet, with a white satin edge, made into rosettes or loops; black lace quillings and small drop buttons; and the inevitable black lace insertion lined with white silk, are all used to trim these coquettish looking little aprons. They are short and rounded at the corners, and the trimming is carried along the bottom and up *one* side; the pockets are generally defined by the trimming.

Peterson's Magazine, August 1863

Fashion is often accused of folly, sometimes worthily, and sometimes unworthily. In this present sultry season she has proved herself especially reasonable, and the ladies have great cause to thank her for bringing in those white muslin bodies which render the heat so much more endurable. These white bodies, covered with an elegant fichu, can be worn with any skirt, and are therefore extremely economical. In our illustration, the skirt is made of black or violet-colour silk, with a trimming of broad black lace insertion, having an irregular edge up each side. The fichu is composed of three rows of lace, or three fullings, with a deeper lace below: but these are also arranged in various ways, according to taste. The hair is fastened up at the back in one large loop, made to appear larger by being frizzed underneath before being formed into the loop by those who have not a superabundance. The flowers and feathers are, of course, only intended for special opportunities, but the rest of the dress is suitable for evening costume on general occasions, more especially if the clear white muslin body worn under the fichu be made high, and finished round the throat with a ruche of narrow lace.

But as it is so useful as almost to be essential to have some dress that may be worn independently of the laundress during the autumn months of the year, we will now mention one well adapted for this purpose. It is a black French grenadine, which, if the right sort be purchased, will be found extremely durable. This may be made with three narrow flounces set on in small plaits at the bottom with a heading, both edges of each being finished with a French hem; the body full in the front, the sleeve shaped to the elbow with a turned-up cuffs and epaulette of the same – each with a quilling of the grenadine edged with the French hem, and the same round the throat; in the front of the waist a bow with long ends edged to match. ... Ladies who have black silk dresses put by, cannot do better than have them made up as underskirts to wear with this French grenadine.

In silk dresses there is now nothing in better taste than those in black and white, some of which are in stripes, and some in checks not large enough to be of a very striking character. These are made with a skirt very long behind. They have no lining, but have a hem four or five inches wide. They are gored, and the breadths are sloped from the front to the back of the skirt, as well at the bottom as the top. We mean, that the breadths of silk are not left even at the bottom, but are slanted from the front one to those at the back. The skirt may be finished with a narrow plaited velvet, or it may have a ruche of black silk laid on about two inches from the bottom – not over, but upon the hem. The body is made low, with a short sleeve formed of one puff, but only slightly full, and with a belt fastened in the front with an ornamental clasp. The finish of this gives it all its peculiarity, and this consists of a fichu made in a new form, which has a very tasteful effect.

Ladies who prefer a long sleeve can have one shaped up to the elbow, the lace frills of the fichu over the shoulder forming a sort of epaulette, equally suitable in either way.

It is a very convenient fashion to have this low body made separate from the skirt a little longer than is required, so that the skirt maybe put on over it, without fear of showing the division, especially when worn with a band. In this case there should be a second body, made in the form of the Postillion jacket, which at once completes the dress for the morning or the promenade, and in this way the diversity may be made still greater by sometimes wearing a sprigged white muslin body, and sometimes one of white pique, according to circumstances or taste.

Another simple, yet rather marked dress, is the following: A Russia leather-colour silk, made with one flounce seven inches wide, edged with a French hem both at the top and bottom, and set on in small box plaits, each plait being five inches apart, the top of each plait stitched down, and either a button or a small bow of narrow ribbon placed upon it; the body cut square in the front, but high at the back and on the shoulders, with a ruche of the silk round the neck; a simple sleeve, reaching not quite so low as the wrist, edged with a quilling of the silk and an epaulette to match. This dress, worn with a lace chemisette, has an extremely good and rather peculiar effect.

The What-Not, August 1863

Fig. 1. – Breakfast Dress of Lilac Cashmere, trimmed with quillings of ribbon and large mould buttons covered with lilac silk. The skirt is open in front, and shows a handsomely embroidered and ruffled shirt. Cap of white lace, trimmed with lace and roses.

Fig. II. – Walking Dress of Brown Silk. – At the bottom of the skirt is a fluted trimming of brown velvet, and long sash like-ends of velvet, finished with tassels, fall on the right side. Body high and plain, fastened with brown velvet buttons, and the rather narrow sleeves trimmed correspond with the bottom of the skirt. White bonnet, trimmed with a tuft of brown feathers.

Gimp is decidedly the most fashionable trimming for dresses; frequently it is employed as braid to form a design round the bottom of the skirt, above the hem; epaulets are made entirely of gimp with a jet fringe, jet heads being also introduced in the gimp network which forms the heading. This style of epaulets is newer than those which are made of the material of the dress, and trimmed to correspond with the rest. Swiss sashes are also made of gimp, likewise ornaments for the seams of skirts; skirts are generally finished off with tassels. When the Swiss sash is worn, made either of gimp, or of guipure lace over white silk, a small basque is also added to the back of the bodice; this is usually arranged with hollow plaits. Three or four rows of black taffetas ruches, about six inches apart, sewn round the skirt in a waved form; rows of black guipure insertion lined with white, or one row of thick silk girdle cord round the edge, are also different fashionable styles of trimming now in vogue for the skirts of dresses.

WALKING DRESS.

Carriage Dress of Purple Silk, trimmed a deep fringe of black chenille with an ornament of chenille running up each breadth of the skirt. The deep postillion basque, cuffs, and jockey, are all made of chenille.

The skirts of silk dresses are all gored; the fashion of ornamenting all the seams, up their entire length, is decidedly on the increase, but this should only be done when the skirt is gored, for the reason that when the seams are left their full breadth some of the trimming would be hidden when plaiting it up to the waist, and this is obviated when the skirt is gored and shaped to the figure.

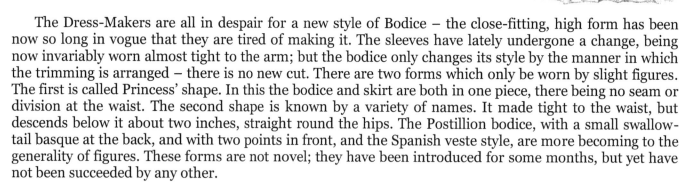

WALKING DRESS.

Carriage Dress of Green Silk, trimmed puffings of the same and insertion of black guipure. The body is square at the neck, with a chemisette of thin white muslin.

Many new taffetas have been made lately with one breadth of a different color inserted in the front; for example, a black and white checked taffetas would have a breadth of Mexican blue taffetas inserted in the front, the checked taffetas being rounded off down the sides as a tunic, whilst the bottom of the skirt would be ornamented all round with a black and blue ruche. This is an excellent style for widening a narrow dress.

The Dress-Makers are all in despair for a new style of Bodice – the close-fitting, high form has been now so long in vogue that they are tired of making it. The sleeves have lately undergone a change, being now invariably worn almost tight to the arm; but the bodice only changes its style by the manner in which the trimming is arranged – there is no new cut. There are two forms which only be worn by slight figures. The first is called Princess' shape. In this the bodice and skirt are both in one piece, there being no seam or division at the waist. The second shape is known by a variety of names. It made tight to the waist, but descends below it about two inches, straight round the hips. The Postillion bodice, with a small swallow-tail basque at the back, and with two points in front, and the Spanish veste style, are more becoming to the generality of figures. These forms are not novel; they have been introduced for some months, but yet have not been succeeded by any other.

For muslin or any very light material, especially for evening wear, plain bodies, half-low and cut square at the top, are much worn. A white muslin chemisette, with narrow plaits, is worn inside. Young girls wear the *chemise Russe* trimmed with insertions and small tucks, with the graceful Swiss bodice in black silk. This bodice is low, with a point in front, and trimmed with pinked ruches: it has no sleeves, but only epaulets, the sleeves of the *chemise Russe* being full and long.

Ball and Party Dresses. – Ball dresses, in Paris, are worn very elaborately trimmed, tunics are universal, cut to the knee in front and sloping down to the back. Underneath the tunic there are four, and sometimes five well-trimmed skirts.

The Art of the Hoop: 1860 - 1869

BODY FOR IN-DOOR WEAR.

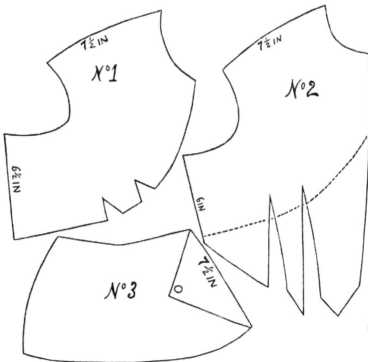

This very pretty model forms a jacket a silk waistcoat of another tint. The sleeve only reaches to the elbow, and is turned up with silk of the same color as the waistcoat. This body may also be of cashmere. The back is completed by a rounded postilion skirt laid in large plaits. This skirt is cut separate.

Diagram No. 1.
No. 1. Front of Body.
No. 2. Sleeve.
No. 3. Sleeve Trimming.

Diagram No. 2.
No. 4. Middle of Back.
No. 4. *bis*. The Postilion Skirt.
No. 5. Side-Piece of Back.

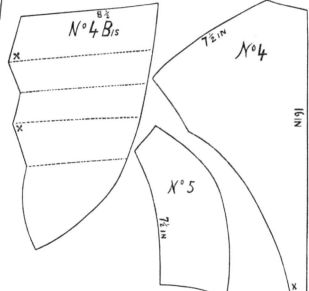

Sleeves are all narrow, not tight to the arm, but about as loose as a gentleman's coat sleeve. For afternoon wear many of the sleeves are left open as far as the elbow, so that the embroidered muslin or lace under-sleeves may be seen. All white under-sleeves should be cut in the same narrow form as the upper sleeves, otherwise they will cause a bulky appearance to the arm, which should be avoided.

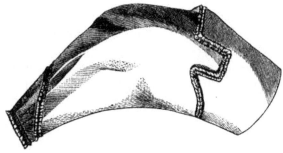

Closed Sleeve For Morning Dresses. – The lining and outer portion of this sleeve are cut the same shape, and are gathered into a plain piece underneath the epaulet. The fullness at the bottom near the wrist is confined means of *three double box plaits*, over which two rows quilling are placed, to keep the plaits in their proper position. The epaulet in the center is rather deep, and cut on each side in a square shape, the whole being trimmed with quillings. The shape of this sleeve is very becoming to any style of figure; it is quite full enough to be pretty, and yet would not increase the width of the figure, the plain epaulet at the top giving the desired sloping to the shoulders.

Peterson's Magazine, September 1863

We spoke last month of the black and white silks, either checked or striped, which were then being much approved, and which are still increasing in favour amongst ladies of the first style and taste. We have just seen a black and white checked silk arranged in a very simple manner, which had the most distinguished appearance. It was made with an ample skirt, and that length behind which approximates to a short train, gored, and had a row of black lace insertion round the bottom. The body, for the house, was merely one of white muslin, and for the promenade, a pardessus of the same silk as the dress, trimmed round with the same insertion: the sleeve was shaped to the elbow, and at the top was a short length of the insertion, with a tassel at each end in the way of an epaulette.

Another elegant dress is made of Pompadour silk, of the palest steel colour, ornamented with small bouquets of flowers, either in the same colour or in their bright natural hues. This is trimmed with two ruches of silk, formed into a chain, and at each crossing tied with a bow of ribbon. The body is the Raffaele, cut square, and low in the front, with a row of the same ruche carried all round the neck; the sleeve that of the bishop shape, with a very small epaulette edged with the ruche. With this dress a shawl of white lama, bordered with black lace insertion and a bonnet of white aerophane, trimmed with green, should be worn.

The dress which appears in our illustration owes all its style to this leading fashion being somewhat elaborately carried out. It is an evening costume, the material being a green taffeta, with six rows of goffered ribbon carried round the skirt, and either two rows of narrow black lace insertion or one wider one between each of the divisions. The bands which cross the body are of the same silk as the dress, ornamented with those black lace flowers and leaves which have lately been so very fashionable.

A soft and pretty shade of dove is a colour likely to be received with favour. We have inspected a dress of this, which had a very good effect, made with bows in black lace insertion an inch wide laid flat all round the skirt just above the hem, and so fastened down. The body was made with a little fulness at the back, the front having the plaits only in the lining, the silk being merely gathered in, a bishop's sleeve, and a bow with long wide ends in front, with a narrow quilling of ribbon round the throat; and a muslin necktie, either with its ends embroidered or made up of white lace insertion and narrow edging. With this may be worn a white lama shawl, or a black silk pardessus, and a bonnet of mingled white aerophane and blue silk.

Dresses composed of coloured silk skirts and white muslin bodies, worn with those Swiss belts or bodies which lace under the arms, are also much in favour. These last are worn over the muslin body, and have the appearance of very low silk bodies, being pointed both at the back and front in the centre of the top of each, as well as at the bottom. Sometimes they are of black silk or velvet, and sometimes of the same silk as the skirt. These bodies are also made in mauve, or violet, or blue, and worn with either a white or a coloured muslin. This season they have a rather peculiar and striking effect, but by the time that another year shall have opened upon us the eye will have become accustomed to their foreign style, and they will in all probability be much more general.

For a very simple and inexpensive dress we may mention those coloured linens which are now being made, checked with white, and which have so glossy an appearance as to be easily mistaken for silk. These, if with a pardessus of the same, make very pretty dresses for young ladies. They wash well, and look well to the end. They ought to be braided either in some slight pattern, with narrow white braid, or three rows of braid half an inch wide, turned up into some little ornamental device at the corner.

A pretty promenade dress is the following: A skirt of cinnamon-colour silk, two rows of ribbon velvet round the bottom of the skirt, an inch and a-half or two inches wide, with one row of black lace insertion between them. A loose jacket, of the shape known as the boating jacket, with a row of the velvet round the edge, and one of the insertions within it; the sleeve shaped to the elbow, and left open part of the way, having a row of the velvet and insertion as a border, and the same as an epaulette at the top of the sleeve.

The What-Not, September 1863

Nearly all the ball-dresses are of *tarlatane*, with under-skirts also of the same. There is rather a rage just now for white and black. For instance, the following pretty dress was lately worn by a young lady. It was composed of a skirt of white *tarlatane*, trimmed with narrow flounces, put on waved, at the bottom of the skirt, and separated by insertions of black lace. The body had a small *fichu* of *tarlatane* and black lace, and was finished off with a scarf of black lace, tied behind. On the front and shoulders, were *bouquets* of natural roses; and the hair was dressed to match.

White *tarlatane* dresses, with a colour underneath, or with *ruches* or pinked flounces, are very becoming for young ladies. Many are made as described, or with wreaths of flowers. For instance one dress of white *tarlatane*, with a narrow gauffered tulle flounce round the bottom, and, above it, two wreaths of myosotis and small roses.

Robe of white *tulle,* over a skirt of white silk. The bottom of the skirt trimmed with two rows of *bouillonné,* and a wide *ruche;* on which are placed, at equal distances, bunches of flowers, surrounded with black lace. The second skirt is trimmed exactly to match; and the third, of *tulle,* and looped up at each side, is trimmed with the *ruche* and *bouquets* only. Over this is a skirt of Chantilly lace, which, like the upper *tulle* skirt, is made shorter at each side. Pointed body of white silk, trimmed with *tulle* to match the skirt.

Dress of *glacé* silk; the upper half of the body made of a different coloured silk, and trimmed with insertion, either black or white, in *blonde.* Round the shoulders, a wreath, formed with *rosettes* of lace and silk alternately. *Coiffure* of ribbon and flowers.

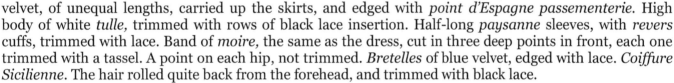

Robe of white *moire antique,* spotted with blue. The bottom of the skirt trimmed with bands of blue velvet, of unequal lengths, carried up the skirts, and edged with *point d'Espagne passementerie*. High body of white *tulle,* trimmed with rows of black lace insertion. Half-long *paysanne* sleeves, with *revers* cuffs, trimmed with lace. Band of *moire,* the same as the dress, cut in three deep points in front, each one trimmed with a tassel. A point on each hip, not trimmed. *Bretelles* of blue velvet, edged with lace. *Coiffure Sicilienne*. The hair rolled quite back from the forehead, and trimmed with black lace.

Gauze dress, with satin stripes, trimmed with *biais* folds, edged with *mauve* and white *chenille* fringe, to match the dress. *Bouillonnées* of white *tulle* between each fold, crossed with wreath of eglantine. Low body, with *postilion* jacket, edged with fringe. *Berthe* of white *tulle bouillonnée,* and trimmed with wreaths of eglantine. A wreath of the same flowers in the hair.

Travelling dresses. *Robe* of *foulard,* trimmed at the bottom of the skirt with five rows of narrow black velvet, edged with "Tom Thumb" balls in *passementerie. Casaque,* the same as the skirt, and trimmed to match. This fits to the figure, and is open at front over a waistcoat of the same. The skirt long, and very full. White straw hat, trimmed with feathers. Black lace veil.

Silk dress, bound round the bottom and up each seam to match the large buttons, with which it is closed up the front. *Pelisse* of black silk, richly braided and trimmed round with a wide insertion placed over a coloured lining. Hood trimmed to match.

The *Louis XV. veste,* cut after the model of the ancient hunting-dresses – a sort of habit body with a round *basque* – is in such favour at the present time, that it is more than probable many of the warm dresses for the coming season will be made in the same form. In velvet, lined with satin, it will have a very charming effect; but, of course, only admissible as an "at-home" dress.

Bodies are still made with points or *postilion basques*.

Passementerie, as we last month prophesied, will be *the* trimming *par excellence*. The *Figaro Epaulette* of *passementerie,* terminating in a fringe, is very graceful and becoming, and just now much adopted.

The body *à veste,* or with a waistcoat, is more than ever in favour. The waistcoat is frequently made of white cloth, or silk cloth; and will be much worn, both in white and in colours.

For example, with a cream-coloured *taffetas,* a waistcoat of white kerseymere; or, with a chocolate dress trimmed with violet a violet waistcoat. With Havana-brown, *groseille* or *ponceau* forms a pleasing contrast. We advise, however, when the waistcoat is coloured, that it be not too bright, as it would produce decidedly a vulgar effect.

The new skirts are made from five and a half to six and a half yards round the bottom, and are trimmed with ribbon, braid, ornaments in *point d'Espagne,* or *guipure passementerie* with or without beads intermixed – the latter being made in an immense variety of styles.

Bretelles and *corselet* of silk, trimmed with two rows of narrow lace, sewn together at the inner edge. The front and back of the *corselet* are made precisely alike. A row of wide lace is placed at the outer-edge of the *bretelles*.

Wide ribbon-sashes are still much patronized; but are no longer seen with such a great amount of trimming as formerly was fashionable. For instance, it is not carried up so high as the waist, but merely round the ends, and to about six or eight inches up the sides. Some of the ribbons made for this purpose are truly splendid. It must, however, be confessed that it is a very expensive fashion, as it necessitates a sash to match each dress, unless a lady is economical enough to content herself with a black one, trimmed with lace or *passementerie,* which is in very good taste, and looks well with any dress. The *ceinture postilion* is made in black velvet with a *plastron* of white *moire antique,* on which is placed silver buttons. This produces a very stylish effect.

Dresses when looped up for out-of-doors wear, have fewer festoons than formerly – four being the fashionable number. One in front, another at the back, and one on each side.

Le Follet, October 1863

Fig. I. – Walking Dress of Leather-colored Poplin. – The skirt is made very long and full at the bottom, and trimmed with a quilling of the same material. The front of the skirt is ornamented with a fine gimp, whilst a heavier gimp of a trefoil pattern extends part of the way up each side. The body is cut with a small basque in front and at the back, and with the sleeves is trimmed to correspond with the skirt. Bonnet of blue silk ornamented with a white plume and lace.

Fig. II. – Evening Dress of Light Blue Silk. – Opera cloak of white cashmere, trimmed with black velvet and black lace.

The newest low bodices are all composed of white tulle or white silk in the upper part of them. The most fashionable manner of making a black moire evening dress would be to make a low bodice first of white silk with two *bouillonnes* around the top of white tulle, and over this a black velvet or moire corslet, the sleeve being formed entirely of white tulle. This imparts a very light appearance to a heavy evening dress.

The fashion of scolloping the dress round the bottom of the skirt instead of hemming it, has become very popular, especially for poplins. For simple morning toilets, the scollops are either bound with braid or velvet of a darker shade than the dress, or sometimes with black silk or velvet; for more dressy occasions, a ruche, or a narrow box-plaiting is placed upon the scollops, and we have seen them also bound with silk, and ornamental buttons placed upon the scollops. With poplin dresses, paletots of the same are always worn; these are short, with a seam in the center of the back, and are cut to fall in to the figure without fitting it too closely; they are generally bound with velvet, or corded with silk – the gimp buttons down the front being very ornamental.

FIGARO BODY AND WAISTCOAT.

We give, this month, diagrams for a Figaro Body in front, with short skirts behind, and under it a body in the waistcoat form. The waistcoat is made of a lighter tint than the jacket.

Diagram No. 1.
Pattern No. 1 is the Front of the Waistcoat.
Nos. 2 and 3 form its Back and Side-Piece.
Pattern No. 1 *bis* is the Front of the Jacket.

Diagram No. 2.
No. 4 is the Middle of its Back.
No. 5 its Side-Piece.
No 6 is the Sleeve. It is gathered in large plaits at top, where it presents the leg-of-mutton shape, while it fits close at bottom.

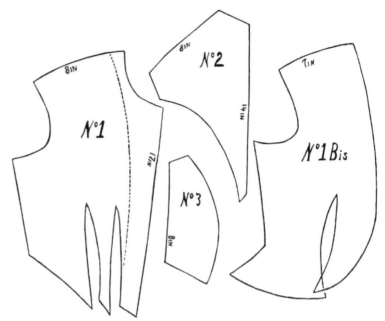

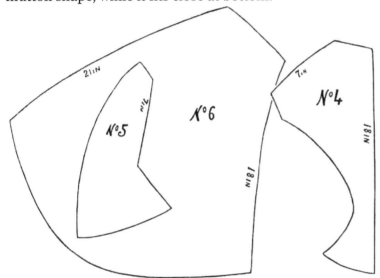

The sleeves may be made of a lighter tint than the waistcoat; but in that case; it must have at bottom a deep turned-up cuff in the Louis XIII. Style, indented at the edge, and made of the darker tinted material like the body of the jacket. This cuff must be six inches, and the points bordered with a narrow black lace. Then also on each of the plaits at the shoulder there must be a dark button set in lace.

We may here remark, for the benefit of amateur dressmakers, and for those who never manage to get their dresses to set high and neatly at the throat under the small linen collars, that a plan has been devised to accomplish this. Instead of cording round the top as heretofore, a small band of the same material as the dress, is arranged in the same manner as the strap which attaches the collar to a habit-shirt. This band being cut separately, and then joined on to the high bodice, will be found easier to fit neatly round the throat than when the bodice is simply corded round the top, and this arrangement also suits admirably with the strap of insertion edged with narrow Valenciennes, and with lace ends now so much in vogue, instead of a collar.

Peterson's Magazine, October 1863

One of the prettiest of the autumn dresses is made of a good alpaca, of a soft brown; the bottom of the skirt being ornamented with a light, but rather diffused pattern, in either chain-stitch, in black silk, or a fine Russia braid. The open parts of the pattern are filled in with a little embroidery in satin-stitch, in violet-colour silk, the loops of the braid or chain-stitch being enriched with a leaf, and the rounds with spots in their interiors. The dress is made with a jacket rounded off in the front, so as to show either a waistcoat of the same material or a white body underneath. The jacket is trimmed to match the bottom of the skirt, and if the white body is preferred, then a band, pointed both upwards and downwards, covered with similar work, must accompany it. The sleeve is shaped to the elbow, and bordered with the same; but it is left open, so as to show the white under-sleeve, which, as we have said in a previous number, is no longer worn full, but shaped to fit the arm rather loosely, and is trimmed to about the depth of five inches with lace insertion or puffings of net. The skirt, of course, is gored, and made with a slight train behind. With this dress may be worn either a shawl or a black silk paletot.

The dress which appears in our engraving is made of either pink or white tarlaton. It has two skirts of equal length, the upper one being looped up on the left side with a cluster of flowers; on the right is a small bow with long ends, headed with another cluster of the flowers. The stomacher is formed of puffings of the tarlaton, and the braces of the same, edged with a narrow blonde; the sleeves are double puffs, with a blonde at the bottom. The hair is ornamented with a group of the same flowers as those upon the dress. As the two skirts of the dress are merely furnished with a broad hem, it is necessary that the under-skirt should have a quilling of some kind round the bottom, to make it spread out. If the under-skirt is of silk, it should have a quilling of ribbon laid on the hem; if of cambric muslin, it should be bordered with two narrow frills set in well-starched box plaits.

A silk dress of the Russia leather-colour should be made in the following way: The skirt gored and long behind, lengths of ribbon velvet, an inch wide, cut of three, four, five, six, and seven inches in length, and laid on perpendicularly all round the bottom, about a couple of inches apart, at the top of each an ornamental button. These graduated lengths of velvet form a pretty wavy ornamental line at the top, and look especially well when the button is relieved with black jet. The body is made to fit the figure, lengths of the velvet being laid upon it, in the fan shape, from the waist upwards, both back and front, each finished with the button. A band of velvet with long ends, widening and pointed at the bottom, must be fastened round the waist with a jet ornament in front. The sleeve is shaped to the elbow, with graduated lengths of the velvet rising upwards over the cuff.

A dress of Humbold violet silk has a very pretty effect made as we are about to describe: The skirt should be cut about an inch and a-half shorter than is required, the lining being of the proper length. On this lining there should be three narrow flounces about an inch and a-half wide, the bottom one of black silk, the next of the same silk as the dress, the upper one again of the black. The bottom of the skirt should be cut into scallops (taking the half-circles from an ordinary tumbler will give the dimensions with sufficient accuracy); these should be piped round. This scalloped skirt, falling over the flounces and fastened down in each division, produces a very pretty effect. Ladies whose dresses have got injured at the bottom will find this style an excellent mode of restoring them, and for economy's sake, they can make the flounces of some other colour, using some discarded dress for the purpose. The body of the dress of which we are now speaking is made with box plaits, both back and front, with velvet braces, narrow at the waist, but wide enough at the shoulder to fall over the top of the sleeve, being cut into two points, each of which is finished with a tassel. There is also a collar of black velvet, pointed both back and front. The ends of the braces are continued from the waist, widening down into long pointed ends, each of which is finished with three tassels. The back also corresponds. The sleeves are shaped to the elbow, and have a turned-up cuff of the velvet. All these different parts of the black velvet are edged either with a narrow black lace or gimp. No white collar is worn with this dress, but merely a ruche of narrow white lace.

Ladies who are wearing the jacket body should all adopt the new leaden button which has been recently introduced, sewn in the inside of the bottom of the jacket. These are added to give such a weight as may prevent the jacket from turning or wrinkling up, to which it has always a tendency, and which is, of course, a disfigurement.

The What-Not, October 1863

Although the winter *toilettes* have scarcely begun to make their appearance, we are able to give some very decided information as to what will be fashionable for the coming season. High bodies will be exclusively confined to morning-dress. For at home, dinner, or evening-dress, *fichus* or lace *vestes* will be worn over low bodies. The *veste camail* or trimmings placed on the body so as to imitate it, is still much in vogue. Many *corsages* for *negligé* dresses will be made with *postilions basques,* especially those trimmed in jacket fashion, so as to form a waistcoat in front.

The dresses made in the *princess* style, body and skirt in one piece, will be much used for visiting-dresses made of rich materials. Full evening-dresses will be as much, or, if possible, more, trimmed than ever.

The Art of the Hoop: 1860 - 1869

Skirts are still made very long and very full at the bottom.

We must not omit to mention that several dresses are made with waistbands, especially those of *taffetas*. Some of these bodies are laced in front, and have ends of the material edged with lace; others form a band in front and *basquine* behind, ending in a scarf (or sash) to match.

Le Follet, November 1863

Evening Dress of Figured Silk, trimmed with rich lace.

Pretty slight figures do well to adopt the sash, especially if it be a long one, for the wide sashes shorten the figure. Short, dumpy figures should, on the contrary, adopt the bodice with the lancers' basque at the back, and with two small points in the front. Young married ladies adopt the *chemise Russe* in white foulard, embroidered with silk and finished off with the hussar sash, which is newer than the Swiss band.

WALKING COAT.

Many ladies, as if tired with the excess of trimming lately disposed over all their dresses, wear now no trimming at all, their dresses being made quite plain, but with an immense train, the skirts and bodices being entirely unornamented. This has a particularly good effect with glace silks, which are again coming into fashion, pearl-gray shot with lilac being the greatest novelty.

Tartans are very popular for dresses. The dress is cut in the Gabrielle form (the bodice and skirt in one piece in front), with a paletot or circular cape to match; the Rob Roy and the Forty second being the favorite plaids.

SPANISH JACKET.

Lonjumeau Body, (*Back and Front View*.) Silk jacket ornamented with braid and galloons. This jacket has a collar and lapels. The Zouave sleeve is fastened at bottom by a lace and tassels. Four tassels on the short skirt behind. This body is accompanied by a silk waistcoat of a color contrasting with that of the toilet.

What we said last month, we now repeat: the greater number of dress-makers are goring the skirts of dresses, with the object of diminishing the quantity of gathers about the hips, and making the figure as flat at the waist as possible. Now, this object can be more easily attained if the petticoats are gored likewise, and those who object to the gored breadths as being liable to be pulled out of shape at the wash, can overcome the difficulty by inserting a piping when sewing up the breadths. This piping or cording will sustain and strengthen the seams, and effectually prevent any loss of shape at the wash.

BRAIDED JACKET: FRONT AND BACK.

Raphael Body, low and square across. Waist round. It is trimmed with black bands between two ruches. A vandyked jockey similarly trimmed. Sleeve oval, that is to say, narrowest at the shoulder and the wrist. Same trimming. Black silk tassels.

DRESS SLEEVE.

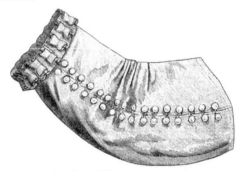

Peterson's Magazine, November 1863

A very pretty and not expensive dress may be made of winsey, trimmed with a lively, handsome-looking plaid. The winseys of an inferior kind ought never to be purchased, as they are nothing more than fabrics of common cotton, while those of a superior quality are extremely durable, and may be worn by any lady. These winseys should be made with a widely-flowing skirt and a band of plaid cut on the bias, of about three inches wide, laid on just above the hem. With this should be worn a pardessus of the same material, cut so as loosely to fit the figure, with a sleeve shaped up to the elbow. A border of the plaid, the same as that upon the skirt, should be carried round the pardessus, which should be made with a small cape, pointed both back and front, and trimmed with the plaid to correspond. The colour of the winsey may be either a deep lavender or a claret, both of which contrast well with the plaid. As this dress is intended for wear in some of the winter months, the pardessus ought to be lined, and ladies would find that an under body or vest knitted in a soft yarn, or one made of the scarlet flannel now so much in use for under-skirts, would render this dress warm and comfortable for even inclement weather.

Another dress, of one of the knickerbocker winseys – by which we mean some that are made with a sprinkling of different colours, such as dark and bright, with a slight proportion of red and black – looks very effective trimmed with a black braid not less than three-quarters of an inch wide. With this braid a pattern of corresponding boldness is formed up each breadth in the pyramidal form, reaching half a yard high, and arranged by the crossings of the braid – broad at the base, but graduated upwards to a point, a loop being left at each turning of the braid. A pardessus of the same material, trimmed to match – that is,

with one of these pyramidal patterns rising upwards from the centre of the back, and a small one descending from the throat down the middle of the back, and corners in the front, with a turned-up cuff, also trimmed with the braid – completes the walking costume. If the pardessus is lined, it will be suitable for many of the bright days of winter.

Knowing that every hour in the day requires it [*sic*] own appropriate costume, and that not one of them can be neglected with impunity, we have thought it desirable, for the usually cold and foggy month of November, to supply one of those warm and comfortable morning robes which may be suitably worn at the family breakfast table. In our illustration the material is scarlet flannel. Up the front is a fulling of the flannel set on with a heading on each side, the edges being pinked. This trimming is carried up the front of the body, which is slightly fulled in, both at the back and front, and carried round the neck. The sleeves are trimmed to match. This sort of dress is usually worn over a white under body, of which the sleeves are visible, forming a good contrast to those of the red flannel; but sometimes these are also made of the same material. Although pockets are not now approved in the fronts of dresses, yet some exceptions are made for the morning toilette; and one of the dresses we are now describing has just been made by a fashionable West End house with two pockets in the front, trimmed at the top with the same heading, and a bow at the side of the waist, having long wide ends, with two rows of the falling at the bottom of each.

The What-Not, November 1863

The Art of the Hoop: 1860 - 1869

Plate I. – Home and visiting-dresses. *Robe* of plush, skirt very long and full; the front breadth set in quite flat, and cut pointed at the waist, so as to form a *ceinture Suissesse*. At the bottom of the skirt is a wide band of velvet edged with *guipure,* and up the front a row of flat buttons to match. *Senorita* jacket, with long tight sleeves, trimmed like the skirt, with velvet and *guipure*. Lace *chemisette,* and under-sleeves. Cap of *tulle* and lace, trimmed with a *bouquet* of flowers. Dress of black silk; at the bottom of the skirt a trimming composed of narrow velvet and quilled silk, forming a wreath of leaves. Petticoat of white *moire,* with a lozenge-shaped trimming in plaid velvet. Small *collet* of plaid plush, with a deep *chenille* fringe all round. Black velvet bonnet, with *fanchon* of plaid velvet, edged with *chenille* fringe, a bunch of flowers inside, and feathers outside the front. Child's dress of woollen material in large checks; at the bottom of the skirt a narrow flounce bound with French merino, the colour of the checks; a wide band of the same above the flounce. Merino jacket braided; waistcoat of Indian *foulard*; undersleeves of muslin.

The corslets will be much worn for full-dress this winter. They are exceedingly charming made in silk, velvet of light colour, or even to match the skirt; some are made with braces, but they are rather too juvenile in appearance to be worn excepting by children. Sleeves of *negligé* robes are as small as ever, just sufficiently large to pass the hand through; but for visiting-dress they are a trifle larger, and cut open up to the elbow.

Plate II. – *Moire* dress, trimmed on the skirt with three rows of English lace – the lowest put plain round the skirt, the two upper ones in wide festoons, the points of the lower festoons joining those of the upper row, and fastened together under a flat bow, also of lace. Low body, trimmed with folds of silk and lace; *bouquet* in front. Sleeves short, and *bouffantes*. Headdress: *bouquet* of lilac, and *tulle* scarf rolled in amongst the hair, and falling in long ends at the back.

Robe of *tarlatane,* trimmed with a narrow flounce of the same gauffered, surmounted by a double wreath of *pompon* roses and myosotis. The upper skirt, which is raised *à la Watteau,* is trimmed to match. Low-pointed body, sleeves, and *berthe,* to match the trimming on the skirt. Wreath of roses and myosotis in the hair.

Bodies of visiting-dresses are made plain; points are generally worn only with more dressy *toilettes*. *Basques* are getting more and more in favour. They are made in many different styles: the old *basque* seems to be reappearing; some are made very long behind, cut up on the hips, and with two points in front; this is novel and rather becoming to stout persons. The little *postilion basques* meet with great success; they are made of *passementerie,* of lace, of stamped velvet, and of material like the dress; the front, a small waistcoat of *taffetas,* or *moire,* of a colour suiting the dress, and trimmed with hanging buttons of gold, *passementerie,* or oven sequins. The *basquine* is often made of black velvet with a white *moire* waistcoat. It can be made also of blue and green plaid velvet, with a blue, red, and white, or plain white waistcoat.

Thick dresses, such as plush or *moire antique,* will most frequently be made in the Princess' form. They will be much trimmed down the front, either with embroidery in fine *chenille,* with *passementerie,* or feathers; the latter, perhaps, is the greatest novelty; the bottom of the skirt must be very full, and, if not made *à la Princesse,* the breadths must be cut a little in a point – indeed, this is quite necessary now the skirts are worn so long and full; it would be impossible to put the whole fulness in the waist.

Veste Postilion of muslin, over a silk lining trimmed with a *bouillon*, edged with worked muslin; the sleeves, quite plain and small, have a *bouillon* round the wrists, up the back of the arms, and round the armhole, with five flat bows of unequal length, forming *epaulettes*. Back of the same jacket, the side-seams and *basque* trimmed to match the rest of the body, with a flat bow behind to match the *épaulettes*. ➜ ↘

Le Follet, December 1863

A Charming Neglige Toilet was lately made for the Princess de Metternich in Paris. It consisted of a plaid green and white poplin skirt, upon which there is no trimming; but the skirt was very long, and measured at least seven yards in width. An embroidered white *percale* waistcoat with a Valenciennes lace cravate in front; a green velvet jacket embroidered at the edge with steel beads; narrow sleeves similarly embroidered with a heavy necklet consisting of a double row of large embossed steel beads round the throat, one row failing low on to the waistcoat; a blonde cap with violet and green flowers and ribbons; no strings. The princess wore green Morocco slippers and white silk stockings, dotted with tiny violets. Plaids are very extensively employed in almost every variety of French toilets. The Rob Roy, the Stuart, and the Macdonald are all in great favor.

Fig. I. – Crimson Velvet Dress, made high in the neck trimmed with fur. Head-dress of lace and flowers.

Fig. II. – Raphael Body Dress of Silk trimmed with velvet. Puffed cambric sleeves.

Dresses are likely to be made with much less trimming than heretofore during the autumn and winter; but the skirts are made more than ever with a train. The widths are gored at the top, so that the skirt may be nearly plain at the hips, and fall wide and full round the bottom. Crinolines are made of a shape to correspond – narrow at the top and expanding gradually downward; petticoats should also be gored to fit well under the dress.

HOUSE DRESS.

House Dress of Fawn colored Cashmere. – The skirt has one deep flounce box-plaited on, and ornamented with large black velvet buttons; four rows of narrow black velvet are put on above the flounce. Body high and plain, and sleeves to correspond with the skirt.

The Art of the Hoop: 1860 - 1869

MORNING DRESS.

House Dress for Morning. – Skirt of gray cashmere, with a loose sacque of dark blue cashmere, trimmed with bands of fur.

The sleeves are now always cut with a seam to the elbow; for afternoon wear they are not stitched up, but are left loose as far as the elbow, where they are caught together with three small bows made of similar ribbon velvet to that upon the dress. The lace of the under-sleeve should be carried up as far as the elbow, and be left to fall through the opening; in all cases, the white muslin under-sleeve must be cut after the same pattern as the upper taffetas one, the shape of the sleeve itself being almost tight to the arm, any fullness underneath it produces a clumsy awkward effect. Epaulets, made of either lace or gimp, are much used at the top of sleeves. A band half an inch wide, of the same color as the trimming upon the dress, is now generally stitched round the top of the bodice, instead of a piping; this band possesses two advantages; it causes the bodice to fit closer and higher around the throat than with the simple cording, and under a fine lace collar it produces all the effect of a neck ribbon.

SPANISH JACKET.

Spanish Jacket. – The skirt, jacket, and waistband are of dark gray poplin. The waistband and jacket are braided in black, and trimmed with black hanging buttons.

For Young Ladies, jackets will be very generally worn, with white muslin chemisettes, and pointed Swiss bands underneath them. The jackets are made in two forms, either they are rounded off in front and are cut straight at the back, being sufficiently short to allow of the waistband being visible, or they have a postillion basque at the back, which proves a very becoming addition to slight figures; but in both forms the fronts are very short and are rounded off. These jackets are generally made the same material as the dress, or should the skirt be minus the bodice, then black silk or a colored cashmere (assorted to match the dress) is employed, and these materials are trimmed either with guipure or black gimp. The chemisette may be made either of white muslin, tucked or puffed with rows of embroidered insertion down the front, or instead of muslin, foulard (white or buff) trimmed with black lace or braided, may be substituted.

The hussar waistband is usually worn over a high white bodice, and is newer and more dressy than the Swiss band, the small gilt or silver buttons adding so greatly to the effect.

The New Petticoats are exceedingly pretty; they are made of a soft woolen material, closely resembling cashmere, and should match precisely the color of the dress. They are self-colored, but to prevent the monotony of both upper and under skirt being of the same shade, there is a band of black or of a contrasting color introduced above the hem of the petticoat, and upon this band there is a tasteful design woven in silk. The narrow black and white striped petticoats made of a French material, with the stripes running downward, are much patronized; many of these are trimmed with narrow scarlet or Magenta flounces; these are gauffred, and sewn on with a heading and edged with narrow black gimp; one or three flounces in this style may be worn according to taste. The black cut velvet forms an inexpensive trimming for this style of petticoat. Knitted under-petticoats will, it is expected, be much patronized during the coming winter; they are made of white and scarlet wool, and prove very warm as they cling to the limbs.

Evening Dresses for Young Ladies are usually made in thin white muslin, over colored skirts, (blue, mauve, or pink,) and are trimmed with either white or black lace. The best taste, however, is to use black lace only when the dress is worn over white, Over the colored under-dresses, white lace should always be employed. Sometimes muslin is used instead of silk as a lining for both skirt and mantle, and although not

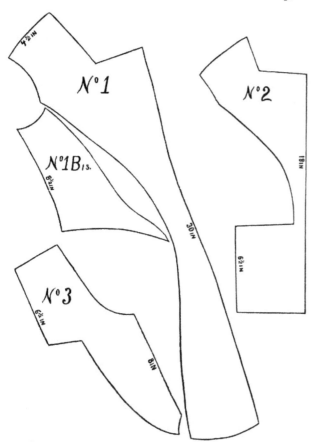

so rich-looking, it is far less costly. A sash should always accompany this style of toilet: it should be long and wide, and fringed at the ends, and the silk of which it is composed must be of a superior quality. The Scudery sash is very popular, and newer than either the Swiss or Postillion belts; instead of being tied with a bow, what the French call a *chou* (cabbage), and which is a sort of rosette, is formed at the top with the silk, and the long ends hang from underneath; this style of sash is usually fastened at the left side.

NEW STYLE BODY.

We give, this month, a diagram, for a body.
No. 1. Front of Body with ends.
No. 1. *bis*. Side-Piece of Front.
No. 2. Middle of Back with postillion skirts, laid in three wide hollow plaits.
No. 3. Side-Piece of this Back.
Peterson's Magazine, December 1863

In sleeves nothing new has appeared. Those shaped at the elbow are still prevalent; although many are made with a gigot top, with a little fulness at the bottom, gathered into a band at the wrist.

The dress which appears in our illustration is intended for the ballroom. The material is white tarlatan, the skirt being covered with puffings of the same; the body also trimmed to correspond. The front is ornamented with sprays of flowers, but for these bows of bright plaid ribbon may be substituted with equally good effect. The head-dress is a small tiara of gold in front, and at the back either a cluster of the flowers or a number of bows formed of the same plaid ribbon. If the plaid ribbon bows are taken instead of the flowers, this will not be found at all an expensive dress for this festive season, more especially as this ribbon trimming can be made very useful for after purposes.

A dress of either French merino or mohair, of the colour of the bright light golden brown of the most perfect of the falling leaves of autumn, is now fashionable. This should be trimmed with three rows of black ribbon velvet round the bottom or three rows of velvet of its own colour, an inch wide. The body should be made with a point behind; the sash from the shoulders in front, of which we have already spoken. The sleeves also wide, like the gigot at the top, with a little fulness at the bottom, to be gathered into a wristband.

A pretty dress is one made of an Alexandra blue French merino, with a flounce five inches wide, quilled on with it heading round the bottom, between each plait the continuation of a ribbon velvet three quarters of an inch wide; sometimes a loop of velvet is substituted between each plait. The body is made to fit the figure, with a point behind. The front is ornamented with those bands from the shoulders of which we have spoken above, being trimmed at the ends, the same as the bottom of the skirt, with some diamonds formed of the velvet. An underskirt, which looks well with this dress, and, is also equally suitable for many others, is a black and white stripe with a crossway band, four or five inches wide, of a large, bold black and white plaid. For some dresses a similar underskirt of black and scarlet may harmonise better. A paletôt of black cloth or imitation skin suits with this dress, and a bonnet of quilted satin of the same blue.

The What-Not, December 1863

Sins Against Good Taste

It is a common objection brought by the Parisian ladies against those of London, that the different parts of their dress do not harmonise with each other, and we are bound to admit that this charge against good taste is too often true. The fact is, that the ladies seldom purchase the whole of any one costume at the same time, or with much reference of the separate portions in point of suitability. In this way expensive articles – even of the first quality, and sometimes even handsome in themselves – injure, instead of helping each other by being worn together. No doubt there are some parts of a wardrobe that should be made serviceable for a long time, such, for instance, as shawls; but even these are made to share the sublunary changes of all other things, owing to the vigorous progression of the English manufactures constantly giving a new impetus to the impulses of trade, by exhibiting a quick succession of novelties. Formerly a shawl might last a lifetime without looking particular in style. The case, however, is different now. Some sorts of cloaks also may be worn longer than others, though of these there is certainly a new shape introduced every season. The burnous may be considered in some decree an exception, its simplicity of form and its Arab origin having given it a sort of standing in the world of fashion; but even here the law of change is marked by the difference of material successively introduced. Still, no matter from what cause, the discrepancy of style in the various parts of a lady's dress is one of the sins against good taste that ought to be reformed. Looking round on any large assembly will supply abundant proof of the truth of what we say. Inconsistency of form and colour – even when the different parts of a dress are of the best quality – must inevitably arise when each article is bought at a different time, and without reference to the form or tints of the others with which it is to be worn. If ladies, instead of purchasing their dresses at various times, would make a point of selecting them altogether, they would find the advantage in a great improvement of style, without incurring any more expense. Many ladies receive their dress-money in quarterly payments, and these should be their appointed shopping times. Those who have not made this arrangement could easily arrive at the same result by reserving the outlay of their purses until the fixed time. At all events, we submit these hints to the consideration of our readers.

It is with this view, however, that we are now adopting a somewhat new plan in our notices of the fashions. Instead of speaking of separate portions of dress as though they could really be independent of each other, we shall describe the whole costume. Not, of course, exclusively, but to a great extent. We are far from recommending that ladies should discard articles of dress that are good, and perhaps handsome in themselves; but we propose that they should select such other portions as may best accord with them, and, in running over our list, they will soon see what they can purchase as accompaniments to what they possess, so as to produce the most harmonious effects. We are very happy to find that these notices of the fashions are found to be reliable and valuable by so many of our subscribers, and hope not to relax in our endeavours to render them even more extensively available and useful.

The What-Not, October 1863

All Things Scottish

Balmorals, Etc. – Much as some of the English fashions have been laughed at and ridiculed by the Parisians, the fair critics are now adopting many of them. Balmoral boots, scarlet petticoats, striped woolen petticoats, scarlet stockings, are anything but uncommon sights in Paris. At Compiegne the guests have all been wearing high-heeled boots. These boots are made in various ways; of brown kid or morocco leather; also of gray morocco. buttoned up the front with steel buttons. the heels likewise bound with steel; also of black morocco and gilt buttons, with gilded heels. But more *recherche* than any of these are the boots made of Russia leather with gilt heels. With this style of boot a red and white petticoat is frequently worn, and the skirt of the dress is raised, when walking out, by the means of cords and rings, so as to form festoons over it.

Peterson's Magazine, October 1863

1864

WALKING DRESS.

Walking Dress of Figured, Stone-Colored Silk. — Black velvet sacque coat, trimmed with pipings of black silk and narrow black lace.

In the make of dresses there is but little new since our last notice; as skirts are still cut with trains, ornamentation becomes less necessary. Chenille fringes are now much used around the skirts of dresses; they should be of the same color as the dress, terminating with round satin buttons. They are frequently arranged upon the skirt, so as to stimulate [sic] a tunic, high in front, and much lower in the back. These chenille fringes, and gimp, with jet intermixed, will form the newest and most fashionable winter trimmings for silk dresses.

No change appears in the shape of sleeves; they are narrow, and in the shape of gentlemen's coat-sleeves. They are sometimes so narrow that they are slit open inside the arm, and fastened, with an open lacing of velvet braid or ribbon, as though to be enlarged. Epaulets, in gimp, chenille, or velvet, are very generally added to them. For dinner and evening dresses, the square-cut bodies and half-short sleeves are preferred, worn with lace cape or fichu.

In black lace, half-low bodices are made, the basquines at the back are formed of several rows of lace; *bretelles* are carried from the waist to the shoulders, and again to the back, the whole being terminated by long, flowing ends of white ribbon, edged with fringe or lace. These form very pretty additions to a simple dinner or evening dress, and can be made girlish or matronly, according to the materials employed.

MARIE STUART CASHMERE HOOD.

This very pretty affair is made as follows. Take a square of cashmere (scarlet, blue, or white), thirty three inches square, and of the shape as seen in the diagram on the following page.

The front is A. From C to C, following the dotted line run a casing of half-inch ribbon on the inside. Trim with silk of the same, or contracting color, pinked on the edges, and quilled, as seen in the design given above.

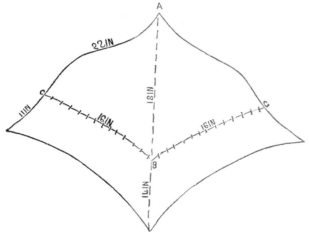

If warmth is needed, line the head-piece with silk, slightly wadded. It will take about one yard of silk for the trimming, cut bias. The lower frill is two inches in width, pinked on one edge only, gathered and put on at the other edge.

The upper frill, of the same width, is pinked on both edges, gathered in the center. Nothing prettier than this, or so easily made, has come out this winter.

The next is a white cashmere jacket, braided in black. The braiding pattern, given in our embellishment, need not be followed, necessarily. Any other pattern, which may be preferred, or may be ready at hand, would do as well. We are constantly giving new patterns for braiding, in order that our subscribers may use them for, this and similar purposes. On certain styles of figures, this jacket is pre-eminently handsome.

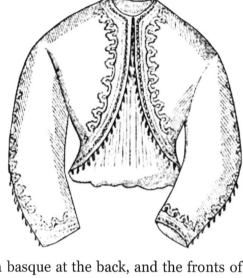

Jackets, for in-door morning wear, are made of either Imperial blue or Monsignore violet cashmere. They are buttoned all down the front, and are cut quite straight, both in front and at the back, reaching as far as the commencement of the plaits of the skirts. They are trimmed, around the edge, with insertions made either of gimp or guipure, and down the front are placed, at regular intervals, gimp rosettes. For traveling and for wearing-out skirts, the military jacket is worn. This is made in cloth, with *revers* in front, which are fastened back with ornamental buttons. There is a basque at the back, and the fronts of this form are sloped or rounded off as they descend.

Raphael bodies still continue popular, and will always look well on certain styles of persons. Our fourth illustration is a very handsome body of this description. The tassels are a particularly noticeable feature of this pattern.

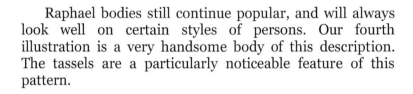

Long, flowing sashes, tied behind or at the side, now take very much the place of the Swiss bands, although these are also still worn. Sashes are made either of the material of the dress, or of the color of the trimming; they are either in ribbon or velvet, or in material piped all round, and are tied in a large bow. With any dress of a sober color, a plaid silk sash of bright tints looks very well, but a black one may also be worn. These sashes are less trimmed than formerly; they have only a plain hem or piping, and, at most, a narrow velvet or ribbon, or a very narrow black lace, sewn all around. A gray or fawn-colored merino dress, with blue silk sash and trimming, is a very pretty style of toilet for a young lady. We also recommend, for sashes, the Algerian ribbons, as a pretty novelty; they are striped of the brightest colors, and remind one of the Algerian shawls so much worn last winter.

Peterson's Magazine, January 1864

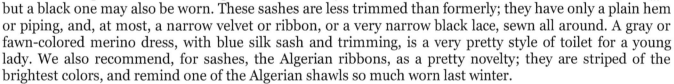

The skirts of dresses being now always gored, with the exception of those evening dresses, composed of very thin fabrics, in which the breadths are merely narrowed towards the top, and being made with partial trains, the trimming is usually rather flat, as being most consistent with its sweep. A dress of violet-colour silk has a very pretty effect made in the following way: Each breadth is cut so as to form one point of a vandyke at the bottom, and the skirt, thus showing a row of points all round, is laid upon a continuation of black silk, the line being covered with a ribbon velvet; over this is laid a graduated succession of lengths of the velvet in six tiers, about an inch apart, each formed into a point at its centre, so as to repeat the vandyke, the upper lengths of the velvet being about two inches long. This style of trimming has a bold and handsome effect. The body is made to fit the figure, trimmed with lengths of the velvet reaching from the centre of the waist to the height of a low bodice, in the form of a stomacher, having a little tassel or pendant ornament at each point where the velvets meet. The sleeve is shaped to the elbow, having graduated lengths of velvet from the shoulder to the elbow, each point finished with the same little tassel or pendant ornament.

The new year brings with it a demand for some costume that may harmonise with its joyous festive gatherings, and we have therefore selected one suitable for its most distinguished occasions. The dress which appears in our illustration is of a bright azure blue, having narrow rows of the same, pinked at their lower edge, their upper one being covered with a narrow black velvet, the whole depth of the skirt. The bodice has a berthe covered in the same way, and the sleeves are trimmed to match. The tunic is of Brussels net, figured with some handsome pattern, bordered with a lace insertion laid over a blue ribbon, and a lace at the edge. The clusters of flowers can be dispensed with, although they add to the elegance of the dress.

The What-Not, January 1864

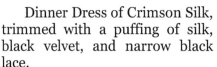

Dinner Dress of Crimson Silk, trimmed with a puffing of silk, black velvet, and narrow black lace.

House Dress of Gray Poplin, richly braided. White lace cap, trimmed with pink flowers.

In the make of bodices there is as yet nothing new; high to the throat and close-fitting, with either a double or single point in front, and a pointed basque at the back, is the usual style. The basque assumes a variety of forms; sometimes it is in three pieces, *a la postillon*, the center being longer than the two sides; sometimes it is square and box-plaited in the center, the plait being fastened down with two buttons. Others are swallow-tailed; if there is a simple point at the back, it is long and rounded. Instead of simply cording round the throat, a crosswise band, about three-quarters of an inch in width, is now also sewn round the top; this will enable the bodice to set higher round the throat, and the collar to fit more closely.

If for a self-colored taffetas dress, trimmed with a contrasting color, this band should be made the same shade as the trimming; it answers then the purpose of a neck ribbon under a lace collar.

EVENING DRESS.

Dinner Dress of Gay Plaid, on a white ground. Skirt, sleeves, and sash, are all trimmed with a heavy silk fringe, of the colors of the plaid.

For Dinner or Evening Dresses, low bodies are very generally worn with a cape or fichu in black and white lace or guipure. For young ladies, silk dresses are often made with a low body, and a small, square-shaped cape of the same material to wear over it; the body is then high, and if wished to be worn low, the silk cape is replaced by a tulle fichu, so that the dress is equally appropriate for walking or evening dress.

There are two different styles of skirts for evening wear. – The first is train-shaped at the back, with an apron in front; the second is a tunic, or double skirt, which is open at the side. When the skirt is ornamented with puffings, they are carried as far as the waist upon the breadth over which the tunic opens. Frequently the tunic is looped up with a right angle at each side, and, in such cases, it is trimmed with the inevitable plaid, which has a better effect at candle-light, and upon white, than would be first imagined.

The Art of the Hoop: 1860 - 1869

HOUSE DRESS.

House Dress of Gray Poplin, trimmed with two bands of gay plaid velvet, with cross pieces of black lace.

In plaids, those which are composed of only blue and green, are preferred for ladies: though children wear the gayest which can be purchased. A great point to remember, in the adoption of plaids, is, never to wear two different ones in the same toilet.

Satin is again very popular for dresses.

SPANISH BODY.

Spanish Basque. – The foundation is of black net, with narrow velvet ribbon crossed upon it, and it is trimmed with a black silk fringe. The sleeves of the dress should always be trimmed to correspond with the basque.

IMPERATRICE PALETOT: FRONT AND BACK.

In the front of the number, we give an engraving of a new winter coat, called the Imperatrice Paletot. In order that our friends may make this stylish article for themselves, if they wish, we give back and front views of it, and also a diagram. The diagram is below, and shows how it may be cut out, and of what size each piece is to be.

No. 1. Front.
No. 2. Side of Front.
No. 3. Sleeve.
No. 4. Back.
No. 5. Side-piece.

We have not given the full length to these pieces, as the size of our page forbids it. The side-piece and side of front should each be lengthened nine inches at the bottom, (the seam under the arm is indicated by a small cut made in each of these two pieces); this being done, the front must be lengthened to agree with the side of front, and the back must be made to agree in length with the side-piece. The sleeve has a small corner cut off the hind arm at the wrist, which will have to be made good. Nothing has come out, this winter, more stylish than this Paletot.

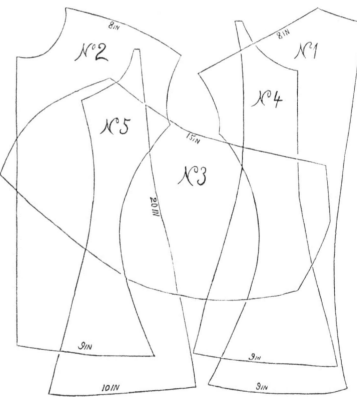

Bretelles are much worn, and they are in many cases very becoming, for they give width to the shoulders and an appearance of slimness to the waist.

Peterson's Magazine, February 1864

One of the most distinguished costumes of the season is a dress of the colour of the golden russet of the autumn grape leaf, trimmed round the bottom of the skirt with four lines of ribbon velvet, edged with white, two and two, crossing each other so as to form a double diamond. The bodice is made high, and to fit the figure, being trimmed with braces, which meet at a point half-way in the middle of the back, form two points on each shoulder, finished with tassels, meet at the waist in the centre of the front, and widen down to about half the length of the skirt, the pointed ends being ornamented with three tassels. These braces, made of the silk, are bordered with the same velvet as the trimming of the skirt, being crossed in diamonds at the ends. With this is worn for the carriage and the promenade a paletôt of black velvet, bordered with minever or grebe.

A dress of very opposite character, but one recommended by its great comfort and durability, is made of twilled serge, a soft warm woollen fabric. In this the skirt is quite plain, the body has a very small postilion jacket, and the sleeves are shaped up to the elbow. To complete this costume for the promenade, a paletôt of the same material is the most suitable. No other trimming is necessary than merely binding with braid of the same colour in the French way – that is, by laying the two edges together, stitching through, turning the braid over and felling it down, thus concealing the stitches and forming a round sort of trimming.

The dress which appears in our illustration is intended for one of those festive occasions which abound at this season of the year. The skirt is of violet-colour silk, trimmed with narrow pinked frills in black silk. The upper part is covered with black net, which may be either plain or figured. The edge is cut into vandykes, and bordered with black lace with a heading of violet satin quilled ribbon. The bodice is of the violet silk, trimmed with the black lace, falls of which hang over and cover the sleeve.

Although jackets have now been for a considerable time exclusively appropriated to morning costume, we must now notice a modification of this most useful and comfortable article of dress quite suitable for wearing in the family circle on all ordinary occasions. This bodice, or jacket, is made separately from the skirt, and does not descend more than an inch and a-half or a couple of inches lower than the waist, being cut evenly of an equal depth all round. The sleeve is shaped to the elbow, and has a small epaulette, round which, as well as round the edge of the jacket, a trimming of chenille fringe is laid on. Sometimes a line of the same fringe is carried round at the height of a low body. The material of a dress made in this style is open to choice. A tartan is very suitable, and the chenille fringe being of colours to match, has a rich effect. An Irish poplin or a French poplin also look extremely well. So too does either a chequered or a plain alpaca. We recommend this adaptation of the jacket into the bodice for its comfort, as well as for a very pretty novelty of style.

A very pretty style of dinner dress is one perfectly easy for arrangement, without much expenditure in trimmings. It consists of a silk dress of any of the prevailing fashionable colours, made low. Over this is worn a fichu, which continues the dress up to the neck, and which can easily be cut by any lady, who may take the upper part of one of her high dresses as a model, shaping it square at both the front and back. This little fichu may be made either of spotted net or of rows of insertion, a fall of lace being carried all round, which, hanging over the bodice, appears to form its trimming. In the last number of this magazine the design for a lace was given suitable for this purpose. A quilling of satin ribbon, about an inch wide, of pink or white or any pretty well contrasting colour, is placed as a heading to the lace, and is also carried round the throat. The sleeves may be either of white, with an epaulette under the lace, or of the same material as the dress. This fichu is a great convenience of the toilette, and can be transferred from one dress to another at pleasure.

The What-Not, February 1864

The Art of the Hoop: 1860 - 1869

WALKING DRESS.

Walking Dress of Blue Summer Poplin, ornamented with gimp trimmings.

The demands of fashion are so numerous, that it is almost impossible to supply them, and so old styles have to be renewed, but nearly always with some slight modification. Basques are striking instances of this fact; but very few years ago basques were universally worn, and now the leading Parisian modistes are adding basques to both high and low bodices. The greatest difference between the basques of five years past, and the basque of to-day, lies not in their length, for they are now made equally as long, but in the manner in which they are cut. Formerly, they were cut out of the same piece as the different parts of the bodice; now they are detached, each division of the bodice being joined only as far as the waist. Flounces are another case in point. If a lady fancies flounces, she may wear them and be fashionable, and if flounces are not to her taste, she may dispense with them and still be in fashion. The only items to be born in mind, if such additions are contemplated, are that they should not be numerous, and that they should be arranged, not straight around the skirt, but waved, and between each flounce there should be a row either of ribbon, velvet, or of lace insertion.

But although flounces are favorite additions, there are many satin and *moire antique* dresses made without any ornament whatever upon the skirt; such materials are rich enough in themselves, they do not require ornamentation; but in these cases, more than usual attention should be paid to the arrangement of the skirt. For evening wear, skirts are all cut with a train, and are gored. As they are not straight around the edge, some little skill is requisite in both cutting and mounting the waistband. They could be sloped at the bottom (in the proportion of half an inch to half a yard) as well as the extra length allowed for the train at the top. In pleating up the skirt, one large pleat should be placed in the center of the front, and another in the center of the back, differing, in this respect, only, that the one at the back should be a double box-pleat, whilst the front one should be single. The wide pleat in the front causes the skirt to flow in a more graceful manner than when two pleats meet together.

CARRIAGE DRESS.

Carriage Dress of Fawn-Colored Silk, trimmed with black lace.

MORNING DRESS.

Morning Dress of Blue and White-Striped Foulard. – This dress is gored at the sides, and hangs full and loose from the shoulders. We give it as a new fashion, not that we think it is neat or elegant.

In the make of dresses there is nothing novel; trains, gored skirts, broad sashes tied at the back, jackets and waistcoats continue to be in vogue. For this style there are two distinct patterns, namely, the postillion bodice with a basque, the jacket being rounded off in front, in imitation of the costume from which it derives its name; and the Oriental jacket, the back of which is plain, and cut straight at the waist, the front being similar to that of the postillion jacket. The waistcoat should be of a contrasting color from the jacket; it is ordinarily made of either cashmere or velvet. A white or red waistcoat, with either a black, brown, or gray jacket; a black velvet waistcoat, with either a blue or a *cuir*-colored jacket, is the Parisian style.

An economical style of retrimming a black silk skirt which has already done a considerable amount of duty, is to procure some blue and green plaid silk, and to piece two crossway bands of it around the skirt. The band should be cut about two inches wide, and commence nine inches from the edge.

Many dressmakers now prefer the long basque at the back, without plaits, as it proves more becoming to the figure. In Paris, the seams of the bodice are frequently ornamented; for example, trimming would be placed from the top of the seam upon the shoulder, and continued midway down the sleeves; the seams at the back would likewise be covered; even the bodices of riding-habits are, in Paris, now frequently trimmed with gimp at the seams.

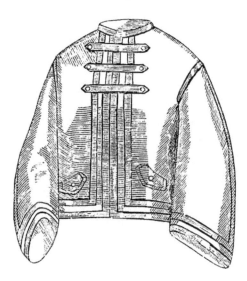

JACKET.

BRAIDED BODY.

Many ladies now suppress the sleeves for dressy demi-toilets; we mean by this the sleeves made of the same material as the dress. They replace them by white ones, which have a very pretty effect at night, and are more convenient for delicate people, as well as for those who are no longer young. This fashion allows of lace being used, which, with the narrow sleeves, was almost impossible.

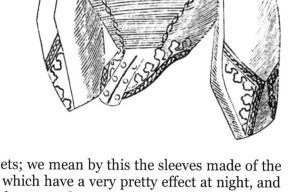

VELVET WAIST.

NEW STYLE BODY.

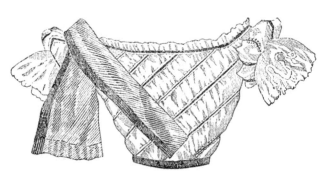

NEW STYLE BODY.

Peterson's Magazine, March 1864

For evening dress nothing can be in better taste than a crystallised silver-grey silk. This requires no trimming round the bottom of the skirt. The bodice is low, made with a small point both back and front, is rounded at the top of the back, and is brought in a straight line from the shoulder to the centre of the front. A puffing of the silk is carried all round a little below the edge, and from this falls a Brussels lace or blonde of about three inches deep. The sleeve is formed of one puff appearing from under the fall of lace or blonde. At the back is a bow of ribbon, in the front a bouquet of scarlet geraniums; a wreath of the same flowers made prominent in the centre of the forehead, being worn on the head.

A second dress, also for festive occasions, is a white crystallised silk; the trimming round the bottom of the skirt being three serpentine lines of silk of that azure blue which lights up so well at night. This is cut on the bias, is about two inches wide, and is laid on only slightly fulled, with a small heading at the top and bottom. The bodice is made exactly the same as the one we have just described, with the mere substitution of the azure blue silk above the lace or blonde. A wreath of convolvolus of the blue, to match, marked with white satin stripes, and a bouquet of the same complete this dress.

For ball dresses the tissues in blue and silver, pink and silver, and scarlet and white, continue much in favour. Added to these, we may mention that black closely sprinkled over with gold stars, or in a pattern of gold stripes, appear to be taking a very prominent place.

The opera-cloak has now for so long a time been worn in white and red, that it would really be quite unnatural for it not soon to approach the end of so durable a reign. Accordingly, we find that stripes may possibly soon supersede these established favourites. The latest novelty is a black and white stripe shimmering with silver, which has a very elegant effect. The cloaks that have a mingling of gold or silver glimmering through stripes of red and black, red and white, or stripes of mingled colours on a white ground, are all open to choice, each of them having a very marked, and some of them a very elegant effect.

Dresses of white leno, with patterns upon them in a variety of colours, should have the cloak to correspond in colour. Thus a white with its design in pink, may be made with three serpentine lines of its own material over a pink ribbon round the bottom, and be worn with a cloak of a pink and white stripe, lined with pink silk. A single rose, to match in colour, laid on the centre of the forehead, completes this dress.

The underskirt has now become an article of dress almost as important as the upper one, since the latter is now made of so sweeping a length as to render it absolutely necessary that it should be drawn up so as to display the former. We have just seen a silk dress of the colour of the golden brown of the autumn leaf, made with an underskirt of the same, or at least its lower part. On this underskirt there are five rows of black ribbon or black silk, put on either by machinery or hand, of about an inch wide, with their own width of distance between them; on the upper one a quilling of black ribbon, just above the hem, and when drawn up in regular festoons all round, showing the bands of black on the underskirt beneath the deep scallops of the upper one, the effect is most especially good. The bodice is made in box plaits, up each of which is a similar black band, the sleeve being shaped up the arm as high as the elbow, having an epaulette at the top trimmed with a quilling of the black ribbon.

Returning again to the subject of underskirts, we will first mention one in scarlet flannel, having a goffered flounce four inches wide, set on with a heading, at each edge of which, just above its hem, is a line of narrow black braid. Above this flounce is a braided pattern, also in black, of from two to three inches wide, of any design that may be preferred. This arrangement forms a really ornamental finish for the bottom of one of these underskirts.

A very useful dress for the present month, for morning wear by the seaside, when its breezes are rather cool, and for the autumn, when it first approaches, is a good winsey of lavender speckled with black. The bottom of the skirt has a deep vandyke of black braid not less than an inch and a-half wide, having on both its edges a narrow braid worked on in loops. The effect is good and striking, and we recommend it the more because any lady can execute this pattern herself without difficulty or tediousness. A pardessus, also braided to match, completes this dress for the promenade, with a straw bonnet, trimmed with velvet either of scarlet or black.

And here let us notice that the trimmings of the skirts this season have gradually been allowed to reach much higher than during the last.

The What-Not, March 1864

Fashions Becoming Masculine. – A letter from Paris says: – "The tendencies of fashion become every day more masculine. If we may judge by certain houses, ladies' garments are becoming mere disguises. We see paletots just like men's, Lancer jackets, fashionable waistcoats, cravats; and, lastly, boots in the Hessian style – all intended for that portion of the human race which ought to be distinguished by gracefulness and modesty!"

WALKING DRESS.

Dress of Mauve-Colored Silk. – Scarf mantle of the same material, trimmed with a ruche of black silk, and with wide black lace.

The New-Fashioned Coat. – The most curious novelty, in Paris, is the coat now worn by ladies. This coat is cut precisely ln the form of a man's coat. But, when worn over ball-dresses, instead of being high to the throat, it is low upon the shoulders. Let our readers picture a garment with *revers,* cut straight as a man's coat, the revers forming a berthe at the back and round the shoulders, with a long coat-tail descending upon the skirt: the tail is in a single piece, and, instead of being divided into two parts, as that of a man's coat, it is separated in the center with a row of buttons upon a broad piping of a different color from the coat. Either blonde ruched or lace generally surrounds the basque. This coat is rarely of the same color or material as the dress; thus, over a white crepe or tulle dress it would be either in sky-blue velvet or lilac moire, with white satin *revers*. Or, over a light green tulle dress it is made of white moire, with light green satin *revers;* another in pink terry velvet over a pink satin dress, ornamented with white blonde.

HOUSE DRESS.

Gabrielle Dress of Leather-Colored Poplin. – There is no seam at the waist, and the fullness is thrown very much back. The dress is trimmed with very heavy cord and tassels. We have seen a black silk dress made in this way, and it is one of the most stylish of the season.

There is nothing decidedly new in the way of making dresses. The small, loose jacket will be much worn with morning and home dresses, and basques are gradually obtaining favor, though they are not yet generally worn.

Braces have also reappeared; they are made very wide, and do not descend quite to the waist, but describe the form of a berthe at the back: they are used especially upon dresses of the Gabrielle form. They are also adopted by young girls over white tucked bodices; in those cases, they are crossed both at the back and at the front, and fall with four square ends upon the skirt.

Vests, Jackets, Etc., are in great variety. The *Sardinian* vest has a small round basque, is worn with a velvet gilet, or under-body, made with a point in front, and laced behind.

The Mexican Jacket is loose in the back, cut open squarely in front, and fastened by small straps and buttons; it is often made of scarlet cashmere, trimmed with black; it is worn with a white cashmere *chemise Russe,* embroidered in black, or with a white muslin body.

Peterson's Magazine, April 1864

In dresses for the ballroom a new but rather curious fashion is now appearing, which we notice that our readers may be acquainted with the leading novelties of the season. An underskirt of white crystallised silk is richly ornamented in various ways in a pyramidal form up the front, sometimes with crossings of silk ruches, forming diamonds, in coloured silk, sometimes with cords of small artificial flowers and leaves, in the same way. Over this is worn a second skirt, not looped up, but cut away. In the centre of the waist it is not more than one quarter of the length of the skirt, and from this point it is slanted away down to the back breadths, which form a sort of slight train behind. Bodices pointed in the front are now frequently preferred to those which are rounded, and in the present style it is cut in a straight line from the top of the shoulder, to correspond with the point of the waist, being trimmed round the neck, as well as round the upper skirt, with a double puffing of tulle interspersed with a flower, or headed with a ruche, according to the choice which has been made for the underskirt.

A much more simple dress is in a style of which we have already spoken in a previous number. It is of two skirts made of equal length in white grenadine, both trimmed with a single ruche of either blue or green silk, the upper skirt being drawn up in festoons, and at the top of each drawing a rosette of the same silk to be attached. The bodice is made with a berthe, also drawn up in festoons, and trimmed to correspond. A white book muslin looks extremely well made in the same way.

In harmony with this opening of the season the costume ought to be arranged, and we have therefore selected one for illustration suitable for most of those occasions in which any dress excepting those for the ballroom may be required. The material is a crystallised silk; the colour admits of some choice, according to the taste of the lady by whom it is to be worn. For the young, and for festive occasions, a pink or a clear light blue are very elegant. A green or the Havanna brown make up to advantage in this style, while for service a black silk, or still better, a black satin are both desirable. The side trimmings are in white lace, which any lady may work for herself on Brussels net; but if time will not allow this, a figured net of some handsome pattern can be purchased, finishing it at the edge with a lace and a ruche of narrow ribbon. A very pretty and easy mode of turning plain Brussels into ornamented net is to work some pretty device in fine crochet, such as stars, or rounds, or sprigs, and to fasten these down at regular intervals. This is useful for many purposes, and would be so in the present instance. The berthe is made to match, with ends crossing in the front. The gloves are white, but sewn with silk the colour of the dress.

Another novelty of the season for evening wear is a dress in which the front is covered with flounces in the front, graduating in length, so that at the top they have only the length of a few inches, while at the bottom they are long enough to reach along two-thirds of the circumference of the skirt, the three or four lowest of the flounces being continued all round. The bodice is made with a berthe covered with frills to match. The materiel may be either a soft slight silk or any light material. This style is new, and has a very superior effect.

As a variety of the above, we may mention that this skirt made in any clear material may have an under-body of the same full in the front and with a bishop sleeve. With this is worn a sort of over-body in black velvet, just fastened at the throat, and cut away at the sides towards the back, where it ends in a small postilion sort of jacket. There are no sleeves, but the edges are finished with a narrow lace headed with a little jet trimming. A silk skirt of almost any colour that a lady's wardrobe may contain worn with a white clear muslin under-body and this black velvet upper one looks extremely well, and it is also an economy, as many ladies have skirts of which the bodies are either fretted or old fashioned.

The What-Not, April 1864

VELVET WAIST.

Black or dark-colored silks are no longer considered in good taste for evening dresses; they should be of a lighter shade. The gray and fawn-colored tissues look best by lamp-light; these may be trimmed with another color. For instance, we have seen a silk dress of silver-gray trimmed round the skirt with a border of blue silk ten inches deep, scalloped out at the upper edge, and finished off with narrow black Maltese lace. The body was plain, and trimmed with two bands of the same blue silk, coming down from the shoulders and narrowing toward the waist; they were also scalloped out and edged with lace. The sleeves, which were pleated at the top and almost tight round the wrist, had a similar trimming at the bottom.

Low dresses are, however, of course, more fashionable for evening wear. A fawn-colored silk dress, trimmed with blue ribbon edged with lace, is a very elegant toilet. The low bodies are made plain, with points in front and behind, and a drapery or berthe of tulle, forming broad pleats, and edged with a piece of the silk.

For evening dresses, young ladies wear striped silk or foulard dresses, with low bodies, and a stomacher of tulle with insertions of lace, or of white pleated muslin, or else the white capes of which we have already spoken; the newest shape of these is round, and bound with a wide black velvet ribbon; for less simple toilets, they are in white embroidered tulle, trimmed with white and black lace, or blonde, and are cut out all round in deep scallops.

Crinolines are worn much smaller than they have been: but, for evening dress, those which are very wide at the bottom are preferred, as the long train hangs better over them.

MORNING DRESS.

Breakfast Dress of White Cashmere, open down the front, and trimmed with facings of light-blue silk. Small square cape.

If skirts are long and very much gored, bodices made with but little trimming, and sleeves rather close to the arm, a dress is in fashion, no matter what modification the taste of the wearer may choose to give it.

Bodices are made chiefly with postillion basques at the back, and a point in front. No waist-band is worn, but the bodice at the sides is carried about half an inch below the line of the waist. The braiding (when the pattern is small) is carried up the side seams of the back, down the shoulder seams, and around the waist, flowing, of course, the outline of the basque.

CARRIAGE DRESS.

Carriage Dress of Gray Silk. – Tight-fitting basque of the same material, trimmed with silk fringe and braid.

WALKING DRESS.

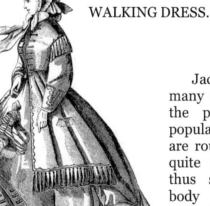

SPANISH JACKET.

Jackets are worn of many different styles, but the prettiest and most popular are those which are rounded in front, and quite short at the back, thus showing the plain body underneath. This under-body, or vest, may be made of the same material as the dress, of silk of the same color, or of a contrasting color, if preferred; or, for warmer weather, a thin white body may be worn.

Peterson's Magazine, May 1864

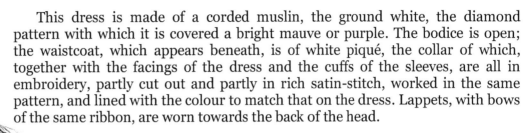

This dress is made of a corded muslin, the ground white, the diamond pattern with which it is covered a bright mauve or purple. The bodice is open; the waistcoat, which appears beneath, is of white piqué, the collar of which, together with the facings of the dress and the cuffs of the sleeves, are all in embroidery, partly cut out and partly in rich satin-stitch, worked in the same pattern, and lined with the colour to match that on the dress. Lappets, with bows of the same ribbon, are worn towards the back of the head.

The double skirt, which, after having enjoyed a long career of favouritism, has been for a time banished, is once again reappearing, and is likely to be more popular than ever. These are variously arranged. The one of which we are about to speak is Parisian, and is in a novel style. The underskirt is of clear white jaconnet muslin; round the bottom are five flounces of about two inches wide. This skirt is made with a slight train behind. The dress itself is of either a bright green or a French blue. The silk upperskirt is cut ten inches shorter than the under one, with a similar sweep as its train, and finished with two flounces of the same silk, also two inches wide. The bodice is low, and its line at the top is straight from the shoulder to the centre of the front, the back being cut to match. An underbody of the white muslin laid in plaits, and finished with a lace edging showing itself at each opening both before and behind. The sleeve is one large puff of the white muslin, with one of the silk left loose and opening over it in the way of a deep frill. ... We recommend this dress most especially to the notice of our readers, as being quite new and the style extremely elegant.

Ladies who admire this style of dress – as we think all who have taste must do – can adopt it in a less marked character, if they wish it to be modified. The underskirt may be of the same material as the dress, of violet or black silk, each of them being trimmed with either one or two of the flounces, and two rows of ribbon velvet above with a white edge, both the upper and the underskirt being made to match. This has a handsome and fashionable appearance, although the white underskirt is certainly more distinguished. In all cases, however, let it be remembered that both the upper and the underskirt must be cut with such a sweep as to form a slight train.

A dress of the spring green silk, made with a single skirt, may be trimmed at the bottom with one row of ribbon velvet an inch wide, with two of half an inch wide just above. The bodice high and plain; a small cape pointed at the back, with long ends crossing in the front, passing round the waist and hanging down from the centre of the back, with ends reaching two thirds of the length of the skirt. This is edged with the narrow velvet, and the long ends have three rows of the velvet to match the bottom of the skirt. The sleeve is a small bishop, with two lines of the wider velvet laid on perpendicularly, having two of the narrow between and two more on each side. This dress, although so unlike the last, is also marked by a peculiar elegance of style.

The What-Not, May 1864

Plain high bodies, with a waist *à l'Empire* – that is to say, very short, with a large buckle – are at any rate as much in vogue as the *basque-habit,* which, on the contrary, lengthens the waist. Frequently on tight bodies the trimming is put on like a Swiss body, and is finished off by long ends behind. The sleeves are still *à coude* and narrow; the trimmings match those on the body, put on round the bottom and up the scam, sometimes to the top, sometimes only to the elbow; and the jockey is also made of similar trimming.

The skirts are as wide as ever, but only at the bottom. To obtain this result, the breadths are cut on the *bias* on one side only. A skirt should be at the very least rather more than five yards round the bottom and two yards and three-quarters at the top. The front breadth is cut slightly on the *bias* on each side; care must be taken to join the *bias* to the straight of the other breadths, excepting that in the middle of the back, which must have the two *bias* together. The breadths should be cut rounded at the bottom, as every dress that is not quite for morning wear is made with a train at least nineteen or twenty inches long.

Le Follet, Journal du Grand Monde, June 1864

EVENING DRESS.

Evening Dress of Pink Silk. – The skirt is trimmed with a box-plaited ruffle of silk, headed with black drop balls. The low bodice of silk has over it another, still lower, of black velvet, from which depend two long velvet ends, one each side, finished with balls and tassels. The sleeves and front of the body are ornamented with bows of velvet ribbon. An inside spencer of black net, trimmed with black lace.

Dresses are now never embroidered down the front, but with bands or borders all round the skirt; sometimes a straight band commences at the waist, and toward the center of the skirt separates into two bands, which are carried in contrary directions to the back. For an embroidered dress, a postillion bodice is very suitable; in front, two bands commence at the shoulders, are rounded off at the sides, and rejoin the basque at the back. The epaulettes and the cuffs should, of course, be ornamented with embroidery. The paletot should be trimmed with fringe which matches the color of the embroidery.

YOUNG LADY'S DRESS.

Evening Dress of White Tarletan for a Young Lady. – The skirt, square bodice, and sash are trimmed with quilling of tarletan, bound with ribbon.

A great variety of fancy materials, both in wool and silk, are already exhibited for the *demi-saison* dresses. Bodies with a round waistband will still be worn, but are more *neglige* than those with points. The favorite basques are those which are made at the back only – the *postillion* shape, but divided into three points; the body has two points in front. The Louis XV. tail is also much seen; it is rather long and square at the bottom; three small folds are formed on each side. Other and more fanciful bodies have very long basques cut all round; they are longer at the back. Rich gimp, or chenille fringes, are still the trimmings generally preferred; but if these ornaments are considered too expensive, let us add that perfectly plain dresses are very *distingues*, and quite admitted by the present fashion.

Organdies, white muslins, lawns, and many other thin dresses have the bodies made lose [sic], and capes of the same material made in any style which may suit the fancy. When the bodies are made high, the lining is usually cut low.

VELVET BODY.

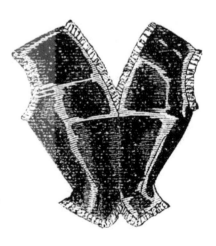

VELVET BODICE.

Crinolines continue *very* small at top, but widening toward the bottom, where many of them form quite a train.

The Art of the Hoop: 1860 - 1869

HOME DRESS.

House Dress. – The skirt is of gray poplin. Jacket of blue cashmere braided in black, and trimmed with tassels.

The "Princess" is the newest style for morning dresses. It is straight in front, with a seam at the back, which runs from the neck to the feet, being sloped or cut out in the back so as to fall into the waist; side pieces are added under the arms; they are very small, but they enlarge considerably as they descend. Should the material not be sufficiently wide, a gore is added to give amplitude to the skirt. These *robes de chambre* are not adjusted to the figure by a sash or waistband, or by any pleat or fullness; still they fall with much grace, by reason of their peculiar cut to the outline of the form. This "Princess" style has been adopted after many attempts at other shapes. The *Gabrielle*, (which our readers will remember is a dress with body and skirt gored and cut in one,) is also popular as a morning dress. A small cape and little pockets on the outside make this quite a jaunty affair.

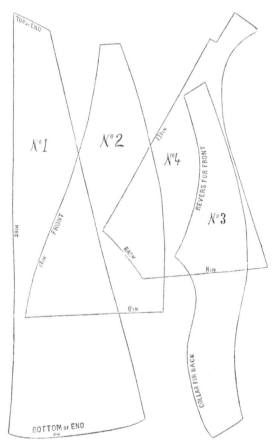

THE EUGENIE FICHU.

This Fichu is intended for an evening or dinner toilet, and makes an admirable finish to a dress, besides obviating the necessity of having any further trimming on the bodice. The Fichu forms a kind of bodice, open in front, and with two long ends before and behind. It may be made in any bright-colored silk, and is covered with white tulle or net, put plain over the silk, with the exception of the back, which is arranged in five puffings from the waist. The Fichu is trimmed round with narrow black lace, and a wide white lace or blonde, divided by a narrow row of velvet. It is further ornamented with black lace leaves applied on the net or tulle. These leaves can be purchased separately, or they may be cut out from old pieces of black lace, the foundation of which is worn out. The dress worn with the Fichu has a trimming at the bottom to correspond. We give both an engraving of the Fichu and a diagram from which it may be made.

Peterson's Magazine, June 1864

The dress which appears in our illustration, as worn by the most prominent figure seated in the chair, is in a style that may be made in two or three different ways. The skirt is of tarlatan, either white, French blue, or of the new brilliant green which is this season fashionable in Paris. The trimming is sometimes a plain ribbon, sometimes a plaid ribbon, and sometimes puffings of tarlatan, of a prettily-contrasting colour. Thus the white tarlatan may have puffings of pink, or blue, or green, but these last-named colours should have them of their own material. If the dress and the puffings are all of the white, then a coloured ribbon underneath them forms a tasteful sort of trimming. Sometimes a plain ribbon is laid on, being fastened down with a stamped-out star of velvet, at regular intervals. The body is covered with a pointed berthe, formed of one fulling of the tarlatan, with a border of the trimming at each edge, and a frill below finished with the same, which, falling over the short sleeve formed of one puff, conceals it from view. The hair is dressed with the Alexandra curls, and either a small plume of feathers behind or a cluster of flowers.

The second standing figure wears a dress of lilac-colour silk, one of the brilliant new dyes. The skirt is made with side trimmings, of either white lace or black lace laid upon white silk. The body is of the stomacher form, trimmed to match. The hair is worn with lappets hanging down from a gold comb behind.

For a summer silk, that which is likely to become the most fashionable is the Indian silk, woven in the double width, soft and glossy. In a cream white, or some delicate tint of dove or silver grey, it is well suited for a bridal costume; but independently of these more especial occasions, it will be found one of the most acceptable of the fabrics of the season. One of these silks, of any soft light shade, may be trimmed at the bottom of the skirt with quillings of either blue ribbon or blue silk pinked at each edge and laid on either as festoons, as a large chain in serpentine lines, or, as the French call it, in teeth. The bodice is made with fronts fastened into the shoulder seam, closed about half-way down, and continued from thence in the form of long strings, which, meeting behind, hang over the skirt to a considerable length. These are trimmed all round with the same quillings as that upon the skirt. The sleeve is small, with an epaulette, and short enough to show the embroidery of the undersleeve round the wrist. Both epaulette and round the hand are finished with the quilling.

A mauve-colour silk dress is very handsome made in the following way: The skirt is a quarter of a yard shorter than the length required, and each breadth is cut into the form of one large deep scallop. The length is completed by the addition of a deep flounce, which is even at the bottom, but follows the indentations of the scallop of the skirt; a ruche of the silk follows the line of the scallop. The bodice is made to fit the figure, and is worn with a black lace cape. The dress may have the flounce of a different colour, according to taste. Mauve and black, or violet and black, look especially well.

This style of skirt will be found very useful for lengthening any handsome dress that may be too short, or that may have got injured at the bottom; but we do not recommend it for any inferior dress, as it is only suitable for a good silk.

The length of the upperskirt requiring that it should be frequently, if not constantly, lifted out of the pollutions of the pathways on which its wearer treads, involves the necessity of the greater attention to the underskirt. We have just seen some novelties of this class which may be acceptable to our readers. The first is a skirt of cambric muslin tucked at regular intervals, so as to leave spaces between on which designs are embroidered in a mixed variety of colours in the forms of flowers and leaves or of slight branches of leaves and berries. These, of course, are very showy. New patterns are also appearing in scarlet or black for the goffered flounce and the running pattern above it, and the goffered frill surmounted with its single line of white embroidery is always in good taste. There is another pretty variety which we recommend to the notice of our subscribers. This is a deep hem in the cambric muslin cut into scallops, which are bordered with a narrow goffered frill, and above the upper line of the hem a narrow pattern either in white embroidery or braid.

The What-Not, June 1864

The Art of the Hoop: 1860 - 1869

Plate I. – *Toilettes de Ville. Foulard* dress, with narrow stripes very wide apart. On the skirt, three *tuyautés* of silk, two inches wide, put on in festoons. *Corsage à basques,* trimmed like the skirt, and open in front over a silk waistcoat, with *basque* with square pockets. This waistcoat is left open from the third button to the neck, so as to show a little lace frill.

Silk dress, with small shaded patterns. The skirt, very long and full, is bordered by a *tuyauté* describing small scollops. A deep fringe of *chenille,* raised with jet, is put on the skirt in the form of a tunic. High body, with square *berthe* of fringe; broad band and buckle.

All young ladies, whether married or single, wear *corselets* with their dresses. The most elegant of these are made with *épaulettes* – that is to say, they are continued very narrow on to the shoulders, where they are fastened with a bow of ribbon or an *aigrette* of *passementerie.* These *corselets* are made in silk or *moire;* some are fastened down the front with buttons, others laced down the back, while some are laced under the arms at each side; this is generally for full dress. They generally have some little ornament round the waist – a *passementerie* or bugles and *chenille* fringe.

We have seen one very elegant *corsage* of this description made for a young English lady. It was of white silk, embroidered in black *chenille,* bugles, and pearls. Each seam had a *chenille* laid along. Round the top and armholes was a handsome trimming of *chenille* and pearls. The waist was surrounded with a fringe of pearls and bugles. This *corselet* was of course intended for full dress. Two skirts were made to be worn with it – one of *tarlatane,* another of silk – and both trimmed to correspond with the body.

The coloured petticoats are extremely handsome, and very richly trimmed. The most *habillés* of these are of white alpaca, trimmed to correspond with the dress with which they are intended to be worn. In many cases, this petticoat if meant to accompany an open skirt, is very handsomely trimmed on the front breadth. Many dresses are made in this way for indoor or carriage wear. The under-skirt just touches the ground. We have seen one of this species, which we will describe for the benefit of our readers.

The dress was of white *foulard,* with hair stripes and leaves of apple green. The skirt open in front over a breadth of white *foulard,* ruched with green silk. The body was cut square, and trimmed with *ruches.* Small coat-sleeves, open to the elbow. Up each breadth of the dress, about half a yard high, was a green *ruche.* With this dress we saw a mantle of *Yak* lace, small circular form, with two deep flounces of lace; and a white *tulle* bonnet, with small *marabouts* tipped with green. The parasol intended to accompany this *toilette* was of white silk covered with *marabouts* like those on the bonnet.

Plate II. – Ball-dresses. Dress of *tulle*. At the bottom of the skirt, plaited silk flounce. Low body, with *berthe* composed of silk and *tulle*. Long sash *bibi* of silk, with fringed ends. A wreath of *muquets*. Necklace and bracelet of pearls.

Tulle dress, embroidered in straw. Two skirts – the second trimmed with a full *ruche* – raised at different places by *bouquets* of wild flowers. Draped body, with *bouquet. Touffe* of flowers in the hair. Necklace with pendants.

Skirts are all worn gored, and are about half the width at the waist that they are at the other extremity. Very few dresses are wider than three yards at the top, and none less than five at the bottom. The fashion of cutting the gores in points will not, we think, be so much in favour as the sloping each breadth at one side. Every breadth but the front one should be gored, the crossway pieces running to the back. This throws the fulness entirely into the train. A small gauffered flounce seems still to be the foundation of every trimming. For ball-dresses this small flounce is lined with stiff net, so as to prevent any clinging of the light material.

We are happy to be able positively to state that the skirts of thin dresses are not worn nearly so long as those of thicker materials. For instance, muslin, *tarlatane,* gauze, or *barège* dresses are never more than two inches on the ground, and rarely that.

It is not improbable that the fashion of wearing one deep flounce may reappear for those dresses which are difficult to gore. Trimmings up the seams are much in fashion. If this style is adopted for ruchings, the *ruches* should not be continued to the waist.

Muslin or thin dresses are worn over coloured *tarlatanes.* This has a very pretty and aërial effect, and is infinitely more economical than silk slips. The bodies of these thin dresses are made high or low; if the former, with a low lining. Plain on the shoulders, and slightly fulled at the waist. The neck is cut with a very small square; in this is a lace drawn to the throat by narrow black velvet. When these bodies are made low, they are accompanied by a *pèlerine* of the same, square, or crossed in front with long ends, fastened behind.

Many thin dresses have a pattern printed on them, to imitate *revers,* ribbons, sashes, &c. In this case, the dress requires no other trimming than the ornament thus simulated.

Those bodies intended for dinner or *soiree* wear are made of Indian muslin, and richly trimmed with embroidered or lace insertion. They are sometimes cut square. When ornamented with *bouillonnés,* these are placed over coloured ribbons; others, meant for less dress, are simply tucked both back and front. The sleeves, made to correspond, are closed at the wrist. White alpaca or *foulard* bodies are also worn, and are generally braided in colour, cerise or blue being the favourite hues. White *Marcella* bodies are generally made with *basques,* sometimes merely at the back, but the newest have a *basque* all round; this is much more becoming to the figure. These jackets are mostly braided with black. We must not forget to mention the *basquine habit,* so closely resembling a gentleman's dress-coat. These have not yet become general, nor are they, we hope, likely to do so, as two things are *absolutely necessary* for their success – one, a really good and youthful figure; the other, a perfect cut. We have seen one of black silk, of a more elegant shape than usual, the *basque* being five inches deep at the side-seams, instead of beginning from the back-seams. This coat was trimmed on all the seams, and round, with bugle fringe and beading. It was quite open down the front, with turned-back *revers.* Small, rather short coat-sleeve, with *revers* and *épaulettes* of *passementerie* and bugles.

Plate III. – *Toilettes de Ville*. Silk dress; trimmed on the bottom of the skirt with two *chicorées ruches* in festoons, and separated by a moss fringe. High plain body; round sleeves, trimmed with *ruches chicorées. Rotonde* of silk gauze, with flounce of *point à l'aiguille;* then a *ruche* and another narrower flounce.

Foulard dress; each breadth trimmed with a double band of silk. Frilling of *taffetas* at the edge of the skirt. *Senorita veste,* trimmed like the skirt on all the seams. Tight seams. *Jockey* hat of straw, trimmed with velvet, and a feather in front.

The silk *paletots* intended for *toilettes de visite,* are made with three seams down the back, nearly fitting to the figure, and with a deep flounce of lace, headed by drop buttons or bugle trimming. The sleeves are wide at the elbow, and small at the wrist. They have *revers* and *Épaulettes* of *passementerie*.

Morning-dresses are generally made with a mantle of the same, either *paletot* or circular cape. We have seen some of the former made without sleeves, so as to allow the sleeves of the body to pass through the armhole, and so serve a double purpose. Though we mention this make, we cannot say we admire it, as it gives a stingy and rather untidy appearance.

The Art of the Hoop: 1860 - 1869

Sashes are worn with one flat loop at the back, or are formed into a small plaited *basque*. They are made in all materials, those of black or white lace being most suitable for thin dresses.

The waistbands now worn are much wider than formerly, and the buckles are, of course, of a corresponding size. We cannot say we consider this in any way a becoming fashion, as it gives the waist a stiff appearance, and very much detracts from the graceful curves of a young and elegant figure.

Le Follet, Journal du Grand Monde, July 1864

Fig. I. – Light Colored Grenadine Dress, trimmed with lilac ribbon, and worn over a lilac silk vest.

Fig. II. – Evening Dress of Summer Silk, figured, and trimmed with green and pink ribbons to match the flowers in the pattern. Raphael body.

All skirts are gored and cut with a train, and each gore is frequently defined with a piping of a contrasting color from the dress; thus a gray alpaca may be piped with green silk.

As neutral tints are more in vogue than decided colors for dresses, the trimmings are frequently of a bright hue, and form a decided contrast to them. Ruches are popular, and so are ribbons sewn flat around the skirt; these latter are waved, and at each breadth where one wave or scallop ceases, and the next commences, a flat bow is sewn. Cords and tassels are arranged in a similar manner; the cord is looped from breadth to breadth, and the tassels fall at each seam; three rows of these ornaments are used.

EVENING DRESS.

Evening Dress of Blue Silk. – Skirt full and very long at the back. Bodice cut in a point, both at the top and bottom, with one broad strap crossing the shoulder. Under-body of thin white muslin.

Petticoats made of plain gray linen, alpaca, coverlet, etc., prettily braided, are very much worn for walking toilet, though many striped materials, (the stripes running lengthwise,) are also worn. These latter should have a fluted ruffle of the same around the bottom.

Close-fitting bodices, with basques at the back and high at the throat, and very narrow sleeves, are the most popular. By young ladies, the round waist is very much worn. When accompanied by a sash with long ends, either in very wide ribbon, or in a material similar to the dress, and edged with a narrow quilling of ribbon, these round waists are quite dressy. But every lady should judge what is best for her figure in the style of making her dresses. A slender figure is much improved by the sash and round waist, whereas a stouter person should always have her dress made with points, both back and front; or now that the basques are so popular, with points in front, and a basque at the back.

HOME DRESS.

Dress of Nankeen-Colored Foulard. – The skirt, jacket, sleeves, and waistband are trimmed with black lace. Puffed under-body.

Deep basques are decidedly coming in fashion once more. In Paris, they are worn all around the waist; but as yet they are worn only at the back in this country. The variety in basques is infinite; sometimes it takes the form of a single swallow-tail, very long and pointed in the center of the back; sometimes of a single square basque; others are divided into two parts which wrap over each other; whilst the latest novelty is the triple basque; this is formed with three "tabs," which are rounded off at the corners, the center end or tab being longer than the side ones; all three are edged with either ruches or gimp.

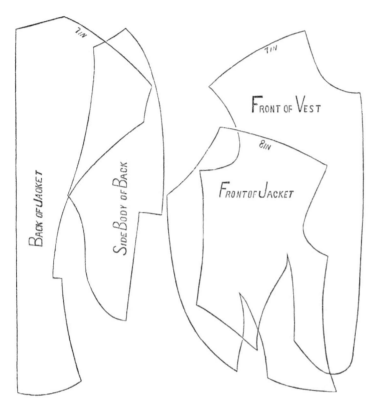

ANDALUSIAN JACKET AND VEST.

To be made of silk, and worn with a muslin skirt for morning and home costume, or as a dress body for thin silks and foulards. It is composed of the front, side-piece, and back of the jacket, and the front of the waistcoat, which is distinguished by a round hole pierced through it; the waistcoat buttons from the top to bottom, the shoulder and side-seams are sewn in with the shoulder and side-seams of the jacket. The jacket closes at the throat and is rounded well off, forming a skirt about six inches deep at the back, which is fastened by two plaits.

Peterson's Magazine, July 1864

The *ceinture* is now one of the most important parts of the *toilette*. For young girls of slight figure nothing can be more becoming than the Swiss *ceinture*, embroidered and trimmed with lace or *ruches* of ribbon, worn over a white *chemisette*. Bands of thick plain ribbon are quite the order of the day. Wide square buckles are worn with them.

Plate I. – Sea-side dresses. *Robe* of mohair, braided with fine braid in a small *grecque* pattern, arranged in large square festoons; in each festoon a *bouquet* of embroidered flowers. *Casaque paletôt*, trimmed to match. The front has *revers* thrown back, so as to show a *ceinture gilet* of silk. The skirt is drawn up over a silk skirt edged with narrow quilling. Brown leather boots.

Poil de chèvre dress. At the bottom of the skirt two crossway folds of silk, edged with *ruches* of lace; over the band of silk are placed bars of silk the same colour as the dress, crossing each other. Plain high body, with *ceinture bernoise* of silk to match the trimming on the skirt. *Capuchon la Vallière* of silk, trimmed with a fringe of *chenille* and jet.

Bodies of *crêpe lisse* are much worn, with skirts of *Chambery* gauze or light-coloured silk. They have a most charming effect trimmed with black braid, and quillings of black and white *blonde*, and are exceedingly becoming. Others are made of thin *nansook*, with narrow tucks, small collar of linen, and wide cuffs, each trimmed round with a very narrow insertion of embroidered muslin; or striped muslin, with *Valenciennes* insertion, and straps of velvet up each side. China crape and *foulard* are both also used for loose bodies. *Foulard*, although not quite so graceful as China crape, is so much cheaper, that it will be more generally worn.

Plate II. – Group. *Robe* of *grenadine*. The skirt trimmed with wide straps of *Yak* lace over silk falling from the waist. *Veste* very short and half-high; trimmed with lace insertion. Sleeves nearly tight; trimmed also with lace. *Ceinture Empire*, with large gold *boucle*.

Muslin dress over coloured *tarlatane*. High jacket-body, with small pointed tails; trimmed round with insertion and narrow edging of lace. Sleeves nearly tight, with pointed *épaulettes* cut up to match the skirt of the jacket.

Robe of *foulard pungee:* a wide *ruche* of cut silk is placed up each seam and round the bottom of the skirt. Greek jacket, trimmed to match the skirt. Waistcoat of plain silk.

Plate III. – Walking and home dress. *Gaze de soie robe,* trimmed with a wide *bouillonné* at the bottom of the skirt, on which, at equal distances all round, are placed crosses formed of lace ends. About a third of the way up the skirt are placed three narrow flounces in large scallops. *Corselet* with *épaulettes,* trimmed with narrow frills of silk, and a cross of lace on each *épaulette*. High body of muslin, plaited with long puffed sleeves. Gauze shawl to match the dress, trimmed with *Yak* lace.

Dress of *Pekin* silk, trimmed at the bottom of the under-skirt with a very wide crossway flounce, over which the upper skirt, which is trimmed round in narrow scallops, falls. Plain high body, buttoned; tight sleeves, trimmed up the back of the arm.

Jacket body. *Garde Française* of muslin over silk; it is trimmed with embroidered insertion, narrow tucks, and scalloped edging. An *agraffe* of *passementerie* placed at the back of the waist so as to fall in the hollow plait of the skirt.

Le Follet, Journal du Grand Monde, August 1864

Going Back to the First Empire. – All the accounts from Paris represent fashions as tending, more and more, to the styles of the first Empire. The waists appear daily to be worn shorter, and the large buckles and wide waistbands without ends are again taken into favor.

Ladies are, it appears, decidedly bent upon imitating the masculine dress in their own attire. We have already had the paletot, a name once reserved to designate an article a gentleman's dress; we have now the boot, the waistcoat, the cravat, and, lastly, the coat. Let us, however, say, at once, that there is a wide difference, at least, in color, between a lady's and a gentleman's *coat*. The shape alone has been imitated, and ladies have taken advantage of the privilege they possess of wearing bright, varied colors and light materials. A few coats have been made of silk, but for the summer they will be worn mostly in muslin, gauze, or grenadine, over silk dresses with low bodies, or of the same material as the dress.

THE COAT BASQUE.

There are so many modifications of the original shape of the coat now in fashion, that it is difficult to give a general rule for the manner of cutting it out, but it must be remembered that it is the coat of the *gentilhomme* in Louis XIV.'s reign, and not that worn by the stronger sex in these days, that ladies have chosen to appropriate to themselves. If made of silk, the coat is copied pretty correctly, as to shape, from the original pattern. It has a turned-down collar, and opens at the throat with revers. It is buttoned over the chest down to the waist, slopes off sharply to the back on each side, and has a long tail or basque behind, generally all in one piece, with sometimes two or three pleats to mark the waist. The sleeves also have deep revers. The coat is generally of one color, with the lining in another, to match with the trimming of the dress. It is ornamented with gimp quillings of ribbon or velvet lace.

The white muslin or gauze coats are really very pretty; the basque is more flowing and wide behind than in the silk one, and trimmed all round with a narrow quilling, over which a colored ribbon is sometime run through the material. This looks extremely well over a dress of colored silk with a low body; it is a stylish toilet for a dinner or evening party, when one does not wish to be quite in full dress. The sleeves of the dress are short, and the arm covered only with the sleeve of the coat. The same style, when the dress and coat are of gauze or grenadine, of a pretty, colored pattern on a white ground, is also very elegant, and suitable for a summer toilet. We give in our present number, a pattern of one of these coats just received from Paris.

THE ADOLPHE COAT.

Our illustration of this very novel and stylish garment so clearly depicts the arrangement of it, than an explanation is scarcely necessary. In Paris, for the last few weeks, both high and low coats have been much worn. Our pattern consists of seven pieces: The front; the back, the side-piece, that fits into the back; the sleeve; the revers for the front of the bodice; the revers for the basque or tail behind; the collar. A row of tiny holes on the sleeve indicates the upper and under portion, the smallest piece being for the under part.

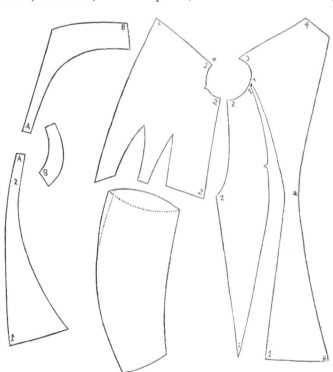

The pattern is cut to fit a medium-sized figure, and it can easily be enlarged or diminished by cutting each piece a little larger or smaller, as may be required. For a very elegant garment, the revers should be in white silk, strapped with black velvet, but if required for a more useful style, silk, the same as the dress, or black silk may be employed. The front of the coat is like a dress bodice, open a little in front, and ornamented with a revers which is carried round the arms and ends in the revers on the basque. A tiny collar finishes the top of the dress behind and just meets the revers in front.

By consulting the diagram, our readers will experience no difficulty in putting the various pieces together. The back is shown with three stars, indicating the center. The side-piece is numbered 1, to correspond with fig. 1 on the back. The front is numbered 2 under the arm, and fits into the side-piece to the corresponding fig. 2. The revers for back is numbered 1, and must be placed exactly over the figures 1 of side-piece and back. The front revers joins at the two letters *A* to the back revers, and the collar meets the revers at *B*. From this diagram, giving the patterns on a small scale, cut full-sized paper patterns.

WALKING DRESS.

Walking Dress of White Pique. – The skirt and paletot are trimmed with black braid and gimp ornaments.

Basques are worn by those ladies who wish a change in the style of making their dresses, who yet think that the *coat* is too pronounced. These basques are always trimmed to correspond with the skirts and sleeves.

Sashes have attained an enormous width – some of them are twelve inches wide. These are frequently made of *moire antique*, but, of course, are too clumsy to tie, and are simply crossed at the back.

WALKING DRESS.

Dress of Dove-Colored Foulard, in the Gabrielle form, trimmed with pipings of black silk and black silk buttons.

Beside the coat, we must mention the white muslin bodice, with two long lappets at the back, and one on each side in front. The lappets are rounded at the bottom, and trimmed with a ruche or quilling of muslin, edged on both sides with narrow, colored ribbon. The shape of the bodice is that of a small pelerine square on the shoulders, pointed in front and at the back over a low body. The pelerine is trimmed all round with the same edging as the lappets. This bodice can be worn over any dress; it is also made of the same material as the skirt, and worn without any other body

underneath; in that case, it is lined up to the trimming marking the pelerine. It would be endless to describe the varieties of white bodices and jackets which are now being prepared for wearing over low dresses in summer. It is affirmed by competent authorities that no fashion will be more generally adopted this summer, and that ladies will wear this style of dress in the day-time as well as in the evening. The difference is, that in the day-time white muslin is worn, and fine gauze or spotted net in the evening. Again, black net or black lace over white net is less dressy than white net and lace combined.

EVENING DRESS.

Evening Dress of White Muslin. – The ruffles are edged with black lace, and black lace insertions are put over rose-colored bands.

White is very much worn – a pretty, cheap dress, that is, cheap in every respect, except with regard to labor, for, to be beautiful, the toilet should always be perfectly fresh.

Peterson's Magazine, August 1864

Plate I. – Walking-dress. *Robe* of *poult de sole*, trimmed at the bottom of the skirt on each seam with three rows of shells formed of ribbon, finished off with a small flat mother-of-pearl button. *Garde-française* jacket, open and rounded in front; the corners of each tail turned back, and fastened together under a mother-of-pearl button. A small shell of ribbon on each side of the front, from which the cord is carried across to fasten the jacket. French cambric waistcoat, with deep pointed collar, trimmed with *Valenciennes*. Tight sleeves, with turned-back cuffs, and *épaulette* formed with one shell.

Foulard dress, trimmed with two rows of narrow lace insertion, placed over a wide ribbon. *Paletôt* fitting to the figure, and trimmed in the same style.

Plate II. – Group. *Robe* of muslin, trimmed on the skirt with three rows of wide lace insertion over coloured ribbon placed in festoons. High body, plaited, and long sleeves. *Corselet* of silk, with square ends behind, trimmed with *guipure*.

Grenadine dress: a plaited flounce at the bottom of the skirt, with an insertion of black silk above; and, still higher up, a wide band of silk, scalloped at each edge, on which are placed leaves of black lace. Low body; square *pélerine* of lace, with open sleeves rounded at the wrist.

Dress of *organdi*: the bottom of the skirt cut in scallops, under which is placed a flounce covered with lace. The dress is in the style *Gabrielle*, with an insertion of lace down each side of the front breadths, and a row of buttons up the front. Low body; long sleeves of *tulle bouillonné*. *Fanchon* of lace, crossed in front, and fastened behind with two long bows and ends.

Plate III. – Sea-side dresses. *Robe* of silk, with small *chiné* flowers: the bottom of the skirt cut in deep oval scallops, with a straight piece between each, bound with plain silk. Under it is a flounce of plain silk, set on in deep folds, and covered with lace. Jacket body, with riding-habit skirt, trimmed like the bottom of the skirt. Tight sleeves; the bottom and *épaulette* made to match the rest of the dress. *Grenadine* shawl, trimmed with lace.

Muslin dress, with *pompadour* flowers: the skirt trimmed with three narrow gauffered flounces, which are carried up the left side, gradually diminishing to the waist. Square open body, half high on the shoulders, trimmed with a narrow quilling. Tight sleeves, trimmed at the wrist and up the back of the arm with narrow frills. Plain muslin *fichu*, trimmed with insertion and *Valenciennes*, crossed in front, and fastened at the back with two rounded ends.

Le Follet, Journal du Grand Monde, September 1864

The Art of the Hoop: 1860 - 1869

BALL DRESS.

Evening Dress of Pink Silk, trimmed with black velvet, cut out in a diamond pattern.

DINNER DRESS.

Evening Dress of Maize-Colored Silk, trimmed with a black fluted ruffle, and two rows of black ruching, put on in a double tunic pattern. White mull body, with a black velvet waist and braces.

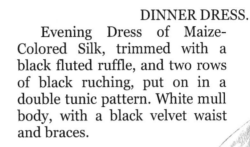

Skirts are not so heavily trimmed as formerly. Many dresses are quite plain, or with only a narrow quilling, or a thick gimp cord around the bottom. Others are cut in large scallops, and simply bound with black velvet, as in our wood-cut, and others again have sewn in the center of each scallop a large velvet rosette. These rosettes are made of ribbon-velvet, and the bodice may be made with a basque, if preferred; but if a sash is worn instead of a basque, it should be bound with black velvet.

WALKING DRESS.

Walking Dress in the hunting-coat style, so fashionable now in Paris. The skirt, it will be seen, is worn looped up, over a striped petticoat, which is vandyked at the edges.

Petticoats are very much trimmed, that is for walking dresses; but for house wear, the pure white with a plain hem, or a few tucks, or a couple of fluted ruffles, will always be in the best taste.

WALKING DRESS.

Carriage Dress of Blue Silk. – The skirt is cut in very long scallops at the bottom, and bound with black velvet. Two rows of black velvet, and a blue and black fringe, are put on to imitate a second skirt. Body trimmed to correspond.

Basques will no doubt be worn before the winter is over. The long coat basque is somewhat *outre* for our notions, but it is quite popular with some of our eccentric fashionables. It can be very much modified, however. Another novelty, but only becoming to very slender figures, is the Empire Sash; it is folded very wide, so as to cover nearly one-half of the bodice, and tied in a very large bow at the back; a long steel buckle is sometimes added in front, either in the center or on one side.

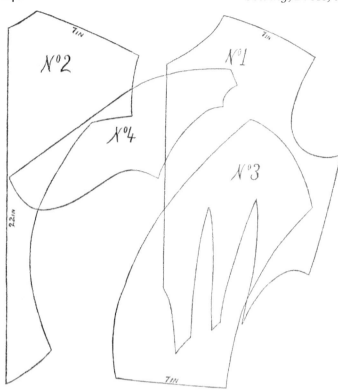

POSTILLION BODY.

Our diagram, this month, is that of one the Postillion Bodies, now so fashionable. This diagram is drawn for a lady of good figure and medium height, and consists of back, side-piece, front, and sleeve. It is, of course, to be made of the same material as the dress, and may be trimmed in various ways, according to taste.

We take this opportunity of reminding our readers, that in cutting out from our patterns nothing should be allowed for seams, as all the necessary allowances have been already made. The sizes of the different parts of the pattern are given in inches, so that a full-sized paper pattern can be cut from this diagram.

The form of all long sleeves is undergoing a small alteration; instead of being cut almost straight, they are rounded at the elbow, narrowing again toward the cuff, but still presenting the effect of an *almost* tight sleeve; this variation, slight as it is, proves more shapely than what we have been wearing.

ANDALUSIAN JACKET.

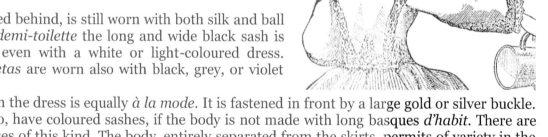

Among the many new patterns of Spanish jackets, that which we give below, called *The Andalusian*, is one of the most stylish. These jackets continue as fashionable as ever.

Peterson's Magazine, September 1864

The wide sash, tied behind, is still worn with both silk and ball dresses. For day or *demi-toilette* the long and wide black sash is generally preferred, even with a white or light-coloured dress. Plaid or striped *taffetas* are worn also with black, grey, or violet dresses.

The sash to match the dress is equally *à la mode*. It is fastened in front by a large gold or silver buckle. *Organdi* dresses, also, have coloured sashes, if the body is not made with long basques *d'habit*. There are some charming dresses of this kind. The body, entirely separated from the skirts, permits of variety in the *toilette;* for, as a change, a *cachemire* or *taffetas veste* may be worn, instead of the body like the dress.

Plate I. – Visiting and home dress: *Robe* of plain silk, trimmed at the bottom with three narrow flounces, edged with velvet and put on in large waves. Between each wave is placed a large heart's-ease, made of velvet, and edged with very narrow lace. High body, with round waist. Up each seam in front is placed a row of very narrow velvet, with a quilling of silk on each side. A heart's-ease, like those on the skirt, forms the *épaulette* and cuff of the sleeve, which is nearly tight to the arm. Head-dress of velvet and lace.

Satin dress, having at the bottom of the skirts a flounce, surmounted by three rows of velvet, and a row of *guipure* plaited so as to form Vandykes. Velvet *casaque*, very open in front and trimmed with *guipure*, forming *revers* and square *basques*. A rich bead gimp is placed all round the *casaque*.

Plate II. – Visiting-dress of *taffetas:* the bottom of the skirt cut in very wide shallow scallops; edged with narrow velvet, above which are placed five rows of velvet spots. Velvet *collet,* trimmed with Thibet fringe and *cachemire galons.* Crape bonnet, with velvet curtain, trimmed with shaded flowers.

Moire dress, trimmed so as to form a very long double skirt, with a row of lace, which is carried a short distance up each seam. Large lace leaves are placed above this trimming. High body; band with two pointed ends behind, surmounted by a bow of ribbon.

The fashion of wearing *vestes* by no means diminishes; on the contrary – *guimpes* and waistcoats are quite the order of the day. For the autumn the *pique* is often replaced by one of white *taffetas,* half open down the front, so as to show a *jabot* of lace.

Long sashes of black or white lace are made very wide, and over a muslin or silk dress form an exceedingly pretty finish to a *toilette.* They are doubly useful, for they can be employed as head-dresses also.

Plate III. – Dress of *taffetas,* trimmed at the bottom with loops of ribbon, surmounted by a thick *chicorée ruche. Paletot* the same as the dress, and trimmed to match ; a group of ribbon loops forming the *épaulette* to the tight sleeves.

Robe of *poult de soie,* trimmed at the bottom of the skirt with two rows of wide Thibet fringe put on in wide scallops – the point of the bottom scallop reaching the middle of the upper one, leaving a large space between each, which is filled in with a double cross-bar of gauffered *passementerie.* High body, with square *basques* in front and behind, trimmed round with Thibet fringe. Tight sleeves; *épaulette* of fringe, and cross-bars of *passementerie* to match those on the skirt. The bottom of the sleeve, which is quite plain, has simply a row of lace falling over the hand.

Many dresses this autumn are made with one wide flounce, crossways, about a quarter of a yard wide. This has a very good effect, especially in striped materials. In this style was a dress of black silk, with satin stripes, very fine, of a rich violet. The flounce edged with a quilling of violet. The bottom of the skirt, which reached below the flounce, was cut in scallops, and edged to match the flounce. *Senorita* jacket, trimmed to match.

Le Follet, Journal du Grand Monde, October 1864

Garibaldi Bodies, made of foulard, mousseline de laine, or cashmere, are again worn. These bodies are not so loose as formerly – and do not droop over the belt – but are made to fit the figure closely. In fact, they are very much like a full high body. The fronts have tucks about half an inch in width, which look well if chain-stitched. The skirt is fastened *over* the Garibaldi bodice. Epaulets are frequently added to the small bishop-sleeves, and around the throat there is an upright band finished off with a strip of white embroidered muslin or Valenciennes edging.

THE BIARRITZ.

This is the fashionable style at the French watering-places, and in the country. The high-laced boots are of russet morocco. The petticoat is of lilac alpaca, with a design in black silk sewn upon it. The dress is of white alpaca, trimmed with rows of black velvet, and looped up with black cord and tassels. The coat is of the same material as the dress, falling open in front, and trimmed to correspond with the skirt. White plaited chemisette, with lilac alpaca waist; gloves of russet leather, and a cane, which is now the universal accompaniment of a walking-dress in France.

THE BRIGHTON.

This exceedingly stylish dress is made of maize-colored foulard. The skirt, and deep loose paletot of the coat shape, is trimmed with a deep fringe. White under-body.

THE SARATOGA.

Under-dress of very dark gray silk, cut in wide scallops around the bottom, and bound with black velvet. Upper dress of light gray silk dotted with black. The edge of the skirt is cut in deep scallops, bound with the darker silk, and trimmed with black lace. Bodice with a plain basque at the back, and trimmed with the darker silk.

The newest style of skirt is the Saratoga. This is stylish, and has the advantage of using two old dresses, if necessary. to make one new one. Of course, the lace can be dispensed with, and the two dresses can be of different colors, provided the colors harmonize. The under-dress should always be of the darkest hue.

Some of the new dresses are cut square at the throat, and are very becoming, but the throat and neck, in this case, should be pretty – and the square quite small, and filled with lace drawn with narrow velvet ribbon tied at the back.

Among the bodices, the one called the Graziella is in excellent taste, and, when made of white muslin, can be worn with a variety of skirts. Imagine a sort of corslet made of black velvet, which reaches midway up the bodice, and descends upon the hips. It has the effect of a small pair of stays, and is laced at the back. It is composed, in front, of six pieces, which are sloped to fit the waist. This corslet is worn over a white bodice, and two black velvet ribbons are carried over the shoulders, where they are tied in a bow with flowing ends. The Graziella bodice is cut in small points round the edge, which produces the effect of basques, and the points are trimmed with narrow white lace, and in the center of each point a small square of guipure is sewn. The white bodice must be trimmed to correspond. To complete this costume, a white skirt is worn, and this is trimmed with lace medallions. For small parties, there is no style of toilet more suitable.

FRENCH GUARD JACKET.

We give, above, an outline drawing of the French-Guard Jacket, one of the most fashionable things now worn in Paris, and so called because it is, in part, copied from the uniform of the French Guards. We also give, on the next page, a diagram from which this stylish affair may be cut out.

No. 1. – Front. – The plait A is made in this pattern only which forms the under part. The skirt will be prolonged from the crosses according to the length of the garment.

No. 2. – Front forming the Facing. – This pattern is laid on No. 1, and forms the skirt with facings. The facings are marked B, in dotted lines.

No. 3. Back, with a seam down the middle and a small plait like a man's frock-coat. The seams of the plait and the facing of the corner are marked C with dotted lines.

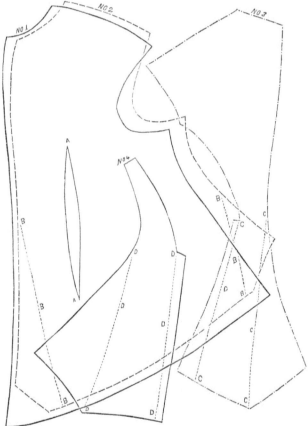

No. 4. Side-Piece. – The middle plait which corresponds with that of the back, and the facing of the side, are indicated by lines of dots marked D.

To form the skirt behind in continuation of the front, place under the waist, on each side, two widths cut in points as for a wide jacket. The points are sewed underneath the side-piece and the back, at the part trimmed with gimp.

The sleeve is cut in the ordinary form with an elbow.

This garment is trimmed either with galloons, with silk cord, or with guipure laid flat.

The war, in this country, has made fashions assume more or less of a military aspect, and this Guard Jacket, we think, will be very extensively worn here. One, almost as military, was in the last number.

Thin dresses are usually made gathered slightly in front of the waist, and a wide waistband or sash is always worn with them. If a waistband, it is at least four inches wide, and is fastened with a large buckle. The breadth of the sashes is also increasing considerably. These latter are now frequently made in one piece with the bodice, that is, the side-pieces of the back are extended to form a sash. The black silk Zouave jacket, made in this style, with a sash from the back, is a useful garment, as it can be worn over any dress.

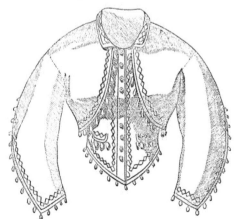

SPANISH JACKET.

Our fourth illustration is one of those dashing Spanish jackets, which still continue the rage, and which, as they can be worn with skirt of a different color, are comparatively economical. This is, to our taste, one of the very prettiest that has come out. It is trimmed with black velvet and buttons.

The mixture of black and white is as popular as ever, and where it is used with discretion, it is very becoming.

White dresses over colored skirts are much worn, and are trimmed with gimp made of straw and with Valenciennes. Straw, both as embroidery and gimp, is in great favor, and is very pretty. It is truly the "gold of the daylight;" beautiful cords to loop up dresses are made with it, likewise plaits which are placed round the edges of hats.

It will be seen that the sleeve has altered less than any other part of the dress. Long basques will be the ultra style for the winter, but many will wear them much modified. Skirts for the street are still most sensibly looped up.

Peterson's Magazine, October 1864

Plate I. – *Robe* of *poult de soie:* a band of velvet covered with lace above the hem, another band is taken up the skirt *en biais*. Crape bonnet, trimmed with velvet and flowers. A diadem of flowers inside. Velvet strings. Long *cachemire* shawl.

Robe of *moire*. Shirt and *veste* trimmed with a *plastron en tablier* of velvet, with *cachemire* braid, fancy buttons, and flutings of velvet. Coat-sleeves with cuffs of velvet.

Little girl. *Robe* of poplin scalloped at the bottom with velvet. Second skirt to match, *drapée*, with large *pattes*. *Veste* to match. Oriental sash, with fringed ends. Cambric *chemisette*. Net, with bows of velvet.

We remark, as the winter season approaches, how much the *basques* are returning into favour; and we may affirm now that *robes*, whatever their tissue, will adopt them generally. It is true it will not be the classic *basque* worn for the last few years; on the contrary, the new *basque* is entirely one of fancy. The *habit*, with square tails, or tails turned back; the long *basques* of the *veste de chasse;* and the *basques de casaque,* with a broad band, are all in vogue.

The *paletots* and *casaques* are now drawn to the waist by a broad band, making them resemble the *blouses*. We hope all ladies of taste will protest against this exceedingly ugly and ungraceful style; though we must admit that, however unbecoming, a now fashion is readily adopted by novelty-seekers.

Plate II. – *Robe* of *poult de soie,* the skirt trimmed with two rows of velvet and *boudettes* placed in flounces. Large *rotonde* of velvet trimmed with lace.

Robe of *taffetas*, with satin stripes; trimmed near the bottom of the skirt with two narrow fluted velvet flounces. *Veste Senorita;* open rounded sleeves. Muslin *chemisette,* with collar and *jabot* of lace. Under-sleeves to match. *Empire* sash, with buckle.

Velvet and cloth are making their appearance, and it is probable that velvet will, as last year, be adopted for all descriptions of *toilettes*. So long as the temperature docs not compel us to envelope ourselves in winter clothing, *pardessus* of the same material as the dress, with *vestes* and *corsages* in all makes, will be seen.

The following *toilettes* are models of elegance: – *Robe* of violet poplin, for walking-dress. The bottom of the skirt is in deep scallops, edged with black velvet. The scallops are sufficiently deep to admit of a *bouquet* of flowers, embroidered with black silk. The rest of the skirt is covered with small black spots at rather wide distances. A fitting *paletôt,* scalloped and embroidered to match the skirt. Coat-sleeve, with a narrow scallop ascending the seam. This *toilette* is accompanied by a bonnet of violet *taffetas,* forming a very pointed tail behind. In place of the curtain is a wreath of small violet feathers mixed with black lace.

Plate III. – Group. *Tulle* dress, with three skirts: the bottom of each has a *blonde* flounce in rounded *dents*. Between each *dent* is a *cogue* of satin ribbon, fastening a large rose. The body is trimmed with a *veste Figaro*, formed of *tulle bouillonnés*. The back of the *veste* has a long *basque* habit, the whole edged with a light wreath of flowers, surmounting a *blonde* frill. *Gilet* of satin, with pockets of *blonde*.

Muslin dress, trimmed *en tablier* with *bouillonnés* and bows. Drawn body. *Taffetas* sash, with ends behind.

Robe of *poult de sole,* the skirt ornamented with a broad *grecque*, composed of small flowers placed at the head of a *Chantilly* lace. Second skirt of *tulle* trimmed to match, fastened up on the side by a broad ribbon, terminating in long fringed ends. Low body, with a *basque* in three pieces behind. *Garniture* of flowers and lace. Short *bouffantes* sleeves.

Tarlatane dress, trimmed with six rows of *chicorées*. Low body. *Bolero* sash, composed of plaited *tarlatane*, fastened with *brandebourgs* and fancy buttons.

Evening-dresses are made with *pans* and *basques* formed of lace and silk. Embroidered dresses will be very fashionable this winter. Satin, embroidered with twisted silk, or *chenille* has a very good appearance.

A *poult-de-soie robe,* scalloped at the bottom and edged with *chenille*. An oak-leaf is embroidered in each scallop. A row of the same leaves is placed upon the front breadth, and continued on the body, *à taille Empire,* with fitting sleeves.

A violet satin dress, with a broad embroidered band over the hem. Then a rich wreath, mounting up each breadth, gradually becoming narrow to the top. The *postilion veste* has all the seams corded.

Le Follet, Journal du Grand Monde, November 1864

MORNING DRESS.

House Dress of Leather-Colored Foulard. – The square coat-body and sleeves are trimmed with black velvet.

But to return to the make of dresses. A combination which is not uncomfortable to economy is that of a dress the front of which, in the shape of an apron, is of a different material from the rest. By this means a rich silk or satin dress, which the present fashion of very ample skirts had obliged to be put aside, may be brought to daylight once more and enlarged. Should it be too short, besides, this also can be remedied. The bottom should, in that case, be cut out in deep scallops, and a flounce of the same material as the front be put on under the edge of the scallops, with a full box-pleat inside each one of them. If the dress be self-colored, the front, of a thinner silk, may be striped; if, on the contrary, the dress itself have a pattern, the front may be self-colored, but always matched in shade to the former. When the dress requires no lengthening, a different style of trimming may be adopted for the bottom – ruches, lace, or fringe.

The front may also be entirely independent of the other part of the dress – that is, two skirts may be worn one over the other, the upper one being open in front. This is prettier in light materials, such as gauze, muslin, or cambric, than the other fashions, the most elegant style being a white muslin or tarlatan dress, trimmed with lace and open in front, over a petticoat of colored silk also trimmed with a fall of lace.

WALKING DRESS.

Walking Dress of Tan-Colored Alpaca. – Deep basque of the same material, with trimmings of alpaca, put on in deep scallops.

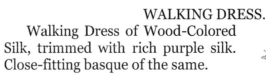

WALKING DRESS.

Walking Dress of Wood-Colored Silk, trimmed with rich purple silk. Close-fitting basque of the same.

WALKING DRESS.

Carriage-Dress of Black and White Plaid Silk, trimmed with black velvet. Coat-body of white silk, with two very long ends, trimmed with black velvet and a quilling of narrow white ribbon.

Carriage-Dress of Dove-Colored Silk, with a coated body, trimmed with black velvet and narrow black guipure lace.

WALKING DRESS.

Buckles, for waistbands, have now attained colossal proportions, but these are generally imitation, and not genuine gold and silver. The chased buckles are more distinguished than the plain dead gold ones, as the workmanship adds to their beauty. The mother-of-pearl buckles are worn with white dresses; and now it is the fashion to wear a buckle both at the front and back of the waist, and if a casaque is worn, both buckle and band are placed *above* the casaque.

Buckles, four to six inches in length, and proportionately wide, are worn by a few, but they look eccentric as yet. Of course, the waistband is very wide, and, strange to say, is worn high around the waist over the coatees and basques now so popular. The buckle is slipped on the waistbands, and the long ends fall at the back. Mother-of-pearl buckles, as well as buttons, are worn – some of these are wide enough for a horse's girth, and are of just the shape.

THE FLORIAN, OR HALF-FITTING PALETOT.

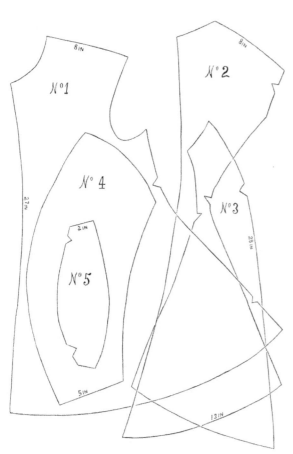

We give, this month, "The Florian."

No. 1. One Front.
No. 2. One Side-Piece.
No. 3. Half of Back.
No. 4. Front of Sleeve.
No. 5. Epaulet.

And, as will be seen, represents exactly one-half of the paletot. No difficulty will be found in joining the different pieces together, if attention is paid to small notches in the edges of the paper shape. The seam of the side-piece to the back is indicated with one notch, which is cut in the paper at the waist; the joining, underneath the arm, to the front by two notches.

As will be seen from the above sketch, the seams, if preferred, may be left open and trimmed round, which is a newer style than closing the seams to the edge of the paletot.

There are notches in the paper shape, which indicate the position of the sleeve; the elbow seam of the sleeve must be placed to the notch at the back of the paletot, and the front seam to that on the front of the paletot.

This garment can be made in a variety of materials – for the warm season of the year it would be very elegant composed of white muslin, lined with colored taffetas, and trimmed with Valenciennes lace.

For morning wear, it should be made of the same material as the dress, trimmed to match.

If made of black *gros-grain*, it may be trimmed down the fronts and round the sleeves with either guipure or gimp. For a silk three-quarters of a yard wide, a length of five yards would be requisite for the paletot. As we have remarked on former occasions, we should advise the pattern to be first cut out in lining muslin and tried on, as it is impossible to issue shapes which will fit every figure. This style of paletot is decidedly the most popular of the season.

Peterson's Magazine, November 1864

Plate I. – Ball-dresses. *Robe* of *poult de soie:* on the middle of each breadth a *bouquet* of flowers and leaves; these *bouquets* are fastened to each other by a cord. Tunics of *tulle* illusion, double, caught up with wreaths of flowers. Low full body, trimmed with flowers and cord. Head-dress of flowers. Necklace and ear-rings of pearls.

Satin dress, trimmed with a flounce of lace, headed with a row of embroidery in beads. Low body; *berthe,* round at the back and crossed in front, and forming two long ends behind, made of satin, trimmed with beads and lace. A diadem of precious stones in the hair. Ear-rings and bracelets to match.

Double skirts are gaining favour. The upper one is generally open up the front and back, to the waist, so as to show the under one, which should be of a different colour. The under-skirt is simply trimmed with a narrow flounce, set on in flat plaits, headed with a *passementerie* cord. The upper skirt, which is generally of satin, is very much trimmed, either with cords, *plaques,* buttons, chains of *passementerie* and beads, and, indeed, all manner of trimmings. However elegant this style may look for tall women, it must plainly

be seen that it cannot possibly be so for those below the ordinary height; and therefore, in that case, it should be trimmed as little as possible.

Plate II. – Dress of *taffetas:* double skirt, trimmed with three rows of cord. The upper skirt is raised at each breadth under a bow of cord with two long tassels. Plain high body, with long *basques*. Tight sleeves, and *épaulettes* formed with *passementerie*. Velvet bonnet, trimmed with feathers and lace.

Poult-de-soie dress, trimmed with a band of feathers, forming deep scallops. Each scallop is filled in with a number of hieroglyphics formed of velvet. Habit-body, with square *basques,* trimmed with feathers.

Skirts are very much trained; cut quite round at the bottom, so as to make them set out. This is certainly graceful for indoors wear; but, as the length of dress is not always in proportion to the size of the apartment, a lady must expect to have her dress frequently trodden upon. However, one thing is certain, that *les modes* of this year are much more becoming than those of past winters; and that, by making some slight modifications, a lady of taste may be not only elegantly but becomingly dressed.

Plate III. – Group. *Robe* of *tulle,* with three skirts, each edged with a thick *chicorée ruche* surmounted by a trimming of velvet and gold. Body full from the shoulders to the front, with *bouquets* of roses and lilies of the valley on the front and shoulders.

Satin dress, trimmed at the bottom of the skirt with a wide band of ermine and a plaiting in festoons. *Veste Russe* of satin, trimmed with ermine. High *chemisette* of *tulle,* with long sleeves trimmed with *blonde* and tassels.

Dress of silk, with a double *bouillonné* of *tulle* at the bottom of the skirt, trimmed with daisies. Tunic of *tulle,* trimmed all over with daisies, and having a small wreath of the same flowers forming an undulating border. Low body, full from the shoulder to the front; trimmed with *bouquets* of flowers.

Basques are gaining favour daily. They are made sometimes in one fashion, sometimes in another; but *basques* of all shapes and sizes are decidedly the fashion. There is, however, one thing against which we must warn our readers – that is, wearing a band over the *basque:* nothing can be more ungraceful. Some have even worn them over *paletôts:* we need scarcely point out the absurdity of such a style. We do not wish to say a word against the band – we have always admired the round body and band – but then let it be the accompaniment of the round body, not an addition to the *basque,* which is quite ornamental and becoming in itself. The mixture of the two is simply absurd.

Sleeves are still worn nearly tight: good news for the winter.

Jackets are the favourite wear for at-home dress. They are, however, admissible even for evening wear, when made of suitable materials. The *veste Russe* is very elegant, made of velvet, trimmed with rich *passementerie* or fur, and without sleeves. The waistcoat, which is generally of light-coloured *foulard,* should have long full sleeves, fastened into a wristband. Some of these jackets are trimmed with a band of feathers, an ornament which is daily gaining favour.

Le Follet, Journal du Grand Monde, December 1864

The Art of the Hoop: 1860 - 1869

DINNER DRESS.

House Dress of Fawn-Colored Silk, with black velvet and embroidery in black silk and jet beads.

The Looped-up Skirts, with a richly trimmed petticoat, are of course still the most worn for walking, and we hope they may always remain the fashion.

Plain waists with moderate basques, or no basques at all, are still retained by those who do not wish to be in the extreme of an eccentric fashion, and these are the majority, too; the dress should always, in cut or trimming, approach the prevailing style.

Skirts for house wear are made shorter in front and at the sides than formerly, but with very long trains at the back. They are also sewn on to the bodies so as to bring every frill at the back, but plain in front.

COAT DRESS.

House Dress of Maize-Colored Alpaca, braided in black and purple. The bodice has a wide coat basque at the back.

COAT BODY.

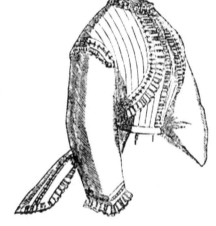

BLACK VELVET COAT.

Coat Bodices are the fashion just now, and the waistbands, with buckles fastened behind, are worn over them. This is an exceedingly unbecoming fashion, except to a youthful or *very* slender figure.

Black Velvet Coats and Bodices of various shapes are popular, for though the material is expensive at first, the one garment can be worn with any number of skirts, If it is made in the coat style, a white silk or any contrasting colored vest can be worn under it, or it can fit the figure closely and button from the waist up.

The Coat Sleeve continues to be worn, particularly for walking dresses and in thick materials. These are made more dressy however by retaining the shape of the coat sleeve, but puffing the material lengthwise. The long, hanging sleeve, with the close-fitting sleeve under it, is being made for occasions when a richer toilet is desirable.

WALKING DRESS.

Walking Dress and Paletot of Gray Poplin, trimmed with blue velvet ribbon quilled, and narrow black gimp. Bows of wide blue velvet are put at the seams of the paletot.

LOUIS XV. PALETOT AND WAISTCOAT.

In the front of the number we give a full-length engraving of the *Louis XV. Paletot and Waistcoat*, one of the most fashionable (perhaps the most fashionable) out-of-door costumes for this winter. We now give here two diagrams, for cutting out the Paletot and Waistcoat: one on this page and one on the next.

No. 1. Front of Paletot.

No. 2. Back of Paletot.

No. 3. Side-Piece of Back of Paletot.

At the bottom of these three portions of the pattern four inches must be added to obtain the proper dimensions.

No. 4. Sleeve of Paletot.

No. 5. Front of Waistcoat.

No. 6. Back of Waistcoat, drawn at the waist behind, and composed simply of silk lining. This back must not come so low down in the hips as the front part; the sides end nearly at the waist.

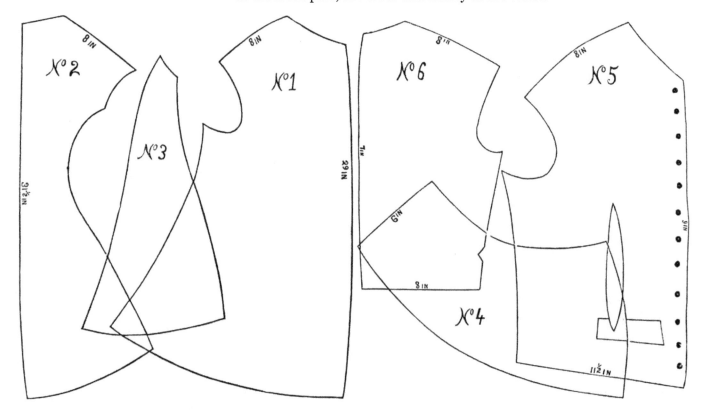

Peterson's Magazine, December 1864

How to Dress the Best at the Least Expense.

To dress expensively is not always to dress successfully. A lady may walk about carrying on her person the worth of some hundreds of pounds in the shape of velvets from Genoa, brocades from Lyons, shawls from India, lace from Brussels, cameos from Rome, with etceteras too numerous to mention; but nineteen times out of twenty she will not look so well as her sister-woman attired in the simplest style, with the strictest economy. If riches were the rule, and restricted incomes the exceptions, then the question of expenditure might be very easily settled; but as the facts are exactly reversed, it becomes the duty of the wife, the mother, and the daughter so to regulate the expenses of her toilette as to enjoy that peace of mind which prudence alone can ensure, in the knowledge that its limits have never been overstepped, however strong the temptations.

But there are other motives which induce frugality in personal expenditure far above the restrictions of a narrow income. Mothers have children to educate; some have the future to provide for, and know that, unless they can spare from the present, want may stand like an armed man in the pathway of the future; while others again would rather follow the example of that Scripture-honoured Dorcas who preferred making clothes for the poor to spending their means in personal adornment.

But whether from necessity or choice, all honour, according to its motives, should be paid to economy in dress; and we shall be very happy to assist those who entertain this laudable ambition with such hints as we are able to offer from time to time.

Let us begin by recommending the looking over of every article that has been laid aside out of sight in drawers and boxes. Many ladies go and buy things of inferior quality, while they leave others of better worth to the depredations of the moths and the mildew at the bottom of their trunks and drawers. First of all, let these be searched out, brushed, and well aired; and here let me say that no article should ever be put away at any time of the year without having been first hung to the fire or in the sun, as there will always be some moisture clinging to it, borne witness to by the after consequences. Taking up one of these, we will suppose that the bodice is the worse for wear, and the lower edges of the skirt dilapidated. In this case the skirt must be worn with a jacket, and the mode of lengthening it must be in accordance with the nature of the material. If of rep, merino, winsey, or any kind of wool material, then purchase as much plaid of colours that will harmonise with its own the best, cut it on the bias, and lay it all round the bottom of the dress. This band of plaid may be of any width necessary to complete the length of the skirt. If the dress should be of silk, then it can be adapted to a modern fashion, similar to that which appears in our illustration, extremely well, no matter how much additional length it may require. Cut off the injured parts of the skirt, and shape the edge into rather bold vandykes, which may be finished round with a French hem; or cut up the edge at regular distance into what the Parisian modistes call teeth, and fold each point inwards, so as to leave the vandyke in the same way, only not requiring the binding round. Under this attach a flounce with very little fulness, fastening down each point of the vandyke in its place, and placing a button between each indentation of the vandyke upon the edge of the skirt. If the silk is of a dark colour, black makes a very good flounce; but as most ladies have by them portions of silks that can be appropriated to this use, the colour must, of course, be settled according to convenience.

When streets and thoroughfares are moist and fluid with mud long dresses are little less than a torment to their wearers; for if they are held up by the hands in one place, they are certain to slip down in another, ensuring both discomfort and destruction. It is essential that arrangement should be made for drawing up the dress. A simple and inexpensive way is to sew on three eyes (the hooks are always useful for other purposes) on each seam, the lowest being a quarter of a yard from the bottom, to pass a worsted cord, which is made for the purpose, through these, bringing the half of them through a ring on one side of the waist, and half of them through another on the contrary side, fastening a button to each, that they may not slip back again through the ring, and attaching ribbon strings to tie when it is necessary to draw up the skirt. This arrangement forms pretty festoons over the under-skirt.

On this account it is necessary that this under-skirt should also be in some degree ornamental. Almost every lady has dresses by her which are no longer eligible, and these being lengthened from the top, may have their worst part cut off from the bottom. To give firmness to these under-skirts, a band of tartan cut on the bias may be carried round; and if the dress with which it is worn should be lengthened as we have described above, then the plaid should be the same, which produces a pretty effect. Another way is to place some wadding (French wadding is the lightest, but it is also the most expensive) all round the bottom of the skirt, and to stitch it with coloured silk in some slight pattern, one suitable for this purpose being given in the Work-Table department of this magazine.

In purchasing a dress, still keeping our regard for economy in view, we think that a chequered alpaca will prove one of the best investments for the outlay of a small amount of money. These look well either in bronze with a gold colour or white cheque, or in mauve and black. The skirt must be gored, the body may be made high, with a point behind, with bands from the shoulders, as we have described in a previous number, crossing before, with a small bishop sleeve, or one shaped to the elbow. Worn with a small linen collar and cuffs this dress has a very pretty effect.

If a little more expense should not be objected to, then we would recommend it plain alpaca of deep-tinted purply lavender. These are often of a superior quality when bought at a tailor's drapers at two shillings or half-a-crown a-yard of the double width. The soft and glossy surface of these alpacas cause them to be much esteemed by the French ladies. It can be made exactly as we have described above. If a cloak is to be purchased at the same time, a tartan looks well with this dress, but in that case it is much more complete by having a crossway band of the same plaid round the bottom of the skirt. One of the most fashionable shapes is also the most economical. It is that which is produced by cutting the material on a slant through its middle, and joining it up again with the two slants together, narrow round the throat, and wide in the sweep round the skirt; but this mode of cutting can only be adopted when the fabric is the same on both sides, or when two cloaks are made at the same time. The points at the back being rounded off, they are shaped into a collar.

The What-Not, February 1864

The sweetest of the spring months brings with it a reminder that it is time again to take up a subject in which we are much interested, and which, involving as it does the welfare of many families, ought to be considered one of even national importance. The American ladies have been accused of causing great commercial panics in their country with their extravagance of dress; and the French ladies often step out of their carriages for exercise and display in the Champs Elysées weary [*sic*: wearing] habiliments that have cost five or six hundred pounds. No wonder, then, that as Ruin walks in at the door, Love flies out of the window. And yet it is altogether a mistake to suppose that a costume is more becoming because it is costly. Taste and elegance achieve greater triumphs where they work with simple materials than where they hold the richest fabrics at their disposal.

Spring-time teaches us to make our selection from some of the light materials of the season. One of these, which we have just been inspecting, is a sort of Swiss muslin, the fabric fine and close, the colour either fawn or lavender, of one uniform shade, without pattern. The bottom of the skirt should be bound with a broad white braid. The bodice is made with a postilion jacket behind, a sleeve shaped to the elbow, with a turned-up cuff, all bound with the white braid, and white fancy buttons. This bodice is not attached to the skirt. For out-of-door dress a casaque of the same material is very suitable. This is made to fit the figure, and just at the back there are two large underplaits, which give width to the skirt. The bodice is covered with the pointed cape, or pelerine, of which we have spoken in a previous number. The whole must be finished with the binding of white braid, but in addition to this the cape may have three or five rows of the braid laid on. ...

We have already spoken in our notice of the fashions, of the corded muslins which have recently appeared. We recommend this as a suitable material for another dress of superior style. The star on a white ground is perhaps one of the most elegant amongst the designs. This may be made with the Raphael bodice – that is, cut square and low in the front, but high behind – a narrow quilling of blue or violet ribbon being laid upon the edge. The sleeve is the gigot at the top, narrowing towards the hand, yet wide enough and short enough to show the embroidery of the undersleeve of clear muslin shaped up the arm, the chemisette being also embroidered to match. The edge of the uppersleeve is finished with the same quilling of ribbon as that upon the bodice. A scarf sash of the same material as the dress, widening towards the ends, with two or three rows of the quilled ribbon across them, is fastened at the left side.

White, the prettiest of dresses for the young, is, we rejoice to say, becoming more and more the mode. The skirt may be made with a deep hem, headed with a line of embroidery insertion; or this may be worked upon the dress with incisions, and a bright violet-colour velvet passed in and out. The bodice should be rather full in the front, with a band to match; the sleeve full, with a wristband to correspond; and round the neck a narrow band of the same, edged with narrow lace. Another way is to have the dress made quite plain, and to wear it with a Medici belt, or a low body of black silk, finishing with a jacket behind, cut square. This is worn over the white body, and has a very tasteful effect.

Another dress, of quite a different style, although economical, is also one of the prettiest of the season. This is a lama, the colour being one of the splendid mauves or violets of the new dye, and not liable to fade.

The skirt ought not to be lined, but merely finished with a hem, above which may be laid a narrow black lace insertion, with a white ribbon under it of the same width. The bodice is made slightly full, with braces of the black lace insertion on the white ribbon over the shoulders, and bars across in the stomacher fashion, both back and front, bordered with a very narrow black lace edging. The sleeve is a small bishop, with wristband the same as the braces. This lama may also be made with the Raphael bodice, just as we have described above, substituting the insertion for the quillings of ribbon.
The What-Not, May 1864

Dressing at Watering-Places. – In spite of the war, ladies dress elaborately at watering-places here, as well as abroad. In the days when Marie Antoinette reigned in France, people were accustomed to blame her for the extravagance which she introduced into the French court; and censure was heard on all sides on account of the foolish, senseless expenditure which the ladies in personal attendance upon the queen were forced to incur. But how paltry such expenditure now appears when we compare it with what is being daily carried on at the present time. In those days the queen and her attendants were, in summer time, dressed, throughout the day, simply in white cambric, and straw hats with long veils. It was only in ceremonious toilets that the queen introduced and carried out her fantastic ideas. But the grumblers of a hundred years ago, what would they say now? Many ladies of the present day would be truly thankful if they had only to think about ceremonious toilets, and be permitted to wear cambric dresses all the day through during the summer season; and the worst feature about the matter is, that one handsome dress daily is not now considered sufficient; there are many ladies who change their toilets four and even five times every day! Fifteen years ago, ladies at the seaside, even in Europe, met each other on the shore in the early part of the day, dressed in morning-gowns with light cloth mantles over their shoulders, and coarse straw bonnets upon their heads. This was laughingly called their *chenille* (caterpillar) costume, but it was a very pictorial expression, for three hours afterward the caterpillar was a brilliant butterfly, fluttering about in the gayest attire.

But now-a-days ladies dress before their bath, then they dress to take their bath – that is to say, their bathing-dress is a fanciful costume, made of white or colored flannel, braided or embroidered in a most elegant design; then for breakfast there is another dress, for the promenade still another, for dinner there is a change for the fifth time, and for the ball a sixth change. And as it would not be thought proper to appear in each dress more than four times, continued variety is wanted, and so much novelty is consequently sought after that both dress-makers and their employers scarcely know where to turn for change of color and style of make.
Peterson's Magazine, September 1864

Dress for Dancing

The first consideration for a lady is simplicity of attire, whether the material be cheap or costly – such simplicity as produces the finest effect with the least apparent labor, and the smallest number of articles.

The next is elegance of make and propriety of color. Fashion generally will determine the former, but the latter is to be left to individual taste.

In the selection of colors, a lady should consider her figure and complexion. If she be slender and sylph-like, white, or very light colors are supposed to be suitable; but if inclined to embonpoint, such colors should be avoided, as they apparently add to the bulk of the wearer.

Pale colors, such as pink, salmon, light blue, maize, delicate green, and white, are most in vogue among blondes, as being thought to harmonize with their complexions. Brilliant colors are generally selected by brunettes for a similar reason.

Harmony of dress involves also the idea of contrast. A pale girl looks more pale, and a brunette less dark, contrasted with strong colors. But as the blonde and brunette are both beautiful in themselves, when the contour of the face and figure is good, a beautiful girl, blonde or brunette, may adopt either style, or both alternately; for a uniform style of dress finally assumes the character of mannerism and formality, which is incompatible with the highest excellence in any of the fine arts.

Ladies should remember that men look to the effect of dress in setting off the figure and countenance of a lady, rather than to its cost. Few men form estimates of the value of ladies' dress. This is a subject for female criticism. Beauty of person and elegance of manners in woman will always command more admiration from the other sex than costliness of clothing.

In having dresses made long, care should be taken that they be not so long as to touch the ground, for in that case they are likely to be torn before the evening has half expired. It is almost impossible to dance, if the dress sweep the floor, without such an accident, except with a very careful and accomplished partner.

Mourning – even half-mourning – has always a sombre appearance, and is, therefore, unbecoming in a ball-room; but since decorating it with scarlet has come into fashion, an air of cheerfulness has been imparted to its otherwise melancholy appearance.

A lady may wear a black dress with scarlet flowers and trimmings. Many ladies, whether in mourning or not, wear black from preference, trimming it with such colors as their taste suggests. A black satin dress looks better when covered with net tarleton or crape; the latter to be worn only when in mourning.

<u>A Complete Practical Guide to the Art of Dancing, 1864</u>

Young Lady's Manual

UPON DRESS AND THE TOILETTE – A CHAPTER FOR YOUNG LADIES.

I have little respect for that philosophy which inculcates a contempt for what some judicious writer terms "the minor morals of society," or the arts and accomplishments which tend to exalt and refined manners and disposition. Foppery is one thing, and a proper regard to dress and the toilette is quite another. Nothing is more ridiculous than the first – nothing tends more to enhance one's self-respect, force of character, and even strength of moral principle, than the other. While I would not therefore (especially in a new country like this) encourage an undue attention to the fripperies and frivolities of mere fashion, I would strenuously urge upon all a due regard to neatness of dress, propriety of deportment, and such a reasonable attention to the person generally, as all tend to render oneself as agreeable as possible to one's associates and acquaintances. I must be permitted to add, that he who doubts the propriety of such advice has yet much to learn of the nature of man, and of the influence of appearances.

I shall now present a few observations and prescriptions, arranged under appropriate heads, which will, I trust, meet the approbation and approval of all sensible and intelligent ladies.

DRESS.

Every lady should study and determine what dress is most becoming and suitable to her style of person. In Paris, the style of beauty, and the peculiarities of every individual, are considered before her style of costume is determined upon. In an English or American ballroom, on the contrary, one dress is too often the fac-simile of all the others; the tall and the short, the lean and the stout, are all robed alike – and all, as they imagine, dressed according to the latest Parisian fashion. This is an error which every woman of real taste will endeavor to correct.

A few general rules concerning dress may be given, which can enable our readers to determine what mode of dress will most effectually display and heighten their charms.

Tight sleeves, without any trimming, are becoming to full forms the medium height, or below it. Upon a tall, slender woman, with long arms, they are very ungraceful, unless trimmed with folds, or a small ruffled cap, which is made to reach the elbow. Upon a very short stout person, moderately wide sleeves are more becoming than tight ones, as they conceal the outlines of the form.

Flounces are graceful upon tall persons, whether slender or otherwise, but never upon diminutive ones. Tucks are equally graceful upon both, and never look out of fashion. A couple of wide tucks, which give the appearance of two skirts, are very beautiful for an evening dress, made of delicate materials. Any species of trimming down the front or sides of the skirt, increases the apparent height.

Capes are, in general, only becoming to persons with falling shoulders.

High neck dresses are convenient, and almost always look well upon a very high-shouldered person, a low-necked dress is more appropriate, and if the shoulders are only moderately high, the neck may still be covered, and the dress finished off about the throat with a narrow piece of lace, turned downwards, instead of a collar. Dresses with loose backs are only becoming upon very fine, and at the same time slender figures. Evening dresses of transparent materials look well when made high in the neck; but upon very young girls it is more usual to cut the dress low, leaving a part of the shoulder bare. A dress should always be made loose over the chest, and tight over the shoulder blades.

Every species of drapery is graceful, and may always be worn to advantage. Long sashes, knotted in front. are more becoming than belts, unless there is much trimming upon the dress.

No dress with long sleeves is complete, without a pair of cuffs. They look very pretty, when simply made of linen cambric, with a double row of herring-bone. Cuffs, with small ruffles, make the hands look small.

To make narrow shoulders look wider, an inside cape, (or cape fastened to the dress,) falling at the shoulders, should be worn.

The effect of a well made tournure (or bustle) is to make the waist look round and delicate. An extremely small and waspish looking waist can never be considered a beauty. It is exceedingly hurtful to those who attain it by tight lacing, and doubly ungraceful, since it prevents all graceful movements. Tying the sash in a point in front gives a roundness to the waist, and lessens its dimensions. To prevent the fulness of the skirt from rising above the sash, which is very ungraceful, the belt should be lined with buckram.

Short cloaks are very unbecoming to short and clumsily built persons – upon others they are generally graceful.

A close cottage bonnet is never out of fashion, and there are very few faces which it does not improve.

The morning costume of a lady should consist of a loose wrapper, fastened with a cord and tassel at the waist, and worn with very plain cuffs and collar.

Shoes should always be worn a little longer than the foot, so that their length makes the foot look narrow, which is a great beauty. A broad, short foot can never be considered handsome. Tight shoes impair the gait, and a large foot is, at any time, preferable to an awkward mode of walking.

ART OF GOOD BEHAVIOR.

Ladies are allowed to consult fancy, variety, and ornament, more than men, yet nearly the same rules apply. It is the mark of a lady to be always well shod. If your feet are small, don't spoil them by pinching – if large, squeezing them makes them worse.

Be as moderate as you can about bustles. While it is the fashion you must wear them, but don't lay them on too thick.

Above all, as you regard health, comfort, and beauty, do not lace too tightly. A waist too small for the natural proportion of the figure is the worst possible deformity, and produces many others. No woman who laces tight can have good shoulders, a straight spine, good lungs, sweet breath, or is fit to be a wife and mother.

The most elegant dresses are black or white. Common modesty will prevent indecent exposure of the shoulders and bosom. A vulgar girl wears bright and glaring colors, fantastically made, a large, flaring, red, yellow, or sky-blue hat, covered with a rainbow of ribbons, and all the rings and trinkets she can load upon her. Of course, a modest, well bred young lady chooses the reverse of all this. In any assemblage, the most plainly dressed woman is sure to be the most ladylike and attractive. Neatness is better than richness, and plainness better than display. Single ladies dress less in fashionable society than married ones; and all more plainly and substantially for walking or travelling, than on other occasions.

In my opinion, nothing beyond a simple natural flower ever adds to the beauty of a lady's bead-dress.

It is a general rule, applicable to both sexes, that persons are the best dressed when you cannot remember how they were dressed. Avoid everything out of the way, uncommon, or grotesque.

How to Do It, 1864

How to Make a Dress.

The number of yards required depends on the width of the material. Ten yards of any material eighteen inches wide, will make a dress for a moderate-sized person, with full body, but no trimming on the skirt. Six yards of French merino, or any other material of that width, will be found sufficient.

Cutting Out.

When you are about to begin to cut out a dress, recollect whether it is to be cut on the cross or straight of the material. This will in some measure depend on fashion; therefore get a fashion book of the month, and study it a little. They are to be had at any of the bookstores. It will tell you if sleeves, bodies, trimmings, or flounces, are cut on the straight way of the material, or on the bias or cross way.

By taking notice of any lady well dressed, that you may meet with, by a little attention you can observe how her dress is made, supposing you to know already something about the making of a dress. Fashion is an imaginary idea, and there is much less change, than many persons think. I would recommend to any one who wishes to see what is going on in the way of a dress, to pay a visit to Broadway any fine afternoon. When that is not in your power, go to any public place where there are genteel people, and make your own observations. With the help of these you will never be far behind the genteel style.

Those who can afford to get a few things made, let them go to a respectable dressmaker, and then, if your means are limited, and it suits you, take your ideas from them, and set to work with courage.

Many dresses are spoilt in the making, by too much fullness being put in the bodies. It is a mistake, to suppose that it adds to the richness of the dress. Anything of a dress is spoilt by being overloaded with trimmings or material.

Waist or Body.

All thin figures ought to wear full bodies; with stout persons it is a matter of taste. Plain bodies require more care in making than full ones. Every small imperfection is sean [sic] in plain bodies. Great care must be taken with seems [sic] in front. They must not look full or puckered; stretch them well and notch them; let the stitches be even; do not draw the hand too tight.

If you have no paper pattern that fits, unpick half an old body that fits well; lay your new lining on your cutting board, with an old body on top of it, and with your piercer prick through both, in the old stitches of your body pattern; prick them well, as the marks are apt to rub out; tack all the body well in the holes round it, before you begin, and be very careful to stitch your body to the tacking thread; take care and attend to this.

Five out of six persons have their dresses made too tight across the chest; it is a sad fault: I have many times seen waists out of reason in length, and the front two inches too narrow; if a penknife were run up the middle, it would burst open; when I have had occasion to do it, I have never found any one willing to have the seam sewn up again; and I feel convinced, that any lady, once wearing an easy dress, would never go back to a tight one; to say nothing of its being healthy and beautiful.

Great care must be taken with the arm-holes; do not make them too large or too small; thirteen inches is a nice size for a person not more than twenty-four inches in the waist; fourteen inches is a large size, only required for stout persons. If you have to alter the arm-hole, never do it under the arm; in nine cases out of ten, it will spoil the dress, and it takes away the free use of the arm; a very small piece cut off round the arm-hole, except underneath, will be all that is necessary. Do not forget, your sleeve must be larger than the arm-hole an inch and a half; when put in, it never looks the least full, and sets better. The seam of your sleeve must not be even with the seam of your body, but half an inch in front of it.

In cording the neck, do not stretch it; hold the cord tight. The waist must, on the contrary, be pulled well, when the cord is put on, or it will never fit; it requires much stretching.

The fit of the body often depends on the finishing of the waist. In putting on a waistband, let it be larger than the body; the fashion at the present moment, I am glad to say, is not carried to the extreme; the waists are moderate in length, and I do hope sensible women will cease to think tight waists are an ornament. Nothing is so beautiful as nature, if we will only let it alone; it is presumption to think we can improve it; so much has been said by all our clever physicians on this subject, that more than a passing remark from me, will be unnecessary.

It is a common error to make the backs of a dress of a different size; both halves should be of the same size; as one comes under, and the other over, they must of course wrap equal, and certainly require to be both alike. Put the hooks not more than one inch apart, and a quarter of an inch from the edge of the back. If the dress fastens in front, make the fastenings the same; and I think a hem down the back, a decided improvement; it takes off the width of the back, for narrow backs and wide chests are what is considered right.

In gathering a body at the waist, if it is at all thick material, guage it with strong silk or thread and large stitches, for it is a small compass it has to be put in; all full bodies are made with quite a straight piece of material, twenty inches long, and eighteen wide; this is half the front, gather it straight at the bottom, and then place it on your tight lining; fix it firmly, and then gather it at the shoulder: but mind and do the bottom guaging first; to make a body with folds, still have your material twenty inches long, and nineteen wide; the selvage must reach from waist to shoulder. Have the piece on a table before you, and make about four folds quite straight; lay them on your lining, push them close together at the waist, and pull them wider apart at the shoulder. I find it makes the folds set better, to cover over half the body lining with a plain piece of the dress, like you would wear a stomacher, and then place your folds to meet it; so that a folded body will be in two pieces, the plain part put on first, and the folds after. In putting folds on a body, let it be on the straight, or a good cross; don't let it be neither one nor the other, which is too frequently the case, and always will, as a matter of course, set badly; do not put your folds into the neck, let them come towards the shoulder, it widens the chest; they had better be laid a little on the sleeves, than pushed all towards the neck.

In making your body lining ready to put on the part, be careful it is very exact and smooth; and mind your body is neat inside as well as out; don't let raw edges be seen; turn them, so that the outside fullness or plates cover what you can, and make the seam under the arm and on the shoulder neat, by sewing them over with white cotton: that is, if your body is lined with white, which it certainly ought to be; do not let your body lining be very stout; it is a mistake with many persons so to do. A stout lining prevents the dress going into the figure, and is not stronger than one of moderate quality. A nice twilled lining at 8 or 10 cents per yard, will answer the purpose. A yard and a quarter is plenty for a moderate sized person. We all admire the gracefulness of the French dressmakers; they are shocked at our body linings, and well know we shall never fit nicely while we use them. They use little or no bone in a dress; if a dress does not fit nicely without bone, it will never fit with. Evening low bodies require a little. The jackets are made to fit without bone, then why not a dress body?

In making jackets you require a pattern; if you buy one on paper, a middle size is best; you can cut it smaller or larger, without injuring the pattern. It is a good plan to fit on a jacket in a common lining and then cut out the material. Never make them very tight, and be sure to give ease in the arm-hole, and width on the chest.

Sleeves: How to make them.

In making sleeves, with one good pattern, strange as it may seem, you can very easily make six different fashions by cutting your sleeve a little longer or a little shorter, and putting on different trimmings, or making some in a band at the wrist, or leaving them loose. The same shape is by a dressmaker altered in the manner I describe, and with a little observation I think can be done. Try and procure a good pattern at first. With taste, one pattern, can be made to look like six.

A trimming on the top of the sleeve is a great improvement to thin persons, and, to my taste, really pretty. It should match the bottom part of the sleeve and body trimming. Let it all match. Most sleeves are now cut on the straight, but cross will do. This must be decided by the wearer, and sometimes by the material. If it is stripes, they do not always look well on straight way; and if a sleeve is tight to the arm, it would hardly fit on the straight.

In making up any open sleeve, lay the material on the lining, cut them both the same size, and tack them together flat on the table. Line the bottom of the sleeve with silk to match the dress, or a piece like the dress, about three inches deep. Put your sleeve together, and let the fullness for the elbow come in the half of your seam. Stitch up your sleeves, and nicely sew them over. Do not leave large turnings. If the material is not soft, you had better stitch up three pieces of your sleeve, and let one side of your lining fell over the three other pieces, and you will find this quite neat.

Don't forget to cut both sleeves at once; that is the outside double, and the lining double. Double your material and lay the two right sides together; you cannot then make up both sleeves for one arm, a very common occurrence with young beginners. One good pattern is absolutely necessary for cutting out your sleeves. Some persons think almost anything will do for a sleeve pattern; it is a mistake; no part of a dress requires a better pattern to cut by.

Skirts: How to make them.

Supposing you have measured over your material, have your inch measure ready to cut the skirt from it. It is a good plan to write down in a little book the number of inches long your skirt is required. Measure it at the back of the dress, and then from the seam under the arm. The slope begins here, and gradually goes to the point.

Lay the skirt on a table, and have both halves exact, pin them together at the bottom, and pull them even at top. A dressmaker would have a person to hold the skirt at the bottom, while she made it even at the top. Put seam to seam. Care should be taken to cut your skirt even, every breadth the same length; and let your seams be nicely pinned before you begin to run them. Make yourself a heavy cushion, to pin your seams to. A common brick covered makes a very good one.

In cutting off the skirt, if the length, we will suppose, should be forty-two or forty-six inches long, leave four inches more for the hem and turnings at the top. Cut the lining for the skirt exact to the material, and mind it fits when finished. Supposing you to have run the seams of the skirt and the seams of your lining, lay the lining on the table, placing the skirt on top, and then tack the seams of your skirt to the lining. Begin at the first seam, and gradually go on to the last seam; stitch up three pieces together, and fell over the fourth; having done this, hem the bottom. Fix your hem all round before you begin, and do not take the stitches through; unless your hem is tacked or pinned, it will be sure to be on the twist, and set badly. Having done this, run on your braid, which must be put on easy, or rather full. Attend to this, or you will spoil the set of the skirt.

If the skirt is to have flounces, they must be put on before you guage the top; and while the skirt is on the table, put a white tacking thread round the skirt where each flounce is to be fixed. Flounces take the same quantity of material if cut either on the straight or the cross. It is a common error to suppose they take more on the cross. For the fullness of a flounce allow one width on the cross to one width on the straight of your skirt; so that if you have six widths in your skirt, you will have six widths in your flounces on the cross.

If there are three flounces of different widths, let the bottom and widest one have the most fullness; three inches more fullness will be sufficient. If the flounces are on the straight, allow eight widths in the flounce to six widths in the skirt. A small cord run in at the top of the flounce makes it look neat. Before running the cord in your flounce, join it round the exact size of the skirt; join round likewise your flounces, and full them on the cord as you go on. Halve and quarter your flounces and also the skirt, and you will find them no trouble to put on.

To cut flounces on a good cross, have the material on a table, and turn down one corner in the exact shape of half a pocket handkerchief, and then cut it through. In turning down your half, try two ways; one way lays flat on the table when folded, and the other does not look so flat, cut through the latter. In silk there is no perceptible difference which way you cut it; but in crape you will very easily observe it. Take any piece you have by you, and try it while reading this. Now begin to turn down your material on the cross, like a gentleman folds his neckerchief; keep folding until you have the number of pieces you want for one flounce, and keep each one pinned to the other as you fold them, so as to leave them all exact in width. Mind the edges measure exact. Supposing you to keep turning each one as you fold it. If the flounces are to be nine inches, cut the selvage the same depth.

Some persons are at a great loss to know how much three or four flounces will take. Supposing you to have three flounces, one ten, one eight, and one six inches deep at the selvage, the flounce of ten inches wide would take not quite one yard and three-quarters; that of eight inches, one yard a quarter and three inches; and that of six inches, exactly one yard; making in all four yards for three flounces; this, you will understand, is for flounces cut on the cross or straight in any material you may wish to use. I should advise you to have paper and pencil and your inch measure, and reckon before you purchase your material.

Trimmings down the front of a dress, when on the cross, should be cut the same as flounces. In trimming the front of a skirt, it is a good plan to cut a paper the length of the skirt, and pin it on the way you intend to trim, and then tack a tacking thread by it. Put tackings wherever you mean to trim, before you begin trimming, and lay your skirt on a table to do it.

Put on all trimmings with a light hand; do not sew them as you would a shirt, it gives them a puckered look. Now mind a good cross, no attempts at making pieces do, unless they are good corner pieces that will join well; you are more sure of making a trimming well, if cut all from one piece.

Before cutting a skirt off, that you wish to put tucks in, have a piece of lining or calico at hand, pin the tucks in it as you wish to put them in your skirt. Supposing you to have pinned your calico exactly like one width of your skirt, take out your pins and measure with an inch measure the exact quantity and then calculate the quantity you will want for the whole skirt. As a general rule, a tucked skirt takes more than a flounced one, and makes less show for the quantity of material used.

When running seams of a silk skirt, notch the selvage all the way up the seams of every breadth, and pass a moderately warm iron over the seams when finished; seams in a merino skirt, require to be run thickly and pressed open; press every join you make in every part of a dress. In guaging a skirt of any kind, guage the four back widths in larger stitches than you guage the three front ones; the rule in guaging is to take as much on your needle as you leave; that is, if you took up on your needle a quarter of an inch, you would leave a quarter of an inch; this size would do for the back gathers, but the front must be smaller.

All seams should be run with silk the color of the dress. It is a good plan to have fine black thread in your work box, to sew waists on and guage the skirts on a dark dress.

General Remarks.

Cut your plain skirt off the piece first, body and sleeves after, leave your trimmings to the last; large turnings are bad and waste the stuff; measure carefully and cut exact. I have met with many who fail in making a dress, owing to their really cutting every part of the body too large, and getting confused; recollect to cut all your body double, that is, the two halves of front, and the two halves of back, at the same time. When you are about to commence a dress, have the following things in a basket or box at your band, viz.: sewing silk, the color of the dress, – one or two reels of cotton, fine and coarse – a pair of scissors, not small – a penny inch measure, you can procure one at a trimming shop; don't cut without a measure, and always measure all that you have bought or have given you for a dress, before you begin to cut.

<u>How to Do It</u>, 1864

1865

Plate I. – Satin dress trimmed with a very deep Thibet fringe, which is so placed as to reach about three inches from the bottom of the skirt: above the fringe is a row of *grelot* buttons of a rather large size. The body is round, with fringe *berthe*, and sash with fringed ends. *Louis XV. redingote* of black velvet, trimmed round and up the seams with *passementerie*. *Brandebourgs* of the same up the front.

Dress of *gros-grain* with broad band of velvet: at the bottom of the skirt and up the front are *pattes* of velvet trimmed with lace. Tight-fitting body, with band of velvet simulating a veste. Velvet *ceinture Empire*, and tight sleeves.

Double skirts are often seen either for visiting, dinner, or ball dress. If closed all round, they are generally looped up; if open, the openings are at the *back*, as well as at the front. In many cases, these skirts are made of different colours and materials, such as *moire*, or satin over velvet, or two shades of the same colour. This fashion of wearing double skirts is much adopted for ball-dresses; the under-skirt generally being white and the tunic of colour. The low body with coat *basques* will be much worn if the dress is of silk. This *corsage* can be made of black velvet handsomely trimmed with jet beads or seed pearls.

Plate II. – *Toilettes de Bal*. Satin dress, open over a white silk covered with white *tulle*, and fastened in puffs by loops of pearls. The low body of satin is also opened in front over white *tulle*, and pearls to match the under-skirt. There are only narrow shoulder-straps to the satin body, the sleeves being formed of a puffing of white *tulle*, with *épaulettes* of pearls, A long garland of velvet flowers mingled with pearls is fastened on the left shoulder, and crossing the body at the waist is continued down the right-hand side of the satin skirt. Flowers and pearls in the hair. Pearl ornaments. *Watteau* fan.

Dress of white *poult de soie antique*, with plaited flounce, on which are placed at equal distances *rosettes* of *blonde* and ivy leaves. Above this skirt is a tunic of white *tulle*, round the bottom a *grecque* formed of ivy-leaves. Silk body, with drapery of *tulle* fastened in front and on the shoulders by *bouquets* like those on the skirt. Silk circular mantle, trimmed with braid and embroidery, and surrounded by a deep fall of lace. The pointed *pelerine* is trimmed in the same way. This cloak has a hood fastened on the head by a bow of ribbon, with very long ends. Ivy-leaves and pearls in the hair. Ornaments of pearls and emeralds.

The wide waistbands so much in favour a little while ago are rapidly disappearing, and giving place to those of a medium size. When the wide ones are used, they are mostly fastened at the back or sides with a *rosette*, instead of a buckle. The sashes are still fastened in the same manner, and have very wide ends.

Plate III. – Group. Dress of *poult de soie antique*, very much gored on the bottom of the skirt. A flounce of *point à l'aiguille*. Above this a drooping *bouillonné* of *tulle*, partly covered by a flounce of black *guipure*; this in turn is headed by *tulle bouillonné* and a flounce of *point à l'aiguille*. Above this is a smaller puffing and a *ruche* of black *guipure*. *Ceinture Suisse* of silk, covered with black *guipure*; *épaulettes* and long sash of the same. High *chemisette*, with long sleeves of figured *tulle*.

Robe of satin, with narrow stripes of velvet. Round *veste*, with small sleeves surrounded with a plaiting of velvet. *Tulle chemisette*. Round belt and buckle.

Tartalane dress, trimmed with *blonde*. Low pointed body, with *blonde berthe*.

White satin dress, with deep flounce of lace, headed by a *cordon* of flowers. Upper-skirt of white crape, raised on each side by long sprays of flowers; on this skirt are placed at intervals single flowers surrounded by *blonde*. Low body, with crape drapery. Behind are two long and broad ends of crape, trimmed round with lace and a cordon of flowers.

We have seen two or three lace coats, intended to be worn over low bodies. One of the low black velvet bodies intended for evening wear had no sleeves, and was pointed at top and bottom. A deep lace was carried round the waist, and formed into the coat *basque* at the back. This body was intended to be worn over white satin dress, trimmed with black lace and pearls.

The *vestes Russes* are much in fashion; they are made for either simple or elegant *toilettes*. We have seen several dresses of *moire* or light satin, made with these jackets, accompanied by the *chemisettes Russes*. These, if intended to be worn with silk or dressy materials, are made of *tulle*, or very fine muslin, with lace insertions; or with frills of lace and open-work insertions, in which are *cerise*-coloured velvets. Some are made of black and white lace, others entirely of English point. If intended for *demi-toilette*, they are in *foulard* or *cachemire*, trimmed with the *cachemire* braid so much in vogue.

There is nothing very new in the form or style of petticoats. For evening wear they are gored and flounced, the one next the dress being of muslin.

For *toilettes de ville* the most elegant *jupons* are made of white poplin or *reps*, embroidered in coloured silks, with a very narrow white or coloured fluted flounce round the edge. For *demi-toilette* they are, of course, more simple both in style and material.

Le Follet, Journal du Grand Monde, January 1865

A very pretty evening dress has just come out in Paris. The material is blue taffetas covered with white gauze; the skirt has a pleating round the edge, and the bodice has seven basques at the waist, two in front, two at the sides, and three at the back. These are short in front, and increase materially in length as they turn toward the back, where they form a point in the center, and are finished off with a sky-blue silk tassel. These basques or straps (so narrow are they) are piped with blue taffetas. There are pointed epaulets at the tops of the sleeves, with a blue silk tassel depending from each point. The dresses for out-door wear are made in the same style, with five basques or tabs separated from each other. A single long basque all round the waist is also worn (exactly like the basques of the time of Charles I.); and above the basque an Empire waistband is added. As both scallops and vandykes are fashionable, these basques are frequently cut out round the edge in one of these forms, and a tassel is sewn to each point. Above the vandykes several rows of narrow ribbon-velvet are sown vertically. This original style of bodice was worn first by the Empress Eugenie.

The Art of the Hoop: 1860 - 1869

Fig. I. – Ball Dress of White Silk, trimmed with bands of crimson velvet, over which falls a broad flounce of white lace. The body is made to correspond with the skirt. Head-dress of crimson ribbon.

Fig. II. – Ball Dress of Lemon-Colored Satin. – The skirt is trimmed with a flounce of white lace and ruchings of satin. The body is finished to correspond. Head-dress of small ostrich plumes.

Sashes, for evening wear, are in great demand; but some who are tired of the old fashion of fastening them at back, now tie them at the side.

An English correspondent says: – "Three things in a lady's toilet are now considered necessary, and to appear without them is to appear unfashionable, and these three things are – a small bonnet, a wide waistband, and a coat-shaped sleeve." If the coat basque is worn, the waistband is usually worn *over* it, but this is so ugly a fashion that we hope it will not last long. The belts are now from four to six inches in width, and, of course, the buckles are in proportion. Jet, gilt and jet, plain gilt, steel, and mother-of-pearl buckles are all worn; but the latter is only fashionable for evening wear.

DINNER DRESS.

Fig. IV. – Evening Dress of Blue and White-Striped Silk. – The skirt opens at the side over a white silk skirt, trimmed with three rows of blue silk, and is faced with blue silk, and trimmed like the body and sleeves with white lace.

A Word about Jackets. – There is great variety in jackets at the present season. The chief novelty about them is, one and all are ornamented at the back. Dressy jackets are made of velvet, cut quite straight, and in no ways fitting the figure. They are trimmed with either guipure or gimp, fringed with beads; upon the center of the back there is a row of large jet beads. Skirts, which button down the center seam of the back, are made to wear with these jackets. Another style, and certainly a very novel one, is a jacket cut to fall into the figure, and with four square basques ornamented with stars of silver beads, the edge being trimmed with silver bell-buttons. The sleeves, which are narrow, and of the usual coat form, have *revers* and epaulets, ornamented with silver beads. This jacket is open all down the front, and is simply held together by means of a chain of silver beads which fastens on to the hanging bell-buttons. A waistcoat (only differing from the masculine waistcoat in length) is worn underneath the jacket. It has two small pointed pockets, starred with silver beads; there is a buckle at the back which is invisible, but serves to tighten the waistcoat to the figure. All the winter paletots, bodices, and jackets, have a small straight collar added to them, which stands up round the throat. This necessitates a small all-round linen collar to be worn also; this is back-stitched, and then edged with narrow lace, and to such collars, as no white is now worn about the face, white muslin cravats are added. These cravats are likewise out after the masculine type, as they have all pointed ends. They are very narrow at the back, and the ends are fringed with either fine guipure or Alençon lace. This pattern is also made in taffetas and moire of all shades, embroidered with chenille, and edged with either a chenille or a jet fringe. The Russian neck-ties are also extremely pretty; they consist of a narrow satin band of any color, bordered with either swans'-down, ermine, or chinchilla.

HOUSE DRESS.

Fig. III. – Dinner Dress of Pearl-Gray Silk, Spotted with Green. – The body has a deep basque, which, with the skirt, is trimmed with narrow ruches of green ribbon.

MORNING DRESS: BACK AND FRONT.

Figs. VII. and VIII. – Front and Back View of an "At Home Dress." – The skirt opens both in front and at the back over an under-skirt of a pretty contrasting color, as a gray upper-skirt over a blue under one, or black over crimson, etc.

The back as well as the front of dresses are now opened and trimmed, as will be seen by our wood-cuts, but this necessitates great expense, as the under-dress should be of a corresponding quality with the upper one, without an old skirt can be used for the lower one. The trimming on the sleeves, the waistband, etc., should be of the color of the underskirt.

WALKING DRESS.

Fig. V. – Carriage or Dinner Dress of Dove-Colored Silk, with a deep coat basque. The skirt and basque are both trimmed with black velvet and Irish lace.

The petticoat is of as much importance, for out-of-door wear, as the dress itself, in these days of looped-up skirts. Of course, linsey, merino, cashmere, or any warm material is worn; but these are always, more or less, ornamented with grave or gay colors, according to the fancy of the wearer. Scarlet, trimmed with black, is popular, but so showy that, if many are worn, they will soon look common. The most stylish ones are black silk, quilted in white of some pretty pattern by a sewing-machine.

The fourth figure is a dress and paletot of steel-gray cashmere, opening down the back over a blue cashmere under-skirt. This dress is made to open or close, with buttons, at the option of the owner.

Tunics are simulated by starting the trimming from each side of the waist, and letting it sweep off, gradually, toward the back, where it forms a trimming around the bottom the skirt.

Peterson's Magazine, January 1865

The question of most interest on the subject of fashion for this month is the style in vogue for ball and evening dress. Amongst the novelties we remark robes of gauze embroidered in gold, or silver, or silk. Nothing is prettier than such flowers on a light, vapoury material, and ladies of elegance can wear such a dress without appearing to be dressed in too simple or girlish a manner. There are some beautiful *tulle* dresses spotted over with butterflies, or flowers formed of feathers, or with silver arrows – very original and exceedingly elegant – but, although needing no trimming, they are expensive.

Plate I. – Ball-dresses. Satin dress, covered with a *tulle* tunic, cut with a train, and spotted all over with rose-leaves, and edged with a wreath of peacock's feathers. The front of the satin skirt is covered with a *bouillonné* of *tulle*, cross-barred with pearl beads, forming large checks. At the meeting of each string of beads there is a *rosette* of peacock's feathers, and a few loops of beads. The tulle is spotted with rose-leaves in such a manner that one leaf comes in the centre of each square.

Robe of gauze with two skirts: the under edged with a wide *bouillonné* of the same, headed with a wreath of flowers; the upper-skirt edged merely with a wreath of flowers. The body and upper-skirt are made in one, so that there is no seam at the back of the waist; but a number of large plaits are carried from the shoulders to the middle of the back at the waist. The body is trimmed round the top with a wreath of flowers, and a *bouquet* of the same forms the épaulette. Small under-sleeves of white *tulle*.

Plate III. – Group. *Robe* of *taffetas*, trimmed at the bottom of the skirt with one wide flounce, pinked at each edge, and set on in large plaits over skirt of *tarlatane*, trimmed with two narrow frills, gauffered, which are placed round the edge of the skirt, and up each breadth; this skirt is raised at each side by two ends of wide ribbon, crossed one over the other. Low body, forming a *veste*, with square *basques*, trimmed with narrow frills.

Poult de soie dress, striped. The front of the skirt is left open *en tablier* over *tulle bouillonné*, crossed with *rouleaux* of satin, forming large diamonds; a small *bouquet* of velvet flowers is fastened to each *rouleau* at the sides of the silk skirt. Low body, open in front, and trimmed to match the skirt. Short full sleeves of *tulle*, crossed with satin *rouleaux*, with a *bouquet* of flowers on the top. Head dress of velvet flowers.

Robe of satin, covered with two skirts of *tulle*, each trimmed with five rows of *bouillonné*, worked with pearls. Low body *drapé*, trimmed with *agraffes* of pearls. *Coiffure*: diadem of pearls.

A dinner-dress of striped satin, white and blue: the bottom of the skirt trimmed with a plaiting of blue velvet. The body has rounded *basques*, trimmed with rich figured velvet, and fastened with buttons Louis XV. Style. The sleeves, which are quite tight, close under cuffs of point lace.

Another, of *taffetas antique*, lilac, embroidered round the skirt with a wreath of grapes and leaves in silk and pearl beads. The sleeves and body are trimmed to match.

Plate II. – *Toilettes de ville*. Dress of velvet, raised at equal distances over a skirt of white satin, trimmed with velvet leaves. The velvet dress is raised under *agraffes* of *passementerie*. Agnes Sorel body, with rounded *basques* reaching below the hips. The upper part of the body is made of satin; the rest of velvet, cut square, with a band of velvet up the front, and round the throat. Tight sleeves of satin, with *épaulettes* and cuffs of velvet.

Robe of *moire antique*, trimmed on the skirt with rich *passementerie à aiguillettes*, arranged in wide scallops. Velvet paletot trimmed with fur open in front over a waistcoat.

For *toilette de ville*, a robe of black *taffetas*, opened at the bottom of each breadth, so as to show a triangle of violet velvet, on which is placed an ornament of *passementerie* and hanging buttons; the edge of the silk cut in large scallops. The body with small *basques* open over a violet waistcoat. The bottom of the sleeve has a similar ornament to that on the skirt. The same ornament forms the jockey.

A *robe* of violet satin, cut in large scallops, edged with a wide band of black velvet. Under-skirt of violet satin, striped with black velvet, forming a long train. *Veste Russe* of plain satin, and waistcoat of striped satin.

Le Follet, Journal du Grand Monde, February 1865

Fig. I. – House Dress of Fawn-Colored Silk, trimmed with embroidered bands and rosettes of the same.

Fig. II. – Carriage Dress of Green French Poplin, trimmed with folds of green velvet.

Large Skirts. – Paris sets the fashions for the world, and the empress sets the fashions for Paris. Eugenie still continues to wear an excessive amplitude of skirt, chiefly displayed at the lower part of the petticoat, for over the hip everything is done which can give slimness of appearance to the rich material in use for afternoon and evening dresses. Most of these latter are made with double skirts, and even visiting dresses have these, either of the same tissue looped up, or of a thinner one dressed over the lower skirt. For the streets, one or two very stylish ladies have ventured to show themselves in dresses made so short as not to reach lower down than the usual colored petticoat, no doubt with great comfort to themselves in walking, but presenting an eccentric appearance, unused as the eye has now become to such a mode.

RAPHAEL-BODY DRESS.

Pearl-Colored House Dress, made without a seam at the waist, cut square in the neck, and trimmed with jet hanging buttons. White plaited chemisette.

The skirts, which open both back and in front, are increasing in popularity.

THE ALEXANDRINA CARRIAGE DRESS.
Carriage Dress of Figured Silk, with light-gray cut-away coat of heavy cloth.

Short waists, plain bodies, wide waistbands, and narrow sleeves, are universal in ordinary toilet. The short waists, however, do not preclude the long coat-tails. The present style of dress is not becoming. It has lost all the flow and grace which it had a few years ago. Skirts gored to be tight around the hips and bodies, cut in half by wide waistbands, are now the ugly fashion. The coat-tails are longer than before, and are now either in one or two, not three pieces.

WALKING DRESS.
Walking Dress of Dark Gray Poplin. – Black velvet basque, and black velvet hat, trimmed with large jet beads.

JACKET.
Jacket of White Merino, trimmed with bands of crimson velvet.

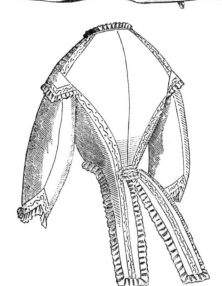

COAT BODY.

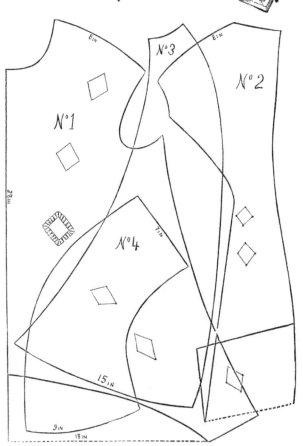

DIAGRAM FOR PALETOT.
We give, here, one of the most stylish patterns for a Paletot, which the season has produced. It is ornamented, as will be seen, with diamonds about an inch square, trimmed with passementerie and guipure. One of the diamonds is represented this trimmed: the others are merely sketched in. It is not necessary to describe the different points.

Peterson's Magazine, February 1865

Plate I. – Ball-dresses. *Robe* of satin, trimmed in front *en tablier*, with wide *ruches* of *blonde* and a row of beads in the centre. These *ruches* are put on in wide scallops; the points of the under-scallops fastened to the middle of the upper-scallops. Tunic of terry velvet falling over the under-skirt, and raised at equal distances by *bouquets* of flowers and feathers. Round low body of satin; terry velvet band, and rich buckle. Spanish *veste*, without sleeves, and trimmed with a *ruche* of *blonde* and beads.

Silk skirt, covered with one of *tulle*, on which is a wide *grecque* formed with small leaves in very fine *passementerie*. A wreath of the same leaves raises the tunic on each side, which is trimmed all round with an elegant gold ribbon. Low round body, trimmed with *tulle* and leaves. Sash of gold ribbon, with fringed ends.

Plate III. – Group. Satin dress, with plaited flounce at the bottom of the skirt, covered with two skirts of *tulle*, raised with straps of ribbon at equal distances. The bands on the upper skirt are headed with *rosettes* of feathers and beads.

Dress of crape, trimmed with partridge's feathers. The body is trimmed with *berthe bouillonnée*, crossed with bands of velvet, and edged with a narrow wreath of feathers.

Foulard dress, with two skirts: the under one trimmed with three rows of narrow ribbon. The upper skirt is raised *à la Camargo*, with wide ribbon velvet; the bows ornamented with rings of mother-of-pearl and light *bouquets* of flowers. Low body, with bows to match those on the skirt, in front and on each shoulder. ... A band of narrow velvet round the throat, tied behind, with long ends reaching nearly to the bottom of the skirt.

For visiting-dress, satin and velvet dispute the palm. *Moire antique* is no longer so fashionable as it formerly was; partly perhaps because with the two former may be worn a *paletôt* or mantle of the same.

Plate II. – *Poult-de-soie* dress, trimmed at the bottom of the skirt with a wide band of velvet and rich *guipure*. High body, with *basques* in folds, and trimmed with velvet and *guipure*. The body is open in front, and trimmed up each side with velvet and *guipure*. Tight sleeves; cuffs and *épaulettes* of velvet and *guipure*. Swiss *guimpe* of muslin, and small stomacher of velvet. At the left side, coming from under the *basque*, are two long bows and ends of velvet, trimmed with *guipure*.

Robe of *moire*, embroidered in velvet butterflies, and drawn up twice on each side, under *pattes* of *passementerie* and tassels. Under-skirt trimmed with two narrow flounces, gauffered. Body with deep *basques*, open over a waistcoat. Tight sleeves; *épaulettes* of *passementerie* and tassels; cuffs and collar of *Valenciennes*.

A visiting-dress of grey silk, having a flounce about half a yard wide, above which is a black velvet ribbon, worked with steel, forming a heading to a wide *chenille* fringe mixed with steel. Higher up the skirt a black velvet ribbon is put on, lozenge shape, with a steel ornament at every point, and a tassel matching the fringe in the centre of each lozenge. High body, with trimming to match, put on in the form of a Russian *veste*.
Le Follet, Journal du Grand Monde, March 1865

Fig. I. – Carriage Dress of Violet-Colored Silk. – The body is cut square in the neck, and is trimmed with a black gimp trimming. It is finished with tassels on the shoulders.

Fig. II. – House Dress. – The skirt is of black silk, with a narrow ruche of crimson silk at the bottom, covered with black guipure lace. The coat-body is of white, with the same trimming as that on the skirt.

Formerly, black or dark-colored silk was considered quite suitable for a small evening party, so that it was made with a low body. This is no longer the case; black or dark-colored silks are now looked upon as suitable for morning wear only, and light-colors are indispensable for an evening dress. The new silks are extremely pretty; many have fine-colored stripes over a white ground; sea-green, Mexican blue, mauve, or rose-color over white looks exceedingly well.

DIAGRAM OF A WHITE SILK COAT.

In the steel fashion-plate [*Fig. II, above*], this month, is a pattern of a White Silk Coat, a very beautiful affair, and particularly appropriate for this season of the year. On this account, we give here diagrams, by which it may be cut out without the aid of a mantua-maker.

The Coat, it will be seen, has colored silk bias-pieces covered by black guipure, is plain and high, and has buttons straight down the fronts. The two long tails are separated behind; they form part of the body as in a man's coat. A silk bias-piece, from an inch to an inch and a half wide, begins from the front forming a small lappet, and borders two pointed lappets, which begin at the side-piece and fall by the side of the long tails. The sleeve is half-fitting. On the top, over the sleeve-hole, there is a long detached jockey, which forms a point before and behind. A bias-piece goes round the bottom and runs up underneath. The skirt is of silk, bordered by a colored bias-piece with black guipure laid on even.

Skirts are still invariably gored, whether cut in the same piece as the body, or separate.

A short time ago it was the fashion to wear *black* belt and sashes with every dress; but now both band and sash are selected to match the dress. Many Parisians, who have objection to wear what everybody else does, directly they saw the deep waistband adopted, appeared in belts not more than two inches wide – made of either moire or velvet, and fastened with small oxidized silver buckles. But the deep band and Empire buckle, the latter made of either dead gold, or gold and black enamel, are up to the present date in the majority. The newest belts are made entirely of gimp and jet; the buckle is likewise of gimp, mounted on a frame-work of jet. These bands and buckles can be worn with any toilet which is not *neglige*.

HOUSE DRESS.

House Dress of Rich Purple Silk, Figured with Black. – Black velvet loose jacket, trimmed with guipure lace. Bows of purple ribbon on the shoulders.

The variety in the style and make of dresses is now so great, that it seems well nigh impossible to say what really is the fashion, and what is not. But of one fact our readers may feel assured, which is, that morning dresses made open in front, and showing a colored petticoat underneath, are decidedly taken into favor. These petticoats should *always* be of silk, however; though when a cashmere upper dress is worn, the under-skirt may be of the same material. Many persons insert a breadth of silk instead of wearing the whole petticoat. The trimming on the upper-skirt must be of the same color as the petticoat.

Morning and afternoon dresses, ornamented down the entire length of the back, are no uncommon sight. Some have buttons and button-holes only, others are elaborately embroidered or braided. When they are worn in the street, the paletots are of the same material as the dress, and also trimmed up the back.

WALKING DRESS

Walking Dress of Cinnamon-Colored Poplin, trimmed with black velvet. The paletot is of the same material, trimmed like the skirt.

CARRIAGE DRESS.

Dress of French Blue Silk, with small black and white figures. The skirt is open on the left side, over a white silk under-skirt, trimmed with two ruffles edged with black velvet. The upper-skirt has a Greek border in black velvet; at the opening on each side the body has a coat basque lined with white silk. For the carriage a small blue bonnet is added to this very stylish costume.

LOUIS XV. PALETOT.

CHAIN-STITCH OR BRAIDING FOR LOUIS XV. PALETOT.

Peterson's Magazine, March 1865

The Art of the Hoop: 1860 - 1869

Plate II. – *Toilettes de ville. Robe* of *poult de soie*, the skirt trimmed round the bottom with a series of medallions embroidered in silk. Plain high body, with two long ends at the back embroidered with three medallions, like those on the skirt, and ending in a wide fringe. Tight sleeves, with medallions to form the *épaulettes*.

Moire dress, with double skirt: at the bottom of the lower skirt are three rows of crossway velvet, fastened on with steel beads. The upper-skirt is drawn up at each breadth under a strap of velvet trimmed with beads. High body, with *basques*, which are trimmed – as are also the tight sleeves – with a narrow crossway fold of velvet, fastened like those on the skirt. ... Black *cachemire* shawl trimmed with wide lace.

As, in the winter, we found the Grecian style revived in *coiffures* and afterwards in *vestes*, we have now to chronicle its reappearance in dresses. The body *à la Grecque* will be very much in favour, especially for young ladies. We are assured that, even for at-home dress during the day-time, low dresses will be much worn – of course, with *guimpe* and sleeves. However, as many ladies will not easily resign the pretty little *vestes* which have been so admired, plain bodies will also be in vogue. They will be made low, and covered with a *veste* of lace, of *tulle* worked with beads, or of embroidered muslin. These are charming when made of lace, and finished off with a lace sash tied behind, and falling in wide ends upon the skirt. They are destined, we believe, during the summer to replace the *pélerine*, which, without contradiction, is less elegant. Already they are fashionable for evening, theatre, or dinner dress. They will be made, also, lined with *taffetas*, of a colour suitable to the pattern or trimming on the dress; and round the edge of the lining will be placed a *ruche* of ribbon to match, over which will fall the border of the lace. Under a *veste* in this style a *chemisette* of *nansook* should be worn, held in at the waist by a wide *ceinture*. These do not exclude the square *pélerine* at present, and perhaps the latter is rather more suitable for elderly ladies. For morning-dress, tight sleeves are still in vogue.

The enemies of crinoline will yet have some time to wait before their ideas triumph. Skirts are made with as much train and as full as ever, and must have well-made crinolines to give them an air of elegance.
Le Follet, Journal du Grand Monde, April 1865

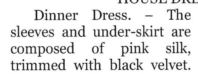

MORNING DRESS.
Morning Dress of Pearl-Colored Cashmere, trimmed with black velvet, and worn over a pink silk skirt. Black velvet jacket, lined with pink.

HOUSE DRESS.
Dinner Dress. – The sleeves and under-skirt are composed of pink silk, trimmed with black velvet. The upper-skirt, and square body, or cape, are made of black and white striped silk, trimmed with velvet.

Crinoline still continues large for evening wear, though for street dress it is quite small.

Jackets of white cashmere, embroidered in beads of various colors, are much worn in the evening; whilst those of scarlet, blue, poppy color, and violet, are very popular for more ordinary wear. Some of these jackets have only epaulets, embroidered and finished with a hanging trimming, and are worn over a white body with long sleeves.

Fig. I. – Dinner Dress of White Muslin, which is trimmed with insertions of embroidery over blue silk. Body very low and square, with thin white under-body.

Fig. II. – Walking Dress of Fawn-Colored Striped Silk, trimmed with poppy color.

Skirts are either entirely plain, or very much ornamented. The pleatings around the edge of the dresses, which have been so long worn, are at length going out of fashion, except for silk skirts to be worn under their dresses.

WALKING DRESS.

Carriage Dress of Gray Silk, trimmed with silk of a darker shade, put on bias, and rows of buttons.

WALKING DRESS.

Walking Dress of Summer Poplin. – The body and skirt in one piece in the Gabrielle style. Gimp trimming, or passementerie, as it is called, is profusely used on this dress. The coat is not separate from the skirt, but is formed by the gimp trimming.

A SPRING PALETOT.

This is one of the newest patterns for a Paletot. It defines the figure in a graceful manner, and has the skirt of moderate length. Our page would not allow us to give this pattern in its entire length, but it may be easily completed by continuing the seams in straight lines. The pattern consists of sleeves, (which is of the most fashionable style,) front, side-piece, and back.

When lengthening the pattern, the front must a length of 28 inches at the front edge, 22 ½ at the seam under the arm, and the width at bottom should be 15 inches. The side-piece should be 22 ½ inches long at the seam under arm, 23

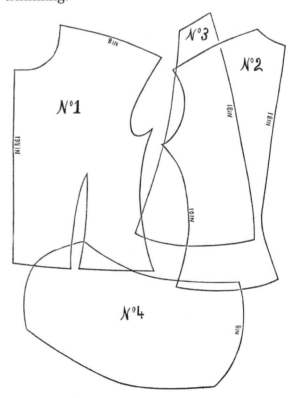

inches at the side seam, and 12 ½ wide at the bottom. The back should have the side seam 23 inches long, and should be 33 in length at the middle, the width at bottom being 16 ½.

This Paletot may be made in black velvet, and trimmed with *passementerie guipure* lace; black cloth, and trimmed with *passementerie* and *grelot*, or ball fringe, in drab or light *Havanna* cloth.

Peterson's Magazine, April 1865

Plate I. – Ball-dresses. Dress of silk, the bottom of the skirt cut in scallops, and trimmed with six *bouillons* of *tulle*. At equal distances round the waist are placed wreaths of flowers, which are carried down the skirt as far as the top of the *bouillons*, and end in *bouquets* of flowers. Low body, trimmed with wreaths and *tulle bouillons*. Ribbon sash, with fringed ends tied in two long bows behind. *Coiffure: Grecque*, and *tulle* scarf.

Dress of *tulle bouillonné*, trimmed with small *bouquets* of flowers, at equal distances, and large rings of gauze *bouillonné*, edged with very narrow wreaths of flowers. Tunic of gauze, edged with a wreath of flowers and drawn up slightly at each side. Pointed low body of *tulle*, and *veste Figaro* of gauze edged with flowers.

We find that all the spring-dresses, even those for *deshabille*, are made with a decided train; they are also, without exception, gored – the only means of obtaining an elegant and graceful fulness. These *négligée* dresses have no trimmings, with the exception of a silk cord round the bottom; or, perhaps, the skirt just cut in festoons, lightly edged with *passementerie*, ribbon, or velvet.

Plate II. – Walking-dresses. *Robe* of poplin, plain skirt edged with silk cord. High body and tight sleeves, trimmed with cords across the front, and bow and tassels on the shoulders. Band and buckle.

Silk dress. The bottom of the skirt trimmed with a flounce, trimmed with *guipure* and bead gimp. High body, with *basques* cut in three pieces, the middle piece being deeper than those on each side. Tight sleeves. The whole of the body trimmed in the same style as the skirt.

Plate III. – Group. Dress of spotted *foulard*. On each breadth, nearly at the bottom, a large shell formed with ribbon; and above these a wide *chicorée ruche*, waved. *Veste Russe*, the same as the dress, and trimmed with *ruches*. Muslin body, with long sleeves fastened at the wrist.

Robe of grenadine, worked with small butterflies. Up each breadth is a band of silk. Muslin body, with *guipure* insertion. Long sleeves fastened at the wrist. Wide band and buckle.

Silk dress, trimmed quite at the bottom of the skirt with a full *ruche*. Over-dress *Princesse* of spotted muslin. High body, with a *ruche* carried from the right shoulder, across the front, and down the left side of the skirt, looping it up as high as the knee. Tight sleeves.

The *robe Princesse* is worn more than any other this season, but with some happy modifications. It is no longer the simple *casaque* without plaits; now the fronts alone are completely plain. Under the arms there are large plaits; the side-pieces are plain down to the waist, but there they are cut across, and the waist is set on in large plaits, so as to give a graceful fullness. This is a charming model, and one much in vogue; but it is very necessary that the crinoline worn with this style of dress should be particularly well made, for so much of its elegance depends upon this.

Le Follet, Journal du Grand Monde, May 1865

Fig. I. – Carriage Dress of Mauve-Colored Silk, with a loose paletot of the same material. Both dress and paletot are trimmed with bands of silk a shade deeper than the dress.

Fig. II. – Dinner Dress of White India Muslin, trimmed with lace, and pink ribbon run through insertion. Over the low body dress can be worn a low paletot of the same material, trimmed in the same way.

Braces are again seen; they are worn at balls, as well as on plain dresses. For the latter, the braces form a small square berthe in front, fringed with chenille and piped with either white taffetas or velvet. The braces are continued down the back with two wide, square ends, which are slashed together with bars made of the same material. Braces are also crossed in front, and form the berthe at the back; they fall with long ends behind, and in these cases the ends are rounded. This style of braces is an excellent contrivance for trimming up an old dress. For instance, upon a gray silk, or even poplin dress, it is easy to arrange either blue or maroon velvet braces embroidered with jet or silver beads, and edged with black lace. These braces cross in front, nearly meet again at the back, and then enlarge in two long, wide coat-tails; with this addition, the dress has an entirely new aspect. For young girls' taffetas, ribbons are used for braces in preference to velvet cut bias.

Short gloves are going out of fashion for evening wear, those with five buttons are now worn with short-sleeved dresses; the bracelets are necessarily fastened at the top of the kid.

EVENING DRESS.

Evening Dress of White Silk, trimmed around the bottom with narrow pink ribbon. The upper skirt is of tulle, looped up with pink ribbons, depending from the waist.

Except in braces, there is nothing new in the make of dresses. The round waist with plain waistbelt, is, of course, still fashionable; but bodies of this style are so very plain in appearance, that for most ladies they require a good deal of trimming.

Dress skirts, for summer, will be very much trimmed, and for this purpose a mixture of colors will be fashionable. On house dresses, a combination of three or four colors are popular. For instance, on the skirt of dresses, a row of blue velvet, a row of black, then a row of red, then one of green, one above the other; these are repeated till they amount to twelve rows. This style should be only adopted by those who have a good eye for color, for unless properly mingled it will have a vulgar look. It was fashionable under the first empire, fifty years ago.

The skirts of dresses are rather short in front, and not very full at this part; the fullness is placed at the back and sides, and all the back breadths are usually gored, so that the skirt may take the train form.

Deep linen cuffs, with butterflies on them, were lately quite the rage. We have just seen some sets with feathers simulated, those in the gayest colors being the prettiest. These feathers are placed one on each side of the sleeve, by the row of buttons, where it seems to lie carelessly, and is nearly as long as the cuff. Each corner of the collar, in front, has a feather of the same color, but much smaller. Some of the feathers are shaded in brown, and in some red, etc., is introduced.

House Dress of Blue Silk, trimmed at the sides with bands of black velvet, and black velvet buttons.

WALKING DRESS.

COAT JACKET.

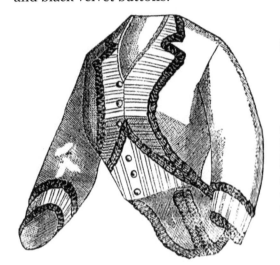

The short *Senorita*, or Spanish Jacket, will be a great favorite, as it is suited to be worn either with a pointed waist, or with the plain belt and buckle.

CARRIAGE DRESS.
Carriage Dress of Gray Silk, trimmed with a band and loops of blue silk and frogs.

PROMENADE DRESS.
Walking Dress and Tight Basque of Fawn-Colored Summer Poplin, and ornamented with black velvet.

The Circular Mantle, which, if well cut, is one of the most graceful out-of-door wraps worn, is still fashionable, though less so, perhaps, than the short sacques and nearly tight-fitting basques. Both sacques and basques, or paletots, have epaulets, which are usually becoming, as they give length to the shoulder.

Gimp is still fashionable for spring dresses, mantles, etc., but it will be found too heavy for light summer materials.

Many basques, etc., open to the waist with revers. In Paris, the newest style is to have the paletots, etc., open down the back, or to appear to do so.

THE PATTI JACKET.

The newest thing in Paris, this spring, is the Patti Jacket, so called after the famous opera-singer, Adelina Patti. It is an exceedingly useful garment, very suitable for out-of-door wear in warm weather, and a capital indoor jacket in the colder months of the year. It can be made in velvet, in cloth, and in cashmere, and should be trimmed at the epaulets and cuffs with gimp ornaments, and with a girdle cord worked with jet beads round edge.

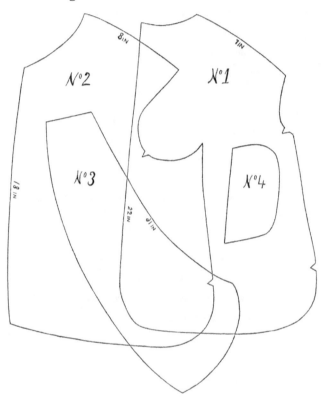

The pattern consists of four pieces.
No. 1. The Front.
No. 2. The Back.
No. 3. The Sleeve.
No. 4. The Pocket.

The place where the pockets are to be sewn, may be judged from the engraving. The seam of the sleeve must be placed at the notch in the front.

This jacket opens at the back, and is fastened its entire length with large jet buttons. The side-seams are to be joined as far as the notch in the paper. It should be observed, that one side of the back folds over the other side. The button-holes are made on the side which folds over, and the buttons are sewn on the other. If fastening down the back be found inconvenient, it would be easy to make this jacket to open in the front, with a *simulated* fastening behind, as the newest jackets, paletots, etc., in Paris are all buttoned down the back.

Peterson's Magazine, May 1865

Plate I. – Walking-dresses. *Robe* of *taffetas*, trimmed on the skirts with a band of silk, worked with beads and edged with very narrow lace. *Paletôt*, the same as the dress; quite short, and fitting to the figure, with *revers* and cuffs to match the trimming on the skirt.

Dress of striped *gaze de soie*. The skirt is trimmed with a double *grecque* detached, formed with a *chicorée ruche* of silk, the same colour as the stripes in the dress. High body and tight sleeves. *Corselet* of silk, with very deep points all round the waist, The whole trimmed with *chicorées ruches*.

In Paris, muslin is pretty well dethroned, for walking-dress, by thin materials, which will not so easily crumple; but it is still as much worn indoors, and in the country. White is now not at all confined to young people; all its importance depends upon the style of trimming.

We have remarked some charming *ceintures*, with long ends, which form a complete trimming for the skirt; and also some bodies simply covered with a lace *veste*, which has this advantage, that it serves for different dresses – *barége*, muslin, *taffetas*, and *foulard*.

Plate II. – Group. Silk dress, with a *corselet* of a deep-coloured silk. This *corselet* is laced under the arms, and is trimmed at the bottom of the lacing and on the shoulders with a *bouquet* of long flat bows. A breadth of silk is fastened at the waist, in front, and another at the back, reaching two-thirds down the skirt, trimmed at the bottom with five stripes, graduated, and headed by a narrow insertion, which is carried up each side to the waist. A deep fringe of silk and beads completes the trimming, The dress has a narrow flounce, set on in wide plaits. White high body and long sleeves, trimmed with insertion.

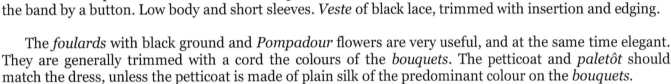

Muslin dress, over a coloured silk skirt, trimmed with one wide flounce, headed with small *pattes* of *guipure*. These are carried up each side of the front breadth. High *chemisette*, with long sleeves formed of insertion and *guipure*. *Corselet* of linen, with small *basques* cut up to the waist, and edged with a very narrow *guipure*.

Foulard dress: the bottom of the skirt cut in scallops, with a band of plain silk below. Each scallop is fixed to the band by a button. Low body and short sleeves. *Veste* of black lace, trimmed with insertion and edging.

The *foulards* with black ground and *Pompadour* flowers are very useful, and at the same time elegant. They are generally trimmed with a cord the colours of the *bouquets*. The petticoat and *paletôt* should match the dress, unless the petticoat is made of plain silk of the predominant colour on the *bouquets*.

An elegant robe *Princesse* of white quilting, trimmed with four narrow flounces of corn-flower blue silk, pinked and placed close to each other. The body, which is cut square in front, is trimmed to match. All the trimmings are sewn on strips of muslin, so that they can be easily taken off when the dress is washed.

Plate III. – Walking-dresses. *Robe* of *taffetas Pompadour*. The skirt trimmed with a *grecque* in black lace, edged with a narrow ball fringe. High body, trimmed with a *plastron* of lace, edged with fringe. Tight sleeves. Wide band and buckle.

Silk dress, cut in scallops, edged with a bias fold, which is carried up each breadth, leaving room for a row of buttons between. Small *paletôt*, the same silk as the dress, and trimmed to match.

Le Follet, Journal du Grand Monde, June 1865

In low bodices there is a great alteration to be remarked in the make. The newest are all cut square and exceedingly low; more than half the bodice being dispensed with in front. Chemisettes are worn underneath, and are made with rows of embroidered insertion, alternating with puffings of muslin. Sometimes a piece of ribbon to match the dress is tacked underneath the strips of insertion; the short sleeve, made of the same material as the bodice, is dispensed with. Whatever forms the square berthe is also carried at the top of the chemisette sleeve, thus giving the low bodice the effect of being only held on by shoulder-straps. To slight figures this style of make is very becoming; but those who are inclined to be stout will find that it too *decollate* an appearance to be pleasant. Lawns and organdies, made in this way, are very beautiful.

Fig. I. – Evening Dress of Thin White Muslin over Pink Silk. – The high bodice has a low lining, and is cut away like a jacket in front. Pink silk sash. The tight sleeves are lined with pink.

Fig. II. – Home Dress of White Foulard, with bouquets of gay flowers. Green silk Spanish jacket, embroidered in gay colors.

Many dresses are trimmed up the seams. Where the dress is much gored this gives an appearance of great slenderness to the figure.

Waistbands are now usually made of the same material as the dress, and are either striped with narrow velvet, or embroidered in beads. These bands can be made by any young lady of taste. Take some rich black taffetas, and cut a wide band on the cross, line it with stiff muslin, and make it pointed at one end – the end which is passed through the buckle; then embroider the right, or taffetas side with white beads, in either a *grecque*, fleurs-de-lys, or palms, in short, in any design easy to trace out in white beads.

A Paris correspondent says: – We constantly see heads powdered with a variety of sparkling dusts, but we confess we ask ourselves frequently, after a careful examination, if the effect given by frizzing the hair, or making it, by ingenious devices, look *crepe* – whether after oiling it, and then dusting it over with any of these powders – we are repaid for the trouble. We hear many around us declare that it is *most becoming*, but to our eye the diamond powder makes the hair look slightly gray, and the gold powder has all the effect of ragged scraps of gold-leaf scattered over the well *crepe* rough hair. Neither is the silver powder happier in its results.

DINNER DRESS AND EVENING DRESS.

Dinner Dress of Light Green Silk, with a black silk over dress, trimmed with bands of green of a shade darker than the under-dress.

Evening Dress of White Muslin. – The square body, as well as the bands which run lengthwise of the chemisette, and head-dress, are all of crimson velvet ribbon.

The most popular jackets, for summer wear, are of the Spanish style, open in front over a chemisette, and without sleeves, a white full sleeve only being seen. Some are profusely trimmed with steel, jet, or colored beads.

White petticoats, elaborately ruffled and fluted, are very much worn, whilst some are braided in colored braids.

CARRIAGE DRESS.

Walking Dress and Sacque of Fawn-Colored Mohair, trimmed with blue.

The Art of the Hoop: 1860 - 1869

PIQUE OR MUSLIN COAT.

This is not intended (as some might suppose) for out-of-door wear, it being too conspicuous for that purpose; but is designed for morning or evening toilet, for which it is very pretty and stylish.

For morning wear it should be made of the same material as the skirt. If it is made of white pique, and worn over a white pique skirt, it should be braided round the sides and up the center of the back with black worsted braid; and a ball or Tom Thumb fringe should be added round the edge. If of white alpaca, three rows of narrow blue or mauve ribbon, arranged in the same way, has a good effect. Black silk can also be used for the coat, and the newest style of trimming for this material is a band of white silk, with strips of very narrow black ribbon-velvet, sewn either slantwise or straight across it; this band is carried all round the coat. Black lace is then used for the edge. Gimp may be substituted for this trimming, if desired.

For evening wear, the coat may be made of white muslin, either plain or embroidered. The simplest trimming is then a narrow frill of muslin, which must be box-pleated. Another style is to sew loops round the edge. These loops are composed of black ribbon-velvet an inch wide, and the same trimming should be repeated upon the white muslin skirt. Black figured net is frequently used for making a coat to be worn over a low dress for a dinner toilet. The best trimming for this net is black lace, and rows of either ribbon-velvet or ruches to correspond in color with the skirt. In all these cases there should be ornaments at the back of the waist, which should correspond with the trimming.

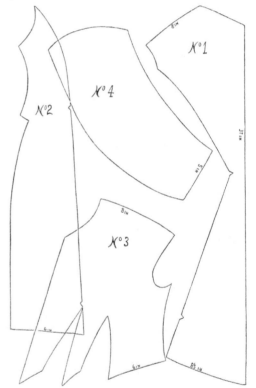

We give a diagram by which to cut out the coat. The pattern consists of four piece, viz:

No. 1. Front.
No. 2. Half of Back.
No. 3. Side-Piece.
No. 4. Half of Sleeve.

Before cutting out the coat in the material in which it is to be made, we should counsel first trying it in lining muslin, as the pattern of the bodice will be found large enough for a full-sized figure.

The tails may be made of any length, but the longer they are the more elegant they will look.

Peterson's Magazine, June 1865

Summer toilettes may be divided into three series – *toilettes* for country and sea-side, visiting-dress, and evening, or summer ball costume; for all these we will now endeavour to give our readers some useful models.

A dress of blue and white shot *linos*, the skirt trimmed up each seam with insertion of Cluny *guipure* about two inches in width; *casaque* to match, also trimmed with insertion.

A *toilette* of silver drab *sultane*. In this case not only the *robe* and the *casaque*, but also the under-skirt of the same material. The dress is nearly plain, having merely a blue cord bordering it, and being looped up at each seam by *pattes* of blue *taffetas*, fastened by three buttons of worked steel. The under-skirt, or *jupon*, has round it a blue plaiting, and is trimmed with *arabesques* of blue, each edged round with a narrow *passementerie*, called *cache-point*, in steel beads. The *casaque* is like the *robe* – that is to say, simply trimmed with a cord, but it is made in the form of a Louis XV. habit, the tails of which are lined with blue, and turned back, fastened with fancy steel buttons.

Plate I. – *Toilettes de ville*. Silk dress in wide stripes, trimmed at the bottom of the skirt with a band of plain silk, cut in wide scallops in the inner edge, the point of each ending an ornament resembling the three-leaved shamrock; this band is fixed on with a row of beads. Jacket open in front, with deep *basques*, trimmed to match the skirt; tight sleeves of plain silk, trimmed simply with a row of beads round the wrist. Muslin *chemisette*, with band and buckle.

Dress of white muslin: above the hem are twenty very narrow tucks on which are placed lozenge-shaped trimmings, formed of a very narrow insertion, edged with full lace; these ornaments reach from the bottom to the top of the tucks. High body, covered with tucks; *épaulettes* and trimmings down the front to match the skirt; long sleeves, nearly tight, trimmed with a wide cuff, pointed. Long sash of very wide ribbon, fringed at the end.

Plate II. – Ball-dresses. *Robe* of *tulle* second skirt of *gaze de soie*, embroidered in *bouquets* of flowers; four inches from the bottom of the skirt is placed a wide bias fold of silk, and over this two narrower. Low body, cut square, trimmed round a fold of silk, and deep fringe of beads. Ribbon sash with long ends, fringed; *bouquet* of azaleas placed on the left side of the sash.

Dress of *tulle bouillonné*: low body, *berthe bouillonné corselet* of silk, with six long ends, cut square at the bottom, falling at equal distances all round the waist; the *corselet* and ends are trimmed with a row of *blonde*, turned back and laid on flat.

Bodies are made with large *basques*; or, indeed, frequently with a short *casaque*, which takes the place of a *corsage*, being made to fit. Bands are sometimes worn over these. We do not recommend this style as being becoming; still it is adopted by some. Russian leather bands and buckles are quite as much in vogue as they were last year.

Plate III. – Dresses for the country. Dresses of *gaze tunisienne* in stripes: the skirt is trimmed with a crossway flounce, six inches wide, put on with very little fulness. Above this is a wide *grecque*, formed with a *ruche* of silk. High body and long sleeves. *Veste russe* of silk trimmed with beads: long sash of silk. *Casquette Louis XV.* of straw, trimmed with a feather and long veil of *tulle*.

Silk dress: plain skirt, high body, long tight sleeves; over-skirt of worked muslin, trimmed with insertion and wide frill. *Revers* on the body and sleeves of embroidered muslin.

Le Follet, Journal du Grand Monde, July 1865

Fig. I. – Dinner Dress of Blue Silk, the skirt trimmed with lace in an entirely new style. Hair dressed with blue flowers.

Fig. II. – Evening Dress of White Silk, trimmed with scarlet ribbon. Hair dressed with scarlet flowers and green leaves.

Sashes are still much worn with thin dresses. The ribbon used is very wide, or else silk pinked, or trimmed with blonde, etc.

For silk dresses cable cord is much used. Black and white cord is frequently used for black dresses. The skirt is usually scolloped around the edge and the cord sewn-on, following the undulations of the dress. Sometimes it is carried up the seams, but then it is put on plain around the skirt.

WALKING DRESS, WITH BONNET.
Carriage Dress of Maize-Colored Foulard Silk, with square coat basque, trimmed with brown silk.

White muslin petticoats will be embroidered with black wool in satin-stitch, instead of being braided as last year. White foulard petticoats, trimmed with black velvet, are much used for house wear.

Steel is profusely used for bonnets, mantles, and dresses. Many of the new gimps and braids are heavily decorated with steel, and these are profusely used to ornament dresses with. Steel beads are studded all over bonnets, parasols, etc.

WALKING DRESS, WITH HAT.
Walking Dress, Petticoat, Basque, and Jacket of Gray Alpaca, trimmed with black velvet and crimson buttons. The skirt is looped high up above the petticoat.

Waists, unfortunately, are shorter and shorter. Those fearful times of the Empire, and since so laughed at, are returning with all their fashions. Hair is dressed upon the summit of the head, and waists are made under the arms, so that even the prettiest, thus attired, become ugly, and one must have inherent taste to be able to look graceful with such fashions. Beauties and the *lionnes* of society leave off crinoline entirely during the day time, and only put it on to go out walking or for a ball. Ladies receive without crinoline, and the dresses open both before and behind over white or red silk petticoats, or striped cashmere of a thousand hues. The thousand hues are made to harmonize with the dress. Thus one of Havana brown would have a petticoat "*a mille raies*" in blue and white. If the dress is trimmed with blue ribbon the sash is also blue, and blue ribbons are passed through the hair. Dresses opening behind are also worn out walking, but then they must be buttoned up behind, and only left open in front.

Old basquines can be modernized by cutting them shorter, especially in front, and by making the sleeves narrow. Some of the new basquines are spangled with steel in the form of small birds.

WALKING DRESS, WITH HAT.

Carriage Dress of Mauve Silk. – Over dress of fine white alpaca, trimmed with a band of mauve silk and white goat's hair.

Small sleeveless jackets are in high favor among young ladies. Those made of black silk are trimmed round with silk of the same color as the skirt with which they are worn. This band of colored silk is about two inches wide, is laid on flat, and then worked over with either steel or gold beads in various devices – stars, lattice-work, diamonds, *grecques*, etc., according to fancy. These jackets are worn over white Garibaldi jackets with full sleeves closed at the wrist.

WALKING DRESS.

Walking Dress of Lavender-Colored Foulard Silk, trimmed with heavy green and white cord. The front of the basque has green silk lapels heavily embroidered.

Peterson's Magazine, July 1865

Skirts are made very full and very long, and the crinolines as large as ever. Some few ladies have discontinued them, but there does not seem the least symptom of their general decrease, excepting for balls and evening concerts. On these occasions they are small below the waist, and so very flexible that the least pressure will compress them; so that they have none of the unpleasantness and inconvenience of the more common makes.

Plate I. – *Toilettes de ville* and for the sea-side. Dress of *poult de soie*, with narrow stripes. There are two skirts, each edged with a girdle cord. The upper skirt is festooned over the lower, at equal distances, by lace *macarons*. High buttoned body, with small coat-sleeves. Lace *macarons* at the wrist and on the arm-holes. Linen collar and cuffs. Black Chantilly scarf. Rice straw Empire bonnet, with wreath of violets. Violet strings.

Foulard dress, with two skirts. *Revers* of silk at each seam of the lower skirt, the opening being covered with straps of silk, fastened by buttons. At the bottom of the second skirt three rows of ribbon, studded with buttons; and at equal distances loops of ribbon looping up the skirt. Low square body, with *revers* like those on the bottom skirt. Loops of ribbon forming *épaulettes*. White muslin under body and sleeves, trimmed with insertions.

The *foulards* with coloured patterns make very elegant dresses when trimmed with coloured silk *ruches*, or bands of Cluny lace, over ribbon. For ladies of a more advanced age they are made with silk or *chenille* fringes, and tassels of *passementerie*. The silk girdle cords make a very pretty and simple trimming for a young lady's dress.

Many bodies of dresses are made with a *basque* either round the waist or merely at the back, and with the skirt separate, so that it can be worn over the *basque* with a band, and thus form two distinct styles of *basque*.

Loose bodies, of a different material from the skirts, are very much worn, and are made of *foulard*, alpaca, Llama, and muslin. The *foulard* or figured alpaca, of the same colour as the skirt, and trimmed with coloured buttons and very narrow velvets, is remarkable pretty. Some of these are made with several loops of velvet fastened on the *épaulette*, and hanging as low as the elbow. These bodies are made either slightly fulled in at the waist, both back and front, by a *coulisse* and cords, or tucked and stitched with some colour. Some have flat tucks both back and front; others merely in front, and drawn in at the waist behind.

The more dressy *corsages* of muslin are made in a variety of elegant styles, with lace or insertion. Many of them are trimmed with loops of insertion down the front and round the armholes. A coloured velvet or ribbon is passed through these loops, and a band or sash with long broad ends accompanies the body. The sleeves are either of the form called "Bishop," and set into an embroidered *poignet*, or puffed all the way down. Some are made of the coat-sleeve shape and trimmed round the wrist.

Plate II. – Group. Dress of white gauze, with cherry-coloured stripes: the skirt scalloped round the edge, with small stars of cherry-coloured velvet between the stripes, made with a very low body, and looped up over another skirt by means of two velvet stars. This under-dress is of white silk, with a velvet *grecque*, and made with a high body and long sleeves, ornamented with a *grecque* smaller than that on the skirt. Lace collar and sleeves.

White gauze dress, with large green spots, very wide apart. Body with *basques*, trimmed round with green ribbon, covered with white guipure. *Epaulettes* and cuffs of the same. Bands of ribbon and lace placed up the skirt, headed by stars of silk.

White *batiste* dress, with two skirts the under-skirt has a hem and twenty narrow tucks and the top one cut with large oval scallops, and edged with a frill of *Valençiennes*; in each of these scallops are three pointed *pattes* of the same lace, with three *rosettes* of *Valençiennes* at the point of each oval. The body is cut in front like a *Figaro veste*, but behind it has a Diana *basque*, with small rounded sleeves, and trimmed to correspond with the skirt; under this corsage is a waistcoat of white muslin, tucked in front and fastened with pearl buttons. This dress is worn over *mauve tarlatane*, and is accompanied by a band of the same colour and a pearl buckle.

Plate III. – *Toilettes de ville et d'intérieur*. Light grey *linos* dress with *mauve* stripes: above the hem a double row of silk violets is interlaced. Silk *corselet* with small *basques* edged with violets or *grelot* buttons. White muslin body, with tucks and insertions lined with mauve.

White alpaca dress with two skirts, the under one has a small blue silk fluted flounce at the edge, and a braiding of blue above; the over-skirt is quite plain and is looped up at each breadth, by loops of blue ribbon and white pearl buttons. Light fitting *casaque* trimmed with a blue *plissé*, and fastened in front by rows of buttons of the same. Blue band worn outside the *casaque*, with large pearl buckle.

The fashion of making promenade *toilettes* with the skirts fastened up over very short petticoats, is now totally discarded; they are still worn looped up, certainly, but fastened in such a manner as to admit of being lowered if required. Walking-dresses are only so made when intended for morning wear, and then the petticoats over which they are festooned are only a few inches from the ground.

For *toilette de visite*, the dresses are never worn thus shortened, as the style of having one skirt looped over another, must not be confounded with the dress looped over the petticoat; as when the dress is made in the manner we have just described, the underskirt is cut quite to the full length, and forms a train at the back.

Morning *toilettes* are generally made *en suite* – that is, dress, *paletôt*, and petticoat of the same; the three being, of course, trimmed to correspond with the skirt. A body of *foulard*, alpaca, or muslin is generally worn under the *paletôt*. Nevertheless there always is a body of the same material, in case of the *paletôt* being required without sleeves. These *paletôts* are generally made with the sleeves arranged so as to hook on to the armhole, the fastening being concealed by an *épaulette*, in case of the white body being desired underneath; as the different sleeve showing through the armhole of the cloak is only considered suitable for very young girls.

Le Follet, Journal du Grand Monde, August 1865

BALL DRESS.

Evening Dress of Very Thin White Muslin, with several tucks, above each of which a rose-colored is run. Ruffle around the bottom of the skirt. Body and sleeves trimmed to correspond with the skirt.

Morning dresses of a plain color are trimmed *round* the skirt, above the hem, with two rows of bright moire ribbon, an inch and a half wide, and with one row *down* every seam where the breadths are joined. The bodice is made with basques at the back, which are edged with ribbon; the ribbon is also carried straight down the center of the back from the neck to the waist, where there is a small strap and two buttons, thus giving the effect of a dress fastened at the back; the epaulets are mere lines of ribbon.

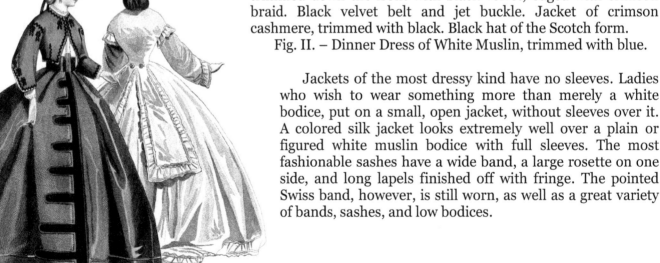

Fig. I. – Out-door Dress. – The skirt is of black alpaca, trimmed down the front with black velvet, edged with crimson braid. Black velvet belt and jet buckle. Jacket of crimson cashmere, trimmed with black. Black hat of the Scotch form.

Fig. II. – Dinner Dress of White Muslin, trimmed with blue.

Jackets of the most dressy kind have no sleeves. Ladies who wish to wear something more than merely a white bodice, put on a small, open jacket, without sleeves over it. A colored silk jacket looks extremely well over a plain or figured white muslin bodice with full sleeves. The most fashionable sashes have a wide band, a large rosette on one side, and long lapels finished off with fringe. The pointed Swiss band, however, is still worn, as well as a great variety of bands, sashes, and low bodices.

A greater simplicity is apparent, we think, in out-door dresses. They are less trimmed, and are almost invariably worn with a plain sacque of the same material as the dress. All walking dresses, if made as long as they usually are, ought to be looped up over petticoats of the same material as the dress, or else some other underskirt, which is very quiet in effect. The more dressy kind of toilets have the skirts looped up with bows of ribbon, or a circle of quilled ribbon. Usually strings are put on the under part of the dress, and tied in such a way that the skirt appears to be fastened by the trimming.

The Art of the Hoop: 1860 - 1869

WALKING DRESS.
Walking Dress of White Alpaca, trimmed with black velvet.

WALKING DRESS, WITH HAT.
Walking Dress of Gray Foulard. – Loose sacque of light maize-colored cloth, trimmed with a gimp. Gray straw hat and maize-colored feather.

A SPANISH JACKET.

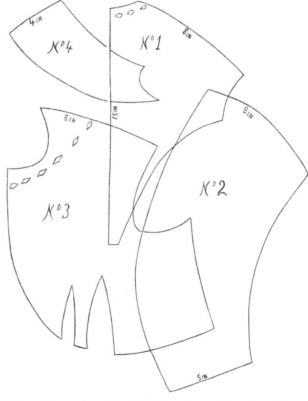

Our diagram, this month, is of a Spanish Jacket. Above, we give two engravings of it; one to be made of dotted lace, or Swiss muslin, the other of the material as the dress with which it is to be worn. The first is trimmed with lace and ribbon, the lace with a ruche of whatever the dress may be with.

The pattern consists of back, side-piece, front, and sleeve. The sleeve is rather narrow, and is of the most fashionable style; it is slightly shaped at the elbow. In cutting out this pattern, the seams are *not* to be allowed for, as all the requisite additions have already been made to the pattern. When the jacket is to be made of the same material as the dress, the corner of the neck is to be rounded off, as shown by the pricked line in the diagram. In a jacket of kind (as will be seen above) a white habit-shirt is worn underneath.

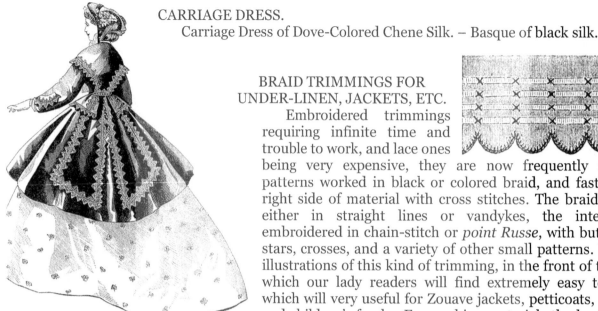

CARRIAGE DRESS.
Carriage Dress of Dove-Colored Chene Silk. – Basque of black silk.

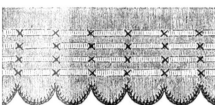

BRAID TRIMMINGS FOR UNDER-LINEN, JACKETS, ETC.
Embroidered trimmings requiring infinite time and trouble to work, and lace ones being very expensive, they are now frequently replaced by patterns worked in black or colored braid, and fastened on the right side of material with cross stitches. The braid is arranged either in straight lines or vandykes, the intervals being embroidered in chain-stitch or *point Russe*, with butterfly knots, stars, crosses, and a variety of other small patterns. We give two illustrations of this kind of trimming, in the front of this number, which our lady readers will find extremely easy to copy, and which will very useful for Zouave jackets, petticoats, chemisettes, and children's frocks. For washing materials the braid should be white, put on with colored cotton or silk.

Peterson's Magazine, August 1865

Plate I. – Group. Spotted *foulard* dress, white and green. Full and long skirt, trimmed with narrow gauffered flounce of green silk, disposed in undulations and rings. High white muslin body, trimmed with bands of black lace insertion. Sleeves to correspond. Long and wide green sash, fastened behind with two falling loops. Trellised and fringed ends.

Mauve silk dress, with low body and short sleeves. The bottom of the skirt is trimmed with shells of white Cluny *guipure*. Above this skirt is a tunic of white muslin, edged with a *guipure* and three rows of insertion, and is raised on one side by a row several *coques* of *mauve* ribbon. White muslin full body, trimmed with edgings and insertions of *guipure*. Bishop sleeves. *Mauve* silk *corselet*, trimmed with lace.

White *Tunisien* gauze dress, with red stripes, trimmed on the bottom of the skirt with a *grecque* in red velvet. Low body and short sleeves, trimmed like the skirt, four buttons on each sleeve. Red band and buckle of *nacre*. Swiss *guimpe*, with long sleeves.

Dresses are made as long and as full as ever, and, as we mentioned last month, if looped up, the under-petticoat should not be many inches from the ground, except for very young ladies. Coloured petticoats will be much worn at the sea-side, When the dress is worn on the shore, the skirt may be festooned all round, but for merely walking-dress on the promenades, it is worn looped up at each side of the front breadth only.

The newest and most elegant way of fastening the dress, is by straps of velvet or silk attached round the waist by a band and buckle. They fall over the skirt, and have a patent hook at the end. Eyes are fastened to the seams of the skirt, and when not required to be looped, the straps – generally five in number – are allowed to hang loosely on the skirt, forming a very pretty ornament. If made in black velvet and ornamented with beads or buttons, they can be worn with different dresses. The one we saw was of black velvet piped with white; at the waist it was about an inch and a half wide; and increasing gradually in width, till at the end it was five inches. The strap was pointed at the end, and trimmed all the way up with graduated *nacre* buttons.

Many ladies who do not care for the encumbrance of two skirts, trim their single one so as to produce the appearance of a double skirt or tunic. This is easily done by putting a flounce on the front breadth, with bands of trimming down the front breadth seams, and continuing them round the skirt. In other cases the trimming is put on in the same manner; but the flounce, on the contrary, is put on all the seams except the front one. Either of these styles gives quite the appearance of an over and under skirt.

We have seen a very elegant dress made in this way. The material was blue *foulard*; a flounce of about twelve inches wide, and put on in large full plaits, was on the front breadth. A broad Persian *cachemire* trimming, the predominant colour being blue, was placed *à la Raphaël* on the body and down the waist; on the skirt, it was on each side of the front breadth, round the skirt, and up the back seam. A small *canotière* mantle of *foulard* accompanied this dress; it was trimmed on the sleeves with the bands of *cachemire*, and the *revers* were of the same material.

The prettiest sea-side petticoats we have seen, are made of a white woollen material, very durable and soft, with bands of colour. One, with which we were much pleased, had a violet band about four inches wide, about three inches above the hem. This band was embroidered in vine-leaves and grapes; the leaves were of white silk, and the grapes formed by bunches of small white buttons. These petticoats should seldom be more than four yards round, as they are rather heavy, and if hanging in folds, would spoil the shape of the crinoline and the set of the dress.

Plate II. – Sea-side dresses. White muslin dress, with an under-dress of silk, the body of the dress being low. The white muslin skirt is looped up on each side of the front, by a bow of ribbon, and the body made high and full, with half-long sleeves. Over this dress is a *casaque* of muslin, lined with silk, and trimmed with *ruches* of silk and muslin frills.

Young girl's dress. Short petticoat of blue silk, trimmed with a row of stars and buttons of the same. White *linos* dress, looped up at each seam by bands of silk, fastened by a star. High body and long sleeves. Small blue silk *pardessus*, with hood and tassels. This jacket is trimmed all round with hanging buttons: it has no sleeves the *épaulettes* being formed of loops of ribbon. Hanging buttons all round the armhole.

Plate III. – White muslin dress, with small gauffered flounce, headed by a band formed of narrow tucks, and insertions of Cluny *guipure*. Bands of the same disposed up the front breadth in interlaced diamonds. High body and sleeves of white muslin, trimmed like the skirt. All these insertions are lined with pink ribbon. *Princesse* tunic of pink silk, embroidered round the edge. *Corselet* of the same, fastened on the shoulders by *épaulettes* of ribbon and lace. Pink bannerettes in the hair. Black lace circular.

Maize alpaca skirt, trimmed down the front with a row of buttons. Two bands of white silk, embroidered in maize, are placed down the front breadth, and, becoming gradually wider as they descend, are continued round the skirt. White muslin body, trimmed with black lace insertions over maize ribbons. Long sash, to match the skirt, fastened behind.

Le Follet, Journal du Grand Monde, September 1865

Decided changes are *predicted* in the make of dresses, but nothing very novel has yet appeared. It is hinted that the enormous quantity of trimming now in used will be dispensed with. We hope so, for it is certainly not elegant.

Fig. I. – House Dress of Buff Alpaca, trimmed with blue velvet.

Fig. II. – Evening Dress of Pearl-Colored Silk. – The skirt is very long, and finished with a puffing of silk at the bottom. The basque slopes very much at the back, and is trimmed with a deep goat's-hair fringe, with pearl-colored silk fringe intermixed.

There is still a great inclination displayed to have all the toilet match in color, skirt, petticoat, basque, parasol, and gloves, are all of one hue. The bonnet may be of a different color, but with trimming which assimilates.

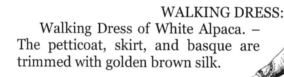

WALKING DRESS:
Walking Dress of White Alpaca. – The petticoat, skirt, and basque are trimmed with golden brown silk.

WALKING DRESS:

Walking Dress of Nankeen-Colored Foulard, trimmed with gimp, and looped up over a petticoat of the same material.

A Pretty Dress. – We have just seen, at a fashionable dress-maker's, a white muslin, scalloped out round the edge, bordered with Valenciennes lace, and looped up over a plain blue silk petticoat; sky-blue ribbons, covered with lace insertion, commenced at the waist and descended each breadth of the skirt, looping it over the petticoat; a half-bodice of blue silk was to be worn over the high, white bodice.

COAT DRESS.

SPANISH JACKET.
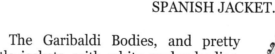

The Garibaldi Bodies, and pretty little jackets, with white under bodies, are as popular as when first introduced for young girls. This fashion is both jaunty and economical, as old skirts, with worn out bodies, can thus be made useful.

The Art of the Hoop: 1860 - 1869

CARRIAGE DRESS.
Carriage Dress pf Gray Silk, trimmed with white guipure over black.

Dresses are no longer caught up with strings. If they are very full dress, they are not taken up at all; but if they are to be taken up, it is done by means of fastenings made in gimp, with two or three tassels hanging from them. Petticoats, similar to the dresses, are most generally worn, but when not the same, must be either white or red with ornaments of black velvet. The striped petticoats have become vulgar, and may only be worn quite in undress.

Sacques still continue to fit the figure rather closely. We do not know as yet what the winter fashions will produce in the way of out-door coverings. Scarfs have been somewhat worn during the warm weather, and, when well put on, nothing can be more graceful.

CARRIAGE DRESS.
Carriage Dress. – The under dress is of blue and white striped silk. The upper dress of blue silk. The under dress has a high body and long sleeves, whilst the under dress has a low body, and only caps for sleeves.

Short waists, with no plaits in the skirt, at the hips, are talked of. This approaches the Empire style, and would accord with the present mode of dressing the hair; but other prophets inform us that double skirts, the upper one of different color or pattern from the under one, and looped up in the Louis XV. style, will be the fashion. Whatever maybe decided on in Paris, the head-quarters of the volatile goddess, will take some time to become universal here.

PATTERN FOR AN EMPRESS SLEEVE.

As the Empress Sleeve is now all the rage in Paris, we give here an engraving of it, and also a diagram by which to cut it out. The sleeve, it will be seen, is very narrow at the wrist, and cut with a seam at the elbow. The sleeve has a cuff composed of two puffings, edged with braid, velvet, or gimp; epaulet in velvet or passementerie. The pattern is composed of three pieces.

No. 1. Upper Part.
No. 2. Cuff.
No. 3. Under Part.

Peterson's Magazine,
September 1865

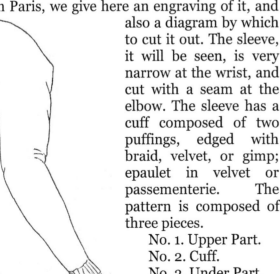

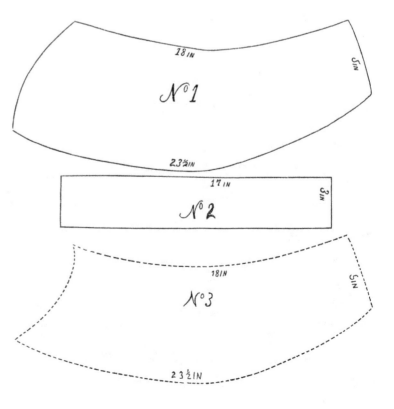

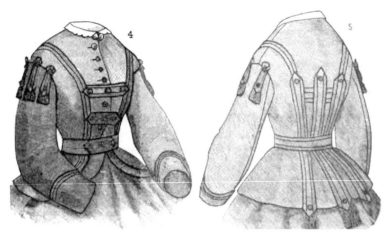

FRONT OF BLACK SILK CORSAGE.
BACK OF BLACK SILK CORSAGE.

Nos. 4 and 5. – *Back and front of black silk corsage*, trimmed with bands of the same, bound with a bright colored silk and edged with fringe. These bands ornament the back and front and extend as bretelles over the shoulders. Coat sleeves trimmed to match.

WALKING COSTUME.

No. 3. – *Dress* of green silk, opened at the bottom of each side, and displaying three gauffered ruffles, barred across with bands of velvet edged with guipure. This trimming extends around the bottom of the skirt and up each breadth, ornamenting also the corsage, which has a series of small basques united by means of straps of velvet. Coat sleeves trimmed to match the skirt. Chip bonnet, trimmed with a black and crimson bird. and a black lace scarf.

Frank Leslie's Lady's Magazine, October 1865

For Evening Dresses, gold cord and gold braid are again in vogue. White silk fringe is also employed on tulle dresses with a most charming effect.

Silk dresses are either very much trimmed, or else quite plain. A small quantity of ornament now looks meagre; but a very full skirt, with a long train without any ornament, is quite elegant, especially if finished with a silk cord around the bottom.

Fig. I. – Ball Dress of Light Blue Silk. – The upper dress is of white tulle edged with lace, and trimmed with pearl beads. The basque waist is of tulle over silk, and the openings are fastened by pearl beads. The head-dress is of the new "Empire" style.

Fig. II. – Carriage Dress of Forest Green Silk, trimmed with black lace over white silk. White bonnet, trimmed with pink ribbon.

There is nothing new in the materials for dress goods and plaids; stripes and small brocaded flowers on heavy silks are all worn; whilst the plain silk is equally fashionable, and if of good quality, probably the most elegant of any. Shot, or changeable silks, have been popular during the summer, and they are very beautiful.

Skirts are still very much gored, and for the house very long. Walking dresses are invariably looped up over pretty petticoats. In Paris, a few of the fashionable women have worn the dress skirts quite plain and short, like those young girls of fourteen years of age. This is sensible, but not so pretty, we think, as the looped skirts, though much money may be saved in this way, as the ribbon, gimp, etc., used for raising the dress is often a considerable item in mantua-maker's bill.

The Art of the Hoop: 1860 - 1869

ALBERT JACKET AND DRESS.

Albert Jacket and Dress of Dark Gray Silk, trimmed with black velvet.

Coat bodies are still worn, and are of every style, but we suppose will soon give place to the basque waist, so much worn some years ago. In fact, many of the dresses are already made so, but they are not very general as yet.

Sleeves are quite close to the arm, and only large enough to admit the hand through at the lower part where the linen cuff shows.

WALKING DRESS.

Walking Dress, Petticoat, and Basque of Stone-Colored Alpaca, trimmed with narrow black alpaca braid. The straps which loop up the upper skirt descend from the waist.

Loops of ribbon are much used for trimming dresses. For example, upon a white muslin skirt, which will be worn over a colored silk slip, a wide waistband is fastened at the side, and the two ends or sashes float at the side of the skirt; at the opposite side a ladder of loops formed with the same ribbon descends as far as the knee. It is a very pretty method of looping up one skirt over another, by making it appear as though it were held up with four ladders of loops. Colored sashes, which contrast with the dress, are worn with dresses which it is desirable to loop up, and they thus form a very ornamental trimming.

WALKING DRESS.

Walking Dress and Loose Basque of Gray Foulard, trimmed with black velvet. The upper skirt is much shorter than the lower one.

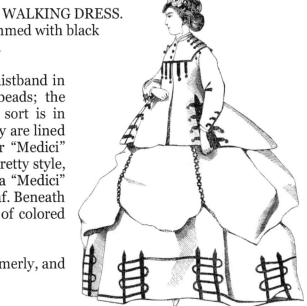

Pretty Style of Waistband. – A very pretty style of waistband in Paris is formed of broad gimp, almost covered with beads; the buckle also covered with gimp and beads. One of this sort is in violet, with gold beads, and others in black and steel. They are lined with self-colored silk. Other bands are made peaked, or "Medici" shape in front, but narrow and straight behind. Another pretty style, but difficult to describe, consists of a band formed with a "Medici" peak, but the lower part cut in and out again like an ivy leaf. Beneath this two long sash ends, peaked, descend. The whole is of colored *gros grain*, edged with a trimming of steel beads.

Belts or waistbands are not so preposterously wide formerly, and are consequently much more becoming.

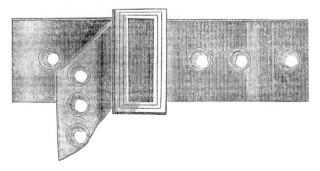

WAISTBAND OF BLACK VELVET, WITH CRYSTAL BEADS AND BUCKLE.

New Styles of Aprons. – Among the new styles of aprons is one rounded in shape, and formed of rich black moire antique, elaborately trimmed in white silk in tambour-stitch, with the addition of steel beads. Another apron, similarly trimmed, is square in shape, with a belt of the same material, and a buckle joined to the apron.

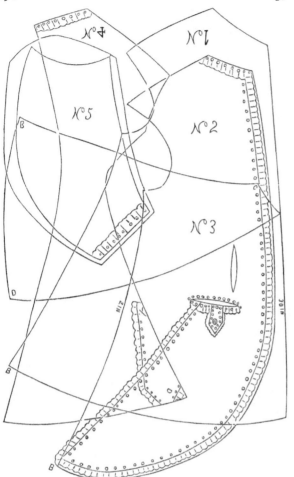

THE EMPRESS JACKET.

Perhaps the most fashionable affair, which has come out for early fall wear, in Paris, is the Empress Jacket, of which we give an engraving above, and a diagram on the next page. This jacket is made of silk, trimmed with Chantilly lace and beads. It sits very close round the waist, is in the waistcoat style in front, and is fastened by a wide band.

The upper part of the front is very open and rounded at bottom; four ornaments are placed behind to simulate pockets.

On account of the size of this garment, Nos. 1, 3, and 4 have been shortened four inches. Our subscribers will only have (after enlarging the pattern,) to prolong the different lines of those parts to that extent to have them of the proper length.

No. 1. Front.
No. 2. Top Part of Front.
No. 3. Side-Piece.
No. 4. Back.
No. 5. Sleeve.

SILK COAT, TRIMMED WITH LACE.

Black Silk Coat, trimmed with square jet buttons, and a profusion of guipure.

Peterson's Magazine, October 1865

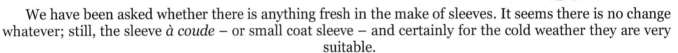

We have been asked whether there is anything fresh in the make of sleeves. It seems there is no change whatever; still, the sleeve *à coude* – or small coat sleeve – and certainly for the cold weather they are very suitable.

Plate II. – *Robe de chambre* of *cachemire* in two colours. The under-dress of white, or very pale colour; plain high body, and long sleeves. The over-skirt is open in front, cut in three large vandykes each side, and plain round the bottom. The body is cut very low, with a narrow shoulder-strap and very deep *basque*; the whole trimmed with Cluny *guipure*.

Poult-de-soie dress, cut in small scallops round the bottom, and up each seam, which are open about twelve inches up the skirt, over points of coloured velvet. Jacket body, with tight sleeves, open in front over a velvet waistcoat.

As to the plain skirts, they are generally scalloped round the bottom, and edged with thick cord, in which is twisted a thread of gold or silver. Linsey and knickerbocker are worn as early morning dress, and these heavy materials are made with a vest and waistcoat, or *chemise russe* of embroidered *cachemire* – the tight high body is not admissible; at least, only with *basques*, and opened in front over a waistcoat, perhaps of embroidered percale or plaited muslin.

We have already mentioned double skirts as fashionable, but we must repeat the information, as every day brings fresh proof of its truth; and when the sleeves and under-skirt are different to the upper skirt and low body, it produces a very stylish effect. What can be prettier than a dress of white silk, with an upper skirt and small bodice of blue green or cerise? By many ladies the *Princesse* or *Gabrielle* make are preferred, as the dress, being cut in one piece, is considered to give a more graceful flow to the train, which is worn as long or longer than ever.

Le Follet, Journal du Grand Monde, November 1865

POPLIN DRESS AND PALETOT.
STRIPED SILK DRESS.

No. 1. – *Dress* of mode-colored silk, plaided with a deeper shade. Three narrrow [sic] bands of orange-colored silk are put on in zig-zag, forming a tunic at the sides, and ornamenting the lower part of the skirt at the back. From the lowest band depends a button fringe. The same trimming is put on above, so as to produce the effect of a long basque at the back and rounded at the sides. The same is repeated for epaulets, and around throat.

No. 2. – *Blue moire antique dress*, trimmed with three narrow bands of white silk, studded with buttons. The upper skirt edged with a fall of guipure lace, headed with a band of white silk, is looped up with a rosette of lace on one side. Round waist, trimmed with five bands of white silk. A scarf of the same material as the dress, and bordered with white silk, is fastened on the right shoulder and is tied beneath the left arm. The scarf is edged with lace. Coat sleeves.

Fig. 7. – Dress *à deux jupes* of garnet silk; the first skirt trimmed at a little distance from the bottom, by two rows black silk ribbon, the upper one having a series of short tabs of the same material, joined to it by small buttons. The second skirt is edged at the bottom with bands of black ribbon, to match the underskirt, and is caught at equal distances by six black silk cords and tassels. Long skirted waistcoat *à Louis XV.*; it is of garnet silk, closing by black buttons, and is edged all round by black ribbon; at the bottom is a grelot fringe; mousquetaire pockets trimmed with black ribbon. Paletot of black velvet, trimmed with bands of passementerie to match the skirt; it is quite open in the front, not covering the front of the waistcoat, to which it is attached by small buttons underneath. The sleeves are trimmed to match the fronts, and are left open at the back of the arm nearly to the elbow, the openings being laced up by a black cord, which finishes by tassels at the top. Bonnet of pink terry with black lace and small bunches of grapes.

Fig. 8. – Suit or dress and paletot of black silk, with plaitings of violet ribbon. The skirt is *à deux jupes*, the upper skirt being very short and cut into large pointed scallops at the bottom, which are edged by the violet trimming. This paletot is open in front, with revers turned back; it fastens by hooks and eyes at the chest only, and is sloped off from this place to the bottom, where it is cut in scallops like the upper skirt; it is of course, trimmed like the skirt, by the violet ribbon. Waistcoat of violet silk, fastened by black buttons.

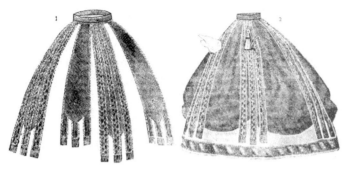

Watteau skirt elevator. This is a very ingenious device for holding up dresses, and is, besides, not inelegant in appearance. The skirt elevator consists of a band to go round the waist, and four wide lapels placed at equal distances from each other. These lapels being double are, in fact, long loops, through which the bottom of the skirt can be passed, as seen in illustration No. 1. Each lapel is trimmed with three strips of black velvet, covered with gimp, and edged with fringe at the bottom. These strips come down a few inches beyond the lapels. Deep pockets are arranged inside the two front lapels, and these are useful for holding a purse, pocket-handkerchief, parasol, or other articles.

Frank Leslie's Lady's Magazine, November 1865

EVENING DRESS.
Ball Dress of Blue and White Striped Gauze, looped up over blue silk with gilt crescents.

BRACES.
Waistband and Braces of Crimson Silk and Black Lace.

BRACES AND SASH.
Braces and Sash of Blue Silk and Black Lace.

Black and white are still favorite combinations for dresses. But if the dress is black, white should be sparingly used, as otherwise the effect will be muddy; but if the dress is white, more black can be employed, as a warm always looks better on a cold color than a cold color upon a warm one.

Fig. I. – House Dress of Crimson Poplin. – The skirt is trimmed with quillings of black velvet. Broad, black velvet waistband, with four long ends at the back. The waistband and trimmings on the sleeves are studded with steel.

Fig. II. – Carriage Dress of Gray Silk, ornamented with Persian trimming. The body is made with a deep basque. Sleeves nearly tight.

Bodices are made quite plain, with a wide (not immoderately wide) belt or waistband, thus shortening the waist, or they fit closely with a very long basque.

Sleeves are almost tight to the arm, and for dress occasions are finished with a frill of lace falling over the hand.

Buttons on dresses are quite large, and are made of jet, mother-of-pearl, coral, ebony, or gimp.

Hoods are made quite soft, and cut with large capes. Both hood and cape are pointed in the center, and are trimmed with velvet ribbon, or full tufted ruches.

The Art of the Hoop: 1860 - 1869

CARRIAGE DRESS.
 Carriage Dress of Lavender-Colored Silk, trimmed with a darker shade of lavender velvet ribbon studded with pearl buttons. Deep coat basque.

WALKING DRESS:
Walking Dress of Russet Poplin, ornamented with Persian trimming. Very deep coat basque.

Petticoats are still an item of consideration in this country, as short dresses are not yet adopted here. White petticoats, worked in black or scarlet worsted braid, are popular. Some persons run several rows of wide, black braid on a white petticoat, and dot this braid with coarse working cotton, which has the effect of white beads. Others work detached sprays of flowers, wheat-ears, palms etc., and others again ornament the skirts with two or three bands of blue, pink, green, black, or straw-colored cambric, or plain gingham. Of course, a material should be selected for this purpose the colors of which will not fade. These bands of colored cambric are also used for trimming, dressing jackets, children's dresses, etc., and can be highly ornamented by forming trellis work, diamonds, etc., with the sewing-machine.

WALKING DRESS.
 Black Silk Basque, lace with black velvet.

Garibaldi bodies are still worn, particularly by young ladies. White silk braid with jet beads, gray braid with steel beads, scarlet braid, and fancy stitches done in purse-silk, are all favorite modes of ornamentation for these bodies.

JACKET.

JACKET.

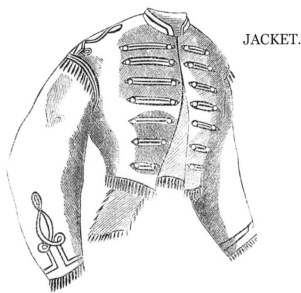
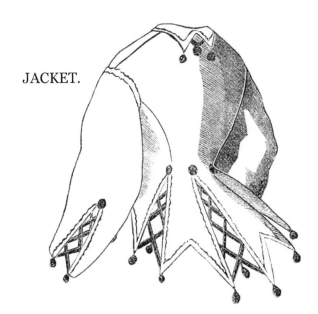

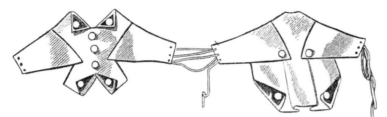

COATEE: FRONT AND BACK.

Back and Front View of a Coat Waistband of Pink Silk, turned up and trimmed with black velvet.

Paletots are worn shorter than heretofore, and usually droop into the figure without fitting it tightly.

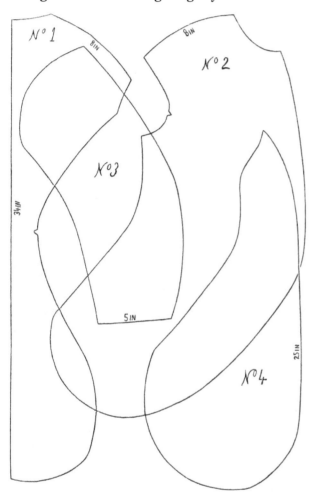

AUTUMN PALETOT.

This very stylish Paletot is made in four pieces. On the next page we give a diagram, by which it may be cut out. The style of trimming is seen in the above engraving.

No. 1. Front.
No. 2. Back.
No. 3. Sleeve.
No. 4. Side-Piece.

Peterson's Magazine, November 1865

A principal feature to be remarked in the make of winter dresses, is the absence of all plaits both in front and at the sides of the skirt. To manage this the dresses are cut in the Princess form, and the bodice and front breadth of the skirt are therefore in one piece. Three large box plaits are arranged at the back of the skirt, but at the sides and front, where it is plain, trimming is laid on to simulate basques. As for crinolines, we are repeatedly told they are "going out;" but the evidence of our eyes assures us of the contrary. In Paris the much abused articles are certainly smaller in front, but at the back they have by no means diminished – rather, we think the contrary.

Dress and paletot of green silk, trimmed with rich steel gimp, put in in half squares three rows deep, and with steel buttons at the ends. The paletot has a fall of black lace. Coat sleeves. ➜

As for the make of dresses, when the material is silk, the bodices are cut plain and to fit closely, with very long basques at the back. The newest cut is the following: The centre basque is pointed, and two small square basques are placed one on each side to fall over it; there are on [no?] basques in front, but a waistband is worn. The sleeves are narrow, in fact tight, as they fit the arm closely; the lower part of them is ornamented with several rows of trimming. A decided preference is evinced for narrow cross-cut bands of colored silk, and in the centre of each band there is a line of gimp, worked with white seed beads. Occasionally these cross-cut bands are edged with a very narrow fringe. The bodice is fastened in front with large buttons, either cut jet or mother-of-pearl. Jewelers are now turning their attention to these large buttons for dresses, and very beautiful ones are produced of precious stones, and particularly of carved coral. Gimp buttons for this purpose are all made with a head, or rather a sort of nail, in the centre, which is invariably of some hard material; buttons covered to match the dress are for the present entirely abandoned.

Frank Leslie's Lady's Magazine, December 1865

Fig. I. – Ball Dress of White Tarletan, made with puffings, which are looped up on one side with an ornament scarlet gimp. Scarlet jacket, richly embroidered, is worn over the shoulders on leaving the ball-room.

Fig. II. – Evening Dress of White Silk, trimmed with the eyes of peacock's feathers, and deep fringe to correspond in color.

Sicilian bands are worn with all white dresses; they consist of a half bodice, straight both in the front and at the back, and with two long ends or sashes, which fall nearly to the edge of the skirt behind. The ends are trimmed with lace, and loops of ribbon are placed between them and upon the shoulders. These Sicilian bodices are very inexpensive; they do not cut into much material, and any odds and ends of lace can be used for trimming them. For autumn wear they will be made of black velvet, and for all demi-toilets will be found most useful accessories.

MORNING DRESS.

Morning Dress of Stone-Colored Cashmere. – Cut in the Gabrielle style, and trimmed with interlaced horse-shoes made of velvet, ornamented with steel.

Sleeves are very close to the arm.
The style of trimming skirts is left to the taste of the wearer. Anything may be in the fashion.

HOUSE DRESS.
House Dress of Fawn-Colored Silk, trimmed with fringe. Jacket of black velvet.

In spite of the predictions abroad, and the example of a few of the ultra-fashionables, long skirts are still the only ones worn in our drawing-rooms. Of course, the looped-up skirts, or skirts made short enough without the necessity of looping, are more in favor as the bad weather increases.

WALKING DRESS.

Carriage Dress and Paletot of Blue Silk, trimmed with velvet of a darker shade and heavy cord of the two shades of blue. The skirt opens at the bottom over white silk to simulate a petticoat.

WALKING DRESS.

Walking Dress and Paletot (when unlooped) of Blue Alpaca. – The skirt has a flounce, and the paletot and dress are both trimmed with black velvet.

Paletots are worn rather short, and sometimes quite loose, and sometimes rather fitting the figure. They are very much trimmed generally, the trimming being carried up the sides and back.

NEW STYLES OF JACKETS, ETC.

JACKET.

PERSIAN DESIGN.

This design in embroidery is for ornamenting the corners and back of a jacket. The palms are done in various colored embroidery silk, interspersed with steel and gold beads.

CARRIAGE DRESS.

Carriage Dress of Blue Silk, trimmed with a bias band of white plush, put on to imitate a double skirt. A deep ruffle at the back beneath the plush band.

Most of the new dresses are made with round waists, and are worn with a rather broad belt. This shortens the length of the waist, of course, and is only becoming to slender figures; but it will be the fashion, and every one will follow it. Even if jackets and basques are worn, the waistband is worn too.

Sashes are now sometimes tied at the side, just *back* of the left arm. This is new and pretty.

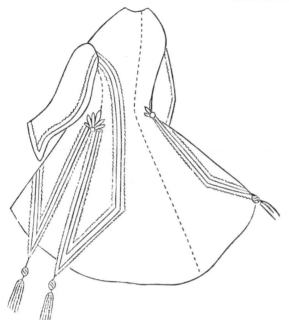

FALL AND WINTER JACKET.

This jacket may be made of black silk, velvet, or cloth, according as the wearer desires a jacket for fall, or for winter wear. It buttons straight down the front, and is fitted to the figure. It is ornamented with two points on each side, proceeding from the side-pieces of the front and back. They are fixed to the garment by the seam under the arm, and fall naturally to the bottom. These points are trimmed with black silk puffing, bordered by a narrow guipure, and terminated by two silk tassels. A similar trimming is applied to the neck, at the shoulder seam, also to the seam of the sleeve and round the wristband. At top the sleeve is round.

We give a diagram, by which it may be cut out, after first enlarging the different pieces to the sizes indicated.

No. 1. Front.
No. 2. Side-Piece of Front.
No. 3. Point of Front.
No. 4. Back.
No. 5. Side-Piece of Back.
No. 6. Point of Back.
No. 7. Sleeve.

Owing to the length of this garment, No. 1 is given six inches too short, and No. 2, eight inches. Our subscribers must, therefore, prolong the lines of those two patterns to have them of the proper length.

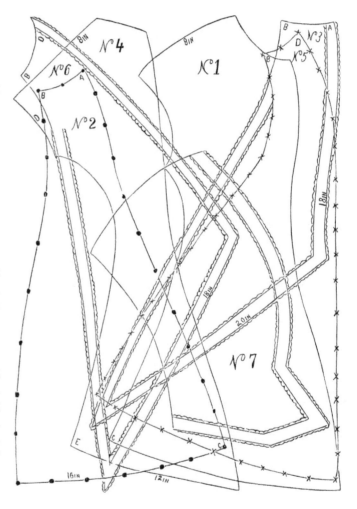

Thibet fringe is much used for trimming handsome silk dresses; and a coarse lace called "Cluny guipure," is very popular for evening dresses, when it is thickly ornamented with crystal or pearl beads. In fact, all kinds of braid is very much used on evening dresses for married ladies.

Good taste in dress will do more than even money. The French women understand this, and hence the supremacy of French fashions.

Peterson's Magazine, December 1865

On the Subject of Dress

The eccentric fashion of dresses composed of two different-coloured materials is gradually gaining ground. Among many we give the following as specimens: –

A dress made in the Princess shape, and with each width cut into a pointed shape, wide at the bottom and tapering towards the top. The widths are alternately of green and havannah silk. Rich ornaments composed of thick gimp cord, and finished off with tassels, are placed at the waist, in the centre of the back, and on the epaulettes. The bottom of the skirt is edged round with a very thick cable cord. This cord is twisted and of the two colours of the dress. The body is fastened in front with large round gimp buttons.

The other is a dress of blue glacé silk. The skirt is trimmed round the bottom with a very deep flounce put on with a heading. The seam is hidden under a very delicate border of black silk gimp spangled with steel beads, and from which hang at regular distances long drooping ornaments of cut steel. Above this flounce there is a second similar to it, and trimmed in the same manner. This skirt is rather short, and a second one is worn over it, but open in front, and forming the train behind. This second skirt is of rich black silk rep; it is trimmed round the top with a flounce as deep as that of the blue skirt, also with a heading but no gimp; it is ornamented with strips of blue velvet pat on slantways at regular distances over the top; the same ornaments come up as far as the waist on each side of the black skirt. The body of the blue dress is plain, and fastened with black velvet buttons. A deep black velvet band with a gilt buckle is worn round the waist. The sleeves are narrow, and trimmed with black velvet round the wrists. A small black silk rep jacket without sleeves is worn over the blue silk body. It is open and rounded off at the sides in front, and has a small square basque at the back. It is trimmed all round with a thick black silk pinked-out ruche. Two long loops of a rich plait of black silk gimp cord fall from the epaulettes, and cross each other over the arm.

For our part we think in dresses made of two different materials one of the two should be black, unless they are of two shades of the same colour, which also looks well; but two contrasting colours have much too gaudy an appearance to be in good taste.

The Englishwoman's Domestic Magazine, April 1865

Ladies who live and dress quietly will scarcely notice a fashion article in August. In spring they may have consulted us as to the proper way of making their new dresses for the ensuing fashion, they may just have condescended to accept our advice on the contending merits of paletot or cape; but now, their summer garments being chosen and made, they are wearing them contentedly, and will not change again till the autumn, unless some extraordinary circumstances occur in the interval. In fact, summer fashions are pretty well settled, but there are eccentric combinations for those who continually crave for novelty, and change their dress forty times during the summer. The number is not exaggerated – ladies of fashion take no less than from forty to sixty dresses for one season by the seaside. The packing up of these dresses, especially the clear fabrics intended for evening wear, is a very complicated affair. The dresses are hung up in high trunks, they are stretched out, and pinned in several places very carefully to pieces of tape, which are arranged inside the trunk in a sort of trellis-work pattern. Thus the dress arrives at its destination uncrumpled and ready to wear. Muslin, however, is so easily creased, and requires such perfect freshness to look nice, that tarlatane and silk gauze are infinitely preferred when travelling has to be thought of. These fabrics, though requiring great care in the management of packing, are, however, less liable to become crumpled than clear muslins.

Dresses of two different materials and colours are very fashionable, but to be in good taste one of the two should be a very quiet, subdued sort of tint, and one only bright. Take the following as an example: – A dress of clear grenadine, striped blue and white. The trimming round the bottom consists of two narrow quillings of the same material. edged round the top by two rows of ribbon of two shades of fawn-colour. The high body and long sleeves are quite plain. Over this dress there is another of light fawn-coloured silk; it is open upon the bosom, and has no sleeves; the skirt is train-shaped, and opens in front like a tunic; it is trimmed all round with a quilling of striped grenadine and two rows of ribbon, to correspond with the trimming of the under-skirt. The bodice and epaulettes are edged with the same trimming.

The Englishwoman's Domestic Magazine, August 1865

1866

THE EUSTACHE JACKET.

It is made of black velvet, and trimmed with embroidered bands and a heavy chenille fringe. A wide belt of black velvet is fastened in front with a fancy gilt buckle. This jacket can also be made of black silk, and trimmed with revers and bands of scarlet or blue silk embroidered with either white or black. The fringe should match the color of the embroidery.

A charming evening-dress for a young lady, suitable for the winter festivities, is of white tarlatane, trimmed with five narrow puffings on the edge of the skirt, looped over with bands of green ribbon, edged with black lane. A second skirt, edged with black lace, is looped up just above the puffs on the under-skirt, by five graduated sashes of green silk, edged with black lace. The corsage is of green silk, with tooth-pick points, both back and front. It is finished at the neck by ruchings of silk, edged with lace and folds of white tarlatane, arranged as in Fig. 5 of our fashion-plate. This dress is highly creditable to the designer, Mme. Demorest, of 473 Broadway, New York.

Another evening dress is of silver gray silk, trimmed with a double box-plaited flouncing of rose Portugal silk, in sections of about eight inches. The flounce is separated by half zones of silver-gray velvet, two and a half inches across, having the interior space barred with narrow velvet. The corsage is a basque, sloping suddenly from the front, and quite long at the back, trimmed to match the skirt, and having much the effect of a tunic

FANCY DRESS.

The underskirt is of gray wool de laine, with a bright Persian bordering. The tunic is of violet de laine, with gay figures and a narrow border of high colors. The overdress is perfectly loose, and caught into the waist by a belt. The long tight sleeves are of gray material, the same as the skirt.

Many of the morning-robes are precisely like those given on the double sheet in December, 1863. For a more eccentric, but still very popular style, refer to page 20 of the present number. ➔

A very novel dress, and somewhat similar in style to the morning-robe in the present number, is as follows: A skirt of blue poplin, ornamented with black velvet horseshoes, studded with steel buttons. Over this is a short and perfectly plain skirt of black silk. A sleeveless jacket of black silk, trimmed with steel fringe, is worn over a blue Garibaldi waist, ornamented with black velvet.

Many of the winter dresses are either laced or buttoned up the back. The edge of the skirt is still cut in scollops, but a thick cord has taken the place of the quilled braid.

Some of the new sleeves are almost tight from the wrist to the elbow, and then puff out very much in the old leg of mutton style.

BODICE FOR WEARING UNDER MANTLES IN COLD WEATHER.

The fulness of some of the mantles now worn causes them to give but little warmth to the chest and arms; the bodice, of which we give the pattern, is intended to wear under these garments. These bodices are buttoned down the front, but not closed under the arms. They are made with or without sleeves, according to the shape of the cloak they are intended to wear with, and either in cloth of the same kind, or in black silk, lined and quilted. Our pattern is made with sleeves; it is bound round the edges with broad silk braid, and fastened round the waist with black ribbons.

Godey's Lady's Book, January 1866

Dresses incline more and more to the Princess shape. All the widths are gored; the skirt is scant and short in front, and forms a long sweeping train at the back. The body is plain, with a round waist, narrower than those of last winter, and fastened at the side with a bow or rosette. These bands often have long lapels at the back. The Princess, or Gabrielle dress, has the body and skirt cut in one. These are made quite plain in front and on the hips, but with three box-pleats at the back. Of course, these are only suitable for high-necked dresses, though we have seen an evening dress of corn-colored silk cut in this way; the body was square in the neck.

The looped-up skirts over fancy petticoats still hold their sway on the streets; our ladies protesting against the short, plain skirt just escaping the ground, because it looks like a school-girl's. The dress looped up on one side, but forming a long train at the back, is very stylish for evening wear; and the under-skirt need be only of a rich material where the upper skirt opens over it.

CARRIAGE DRESS.

Carriage Dress of Fawn-Colored Poplin, trimmed with blue ribbon. Black lace sash.

Round waists are still the fashion, worn with belts. Basques are sometimes made, and form a pretty variety. These light bodies, with the close sleeves, have been so long worn that it was to be hoped that some folds, or any other addition to the dress would be made to relieve the stiffness, but the style, because it is an ugly one, we suppose, has not changed.

Basques are, sometimes, added at the back only. These basques may be made separately from the dress, the body put on a narrow band, and then worn, or not, at pleasure. The universal belt, or waistband, conceals the ribbon, and the basque looks as though it was cut with the bodice.

Sleeves are long and nearly close at the hand. Sometimes a *very small* epaulet ornaments the sleeve at the top.

HOME DRESS.

Home Dress of Green Silk, trimmed with three ruffles at the bottom, black guipure lace, and white lace, put on in the horseshoe form. Striped basque, with a hood, confined at the waist with a green silk sash, ornamented like the dress.

Cords placed at the bottom of the skirts, on the shoulders and sleeves, are ornaments frequently preferred for rich, plain silks.

Broad stripes are very fashionable, but very unbecoming to short, stout figures; and then not one dress-maker in a hundred knows how to fit a body with stripes to look well.

Peterson's Magazine, January 1866

The Art of the Hoop: 1860 - 1869

LATEST STYLES.

Fig. 1. – Visiting costume. Dress of steel-colored silk spotted with black and trimmed with applications of black velvet cut out in bunches of leaves. *Paletôt* of black velvet trimmed with crochet trimming and jet ornaments.

Fig. 2. – Walking costume for a young lady. Dress of black silk. Sacque of purple velvet cloth, heavily trimmed with black braid and pendent chenille ornaments. Derby hat of gray felt, trimmed with bands of purple velvet; on one side is a short gray plume and a bird with gay plumage.

Fig. 3. – Evening costume. Dress of rich white silk, trimmed with crystal ornaments.

Fig. 4. – Walking suit for a young lady. Dress of ruby poplin. Sacque of gray velvet cloth, trimmed with photographic buttons and gray silk cord.

One of the prettiest corsages is made tight-fitting and round in the waist. Seven sash-like ends caught together by a lacing of beads, cord, or velvet are then set on, and form a very dressy waist. This style looks particularly well in velvet; it is also a very nice method of refashioning an old garment.

Another charming novelty in the dress line is of rich blue silk cut square in the neck both back and front. The space is then filled in with white corded silk or satin edged with black lace. The sleeves are almost tight, and slashed with puffings of white satin or silk showing through. The skirt is trimmed with a heavy cable cord arranged in scallops to simulate a tunic skirt.

A very nice arrangement is to have a dress-body cut plain to wear with a belt and a basque made separate and sewed to a band. It can then be worn at pleasure, and, as it fits on under the belt, it has all the effect of being made on the dress. Sometimes the basque is perfectly plain, at other times it is slit up to the waist in the back, or else made with three tabs or tails.

Sleeves are still of the coat form, the novelty being in the trimming, which is now arranged in a spiral form round the sleeve, or ladder-like on the outside of the sleeve from the waist to the shoulder. The only new sleeve is perfectly straight and hanging. Sometimes it is caught together at the end as if fastened round the wrist, though it hangs perfectly free. This style of sleeve requires a lining of either white satin or silk; it also calls for a tight sleeve of the same material as the dress, or a full white sleeve.

ROBE DRESS.

Robe dress of purple poplin, richly ornamented with applications of black velvet studded with small steel beads and buttons. The pendent straps are of ribbon tipped with velvet.

Now that the winter festivities have commenced in earnest, the most important subject for fashionable consideration is that of evening dresses. Although extravagant expenditure prevails to a great extent in the getting np of evening *toilettes*, still we have seen some very beautiful, and, we may say, inexpensive evening dresses recently imported.

The majority of them are of white tulle or tarlatane, ornamented with bands of book muslin or *crêpe* edged with lace, and arranged in fanciful devices. The trimmings are of the most vivid shades of rose, buff, blue, yellow, pearl, lilac, and green; sometimes these bands are interwoven with black lace insertion producing a most charming effect. Our readers will understand that but one color is used in a dress, but the different styles are reproduced in the shades we have mentioned. On page 122 ↗ we give an illustration of this style of robe, which will give an idea of the style of trimming, though, of course, the lightness and beauty of the dress cannot be produced in a wood-cut.

EVENING DRESS.

Evening dress of white tarletane, trimmed with bands of green book muslin edged with lace. These bands are woven in with black lace insertion, forming an elaborate Grecian pattern. The same style of trimming is arranged on the corsage.

The next important subject is the making up of evening dresses. There is no marked novelty that we are able to discern. In most cases dresses are made low in the neck with very short sleeves, and frequently cut square both back and front. The angel sleeve, worn a few years ago, has been resuscitated, and is much admired for its airy lightness. It is merely a veil of blonde, *crêpe,* or tarlatane laid in plaits half way round the sleeve and falling free. The length varies from a half to three-quarters of a yard. Corsages are generally made tight and with long points back and front, or else the waist is round and worn with a broad sash made of some light material. Tabs or short tails have also appeared on some of the new evening dresses, but are more admired for their novelty than their beauty.

Skirts are all made with a train and very full at the hem, the fulness, however, decreasing at the hips. Silk tunics over tarlatane skirts are exceedingly popular.

We would suggest that if the underskirt be of tarlatane, that it should be gored and lined with a thin muslin or a coarser tarlatane. It will lose none of its lightness, there will be less fulness about the hips, and the dress will be much more durable.

WALKING COSTUME FOR A YOUNG LADY.

Dress of blue silk poplin. Black velvet *paletôt*, embroidered with jet beads and bordered by a narrow band of Astrakan. Triconne of black velvet, turned up with blue velvet, and trimmed with a blue feather.

Double skirts are now very popular, and one of the most stylish modes is to have the skirts of a different shade or color. For instance, an underskirt of rich Mexican blue silk with an overskirt of mode silk, an underskirt of violet silk and an upperskirt of mauve, or a pearl-colored skirt enlivened by an upperskirt of Solferino. The edges of both skirts are generally waved and trimmed with a rich cord or *passementerie*. The best style of corsage for this dress is a vest with sleeves and a sleeveless jacket. The vest should be of the shade of the underskirt, and the jacket the same as the overskirt.

Another style of dress greatly in favor is the Princesse. This is tightly gored in front with large double plaits at the back of the skirt, each plait being ornamented with tassels or gimp ornaments.

Godey's Lady's Book, February 1866

An Afternoon Dress has just come out in Paris, made of black and blue striped satin, without any trimming upon the skirt, but with a tunic or second skirt made of blue-velvet, opening in front, and simply trimmed with small *rouleaux* of blue satin. The bodice, which was entirely of blue-velvet, was cut in one piece with this tunic. At the top of the sleeves there was a small velvet frill bound with satin, and underneath the frill a tight sleeve, made with the striped blue and blue [*black*?] satin.

Bodices, for the present, for both in-door and morning dresses, are worn high and plain, just as they have been during the last eighteen months; the coat-sleeve remains unaltered, except that it is cut narrower and closer to the arm; the epaulets have given place to mere shoulder-straps, and even the cuffs, in several instances, are abolished.

The Art of the Hoop: 1860 - 1869

Dresses in Paris are made with decidedly narrower and shorter skirts than have been seen for many years.

CARRIAGE DRESS.

Walking Dress of Gray Silk, with Black Velvet Paletot, trimmed with gimp and cord.

The tendency of fashion shows that the tunics of our great grandmothers, without any pleats at the waist, made in one piece with the bodice, and looped up over handsome silk petticoats, are the style to which we are inevitably drifting.

Crinolines are reduced, but by no means abandoned; they have entirely disappeared from round the hips, but the lower part of the skirt, besides being longer, is more ample than ever.

WALKING DRESS.

Walking Dress of Black and White Striped Cashmere, made in the Gabrielle style, and looped over a white cashmere petticoat.

Skirts are worn as long and as wide at the bottom as they have been heretofore, notwithstanding the prediction that short, narrow ones would be once again in favor, as they were worn about thirty-five years ago. Skirts are but little trimmed, and often not at all. The Gabrielle style is quite popular for more ordinary wear. A few double skirts have also made their appearance, but these are not general. The fronts of dresses have but few pleats in them, as all skirts are very much gored.

Short waists are now the fashion; and belts of moderate width are always worn with them.

PATTERN FOR BODICE: BACK AND FRONT.

Basques, like the skirt, fitting close to the figure, will be again popular as the spring approaches; and when these are now worn, a belt is always fastened over them.

Sleeves are trimmed from the wrist to the shoulder, sometimes the trimming winds around the arm in a spiral manner.

Loose sacques and jackets are popular over the bodies of dresses, or over white bodies.

Striped petticoats, scalloped at the bottom, and bound with braid, are as new as any we have seen, except the imported ones, when the Persian trimming is employed. Generally the stripes are black and white, though sometimes red and white, mauve and white, or blue and white, are preferred. These petticoats, however, do not suit all styles of dress, as the black and white do.

TRAVELING PALETOT.

We give, this month, a pattern for a new style traveling Paletot, which is easily made, with the assistance of the diagram on the next page.

This traveling Paletot is of cloth, trimmed with two rows of black velvet laid on flat. The garment closes straight in front, and it is open at the side. Under the opening is placed a gore of cloth, trimmed with three narrow velvets, which begins under the arm and widens as it descends to the bottom of the garment.

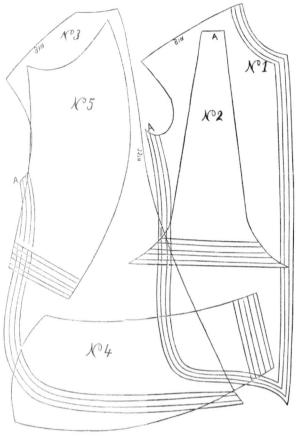

The sleeve has an elbow; it is long and half-tight at the bottom. A cuff is simulated by three narrow velvets.

On the next page we give the diagram, by which the Paletot may be cut out.

No. 1. Front.
No. 2. The Gore.
No. 3. Back.
No. 4. Front of Sleeve.
No. 5. Back of Sleeve.

To enlarge the diagram, measure the angles, and them make the sides as long as they are marked. Thus the back, in this diagram, is thirty-eight inches.

Peterson's Magazine, February 1866

EVENING ROBE.

Dress of white tulle, ornamented with bands of green *crêpe* edged with black lace. The flowers on the skirt are formed of green *crêpe*, with foliage and branches worked with floss silk.

Many of the tulle dresses are made with double skirt with a tunic forming a third skirt.

Long sashes with wide bows placed in the centre of the back, the ends falling nearly to the edge of the skirt, is one of the novelties instituted by the Maison Tilman.

Skirts are made very long and laid in double box-plaits. Corsages are quite low. Puffs are being inserted lengthwise in the coat sleeves.

Home and promenade dresses, if not made in the Princesse style (that is, body and skirt in one piece and tightly gored), have the skirts gored.

The Pompadour or square corsage is unquestionably one of the most fashionable styles. A really charming fashion is the little sleeveless jacket. It is cut away very much in front, in the Senorita style, and in the back it is short and perfectly straight. It is exceedingly becoming and stylish, and can be worn over a waist of colored silk or white muslin. We give preference to the muslin or illusion waist, and suggest that the sleeves should be puffed, or else fully trimmed.

The prettiest and most desirable style of fancy petticoat is of white moreen trimmed with black velvet. For instance, a band bordering the skirt with the upper edge out in points, between and above each point is a large velvet button. The beauty of the trimming is enhanced by twisting a white silk cord fancifully

The Art of the Hoop: 1860 - 1869

around the points. Black reps or poplin, though, of course, not so rich as the velvet, makes a very effective trimming, and answers every purpose.

WALKING COSTUME FOR A YOUNG LADY.

Dress of light purple silk poplin, with *paletôt* of the same, trimmed with bands of black velvet and small jet buttons. Hat of purple velvet, with long veil of purple *crêpe* lisse.

White muslin jacket, trimmed with *point appliqué* lace, loops of pink ribbon, and pink ribbons.

Godey's Lady's Book, March 1866

Dresses are being made much as they have been for some months past. Unquestionably, if crinoline is not wholly abolished, its dimensions are becoming rapidly restricted. Now the general tendency, on all sides, to diminish skirts is so very marked, that very wide skirts, as distinct from trained, are remarkable for their want of distinction.

Skirts are made as long as ever for home wear. The looped-up skirts are more fashionable than ever, from the fact of their being economical; they are made of every conceivable material and color, from solid scarlet to plain white moreen, and trimmed in every manner. Bias bands, stitched on with the machine, are neat and elegant; and we have seen some trimmed with fur; but fur never was intended to be put to such a use as that.

WALKING DRESS.

WALKING DRESS.

Paletots are quite short in front, but certainly a quarter of a yard longer in the back. The front is cut almost straight across, and the back of the skirt forms nearly half circle; again, some are cut straight around, and slashed up as far as the waist, both in the buck and on the hips. For walking and traveling wear they are made of the same material as the skirt and petticoat, and trimmed in every way.

They are pretty, of a thin material, ornamented with a rosette of bias silk on the shoulders, with two cords of silk to the waist, with another rosette like the one on the shoulder.

Embroidery is not as much used as formerly; as spring advances, and thin dresses are needed, it will give place to fringes, etc., which are made much prettier than in their last reign. However, gold and silver trimmings are not used in that profusion that they were in the winter.

Buttons of immense size are the fashion; but if Egyptian mode should take, the round button will have be dispensed with and the triangle substituted in its stead.

NEW STYLES OF BODIES.

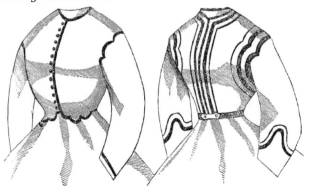

Round waists still hold their places. They can be worn with belts of ribbon, leather, or silk, folded and tied to form a rosette on one side.

Basques are still worn. The prevailing number of points for dresses is three – one only of which is seen behind. They are deep and rounded, some being trimmed with white guipure.

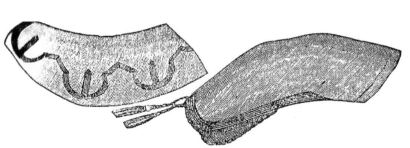

Sleeves cannot be said to have changed much; coat-sleeves are very plainly made.

NEW STYLES OF SLEEVES.

Jackets are very much worn. A self-colored velvet jacket is very useful on many occasions; such a thing is now usually trimmed with small gold hanging buttons, which sometimes take the form of bells, and sometimes of elongated pears and small flowers. Many Senorita-jackets are vandyked round the edge and dotted all over with beads; others are made of either pearl-gray or groseille-satin, and bordered with Cluny guipure, worked with pearls.

A SENORITA BODY.

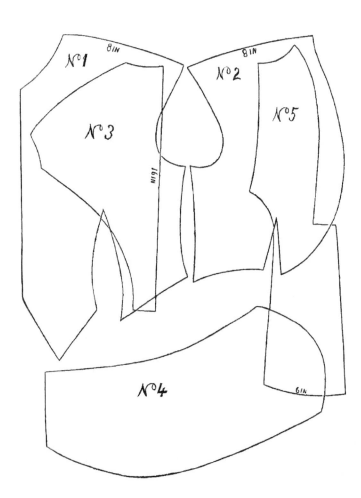

We give, this month, a pattern of a Senorita Body, rounded off in the front, and forming a large square Postillion Jacket at the back, at a Waistcoat to be worn underneath: the style is shown on the two figures above, except that, as some ladies may not like the square form of the waistcoat, we have given it with double points at the waist, (for which see diagram on next page,) which will, we think, be most worn. The pattern is for a lady of medium height, measuring 34 1/2 inches round the chest. We have given the pattern complete, consisting of back, side-piece, with its postillion skirt, front, sleeve, and the front of waistcoat, which is sewn in with the shoulder and side-seams of the body.

Skirts are made as long as ever for home wear. The looped-up skirts are more fashionable than ever, from the fact of their being economical; they are made of every conceivable material and color, from solid scarlet to plain white moreen, and trimmed in every manner. Bias bands, stitched on the machine, are neat and elegant; and we have seen some trimmed with fur; but fur never was intended to be put to such a use as that.

Evening dresses are passing through a remarkable change. The bertha, instead of passing round the edge of the bodice at nearly the same width all round, now, rather than otherwise, assumes the shape of a scarf. Tarletanes and thin muslins are composed of many diaphanous skirts over a puffed under-skirt. The bodies are slightly pointed back and front. Jackets, made of lace, will be stylish and pretty for spring wear. They can be made in either shape of either black or white dotted net, and trimmed with black or white thread or Cluny laces. Some sew colored ribbons under the edge, giving them a bright and more finished look. Buckles, ear-rings, and brooches of immense size, are popular; those made of silver are the prettiest, as the others, unless of gold, have such a cheap look. Clasps, for short sleeves, are also worn.

Peterson's Magazine, March 1866

ROBE DRESS.

De laine robe of a delicate pearl ground, ornamented with large and small bouquets of bright-colored flowers, apparently caught on the dress by rosettes of variegated ribbons. The Zouave is trimmed with a bright border.

A charming promenade or travelling suit is of cuir-colored cambric or linen, bordered with a band of a darker shade edged with a waved design in black. The *paletôt* is in the Louis XV. style, half tight, fitting with large flap-pockets at the back, stamped with three large buttons. The front is made to resemble a long waistcoat, and is trimmed with pockets and narrow borderings of black. We recommend this style of *paletôt* for all kinds of suits. It is also very stylish made of black silk, and admits of much ornamentation.

ROBE DRESS.

Skirt of steel-colored de laine, stamped to resemble an embroidery of jet beads. Garibaldi waist of blue de laine, stamped to simulate braiding.

Full suits of Winsey will be worn for travelling. These suits consist of a gored petticoat trimmed with a black and white stamped velvet, which, can now be had from one to five inches wide. The dress skirt should be trimmed with straps about six inches long, which ornament the dress when flowing, or loop it when required. With the dress is worn a short, loose sack of the Winsey, ornamented with large pearl buttons.

All dresses are made *en traine* at the back, and short enough in front to show the tips of the boots.

Bodies are made round and worn with a belt about three inches wide, shaped to the figure, dotted over with beads, and fastened at the side with a small rosette.

Expense is frequently the objection made to many of the new styles we give, but our subscribers should bear in mind that the same ideas may be carried out to suit modest purses, and at the same time be very attractive. An old garment may be remodelled by one of our plates, and be made quite fashionable.

With regard to stuff petticoats, if the Winsey or Moreen extends up half a yard, it will be found quite sufficient, the rest can be eked out by an old dyed silk, which will answer every purpose, feel lighter, and be decidedly less expensive. An entire skirt of white moreen, of coarse texture, trimmed with three straight rows of narrow black velvet, costs in the stores sixteen dollars. A much handsomer skirt can be made for six dollars if economy will lend a hand, and bring out some old silk or alpaca for the top of it.

Godey's Lady's Book, April 1866

WALKING DRESS.

Walking Dress of Silver-Gray Silk. – Basque to match, cut not to fit the figure closely. The skirt trimmed with blue silk, and inserting of black laid over it flat. The basque trimmed round the neck to match the skirt, with lapels in front, finished with three tassels of blue and silver.

Black dresses, striped with white, and white dresses, striped with black, have been so long in favor, that we are not surprised to hear that the white stripes are at last to be superseded by gold ones. It is a pleasant change, for white in winter certainly looks very uncomfortable. These dresses are trimmed with black silk and with narrow silk braid, which matches the gold stripe.

As a fact, wide waistbands are going decidedly out of fashion; and the rosette, which we mentioned in our last number, gains favor every day. As the season advances, too, they must be very popular, being made of the same colors as the dress.

HOUSE DRESS.

Home Dress of Emerald Green Silk. – The skirt gored and wide, bound with a large cable-cord, trimmed with long hanging buttons of black jet; and smaller ones on the sleeves at the hand, and the same ornamenting the waistband.

Skirts were never so thoroughly trained – indeed, it appears to be the rule to have the bottom of the skirt three times and a half wider than the hips. This tendency to narrow and lengthen the skirt has given the impetus to the Gabrielle. Pockets are often placed at the back of the skirts to these dresses.

Waists remain high and plain – the only difference is, that some have them with two points. The waist is often cut on the cross instead of lengthwise of the material, thus ensuring a more satisfactory result; but we would advise our readers to try this on something of no value first, as it would be a waste of material should they fail with the other.

BRAIDED BODY.

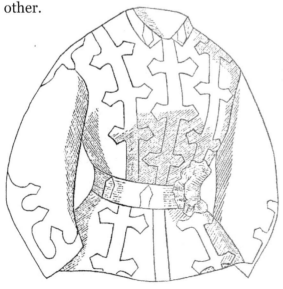

Jackets are more popular than ever, and are frequently seen upon all occasions. The Raphael jacket is a novelty which has lately appeared. It is buttoned straight down the front, does not fit the figure, and is cut out squarely at the top, so as to admit of the *guimpe* underneath being seen. For dressy occasions it can be cut short; but it is generally worn as long as a paletot. It is made of heavy materials, such as velvet and cloth, and the trimmings are of the most sober description.

Peterson's Magazine, April 1866

Thin dresses are to be gored this season by being mounted on a stiff lining. The seams of neutral tints will be corded heavily with a contrasting color.

Many robe dresses have also appeared of entirely new designs, and more suited to the popular taste than those of previous seasons. Though we could not forbear admiring the artistic and exquisite designs of last year, yet they were generally of such gigantic proportions and of such bright colors that few persons could wear them.

ROBE DRESS.

Skirt of fawn-colored de laine, bordered on the edge by a wide band of rich blue, headed by a narrow stripe of gold-color and black. Above this band are festoons of gray flowers, caught up by medallions. Over the plain fawn-colored corsage is a jacket of black de laine, trimmed with a band of gold-color and black.

A very effective robe, styled the Madeline, is gored and cut without plaits at the waist, skirt and body in one piece. It is made of white mohair alpaca, spotted with black and trimmed with bands of Mexican blue silk studded with jet buttons resembling nails. The great feature of the dress is in the side bodies, which are continued down upon the skirt forming coat tails rather than sashes. They are fifteen inches in width at the base, and have simulated pockets. The tails or sashes are repeated in front but are shorter and not so wide. The silk forms a narrow border to all the edges and round the bottom of the skirt. This style of dress is suitable for silk, goats' hair, alpaca or any kind of wool goods. The same design answers also for *piqué* or cambric, but for wash goods we think it better to simulate the sashes by braid, wash-ribbon, or cambric of a contrasting color.

EVENING DRESS.

Dress of white tarlatane, richly trimmed with a waved band of maize tarlatane, edged with black lace. The sprays are embroidered with black and white floss, and the flowers are formed of maize-colored tarlatane.

Coat sleeves seem to have taken a new lease of life. They are, however, varied in different ways. Some are capped by a large puff trimmed with straps of velvet worked over with jet or crystal beads. Others have a short flowing sleeve sewed in with an almost tight coat sleeve. Another style is plain on top but the outside half of the sleeve is laid in four plaits meeting in the centre of the wrist, which is sufficiently wide to pass the hand through. The trimming consists of velvet loops and cameos.

Sleeveless jackets, now so much in request, are made up in various styles. Some are rounded in front, others straight. Many are cut with a point on the shoulder forming an epaulette, though the straight shoulder is equally fashionable. The novel and tasteful decorations of two we would like to photograph on the minds of our readers. One is of pearl-colored silk of a charming shade, chain-stitched with white and trimmed with a border of ruby velvet buttons studded with steel, nestling in a bed of soft, white, downy feathers. Another is of rose-colored silk chain-stitched with black and trimmed with lozenges of rose-colored silk richly ornamented with embroidery and beads.

Godey's Lady's Book, May 1866

Sleeves still continue in the old coat fashion. We do not know why, unless that they are both comfortable and convenient. Thin dresses will have loose sleeves, however, and in the same style as was formerly termed "Angel."

Sashes, with wide ends, are very much worn at present with dressy out-door toilets, and likewise with evening toilets. They have usually three ends to them, and the richest are made of velvet.

DINNER DRESS.

Evening dresses are rather giving place to those suitable for the sea-side. We only wish we had space to detail some of the prettiest which we have seen. Many of these are made in white or colored Brussels net, which proves more durable than tulle. Large diamond bullionnes, about three-quarters of a yard up the skirt, which is made without goring, is a very favorite style. One of this kind, made in pink, was linked at the point of every diamond by a large pearl; another, in white, caught together by gold coins.

A very stylish tulle skirt was gored plain first, and on this bullions, arranged lengthways, and graduated narrow at the waist and broad at the hem. Ribbon velvet was placed between each puffing, and a narrow box-pleated flounce round the edge. A very stylishly made black tulle had the back and front breadths robed. This was done by puffings of tulle dove-tailed, a row of pleated tulle dotted and edged with real straw trimming arranged between each, and on either side of the entire trimming. Of course, the points were placed downward. On the bottom of the skirt, at the side, a large vandyke, point upward, was described by a similar trimming of puffed tulle and straw, and this nearly went round the rest of the skirt, but not reaching above the knees.

The fashion of trimming the backs of the dresses is increasing. Long sash ends are simulated with good effect. Thus on a gray silk dress, a blue silk sash terminating with long fringe, will be simulated on the back breadths of the skirt. Crinoline is at last disappearing in evening toilets, although it is still seen under promenade and morning dresses. But for evening wear, starched petticoats are now adopted instead of steel cages. These petticoats are made quite plain round the hips, and have several flounces from the knees downward. About four those skirts are worn at one time.

Waists are made in so many ways, that not one in particular can be called most fashionable. Very many of the dresses are cut in the Princess form; and it seems to be a favorite, although it requires a very round figure to adopt a fashion so trying.

WAIST OF DOTTED NET.

Black nets are also much trimmed with satin pipings. One in this style had a tunic described by three rows of white satin piping placed on the skirt. Another row of satin piping headed a box-pleated frill, bound at both edges with white satin, and carried all round the hem. In the center of the space between the tunic a bunch of bows and ends of black net, edged with white satin, and fringed, were very prettily arranged. Two similar knots of bows were placed one on each side of the tunic as it turned off near the hem. Cameos ornamented the bows.

Peterson's Magazine, May 1866

The Art of the Hoop: 1860 - 1869

ORGANDY ROBE.

The ground is white, striped with a delicate shade of violet, while the front breadth is brocaded with bouquets and garlands of flowers of the most brilliant hues. The same style of robe may be had in different colors.

Low corsages are frequently cut heart-shaped both in front and back, or cut straight down and turned over in *revers,* the space being filled in both back and front with puffings of tulle.

It is no unusual thing to see long sleeves with low dresses in the Louis XVI. style. A happy idea in the way of a trimming consists of velvet laid square across the corsage both front and back, separating at the arm, and half passing over and half round the under part of the sleeve.

SUMMER ROBE FOR A YOUNG LADY.

Skirt of white organdy, dotted with black, having on each breadth a wide stripe of green, with a design in black and white running through the centre. The Garibaldi waist is of plain green organdy. This same style of robe is reproduced in all the desirable light colors.

We find also a charming assortment of fancy jackets, most of them sleeveless, but finished on the shoulders by an epaulette. A very stylish little affair, called the Jarnac, is of white Cashmere dotted over with black beads and trimmed with a fringe of jet and gold. Another, known as the Metternich, is of a basket-work material formed of thick cords of blue and white silk woven together. It is open In front, describes two points at the waist, curves upwards on the hips, and descends in a basque at the back. The trimming is a fringe of gilt and crystal.

SPRING COSTUME.

Jacket of white alpaca, trimmed with narrow bead trimming and jet pendants. The collar is one of the latest styles, being merely a tiny standing band at the back, and falling points in front.

We are at last able to recommend a reliable fluting machine. It consists of two corrugated wheels turned by a crank, and heated by means of a lamp placed underneath. The material runs between these wheels, and passes out in perfect flutes. We know this machine to be good, as we have used it.

Godey's Lady's Book, June 1866

Evening dresses at no one time have confined themselves less to one fashion. They nearly all have a pieced up look that is astonishing – so many dresses look as they were originally two. They are much wider round bottom than ever, and are very much trimmed.

THE SICILIAN ROBE.

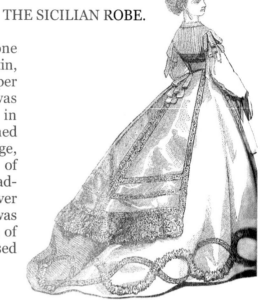

The prettiest Ball-Dress we have seen for some time, and one very suitable for a bride's *trousseau*, was made of pink satin, covered with white tulle, spangled over with silver stars. The upper skirt was trimmed round the edge with a light silver fringe, and was looped up at the left side with a chain of pink roses graduating in size as they approach the waist. The pink satin bodice was trimmed with a drapery of white tulle folds, edged with silver fringe, somewhat narrower than that round the skirt. There were tufts of roses on each shoulder, and one in front of the bodice. The head-dress consisted of a silver band and of a spray of roses, with silver leaves at the left side. A white tulle veil, spangled with silver, was fastened in with the comb, and confined again at the termination of the chain of roses which decorates the skirt. The comb has a chased silver top.

Jackets are now made in many very coquettish shapes. They are mostly sleeveless, and or ornamented with either Cluny guipure, or embroidery, and are made in either cashmere, foulard, or silk; some, also, are made in the new basque shape of muslin for morning use.

WALKING DRESS, OR IN-DOOR TOILET.
Home Dress of Pearl Gray Silk. – The trimmings of velvet laid in scallops, and edged with guipure lace. Bonnet of purple silk, trimmed with lace.

Dresses with *simulated* double skirts are likely to be more popular than ever. The upper skirt is seldom straight; as generally the trimming describes scallops, or vandykes, more or less accentuated. The prettiest form is the tunic, which is very short in front and very long at the back. The trimming which simulates this tunic, whether it be cross bands or velvet ribbon, should be edged either with narrow black lace or with fringe. These additions impart reality to the otherwise false tunic.

Peterson's Magazine, June 1866

This very pretty apron is made of white mull muslin, and is trimmed with several rows of narrow black braid. It fastens at the back with small buttons. If required for everyday wear, it can be made of brown Holland; and chain-stitch worked in single Berlin wool, either scarlet or black, can be substituted for the braid.

The newest bretelles are formed of alternate squares of Cluny insertion and colored ribbon plaited together to form a checked pattern. These braces pass over the shoulders, and are caught on a belt of silk covered with Cluny, which is fastened at the side with a rosette. This little novelty called the Navarette, is frequently strapped across the chest and at the back by a band of Cluny and ribbon.

BASQUE CORSAGE.

Suitable for Silk Reps or Alpaca.

Our Fashion Editress can furnish the plain pattern of this corsage for 50 cents, and the trimmed pattern for $1.

Jackets of Cluny and black guipure made half-tight fitting and worn over the same shape in colored silk are exceedingly stylish. Most all summer dresses are made with jackets, some worn with a waistcoat in the Louis XIV. style, and others sleeveless and worn over a white waist.

Tablier dresses are much admired; in most cases the skirt laps over the apron or tablier, and is scalloped and trimmed with rosettes of lace or ribbon. The tablier being underneath has much the effect of an underskirt. Flowers are substituted for the rosettes when the dress is intended for evening wear.

ROBE DRESS.

Walking-dress of coffee-colored percale, ornamented with fancy borderings of black woven in the material. The corsage is made with a deep basque, which can be removed when the dress is worn in the house.

ROBE DRESS.

This very tasteful robe is of white organdy, sprinkled over with scarlet rose-buds and green leaves. The skirt is made with a deep flounce, headed by a band matching the flowers thrown over the dress.

Godey's Lady's Book, July 1866

Striped dresses are confined more principally to textures, like foulards, than any others, because the skirts are not necessarily gored – although some improperly have even these gored. Skirts are generally made long; but those intended for the street not so long as formerly, as nearly every one now wear their dresses looped up. White muslin dresses will be much worn this season, both plain and trimmed with colors. Silk petticoats, too, are very fashionable with white muslin dresses looped over them with rosettes, etc. This seems a divergence from the old rule of wearing the best outermost; but it is the fashion to reverse the order.

For a simple every-day toilet there is nothing prettier than a black silk skirt, scalloped out round the edge and looped up over either a Mexican blue or a mauve cashmere petticoat. The petticoat does not require any trimming – not even a fluted flounce. Those who are compelled to be economical make the lower half only of the petticoat of cashmere, and the upper half of twilled calico; the *chemise Russe* is made of cashmere to match the petticoat.

CARRIAGE DRESS.

Silk paletots are to be seen trimmed with white Cluny lace; they are conspicuous, but somewhat lighter-looking than those that are loaded with jet.

WALKING DRESS.

Jackets, made entirely of lace, are one of the novelties of the year. They are in black-and-white guipure, and worn half tight over jackets of the same shape in colored silk. These lace jackets have no sleeves. A very pretty muslin Garibaldi, made with braces, waistband, and trimmed on the sleeves, from the shoulders to the wrist, of blue silk is very pretty; scarlet is also much worn.

Peterson's Magazine, July 1866

Gored dresses which have been so persistently fashionable for such a length of time, are, if possible, more in favor than ever. In fact, everything is gored. In front and at the sides the skirt should just clear the ground, while the back should slope into a decided train.

The Princess robe necessitates a seam down the front of the skirt, which by some persons is very much disliked; other methods are, therefore, adopted. For instance, in some skirts we find the front and back breadths perfectly straight, and only the side breadths gored. This style we recommend for muslins and lawns. Another style has a bias seam directly down the back, which forms an admirable train, and is very generally adopted, particularly for evening dresses. Skirts to be worn with jackets are formed entirely of small gores, and fit the figure the same as a Princess dress, but have the advantage of a seam at the side instead of down the centre of the front.

NEW STYLE OF DRESS.

Dress of white alpaca, trimmed with blue silk cord to simulate a basque. The skirt is richly ornamented with blue silk cord, and loops of blue velvet.

The Greek style of dress is fighting hard for ascendency, and for evening is exceedingly stylish. Imagine a rose-colored silk skirt, with overskirt and body of white silk. This overskirt is in the *peplum* style, laid in deep box plaits at the waist. The skirt in the front and back is but half a yard deep, but slopes gradually down to the sides, which hang in quite deep points finished with tassels. We should also add that the skirt is slit up on each side to the waist. The trimming consists usually of velvet bands or rows of stiver or gold braid. The corsage is cut square both back and front, and laid in very deep box plaits, and the sleeve is very short and perfectly plain.

These Peplums have lately been introduced for promenade suits. The Greek, which we have already described, is generally reserved for ball *toilette*, while the Directoire is for street or home wear .The distinction is that latter describes a deep point at the back and front, and hollowed out on the sides. It is slit up to the waist both in the back and front, the points being trimmed with acorns or tassels. Wide waistbands are frequently worn with these dresses; they are fastened at the side by a large rosette.

The loose sack is still a favorite, and for a suit is generally made sleeveless; the dress sleeve being all that is required. With tight fitting *paletôts* square or pointed pelerines are very popular. They are trimmed with Cluny lace, beads, or embroidery.

GRENADINE ROBE.

The ground is of a lovely peach blossom hue, with rich designs in a darker shade; corsage made plain and lined with silk. The belt is of Cluny, lined with silk, and fastened at the side with a rosette with fringed ends.

To all those who wish to pay homage to that fickle goddess Fashion, but are obliged to retrench as much as possible, we recommend the removable basques. They have all the effect of a street basquine, and are made in various ways; some slope off suddenly in front and extend down at the back one-half or three-quarters of a yard. They hook round the waist and are belled on with a wide waistband. The delusion is complete, and thus a very stylish walking costume is obtained without much increasing expense, and in a very short time. We have mentioned these little accessories before, but we enter more into details as they are so extensively patronized, and possess so many advantages. They are very convenient for travelling dresses and *piqués*, and when made of silk form an exceedingly effective and elegant *toilette*. Some are slit up to the waist at the back, and others are cut on each hip.

Cut skirts are very much worn, the upper part which reaches just below the knee is cut in points or scallops, and falls over the lower part of the skirt, which is set on underneath like a flounce. We should also add, that the upper part of the skirt, besides having two breadths less than the other, is also slightly gored, and is quite plain in front, all the fulness being thrown to the back. Wash dresses are trimmed with straps of insertion through which bright ribbons are run. Sometimes they are carried down the front covering the seams, or else they are arranged to simulate a basque or tunic skirt.

Sleeveless jackets continue quite the rage, and when intended to wear over a white dress, are generally of some bright-colored silk, such as pink, cerise, violet, blue, or green. The long sleeves of the dress should be puffed and confined by bands of silk matching the jacket. The trimming is generally Cluny lace or crystal fringe. These colored jackets are also very effective over a pearl-colored skirt; in this case, however, the skirt should be trimmed with ribbon or silk matching the jacket.

For morning wear at the sea-side, Senorita or Zouave jackets made of scarlet cloth or cashmere trimmed with black, or blue trimmed with white are very popular. Unless in midsummer, it is generally requisite to have something a little warm over the shoulders in the early morning, and for this purpose these little jackets will be found very convenient besides being very effective.

A very pretty dress from the Demorest establishment is of white coutil, tightly gored, and cut square at the neck, but merely to the depth of one finger. The trimming is a white wash ribbon, embossed with a Grecian pattern formed of black dots, and arranged to simulate a tunic skirt. Large pearl and jet buttons are carried down the centre seam of the dress in front.

Godey's Lady's Book, August 1866

HOUSE DRESS.

The skirts of dresses are more gored than ever. The front width is gored on each side all the way up from the bottom, and the remaining widths, with the exception of the one in the back, (which is perfectly straight,) are gored on the bias, making the skirt sit almost close to the figure. There must be no more fullness allowed in the front than absolutely necessary, and only one large box-plait at the back. Town dresses are all looped up, and almost invariably over white skirts.

The fashion is again coming up of cutting the front of high-necked waists with little lapels, which are turned back, and are worn with a lace bodice inside. A great many dress-makers cut the skirt of the basques off, and with the body plain they can be attached at pleasure.

WALKING DRESS.

Round waists are much worn, and with the skirt gored, and a belt-ribbon, they have the effect of the Princess shape.

Narrow stripes are quite fashionable; but stripes should never be gored, as it gives a garment a pointed look, which is ugly.

Evening dresses are made, when low in the neck, about four inches deep, and are filled up above by a tucker, which is formed of lace, inserting, etc. Grenadines and organdies will be very fashionable for the fall. There is a new muslin out this summer, which is called by some Tarletan muslin, and looks like it, too; it is very light, and makes a stylish dress. Lace capes and jackets, both black and white, are very much used for evening wear.

Braces are very much worn, and are made in guipure and velvet, and guipure and silk, which are worn over high or low white bodies. They are particularly suitable for young ladies, and it is not necessary for them to be like the dress. These braces are made of squares of guipure, alternating with squares of the silk. They are of an equal width all their length, and are joined to a round waistband about four inches deep, made in the same manner, and fastening on the side with a big rosette of silk and guipure. When these braces are in light blue or pink silk, they are very coquettish; but in black velvet or silk, they have the advantage of being suitable to be worn with any toilets.

CAPE MAY IN FULL TOILET.   CAPE MAY IN BATHING TOILET.

Cape May and its Toilets. – Our subscribers know, we suppose, that Cape May is one of the most popular sea-beaches on the Atlantic coast. One of our artists has just been there, and has illustrated the toilets he saw. In one picture, we have the belles and beaux, in full dress, when walking or flirting on the beach; in the other, we have the same persons when in bathing costume. Those who have never been at Cape May will have a hearty laugh, we suspect, over the metamorphose. We, who have often been at the Cape, can testify that the picture is not exaggerated.

Peterson's Magazine, August 1866

The short dresses are made in the following manner: – They are from four to four and a-half yards wide round the bottom, being generally formed of material about one yard wide. Three widths are gored, and in the centre at the back two of the slanting sides are joined together; but this is an exception: the other widths are generally joined one straight side with a slanting one; the front width is out apron-wise – slanted off on either side. The way to cut the widths is to fold them across slantways, and to cut them from the top on one side to the bottom on the other, as for a chemise. This process can, however, only be employed when the material has no wrong side and no top and bottom pattern, otherwise one-half of each width could only be used for the body, the sleeves, and the trimming.

The under-skirt, longer than the dress, is exactly of the same width and shape; neither has any pleats whatever, not even at the back. They are, in fact, cut much after the pattern of a lamp-shade, narrow at the top, and gradually widening towards the bottom. The short dress may be of the Princess shape, now beginning to be called by an old name, *fourreau*.

A pretty autumn fashion is that of the tiny jacket without sleeves, to wear over a white bodice. Not only has it no sleeves, but it has no armholes even, being open from under the arm to the waist; the back and front are only joined together by the waistband. The jacket is rounded and open in front. It is made of red cashmere, trimmed with white or black guipure; or of mauve, pink, or blue silk, trimmed with the same. This style of jacket only looks well over a pretty white muslin bodice with long sleeves. Any fancy belt or waistband can be worn with it.

The Englishwoman's Domestic Magazine, September 1866

The fashion of festooning dresses has given rise to a new style of dress. We refer to the *robe fourreau*, which at first did not take well at all, but is now universally adopted by Parisian *modestes*. The dress skirt is cut quite short and worn over a petticoat of good walking length. The latter is generally gored and trimmed with an elaborate design in velvet or braid sprinkled with beads. The dress skirt is cut in bunches of scallops to simulate looping, and ornamented on the top of each festoon by an *appliqué* ornament of silk or velvet. A *paletôt* or basquine with hood made of the same material as the dress completes the costume. When a very dressy costume is required, the underskirt is of silk, while the upper is of poplin or some similar material. It must be remembered, however, that as this style of dress is somewhat conspicuous, the only colors suitable for the street are the dark shades of mode, brown, and flax gray; the latter is the new color of the season.

FANCY APRON.

This apron may be made in silk, alpaca, or Holland. Silk trimmed with a ruche of the same, and stitched by the sewing machine, with colored silk, and the design worked in colored braid, will make a very stylish apron. Alpaca will be less costly, and look very well. Holland, braided with scarlet, and the ruche stitched with scarlet ingrain cotton, will make a serviceable apron for morning wear.

Aprons are again becoming fashionable. For morning we see the dainty little bib apron of white muslin edged with a tiny fluted ruffle. Some are made with the skirt frilled on to the band or bib, while others, again, are gored; the bib and centre piece of the apron being in one piece. The latter is decidedly the newest and best style, and makes up charmingly in black silk. The Pompadour apron, another novelty, is plaited on to a pointed waistband. The edge of the apron is cut in three deep festoons trimmed with Cluny lace and ornamented with a bow placed on top of each festoon.

A very good style of peplum, which may be modified for street or evening wear, is as follows: It is open at the sides where it falls in deep points finished with long tassels, the front part of the peplum is much shorter than the back, and it is finished with a rich trimming laid on in a Grecian pattern. For the street it would be of heavy black *gros grains* trimmed with jet *passementerie*, and for evening it would be of light silk richly ornamented with Cluny lace, and edged with silver bells.

Many dresses of solid silk are trimmed with bands of striped silk, and have tablier or apron pieces of the striped silk. The body is a long basque cut with three long and well accentuated points edged with a band of cameos and hanging buttons. The front is a short waistcoat of striped silk.

A rich dinner dress is frequently made of a striped or figured silk made rather short and worn over a skirt of solid contrasting color. Three bands of ribbon or velvet are fastened at the waist on either side, and apparently festoon the skirt at the lower edge.

For evening dresses the corsages are growing shorter and shorter, sleeves are almost non-existent, and a very wide sash known as the *enfant de chœur* is worn round the waist and tied in a bow at the side. The style is extremely *decolleté*, not at all picturesque, and so absurd and ugly, that we hope it may not be adopted.

If the *decolleté* or very low dresses are admired, we would suggest that the neck should be veiled by a tulle scarf thrown over the shoulders, or a tucker of tulle sewed to the dress and drawn up to the throat by a ribbon or velvet.

Ladies Clothing. – It has been ascertained that a linsey dress, a thick cloth cloak, a scarlet flannel upper petticoat, a steel skeleton skirt, a flannel under petticoat, and all the rest of the clothing worn in winter by a young lady of eighteen, of the average height, weighs upwards of fourteen pounds. Few ladies have enough to do with weights and scales to have a clear idea of the weight represented by fourteen pounds. If they will take the trouble to carry a seven pound weight in each hand up and down the room for five minutes, they will soon be convinced that such a weight is far too great to be carried about in the shape of clothes. There can be no doubt that it greatly wastes the strength.
Godey's Lady's Book, September 1866

The skirts of dresses no longer have any pleats in front. They are as wide as ever around the bottom; but very narrow at the waist. Every width is gored, with the exception of the one at the back; and the pleats are at the back only. Crinolines, usually, are not so wide as some have worn them, but maintain a happy medium, which is comfortable without being vulgar. The newest ones have no steels above the knee. The skirts of dresses have very long trains, which is kept out by stiff facings and starched ruffles sewed on the crinoline.

WALKING DRESS.

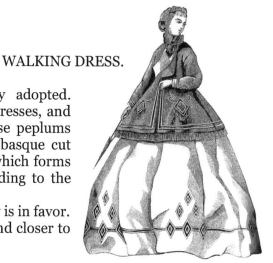

WALKING DRESS.

Round waists are universally adopted. Peplums are frequently made to dresses, and are worn or not at pleasure. These peplums are nothing more or less than a basque cut from the body, with a waistband which forms the belt. They are trimmed according to the taste of the wearer.

The open Watteau style of body is in favor.

Sleeves are longer than ever, and closer to the wrist.

Evening dresses are made very low in the neck, so low, in fact, that they are scarcely wider than a broad belt. Of course, they are fitted so as to come, at least, to the top of the shoulder with a tucker, which is composed of lace inserting, and a velvet which runs through it. The skirts have immense trains, and these trains are very difficult things to get it to hang correctly. Remember one thing, always have your skirt cut over the crinoline you intend wearing with it. This saves a great amount of trouble.

Moire waistbands, with long sash ends, are now frequently embroidered with either crystal beads or with steel spangles. They are fastened at the side with a rosette, and are now considered more stylish than the plain ones clasped in the center of the waist with a buckle. Wide scarf-sashes, fringed with Lama, are worn with dresses trimmed with Lama fringe.
Peterson's Magazine, September 1866

Sleeves are of the coat shape, some varied with a large loose puff at the top sewed into a straight band. For full dress, the flowing sleeve is considered the most *recherché*. The outside of the sleeve measures one yard in length, while the inside seam is but the length of the arm. It is merely caught together at the lower edge, and hangs free; underneath it is generally worn a tight coat-sleeve.

Most all skirts are gored, but the tightly gored are in the ascendent. Of the latter style we notice one of aluminum gray, with rows of Cluny and Magenta velvet running down each seam. The front ones are trimmed down for the space of three-quarters of a yard, and connect with the next, which is somewhat longer by an arch formed of the trimming. This trimming continues all round the skirt, but is not connected on the front breadth. The waist is a Peplum basque, finished with long tassels.

The Art of the Hoop: 1860 - 1869

PROMENADE SUIT FOR A YOUNG LADY.

The whole toilet is made of poplin striped black and white. The plain skirt is looped up at equal distance by white silk tabs edged with black braid and fastened by a cameo. It shows a flounced petticoat, edged and headed by black braid. The long *paletôt* is entirely bordered with black braid, and buttoned with cameos. Two long white silk tabs, edged also with black braid, cross each other on the shoulder, and descend down the bottom of the garment, being fastened with cameos. White silk cuffs and collar.

Jackets are worn of every conceivable shape. The greatest novelty in this line is the Sultana, which not only is made without sleeves, but has no side bodies. The best idea we can give of it is to compare it to the front and back of a Senorita, or short Zouave jacket, joined near the waist with a narrow band. It is made of silk or cashmere, dotted over or embroidered with beads, and finished with guipure or Cluny lace.

Negligé jackets are made perfectly loose, quite short, and finished with revers, They are generally of fancy cloth, trimmed with large buttons, and the revers faced with a bright color.

Armenian jackets resemble the Senorita as are sleeveless, the exception is that they are shorter. The Selica jacket, another novelty, is cut square in front, and buttons down for about four inches. The lower edge of the jacket describes an arch both back and front, and falls in points beneath the arms.

Most of these jackets necessitate an under waist of some kind, and for morning or *demi-toilette*, the waists are made either of white alpaca, cashmere, or Foulard, ornamented with rows of feather-stitch, executed in black silk, or else a delicate braiding. Many persons much prefer these materials, as they remain clean for a long time, do not rumple, and will do up admirably.

The Macbeth jacket, lately brought out by the Maison Tilman, is of silk, velvet, or cashmere. In front it is round like a Senorita, the back is a basque cut in deep turrets. The trimming consists of a band of velvet studded with beads or buttons and bordered on the sides by Cluny lace. The same trimming is arranged both on the top and bottom of the sleeve.

Skirts continue to be festooned on the street, and the newest arrangement is the dress-looper just introduced by M'me Demorest. For each breadth there is a little cord three inches long, finished on each end with a little sheath-like attachment, which is adjusted on each breadth, and festoons the dress most gracefully.

Others again merely tie up the skirt at the back, *à la lavense* or washwoman style. When the skirt is tied up with a large sash, it suggests the idea of the priests' cassock, and from this the knot has been christened the "Bishop's bow."

Godey's Lady's Book, October 1866

CARRIAGE DRESS.

The skirts of dress for home wear are very long. All the widths are gored, and are very wide – quite six yards. The hoops are very small at the waist, and very wide at the bottom. Some people have ruffles, made of muslin, sewed on the hoops to support the dress-skirt.

Although short dresses are slowly coming into favor, looped-up skirts prevail for the present, and skirts are to be seen on the most fashionable promenades, either looped up, or the trimming so arranged as to simulate that effect.

White silk petticoats are, also, embroidered with black purse silk, and are trimmed with black chenille fringe. As plain white silk petticoats have been very general since the commencement of the season, many ladies, who are economically inclined, are now freshening them up by the addition of either black chenille fringe or colored chenille, tipped with crystal drops. These petticoats are not always very costly, for they can be made of slips which have been used under ball-dresses; the train (indispensable with an evening toilet) is cut away, and the upper part remains usually very fresh.

All skirts are now tied at the back with sashes; the fashion is spreading, and, instead of plain sashes, the ends are now ornamented.

WALKING SUIT.

Jackets for *neglige* are still cut in what is called the sailor form, which is so convenient; *revers* are now added in front, and the jackets are made of more fancy materials, such as Pyrenean cloth, striped scarlet and white, with a thin, gold line, the *revers* in front of scarlet cashmere, and at each point of the collar there is an anchor, in mother-of-pearl or gold. Soft white flannel, dotted with black chenille, trimmed with black velvet *revers* and oxidized silver buttons, enameled with black, is another style.

Petticoats are a costly novelty now-a-days. They are made of every conceivable texture, and are trimmed to match. Some are ornamented with bands of Oriental embroidery, worked in silks of divers hues, while others are trimmed to match the over-skirt. The latter is in the best taste.

Peplums are the novelty of the year, and are very pretty on many occasions. Nothing is more elegant than them little red peplums, enriched with Algerian embroideries, passementeries, black braiding, applique of black or white guipure. The peplums are lined with silk of different colors; thus a peplum in coral color, braided with black, should be lined with black silk. The first peplums had coat sleeves like paletots; now they are worn with large pointed and flowing sleeves, open nearly from top to bottom, and show the sleeve of the dress, or of a white bodice. Now the flowing sleeve is being worn, but with a tight under-sleeve to keep out the cold. Those flowing sleeves are very graceful; they are finished on at the bottom with a tassel similar to that hanging from the points of the peplum.

White peplums are encircled with lama, white silk, or crystal fringes. The Benoiton knot fastened behind red peplums, is entirely made of gimp or black lace. The knot of the white peplums is of white moire, embroidered with gold or jet. White peplums are worn in full dress, and as an opera cloak.

For ball dresses the peplum is generally fastened to the bodice, while with walking toilets it is only fastened with a waistband worn over the body. The antique peplum is made of crepe, fastened on the shoulder with a cameo.

Evening dresses, unless for large parties, are almost universally made of white muslin. There is no particular fashion, however, for them in point of trimmings. Colored silk under-skirts are much worn, with sashes the same color as the skirt.

Peterson's Magazine, October 1866

PEPLUM PALETOT.

Made of gray cloth, trimmed with black braid and jet buttons. The points of the peplum both back and front are finished with large jet drops.

The other style of Peplum is the Directoire, and is just the opposite to what we have described. In front and at the back is a long accentuated point slit up at the waist, and the sides are hollowed out. A good idea of this style may be had by referring to the Peplum *paletôt* on page 383. [*described above*] ↗

For travelling or home wear the Peplum basque mounted on a band is generally adopted. This *basque Independante* is worn with a plain waist, and is, of course, made of the same material as the dress. A fancy waistband is worn with it, and in this way one dress may be made to serve the double purpose of house dress or an acceptable out-door costume. Both of the illustrations given this month may be arranged in this way.

Dresses with short, round waists are very fashionable, and the Empire style is universally adopted, that is, the waist is almost under the arm, it is so short. Broad waistbands are worn, and the sleeves are puffed and separated by wide bands. This style – the gored dress and the Peplum – are the three principal modes for the winter.

As some of our readers do not fully understand what Peplums are, we will again describe them. Peplum skirts or tunics are of two kinds, the Greek, which describes a curve or arch both back and front, and falls on each side in a deep point slit up to the waist. The points are finished with long tassels, the trimming is invariably carried up the sides, and the back is always longer than the front. Sometimes the Peplum skirt is but a quarter of a yard below the waist in front, and in other cases it is as long as an ordinary over-skirt. A very good style of trimming is a band of silk or velvet studded with large buttons, having the effect of nails. Some of the newest Peplums do not meet at the sides by two or three inches, and are then tied together by ribbons or are connected by a border of velvet.

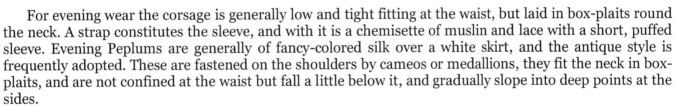

GORED DRESS, WITH PEPLUM BASQUE.

The material is a black and white striped poplin, trimmed with a black and white mixed braid. The epaulettes are formed of very heavy black and white silk fringe. The sash and the points of the peplum are finished with large silk tassels.

For rich dinner dress, sleeveless jackets of Chantilly are much in vogue. They are made with an epaulette, and are worn over colored silk dresses. Loose sacks of Cluny lace are also very much admired.

For evening wear, most bodies are cut low, and trimmed with a rich crystal or pearl fringe. Some are made with removable basques cut with deep points and trimmed with crystal fringe.

A rich waistband worked with crystal or pearl, and fastened with a clasp of filigreed silver, is worn with them. The neck is covered by a chemisette of muslin and lace, which fits close to the throat. The lace on the chemisette is usually lined with a ribbon matching the dress in color.

For evening wear the corsage is generally low and tight fitting at the waist, but laid in box-plaits round the neck. A strap constitutes the sleeve, and with it is a chemisette of muslin and lace with a short, puffed sleeve. Evening Peplums are generally of fancy-colored silk over a white skirt, and the antique style is frequently adopted. These are fastened on the shoulders by cameos or medallions, they fit the neck in box-plaits, and are not confined at the waist but fall a little below it, and gradually slope into deep points at the sides.

Godey's Lady's Book, November 1866

Evening dresses are so varied, in point of trimming, the best that we can do is to give a single description. The following toilet will be found both novel and effective: A white tulle dress with a tunic out like a *manteau de cour* over it. This tunic is also of tulle, and is trimmed with two rows of small, well-curled white feathers, and between the rows with large, white daisies studded at regular intervals on the tulle. This decoration is carried up the sides as far as the waist; another tunic, ornamented to correspond, is added in front, and the trimming of daisies and feathers, crossing at the sides, looks extremely well. The bodice is a peplum of blue Oriental silk, fitting close at the waist, and falling on the skirt in two pointed and separated basques, each terminating with a tassel; the peplum takes the same form in front, only it is somewhat shorter. White muslin peplums are *bouillonnes* or tucked in horizontal lines, or else striped with either guipure or Valenciennes insertion, and afterward trimmed round the edge with Valenciennes lace.

PEPLUM.

Peplums have become more comfortable since they have been made to be worn as mere basques, long and fastened with a waistband. This shape is convenient and economical, because it allows one to wear a dress without any paletot or casaque; it is sufficient to add a peplum mounted on a waistband to one's bodice to have an acceptable out-door costume.

WALKING DRESS.

Waists are invariably made with either basques, or plain and round; sometimes they are cut with revers, which are not suited however to all figures.

WAIST.

Jockey Jackets, as they are termed, are still much made in silk and lace, especially blue, the whole rendered in stripes. These are like Garibaldis in appearance, but fit the body, are set into a band, have an ornamental band, collar, and cuffs *en suite*. The sleeves are shaped and also striped. A muslin jacket striped with Cluny insertion, and with the basque fluted, of double muslin, is pretty.

Sleeves, for the street, are made narrow and long. House jackets are made occasionally without any. Some new garments have come out with wide sleeves, but they are not popular.

HOUSE DRESS.

Skirts, which are looped up, are now frequently fastened at every festoon with large daisies, imitated in silk, pinked out at the edges. The front and back are looped up with separate drawings; the front is all drawn up in the usual manner, but the back is tied up in two parts only, so that it falls on the petticoat, as though it were the two wide ends of the sash. This style of fastening up the skirt at the back does not look ungraceful, although it reads so. Petticoats are worn in muslin-de-laine and poplin.

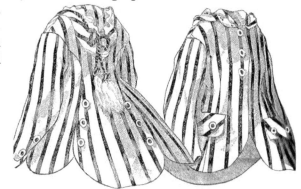

BACK AND FRONT OF A NEW BASQUE.

LADY'S KITCHEN-APRON.

Lady's Kitchen-Apron of Holland, escalloped at the pockets and edge, and sewn over with scarlet wool in button-hole stitch. This apron is ornamental as useful.

Peterson's Magazine, November 1866

Morning dresses are made of a loose princess shape, and very short. Walking dresses are short also, but are worn over long petticoats.

A curious thing we notice in the present fashions is that a short skirt is often worn *over* instead of under a dress. For example, a dress of white and blue striped glace silk, with a high plain bodice and long sleeves; over this is worn a shorter skirt of plain blue silk, rounded in front and at the back, and caught up on each side with tassels of blue silk edged with white chenille and narrow black lace; the bottom of the skirt is trimmed with two strips of white moire antique, edged on either side in the same manner. A square plastron of plain silk is placed over the striped bodice. The epaulettes are blue, the waistband is white, edged with black and white, and has small lapels finished off with fringe.

A dress of pearl-grey poult de soie, trimmed with a deep border of black lace, disposed so as to simulate a court train, over the skirt; the same lace is placed in a treble curved flounce over the front width; it is but very slightly gathered. The bodice is fastened with grey gimp buttons edged round with black lace.

Though ball toilets are not yet seen, we have several *evening* dresses to take note of. Soirées and dinner parties are frequent at this time of the year.

An evening dress for a *mother* is made of nasturtium-coloured satin; in front and at the sides the edge of the skirt barely touches the ground; at the back the widths are all gored, and form a long train much resembling in shape a pigeon's tail. The trimming is composed of black lace, embroidered with tiny jet beads disposed in revers all round the long widths of the train, and of triangular lace patterns placed round the bottom of the skirt and open the front width. The bodice is demi-high and trimmed with lace and jet; the sleeves, *à la Juive,* are lined with white silk.

Evening dress for a young married lady: – Under-dress of plain pale pink silk; upper-dress, covering merely the back and bides of the first, and open in front, of white silk, with wide strips of pink satin, trimmed with a cross-strip of pink satin, edged with narrow white lace and pearl beads; low bodice of white pleated muslin; corselet of the same material as the upper-skirt, edged with narrow cross-strips of pink satin, white lace, and pearl beads. Coiffure formed of strings of pearls, with a small bunch of pink roses placed upon the left side in the Pompadour style.

An evening dress for a young (unmarried) lady. – Short dress of light gray glacé silk cut out round the bottom in square tabs, edged round with a ruching of pinked-out gray silk; under-skirt of bright light blue silk; low bodice of white pleated muslin; corselet of grey silk, with braces fastened upon the shoulders with large rosettes of grey silk.

Silk tissues seem likely to be more generally worn this winter than clear materials, even for ball dresses; the train is more and more lengthened, and is quite indispensable for evening dresses.

The bodice, separate from the skirt, can become quite an important article of the female toilet; with evening dresses it, is worn of pleated muslin; for the daytime it is made quite after the same pattern as the white ones that were worn in the summer, only the nainsook and jaconet are replaced by silk or velvet, and the strips of embroidery or guipure by trimmings of satin or fancy braid, studded with beads.

The most fashionable are velvet bodices, ornamented with cross stripe of silk or satin, worked with a pattern in soutache and beads.

For the morning bodices of bright blue, red, violet, or white cashmere are worn more than ever; they are trimmed with soutache and jet. Some are covered with narrow bouillons; over all the front part the bouillons are divided by stripe of black silk braid, studded with jet. This is a pattern very becoming to thin people.

Black cashmere bodices may be worn in mourning; they suit some figures better than the plain tight bodies which are made to modern dresses.

The Englishwoman's Domestic Magazine, December 1866

MORNING DRESS.

Made of scarlet poplin, cut in the Princess shape, without any plaits at the waist. It is half tight fitting, and closed down the front with small jet buttons. The trimming, simulating a long tunic, is composed of black braid and narrow poplin tabs edged with black and fastened by jet buttons. The pockets and coat sleeves are ornamented also with black braid and jet. The pointed collar is made of black velvet, and completes the costume.

Short dresses are now all the rage in Paris for promenade costumes, and as the skirts shorten hoops decrease. Those short dresses are much talked of here, but so far have been adopted but by few. Ere long, however, we will be obliged to doff our trains and don short clothes. We think for the street this will be a very sensible idea, for the looped dress is in fact nothing more than a short dress, but vastly more troublesome. It is almost impossible to loop a train, and the effect of trimming is entirely ruined. The plan to be adopted is, in the first place, to wear exceedingly small hoops. The petticoat is just to clear the ground, and to have but little fulness. The dress will be of the same material as the petticoat, but a quarter of a yard shorter, the edge being cut in turrets, scallops, or points. This style will first be adopted for travelling, and, if well received, will be the conventional promenade costume.

FASHIONABLE JACKETS.

Sleeveless jacket of pearl-colored silk, trimmed with black velvet and steel buckles. This style of jacket will look well in velvet trimmed with Cluny lace.

Jacket with hood for morning wear. It is of white cashmere, or cloth trimmed with scarlet and braid and buttons. The hood is lined with scarlet silk, and finished with scarlet and gold tassels.

Fancy underskirts of all kinds are in great requisition. The preference is given to either black or white, though very beautiful ones have appeared in striped materials, also in plain scarlet. The latter will be more in favor later in the season, and will be very generally adopted for skating.

The latest style of collar we hear of is said to be like a gentleman's turn-down collar reversed, the difference being that the edges are turned up from the bottom instead of turning down from the top, If the collar is white, the turned piece is of a bright color, and if the collar is colored, the point turned up is white.

Godey's Lady's Book, December 1866

Evening dresses are a good deal worn with two skirts, the under one of which is silk, and the upper one muslin, or else reversed; but the upper one is always looped up with knots of ribbons or flowers. Peplums are much worn on ball-dresses; they make them of crape embroidered in silk, over covered with a rain of gold, or silver beads. The prettiest we have seen is of white crape, spangled with coral beads, with a coral fringe all round. Those striped with stuffs they call *sultane*, and which are imitations of Eastern materials, are employed to make very dressy day peplums.

The Art of the Hoop: 1860 - 1869

EVENING DRESS.

The skirts of dresses, for home and evening wear, measure as much as two yards and one nail in length, and, as a natural result, are very much gored. The slope, too, which is so important, must not come alone from the top, but the bottom of the skirt, also. Walking-dresses will be made with petticoats to match; but instead of the upper-skirt being looped as formerly, it will be cut short, and trimmed to correspond with the under-skirt.

The arrangement of this new style of toilet (with two skirts, so to speak) will be as follows: First, a petticoat will be made to reach as far as the knee with any material that is convenient; to this will be joined a deep border of the same material as the dress. This border is plain at the edge, and if any trimming is desired, it is placed above the straight hem. The second, or upper skirt, is very narrow round the hips, and is cut out at the edge in large round scallops. This edge is occasionally varied, according to taste, by cutting it in squares like the top of a battlement, or in vandykes or festoons; but, whatever form it assumes, it is always bordered either with velvet, gimp, or a narrow silk fringe.

WALKING DRESS.

Cut skirts are quite fashionable now, and, when not too deep, are called the Marie Antoinette flounce.

Round waists are frequently cut square in the neck, or else pointed; pleated bodies are not unfashionable. Anything makes an agreeable change to the old and very stiff bound waist.

Peplums are worn with everything, either made of the same material as the dress, and with the dress, or else cut separately, and of a contrasting material and color.

Sleeves are not any longer than usual, but are much closer, so much so that before long they will grow enormously wide. They have already made their appearance among us in cloaks over one yard in width.

TUNIC PEPLUM.

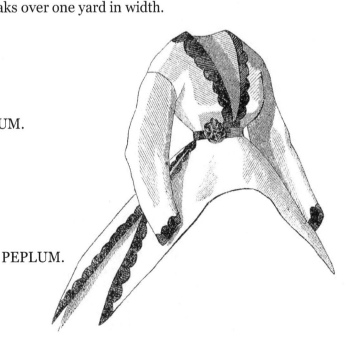

PEPLUM.

Peterson's Magazine, December 1866

Hints on Dress

The following hints are given for the benefit of those who are obliged to exercise economy in expenditure, yet appear well dressed, a combination very common, and not nearly so difficult to accomplish as many imagine: –

1st. Never buy conspicuous articles of dress, or colors which are not likely to harmonize generally with others. On your means you must, of course, purchase things which will last more than "one doing up," and it would be a pity to have dresses which would be recognizable, however altered or retrimmed, as that would completely do away with the pleasure of variety. And though brilliant colors may be arranged so as to look very beautiful in dress, you will find it wiser to select quiet shades which will never jar with each other. Your dress need not, however, be grim-looking on this account, as a little exercise of taste will show you how to relieve it – by a tiny knot of bright ribbon, a pretty little tuft of gay-colored feather in your black or gray hat, or such-like pleasing little reliefs.

2d. Do not spend money on evanescent fashions, or in the various etceteras which run away with so many young ladies' pocket-money. Many articles of dress are very graceful and pretty where a girl has money to spend on what will probably be out of fashion next month, or too much run upon to be any longer lady-like. I allude to such things as expensive neck scarfs, fanciful patterns of collars and cuffs, especially lace ones, elaborate bed-room slippers, etc. Your dress need never be unfashionable, but you should not attempt to make yourself conspicuously fashionable.

3d. Try to have a system in your dress, or what I may almost call a style of your own, modified to some extent by the fashion of the day. I have a friend who always makes a rule of wearing plain skirts, even though others are generally being trimmed. I merely mention this as an instance of what I mean. Far from being remarked for dressing poorly, the young lady in question is generally admired for her "simple but *distingué*" style of dress. She certainly possesses a tall and graceful figure, and always has an ample allowance of material in her dresses.

To enter now into a few particulars for your benefit. You will always find it a comfort to have a good black silk dress in wear, unless your friends think you too young for black. Some people will advise you to buy very few dresses, but all of the best material. I do not think this is your wisest plan. You are so young that you do not require to wear rich material to look well dressed, and the present fashions change so quickly in material as well as in make, that you would often feel yourself hampered by having an unworn-out dress which you felt it your duty to wear, though it no longer looked new. For morning wear, I think you would find scarlet or blue flannel Garibaldi's or bodices, becoming and serviceable. With these you can wear a gray or brown linsey skirt, without looking at all dingy. A neatly-fitting black or dark silk dress, for hotter wear, will last long with care. If some of your friends ever give you the choice of a Christmas or birthday present, you cannot do better than choose a good dark silk. Light silk dresses, however good in quality, are never serviceable.

For ordinary walking dress, I think nothing so pretty for young girls as short jackets of thick, rough cloth, black, gray, or dark blue. For better, fine black plush makes exceedingly pretty jackets, which are exceedingly serviceable; I mean the plush made expressly for cloaks.

You would find a black net evening dress very useful, if you are not too young for it. There are very pretty and inexpensive gauzy materials which look quite handsome enough for young girls' evening wear. Lavender or light gray, with a bright-colored spot on it. Is very pretty. White tarlatane or grenadine muslin dresses with colored patterns on them, are to be had very cheap at almost any of the large shops. They last quite as long as the much more, expensive silk grenadines, and look, I think, quite as pretty. For half-dress, evening wear, you will find a pink or pale blue mousseline-de-laine Garibaldi very useful and becoming. Plain white muslin dresses, I think, are expensive, as they must have trimming of some kind to set them off, and so quickly lose their first freshness.

I have not spoken of under-clothing, as you are almost sure to have a pretty good stock to begin on. If you require to buy any, you would, of course, do well to have it made at home. Do not think it necessary to have a great quantity; half a dozen is quite enough for a set of linen – and very simple trimming both neater and more serviceable for young girls. Always wear small plain linen collars in the morning, and a little lace tucker in any high evening dress. Lace collars and sleeves are very dear, and not suitable for you.

Be very careful to pay for everything as you buy it, and close your accounts every quarter at least. If you let one quarter run into another, you will soon exceed your income.

Godey's Lady's Book, February 1866

The Economies of Dress.

Among the useful pursuits and home amusements to be derived from a knowledge of needlework, there is no one by which a young lady can so easily and essentially profit herself and assist her family, should they need her help, as in the art of making her own dresses. The high prices now charged by mantuamakers are more than a young woman of moderate means can prudently or conscientiously, spend on her outside articles of dress; and yet she does not like to appear in ill-fitting apparel, as "a fright or a dowdy."

Young ladies, if you will take up this neat work of making your own dresses, you will find it a very simple process. We suppose you to have some readiness with the needle; you have hemmed pocket handkerchiefs, stitched up seams, and gathered ruffles. If you can do these neatly never fear any difficulties in making a dress by the aid of the hints we shall now give, and the plates and directions to be found in the Lady's Book.

Take one of your worn-out dresses that fits you exactly, rip it up and lay the several parts on your new material, cut carefully and exactly, baste the different seams together, and try how it fits. At first you may have a little difficulty, but never be discouraged; try on again till it fits. Experience, the best of teachers, will in due time give you precision and skill, and you will find dresses of your own make fit better than those made by a stranger, as no hired skill can be stimulated by so strong an interest as you feel for yourselves. As to the trimmings, that is fancy work in which you will improve your own taste, and show your judgment. A dress loaded with trimmings makes a dowdy of its wearer. The real lady subordinates her attire to her own style, character, and condition.

Godey's Lady's Book, December 1866

SEWING MACHINE!

This invention may well be called the sister art of the printing press, for it gives to one-half of humanity a new inlet for light to the mind; the needy mother of families has leisure for mental culture beyond the material and the finite. It was of no use to the woman, whose days and nights were devoted to the benumbing toil of earning a scanty pittance by setting stitch upon stitch with her sewing needle, that the press scattered books and papers broadcast over our land. She had no time for reading. Book learning was beyond any woman's home circle of enjoyments, when she had half a dozen or more in the family to make and mend for besides doing "the work of the house." The *Sewing Machine* has changed all this, in such measure that the great majority of American women have now time to read and to think, if she choose; and what mother will not choose that which enables her to guide and inform her children.

In another class, that of families or ladies in "genteel poverty," where a certain appearance must be maintained with restricted means; how many mothers, wives, sisters, daughters, have had to sacrifice mental enjoyments and even health to that wearing needlework, which now is done by the *Sewing Machine*! This help gives the intelligent, delicate lady time for improvement of health and mind, and thus our homes are made better and happier; life is prolonged and comfort increased by the *Sewing Machine*.

The great variety of these useful inventions gives scope for choice; no doubt there are several good patents; but we commend only the one we use in our family and know to be *very excellent*, that of

WHEELER AND WILSON'S*

Highest premium Lock Stitch Sewing Machines. These are adapted to all kinds of family sewing, and work equally well upon silk, linen, woollen, and cotton goods, with silk, cotton, or linen thread. They will seam, quilt, gather, hem, fell, cord, braid, bind, and perform every species of sewing, making a beautiful and perfect stitch, alike on both sides of the article sewed.

*704 Chestnut Street, Philadelphia.

Godey's Lady's Book, December 1866

1867

TARTAN DRESS.
Gored dress in "42d" plaid, trimmed with velvet, short plush, or gray Astracan in milestones around the bottom of the skirt, and in a design to match upon the top and bottom of the sleeves. The belt is composed of the ornamental material.

MORNING OR HOUSE DRESS.
Full gored dress of green poplin or empress cloth, trimmed with bands of green velvet, and silk ruching in black and green, put on in scallops, and forming a heading round the bottom of the skirt, and an elegant finish to the front of the skirt, and also upon the high body. Shaped sleeves, trimmed with cuffs and cape to match.

Walking dresses are now made short cut off just below the knees, exhibiting either white or colored petticoats beneath. They are generally finished with deep points or scallops at the bottom. This would be an extravagant fashion (as these dresses can only be worn in the street), were it not that it affords a very good opportunity to make over old dresses which are worn about the bottom. An old silk or poplin can be cut off for nearly a half a yard about the lower edge of the skirt, scalloped and trimmed, worn over a balmoral or white petticoat, thus making a very serviceable walking dress for some months. When these dresses are worn with small, modest hoops, they are not unbecoming. It remains to be seen whether they will constitute a permanent fashion. One advantage is gained in the fact that it saves the inconvenience and trouble of looping up the long trail usually worn in the house. This looping up, by the way, has been proven to be very injurious to nice fabrics, especially silks, which may serve to account for the change that has been made.

NEW LEG-OF-MUTTON SLEEVE.
The upper part of this sleeve is composed of one immense puff, gathered into a strap, the pointed end of which is fastened over in front with a button. The lower and plain part of the sleeve is ornamented with straps and buttons.

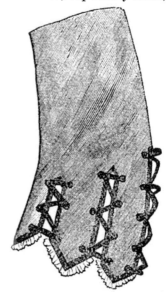

NEW DAIN FLOWING SLEEVE.
A handsome sleeve in any rich, thick material which will admit of an elegant under-sleeve. The lower part, it will be seen, is half flowing, cut up in graduated lengths, and crossed with bands of velvet fastened with buttons. A white satin quilling projects from the inside edge of the sleeve.

Arthur's Home Magazine, January 1867

The Art of the Hoop: 1860 - 1869

MORNING ROBE.

Brown cashmere robe, with deep band of blue on the edge, and a rich bordering in brilliant Persian colors.

The fiat has gone forth – short dresses are to be fashionable, and hoops are to be reduced in size. Already do we see a number of short-skirted, collapsed individuals perambulating our streets, but so far the custom is not general. It is, however, struggling hard for supremacy, which it is bound ere long to obtain.

Short skirts are not to be reserved for the street only, but are also destined for the ball-room. This is doubtless a wise proceeding, for a beautiful *toilette* frequently comes from a dance completely *hors de combat*, or, in other words, in tatters only fit for the rag bag.

Trains are to be by no means discarded, but are intended for home wear, dinners, and receptions. With long skirts ample crinoline must of course be worn, to give a graceful sweep to the dress.

Coat tails and basquines are now generally simulated by trimmings. It requires less material, gives less fullness round the hips, insures a better fit, and the deception is complete.

Peplum dress for evening wear. It is of white silk, bordered with scarlet velvet, and trimmed with cameos and gold acorns.

Dinner-dress of blue silk, made square, and trimmed with a puffing of velvet. The waist is cut very short, and worn with a wide sash of blue velvet.

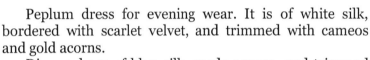

The generality of sleeves are made quite close at the wrist; so small are they, as scarcely to admit of an undersleeve. Deep cuffs are worn, the edges slipping under the sleeve and simulating an undersleeve without the bulk. For dressy occasions, a rich lace is basted on the edge of the dress sleeve.

Godey's Lady's Book and Magazine, January 1867

No very decided change has taken place in the style of making dresses since our remarks of last month. Short dresses, in all varieties, are worn out-of-doors. Nothing can be more sensible than this fashion – for what is more untidy than the long trailing skirt in the street, or more annoying than to be obliged to hold up yards of silk or muslin whilst walking? These short skirts have another advantage, for partially worn out dresses can be cut and gored to look like new. The petticoat or under-skirt may be either of the same material and color as the upper one; or, if preferred, of a contrasting color.

HOUSE DRESS.

Polonaise Dress of Green Silk, trimmed with blue velvet, cut bias, and laid on as in the design; trimmed around with black thread lace. A white lace bonnet, trimmed with pearls and green leaves.

Long trains, for the house, are still worn; in fact, they are larger than ever. Nothing can be more graceful than this style of dress; but in small crowded rooms they are difficult to manage. Eugenie, who is the arbiter of fashion in Paris, is endeavoring to introduce short dresses for dancing; leaving the long, graceful skirt for matrons, and those who do not dance. It will take some time to reconcile our belles to this fashion; but it is so obviously comfortable that we have no doubt it will be adopted.

Bretelles or Braces, on evening dresses, are very much worn; they have usually long flowing ends at the back, like wide sashes.

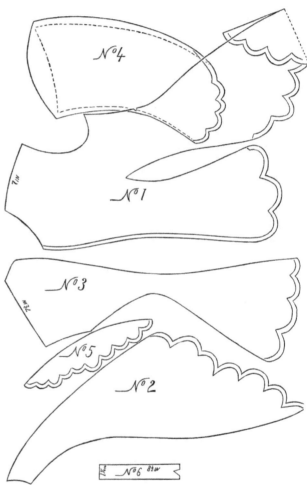

A well dressed woman need not be necessarily expensively dressed. It is the style and fashion, not the mere material that makes elegance of attire.

Peplums are much worn for party dresses, (but not when bretelles are worn, of course,) made either of light-colored silk over white, or of white trimmed with ribbon and straw.

THE NEW STYLE PEPLUM.

The most fashionable article of the season is the Peplum, engravings of which we have given in former numbers, and a pattern and diagrams of which we give here.

No. 1. Front.
No. 2. Side-Piece.
No. 3. Back.
No. 4. Sleeve.
No. 5. Jockey.
No. 6. Collar.

For winter wear, the Peplum should be made of cloth, or velvet. While this garment is always substantially of the same pattern, it often differs in details. The design we engrave is, however, the very latest. The diagrams give the shape of the several pieces, with the sizes marked; and from them a paper pattern may easily be cut. In former numbers we have given directions how to do this, and do not think it necessary to repeat the directions here. A good deal depends on the size of the lady for whom the pattern is to be made; and it would be well to fit the paper pattern to the person before cutting into the silk or velvet.

Peterson's Magazine, January 1867

Crinoline is declared to be doomed. Certainly it is greatly reduced in size during the last two months, and possibly it may disappear altogether.

WALKING DRESS.

Skirt of purple cashmere. Dress of gray poplin, turned up in front, and fastened in a knot at the back. Half tight-fitting sack of heavy spotted plush cloth. Boots of black and white checked cloth.

The short skirt is now a clearly-established "fashion" among us. The walking dress is now cut not only looped above a false under-skirt, a broad band of the same material sewn on a little above and inside of the festoons, doing duty for a jupon, but simple tunics, variously cut and shaped, hang over a short under-skirt, which only reaches the ankle. The feet of the wearer are protected from too much exposure to observation by Polish boots, ascending about four inches and a half up the leg, where they are cut to a point in front, and ornamented with tassels.

The Art of the Hoop: 1860 - 1869

THE EMPRESS WALKING DRESS.

This is a still later and more elegant style of short dress. It is made in purple velvet, trimmed with narrow bands of ermine or swan's-down. The dress is scalloped out wide over a white mohair petticoat, trimmed with a flat (Marie Antoinette) plaiting. It is edged with fur, the plaiting having a heading of jet. The peplum basquine is also bordered with fur, and is particularly graceful in style. It is open on the back, as well as upon the sides.

Some of the petticoats are fluted like a piano-forte silk, others are plain. In Paris, blue scarlet, and mauve merino skirts are in vogue. The tunic is either black or gray, and the tight-fitting jacket, with peplum ends, either corresponds with the petticoat or the dress, according to the taste of the wearer. Some dresses have the body *en suite* with the dress-skirt or tunic, and the sleeves and peplum to match the petticoat. Most of the short skirts that we have remarked in London, are of black *glacé* or *gros grain*, the whole toilet of the same material. Some of the tunics are straight at the hem, much shorter in front than behind, with a graceful slope. Others equal in all parts, and ornamented simply with a few rows of ribbon, velvet, or braid.

THE PARISIAN WALKING DRESS.

This illustration represents one of the most stylish models of the new short dress – the novelty of the season. The dress and peplum *sac* are of the same material – black wool poplin. The sleeves and petticoat are of scarlet wool. The trimming is black jet braid, put on in bands, and loops upon the edge, which is cut out in battlement, both upon the *sac* and skirt. The pendant ornaments in the spaces upon the petticoat are black, edged with narrow fringe.

THE "ITALIA" DRESS.

Skirt and short open jacket of granite gray poplin or cashmere, trimmed with bands of poppy-red silk, striped with narrow black velvet, the ends fastened down with small red crochet buttons. The skirt is ornamented down the sides, round the bottom, and in bands across the front breadth. A belt is attached to the skirt, and a strap unites the two sides of the jacket. The sleeves are trimmed upon the back and at the wrists to match the rest of the dress. A white waist, embroidered and edged with lace, is displayed by the open jacket.

The favorite mantle shape is the peplum, with a loose paletôt back – that is, short before and behind, but presenting two long vandyked peaks below each hip. These may be made short, like jackets, or as long as shawls. Peplums added to the dress are much worn indoors, and look very stylish. A very low corslet, with shoulder-straps is also stylish.

THE "ADELAIDE" SLEEVE.

A full sleeve, with a deep, plain cuff and cape, ornamented with pendant straps, loops, and buckles at the back as well as upon the front of the sleeve.

POMPEIAN SLEEVE.

Plain shaped sleeve, ornamented with velvet, put on in a circular design, from the centre of which is suspended a tassel both at the top and bottom.

PUFFED SLEEVE.

A small shaped sleeve, ornamented with side puffs divided by straps of silk, with lines of jet running through the centre. A strap of silk, studded with jet bead buttons, ornaments the back of the sleeve.

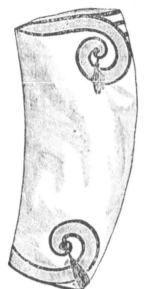

Arthur's Home Magazine, February 1867

PROMENADE SUIT.

Petticoat of blue poplin, trimmed with black velvet studded with steel ornaments. Gored overskirt of black poplin trimmed round the point on each gore with a bias fold of blue satin studded with steel beads. Basquine of blue poplin, trimmed to match the skirt. Bonnet of blue velvet, sprinkled over with steel beads.

We seem to have the two extremes in dresses, for long dresses are longer than ever before. All the breadths, with the exception of the back, are gored. The back width is straight and laid in a large double box-plait at the waist, and the dress should be made to hook underneath this plait, which is decidedly better than having a slit at the side which is apt to fly open and show the petticoat. The breadths are sewed together with cordings or pipings of two colors, each piping being as large round as a lead pencil. If the dress is striped, the pipings may be of the colors of the stripes, or else of white or black and some high color. They are also carried all round the edge of the skirt, which is frequently scalloped or waved. Satin folds are very much in favor, and, as to beads, people are running wild on the subject. No dress, sack, or bonnet, is considered complete unless well peppered with beads.

In Paris we find all the gored dresses worn with body and skirt separate, which does away with that very objectionable seam down the front of the dress. A belt, fancy basque, or a band worked with jet and fancy pendent straps is worn round the waist.

Fig. 5. – Evening-dress of white silk figured with high colors. It is trimmed with a basque formed of long points, which may be removed at pleasure.

Fig. 7. – Evening toilet. Dress of pearl-colored silk, gored, and high in the neck. Peplum of striped pink silk, belted in to the waist with a pearl-colored belt. The Peplum is edged with a band of plain pink silk, finished with silver braid.
Godey's Lady's Book and Magazine, February 1867

Not to dress well is to do one's self a real injustice. It is not necessary to spend much money in order to dress well. What is wanted is taste and a knowledge of the latest styles. It is astonishing on how little money a Parisian manages to dress; and yet no women in the world are better dressed than the Parisians.

THE HUNGARIAN.

THE ATHENIAN.

THE EUGINE PALETOT.

We, this month, render our series of winter Paletots more complete by presenting our fair Subscribers with the pattern of the Eugenie Paletot, or out-door jacket, shown above. It is cut to fall nearly square, that is to say, it only defines the waist in a very slight degree.

It is, for a well-proportioned figure, measuring about 34 1/2 inches round the chest. We have given, on the next page a diagram, showing the back, side-piece, front, and the top part of sleeve, which our readers can easily complete to its full length, according to taste. On the front we have marked, by pricked lines, the form of the fish which has to be taken out in the chest; but by omitting this fish, and cutting the skirt a little shorter, a Paletot like the other figure above will be obtained. Both of these are very pretty affairs.

Peterson's Magazine, February 1867

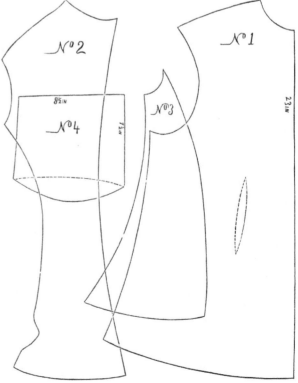

It is yet too early to decide what will be the prevailing modes for spring. We make from foreign papers a few extracts as to some of the novelties in the *"beau monde."*

This graceful jacket is made of black velvet or silk, trimmed with jet and chalk beads. The edge is finished with a rich fringe of chalk and jet beads, matching the other trimming. The jacket is closed halfway down, showing the whole waist underneath. It then slopes suddenly off to the back, where it springs into a basque. A wide waistband encircles the waist and falls behind in two large bows.

The short dresses are gaining more acceptance than ever, but chiefly in black, and the short tunic is exchanged for a longer skirnoors. [*sic: skirt indoors?*] Jet beads are sometimes used on these. All trimmings go down the seams, ending a quarter of a yard above them in medallion, or fan-shaped piece.

SHORT DRESS. – No. 1.

Dress of garnet poplin, scalloped out over a black silk petticoat, bound with black velvet. The scallops are simply bound with braid, and ornamented in each space with jet buttons. Leaves are cut out of poplin, and bound with braid, and arranged in the form of a star at the point of each of the festoons. Black velvet paletôt trimmed with jet passementerie, buttons, fringe and tassels. The scarf ends upon the cloak are simulated by silk embroidery and silk and jet buttons.

EMPRESS DRESS.

Gored dress of rich black corded silk, ornamented with wide bands of black velvet edged with jet, and forming side sashes, and two rows at a distance from the bottom of the skirt, which is finished by a cord. Black crochet buttons mixed with jet down the front, and down the back of the sleeves, which have short straps of velvet simulating button-holes. Straight caps, cuffs, and belt of velvet edged with jet. End and buckle to the belt instead of rosette, matching the trimming upon the skirt and sleeves.

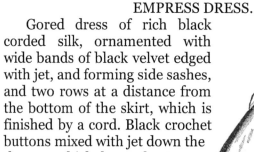

"VICTORIA" SLEEVE.

This sleeve is shaped something like the old-fashioned "leg-of-mutton," but it is sufficiently loose at the wrist to slip over the hand; and at the top there is a pointed cap; which subdues the fullness and makes it less perceptible. It is a good sleeve for silk or merino, but not for any very thick material.

THE "VIOLET" SLEEVE.

A plain sleeve, shaped to the arm and trimmed in points to simulate a cap and cuff upon the top and bottom of the sleeve. Ornamental buttons of onyx, pearl, jet or gilt, occupy the spaces.

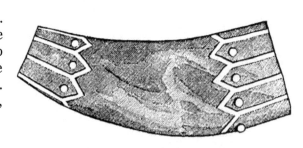

The Art of the Hoop: 1860 - 1869

Silk dresses are garnished with bands of silk edged with satin in two inch broad strips down the seams, may have a double piping of satin and silk. Flowers made of satin with a centre jet button are greatly used, three placed at the end of a straight seam trimming. The same ornament is carried out on mantles, which are striped lengthways with broad silk bands, or more simply garnished, with very narrow ones. The present fashions glory in extremes. Either the trimming is very simple, or extremely rich and profuse. In the latter case it consists of a perfect mass of jet beads, finely cut, and mingled with delicate braid work. Jet ornaments are still the height of the fashion. Silver is now very little worn.

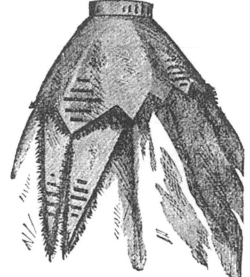

DRESS PEPLUM.

This simulates a double peplum upon the hips, the lower point being very deep and open, so as to form a double point, to which tassels are attached. The trimming consists of fringe and narrow straps of gold or silver ribbon, and small gold or silver tassels. The belt is ornamented with straps to match. This is beautiful in blue or yellow silk over a dress of white tarlatan or white organdie muslin.
Arthur's Home Magazine, March 1867

It is stated that California silk far exceeds in quality that grown in Europe. The climate is much more favorable to the growth of the mulberry.

SPRING COSTUME FOR A YOUNG LADY.

Dress of steel-colored silk, open at every breadth, disclosing an underskirt of rich blue silk. Each breadth is richly embroidered in blue silk, and trimmed with a quilling of ribbon. The corsage is embroidered to suit the skirt, and finished with a wide blue belt, fastened with a steel buckle. The hat is of gray straw, trimmed with a long and full blue feather. Parasol of blue silk edged with gray.

Short dresses, which have caused so much perturbation in the feminine world, have now become almost indispensable. They grow shorter and shorter: but do not be frightened, dear readers, we are not coming out as ballet dancers; though the upper skirt is short, the petticoat is of a suitable length.

You can always detect an American girl in Paris by her outrage on fashions. If hoops are in vogue, our American girl will have the largest; if small bonnets are the rage, she will have the smallest, etc.; but a sure mode of detection is the waterfall. Our ladies subject themselves to the laughter of all Parisians by the enormous piles of material they place on the backs of their heads. You can always tell them.

Evening peplum. An admirable style for an evening dress. It is of white silk, bound and trimmed with blue velvet and gold. At the back the peplum falls a quarter of a yard longer than in front.
Godey's Lady's Book and Magazine, March 1867

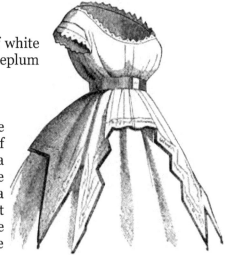

Evening dresses are made with low waists, and crossing over the left to the right of the waist, is frequently worn a broad ribbon or scarf of tulle, on which is sometimes placed a small wreath of ivy-leaves, a cluster of pink roses, or some other flower corresponding with those worn in the hair. One charming dress of white spotted muslin, for a young lady, has recently been made with an "infant waist." A light scarlet sash was to be worn around the waist; coral cameos in the center of the shoulder-knots, a row of large coral beads around the waist, and a comb, ornamented with coral, in the hair, completed this beautiful toilet.

WALKING DRESS.

Carriage Dress of Pearl-Gray Silk, trimmed with black velvet and bands of crimson satin.

Small crinolines, for the street, are now indispensable, if you would be in the fashion.

The brocaded silks, are too heavy for spring and summer wear, and will be replaced by chene, plain or small striped, or plaid silks. Black silk dresses are always popular, because they are always so useful. One celebrated dressmaker in Paris made over one hundred black silk dresses in two months.

The waists of dresses are still short with a belt of moderate width, and but little trimmed. Over the tight sleeve the wide Venetian sleeve is frequently worn. For the house, the trains are still long; though on the street nothing is seen but the short dresses, which do not touch the ground. *All* skirts are very much gored.

NEW STYLE DRESS.

House Dress of White Silk. – The bottom of skirt is trimmed with a broad band of blue satin, as well as the body and front of the skirt. Tight white sleeves, trimmed in blue. Over the white dress is worn a blue satin peplum, with deep Venetian sleeves, and is trimmed with a mixture of black and white blonde.

NEW STYLE DRESS.

BODICE.
Peterson's Magazine, March 1867

The following is a simple, charming toilette a young girl; the material is gray cashmere, the petticoat is plain, but the skirt, which is shorter, is cut out in square scallops round the edge, and trimmed with a double row of cerise satin galloon, goffered. The skirt is fastened the entire length of the front with cerise silk buttons. The bodice consists of a gray corslet and narrow braces,

The Art of the Hoop: 1860 - 1869

both trimmed with cerise satin. There is no band, the waist being simply corded with cerise satin. The short *paletôt-sac* is made of gray cashmere, lined with gray silk, and trimmed all round with a double row of cerise galloon. On the left shoulder there is a tasteful bow, consisting of three loops and two flowing ends. This stylish costume can be copied in poplin, and trimmed with black velvet, or in any fancy material, and ornamented with black braid. It is always fashionable and ladylike.

SPRING FASHION.

Dress of steel-colored silk, open at every breadth, disclosing an under-skirt of rich blue silk. Each breadth is richly embroidered in blue silk, and trimmed with a quilling of ribbon. The corsage is embroidered to suit the skirt, and finished with a wide blue belt, fastened with a steel buckle.

SENORITA JACKET.

Breakfast jacket of scarlet cashmere, ornamented upon the breast, and epaulets with butterflies with spread wings cut out in velvet and embroidered with gold and red and blue silk. There is a slight spring at the back of the waist, which deepens into a point, ornamented with butterfly to match.

Dresses made expressly for afternoon driving or visiting, are cut *en redingote*. A pearl gray poplin *redingote*, trimmed up the seams of the skirt with narrow cross-cut bands of white satin, is the fashionable outdoor toilette for a youthful married woman. Lace is again worn on afternoon dresses intended for weddings, visits, and other ceremonious occasions, and is usually arranged above the pleating which borders the skirt. *Basquines* fitting the figure are again very popular; they are so much more graceful and becoming than the short loose paletôt, therefore their reintroduction is easily understood.

The prettiest form of short dresses is the skirt straight round the edge and cut up at the sides; this style harmonizes best with the short straight paletôt, likewise cut up at the sides.

THE BELLE OF THE BALL.

This elegant toilet is draped over Bradley's new Empress "Invisible" Trail, the proper hoop-skirt for a narrow gored dress. The robe is of white corded silk, with peplum ornamented with black lace, black velvet sash ends, and opal buttons set in silver. The body is cut very low in front, and trimmed with black lace ruching. Small square lace chemisette. The figures in the background show the new short skirts, the new style of peplum, the shortness of the waists, and the height to which the hair has attained at the back of the head.

Arthur's Home Magazine, April 1867

Though the general appearance of a lady's dress has changed very much since last year, still all the predictions respecting fashions have not been verified. Crinoline, for instance, which was to have been entirely proscribed, has obtained a new lease, subject, however, to some restrictions.

For street wear it is to be of very small proportions; but long dresses, with the anaconda-like appendages called trains, require some support, and with these the limits of crinoline are extended, only, however, on the lower edge; the upper part must fit the figure quite closely.

SPRING DRESSES.

Fig. 1. – Black alpaca dress, trimmed on the skirt in a Grecian pattern, formed of narrow black velvet, fancy braid and lacings of cord. The skirt is tightly gored, but cut separate from the waist, which does away with the objectionable seam down the front of the skirt.

Fig. 2. – Short dress of gray mohair, cut in deep points, and bound with gray silk. The underskirt is of blue mohair. The plain corsage with long sleeves is of blue silk; over this is a low sleeveless corsage of gray mohair laid in folds.

Fig. 3. – Dress of gray silk, worn over a petticoat of the same material. The skirt is looped up by fancy sashes, trimmed with narrow green velvet ribbon and green velvet buttons. The sleeves are trimmed to suit the skirt, and the corsage may be likewise ornamented, if desired.

Fig. 4. – Short dress of buff mohair, tightly gored and trimmed down the front with large black velvet buttons. The edge of the skirt is cut in very deep points ornamented with straps of black velvet and jet buttons. It is worn over a petticoat of black silk trimmed with a deep plaited ruffle.

Fig. 5. – Walking suit. Petticoat of gray alpaca. Overskirt of blue alpaca, cut in deep points, and bound with blue silk. The basque is of gray alpaca, cut in points, and bound with gray silk.

Dresses are, for the most part, tightly gored, without any plaits whatever, and when worn short, and fitting closely over very small hoops, the wearers, to use the expression of a French writer, resemble perambulating sausages.

A new style of skirt is being introduced by some of the Parisian modistes, and, if possible, it is a little uglier than *le saucisson*. It consists of a narrow skirt without train, just touching the ground at the back. The seams are only slightly gored, and the skirt is mounted on the waist by a large plait before, behind, and on each end.

The sleeves, *à la Juive*, hanging in long lapels from the shoulders, or from the elbow, are also fashionable. The undersleeve is generally of the same material as the flowing sleeve. If two skirts are worn of different colors, the tight sleeve is of the color of the underskirt, and the flowing sleeve is like the upper skirt and corsage. This style of sleeve is also used for wraps –

Godey's Lady's Book and Magazine, April 1867

EVENING DRESS.

Evening Dress for a Young Lady. – It is cut without a seam at the waist, is of pearl-colored silk, trimmed with pink silk, edged with a narrow jet gimp. The body is very low, with a low, white under body and sleeves.

NEW STYLE PARTY DRESS.

New Style of Ball-Dress for a Young Lady. – It consists of a pink silk under-dress, with a deep fluted ruffle, and a full tulle over-skirt, looped up with bands of pink ribbon, on which are placed wreaths of roses. The body is low and square, and has short, puffed sleeves. This style of dress has become very popular in Paris with ladies who dance, as it obviates all the difficulties of managing long trains.

Short ball-dresses, as will be seen in our illustration [*page 244*], are introduced for ladies who dance; and though not as elegant as the long trains, they recommend themselves to all sensible people.

For the house, skirts are still made with very long trains and excessively gored; no fullness is seen in front, or at the sides of the skirt; but either one very large plait, or three smaller ones, is placed at the back.

WALKING DRESS.

Carriage Dress and Peplum Sacque of Brown Silk, trimmed with heavy jet fringe.

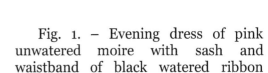

Walking dresses are made in the greatest variety of styles, and look very picturesque over bright-colored petticoats. Yet we think that the petticoat will disappear, and the short dress, just escaping the ground, take its place. To have a walking dress stylish, the jacket should always correspond in shape; thus, if the skirt is cut in points, the jacket should be cut in points also; or if the dress is square, back and front, and looped up at the sides, the jacket should be square too.

Jackets are cut square in front instead of round, as formerly. Many are fastened down the front with bars of gimp or braid. Others are made without sleeves and are left open, so that the waistband and bodice are plainly visible. These small jackets are either made of the same material as the dress, or else of light-colored cashmere, embroidered with silk of various colors, or with gold.

Waists of dresses are still made quite plain and short; but the long loose sleeve will be much worn during the coming warm weather.

Peterson's Magazine, April 1867

Fig. 1. – Evening dress of pink unwatered moire with sash and waistband of black watered ribbon starred with cluny, lace and cut with a train.

Fig. 2. – An opera or dinner dress of white corded silk, edged round the bottom of the skirt with a thick braiding of pink satin.

Fig. 3. – Evening dress of white tarlatane, ornamented with double ruches of the same, box-plaited and pinked-out. Peplum tunic, trimmed to match.

Fig. 4. – Walking dress of gray poplin, trimmed with bands of gray velvet and ornaments made of gray silk cord and chenille. The peplum is cut up on the sides, and trimmed to match.

SPRING WALKING DRESS.

Skirt and jacket of gray mohair, the skirt partially gored, the jacket cut out in nearly square lapels, which, however, are divided so as to allow the trimming to be seen upon the seams of the skirt. This trimming consists of black galloon, and extends down the entire length, forming darts on each aide. It is repeated upon the lapels of the jacket and upon the back part of the sleeves.

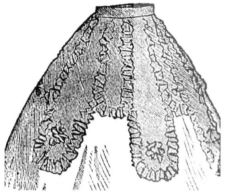

SASH PEPLUM.

A very dressy peplum, to be worn over white thin dresses. Five sashes, rounded upon the ends and extending down upon the skirt, alternate with short rounded basques, the whole trimmed very effectively with pinked-out ruching and rosettes of the same. The belt also is fastened with a rosette.

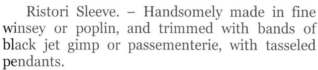

DRESS PEPLUMS.

This is open on the sides and cut out in crescents, which are trimmed round with lace and ribbon, and united together with rosettes of lace with a silk button in the centre. The peplum is attached to a trimmed belt, and has a simulated pocket in front. The trimming is black lace.

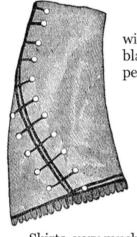

Ristori Sleeve. – Handsomely made in fine winsey or poplin, and trimmed with bands of black jet gimp or passementerie, with tasseled pendants.

Henrietta Sleeve. – A handsome sleeve in silk, poplin, or foulard. The seam is under the arm, but a trimming of lace headed with gimp, is put on in scallops upon the front of the sleeve, each point finished with a lace rosette.

Arthur's Home Magazine, May 1867

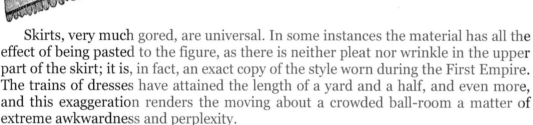

Skirts, very much gored, are universal. In some instances the material has all the effect of being pasted to the figure, as there is neither pleat nor wrinkle in the upper part of the skirt; it is, in fact, an exact copy of the style worn during the First Empire. The trains of dresses have attained the length of a yard and a half, and even more, and this exaggeration renders the moving about a crowded ball-room a matter of extreme awkwardness and perplexity.

Some skirts are trimmed with a sash kind of piece, which widens as it descends from the waist, and is cut round at the ends; there are several on the skirt, lengthening as they approach the back. Some of these sashes end in points, trimmed with tassels, some are triangular, and others ornamented with a rosette.

DINNER DRESS.

House Dress of Black Silk, over a blue silk petticoat. The tight sleeves are of blue silk, with black silk lozenges on them; and the loose sleeve is of black lined with blue.

Seasonable Dress. – We adapt our dress to spring, summer, autumn, and winter, but often with very little success, at least as far as comfort is concerned. It seems to be forgotten that a little extra looseness of dress will produce coolness, and that a thin covering in the heat of the sun fails to protect us from the heat. Thin, dark clothes, in a hot summer, are especially uncomfortable; and a black hat, however light, is in some places enough to roast the brains when exposed to the full power of the sun's rays. Remember, as a rule, that light-colored clothes keep the heat in the body when the air is cold, and when the sun is warm, keep the body from reaching the heat better than dark. Remember, also, that a woolen or cotton covering keeps the skin at an equable temperature better than linen.

CARRIAGE DRESS.

Carriage Dress of Chene Silk, trimmed with pipings of green silk. The peplum can be worn with the dress or not, at pleasure, as it fastens on under the belt.

Sleeves will be wider as the warm weather approaches; and we shall soon how our graceful, old-fashioned Pagoda sleeve back again.

The waists of dresses are made quite plain and high usually, though those which are cut square in the neck are popular with young ladies.

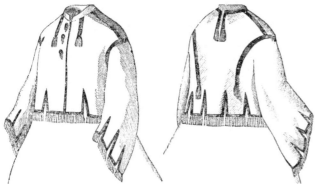

NEW STYLE JACKET – FRONT. BACK.

An entirely new fashion has recently been introduced in Paris; it is the adoption of complete Breton costumes. Some have as yet but partially adopted them, and wear the jacket belonging to the costume only; but more daring ones have accepted the entire dress with the exception of the cap. At a fashionable reception, lately, the hostess wore – first a short petticoat of dark-blue cloth, bordered with embroidery of various-colored silks, and above that a second skirt in the same style, with this difference only, that the embroidery was edged at both sides with a wide band of black velvet. The bodice was low, with immense arm-holes simulated by embroidery and velvet; the sleeve was quite plain at the top, but opened at the elbow to allow a white, full sleeve, which fastened at the wrist, to be seen. A *guimpe*, made of tucked nainsook muslin, with a plain turned-back collar, concealed the shoulders.

Peterson's Magazine, May 1867

Aprons are in vogue again, and are said to be even attached to the ball dresses. The deep flowing sleeve it is said will replace the close fitting one which has been so fashionable of late.

EVENING DRESS AT HOME.

Dress of white foulard delaine, trimmed with upright bands of blue ribbon, enclosed with double ruches of blue ribbon, so as to form a border for the bottom of the skirt. A belt and square trimming for the waist, and simulated cuffs for the bottom of the sleeves. Shakspeare collar of cluny lace.

Walking dresses cut short and variously trimmed are now almost universally worn in the street. They usually consists of two skirts, the upper one, and perhaps upper and lower, closely gored. For convenience and economy, this fashion cannot too highly commended. For travelling suits this summer they are most popular made either in light poplin or other plain material. A very fashionable trimming for either walking or house dresses just now is satin, laid on in folds around the skirt, or in perpendicular pleats.

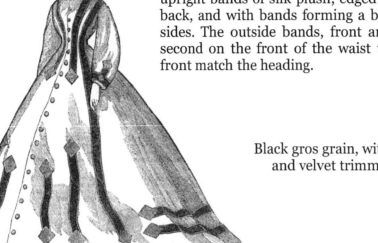

THE "VERONESE" ROBE.

This dress is gored without plaits at the waist, and trimmed with upright bands of silk plush, edged with a narrow heading at the front and back, and with bands forming a border for the bottom of the skirt at the sides. The outside bands, front and back, extend over the shoulder; the second on the front of the waist to the shoulder. The buttons down the front match the heading.

Black gros grain, with jet and velvet trimmings.

For the walking dresses cashmere and poplin are the fashionable materials. For example, a pale gray cashmere petticoat will be worn under a skirt to match, bordered with either a cross-cut band or three pipings of cerise satin; these are laid on as festoons, and above them, at the commencement of every festoon or scallop, there is a trefoil formed of cashmere and edged with cerise satin, a cerise button being placed in the centre of the leaves. The short loose paletôt is ornamented to correspond. The same style is also made in blue cashmere and trimmed with black satin when it has a very distinguished effect.

GOATS'-HAIR DRESS FOR COUNTRY WEAR.

Dress of dark gray goats' hair tissue, trimmed with dark green ribbon, put on in squares crossed at intervals and barred with straps of the same, fastened with small crystal nails or buttons. The trimming is repeated upon the waist and sleeves.

Arthur's Home Magazine, June 1867

Maltese lace, which is somewhat on the Cluny order, but finer in appearance, is now much used for trimmings. The newest colors for dress goods are the Waters of the Nile, a dull, dead mixture of gray and green, arsenic green, a very bright, beautiful shade, but very trying to most persons. Sulphur, a yellow as bright as canary, is another fashionable shade, but only suited for evening wear.

NEW STYLE OF DRESS.

Long skirt of blue silk, with over-dress of blue grenadine, trimmed with black ribbon or velvet. This same style may be made up as a short walking-dress.

MORNING-DRESS.

Dress of white cashmere, finished on the edge with a deep plaiting of white silk, caught down by a band of blue velvet. The fancy pieces on the velvet band are of white silk, studded with crystal beads. The trimming on the back of the dress is composed of white silk, blue velvet, and crystal beads.

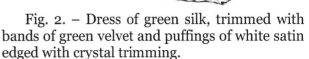

DRESSES FOR A WATERING-PLACE.

Fig. 1. – Underskirt of pearl-colored silk, trimmed with bands of cherry velvet. Overskirt of pearl-colored grenadine, trimmed with mixed black and white Cluny and bands of cherry velvet.

Fig. 2. – Dress of green silk, trimmed with bands of green velvet and puffings of white satin edged with crystal trimming.

Fig. 3. – Gored dress of blue silk, trimmed on the edge of the skirt with bias bands of blue satin. The points on the upper part of the skirt are formed of bands of blue velvet edged with a narrow white fringe.

Godey's Lady's Book, June 1867

No long dresses are now seen on the street; but in the house, and more particularly for evening wear, very long trains are worn. What the short walking dresses lack in style, they make up in convenience. A basque or loose sacque, (which is much the most popular,) like the dress, is considered indispensable. A very stylish walking suit consists of a blue-and-black striped silk skirt over a plain blue silk petticoat, the latter trimmed round the edge with a tress or plait of black velvet. Similar plaits are used to loop up the skirt in festoons. The short, loose jacket is of plain blue silk, to match the petticoat, and opens over a striped black-and-blue waistcoat. The sole ornament to the jacket is a shoulder-knot of black velvet, placed on the left side.

HOUSE DRESS.

House Dress, or Walking Dress, as Preferred. – The skirt is of blue summer poplin, made long, with straps depending from the waist, in which button-holes are made; on the skirt are buttons to correspond with button-holes on the straps; by using these the house can be converted into a walking dress without trouble.

WALKING DRESS.

The Above House Dress Converted into a Walking Dress.

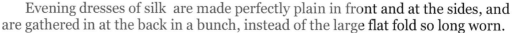

Evening dresses of silk are made perfectly plain in front and at the sides, and are gathered in at the back in a bunch, instead of the large flat fold so long worn.

White dresses, especially tarletan, are trimmed with numerous narrow flounces, some with only five, others ascending as high as the knee. When a very dressy toilet is desired, wreaths of leaves, or pretty small flowers, just above each flounce, is a great addition.

WALKING DRESS.

Walking Dress of Green Foulard over a Green Silk Petticoat. – The upper skirt is cut in points, and trimmed with black cord and black jet tassels.

CARRIAGE DRESS.

Carriage Dress of Blue Silk. – The skirt is very much gored, and has a ruffle around the bottom one-quarter of a yard deep. The front is trimmed with ruchings of silk and lace. Black silk paletot, embroidered in jet. Small black bonnet trimmed with blue flowers.

Small basques are sometimes added to the waists of dresses – not so large as the peplum basques, which were so fashionable last year, but quite small, not over three-eighths of a yard deep, and cut in large points; these points can be finished with jet tassels; from some of these basques long-pointed, sash-like pieces depend. We have seen a stylish black grenadine with a Magenta-colored figure in it, the small basque of which was of Magenta-colored satin, trimmed with jet. It was cut in points in front, and trimmed with jet tassels, and from the back three long straps descended nearly to the bottom of the skirt, the center one being the largest. This basque was about three-eighths of a yard in depth, and could be worn or not, as desired.

Peterson's Magazine, June 1867

SHORT WALKING DRESS.

This is made of light brown summer poplin – the amber shade – and trimmed with bands of blue silk dotted with amber beads. The short skirt is made distinct from the petticoat, and open on the sides, where it is fastened across with straps of silk dotted with beads. The body is high, the sleeves plain and shaped to the arm, and trimmed to match the skirt. Bonnet of blue crape, with amber fringe and blue strings.

THE ROBE VIOLETTA.

This is suitable for a dinner dress. It is made of white silk, striped with mauve satin, and gored without plaits. The overdress or tunic, with bodice attached, is of white silk, scalloped out and edged with a notched-out quilling of mauve satin. Buttons covered with satin ornament the front of the tunic.

THE ROBE ADELAIDE.

This charming dress is made in dove colored silk, striped round the bottom with narrow alternate kinds of blue and cerise velvet. These are headed by a black silk braid, put on in festoons, and carried up each side of the front breadth in a chain, which extends over the shoulders and down each side of the back breadth. The body is striped to match the skirt, and giving the effect of a tunic to the skirt.

THE ROSE OF SHARON SLEEVE.

This is a pretty sleeve for a gray barege or pearl-gray summer silk. It is elegantly trimmed with cross-cut bands of blue silk or satin, and rosettes of the same shade as the material, notched out.

THE IDAHO SLEEVE.

A handsome and suitable sleeve for gaze de chambéry, or any pretty summer material. The lower part of the sleeve is cut out in scallops on the back, and trimmed with a ruching of silk, which extends to the top and around the wrists. The scallops are united, but the indentations are left open, so as to display the lace underneath; and black velvet bows with straps and buckles, constitute additional ornaments.

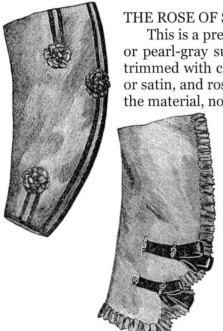

ROSINA CAPE.

A new and pretty cape in lace or muslin, trimmed with frills or lace. It is of the pelerine shape, with short basque at the back, and belt, which fastens with a rosette at the side. The shape is peculiar in front, closing over the upper part of the neck, but slanting from the sides. When the cape is made of lace, the trimming is barbe lace dotted with pearl beads.

Arthur's Home Magazine, July 1867

NEW EVENING DRESSES.

Fig. 1. – is of light sea-green silk, trimmed with bands of straw worked with black, and arranged to form a *tablier*, or apron piece in front. Large jet buttons are placed between the bands. The front of the dress is formed of rows of Cluny, and bands of straw. A garland of roses with leaves is caught on the shoulder, and is carried some distance down one side of the skirt.

Fig. 2. – Petticoat of blue silk, trimmed on the edge with three tarlatane ruffles. The overdress is of tarlatane or crèpe, either blue or white, drawn lengthwise.

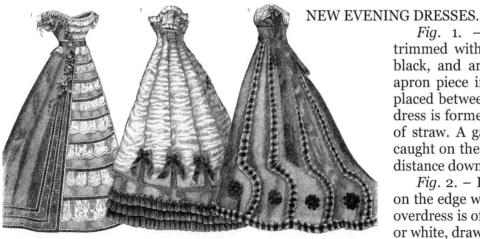

Fig. 3. – Dress of white silk, tightly gored, and trimmed with quillings of pink silk or *crèpe*, arranged as shown in the plate. Rosettes of ribbon or velvet are placed between the rows of quillings, in puffs. The edge of each gore is cut in a square bound with velvet, and finished with a bow or bouquet of flowers.

A new style of peplum, very much in favor at the Demorest establishment, is open down the front, and measures eighteen inches, it then gradually slopes to the sides, which are twenty-seven inches in length; these are also slit up to the waist. At the back the peplum slopes up from the sides, and then down to the centre of the back, which forms a point of twenty-one inches from the waist. It is also open at the back, and each opening or slit is strapped across with fancy velvet or jet bands and buttons for the distance of six inches. The rest of the trimming consists of a binding of satin or silk, and a graduated band down each opening. The edge maybe finished with a fringe or left plain.

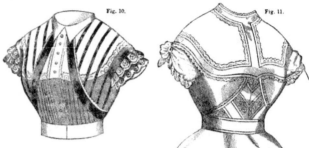

Fig. 10. – Sleeveless jacket of white grenadine, striped with narrow violet ribbon and bound with a strip of bias violet silk. The sleeves are furnished with Cluny lace.

Fig. 11. – Fancy white waist trimmed with Cluny lace and inserting.

Godey's Lady's Book and Magazine, July 1867

Small lace jackets, of the Greek or Spanish form, are very much worn over low-necked dresses. White, black, and colored cashmere jackets, dotted over with beads, are very much worn; they are especially nice for wearing over thin bodies on cool days.

EVENING DRESS

Evening Dress of Gold-Colored Satin, with a basque and body; trimmings of fancy black cords and tassels.

In-door toilets are still made either in the redingote or the empire shape, without pleats, with only one large pleat behind. Sashes are much worn; they are very wide, and fastened very low down. These sashes are worn even with walking-dresses under a paletot.

Wide sleeves are gradually gaining favor, but they usually have a close sleeve of the same material underneath. The Hungarian sleeve is very popular. It is straight and open to the top of the arm, but is slashed together again with silk cord.

WALKING DRESS

Carriage Dress of Fawn-Colored Silk. – Paletot of the same material, with Hungarian sleeves, and trimmed with bias bands of brown silk and large buttons.

PETTICOAT, WITH PATTERN FOR TRIMMING.

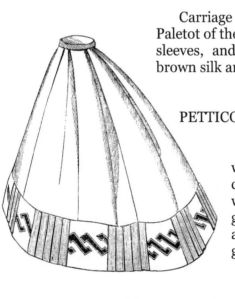

Some under skirts are trimmed with very narrow flounces, put on with a heading, pinked out and gathered. This is an old fashion which comes back to us again. Deep pleated flounces have been so much worn during the winter that ladies are already tired of them. Small gathers are now occasionally to be seen on the hips, and these gathers are now occasionally to be seen very close together at the back. Small gores are inserted into the lower part of the skirt to widen it.

Peterson's Magazine, July 1867

The Art of the Hoop: 1860 - 1869

THE LISBON DRESS.
May be made of lustrous alpaca or taffetas. Trimmed with fine braid silk or velvet.

The form of skirts is definitely fixed; the short costumes are worn for morning promenades in town, and for both morning and afternoon in the country; for visiting and dinner dresses the skirts are cut with long narrow trains, while for evening toilettes the trains are immoderately long, something unprecedented in dimensions. But the skirts, if longer, are decidedly much narrower; at the top they are quite plain, although a few ladies still insist on having a pleat about ten inches wide in front, and another equally wide at the back. The usual width round the bottom of the skirt is now only six yards, which is a decided improvement, for instead of sixteen, and even seventeen yards of wide-width silk being required for a dress, it is now possible to cut out a very fashionable robe from thirteen yards of materials. This fact will be good news to those with whom quantity is an object, and they unfortunately are the majority.

TULLIP SLEEVE.
A graceful flowing shape, the bottom being cut into sashes, and trimmed with gimp and fringe. A bow of ribbon is clasped with an aigrette between the sashes. Grenadines may be made up in this style.

TULLIP PEPLUM.
Corresponds in effect with the Tulip Sleeve. It is trimmed in the same mode, and forms a tasteful finish to the skirt of grenadines or bareges.

DRESS PEPLUM BASQUE.
Back and Front Views.
A very dressy Basque in silk or satin, trimmed with lace and pearl or amber beads. Upon the hips it is cut out in two short points, and also ornamented with lace rosettes. It is finished with a trimmed belt, fastened with a rosette.

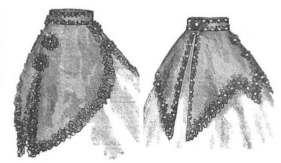

SLEEVELESS JACKET.
Fitting close to the figure, trimmed with narrow lace with heading of velvet or galloon.

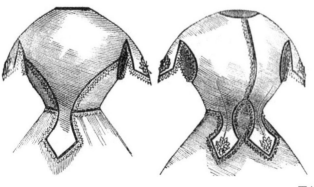

TARSCHA SLEEVE.
Intended for thick summer fabrics shaped to the arm and decorated with bunds of silk of a darker shade of color and small jet buttons just large enough at the hand to show a cuff or ruffle of lace.

Wide square pockets form an ornamentation greatly in favor at the present. They are frequently added to short, loose paletôts, so that each side of the jacket there is a long end which descends below it and terminates with rich silk fringe. This pocket is simulated on dresses with cross-cut bands of a color which contrasts with the dress, and which commence at the waist. The fringe is placed across the end of it, and the pocket has the effect of being fastened down to the skirt at each side with a large button.
Arthur's Home Magazine, August 1867

One of the newest styles for making up dresses is as follows: A plain skirt of gray silk, a shorter skirt of blue silk with oval openings cut slantwise at the sides of the front breadth. Gray silk is then pulled through these openings to form a puffing, and the whole is ornamented with crystal or jet. The outside of the sleeves should be ornamented with these *crevés* or openings, and the shoulders richly trimmed with crystal or jet ornaments. This style is suitable for either a short or long dress.

ROBE DRESS.

White percale robe, dotted with bright blue. The lower part of the skirt is ornamented with a rich bordering of black and blue. The same design can be obtained in various colors.

Everything continues to be tightly gored, even muslin and *barège* dresses; the latter require a thin book-muslin lining, and the lawn or muslin dresses generally have a few shallow plaits or a little fulness at the waist.

Skirts, though very long, are decidedly narrower – the usual width being five yards. In most instances they are perfectly plain round the hips, a style not generally becoming, and for stout persons we would recommend a deep box-plait directly in the front and back. The plain appearance of the skirt is sometimes relieved by a fanciful little affair called an African basque. It resembles, somewhat, a Freemason's apron, but instead of fitting closely to the waist, it is hollowed out at the upper part and hangs festoon-like, being caught to the belt on each side. This is generally of silk of a color contrasting well with the dress, and the trimming is either beads or Cluny. The same thing is also worn at the back of the dress. As this novelty will be better understood by illustration, we will give it in our next number. [*shown below, page 257*]
Godey's Lady's Book and Magazine, August 1867

WALKING DRESS

Walking Dress of gray Alpaca, trimmed with black velvet, put on in the diamond shape.

Small flounces are again worn, as we predicted early in the season.

Trains are longer than ever, but only sufficiently wide to look well without hooping – none being over six yards at the bottom. All skirts are very much gored; but almost all have one large box-pleat at the back, or a few gathers – the perfectly plain ones being very unbecoming.

CARRIAGE DRESS.
Carriage Dress of Blue Silk; the tight sleeves are trimmed with bands of jet. An over-dress of black silk, without sleeves, cut in scallops, and trimmed with jet fringe.

Dresses entirely without pleats have by no means such uniform success. Ladies perceive that this style of dress is not becoming, and they almost all prefer to wear skirts with a few pleats at the back and sides. The short dress is worn mostly by young ladies, and, to be in good taste, they must be accompanied by under-skirts much longer than ordinary petticoats. Very few white under-skirts are seen with walking toilets; they are either of the same material as the dress, or of some material of a different color.

PEPLUM AND BODY.

Peterson's Magazine, August 1867

Instead of looped-up dresses over fully-trimmed petticoats, a preference appears to be evinced for *redingotes* or gored skirts buttoned down the front and almost entirely covering the short petticoat, which is invariably the same shade as the *redingote*. The redingote does not fit the figure quite closely, but, as a wide fringed sash is worn over it, it is drawn to the figure. The petticoat is trimmed either with a fluted flounce or with live cross-cut bands. If a toilette is desired in two colors – say gray and blue – gray bands are arranged on a blue petticoat, the *redingote* is gray, and the wide sash is blue. The *redingote* has pleats in the back.

No. 1. – THE PALETTA DRESS.
No. 2. – THE MAGINETTE DRESS.

No. 1. – A tasteful home dress for a young lady from fifteen to seventeen years of age. The material may be blue or green chambery, plain waist and gored skirt, and the trimming, bands of the same fabric of another color, stitched down upon each edge. Pearl or jet nail-heads ornament the points, sleeves, and front. A lawn or muslin may be made in the same style.

No. 2. – A striped cambric is represented in the cut; by choice of this material we are enabled to show exactly how the gores of the skirt are joined together. It will be seen the front width is gored upon each side; the back waist corresponds to this. There are four remaining widths, two upon each side making six in all. The bias sides are joined upon the hips, which brings a straight side to the edge of the front and back breadths. The waist is plain, and the peplum attached to a separate belt, so that it may be worn or not at pleasure. The effect of a double skirt is produced by the trimming, which consists of fine mohair, braid, or cotton galloon, and small jet buttons.

THE BRISTOL DRESS.

An elaborate walking suit of mohair. A more expensive material may be used if desired. The under-skirt, peplum, epaulettes, and points upon the sleeves are of steel gray. The trimmings are outlined with black galloon, and the peplum and points of the upper skirt are bound with the same. The over-dress is a yellow or Havana brown. A row of brown diamonds on lower skirt, and a row of steel gray upon the upper. The peplum has five points.

Walking dresses, we are told, are more in favor and gayer than ever. The favorite colors are Empress blue and the new *cuir*, a shade difficult to describe, as it has a reddish hue on it; these are the two fashionable colors in Paris at present.

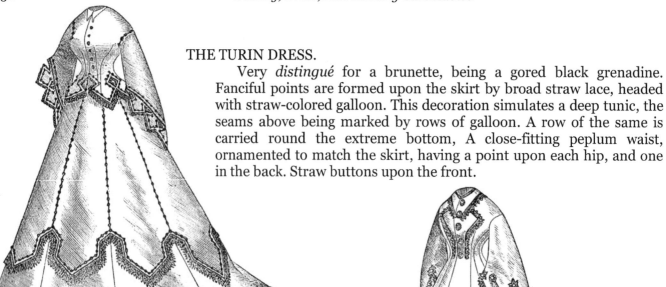

THE TURIN DRESS.

Very *distingué* for a brunette, being a gored black grenadine. Fanciful points are formed upon the skirt by broad straw lace, headed with straw-colored galloon. This decoration simulates a deep tunic, the seams above being marked by rows of galloon. A row of the same is carried round the extreme bottom, A close-fitting peplum waist, ornamented to match the skirt, having a point upon each hip, and one in the back. Straw buttons upon the front.

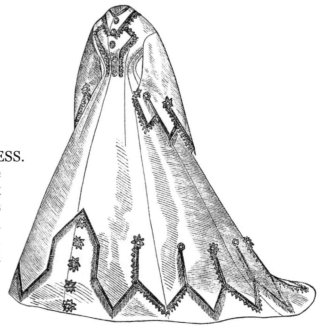

THE SAVOY DRESS.

An ash-colored summer silk or delicate chêne Gabrielle. The decoration consists of guipure and black silk fringe, headed with jet passementerie. The uprights are headed alternately with a large ornamental button and lace rosette. The trimming upon the waist simulates revers, and an empress collar. Buttons on the waist, and rosettes upon the front of the skirt.

Arthur's Home Magazine, September 1867

One of the latest confections in the shape of a ball-dress, is of white tarlatane puffed for the space of a quarter of a yard on the edge of the skirt, each puff being separated by a band of straw. A second skirt is ornamented with a double *Grecque* of straw. The corsage is trimmed to suit, and a tarlatane sash, also ornamented *en Grecque*, is fastened on the shoulder, and ties on the opposite side below the waist. This is a simple but very charming dress for a young lady.

Another very pretty dress is of bright green tulle embroidered with straw. Above the tulle skirt is a new style of peplum measuring on the right hip but one-half yard, and extending down to a very deep point almost to the edge of the skirt on the opposite side. It is formed of puffings of tulle and bands of straw let in as an inserting, and trimmed on the edge with a deep straw fringe. The corsage is of puffed tulle ornamented with a *berthe* formed of the most delicate straw and crystal beads, headed by a band formed of wheat-ears. The necklace of green velvet is elegantly ornamented with straw, and tipped with fanciful straw pendants. It is tied at the back with very long streamers of green velvet.

EVENING TOILETTE FOR A YOUNG LADY.

The fancy corsage is formed of lace and ribbon, and may be worn over any plain waist. The necklace is of black beads, hanging from a band of black velvet, which is tied at the back with bows and long ends.

Wide sash ribbons are now quite the rage; some are twenty inches in width, and the bouquets thrown over them have, at a short distance, the effect of an exquisite painting. They are mostly of white grounds, brilliant with gorgeous blossoms, swelling buds, and plume-like grasses, forming a rich mosaic, always beautiful and attractive. These charming accessories to the toilet are tied at the back with large bows and ends, and are even worn in this style by married ladies.

From good Parisian authority we learn the crinoline is not to be discarded; and those *élégantes*, by whom for a while it was ignored, now regard it as indispensable. Not the crinoline of former days, which required space, and then gave the wearer the appearance of an enormous church bell or balloon. It is the modified crinoline, merely sufficient to give style and support to the long trains now in vogue, and to take the place of the numerous skirts which are immediately adopted as soon as crinoline is dropped and generally prove so injurious.

Fig. 9. – African basque. Our illustration represents the new style of basque. It may be of any kind of silk or satin, trimmed with velvet, lace, or beads. The same ornament can also be worn on the back of the dress.
Godey's Lady's Book and Magazine, September 1867

The unbecoming, convenient short dresses are still worn, but scarcely any two look alike, the style of making and trimming are so different. Sometimes the skirt is sufficiently long to dispense with the trimmed petticoat, and trimmed with three or four bias ruffles or folds; sometimes the petticoat is of the same color material as the dress, sometimes of a pretty contrasting color. Then the upper skirt is often looped up with bows or rosettes, or rounded off at the sides, or tied at the back with a bow and ends. Handsome silk petticoats, prettily trimmed, are also worn under long skirts, which are simply fastened at the back by means of a wide sash, which forms a loop through which the skirt is passed. This is a most convenient style of wearing dresses with trains out-of-doors.

The wide, loose sleeve has not been as much worn, during the summer, as was expected; and as the autumn approaches the close sleeve will most probably be the most popular. Still the Jewess sleeve is very suitable for dresses of heavy material, and paletots, and is by some very much liked; it is a wide, open sleeve, made round, slightly pointed, and very long.

The Redingote, a style of nearly half a century ago, is again coming in fashion. It is an over-dress, cut in the Gabrielle style, buttoning all the way down the front, without a seam at the waist, and is just long enough to show the silk petticoat underneath. A small pelerine cape, of the same material, is worn with this dress.
Peterson's Magazine, September 1867

No. 1. – THE EDISTA. No. 2. – THE FALCASETTE.
No. 1. – An evening costume of pale pink silk. The skirt is gored. Upon each side of the front width is a triple row of white Angola fringe, headed with narrow black velvet curving into broad scallops. A low-necked surplice body and angel sleeves, ornamented with velvet and fringe. Tulle under-waist, with long puffed sleeves.

No. 2. – A superb carriage dress of Bismarck *poult de soie*. It is a Gabrielle, having a pointed peplum, and yoke simulated by bands of Bismarck satin, studded with nail-heads. Four rows of folds are carried down each side of the skirt and down the centre of the back. A single fold upon the front, and sleeves trimmed with satin folds and nail-heads.

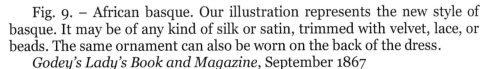

The latest fashion is to loop the upper skirt at one side only. For example, a petticoat of brown silk, with a skirt of pearl-gray silk above it. The skirt is scalloped out round the edge and looped up at the left side with a gray rosette, from which two pointed sash-ends, each terminating with a long gray tassel, depend. For outdoor wear a short gray paletôt without sleeves is added, the long coat-shaped brown sleeves doing away with the necessity of any other covering for the arm.

A great many of these *escalier* toilettes are made in yellow and black. The lower half of the skirt and the front breadth are black; the tunic is yellow, trimmed with black crossbands and black fringe. The ultra-*élégantes* wear the black silk studded all over with small gold beads, and substitute gold for black fringe; and as the ambition of ladies is now to be *brunes* instead of *blondes*, and but little difficulty is apparently found in a sudden conversion of complexion, this mixture of color is very becoming.

We note some general observations in the foreign papers. Concerning the very popular walking dresses we are told that as the short costumes are pronounced to be the most comfortable for outdoor wear, there is no doubt but that they will enjoy a long reign. Train-skirts looped up by means of the thousand and one devices (not one of which, by the way, ever answered satisfactorily), are now regarded in Paris as most unfashionable and ungraceful drapery.

SEPTEMBER WALKING-DRESSES.

Fig. 1. – The short dress is made of buff crape Eugénie, over a white mohair skirt, trimmed with upright straps of black velvet. The skirt of the dress is festooned round the bottom, and ornamented with pointed straps of the material, edged with black velvet and a narrow quilling of buff silk or ribbon. The buttons are white agate. The straps extend up the skirt at the sides only.

Fig. 2. – There are several novel features about this costume, one of which is the cut of the paletôt, the sleeve being joined to the back down its entire length, and open upon the front. The skirt is gored and cut all in one, although the trimming very naturally simulates two skirts, and is very pretty and effective. The material is black and white chene poplin, the trimming black velvet, put on in narrow straps, fastened at each end with small cut-steel buttons. The paletôt is cut out in squares; the trimming gives this effect perfectly upon the skirt.

Peplums are still the rage in Paris, and no shape seems to look peculiar. Sometimes they are nothing more than small tabs round the waist, while others are long and deep, with another and a smaller peplum at the top. Some are worn short in front in a point, wide ends coming from each hip like a sash, forming again in a point quite at the bottom of the skirt, and trimmed all round with blond.

CZARINA ROBE.

This elegant robe is made of French gray corded silk, ornamented with bands and Maltese crosses, formed of Bismarck satin edged with a very narrow black lace. The satin is arranged so as to ascend and form a very wide band in front of the skirt, but rounds off toward the back in a narrow border, which extends all round the bottom of the skirt. The crosses are employed as ornaments for the tops of the sleeves, and to occupy the space left at the lower part of the skirt in front. They are very effective. Sash ends, the top representing a Maltese cross, are also attached to the back.

Another very fashionable style is the decoration called *escalier* or "step," and with dresses thus ornamented there is no petticoat worn; crosscut bands of silk, several shades darker than the dress, are laid upon the skirt to simulate a second skirt. For example, myrtle green is used upon light green and black upon Bismarck silk, the fringe bordering the *escalier* matching the dress in color. The small *escalier* paletôt is very original; it is round at the back, and in front is cut out in steps, consequently the front of the paletôt is considerably longer than the back; cross-cut bands of silk and fringe are the usual decorations for this out-door covering.

THE ROSINE PEPLUM SKIRT.

A new and pretty peplum skirt, made in colored silk, and trimmed with folds and rosettes of satin or velvet, lace, and silk tassels.

Arthur's Home Magazine, October 1867

As the empress is decidedly in favor of short dresses for promenade and travelling purposes, we willingly follow her example, and invite attention to a few of the latest styles. Many are cut in the Princesse form, with a corselet, which is sometimes pointed as a Spanish waist, or assumes a square neck back and front with shoulder straps. The latter style is known as *la paysanne*. These corselets are worn over waists and sleeves of a contrasting color, generally the same as the underskirt, which is now very frequently simulated. A simple style of trimming consists of a bias band of silk studded with large beads, and finished on each edge with black lace. This is run up each seam and round the edge of the skirt, which is usually cut in some fanciful style. For instance, we sometimes see every other gore a sharp deep point, while the others have the points cut off halfway up, and are perfectly square. The edge is often finished with a fringe which though objectionable in a long dress, from its tendency to collect dust and small objects when walking, is on a short dress a very desirable trimming. Plaits also form a very *recherché* decoration; they are composed of bias bands of silk or velvet, lined with paper muslin, and braided to stand up in points.

A very good style of short dress is open for the space of three inches at every gore, and laced together with silk cords tied at the end of each gore with bows finished with tassels. The edge of the skirt is trimmed with a band of a contrasting color laid underneath; the spaces between the gores are also lined with the same, and thus an underskirt is simulated at a great saving of expense.

FALL PROMENADE SUIT.

Dress of gray silk poplin, trimmed with velvet of a darker shade, formed into graduated leaves. The dress may be trimmed to simulate a *paletôt*, or a separate basquine or *paletôt* may be made of the same material as the dress, and trimmed with velvet leaves. This is a good model for silk, and would make a charming evening toilet.

The elegant flowing robes, or, as they are called, robes *à queue* are certainly the most graceful and suitable costumes for evening or full reception *toilette*. They seem to increase in length, the trains sometimes measuring five feet. In front they are perfectly plain; at the back they are frequently laid in plaits to admit of a bustle or dress supporter, which we understand is to be again resumed.

In many cases, where the dress is not gored tightly, it is caught to fit the figure by rows of French gathers, which have a very pretty effect, particularly on a thin dress. A good style of belt for a silk dress is formed of a series of leaves overlapping each other. These may be formed of velvet or of silk, embroidered with beads.

Evening dresses are now frequently made to fit tightly over the hips, and are then trimmed with a fringe of flowers. A floral *bèrthe* is also worn, and the effect is exceedingly light and pretty.

Many of the new morning dresses are made as a pardessus or coat. They are cut slightly into the figure, and can be belted in or hang loose at pleasure. Some are closed in front, and are cut to resemble a peplum or short overskirt, the edge being fancifully notched out. Others, again, are closed down the front almost like a walking coat.

A new style of peplum is cut in one piece with the body and the ends at the sides looped together. One of the newest sleeves is very long and hanging; it is slashed up on the outside, and the ends are tied together.

Godey's Lady's Book and Magazine, October 1867

Dresses for out-door wear are more conspicuous than ever for color in Paris. Red and golden-yellow are to be seen everywhere; and fringe has become very general round the edges of skirts. We do not like this fashion. When the costume is a short one, there is no objection to fringe as a trimming; but when bordering a long train-skirt, it is apt to catch at any incidental fragment that comes in its way, and then it serves the purpose of a broom rather than an ornament to a lady's dress.

WALKING DRESS.

Walking Dress of Gray Poplin. – The petticoat is of gray poplin, fluted, and trimmed with black velvet points. The short, plain skirt is looped up carelessly on one side. Body with a rolling collar of black velvet, and waistband of the same.

Short dresses are still in great favor, though the petticoat, or under-dress, is made larger than earlier in the season, just escaping the ground. The long skirts are *very* long, very much gored, but only moderately trimmed.

CARRIAGE DRESS.

Carriage Dress of Blue Silk; skirt quite plain. Black velvet paletot, trimmed with braid and fringe, and a pointed hood lined with blue silk.

Crinolines cannot be abandoned whilst skirt are made so long and narrow, requiring something to throw them away from the feet. But if "cages" or steel-hoops are worn, they are very small, just supporting the dress, and without any hoops at the top. In Paris, "hoops" are abandoned, but crinoline is worn with one or two plaited flounces at the bottom.

Crinoline is made of horse-hair, and looks like common embroidery canvas, and is much heavier to wear than the hoops. Under short dresses, frequently only cambric petticoats with a ruffle, are worn – the hoop or crinoline being dispensed with.

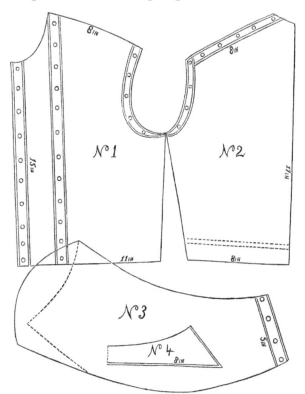

GARIBALDI WAIST IN BLUE FOULARD SILK.

We give, this month, a diagram of a Garibaldi Waist, which is to be made of blue foulard silk, and trimmed with rows of white beads and with braid. It consists, as will be seen, of four pieces, viz:

No. 1. Front.
No. 2. Back.
No. 3. Sleeve.
No. 4. Collar.

These are to be enlarged to the sizes marked on each piece. Cut a paper pattern, in this way, of the full size; try it on; and make needed alterations: then cut into your silk.

Peterson's Magazine, October 1867

The walking dress is another extremely sensible thing, and very pretty and becoming, too. We think none of our friends need be fearful about cutting their good materials into short robes. They are so convenient, so comfortable, and withal so pretty, that we are sure it will be long before they will be abandoned.

No. 1. – CARRARA DRESS.
No. 2. – HIPPOLYTE SUIT.

No. 1. – A handsome garnet merino; double skirt simulated by a ruching of black silk studded with jet nail-heads. A similar ruching is carried down front, back and each side from the belt. Upright ruchings are carried up from the bottom of the skirt in each hollow point. The waist is yoked with the same trimming, and a row carried round the wrist of each sleeve.

No. 2. – This is composed of apple-green silk. The upper skirt is raised in a series of festoons, a row in the centre, and one upon each side of the front, by buttons or aigrettes of pearl and steal. The bottom is finished with two rows of green fringe, headed with rich steel passementerie. A loose sack with hanging sleeves. The dress has close sleeves, trimmed with a fall of fringe upon the outer seam to the distance of four or five inches, and passementerie extending to the shoulder. Epaulet of fringe. Under-skirt of green and white striped poplin, trimmed with two wide bands of green silk.

No. 1. – THE ST. ORME DRESS.
No. 2. – THE DIRIGO DRESS.

No. 1. – An exquisite mode for worsted or silk goods. It should be made of two shades of one color. For example, golden brown, and trimming at least four shades darker. The design represents taffetas. The ornamentation of the skirt is formed by box-plaited folds of the lighter shade set on with a pinked-out ruching of dark brown. A rosette, with an aigrette or button in the centre, is adjusted at the top of each fold. The bottom of the jacket is divided into sashes, each finished with a ruffle and rosette of dark brown. The ruching is disposed upon the sleeves and shoulders to form cuffs and epaulets.

No. 2. – This is made of handsome green Lyons poplin – a medium shade. A plain waist and gored skirt. A hand of black silk or velvet, the upper edge cut in deep scallops or curves, encircles the skirt about eight inches from the bottom. The lower edge is straight. This band is outlined by a narrow black velvet. A row of jet nail-heads follows the direction of the curves, and above these two rows of narrow black velvet. A cuff to match upon a plain coat-sleeve, surmounted by an epaulet; a sash of poplin, bound and trimmed with black velvet and nail-heads. This style is suitable for a young lady of eighteen and upwards.

Trains are worn in the parlor as long, and longer than ever. Wide sleeves, inconvenient but graceful, are coming in again. Vandykes have long been fashionable round the edges of skirts and short paletôts, but now they are used with good results round these sleeves, which daily gain favor both for bodices and jackets.

THE LINDEMAR WAIST.

This is a superb mode for black silk and reps. It is finished at the bottom with a basque of lappets, the sleeves being shaped to match. The edges are bound with satin or velve.t A row is placed in addition across each point above the binding, and below the latter fall sections of rich silk or jet fringe. A jet button, with a pearl or onyx centre, in each lappet, and a row of the same down the front.

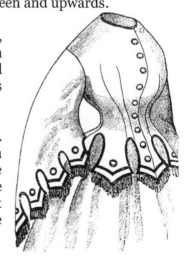

THE MALMAISON COAT.

This *petite cotte* is open, with revers, and has a basque at the back, which is divided into lappet of irregular length. In front the skirt is cut square across, and forms a Louis XIV. waistcoat. The sleeves are shaped to the arm, and ornamented with simulated revers at the wrist and a little pointed cap upon the top.

THE PEPLUM BREAKFAST JACKET.

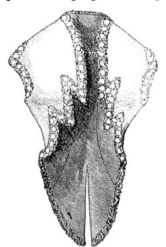

A very becoming sleeveless jacket for morning wear, cut in steps down the front, and in a long peplum point at the back. A little cap divided in the centre, forms an epaulet upon the shoulders. This jacket may be made in silk or velvet, trimmed with cluny lace; or in cashmere, ornamented with bands of silk, studded with small steel, silver or gilt buttons. It will be found a useful adjunct to summer dresses for cool mornings.

THE SASH PEPLUM.

This is the newest style in these pretty accessories to a handsome toilet. It is made with four sash ends, which are placed between the points and extend several inches below them. The sashes are studded with buttons. The trimming consists of *rouleaux* of silk or satin edged with narrow black lace. There is a belt attached, also studded with buttons, and fastened with a lace rosette.

THE JUDISA SLEEVE.

An exceedingly elegant flowing sleeve for poplin or Empress cloth. The scallops are bound with velvet, and the white band simulates velvet of a contrasting color; or, if preferred, passementerie. It is separated on the upper side only, and requires a handsome under-sleeve. The bows uniting the two sections are of velvet or ribbon the same color with which the scallops are bound. They should be fastened with aigrettes to match the passementerie.

Arthur's Home Magazine, November 1867

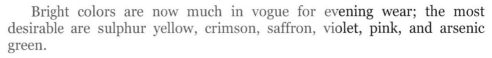

Bright colors are now much in vogue for evening wear; the most desirable are sulphur yellow, crimson, saffron, violet, pink, and arsenic green.

DINNER-DRESS.

Dress of pearl-colored silk, trimmed with a band of Magenta silk, cut in points on lie edge and trimmed with black lace. The leaf-shaped apron in also of Magenta silk, trimmed with black lace.

The salient novelty of the season is to be found in the showrooms of Mme. Demorest. We refer to the new promenade skirts, which we think destined to meet with the entire approbation of the ladies. Indeed, so pretty are these skirts, that many persons are matching them with sacks, and thus forming a pretty and decidedly comfortable travelling suit. This sensible novelty is woven in the gored shape without seam, and produces a most graceful *ensemble* over a small hooped skirt. It is all wool, warm without weight, and is either trimmed with a fluted ruffle of the material bound on each edge with a contrasting color, or else it is very elegantly braided. When once worn it will be deemed indispensable to comfort, and we pronounce it the best skirt which has yet been introduced. The juveniles, too, have been remembered, and they may also enjoy this winter a good warm ornamental skirt, which we learn may be washed as a plain piece of cloth. The prices range from six to ten dollars, children's skirts half price. The name, we think, should be altered to *Le jupon indispensable*.

WALKING SUIT.

Walking suit of rich brown poplin, trimmed with black and white velvet, arranged to simulate a notched edge. The upper skirt and sack are really notched or cut up, and trimmed richly with velvet. The sack is a very good model for cloth, and would look very well decorated with fancy silk braid.

At the Maison Tilman we find all the dresses gored: in front they fit the figure closely, while the back is laid in deep plaits.

Hoops are very close around the hips, but sufficiently large at the lower edge to support the dress.

Godey's Lady's Book and Magazine, November 1867

The French Empress, confessedly the leader of fashion, never falls into exaggeration in her dress, as some even the ladies of her own court do. She is never seen, for example, in a dress which fits the figure closely and without a pleat below the waist. Her skirts are always full at the back, and then at the side there is invariably a sash or some trimming, which takes from the very bare effect produced by a plain, pleatless skirt.

WALKING DRESS

Walking Dress of Brown Poplin. – The under-skirt is trimmed with black velvet ribbon; the short upper-skirt and paletot is also trimmed with one row of black velvet; and this skirt is looped up at the back with a long loop and bow of wide black velvet.

The mixture of gray and brown is now most popular, especially for dresses composed of *sultane* and mohair; and these pale gray costumes are almost invariably trimmed with cross-cut bands of Havana-brown silk.

EVENING DRESS, AND CAPE.

Evening Dress of White Silk, chened with pink roses and green leaves. Around the bottom of the skirt is a loop pink fringe, put on in vandykes, headed by a narrow band of green silk. Pink silk jacket, vandyked and trimmed with fringe. White tulle sleeves puffed.

Upon dresses of glace silk or foulard of a light color, with low bodices, small paletots, entirely made of guipure, are worn, ornamented with ribbons of the color of the dress. Ball-dresses of white tulle are made with long scarfs, and trimmed with garlands of flowers. Although spangles and glass beads are still too much the order the day, good taste is beginning to reassert itself.

It is the height of the fashion to dress unlike any one else; so no lady need appear in an unbecoming costume, if she has good taste; and two old dresses can be made to look as good as one new one at a very small expense. There are some rules to be observed, however, with all this licence. For street dresses, the skirt must be short; and for the house, particularly afternoon or evening dresses, it is just as necessary that the skirt should be long, for evening wear *very* long. Crinoline must be small, some even wear none at all; but with a long dress it is almost indispensable, for not one woman in a thousand knows how to wear yards of silk or muslin around her feet gracefully; it is like going about in a perpetual riding-habit. But the bodice may be high to the throat, or low, with a bodice like the under-skirt, fitting high; and the sleeves may fit closely to the arm, or be made loose in any of the numerous patterns of flowing sleeves. Much trimming, or little trimming, may be used; narrow ruffles, or bias bands, or ruches, or gimp, may be employed as ornaments, and disposed of either in the simplest or most fantastic way; in fact, there is the greatest field for exercising individual taste. Gilt, or enameled ornaments, coral beads and jet, are all fashionable as trimmings. Then the paletot may be made straight and loose, or cut more to the figure, and drawn into the waist with a broad sash tied behind; it may be either long or short, of the color of the dress, or of the petticoat.

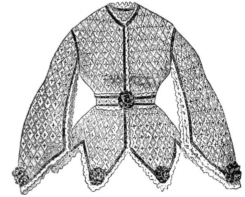

BLACK LACE BASQUE.

Black Lace Basque, trimmed with a bow and rosettes of orange-colored velvet.

THE PALETOT GALILEE.

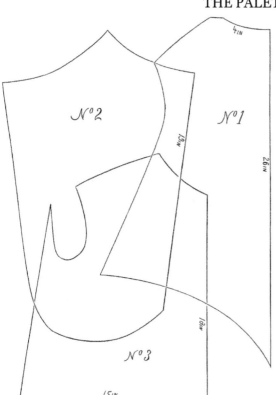

Our diagram represents exactly one half of the "Paletot Galilee." It consists of three pieces: the front, the back, and the sleeve. The front and back are joined together without any side-pieces. There is no upper part to the sleeve, which is sewn to the back of the Paletot in its entire length, being quite open in front. The sleeve describes in the center a well-accentuated point, which is finished off with a tassel. The Paletot Galilee is made both in rich black silk and black cashmere. It is embroidered at the bottom of the sleeve, and in the center of the back, with fine black *soutache* and jet beads; round the edge it is bordered with embroidery and jet. It is also made in white for evening wear; it is, in fact, the fashionable jacket of the season. The sleeves are lined with either white or cerise silk, if a very elegant Paletot is desired. If it is made of cashmere, it is lined throughout with silk.

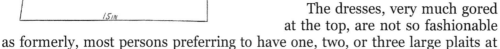

The dresses, very much gored at the top, are not so fashionable as formerly, most persons preferring to have one, two, or three large plaits at the side and back, others liking the small gathers at the back. Many silk dresses, cut with trains, are trimmed with narrow pinked-out flounces, sewn on one above another. If a sash is worn, it is trimmed to correspond, only there are fewer rows of trimming. Other train-skirts are trimmed so as to look like a double skirt; and many are cut out in round scallops, in the form of a tongue, and these are bound with satin of the color of the dress, or of satin or silk of a contrasting color.

Peterson's Magazine, November 1867

Gored skirts are made with long trains for full dress. They are gored to fit plain in front and at the sides; but the two back widths are left entire and plaited or gathered in at the waist in order to give the proper fullness to the train. In very long trains these back widths are sometimes cut off square to prevent them from curling up as pointed trains are apt to do. The front and sides are quite short – gradually sloping longer toward the back, giving a graceful sweep to the train. When two skirts are used the upper one is looped up at the sides or caught up in a loose knot behind, *à la benoiton*.

Indoor dresses for demi-toilette have plain gored skirts just long enough to escape the floor.

Promenade Dresses.

Fig. 1. – Gored dress of gray poplin, trimmed with black and white dotted ribbon, arranged in the form of a cross on a pedestal, and alternately reversed, as in the engraving.

Fig. 2. – Dress of violet silk, trimmed with violet velvet ribbon and crystal beads, with belt to match.

Fig. 3. – Short dress and under-skirt of brown and white mousse marine, trimmed with bias folds of brown silk, edged on one side with a white silk cord. The skirt is looped up a little on one side. From the belt three leaves fall like a sash nearly to the bottom of the dress, as seen in the figure.

Coat sleeves are still worn and are gradually narrowing to the tight sleeve of the Empire. Flowing sleeves are only suitable for full dress. In their proper sphere they are graceful and becoming, but are in bad taste for home dress, where comfort and convenience are the great consideration. They are cut quite short on the forearm, sloping gradually away to a point at the back, and are very much trimmed inside. Puffs and caps at the top of the coat sleeves are but little used.

Crinoline has grown beautifully less until it is as small as can possibly be worn. The standard skirt for ordinary toilette measures only two yards round the bottom, and those for ceremonious occasions only three yards, which of course affords but little assistance in managing a train.

Harper's Bazar, November 2, 1867

Dress looped up à la blanchisseuse.

The accompanying arrangement for looping up trailed dresses is both simple and convenient, and is far superior to any means for the purpose yet adopted. By this means the long robe is at once converted into a graceful walking-dress, and the whole contour of the bottom is preserved. It is only necessary to lay the front in a pleat and fasten the side breadths behind by a button and loop, or hook and loop, as seen in the first illustration; after which the back breadth is drawn up through the opening, and suffered to fall over in a puff, as seen in the second figure.

House dresses, if made with trains, must be very short in front and at the sides, as nothing more completely destroys the effect of a train than holding the skirt up in front, nor can any thing be more awkward than for a lady to continually trip herself by stepping on her dress. If long dresses are worn in the street they can be stylishly fastened up in the *blanchisseuse* fashion, so as to have precisely the effect of a short dress. The redingote style is introduced in dresses intended entirely for the house. These have surplice waists lapped on the breast and worn with a belt. The skirt also crosses over and has two rows of large buttons down the front. Chemisettes worn with these waists and with the "Pompadours" are now left open instead of closed, and are made of cluny and guipure lace.

Half-Flowing Sleeve.

Sleeve of pearl silk, trimmed as shown in the illustration with bias fold of brown silk and passementerie drop fringe. The close sleeve is trimmed simply with a bias fold.

Bell Sleeve.

Bell sleeve of lilac cretonne, trimmed with violet worsted braid in the manner shown in the illustration. ... The under sleeve is of puffed lace and lace insertion.

Coat-Sleeve with Point Trimming.

Sleeve of black silk, trimmed with three bias folds of the same, edged on both sides with satin piping, and finished with satin points as shown in the illustration.

Harper's Bazar, November 9, 1867

Velveteen suits are very fashionable this fall; but this is another caprice that we deprecate. The plainest walking-suits of this material cost sixty dollars, and many of those exhibited cost ninety or a hundred dollars, and after all are only cotton velvet. The same money would buy a suit of poplin or winsey – not quite so showy perhaps as velveteen. but at least not an imitation.

Home Toilettes.

Fig. 1. – Gored dress of Bismarck poplin. Skirt cut with a small train, and trimmed up the front with satin rouleaux, or piping, plaited, of a somewhat darker shade than the dress, and in the back with bias folds of the same satin, fastened at the ends with jet buttons. Waist and coat sleeves trimmed with satin folds and rouleaux to match the skirt.

Fig. 2. – Gored dress of pearl velours, trailing slightly, with peplum of the same material. A long sash of pearl silk is fastened at the right side, and falls nearly to the bottom of the dress. The sash and peplum are trimmed with silk fringe, with tassels on the lappets of the peplum and on the waist, as seen in the illustration. The skirt waist and coat-sleeves are trimmed with bias folds of pearl satin.

Fig. 3. – Dress and peplum of violet silk, trailing slightly, and trimmed with violet cord, fringe and tassels, and jet beads. The trimming is put on the skirt to simulate an over-skirt. The peplum is closed in front.

The attempt to have materials and of a uniform color has led to the introduction lace of various colors. These laces have a tawdry appearance, and are as much to be deprecated as the profuse use of gilt.

Low necked bodices or corselets of gros grain, with epaulets, and long lappets at the back, are trimmed with bias folds of the same material, studded with jet nail-heads. They are worn over Empress cloths and self-colored merinos.

Harper's Bazar, November 23, 1867

THE ADELAIDE DRESS.

A gored dress, for indoor wear, of brown poplin, trimmed with vertical bands of black velvet or galloon edged with brown silk cord, and studded with bronze buttons. The bands at the back, corresponding to those on the front, extend down the entire length of the dress.

Cloth costumes are already prepared for cold days; they are of a light make of cloth, and marine or sailor blue is the color universally selected for them, on account of its durability. It is trimmed either with flat braid or narrow bands of fur. The following is a novel and very distinguished style of making up one of these blue cloth dresses: The skirt is made short enough to escape the ground, and is trimmed to simulate a tunic opening at the left side; this is managed with a cross-cut band of black silk and a large sculptured ebony buttons.

CORDELLA DRESS.

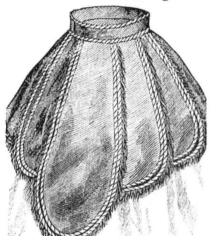

Two shades of thick brown mohair, the light forming the dress itself, and a darker shade the trimming, which is cut out straight upon [one] edge, and the other pointed. A row is placed round the bottom, headed with narrow black velvet. Sashes divided by black velvet buttons are set upon the side and back seams, and two lappets in front. A similar design is carried up over the shoulders. Belt and cuffs of trimming.

THE NETTLETON BASQUE.

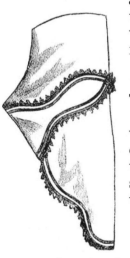

This may be cut in shape with seams upon the hips, and have the sashes described by gimp and fringe like the sleeve; or each sash may be cut by itself and the trimming extend along the edge to the extent it will be likely to show. These are nine sashes, graduating in length from each front towards the back. It will be necessary to fasten these sashes together a little distance below the belt, to keep them from flying up.

THE NETTLETON SLEEVE.

Very stylish for a dress of Eugenie blue silk, the ornamentation to be composed of blue and silver gimp and narrow blue silk fringe. It is a plain flowing shape, cut in broad scallops at the bottom, and so trimmed as to resemble lappets or sashes, one set upon the edge of the other. The underside is trimmed in the same way. A row of gimp, heading a row of fringe an inch wide, is requisite to indicate each section.

THE AGNES SLEEVE.

This is a flowing sleeve open to the bend of the arm, and ornamented with a cap, which passes over the under side of the arm, and is joined upon the back, near the top of the sleeve, by a rosette of lace. The Agnes may be made in silk or poplin, and trimmed with lace and jet, or gimp and jet. The lower part should be lined with silk, and a narrow ribbon quilling added to the inside edge.

THE LAVINA SLEEVE.

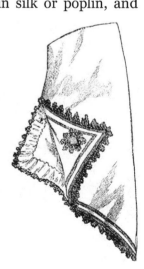

A style quite elegant for rich materials, such as heavy silk, satin, or moire. The outer side describes a lap or point of the sleeve, turned up; but as the fabrics mentioned are not, except in the first instance, perhaps, double surfaced or alike on both sides, this lap will have to be cut out to match with the shape of the sleeve and set on, the seam being hidden where it folds. The lining requires to be rich, and finished upon the edge with a broad quilling, as it shows upon the under side so conspicuously. The trimming consisted of embroidered galloon or passementerie and heavy guipure lace.

Arthur's Home Magazine, December 1867

WINTER PROMENADE SUIT.

Dress of heavy black silk, trimmed with narrow velvet and jet buttons. Coat of black velvet, with pelerine of quilted black satin. The revers are also of quilted satin, and the trimmings and the muff are grebe. Hat of black velvet, trimmed with black velvet and gold flowers.

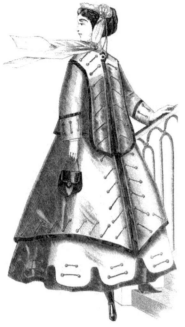

For travelling and promenade suits, we recommend the twilled winseys trimmed with mohair braids and fanciful bands of silk. Many of the sacks made *en suite* are either tied in at the back with a ribbon or fastened with a fancy strap. Sashes of every description are worn, mostly fastened at the back with long pendent ends.

PROMENADE SUIT.

Purple silk, trimmed with purple velvet, purple cord, and velvet buttons. The sack is of the same material as the dress. Bonnet of purple velvet, made with coronet front, and trimmed with velvet and feather ornaments at the sides. This same suit would make up effectively of linsey, trimmed with silk or plush.

The newest ornaments for looping dresses are gilt or jet rings; two are attached to the belt, two larger ones are then joined on, and to these are fastened one ring still larger, through which the skirt is pulled, thus making a festoon.

Fig. 9. – Silk bodice for a young lady. Our pattern was made of black silk, bound with black velvet and edged with pointed jet grelots, but it also looks well in colored silk. It is intended to be worn with a high white muslin dress, or with a muslin bodice and colored skirt.

The most elegant robes ever introduced into the realms of fashion are the evening silks embroidered in colors. Imagine a rich heavy silk of the lovely shade of blue known as *Céleste*. On this is a waved lace-like border in white, while on every breadth bloom the most gorgeously tinted flowers, mingled with drooping leaves and grasses executed in very heavy embroidery, similar to that on the Canton *crêpe* shawls of former days.

An equally elegant robe is a golden cuir ground, with clusters of poppies, corn-flowers, and wheat-ears, bound and tied with a violet ribbon. We can but tell our friends that such things are to be found, but to give an idea of their beauty is quite impossible. We have never before seen anything approaching them in elegance. The prices range from $200 to $400 the robe.

Fig. 1. – Dress of gray reps trimmed with bands and points of golden brown satin studded with steel buttons. The front of the dress is trimmed the same as the back.

Dresses are still gored, but a small plait is laid under at each seam, which gives ease to the skirt. The back breadths are either straight or but slightly gored and caught to the belt by two rows of gathers or a triple box-plait, as in Fig. 1, page 529.

The Art of the Hoop: 1860 - 1869

Fig. 3. – Dress of blue Winsey, trimmed with fancy braid and Tom Thumb fringe.

Colored silk underskirts with overskirts of black silk are much in favor. The underskirt is either plain, or finished with a little plaiting of the same; the overskirt is cut up in front in the form of strips, which are edged with fringe; the back is merely notched or cut in turrets.

Small hoops are still worn, but with a trained dress, a stiff petticoat flounced at the back is requisite, or else the back breadths of the dress are faced up much higher than the front.
Godey's Lady's Book and Magazine, December 1867

The Redingote style of walking dress is very popular. The dress can be worn rather short over a colored petticoat, or made sufficiently long to dispense with it. The body and skirt are cut in one, like the Gabrielle dress, and either buttons all the way down the front, or at the sides. In the latter case, the body buttons like a gentleman's double-breasted coat. Some are made with and some without *revers*. The dress or the petticoat should be made just long enough for the highly ornamented boots to be seen. Another avenue for coquetry has been opened in these boots. Many persons wear them of the same color as their dresses – though black boots are really much the most becoming to the feet. The boots are stitched in various colors, and the heels are very high.

WALKING DRESS

Carriage Dress of Lavender-Colored Silk, embroidered in black. The under-skirt is quite plain, the upper-skirt is open at the seams and tied carelessly at the bottom; the paletot is square, with long Jewess sleeves.

WALKING DRESS

The short dress for walking or morning wear is fully established; but long trains are equally fashionable for evening wear. For ordinary house dress the skirt is made long, but not of the exaggeration of an evening dress. The varieties in style of the short costumes is marvelous – no two dresses are just alike, and any amount of coquettish taste can be displayed if the wearer chooses.
Peterson's Magazine, December 1867

Opera Toilettes.
Fig. 1. – Gored under-skirt and low corsage of white satin, tunic of white poult-de-soie with satin stripes, bordered with a broad bias satin fold. Under-skirt trimmed with fourteen satin rouleaux. The tunic reaches to the shoulder and forms a corsage behind. Empire coiffure, profusely ornamented with foliage. Necklace and ear-rings of brilliants. White kid gloves, white fan, and point lace handkerchief.
Fig. 2. – Pearl-colored dress, with satin overskirt, trimmed round the bottom with a pleated tulle flounce, with a band of Solferino satin between each pleat. Over-skirt of the same satin, trimmed with a narrower flounce.

Marie Antoinette fichu, with short lappets falling on each side. Coiffure composed of a Louis XV. cap, formed of a shell of tulle, in which are set flat shells of satin and velvet, with crystal grelots. Pearl necklace and ear-rings. Hair rolled back from the front and falling forward from behind the ears in long crêped locks.

Fig. 3. – Blue dress of poult-de-soie. Waist covered with a corsage of puffed tulle. Coiffure similar to that of Fig. 2, composed of roses, spangled with gold. and satin shells. White cashmere opera-cloak, trimmed round the bottom and on the sleeves with satin point. Chignon rolled loosely with long crêped locks falling forward from behind.

Fig. 4. – Young girl. Tulle dress, puffed all the way down from the corsage. Pink under-skirt of taffetas, trimmed round the bottom with bias folds of pink satin, on which are scattered a few sprays of leaves to match those of the coiffure. Under-waist and sash of pink taffetas. Coiffure similar to the last, of pink roses and leaves, and satin shells. Short Eugenie curls over the forehead. Narrow pink ribbon tied loosely round the neck.

Harper's Bazar, December 7, 1867

Corsages of evening dresses are merely *corselet ceintures*, or girdles of silk, over lace or tulle chemisettes. When an over-skirt of silk is worn, the girdle and skirt are cut in the Gabrielle style, without shoulder-straps. When separated from the skirt the corsage extends over the shoulders, and is exceedingly low and square in front and back. Puffs of tulle fill out the squares to a proper height. Belts and sashes have entirely done away with pointed waists. Some dresses just imported, instead of being laced, are buttoned behind with large flat button-molds covered with the material of the dress.

Skirts of all kinds of material are gored with long trains. The front and sides are flat and close-fitting. A handsome train of medium length is formed by sloping the skirt gradually until the back widths are a yard longer than the front. An imported bridal dress measures three yards from the belt to the edge of the train, and the back widths of a white Antwerp silk are four yards long. Trained skirts are not pointed, but rounded gradually, or cut off square. Double skirts are made of two materials, the under one of rich silk with an over-skirt or tunic of lace looped at the sides, the front forming an apron, or a gauze or tulle trained skirt with long peplum or tunic of silk. The under skirt is not trimmed.

Evening Dresses.

Fig. 1. – Dress of mauve taffetas, with very long train, trimmed with a deep flounce surmounted by a ruche of violet taffetas. Neck cut square, with under-waist of puffed tulle, edged with two rows of violet velvet on rich point d'Angleterre. Short puffed sleeves, with bands of violet velvet separating the puffs. Belt of violet taffetas. Coiffure of violet ribbons.

Fig. 2. – Dress of white poult-de-soie. Gored skirt, trimmed round the bottom with a coquille of corn-colored taffetas, corselet-ceinture of corn-colored taffetas, confined by bretelles of pinked taffetas, forming a ruche which encircles the top of the corselet. Large rosette, and double lapels bias on the sides. Under-waist low in the neck, with short puffed sleeves confined by a corn-colored band. Coiffure composed of an artistically wrought jewel. White gloves.

A ball dress is of white satin. Long trained skirt with three broad rouleaux of gros grain above the hem. Over-skirt of white gaze Chambery. This is long and bordered by tinsel ribbon three inches wide. The skirt is looped up at each side with tinsel cords and tassels. Low satin bodice, above which rises a chemisette of Chambery. Short sleeves.

Harper's Bazar, December 14, 1867

Walking dresses, with sleeves and large cape, are made of plush or of velveteen, simply notched at the edge and bound or corded. When made of cashmere they are lined and wadded, and trimmed with silk quilted in diamonds. Others are braided or embroidered in bright colors, or ornamented with a satin or velvet appliqué of leaves edged with narrow serpentine gimp. Velveteen and silk velvet are bordered with ermine, astrakhan, or chinchilla. Satin crosscut bands corded with white or very narrow folds stitched in the centre, and pleated rouleaux are used for trimming poplin walking dresses; but all satin trimmings fray and soil easily, lose their gloss, and look shabby, and are consequently not serviceable for children's use.

Boulevard felt skirts are made in all sizes and handsomely trimmed with braid or Amozine embroidery.

Fancy aprons of silk, of alpaca, or of white linen, or diaper, are gored with bretelles over the shoulders, and embroidered or braided.

Home Toilettes.

Fig. 1. – Dress of black silk, trimmed with bias folds of black velvet, black velvet buttons, and black silk fringe.

Fig. 2. – Dress of gray Irish poplin, trimmed with gray satin rouleaux and silk tassels of same color; with simulated button-holes of gray braid.

Fig. 3. – Dress of brown empress cloth, trimmed with bias folds and lappets of dark brown silk, and brown buttons.

Fig. 4. – Dress of purple silk, trimmed with bias folds of black velvet, narrow black lace, and black and purple fringe, in the manner shown in the illustration.

Harper's Bazar, December 21, 1867

Valenciennes Tulle Waist.

This waist is made of a new kind of tulle simulating the texture of Valenciennes lace, whence its name. The trimming consists of a lilac ribbon, an inch in width, laid under a puff of plain tulle, which forms a frill on each side about half an inch in width. For this trimming take a straight strip of tulle three inches wide and twice as long as is desired for the puff; hem each side narrow, and gather it so as to form the before-mentioned frill on either side. The neck and sleeves trimmed with bows and ends of lilac ribbon.

Harper's Bazar, December 28, 1867

Making the Short Walking Dress.

Every lady, we believe, aspires to be well dressed, and to follow, to a moderate extent, the prevailing modes. We do not advocate extremes, and would not advise any one to follow blindly every foible that appears; but when a desirable fashion is introduced, it is well that it should be adopted. One thing, however, should always be remembered, that every new fashion mast be modified to suit the years and style of the wearer. The subject under consideration is the short walking dress, which has taken so wonderfully of late. As we must all adopt it, sooner or later, let us go to work and assist those who are not able to give the exorbitant prices now demanded by dressmakers.

By following our directions, we think there will be little difficulty in cutting one of these dresses. The measures we give are for a medium-sized person, and will be found a good guide, but, of course, must be varied to suit the size of the wearer. Garments old in the service we have no doubt will be brought out and remodelled into fashionable costumes.

The lower skirt must by no means touch the ground, but should be of sufficient length to appear well when walking. It is composed of eight breadths, the back and front being without seam down the centre. The front width measures thirty-nine inches in length, is twenty-four inches wide at the lower edge, and slopes on each side up to the waist where it only measures six inches. The back breadth is precisely the same width, but is forty-one inches long. The three intermediate ones are alike, being twenty two inches wide at the lower part, and slope on one side up to three inches. The breadths are sewed together so that the gored side is always nearest the back of the dress.

The upper skirt is composed of eight smaller gores, and, as in the lower skirt, the front and back widths are without seam down the centre. These breadths are the same in width, sloping on each side from nineteen inches to the waist, which is but six inches. The front breadth is thirty-one inches long and the back thirty-three. The other widths are thirty-three inches long, and slope from eighteen to three inches. The edge of the upper skirt is notched or dentated in fancy motifs or designs. For instance, points with the ends cut off forming squares, turrets, slanting teeth, scallops, lozenge-shaped ends, graduated steps, the sharp points known *folies*, and many other inexplicable designs, that fancy alone dictates. The tips of the points or ends are generally finished with fringe or jet trimming made on the material, with bugles and beads.

The lower skirt generally has a plain edge trimmed with a fold of velvet or satin studded with beads, or else it is finished with a Marie Antoinette ruffle a quarter of a yard deep, sewed on in overlapping single plaits. In Paris the latter style is the one most generally preferred.

Godey's Lady's Book and Magazine, February 1867

Mr. Worth's Influence.

The New Style of Skirt. – The great dress-maker Paris, our readers should known [sic], is a man. To have their dresses made by Mr. Worth is the ambition of everybody in the French capital who can afford it. Worth has just introduced an entirely new kind of skirt, one very long the back, and very short in front. Skirts, which are made with a petticoat to match, are only scalloped or vandyked in the front; at the back the edge of the skirt falls in straight line over the petticoat. There is endless variety in the form of what are called *dents* in France, and for which expression there is, we believe, no equivalent in English which expresses the meaning in a single word. By *dents* are understood the scallops, vandykes, and three sides of a square, (styled battlements,) into which it has become the fashion to cut out the edges of all skirts and petticoats. There are, likewise, the large lozenge-shaped dents, the small and very pointed *dents* called *folies*, the round *dents*, more or less scalloped or hollowed out, (and when these last named are used, the trimming is usually carried up to the center of the skirt;) and, lastly, there are the *dents grecques*.

All the taste and fancy which a dress-maker may possess are expended, now-a-days, on the cut and trimmings of the skirt: but little attention apparently paid to the bodice, in the style of which there is no change; in fact, many of the fantastic toilets, which are in great demand at the present moment, are made without bodices to match, a *chemise-russe*, or a Garibaldi, replacing the legitimate bodice. If a short dress is ordered, in either *gros grain* or velvet, then a low, square bodice, with braces to match the skirt, is made, and this is worn either over a high white bodice, or over a silk bodice of a totally different color. The most charming effects have been obtained, in this very fantastic style of ladies' costume, by a skillful mixture of poplin and cashmere.

Peterson's Magazine, February 1867

Traveling Dress.

The season of preparation for travel has again arrived. The most desirable materials are spotted Winsey, a somewhat glossy mottled fabric different from the ordinary materials known by that name; another is *crêpe* poplin, a rather thin *crêpy*-looking material, trimming up very effectively; then a material resembling Pongee, to be had in the most desirable shades of Bismarck, cuir, and mode. Besides the above, there is *Mousse Marine*, resembling a striped mohair; the Sulline, a kind of poplin covered with tiny stars; the Sultane, a mohair striped with satin.

For travelling costume short dresses are universally adopted, and the two skirts are generally simulated by trimming, as it is a saving of trouble, material, and expense, and is decidedly more comfortable.

The dresses are all gored and made with loose sacks, some with close coat, and others with long hanging sleeves.

At all our principal stores costumes of this description may be obtained ready made, or else material can be selected and the suit is made up according to the wishes of the wearer. This is certainly a great convenience, and in most cases it is less expensive than when attended to by a regular dressmaker. These *toilettes* are generally trimmed with bias silk cut in fanciful devices and edged with braid, or else pipings or folds of satin. The edge is generally notched out and bound to match the dress. Satin is decidedly the most fashionable trimming that we have, and it is used on everything. In black it has appeared with a linen back, which gives it firmness, adds to its durability, and lessens the price about one-half. This material can be purchased on the bias, and is extensively used for dress and sack trimmings.

In New York the most elegant materials are being made up for short walking-dresses. Though black silk suits are very much in vogue, light goods very elaborately and gayly trimmed are equally desirable. They are considered the most fashionable style of dress for visiting and receptions, though in Paris they have been entirely abandoned for dressy occasions, and are merely reserved for walking and travelling. This we think a very sensible decree, for while the short skirt is decidedly too convenient to be rejected for street wear, it has not the grace of a trained skirt, and is not adapted for evening or *grande toilette*.

Godey's Lady's Book and Magazine, July 1867

The variety of wool materials suitable for tourists is greater than usual, and since last month goods have fallen very much in price. Mohairs of good quality and of every imaginable shade can now be had for 53 cents a yard. All that is required for a costume is a short skirt, very narrow, say four yards wide, trimmed to simulate two skirts. With this a short loose sack with coat-sleeves is worn. All this can be obtained out of seven yards of material, so that a travelling dress may be made up at very little expense.

The most convenient travelling petticoats are of a cotton and wool material, striped gray and white, the width of the stripes varying from a straw to three inches. These skirts, when tightly gored and trimmed with applications of silk and velvet, are exceedingly pretty. The material costs 63 cents a yard, and it requires but three and a half or four yards for the skirt. Some are decorated with bands of cloth, cut out in scallops and embroidered with silks of various colors; others, again, are ornamented with bands of imitation Cluny and medallion of bright-colored cloth. Another effective trimming is formed of narrow silk bands arranged as ladders. The edge of the skirt is generally notched out in some fanciful style and bound.

Godey's Lady's Book and Magazine, August 1867

1868

Fig. 1. – Walking costume of light Bismarck velours, trimmed with bands of satin of the same shade, and Bismarck velvet buttons. The quillings may be of the dress material or of satin, the later of course would be the most elegant. The dress can be made with two skirts, or the trimming can be laid on to give the appearance of a second skirt.

In former years travellers, on their return home, were immediately struck with the antiquated appearance of their friends. This is no longer the case; they now find that we are posted up on all the latest novelties, and are as well dressed as most Parisians.

WALKING DRESSES.

Fig. 1. – Dress of wine-colored reps, trimmed in the sash form at the sides, with velvet to match, and large fancy buttons. The trimming is arranged on the skirt to simulate two skirts. The effect is increased by having the portion of the dress below the trimming of a darker shade of the silk.

Fig. 2. – Dress of frog-color winsey, trimmed with bands of black velvet laid in steps on the front of the dress. The corsage is trimmed to match.

Fig. 3 – Dress of noisette (a new shade of brown) velours, trimmed with narrows of jet gimp and a silk fringe tipped with jet. To give the dress more the appearance of two skirts, the lower part is of silk of a darker shade. The sack is of velours, to match the silk, and the tight sleeves are of silk.

Fig. 4. – Walking dress, made with two skirts. The material is blue poplin, trimmed with velvet straps of different lengths pointed at the ends. The over-skirt is laid in very full plaits at the side, which gives a very graceful effect. At the back is a wide sash of the material bound and trimmed with velvet, and tied or arranged in four loops and two long ends. This costume is intended for a miss.

Fig. 5. – Walking suit of gray poplin, trimmed with four plain bands of bias satin slightly darker than the dress. The appearance of a second skirt is given by four more bands of satin fastened up at each side by a bunch of leaves formed of satin. The corsage is trimmed to correspond. The dress would be improved by having a poplin sash, bound with satin and ornamented with leaves, tied in large loops at the back.

Now it frequently happens that it is not convenient to change one's dress for the promenade, and to let it drag proves fatal to a good material. It was therefore necessary that Dame Fashion should invent some new method for looping a trained skirt. The result of her cognitions proves admirable; she gives us a new style of festooning quickly arranged, and the same time graceful. We will try to describe it. Take hold of the skirt each side of the front breadth about halfway down, then raise it in a smooth fold to the height of a short dress; carry the fold to the back, where the two sides, or the fold from the sides, are pinned together. The long portion of the skirt which hangs down at the back is then drawn over where the skirt is pinned together, and forms a bag-like loop. In our next number we will give a cut which will probably explain our ideas better.

The rings for looping dresses spoken of last month, are to be had in gilt or jet, arranged thus: Two rings about an inch and a half in diameter, with a bar down the centre are run on the belt, from these are chains or else two larger rings, which are attached to a large ring about four inches in diameter. They are now used as ornaments for sashes, the long ends being passed through the rings. Modistes are making them of velvet or satin to suit the dress, and powdering them with fancy beads. They are exceedingly stylish ornaments, and are frequently worn at the side of the dress.

Fig. 3. – Gray poplin dress, with fancy corsage and sash of green silk, trimmed with chenille fringe. The sash is finished on the end with a very deep silk and chenille fringe.

Madame Demorest has brought out a variety of new sleeves and fancy basques. The Nina is a sleeve almost close at the wrist, but cut above the elbow in long leaf-like points. Another is a close sleeve, but so arranged that it simulates a hanging sleeve with close undersleeve. This is quite pretty, and requires but little material. The Batinea is very wide in the upper part, and is laid in a box plait to the elbow, where it is cut square and shaped in the coat style. From the elbow to waist the outer edge is cut in scallops, and flat bows with buckles in the centre are placed between the scallops.

In basquines, or fancy girdles intended for evening wear or suitable for home dresses, we find the Brabant. This is a belt richly ornamented, attached to a basque a quarter of a yard deep on the hips and extending at the back into two sash ends a yard in length. The front is sloped into an end three-quarters of a yard deep. The edge is waved and elegantly trimmed with cluny lace and fringe. Another style resembles the preceding in front, but in the back is merely a basquine nine inches long. The Viennois is formed of eight gores; two small ones on each hip pointed and measuring three fingers from the belt to the end of the point. The others are also pointed and much longer, measuring about five fingers. Each gore is covered with trimming, and the edge is ornamented with bugle gimp and fringe. The Montmartre is a very stylish garment. It is cut with twelve gores; first one gore a quarter of a yard long, cut straight on the lower edge; then a long sash, also cut straight on the lower edge; then two like the first; then a long sash and a short gore form just one-half of the basque. We should add that the gores are sloped on each side, the short ones sloping from five to two inches; each seam is trimmed, also the edge. The ends of the sashes may be trimmed quite elaborately.

↖ Fig. 5. – Dinner or reception dress of luminous green silk, trimmed with a band of white satin and narrow green fringe. This trimming is arranged to simulate a double skirt. The straps are all of white satin, and the buttons of green velvet.

Fig. 4. – Dress of black silk, trimmed with bands formed of black and white satin run in together. The basque is quite novel, and will look well in any material.

Sashes have become very important items in a lady's *toilette*, many of the fancy ones costing from fifteen to thirty dollars. Some of them are thus arranged: The belt consists of alternate folds of the dress material, and satin caught at the back by a bow bound with satin; the streamers are also bound with satin, and are tied in a knot at the end, and finished with a long tassel, or else the ends are square and ornamented with a rosette or bow made of satin. We also see them of wide ribbon, velvet and satin arranged *à l'Ecossaise*; that is, caught on the right shoulder and tied under the left arm. This is a good style for evening wear, or for children.

Godey's Lady's Book, January 1868

Bretelle belt of blue taffetas, composed of three lappets in front and three behind, bretelles, and belt, all edged with black guipure. This beautiful belt is of an entirely new shape, and is easily made. It is worn over a muslin or lace waist for opera or dinner toilette, and also sets off a Cashmere or silk waist of a harmonizing color.

Harper's Bazar, January 4, 1868

A New Year's reception dress prepared, by one of our most tasteful modistes is of gros grain of the delicate shade known as pistache. The long, full-trained skirt is plain about the hips and front, but is gathered at the back in several rows of French gathers. The front width is cut off at the knee and finished by a wide flounce set on in box pleats. Large velvet leaves, embroidered with floss, and shaded from a dark green to the lightest shade, form a heading to the flounce. Similar leaves, alternating with others of gros grain, bound with white satin, are arranged around the skirt about ten inches from the edge. The long sash-ends are ornamented with three leaves at the points of which are acorn pendants of green and white. There are two waists to this dress – a plain high corsage with flowing sleeves, and a low round waist with bertha of folds and short puffed sleeves.

An appropriate toilette for a married lady receiving New-Year's calls has just been completed. It is of Lyons velvet, of a rich maroon color. The front widths of the skirt are left open, disclosing a white satin under-skirt. Two wide ruffles of point appliqué lace are sewn on the front width of the petticoat. A thick satin cord surrounds the velvet skirt. The corsage is round at the waist and short on the shoulder. A revers or surplice collar leaves the throat bare. The revers is faced with white satin, and edged with maroon-piping and appliqué lace. Chemisette of tulle, and under-sleeves puffed from wrist to arm-hole. Long flowing sleeves lined with white.

A very appropriate and far more simple toilette for a young lady is of white French poplin, gracefully made and trimmed. It is gored in the Princesse style. The skirt measures two and a half yards from belt to edge of train. The front width is cut entire and plain. A Spanish flounce, beginning at the front seams, half a yard wide, becomes gradually narrower toward the back. Three rows of blue satin pipings an inch thick are sewn above the flounce. A finger-length above these are three other rows, to which are added a netted fringe with blue crocheted pendants. High corsage and coat sleeves. Blue satin pipings arranged about the shoulders with a bertha of fringe. Similar trimming on the sleeves and sash. Large buttons of blue satin with a pearl rim. Point lace collar and under-sleeves. Jewelry of turquoise and pearl.

Harper's Bazar, January 11, 1868

For the convenience of dancers short ball dresses are coming into favor. The trains now so necessary for full dress are objects of censure to gentlemen, and occasion a good deal of annoyance to their wearers. The new Pompadour trains are more easily managed, as they are left open in front and may be thrown over the arm in a crowd.

A morning dress for sea-voyages is of Petersham cloth, a kind of tufted French flannel, in alternate blocks of purple and white, with a purple tuft, somewhat resembling Astrakhan cloth. The garment is cut in a loose Gabrielle, confined at the waist with a belt of the same material. A pointed hood, lined with purple silk, is attached to this wrapper, making it a comfortable dress for deck-promenades on ship-board. The price is $30.

Bretelles of black velvet and guipure lace are fashionably worn with self-colored dresses of empress cloth or velours. Sailor collars of fine linen, deeply pointed at the side, are pretty for morning wear.

Harper's Bazar, January 18, 1868

Double skirts are very much worn. When gracefully made they take away the stiffness of a gored dress. They are bordered around the edge when short, but when left long, following the train of the lower skirt, they are only scalloped at the front seams, and looped up, forming an apron.

Pelisses and redingotes require five yards of material, seven-eighths of a yard wide. They are lined with flannel or cloth, and occasionally with fur, and are worn without other wrapping.

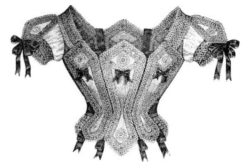

Pompadour Basque Waist.

This waist is of muslin, guipure insertion four-fifths of an inch wide, guipure edging three-fifths of an inch wide, small needle-work rosettes edged with lace, and blue ribbon one and two inches in width. ... With the ribbon make short loops at the top and long loops with ends at the bottom of the waist. Put on the frilled edging, the rosettes, and the bows of narrow ribbon. Lay a strip of muslin doubled along the edge of the left front, sew small buttons thereon, and cover it with blue ribbon, making corresponding loops on the right side. The sleeves consist of a strip of muslin, about three-quarters of a yard long and four inches wide, puffed and confined by a band of insertion and edging, with a lappet, similarly trimmed, and a ribbon bow the top.

Bodice with Lappets – Front.
Bodice with Lappets – Back.

This bodice is made of narrow silk braid, notched on the edges and studded with beads, black watered ribbon an inch and a half wide, black lace two and four inches wide, studded with beads, jet buttons, and jet grelots.

Harper's Bazar, January 25, 1868

Velveteen is very much worn, not only for paletots, but for entire walking costumes. These velveteen dresses are made sufficiently long to come to the top of the instep, not showing any under-skirt, and are without any trimming whatever. We have seen two beautiful ones, one of a rich dark blue, and the other of violet. These are, of course, most suitable for young ladies; whilst gray, brown, and black, can be worn by a woman of any age. Black silk skirts, worn over bright-colored petticoats, or trimmed with some brilliant color, are also favorite walking dresses.

PATTERN FOR A TRAIN SKIRT.

Ladies frequently complain of the difficulty of getting a good-fitting skirt to wear under a train. We give above an engraving of one, and, on the next page, a diagram by which a paper pattern may be cut out.

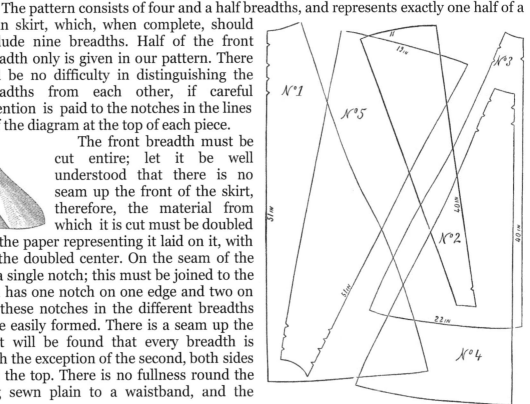

The pattern consists of four and a half breadths, and represents exactly one half of a train skirt, which, when complete, should include nine breadths. Half of the front breadth only is given in our pattern. There will be no difficulty in distinguishing the breadths from each other, if careful attention is paid to the notches in the lines of the diagram at the top of each piece.

The front breadth must be cut entire; let it be well understood that there is no seam up the front of the skirt, therefore, the material from which it is cut must be doubled down the center, and the paper representing it laid on it, with its straight edge over the doubled center. On the seam of the front breadth there is a single notch; this must be joined to the second breadth, which has one notch on one edge and two on the other; by making these notches in the different breadths match, the skirt can be easily formed. There is a seam up the center of the back. It will be found that every breadth is straight at one side with the exception of the second, both sides of which are sloped at the top. There is no fullness round the waist, the skirt being sewn plain to a waistband, and the overplus material put into one large box-pleat at the back. This pattern will suit a figure of moderate height – five feet three and a half inches: but should any shortening or lengthening be required to suit an individual figure, it must be allowed for at the bottom, and not at the top of the skirt.

Skirts are still very much gored, and are being more trimmed. Narrow flounces, about three inches deep, or one flounce a quarter of a yard deep, are among the newest trimming.

WALKING DRESS.

Walking Dress of Black Silk. – The under-petticoat is trimmed with bands and bows of black silk. The upper-skirt is looped up with black silk bows, and trimmed with a fringe. The short paletot is ornamented to correspond.

One of the most stylish walking costumes which we have seen is of black velveteen, worn over a rich black silk petticoat with a flounce. The velveteen dress is cut in the redingote, or polonaise style, slightly full in the back, and fastened around the waist with a broad silk sash edged with fringe. The dress is larger at the back than in front, and is fastened at the sides. Some wear the skirts of these redingotes open in front.

Sashes, as we observed in our December number, are very much worn. If the ribbon-sash cannot be procured, silk of twenty or twenty-two inches wide is usually taken, cut in two and pinked, and used for the purpose. Some of these sashes have small bows on each end, others are gathered together at the ends, and finished with tassels.

Peterson's Magazine, January 1868

Gored morning dress of white alpaca, trimmed with a blue velvet garniture. Sash of blue velvet, carelessly knotted at the side. The wrapper is open in front, showing a blue silk petticoat.

A lady requests us to publish fashions for ladies of forty or fifty years of age. Leave off some of the trimmings of our dresses, and you have them. By the way, it is ladies of about forty or fifty with us that wear the most expensive dresses.

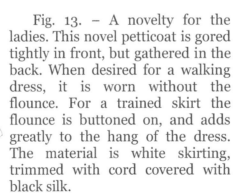

Fig. 13. – A novelty for the ladies. This novel petticoat is gored tightly in front, but gathered in the back. When desired for a walking dress, it is worn without the flounce. For a trained skirt the flounce is buttoned on, and adds greatly to the hang of the dress. The material is white skirting, trimmed with cord covered with black silk.

Walking dresses are frequently made available for other purposes by the addition of a train, which is plaited on to a band at the waist, and buttons down the side seams. Another style is arranged as the petticoat on the extension sheet, Fig. 13. ↗ The flounce may either match or be of a contrasting color.

A very good style of short dress is gored to fit the figure very loosely, and is then caught in to the waist by a ribbon sash ornamented by velvet rings. [*see Fig. 2 on the next page*]

Figs. 2. and 3. – (Front and back view.) Walking dress of Bismarck poplin, trimmed with velvet of a darker shade. The overdress is gored loosely, and is drawn into the figure by a poplin belt bound with velvet. The rings through which the sash is passed are formed of Bismarck velvet studded with jet. For home or evening wear rings of gilt might be arranged in the same style. A ring of velvet, corresponding with those on the sash, is placed on the belt in front. This is a very good costume, and can be made up with trimmings to match, or of a contrasting color. It is suitable for Winsey, poplin, alpaca, silk, or velveteen.

↙ Fig. 4. – Long dress, looped to simulate a short walking-dress. Underskirt of black merino, trimmed with a band of Oriental bordering. The upper skirt is of poplin, looped according to the directions given in the chat of last month. The sack is of black poplin, trimmed with very elegant silk bordering in the Oriental style.

Among the pretty things that were to be seen at the [Paris] Exposition, was a white silk dress, with peacock's feathers embroidered upon it so admirably, that at first sight almost every one was deceived by the resemblance; also an apple-green silk dress, embroidered with silk and pearls so as to produce the effect of velvet and lace; some splendid *guipure de cluny* over silk; and specimens of embroidery in colored silk, straw, and other materials, some of it evidently after Japanese models.

Fig. 5. – Dinner-dress of ashes of roses silk, trimmed with Magenta silk. The Marie Antoinette fichu is continued down in sashes on each side of the skirt, and caught together by rosettes of the dress silk. The edge of the skirt is ornamented by bands of Magenta velvet laid in festoons, and trimmed with Tom Thumb fringe. A still more elegant dress is obtained by continuing the sashes all round, forming, as it were, a second skirt. As the dress is cut with a long train directly at the back, the sashes should be graduated in length.

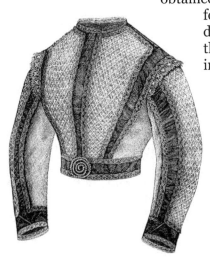

The great dress novelty is still the waistband rings, through which sashes are hung in elegant folds behind.

Fig. 12. – Bodice of white muslin; the fronts and upper part of the sleeves are covered with white guipure tulle, trimmed with lace and strips of colored satin ribbon. The waistband, of ribbon edged with lace, is fastened under a lace rosette.

Godey's Lady's Book, February 1868

Promenade and Demi Toilettes.

Fig. 1. – Dress of Metternich green velours, trimmed with wide black military braid, set on in blocks round the bottom, and simulating lappets with buttons on each breadth of the skirt. Short paletot of the same material as the dress, and trimmed with wide braid and buttons to match the latter, the braid simulating a bertha on the upper part of the paletot. Bonnet of Metternich green velvet, with grebe trimming, and fall of black lace over the chignon.

Fig. 2. – Under-skirt of purple gros grain, trimmed with three rows of wide black galloon. Fourreau of black gros grain, festooned with the same galloon, down the middle of which passementerie buttons set. Castellated, scalloped trimming, bound with and surmounted with galloon, adorns the breadths of the fourreau. Short paletot of black velvet, trimmed with heavy silk fringe, galloon, buttons, and velvet scallops. Bonnet of purple velvet, with deep fall of lace over the chignon, and a gilt band with cut steel ornaments in front. Astrakhan muff, without tassels.

Fig. 3. – Gored dress of Mentana red poult de soie, with ladder trimming on the sides, consisting of satin folds of the same color, edged with black guipure lace and studded with passementerie buttons. The same satin folds and buttons form a graduated turret trimming around the back and front, as seen in the illustration. The bottom is trimmed with a heavy satin cord, surmounted by scalloped satin, edged with guipure lace. High waist and close sleeves, trimmed to match the skirt.

Ball and Evening Dresses.

These dresses are all gored, with very short waists, and are worn over a chemisette of puffed or figured lace; a puffing of lace being likewise set in the arm-hole.

Fig. 1. – Dress of green taffetas, with a narrow flounce of the same material round the bottom; this flounce is surmounted by three puffings of white lace, separated by satin rouleaux. Short over-skirt of light-green taffetas, with broad, pointed flounce, covered with white lace, over which satin rouleaux intersect each other in a sort of trellis. Two long sash ends fall in the back of the skirt. The low corsage is trimmed round the neck with a narrow frill of taffetas, surmounted by a satin rouleau. White roses complete the trimming.

Fig. 2. – Dress of pink taffetas, with short over-skirt of white muslin, both trimmed with a muslin quilling.

Fig. 3. – Dress and over-skirt of lilac silk; the latter bound with lilac ribbon and edged with broad black lace. Black lace bertha.

The Pompadour colors, blue and pink together, are in vogue for evening dress. A Parisian ball-dress has an over-skirt of blue crape dotted with silver, on white crape. Knots of pink satin sprinkle the skirt, and bouquets of pale roses from an apron and bertha.

Satin is very much used in conjunction with tulle, not only beneath it as transparent, but as peplum over-skirts, as tabliers or aprons, and as open trains over two or three tulle skirts. It is made into berthas and sashes, and the Marie Antoinette fichus that form a noticeable feature in the best toilettes of the season. It is also arranged in folds with pearl trimming and blonde lace to form braces or bretelles for low-necked dresses of gauze and self-colored silk.

White crape is used for trimming ball-dresses. It is scarcely so becoming as tulle, but is preferred on account of its novelty and its peculiar glistening in the gaslight like hoar-frost. A beautiful evening dress, worn by a blonde, is of a delicate new shade of green *faille* (another name for poult de soie moiré), with white crape bertha and tunic, with reversed plaited puffs around the trained skirt.

Harper's Bazar, February 1, 1868

EVENING, OPERA, AND BALL DRESSES.

Fig. 1. – Evening dress of pink satin, over which a black lace bedouin is worn as a fourreau. As is shown in the illustration, the bedouin is arranged without any fullness round the waist, and is fastened behind, where the ends are looped together. The bedouin can also be worn as a fourreau in the style of Fig. 3, with the ends sewed together. Low-necked corsage, around which is a deep frill of black lace and a quilling of pink satin ribbon. Short sleeves of puffed satin. Pearl bracelets. White kid gloves. Belt of pink satin to match the dress.

Fig. 2. – Opera dress. Pompadour gored dress of blue silk. Close Watteau sleeves, reaching only to the elbow, and finished with an under-sleeve of puffed lace. Spanish mantilla of black figured lace, trimmed with a lace frill, and pointed at the bottom, and finished with silk tassels. The mantilla also serves as a head-dress, being confined on the head by a diadem of flowers. It is fastened in front by a flower of the same kind as those used for the diadem. White kid gloves and white fan.

Fig. 3. – Ball dress of white tarlatan, trimmed round the bottom with four puffings of tarlatan. Fourreau of white lace, trimmed with 3 narrow rouleaux of pink satin. Bertha of puffed lace and rouleaux of pink satin. Broad sash of pink satin ribbon, tied in a bow behind, and looping up the fourreau as shown in the illustration. Low corsage of white tarlatan, with short puffed sleeves, trimmed round the bottom with a frill of narrow edging. Pearl necklace, ear-rings, and bracelets. Chignon of curls, wreath of pink roses in the hair.

A pretty addition to a solid-colored silk dress is a sleeveless jacket of Brussels lace with satin pipings arranged in scallops. Beaded lace edge with jet pendants. Long sash of lace.

High Waist with Simulated Fichu.

The waist is ... of brown velours trimmed with a bias fold of brown silk simulating a fichu. This fold is edged on each side with black lace. The sleeves are likewise trimmed on the top and bottom with a bias fold of silk edged with lace. A brown silk belt with sash ends completes the dress.

Dress with Velvet Rolling Collar.

Marie Antoinette Dress.

This dress is of brown silk. The waist is plain and high, but is cut out in the shape of a heart in front. The sleeves have a puffing at the top, ... Below the puffing the sleeves are close to the elbow, where they are terminated by two deep frills of lace. The puffing is trimmed with a bias fold of the same material as the dress. A white lace fichu and a belt and bow of brown silk complete the waist.

Harper's Bazar, February 8, 1868

Evening and Opera Toilettes.

Fig. 1. – Empire skirt of pearl-gray poult de soie. Corsage of white tarlatan, gathered all round into cherry silk, edged with narrow lace, and Middle-Age sleeves in two pieces, with white puffing at the elbow. Lace cuffs. Broad corselet-ceinture of cherry silk, knotted at the side. White kid gloves.

Fig. 2. – Dress of tea-rose poult de soie, covered with an opera cloak of white silk, trimmed with white galloon embroidered with gold. This cloak is loose and open up the middle of the back, the opening being finished at the top with a Gothic ornament. The collar is trimmed with heavy silk tassels, matching the galloon. The close sleeves are likewise open in the back, and are trimmed in the same manner. White kid gloves.

A breakfast-suit for a Southern climate is of thick nansook. A short, round jacket is worn over a puffed waist. The skirt is long and gored. Two standing ruffles of Valenciennes trim the neck and wrists of the jacket. Bands of cambric insertion and Valenciennes, arranged diagonally in square blocks, are inserted down the front. An outside breast-pocket is ruffled with lace, and a monogram is embroidered in the centre. Two box-pleated ruffles are on the edge of the skirt, above them is a row of lace blocks or medallions.

PROMENADE DRESSES.

Fig. 1. – Dress of dark brown silk. Short fourreau and paletot of brown poplin, trimmed with mother-of-pearl buttons. The fourreau is caught up on each side with bands.

Fig. 2. – Dress and paletot of purple velours, trimmed with bias folds of brown satin, which simulate an over-skirt on the dress.

Fig. 3. – Dress and paletot of gray empress cloth, trimmed with black satin piping, which simulates an over-skirt in the manner shown in the illustration.

Harper's Bazar, February 15, 1868

Visiting and Reception Toilettes.

Fig. 1. – Suit of bright blue poplin, composed of skirt and redingote. The skirt is trimmed with a bias fold of black satin, forming a Greek figure, with a black galloon set zigzag between the narrow interstices. The broad sash is trimmed in the same manner, and is confined at the top by three jet sash rings, fastened together with black and white cords. The redingote is trimmed round the edge with a bias fold of black satin. Black velvet bonnet, trimmed with blue satin and blue velvet flowers.

Fig. 2. – Dress of mauve satin, trimmed with bias folds of a darker shade, finished at each end with a button covered with the same satin as the fold. On each side of the front breadth, nearly under the arm, these folds simulate broad sash ends, ending in lozenges, and the end of which is trimmed with buttons and fringe. The high waist is trimmed with a simulated bertha of bias folds and net fringe; the bottom of the sleeves has a similar bias fold, running up toward the elbow, and finished with fringe.

Harper's Bazar, February 22, 1868

Home and Evening Dresses.

Fig. 1. – Dress of brown silk, with high waist and peplum, formed of lappets edged with satin piping. Skirt with small train. Close sleeves. Lappets edged with satin piping, to match the peplum are set round the arm-hole.

Fig. 2. – Evening Dress. Under-skirt of white silk. Over-skirt of white tulle, with four rows of puffing round the bottom of the skirt, separated by rows of narrow green satin piping. Fichu of blonde, piping, rosettes, and bows of green satin, with long sash-ends behind, which are crossed over each other.

Fig. 3. – Dress of white cashmere. Fichu of white blonde, trimmed with gilt flowers. The long sash-ends of the fichu are crossed at the side.

Loose, square breakfast jackets are giving place to bodices with tight-fitting sleeves and a sash worn at the side. Another style has a small basque attached to the waist instead of a sash.

Jacket with Fur Trimming. – Back.
Jacket with Fur Trimming. – Front.
Harper's Bazar, February 29, 1868

Hungarian jackets, embroidered in gold, have been the fashion in Paris ever since the Emperor of Austria was there. The jackets are adapted for female wear, and are made in black, dark-blue, and also in Sevres blue cloth, and are ornamented with broad old braid, framed in a design carried out in gold soutache. They fasten at the side with a row of small chased gold buttons, and the wide sleeves are almost covered with gold soutache. They are very stylish, and regarded as dressy garments, notwithstanding their being made of cloth. They are known also as "Elizabeth Paletots," are made in white and in deep crimson cloth, and then are intended for carriage or evening wear. They will quite take the place of the Breton jacket.

DINNER DRESS.

Fig. VI. – House Dress of Blue Silk, made in the Gabrielle style, buttoned down the front, and with a deep flounce at the back. It is trimmed with white Cluny lace and floss tassels.

Redingotes are a good deal worn; but it is difficult to make them sufficiently warm for our cold winters. If too heavily wadded, they do not look graceful when tied at the back with the sash.

Nearly all dresses not made in the Princess fashion, that is, with the bodice and skirt cut out all in one piece, have round waists. But a great many waistbands with basques are worn, and quite change the appearance of the dress. These waistbands are made in different styles, some with long lapels forming a sash.

One of the newest is the *Bayadere* ceinture, it has a rounded basque in front and at the back, and long lapels finished off in points on either side.

WALKING DRESS.

Fig. VII. – Walking Dress of Bismark-Colored Poplin. – The petticoat of the same material as the dress, is quite plain; the front of the upper-skirt crosses the back part, which is made separate, and buttons over it. The loose sacque corresponds.

WALKING DRESS.

Walking Dress of Gray Merino; the under and upper-skirts, sacque, and sleeves, are all scalloped and trimmed with black velvet. Black velvet trimmings, in the shape of leaves, ornament the sides.

Pockets, slit open lengthways on either side of the front width, are always ornamented with lapels, or else concealed under the trimming placed upon the seams of the front width. No pockets are made to ball-dresses; there must be one in the under petticoat.

There are still various ways of cutting dresses, because the same cut does not suit all ladies. Some prefer a skirt perfectly plain; others will not give up having a few pleats or gathers at the back. So far all this is allowed by fashion, and depends on personal taste.

WALKING DRESS.

Walking dress of Violet-Colored Cashmere; the petticoat is of violet cashmere, trimmed with bands of black silk. The upper-skirt and sacque are trimmed with black cords and buttons.

The Pompadour style is also becoming very popular, thus producing quite a revolution in dresses. The bodice is low and square, and the dress made with two skirts, is looped up at the sides, thereby forming large festoons. The chief points of difference between a dress of to-day and one of a hundred years ago is, that the two skirts are made of the same material, and that the sleeves are narrow instead of being wide; also that the waists are not so long as they were worn at that epoch. The cut of the back of the bodice is precisely the same, the lower half of the center-piece is extremely narrow, consequently the side pieces are wide in proportion.

Peterson's Magazine, February 1868

Fig. 1. – A very stylish short costume of black velveteen and Bismarck satin. The front is trimmed to correspond with the back.

Fig. 2. – Dinner-dress of heavy green silk, made *en train*. It is trimmed with Cluny lace, and leaves and rosettes formed of green velvet. The body is low, and worn over an illusion waist trimmed with pipings of white satin.

Fig. 3. – Rich reception dress of black satin, trimmed with pipings, jet beads, and heavy jet and silk fringe. It is made to display a petticoat of blue silk striped with black satin. The appearance of the dress may be changed by wearing it over different colored skirts.

Fig. 5. – Dress of purple silk, trimmed with bands of velvet and tassels arranged in a graduated pattern. The sash is of wide ribbon, knotted at the back. Fancy jacket of black velvet, trimmed to match the skirt.

This style of jacket would make up well in silk, cloth, poplin, or *piqué*.

Fig. 6. – Walking dress of Bismarck poplin, made with two skirts, and trimmed with bands of velveteen of a brighter shade, arranged in a pattern. The sack is of the dress material, trimmed to correspond. The gloves match the trimming of the dress.

In making up dresses, skirts are gored quite plain in front and at the sides, but drawn up in larger gathers at the back. These are held up by on row of gathering not gauged down as it formerly was. Trains attached to a belt are also being made.

Short dresses continue popular for street wear, and are fast gaining ground, as of late they have been adopted for evening and ball costumes.

The disadvantage of long trains consists in the fact that but few of the many ladies wearing them know how to manage them gracefully, and they become not only an annoyance to the wearer, but also to those by whom she is surrounded. For receptions and carriage wear, the open train is still in vogue.

A great number of dresses are now made like open Redingotes, and are very elegant as well as being more dressy than a complete high bodice. Lace is sewn around the opening in front, and a large locket suspended on velvet is worn round the throat. This style of *toilette* looks well on those occasions when full dress is not required.

Fig. 5. – Morning robe of gray poplin, trimmed with leaves of cherry-colored silk. It is gored loosely, and caught to the figure by a belt of cherry leaves. If it is desirable to have a plainer dress, the leaves may be of gray silk, bound with cherry or blue.

The "Boulevard skirts," which have been so universally admired during the winter, are to be improved for spring and summer wear by having hoops inserted through the slides on the under side. This addition will dispense with the extra weight of a hoop-skirt, and answer the purpose of the latter fully as well. The hoops may be easily removed and replaced when the garment is to be washed. The idea has already received great approval, as ladies are not slow to recognize anything that adds so vastly to their comfort, and is really so much of a convenience.

Fig. 3. – Dinner-dress of Dagmar blue silk, trimmed with ruffles of a lighter shade, edged with a narrow twisted fringe. It is worn with a Marie Antoinette fichu, which crosses in front and forms long sashes at the back. It is made of the dress silk, trimmed with a lighter shade and narrow fringe.

In Paris, a novelty to be worn by a lady of very slight figure and pearly complexion, is an overdress of white down, to be worn above a body and skirt of puffed tulle filled in with little scarlet feathers. The headdress is a crown of vivid scarlet plumage, with a white marabout tuft topping the front puffs of hair. This is a very costly, fancy, and exquisitely lovely affair.

The way a new style of skirt that has come into fashion was invented, is thus described: –

"A Brooklyn hatter, for amusement, promised his wife that he would make her a skirt – such as never was before known. He took some felt, and adopting the beating process by which felt hats are made, he stretched the material over a frame and beat it in successive layers till a thick, full-sized seamless skirt was made, impervious to rain or damp, warm and not heavy. It was regarded as a wonder by the ladies of New York, and more were demanded, until an immense factory has been opened, one hundred hands employed, and the demand cannot be supplied."

Godey's Lady's Book, March 1868

Evening Dresses.

Figure 1. – Evening dress of blue tarlatan, trimmed round the bottom with narrow flounces of the same material. Short fourreau, cut in points and trimmed with piping and blue silk fringe in the manner shown in the illustration. Low corsage and short sleeves. Bertha cut in points and trimmed with piping and silk fringe to match the fourreau. Frill of lace round the neck round the neck of the corsage.

Figure 2. – Evening dress of white tarlatan, trimmed as shown in the illustration, with clusters and long sprays of lily of the valley. Under-skirt of white silk, trimmed with satin piping. Low corsage and short sleeves. Under-waist of puffed lace.

Figure 3. – Evening dress of pink tulle, trimmed round the bottom with narrow folds and fringe. Under-skirt of white silk. Sash ends of pink tulle, trimmed with fringe, and confined by rings. Low corsage and short sleeves. Low necked puffed lace under-waist. Bretelles of the same material as the corsage, with ends crossing each other on the shoulder, through a ring, and trimmed with fringe. Similar ends ornament the front of the corsage.

[*at a ball at the Tuileries*] The Princess Murat appeared in mauve satin over a puffed skirt of white tulle. The puffings were separated by slender rouleaux of mauve satin. The dress itself was bordered with seven of these little rouleaux, and was caught up on one side only with a diamond agrafe. Diamond bandeaux in the hair.

Madame Worth, the wife of the celebrated man-dressmaker, was remarked for the immense size of her *paniers*, which called to mind those of Queen Marie Antoinette. Whether this is a presage of the fall of crinoline, none can say positively, for the use of *paniers* has not yet been adopted outside of women of the greatest elegance. The skirt of Madame Worth was looped behind by a long spray of smilax, which extended from front the like a chain.

Harper's Bazar, March 7, 1868

Marie Antoinette Fichu.

This fichu is especially suited to mourning toilettes. It is made of black silk lace, insertion, and two widths of black satin ribbon the fichu consists of a piece of black lace, three quarters of a yard square, bordered with black lace insertion, an inch wide, through which is run a narrow black satin ribbon, and black lace two inches wide. This square is then doubled in a triangular shape, so that the lace on one corner just reaches the insertion of the other. The lace is pleated along the fold, leaving the front corners loose, and a bow of satin ribbon with long ends is set over the pleats in the middle of the back, with ribbon loops, an inch and a half apart, on each side. The lower one of these loops is an inch and a half long, and each of the others a quarter of an inch shorter. Lace sash-ends, trimmed to match the fichu, are set on in front.

Harper's Bazar, March 14, 1868

Two yards and a quarter from the belt to the edge of the shirt makes a train of good length for a lady of medium height.

The combination of redingote and Gabrielle which you suggest is not worn.

Harper's Bazar, March 21, 1868

Radical changes in dress are usually introduced in the fall. Modistes tax their ingenuity to devise novelties and variety for the gay winter season. In the spring the most successful features of the fall modes are remodeled and adapted with the necessary variations to lighter materials. For instance, the Marie Antoinette type of dress alluded to in the first Number of the *Bazar* has been worn during the winter, but more particularly for full dress. It will now be more generally adopted, and made up in all kinds of material.

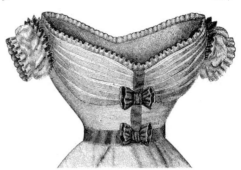

Low-Necked Waist for Evening Dress.

The original of this waist is of gray silk gauze. The trimming consists of folds of the same material, arranged in the form of a bertha, bordered with gray satin, and ornamented with gray satin bandeaux. The waist is trimmed, besides, with bows of blue satin and epaulets of gray and blue satin. The same pattern may also be used for making waists of other materials, such as light wash goods, silk, or other light stuffs, the trimming being chosen to suit the dress.

The style of corsage prevalent during the winter, with short shoulders and round waist, will be used with slight modifications for spring dresses. Our best modistes, however, never go into extremes, and at present fashion does not exact either a very short or a very long waist, but one fitted in accordance with the figure. Broad shoulders that need to be contracted are shaped with short seams, and the sleeve is placed very high; but if the figure is too slight, it is amplified in appearance by cutting the corsage long on the shoulders. It was formerly considered necessary, in order to make the back sufficiently narrow, to place the shoulder-seam two or three inches behind the line of the shoulders. Now it exactly describes that line, and may be seen from the front. Side bodies are made quite narrow. The waist is not so high at the throat as has been the fashion lately, but is still finished by a bias band, or a fold scalloped, or pointed and bound.

The Pompadour corsage is still in favor, together with *revers*, or rolling collars. The old-fashioned surplice waist open to the belt, and held together with a brooch, is revived for thin materials that are made full and gathered into a belt. Double-breasted garments are lapped in a deep point or sloped on the bias in the redingote style. Bretelles are also used.

The chemise Russe for morning wear is prettily brought out in cashmere and delaines of rich-colored grounds, with gay Parisian patterns stamped on them for trimming. Gay Turkish jackets are in white delaine, and in black spotted with gilt or with crimson, with bright borders. $5 is asked for the cashmere patterns.

Skirts of walking dresses are made slightly longer, almost touching the ground. They consist of eight gored widths similar to those used for trained skirts, but not so wide. Short overskirts are looped at the sides, or left open, the front forming a rounded apron and connected with the back by bands or clusters of ornaments. Black silk is in favor for spring suits. A good corded silk for this purpose, three quarters of a yard wide, may be bought for $3 a yard.

We are not informed of any decided change in trained dresses. There is a tendency to greater amplitude, but the fullness is still confined to the back of the dress. Usually there are seven gored widths in the front and sides, and a full one gathered in at the back. With very stout figures two full widths are used. A small pleat laid over on the gored seams adjusts the skirt into the waist. The plain width is gauged. The lap at the fastening should be over the second seam on the left. The pocket is concealed beneath the opposite seam on the right side. Small fancy pouches for the handkerchief are attached to the belt, or made to hook on the corsage.

Our correspondents write that they are weary of the coat-sleeve; but we are compelled to say that it has as yet no formidable rival. True, it has been worn a long time; but it is graceful and convenient, and susceptible of great variety of trimming. Four bands of bias satin, an inch in width, placed horizontally on the upper half of the sleeve from seam to seam, one band at the arm-hole, the lowest at the wrist, and the other two at regular intervals between will make a stylish trimming. This is exceedingly becoming to a long arm, as it shortens it in appearance. Another pretty style is to put a puff of silk around the elbow. Cuffs are pointed and very deep. Tight sleeves are being made for spring walking dresses. Very broad cuffs are worn with these, and a slight heading like an epaulet. Wide, open sleeves cut square at the end are worn over tight-fitting sleeves of the same material, or full puffs of muslin or of lace. The Moyen-Age sleeve is closed to the elbow, where it opens and hangs in a straight line below. It is sometimes caught together at the end. The Marie Antoinette sleeves are puffed to the elbow, and finished by a wide ruffle of the material, or fringe, or lace.

Harper's Bazar, March 28, 1868

HOUSE DRESS.

Short House Dress of White Alpaca, trimmed with black velvet.

COAT BODY.

The three back widths of dresses are no longer gored, the front and side widths are still very much so.
Peterson's Magazine, March 1868

Short walking suits still continue popular.

The way of looping up long dresses gracefully is, in fact, the great problem over which our Parisian mantua-makers are now puzzling their wits, as it is necessary sometimes to wear a trained dress in walking. The simplest mode is to sew buttons and loops upon the seams of the gored widths; but this method is not considered ornamental enough for very elegant dresses. Bows and lapels of velvet and ribbon are used in various ways for lifting up the dress, and trimming it at the same time. We have noticed in particular a very gracefully arranged dress of pearl-colored poplin. Upon each shoulder there was a bow of velvet of the same shade without lapels. To each bow was fastened a strip of the same velvet ribbon; these strips were crossed over the bodice in front, and then fixed under the velvet waistband; from thence becoming much wider, they were continued over the skirt and tied half way up, in the middle of the back. The bow had very short lapels. To loop up the skirt it is pulled up over the bow, so as to form a deep fold, which is made to hang over the ribbon in a sort of puff. This is a more ornamental mode than *à la blanchisseuse*, a fashion which appears to have been borrowed from the washerwomen of the Seine, and which is perhaps more effectual, but less elegant.

Fig. 1. – Visiting-dress of black gros grain silk, trimmed with bands of black satin, edged by a plaiting of silk. The trimming extends across the front and back of skirt. The waist is made plain, with a peasant waist made to match the trimming on the skirt. The sleeves, and around the armholes are trimmed to correspond. This dress can be made in any color.

Fig. 2. – Morning-dress of stone colored de laine, trimmed with blue velvet and small steel buttons. The velvet is placed around the bottom of the skirt in graduated lengths, the upper ends being pointed. It is also put above in points, which gives the appearance of two skirts. The French sack is cut pointed, back and front, and trimmed to correspond. The same trimming extends around the armhole and bottom of sleeve.

Fig. 3. – Dress of white *piqué*, trimmed with flat white braid, put around in scallops, to form an upper skirt. Four sashes of the *piqué*, cut in scallops, and bound with the same kind of braid, commence on the corsage and extend down the skirt below the scallops. A belt of the same material completes the costume.

Fig. 4. – Reception-dress of luminous green silk, trimmed with black thread lace to simulate a tunic. A rouleaux of a darker shade of green satin heads the lace, and extends from the waist to the top the scallop, where it is finished by a rosette of satin ribbon with ends. The corsage is trimmed with lace, to form a square neck. The peplum basque made of the silk, trimmed to correspond. A belt the same with a rosette completes the toilet.

In white Llama lace we see "Marie Antoinette" skirts to be worn over colored silks; also fichus to correspond. Tunics of the same with short, open skirt, high bodice, and long, loose sleeves. Also sashes with long lapels; these can be worn over colored silks or grenadines, and are very *distingué* for evening or watering places.

Fig. 11. – Dinner-dress. The underskirt is of apple-green silk; upper skirt, upper part of waist, and sleeves of black silk. The peplum corsage, of green silk, is cut in points, the side ones being deepest, and looping up the overskirt at each side. The corsage is trimmed with a plaiting of the silk, edged by a narrow black velvet; the same extends around the wrist of the sleeves.

Mantles of the scarf-shape are worn to correspond with the dress; also short jackets. One we notice is quite short, with a cape hanging over the shoulder like a bretelle, and crossing, with long ends finished by a tassel. It is said capes will be worn for travelling in place of sacks; they are convenient, but are so easily made, and so inexpensive, that they soon become common and are abandoned.

Model wives formerly took a "stitch in time;" now, with the aid of sewing machines, they take one in no time.
Godey's Lady's Book, April 1868

Evening Dresses.

Fig. 1. – Under-skirt of pink silk, trimmed round the bottom with two rows of quilling of the same material. Over-skirt of white Swiss muslin, trimmed round the bottom with a broad quilling of pink silk, and around the neck and long open sleeves with a narrow quilling of the same. Chemise Russe and short sleeves of pleated lace.

Fig. 2. – Under-skirt of white satin, trimmed with several rows of blue satin piping. Robe with train of blue satin, open in front, lined with white silk, and bordered with silver lace. This robe is fastened on the right shoulder with a silver clasp, and is confined by a similar clasp just below the waist on the left side. Chemise Russe and puffed sleeves of lace. Pearl necklace and bracelets.

Fig. 3. – Under-skirt of white tarlatan, puffed in diamonds, with a large wax-bead in the centre of each, and edged round the bottom with a narrow flounce of green crape. Over-skirt of green silk, trimmed with a quilling of green crape. Belt of green crape. Chemise Russe of puffed lace.

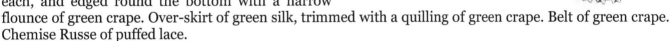

During the summer it will be found a comfortable plan to dispense with the regular corsage of the dress, and wear white waists under blouse wrappings. Let the skirt of the dress, however, be ample and perfect. It is poor economy and bad taste to scant, the material of the dress in order that there may be a greater abundance of trimming. No matter how plain the skirt, let it be complete; then there is a comfortable sense of security in case of accident. There is a tendency toward superfluous ornament. Let economy begin with the trimming, and ladies will not so often be surprised to find their mantua-maker's bill exceed the amount paid for the dress. We deprecate the idea adopted by some of sewing a band of the same goods as the redingote around an old skirt, or one made of cambric. At every breath of wind that moves the redingote the wearer fears that the sham will be discovered, and she convicted of an effort at display that she will not care to acknowledge. Short dresses with gored widths require so little material that it is best not to abridge, the real garment, but rather to dispense with all elaborate ornament.

A morning dress of white percale with a black stripe is made a long, loose sacque, cut off at the knee, and finished out to the proper length with a broad ruffle. Large pearl buttons down the front. A white linen cord and tassel confine it at the waist. Coat-sleeves and Shakspeare collar. Price, ready-made, $15. Another breakfast dress of white cambric has a gored sacque with tucked front and a fluted puff going up over the shoulders and down the seams of the side-bodies. A row of Cluny insertion is on each side of the puff. The long, trained skirt has a puff and insertion above the hem. Coat-sleeves with a puff on the outside seam. Bands of blue chambray are sewn under the insertion, a better plan than to use ribbon, as it does not have to be removed when washed.

Dinner Dresses.

Fig. 1. – Dress of green silk, trimmed with green velvet and green tassels. Peasant waist of the same. Under-waist, with high neck and long sleeves, of puffed Swiss muslin and needlework.

Fig. 2. – Dress of lilac silk, trimmed with lilac satin, two sizes of tassels, and silver leaves. Chemise Russe and puffed sleeves of Swiss muslin.

Fig. 3. – Dress of brown poult de soie, trimmed in the manner shown in the illustration, with brown velvet and black lace. High neck, and long, close sleeves.

IMPORTED WALKING SUITS.

Some spring suits just received from Paris are made with seven breadths in the skirt, all of which are gored. The front width is but slightly sloped. Two gored breadths form a bias seam in the back. These dresses are all in light neutral tints, trimmed with a more decided color in contrast, or a darker shade of its own. The most expensive suit, marked $200, is a repped chameleon silk, a delicate tan color, that seen in one light has a bright pink tinge. The skirt cut in the manner just described is untrimmed save by a thick silk cord around the edge, and measures three and a half yards at its greatest circumference. The over-garment is a tight-fitting basquine, with side-bodies and a seam down the middle of the back. The front and back are longer than the sides, and are square instead of sloping. Two cross-cut bands of silk, with a satin cord on either side, surround the basquine and sleeves. Heavy bullion fringe finishes the garment. Material for waist and sleeves is furnished.

Harper's Bazar, April 4, 1868

Polonaise or Redingote.

This sleeveless Polonaise or redingote must be of the same color as the dress, although the material may be different. The suit in the illustration consists of a short dress of brown poplin, trimmed with brown silk rouleaux. The paletot is of brown taffetas, lined with silk, and trimmed with bias silk folds of the same color. The waist is confined by a narrow belt, with wide loops and ends behind.

At the spring opening of French dresses by one of our leading modistes we were surprised to notice the entire absence of the redingote or polonaise. This garment is, however, in such favor here that it will not be abandoned this season, though it is no longer cut so full as the original pattern, but is half adjusted to the figure by side bodies, and is worn with a fichu or scarf.

All the short suits exhibited had two skirts, the under one cut in the way we have lately described, and bordered with a flounce or with three narrow frills. The upper skirt is gored flat in front, with the back widths fulled in at the sides, and puffed or festooned to give a very full appearance, as of the tournure or bustle. There is no longer any doubt that the panier style is about to be revived, or that it will be generally worn, since it is precisely the opposite of the scant drapery over small crinoline that has so long been in favor.

The most admired short suit was a chameleon silk of beautifully blended rose color and mauve. The lower skirt was of inch-wide stripes, a solid brown alternating with a changeable stripe of the same width. A pleated ruffle at the bottom was of the chameleon silk cut in squares and bound with the stripes. The up or skirt was trimmed with a narrower ruffle, and festooned in the back. A half-adjusted basque, with long mantilla fronts, was the over-garment. The price was $300, with material for waist and sleeves.

THE EMPRESS EUGENIE AT THE LAST COURT BALL.

The dress of the Empress, of which we give an illustration, was strikingly magnificent and original. It was composed of two tulle skirts, the under one laminated with silver, and the over one with gold, in narrow stripes converging toward the waist and producing the effect of rays. In front of the skirt was a sort of little apron of white satin, fringed with marabout, and completely covered with peacocks' feathers, arranged in horizontal lines. The apron seemed held at the sides by bouquets of diamond flowers. Around the waist was a bertha of white satin, fringed with gold and marabout, and ornamented with a cordon of large emeralds, encircled with diamonds. The long Hungarian sleeves, of tulle, were spangled with gold. The belt was of gold confined by a diamond agrafe. The Empress wore on her neck a simple black ribbon velvet, with long ends (dog's collar) studded with fine emeralds. Her head was adorned with a splendid green peacock's feather, thrown on one side across the back hair; a diamond crescent glittered in the middle of the forehead, and several small peacocks' feathers were mixed with the curls of her chignon behind. The effect was imperial and splendid;

Harper's Bazar, April 11, 1868

Organdy grenadine, or Chambery gauze can be used for a summer wedding dress. White morning dresses are gored, with full train, and sloped to fasten at the side, like the redingote. Muslin house dresses may be made with a demi-train, but not short. Very small hoops are worn at present. There are indications that the tournure or bustle will be revived. An inch and a half is the usual width at the waist between the seams of the back, but this depends somewhat on the figure. The side seams should be directly under the arm. The gauging of the skirt reaches three or four inches. A medium belt is from an inch and a half to two inches wide. The "chemise Russe" is a kind of blouse gathered into a belt; not so full as the Garibaldi. The military style of trimming is with graduated parallel lines of plain folds or of braid.

Harper's Bazar, April 18, 1868

[*at the Paris opera*] The Pompadour was the reigning style in all the dresses. A few young girls, however, wore corsages *à l'Italienne* or *à la Raphael*; the first very low, and composed of a plastron, with bretelles of the same stuff us the dress, with a half-high under-waist, the whole shirred all round. The under-waist is of white muslin or gauze. The Raphael corsage is in the same style, except that the plastron is cut square instead of curving upward like the preceding. The distinctive character of these Italian corsages is that they always have long sleeves.

A stylish [*walking*] suit of gray woolen serge, with a silk diagonal reps, has a plain under-skirt with an over-skirt made *en paniers*. Of the six widths in the upper skirt only the front one and those each side of it are gored. The three full back widths are almost as long as the under-skirt, and are caught up in a large *panier* puff by a draw-string extending across from the side-seams. The gored front breadths are cut out in deep points. The paletot is short in the back, with long rounded fronts, crossed on the breast with the two lapped ends visible. A belt and sash ends at the side. The paletot, upper skirt, and coat-sleeves are trimmed with fringe and satin folds. Price $100. Material is furnished for the waist.

Arrangement for Looping up Paletots, Dresses, etc.

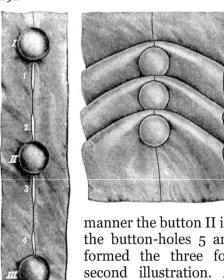

Long cloaks are now often looped up in order to show more of the dress; paletots and dresses are looped up in the same manner. The accompanying illustrations show a simple and easy way of doing this by means of buttons. In sewing up the seams which join the breadths of the dress-skirt or paletot, leave open a portion of the seam in order to form the button-holes, and afterward open the seam and stitch it down on the right side. Then sew on the required buttons as shown in the illustration, so that two button-holes shall lie under each button. In buttoning up the dress, put the button marked I backward through the button-hole marked 1 and forward through the button-hole marked 2. In the same manner the button II is brought through the button-holes 3 and 4, and the button III through the button-holes 5 and 6, by which are formed the three folds shown in the second illustration. Additional buttons and button-holes may of course be furnished each seam if desired.

A neat way of making a black silk walking suit is with gored under-skirt; fuller upper-skirt, with bands inserted in each seam, to which each width but the front is sewn after having been gathered lengthwise. This gives a full puffed appearance, which is now very fashionable. The band is an inch and a half wide, cut bias, and may be trimmed with pipings of the silk with tiny buttons between, or inserted points of satin, or with a pleated rouleau. The sleeveless tight jacket cut short behind with long lapped points, and worn with a sash, is a good accompaniment.

Harper's Bazar, April 25, 1868

With train skirts the cage or crinoline is now suppressed; either two muslin or fine twill petticoats are worn instead. These are made very plain in front, and very full at the back, and are bordered with a deep flounce, which serves to prevent the train from falling in and clinging about the feet. The fashionable dress-makers now add a piece of very stiff muslin at the top of the skirt, commencing at the hips. This forms a sort of bustle, as the very scant skirts, plain all round, were found to be generally unbecoming, and in consequence Fashion decrees a sort of shy attempt at hoops. The rosette of the sash now reaches considerably above the waist, and the very wide ends that escape are so ruched that they have the effect of panniers, which it seems an ambition to achieve.

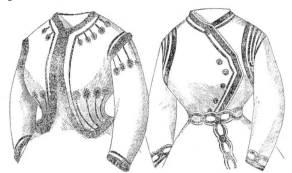

JACKET. BODY.

In Paris they are wearing black sashes, worn across the body of the dress, from the right shoulder to the left side, and the ends, which are very broad, and hang half-way down the skirt, are exquisitely painted in body color. The design of one is given: it was a bunch of primulas with green and brown leaves, well grouped, and the effect was most beautiful. A black wooden fan had been painted in the same manner, with the same design to match. Any one who paints flowers nicely could do this, and they would be well repaid for their trouble.

The Art of the Hoop: 1860 - 1869

MARIE ANTOINETTE FICHU.

This fichu is at present most fashionable over both high and low dresses. It is made in black and white net, either plain or figured. We give above an engraving of a Fichu of plain Brussels net, trimmed with two rows of Cluny lace as far as the waist, where one row tapers off, and one only is continued round the ends. Oval medallions of Cluny ornament the ends of the Fichu, and five little tabs of insertion, edged with lace, are placed round the back of the neck. The Fichu should be cut in one piece. It will require two yards of net, twenty-four inches wide, for the foundation, one yard of insertion, twelve yards of lace, and three yards of edging. We annex a diagram, from which a paper pattern, full size, may be cut.

Peterson's Magazine, April 1868

Skirts still continue gored; fashion as yet shows no inclination to change. They are mostly cut to the fancy of the wearer; some persons desiring some fulness, and not caring to cut up material in tight gores. Others remodelling old dresses, find the tight gores more convenient. But the style most universally adopted has gathers in the back. The trains are even longer than they have been, if that is possible.

Fig. 2. – Underskirt of black silk, trimmed with three bands of satin; overskirt of green silk. The side gores are cut pointed, the edge scalloped and bound with narrow braid; these extend up to the waist. The skirt is cut the full length, and looped up with satin bands terminating in loops. Sack of black silk, trimmed to correspond.

We cannot resist describing a walking suit, it is so extremely simple and stylish. It was made of gray silk poplin, trimmed with knotted fringe, to simulate two skirts, headed by three satin folds; the sack was trimmed to correspond. As satin trimmings can now be purchased in all styles, this makes a very easy and inexpensive trimming.

Fig. 3. – Dress of silver gray silk, trimmed with a plait of blue satin, headed by leaves of the same. The trimming extends down the sides, and across the back and front of the skirt. Waist and sleeves trimmed with bands of blue satin, finished by small bows. Belt of the same, with satin points around it. ➔

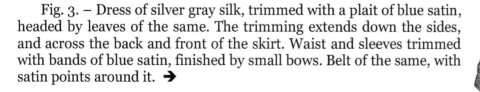

In outside wrappings, sacks, tight and partly tight-fitting basques, and scarf mantles, are the favorites. The principal feature in all, and in fact everything, is the sash. Of a large number which we saw, all had sashes, either fastened at the side or back; these are elaborately trimmed.

Fig. 4. – Dress of mauve-colored silk, trimmed to simulate two skirts; the trimming consists of a row of chenille fringe of a darker shade, headed by a silk braid put on in a pattern, and a row of small buttons between. The same braid extends around the bottom of the skirt. Low corsage and Marie Antoinette fichu trimmed with lace.

Fig. 5. – Dress of lilac silk. The bottom of the skirt is trimmed with one flounce, which is deeper in front than back; it is headed by cross-cut bands of satin. The waist is cut like a jacket, with three points in back; the sides extend down, forming sash ends, and is trimmed with satin. The sash at the back is gathered and fastened by three bows, the ends finished by a chenille fringe.

Sashes are a great feature of the dresses, and are worn in a multitude of styles, and frequently form the only ornament to the dresses. We will notice a few of the most *distingué*. The Metternich sash is made of green moire ribbon, and ornamented with a tiny golden horn, and other attributes of the chase. The Impératrice is of blue satin, with delicate silver bees, and tiny silver chains. The Bergere sash is a novelty for evening wear. It is tied with two large loops, and a miniature shepherdess's hat in silver is placed on the loops. There is no rule as to the length of sashes, but it should be observed that when sashes are made of ribbon they are very long, and when of the same material as the skirt, they are short. So popular are they, that they will even be worn with wash dresses made of the same material bound.

Fig. 9. – The new style of sash rings now so universally worn. These rings are sometimes worn at the back and sometimes at the side of the skirt, the waistband passing through two of them, the bar across the interior of the ring keeping the band straight. Net and lace tunics are also looped through these sash rings. They are made of gilt, large pearl beads, jet, steel, and of velvet embroidered with jet beads.

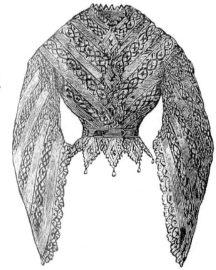

Fig. 17. – Black net bodice. The material of which this bodice is made is black guipure, and them trimming consists of insertion formed of velvet and studded with jet. There are lozenge-shaped ornaments down the front, composed of velvet, edged with narrow guipure; similar lozenges are reproduced below the waistband. The sleeves, *à la juive*, are striped crosswise with guipure and velvet alternately; lozenges form epaulettes, and are continued down the sleeve, as though they looped it up halfway down the arm.

The Art of the Hoop: 1860 - 1869

PERCALE MORNING ROBES.

Fig. 1. – Robe of green percale, with a border of black and white up the front. Short French sacque, trimmed with the bordering put on in squares at the sides; the pockets are formed of the same.

Fig. 2. – Morning-robe of white percale, with bands of gay colors extending down each side of the skirt; bands of the same trim the basque, which is also fastened at the waist by a belt.

Godey's Lady's Book, May 1868

VISITING AND DINNER TOILETTES.

Fig. 1. – Polonaise of black velvet, trimmed with rich passementerie and black silk galloon. The open sleeves are trimmed at the top and bottom with a bead fringe, and show the sleeves of the dress through the opening. The left front of the skirt of the paletot is longer than the right which is cut bias. Dress of black gros de France, trimmed round the bottom with black passementerie, galloon, and heavy silk cord, and looped up on each side with a large passementerie fastening, showing the under-skirt of blue silk, which is also tr mined with wide galloon.

Fig. 2. – Dress of men satin, with short tunic and low bodice, trimmed with a puffing of tulle and gold cord. Belt edged with gold cord and white lace, fastened on the left side with long sash ends. Skirt trimmed in front with three tabs of white lace, puffed in the middle and edged with gilt cord; one of these tabs runs from the top of the skirt downward, and is furnished with tassels; the others run from the bottom of the skirt upward. Lace rosettes with a gold button in the centre complete the trimming. Under-waist of pleated tulle, trimmed with gold cord. Short puffed sleeves, also adorned with gold cord.

Harper's Bazar, May 2, 1868

ANSWERS TO CORRESPONDENTS.

For a demi train make a gradual slope of half a yard from the front to the back breadth. One wide ruffle from the knee down is a favorite style for lawn skirts. The skirt proper should be slightly sloped from the waist to the knee. Narrow ruffles at the bottom of the skirt are also used. Silk skirts should be lined throughout with glazed cambric, and faced with wigging half a yard deep. For trained skirts of rich materials alpaca of the precise shade of the dress should be faced over the wigging an eighth of a yard deep. The trimming of sashes is a matter of taste. They are quite pretty trimmed only across the ends. They are usually draped about the hips with trained dresses, but this is not absolutely necessary. One dart is usually taken in a loose Gabrielle front. Any lace handsome enough for a bridal veil would be very expensive, as the whole veil must be made of it. Tulle, trimmed with a ruche of the same, is a favorite style, and is appropriate both for elaborate and plain dresses. Boots are made of the same material as the traveling dress. Thick twilled serge is the most appropriate. A plain buttoned boot – half high Polish – is made of Grison's kid for traveling.

The Marie Antoinette fichu is worn at this season over a long blouse or redingote. In summer it will be a sufficient wrapping of itself. The short dress worn with it should have two skirts; the upper one gathered up at the seams to form a frill of a bunchy appearance.

The morning dress of which you speak is simply a loose sack, with a sloping seam in the middle of the back and under the arms. A loose Gabrielle may be made in the same way.

Harper's Bazar, May 9, 1868

The walking suits this year consist chiefly, as in the last, of a skirt and paletot of the same material. The skirts are not quite so short or so narrow as those of last season, but almost touch the ground, and are longer behind than in front. The front breadth is almost plain, with one large box-pleat; the back breadths are straight, and gathered, with a small pleat on each side of the gathers. The paletots are either close-fitting or sack-shaped. A belt with a bow or rosette and broad sash ends is worn over the paletot. This belt is made either of the same material as the paletot, with trimming to match, or of silk, satin, etc.; the ends do not fall below the bottom of the paletot itself. Fichus, crossing in front, are also worn either over the paletot or instead of it; these are very stylish and becoming to young girls. Walking dresses may be either of black silk, or of the many light-colored worsted or linen goods suitable for summer wear. Close sleeves are still in favor. The trimming consists of narrow or wide flounces, quillings, bias folds, and lappets of different shapes, either of the same stuff as the paletot, bound with silk or satin, or of the latter materials. Many suits have no other trimming than a broad hem, with one or more rows of stitching in silk twist of the same color as the dress. The buttons generally match the suit in color, and are covered with silk or satin, embroidered in point russe or satin stitch; these buttons may be made more durable by winding them over with silk twist. We proceed to give a description of the home and walking dresses in the accompanying illustration.

Fig. 1. – Dress with train of brown poult de soie, trimmed with bias folds of brown silk bound with brown satin.

Fig. 2. – Dress with train of mode Panama cloth, trimmed with bias folds of brown silk. Belt with lappets of brown silk, bound with brown satin. The bias folds are bound in a similar manner.

Fig. 3. – Walking dress of lavender gros grain, trimmed in the manner shown in the illustration with lavender silk flounces and bias folds. The belt and bow are trimmed to correspond with the dress. The paletot and fichu belonging to the Maria Theresa and Norderney dresses (see page 473 [*below* ↘]), the patterns of which are given in the present Number of the Supplement, may either be worn with this dress.

Fig. 4. – Dress with train of pearl-gray silk, trimmed with satin, silk fringe, tassels, and buttons of a darker shade, in the manner shown in the illustration.

Fig. 5. – Dress with train of brown poplin, trimmed with brown satin piping, black lace, and brown buttons.

Maria Theresa Walking Dress. – Front.
Norderney Walking Dress. – Front.
Norderney Walking Dress. – Back.
Maria Theresa Walking Dress. – Back.

The Parisian models imported for the coming season are in the Watteau or Pompadour style, or *à la Marie Antoinette*.

The Watteau is in imitation of the pastoral dress worn by court shepherdesses in the days of Louis XV., when they enacted idyls at Trianon and Fontainebleau. It is a close copy of the original costume, with its square Pompadour neck, its velvet necklace and cross, the merest atom of sleeve, a belt and sash looped with eglantine, and a festooned over-dress with striped petticoat, short enough to display clocked stockings and slippers with large rosettes. This fanciful attire is surmounted by a Louis Quinze hat turned up at the left side, and a cardinal pelerine with long pointed hood.

Differing from this is the Marie Antoinette, with its high-necked fichu folded over the breast, sleeves puffed to the elbow and frilled, slender waist and paniers, with skirts trimmed with innumerable ruffles and ruches. The broad-rimmed garden hat of chip is trimmed with field flowers, and completes a costume peculiarly becoming to youthful faces and slender figures. The Watteau is better suited to maturity and embonpoint; but like every thing else, they are worn indiscriminately.

Traveling Costume. – Belt with Pocket and Strap for Shawl. Short dress and tight-fitting paletot of gray silk serge. The skirt is trimmed with a wide bias fold of the same material, pleated and set on in waves, as shown in the illustration. The bottom of the paletot is scalloped and bound with brown silk.

An elaborate Watteau suit, marked $225, has a satin under-skirt of striped gold and maroon. It is cut off at the knee and finished with a deep flounce. The Watteau jacket forming the overdress is of narrow repped silk. It is trimmed with a wide pinked ruche of the same and looped at the sides and back to form puffs. These puffs are lined with crinoline to make them project. The wide sash ribbon has three stripes like the petticoat. It is arranged in a fan-like quilling with butterfly bows on the ends.

Harper's Bazar, May 23, 1868

First we have a house-dress of gray foulard silk, or any other suitable material, trimmed down the front with bands of black velvet, arranged to look as if the ends had been passed through a buckle. The front and back of the body, and the sleeves, are trimmed to correspond: so also are the belt and sashes. One row of black velvet passes round the bottom of the skirt. Our illustration shows the back as well as front of this dress.

Another is an evening-dress, which may be made either of white silk, white mohair, alpaca, or tarlatane. It is ornamented with a coral pattern, which should be worked in rich silk on any of the materials except the latter, and there zephyr might be used. This is really one of the most charming costumes of the season.

WALKING DRESS.

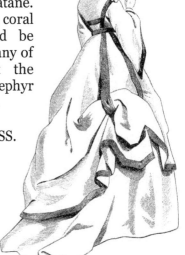

Fig. VI. – Walking and House Dress of White Alpaca. – The under-skirt is plain, the upper, and longer one, trimmed with a bias band of pink silk, and passed through a long loop of pink ribbon, as occasion may require. Sleeves and waist are also trimmed with pink ribbon.

Peterson's Magazine, May 1868

Fig. 1. – Dress of white grenadine, made with two skirts; the front breadth is puffed lengthwise; a narrow Cluny lace finishes the puffs at the seams; four puffs extend down each side of the back breadth. The upper skirt is looped up at each side by an illusion scarf, which is looped up over the front breadth, and is finished by a bow of green ribbon. Sash of green silk, edged by Cluny lace, and trimmed with two lace bows. Low corsage, trimmed with green silk and Cluny lace.

Fig. 3. – Dress of green silk, made with two skirts. The lower one is edged by two small flounces, headed by four narrow rows of braid. The upper skirt is cut in a deep scallop in the front, trimmed with three rows of braid. The upper part of this skirt is trimmed with three rows of braid, making it have the appearance of three skirts. Low corsage, trimmed to correspond. Sash of the silk.

One of the prettiest new models we have seen for evening toilet is the Spanish corselet of satin or *poult de soie*. This corselet can be made of any color; but we particularly admired one of cerise-colored satin, which was worn with a white dress. This bodice is made somewhat like a low zouave jacket, not coming down any further than the waist. It is open and rounded off at the sides, and then laced together with silk gimp cord of the same color as the satin, and finished off at the bottom with gimp tassels falling over the skirt. There are no sleeves, but epaulettes ornamented with a bow of gimp cord and tassels. Of course, a white bodice or chemisette must be worn under the Spanish corselet, and short white sleeves show under the epaulettes. A sash with long wide lapels fastened it at the back, of the same material as the corselet is worn with it.

EVENING DRESS.

Evening dress of white silk. The skirt is gored; in the back a deep flounce of the silk is plaited on; a puff of white illusion extends around the bottom of skirt; a deep puff heads the flounce in the back, and extends across the front; the same puffs extend up the front to the waist, divided by sprays of heartsease and leaves, and finished by a large rosette, with a bouquet in the centre. The corsage is cut low and square, with flowers forming the bretelles, and extending down the back of the skirt, where they are fastened by a rosette. The sleeves are of one puff, with flowers through the centre; the belt is fastened by a rosette.

Never have we seen so many suits of black silk at this season as now; they are the favorite for street wear, also for travelling, especially for married ladies, as they are more serviceable than most of the travelling dress goods. Most of the suits are made with the Redingote. We saw one with a band of silk about four inches broad, bound on each side with satin; the band was cut in squares about one inch apart, each one being bound with satin. These squares were lined with blue silk; one of these bands extended around the bottom of the skirt, around the Redingote and sleeves; one formed the belt, and the sash was made to correspond. This is an inexpensive trimming, but very troublesome, as satin bindings are very tedious to put on.

Fig. 2. – Walking-dress of gray silk, made with two skirts. The lower one is cut in small points and trimmed with a band of satin. The upper skirt is cut in turrets, trimmed with satin; a second row extends above this, which is finished at the sides by chenille fringe. A silk cord and tassel are sewed on at the sides. Sack of black silk, cut in points, trimmed with chenille fringe, a satin fold, and small satin buttons. A plait of satin trims the front, back, and sleeves.

There are very few styles by which the skirts of wash dresses can be made and trimmed. The cut-off skirt with narrow flounces on the edge, or a plain skirt with small puffs, for flounces around it, is the favorite.

Fig. 4. – Walking-dress of black gros grain silk, trimmed with two narrow flounces. Redingote of the same silk, trimmed with a satin fold; the trimming extends up the sides and in the back, giving it the appearance of being cut. Sash of black silk, bound with satin, the ends ornamented with a satin fold and edged by fringe.

Godey's Lady's Book, June 1868

It is customary to gore all the widths of a short dress, but the back widths are sloped less than the three front widths.

Demi Toilettes.

Fig. 1. – Dress of light green foulard, with low bodice, worn over a puffed Swiss muslin under-waist. Over-skirt caught up on the left side of the front with a large satin bow, and trimmed with long rounded tabs, bound with green satin, which simulate a sort of peplum. The waist and belt are trimmed in the same manner. Under-skirt of white foulard.

Fig. 2. – Dress of gray poplin, trimmed with bias folds and buttons of gray silk. Marie Antoinette fichu of the same material.

SUMMER DRESSES.

We are told that the Empress Eugénie has shortened her trains several inches, and that the ladies of her court are fast following her example. The fashion has not yet been adopted on this side of the water. American ladies, loath to part with what they have cherished against so much opposition, are having their summer dresses made with the graceful, sweeping trains worn during the past season, The skirts, however, are not gored to fit so plainly over the hips as they have been of late. Many ladies prefer to have the front widths plain and all the breadths slightly sloped; but the very newest dresses have three front widths alone gored, while the others are straight and gathered at the back.

We hear many objections made by ladies who do their own sewing to goring thin dresses, but modistes say that by taking a little care not to stretch the bias edges of the goods, or to pucker the sewing, the gored seams will hang as well in thin materials as in the thickest silks. It is said also that the bias seams of muslin skirts can not be ironed properly. This is the fault of the laundress who attempts to smooth the seams by pulling them on the bias instead of the way of the thread. In the furnishing houses thin goods are ironed with great precision, and the process at the same time seems very simple. Gabrielles of sheer muslin, every seam of which is sloped, are perfectly smooth and shapely.

Double skirts, such as are seen on walking dresses, are worn with thin trained dresses. The upper skirts are made with apron fronts and looped up with immense puffs at the back. It is especially stylish to catch them up directly behind almost to the waist, a grotesque fashion that we thought at first sight was certainly a ludicrous mistake of the modiste. Short sashes with four broad loops and two fringed ends hanging very little below the loops are worn with these skirts. The long sash is already *passée*. Sometimes a long tunic or a kind of court train is formed by leaving the upper skirt open in front and gathering the fullness in from the hips backward.

Waists are plain blouses gathered into a belt, or with shirred yokes. A pretty design for solid colored organdies is to make the puffs of the yoke run diagonally from right to left. The old-fashioned surplice waist is again in vogue. This is the simplest form of bodice, and is becoming alike to stout and slender figures. It is easily made by the blouse pattern. The back is precisely the same. The fullness in front is made by gathering at the shoulder the piece that is usually cut out at the neck. The front is then left in a straight line and fits true.

We find it very difficult to discover any thing new in sleeves. French dresses imported for summer have invariably the coat-sleeves so long worn. It is elaborately trimmed up the outer seam, or with innumerable horizontal folds from the wrist to the shoulder. The ruffled Marie Antoinette sleeve is being made here, and is appropriate with the present costume; but we have not seen it on any of the many Parisian dresses shown us.

Waist with Fichu.

Waist with Simulated Fichu.

Among the many pretty things that add variety to summer toilettes we are shown fancy aprons of black lace with bretelles and sash. They are looped at the sides with large rosettes of ribbon the color of the dress with which they are worn. They are made only in the French woven laces, that imitate admirably real thread lace. Most fastidious ladies consider it admissible to wear fancy jackets and aprons of imitation laces, since they are only a transitory fashion.

Harper's Bazar, June 6, 1868

ANSWERS TO CORRESPONDENTS.

Brussels net and guipure insertion are made into black waists, to be worn over trimmed underbodies of linen.

White piqué is more dressy than figured. A muslin frill an inch and a half wide, needle-worked in scallops at one edge and sewed on in box-pleats or simply gathered on a cord, will trim a piqué prettily. The waist should be tight fitting, with button-holes worked up the front. Piqué is too thick to gather into a belt.

Plaid silks are not admired for short dresses. Make your dress long. Gore the front width. If the skirt is a yard and a half long, it will require all your fullness of five and three-eighths yards to be wide enough at the bottom. Gore it to fit closely to the waist in front and at the sides. Leave the back width full. With the pieces that are left you may be able to make a new waist by joining them so that the plaids fit accurately. The narrow ruffles of black silk will trim the skirt prettily, either as long or short dress. A fichu three inches wide in the back tapering down to a point at the belt will trim the waist; edge with a ruffle. It is sewn on the waist, is shaped like a bertha in the back, and bretelles in front. Short dresses are worn for visiting. Long dresses require a carriage. After the seams at the back are sewn they should be from two to three inches apart – according to the figure – two inches for slender waists. Two darts are made on each side of the front. The back breadths of the piqué should be gored, as there is a tendency to make all skirts fuller. The seams need not be corded; but that is a matter of fancy. If the bretelles are of the dress material the ends are concealed under a belt. If of lace and velvet, short loose ends fall a few inches below the waist.

Harper's Bazar, June 13, 1868

Promenade and Home Toilettes.

Fig. 1. – Short dress and over-skirt of lilac silk barege, trimmed with a pleated flounce of the same, lilac satin folds, and lilac silk tassels. The over-skirt is puffed from the bottom to the waist. Gray straw toquet with lilac gauze veil. Lilac parasol.

Fig. 2. – Gored dress of green silk, trimmed with green satin points and piping and chenille tassels.

Fig. 3. – Dress of ray and violet figured foulard. Over-skirt of violet silk, bound with satin of the same shade, and trimmed with satin piping. The embroidery in the scallops of the over-skirt is wrought with black opaque beads in satin stitch.

Fig. 4. – Dress with double skirt of white alpaca, trimmed with blue ribbon.

Fig. 5. – Dress of gray silk serge. Bretelles and sash of black silk trimmed and bound with black satin.

THE PRINCESS DE METTERNICH AT THE OPERA BALL.

The Princess de Metternich wore the most ravishing toilette that it is possible to imagine – over a dress of white tulle puffed, a tunic caught up à la Pompadour, of pink gros grain, glacée with white. This tunic was confined by fanciful bouquets and trains of rose geraniums; the sash of white tulle was caught up behind in a *pouf* by clusters of rose geraniums. Corsage bordered with rose geraniums. Diadem of olive leaves in the hair; and a double row of diamonds around the neck.

Kitchen Apron.

This apron is cut gored, and is wide enough to protect the skirt of the dress. It is buttoned together behind, as shown in the illustration. This apron is also suitable to wear in the garden when gathering fruit or vegetables. The bodice is joined to the belt, and requires neither pins nor strings to fasten it on the upper edge, as a few whalebones hold it in its place. The original is of white and pink striped percale, finished with a large pocket, and trimmed on the outer edge with a percale ruffle. ... hem the apron on the outer edge, and put on the button and button-hole as shown in the illustration; then take up the darts in the bodice, run pieces of tape on the wrong side for the whalebones, sew on a button and work a button-hole on the ends, and join to the apron as shown by the figures on the pattern. Conceal the seam by a facing on the wrong side, and sew on the ruffle, which consists of a strip of percale about an inch and a half in width, which is gathered on the apron with a cord. Hem on the upper edge the slit cut for the pocket, lay in pleats from X to •, sew the pocket on the apron as shown by the figures, and finish with a ruffle. Finish the back of the belt with a bow and ends.

Bismarck is no longer fashionable. The brown we alluded to as in demand for traveling dresses is a dead leaf color, and not the reddish tinge so much worn in the winter. A simple but stylish traveling dress has a gored skirt of brown cashmere, with a six inch flounce set on around the bottom. It is bound at the lower edge and may be gathered at the top or in box-pleats. A fold of the cashmere two inches wide, piped with satin, conceals where the flounce is sewn on. The polonaise is of worsted poplin, striped brown and white. It buttons all the way down the front, and is looped up at the sides by three large pleats, with a brown button on each pleat. The trimming consists of three rows of brown braid with a cord fringe at the edge. Coat sleeves.

Harper's Bazar, June 20, 1868

High bodies are often trimmed squarely with deep pendant fringe. Fringe is very much used as trimming; but just now no one thing can be said to be much more in vogue than another, for individual taste was never allowed a larger scope.

WALKING DRESS WITH PANNIER: THE NEW STYLE.

Fig. VII. – Walking Dress of Green, Summer Poplin. – The under-skirt is of a good walking length, without train, and quite plain. The second skirt is not so long, much shorter in front, and cut in bias battlements. The sacque is cut with a deep skirt, which is looped up with bows and ends of ribbon in the new *panier* style.

WALKING DRESS WITH PANNIER: THE NEW STYLE.

Fig. VIII. – Walking Dress, also in the new style. The under-skirt is of blue silk, just long enough to escape the ground; it is quite plain. The upper-skirt is of gray alpaca, cut much longer, and looped up all around with large mould buttons covered with blue silk. A wide short sash is tied at the back.

Evening dresses are to be made quite flat in the front breadth, which is usually trimmed differently to the rest of the skirt, and more simply; all the adornments are thrown backward, where there is a great deal of fullness. Thus, in fact, only half the figure is attired *en grande tenue*. When a lady is seated one only perceives a simple toilet; upon rising, all the art and coquetry of the dressmaker are displayed. Well, one never looks for common sense or utility in the fashions we do not make, we only chronicle the fashions.

Peterson's Magazine, June 1868

An evening dress, suitable for a watering-place, is of pink tulle, trimmed with narrow flounces upon the first skirt, and with a lace apron upon the front part of the second skirt. This apron is fastened on either side with the ends of garlands of roses, which slightly loop up the skirt at the back. The low bodice is ornamented with a Marie Antoinette bertha of white lace, which is crossed in front, and tied in two long, rounded lapels at the back.

Fig 1. – Robe of white organdy, with bands of blue around the skirt, with gay-colored flowers between. The flowers above and below the band are of a delicate blue. Plain corsage, trimmed with bands of same.

Fig. 6. – Robe of sea-green organdy, with a border of leaves and bright flowers extending up in squares on each breadth. Plain corsage, trimmed with bands of the bordering; the belt is also made of it.

The Art of the Hoop: 1860 - 1869

Fig. 1. – Dress of lilac silk, trimmed with black lace headed by a heavy plait of white satin, which also extends up each side of the front gore to the waist. Plain waist, open at the throat, displaying muslin chemisette. Coat sleeve, with satin cuff; chenille fringe forms the epaulettes. Belt of white satin, with long sash of same, knotted twice on the skirt; the sash is bound with lilac. White llama lace shawl. Bonnet of white chip, trimmed with lilac flowers and green leaves.

Fig. 2. – Dress of light green grenadine, trimmed with silk and fringe of a darker shade. A row of fringe extends around the bottom of the skirt, headed by a silk band; the ends of the bands are finished by fringe. A piece of the silk is cut to fit the dress and extends across the back, finished at each side by a rosette and ends; a similar piece, only narrower, extends across the front gore fastened by a rosette. Full corsage, trimmed to correspond; belt and rosette of silk. White straw hat, with a wreath of pink roses and leaves.

Fig. 3. – Dress of white alpaca, made with two skirts, each bound with Bismarck satin. The bias fold of satin extends down the sides; it also extends around the back of the skirt from the waist in front, so as to simulate a third skirt. The waist is trimmed to correspond. Coat sleeve, with deep cap. Hat of white chip, with Bismarck satin trimming and small plume. Parasol of Bismarck satin lined with white.

Fig. 4. – Dress of French muslin; the front breadth is plain from a quarter of a yard below the waist. The puffs extend down that far, then gradually slope off, forming *en tablier*. They extend all around the skirt, and are finished by five bands of ribbon, each band being finished by a bow of the same. The waist is puffed to form a square neck, and trimmed with ribbon and lace; the sleeves are trimmed to correspond.

Fig. 5. – Dress of white grenadine; the front breadth is gored; the back breadth cut longer, and slightly fulled into the front. A row of blue satin leaves forms the trimming; a row of the same also extends around the bottom. Low corsage, with puff around the neck, edged on each side by satin leaves; rosettes on shoulders. Broad blue satin belt, edged by wide chenille fringe; rosette and long ends in back. A second sash is fastened in front, and knotted half way down the skirt in the back, and then let flow, forming four ends in all. Bandeaux of blue velvet leaves tied under the chignon with long ends.

Fig. 2. – Dress of white grenadine, over an underskirt of blue silk trimmed with a gimp, and tassel fringe, which is put plain around except at one side, where it describes three scallops. The overdress is looped up at the side with two blue rosettes. Plain bodice, trimmed with blue silk bands, edged by a narrow Cluny lace; coat sleeves, trimmed to correspond.

Fig. 3. – Dress of lilac grenadine, trimmed with bias bands of silk of a darker shade; the bands are pointed around the bottom and trimmed with a narrow braid. Plain bodice, with revers of silk; the same trims the sleeves.

Fig. 4. – Walking-dress of pearl-color mohair, with two skirts; the edges of skirts are cut in scallops, and bound with satin; a bias band of satin heads the scallops. Sacque with mantilla ends trimmed to correspond.

Several new walking suits have been lately made up to serve for travelling dresses. They are made to just clear the ground, and with two skirts, the upper skirt from twelve to eighteen inches shorter than the lower one; they may be plain at the bottom, scalloped, Vandyked, or cut up in almost any style fancy may dictate. The underskirt is made of a different color from the dress, and the Marie Antoinette fichu (more worn than sacque or Redingote for the summer) is of the same color as the underskirt and trimming. The upper skirt of the dresses are looped up in puffs at the back, to give the effect *en paniers*, spoken of in our last. They are not generally adopted as yet, but there are few persons who do not desire to imitate them in some manner, and are willing to wear the dress so looped when they would not wear the regular paniers.

The newest style of gored dress is the Polonaise, with the fronts opening in a slanting direction from the left shoulder, and continuing down the skirt. The dress can be trimmed down the skirt where it is open, as plainly or elaborately as fancy may dictate. The other side of bodice is also open, the trimming extending around the neck. This style of dress can be worn with a plaited muslin or lace chemisette. For morning wear, dresses are mostly made high in the throat, but for afternoon *toilette* they are made as described, or with square neck, when a fichu is not worn. So popular are the latter, that there are over twenty different varieties. Tulle scarfs are also very much worn. In our next number we will give some models to arrange the scarf by; they are very simple and graceful, and add much to the effect of the dress at a trifling cost. For persons who do not desire a separate fichu, the fichu style is desirable. The dress is made of plaited muslin, bordered by an embroidered flounce or lace, in the form of a fichu, which becomes narrow on the shoulder, like a simple suspender, crosses in front, and extends a little beyond the belt, to which it is fastened like a small skirt, and elongates itself on the skirt behind in a long skirt, and ending in a point.

Fig. 5. – Morning dress of white *piqué*, trimmed with bands of pink Chambray scalloped on one side down each breadth. These can be edged by a narrow white braid, or stitched on by a sewing-machine. Tight coat sleeve, trimmed to correspond.

Morning dresses are mostly of white, trimmed with embroidery, or colored braids. We have seen a very elegant morning dress of white Nainsook, trimmed with sashes on each breadth. These sashes were ornamented with rows of Cluny lace insertion, and edged by a lace; this lace can be lined with a color if desired. Another of white foulard, trimmed with bands of blue silk, edged by lace to simulate two skirts; large blue buttons up the front of skirt and waist. Sash fastened at left side.

Fig. 4. – Morning robe of buff organdy, from Stoddart & Brother, with two borders of shades of brown extending down the skirt. The waist is made in the basque form, fitting loosely to the figure, and trimmed with a bordering to match the skirt.

For plainer and more serviceable dresses, we have the percales, *piqués*, and lawns, before spoken of; a lawn robe made in fashionable style for morning wear, can be seen on our second page of extension sheet from the establishment of O. Stoddart & Brother. For a really serviceable dress for both ladies and children, nothing can be nicer than the unbleached linen; they are generally made in a tight-fitting Polonaise, with sash, and ornamented with a coral pattern worked in scarlet wool. Both the linen and embroidery wash nicely, a very important item in a housekeeper's morning dress.

Godey's Lady's Book, July 1868

Foreign correspondents advise that the rumor of the probable abandonment of trains is not without foundation. Already many fashionable Parisiennes have appeared in what are called round-skirted costumes. These are neither very long nor very short, but are a return to the medium-length skirts worn before trains were adopted for full dress, and short dresses considered indispensable for the street.

Peasant Waist with Sash and Tunic. – Back.
Peasant Waist with Sash and Tunic. – Front.

A black velvet waistband, resembling the peasant waists formerly worn, is beaded with jet. At the back and sides are cords and tassels for looping up the skirts of the dress.

Chambery gauze is the favorite material of the season for full dress. It has all the lustre and light gossamer appearance of grenadine, but is more substantial, and does not so soon become limp and stringy. White is especially desirable for evening dress, trimmed with satin bands of a bright color piped with white. Stripes of butter-cup color, of violet, wood color, or grass green alternating with white, are made with long skirts scalloped at the edge, and bound with satin of the same shade as the stripe. The scallops must be faced with white net to stiffen them and prevent curling up. The net facing is not hemmed at the upper edge, as it is held securely by the binding. A blue and white Chambery gauze has all the widths of the skirt but the front one, cut in sharp scallops two inches deep and bound with blue satin. The scallops extend up the side seams, overlapping the front breadth. A Marie Antoinette flounce, widening to the knee in the centre, extends across the front width. Low waist and fichu. A solid white Chambery has a box-pleated flounce, bound on both sides with lavender. Three bands of cross-cut satin – lavender piped with white – descend from the belt sweeping around toward the side. Similar bands put on in crescent shape form a tablier trimming in front. The low corsage has Grecian folds on the breast alternately of satin and Chambery. Shallow bands for sleeves.

A unique addition to dressy toilettes is a kind of apron which almost forms a third skirt. It is cut long and rounding in front, sloping upward at the sides to the back, where it is held by a rosette or bow with sash ends. The upper skirt is raised at the sides and back in large puffs, and trimmed like the apron with cross-cut bands of satin. The lower skirt is plain.

Dress with Double Skirt – looped up.

This dress is of gray foulard, trimmed with pleated ruffles of the same material. The short upper skirt is looped up in the manner shown by the illustration. Under this is arranged a piece of the material of the dress, which is finished by a wider pleated ruffle on the bottom, and is so arranged as to simulate a second skirt looped up.

As to the ladies' dress, I assure you I feel the greatest difficulty in trying to describe it. Marie Antoinette fichus and loose jackets, confined by a band round the waist and a sash at the back, are all the rage; so are short dresses. Very few dresses are allowed to trail on the ground, and all kinds of devices are used to loop up the long ones. The best of all plans is to have loops and buttons put at each breadth, outside the dress, at a sufficient distance apart to prevent them touching the ground; but some of the belles arrange them so artistically that they remind one of the Watteau beauties. Loops of ribbon are worn at the back, from one hip to the other, and through this the fullness of the dress is caught, and with a little further looping at the side the effect is excellent. Paniers, that is, hoop petticoats, are, they say, all the rage in Paris, and the fashion is slowly creeping over to us, and shows itself just now in the excessive fullness and bunchiness of the dresses at the back. Plain blue and pink camlet petticoats, with short striped dresses of the same worn over them are very much in vogue; every thing is worn in suites, that is, petticoat, dress, jacket, or Marie Antoinette fichu alike, with a bonnet of exactly the same shade; contrasts seem quite abandoned by us all.

Dress with Figaro Mantelet.

This dress and mantelet are of gray silk, and are trimmed as shown in the illustration with black lace insertion three inches in width. The mantelet is fastened in front by means of a bow and long ends of gray ribbon.

ANSWERS TO CORRESPONDENTS.

A trained skirt two yards and a halt wide around the bottom. The flounce may be either ten inches or half a yard, according to your own fancy. The skirt must be sloped from the flounce upward or it will be too full at the waist. Leave the two back widths of the silk skirt full. Make but few pleats at the back. There must be some fullness but should not be a great deal.

Wrappings of the same material as the walking dress are invariably worn here. It is positively a rare thing to see the mantle and dress of different material.

Harper's Bazar, July 4, 1868

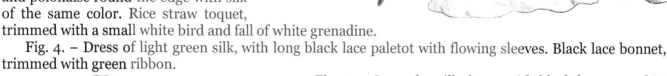

Promenade Toilettes.

Fig. 1. – Round dress and scarf mantilla of lilac foulard, embroidered with violet silk. Lilac crape bonnet, trimmed with lace.

Fig. 2. – Under-skirt of blue and white striped foulard. Short over-skirt, looped up by means of two lapels, and scarf fichu of blue and white figured alpaca, trimmed with a pinked frill of blue silk. White lace bonnet.

Fig. 3. – Round dress and polonaise of Sultan red foulard, with skirt embroidered round the bottom and polonaise round the edge with silk of the same color. Rice straw toquet, trimmed with a small white bird and fall of white grenadine.

Fig. 4. – Dress of light green silk, with long black lace paletot with flowing sleeves. Black lace bonnet, trimmed with green ribbon.

Fig. 5. – Lavender silk dress, with black lace over-skirt and Marie Antoinette fichu. Black lace bonnet, trimmed with lavender ribbon.

Summer Toilettes.

Fig. 1. – Dress of lilac silk cut square in the neck, and trimmed with a pleated flounce of the same material. Bias folds and buttons of lilac silk simulate an over-skirt, closed on the right side. Chemisette of pleated lace.

Fig. 2. – Dress with over-skirt and high corsage of maize foulard, trimmed with flounces, bias folds, and rosettes of the same. The upper skirt is open in front, and turned back on both sides. Sash with ends trimmed to match the skirt.

Sea-side and yachting jackets of white serge are made short, close-fitting, with nearly tight sleeves, and are buttoned with shell-shaped buttons of a color to match the silk with which they are trimmed. These jackets display a good figure to advantage, and are sought after during the

The Art of the Hoop: 1860 - 1869

boating season. The trimming is a fold of blue or scarlet gros grain, with fluted shells of the same pendant as a border. A blue serge jacket, bordered with white, is made with pointed revers, disclosing a habit shirt.

The Moorish jacket is piquante and gay. It is made of black crape cloth, with sleeves, rounded in front to show a lace bodice. The back has pointed basques. The front and basques are braided with gilt, in arabesque patterns. Ball fringe of black and gilt on the edge.

Harper's Bazar, July 11, 1868

ANSWERS TO CORRESPONDENTS.

Make your dress with but one skirt, as you are short and stout. If you have material enough, put a flounce round the skirt, cut bias, eight inches wide, with one-third of the length extra for fullness. If you have not enough for this put two cross-cut bands about a quarter of a yard from the edge of the skirt, with a row of cord fringe beneath.

Make the breadths less sloping toward the top, in order to give them more fullness. The skirt should be gathered – slightly in the front breadths, and very full at the back. Both organdy and ribbon sashes are used. Organdy sashes are ruffled or bordered with lace. Sometimes the trimming only extends across the end and a quarter of a yard up each side. If the material is solid colored, a bunch of tucks at the end of the sash is very pretty.

Harper's Bazar, July 18, 1868

WALKING DRESS.

Walking Dress of Blue and Pearl-Colored Striped Mohair. – The lower skirt is trimmed just above the hem and up the sides in points with a pearl-colored and black worsted lace. The upper skirt is looped up at the sides; and with the small sacque, which is straight at the back with pelerine ends in front, is also trimmed with worsted lace. The sleeves of the dress are plain and close; but the sacque sleeves are long and pointed.

All walking dresses are looped up somewhere, usually at the sides, but sometimes at the back. But the variety in the style of walking dresses is astonishing; and the skirt can be either looped up nearly to the waist, or caught up in one or two small plaits quite near the bottom. But the very newest style is certainly to loop them up near the hips.

WALKING DRESS.

Walking Dress. – The under-dress is of lavender-colored silk, trimmed with a leaf trimming of the silk, bound with white; the sleeves and body are of the same silk. The upper-dress is of gray poplin, cut round in front and in points at the back, and trimmed with rich fringe; the fringe in front has a deep heading, and is heavier than that at the back. The body to this upper-dress is cut low and square, and the sleeve long and square; a wide sash with fringe on the ends tied behind.

The *panier*, or as we should say in English, the pannier, is a mysterious support made of horse-hair and whalebone, and worn at the top of the crinoline, that brings back to memory the *tournues* of some twenty years ago. To speak more accurately, however, it is a sort of *bustle*; and is a revival of the fashion of Marie Antoinette's day. A wag has said that the name is well chosen, for that a woman in one of these dresses does not look unlike a donkey, with a pair of panniers on each side. A lady, in whose taste we have great faith, however, declares it the prettiest fashion of her time. Dresses, made in this style, have the skirt plain in front only, but rounded off at the back, so that the folds of the dress may show off to advantage the outline of a slender waist. Sashes and scarfs loop up the bottom of the dress in large puffs, and show the under-skirt, which should be as pretty and as much ornamented as the dress itself.

Of course, the pannier dresses, though the newest, are not the only ones worn. Many ladies do not like them. Gored dresses, consequently, still hold their own, and will make a strong fight for it. We give, therefore, in this number, some of every style. But, in the end, say by next winter, perhaps even by next fall, the pannier dresses will, probably, drive all others out of the field.

CAPE WITH SASH.

The large sashes make an evening dress look very pretty. They are mostly tied very low down upon the skirt, and so as to loop up the upper-skirt slightly at the back, quite in the Louis XV. Style. For more ordinary wear, the sashes are usually short, with large bows and fringe on the ends.

House dresses are still made with long trains, full at the back and trimmed with flounces and sashes, or with bows of ribbon caught here and there.

Fringe and Lace are both much used as trimmings, the former on walking dresses, the latter on house and evening dresses.

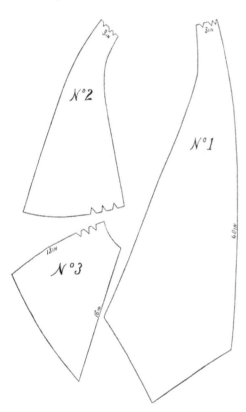

MARIE ANTOINETTE FICHU.

The short, ungraceful sac-paletot is at last to be replaced. The two new forms of out-door covering are the Marie Antoinette Fichu and the Lamballe Mantelet. The former crosses in front of the chest, and the ends are looped over at the back of the waist; the Lamballe is a small cape, with short ends that are left to hang at the sides. As the Marie Antoinette Fichu is likely to be the more popular of the two, we this month present our readers with the cut paper pattern of one. It represents exactly the half of the fichu, and consists of three pieces – the back, the front, and the long sash end. Notches will be found on the edges of the paper, showing how the different pieces are to be joined. The fichu may be made and trim med in a variety of styles. For morning wear, can be cut out of the same material as the dress, and trimmed to correspond with it; in black taffetas, either embroidered or braided, and bordered with fringe, is extremely stylish, as well as useful. For evening wear, it is very fashionable, in either black or white lace, in the new hand-embroidered tulle, and in white muslin, richly trimmed with Valenciennes lace, as in the illustration.

A becoming dress is a wonderful restorer of good humor. An ugly dress makes people doubt if even a pretty woman is handsome.
Peterson's Magazine, July 1868

The trains of evening dresses are a little shorter than they have been. The example of moderation was first given by the fair Empress Eugénie herself. Not that they are short now, far very far from it; many, many inches can be taken off before they will even think of approaching that stage. The dresses worn the last season at a crowded party, where dancing was done, were the next morning fit to be thrown away, and the floor of the room used was literally strewn with strips of lace, tulle, and gauze.

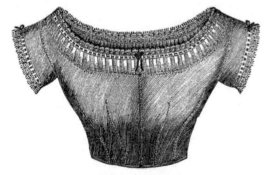

Fig. 16. – Low under-bodice for ladies. This bodice is made of white silk, lined with cambric. It is edged at the top with a strip of plaited muslin bordered with guipure insertion and lace. The sleeves are trimmed in the same manner. A piece of black velvet ribbon is drawn through the strip of insertion. The bodice may also be made of cambric.

The Art of the Hoop: 1860 - 1869

Fig. 1. – Walking-dress and polonaise of black *gros* grain silk. The skirt is looped up at each side, and forms a puff across the back. The front breadth is plain, cut in a deep point, and trimmed with fringe and braid. The underskirt is of lilac silk. The polonaise fits the figure, buttons over to the left side, and is trimmed with an open gimp lined with lilac silk.

Fig. 2. – Dress of Metternich green silk, with two skirts. The underskirt is of a darker shade, trimmed with braid. The upper skirt is scalloped on the edge in the back, and looped up at the sides so as to puff in the back. The front breadth is cut in a scallop, trimmed with a bias ruffle and puff. Marie Antoinette fichu, with the ends falling in front, and trimmed with a ruffle. Fancy headdress of white lace and flowers.

Black grenadines are very much worn for both street and house dresses, trimmed with colors. We have seen several walking suits made of it, the dress just long enough to clear the ground, trimmed with four or five small ruffles bound with silk of any pretty contrasting color, the Redingote trimmed to correspond, with a sash of ribbon or silk of the same color, or of the grenadine bound with silk of the same color as the trimming.

Fig. 4. – Dress of pearl-colored silk, with two skirts trimmed with plaited ruffles of the same. The upper skirt is looped in the back; the lower one is trimmed with a second ruffle in the back, giving the dress the appearance of three skirts. Black silk basquine, trimmed with chenille fringe braid and buttons. White chip bonnet, trimmed with white ribbon and violets.

Fig. 5. – Dress of stone-colored grenadine, made with two skirts. The upper skirt is cut in deep points, trimmed with blue silk braid; the lower one is trimmed with large bows made of blue silk, and trimmed with chenille fringe. The sash and rosette in the back are made of blue silk.

As mentioned in our last, white muslin dresses are again very fashionable; they are more serviceable than tarlatane, and certainly nothing can be more becoming for young ladies. The two following will serve as models: The first is a dress of embroidered muslin, over a skirt of rose-colored *glacé* silk. The skirt is train-shaped. The muslin bodice is covered with a pretty corselet of rose-colored silk, embroidered with silver, and trimmed with white satin rouleaux, and white blonde. A lappet ornamented in the same manner fastens the draperies of the muslin bodice. The corselet is open in front, and fastened with silver cords. The wide sash corresponds with the corselet both as to material and trimming, and forms a large bow at the back, about midway up the skirt.

The second dress is of clear white muslin, and is also train-shaped. The skirt is trimmed round the bottom with a deep flounce, headed by a ruche of buttercup-colored satin. A wide sash is of the same material; it is fastened with a large puff at the side. The outline of the low bodice is edged with small bunches of golden-tinted buttercups, with delicate black foliage. If a simpler style is preferred, the best way to make up a clear white dress is a train-shaped skirt of moderate length, with a deep flounce, headed with a thick ruche. Low bodice, with a bouillon and lace border round the top. Bows or flowers on the bosom

and shoulders, and a wide sash – for sashes are indispensable this season with white dresses.
Godey's Lady's Book, August 1868

Robes for the most part are worn to show the feet in front, the back being slightly raised from the ground. The front breadth is still quite plain, the back gathered or puckered up. Puffs or *bouillonnés*, horizontal and perpendicular, are much *en vogue*; these can also be arranged to suit the fancy of the wearer; in fact any trimmings of the last quarter of a century adapt themselves easily to the present fashion. A band of the material, two to four inches in width, exclusive of the hem, put on with a deep beading fancifully arranged, is placed above the flounce, which also forms the bottom of the skirt in conjunction with the puffs. Muslins, grenadines, etc., are particularly adapted for this style, as these are made with a border specially designed to carry out this effect. The *fond* of these dresses is white, covered with a small pattern, the border being always in keeping with the same, although more color and design is necessarily introduced into it.

One of our best furnishing houses is making a specialty this season of calico morning dresses that are sold at $4 50 and $5 when completed. Such as you allude to are made sacque-shaped, the body and skirt in one, with a sloped seam down the centre of the back and under each arm. Coat-sleeves and turn down collar. Pearl buttons down the front. Pockets with flaps slit downward. Bind the skirt with braid that has been well shrunk. Bias hems and facings are seldom well ironed, and the plain binding is quite sufficient on thick calico. A band of striped calico of the color of the figure in the dress will serve for trimming, or a wide braid of white mixed with a color. Border the sleeves top and bottom, also the collar, pockets, and belt. Fasten the belt permanently at the back, making a pointed lap in front buttoned with two buttons.

Cut the plaid muslin as a sacque by the same pattern as the calico, but half a yard or three-quarters shorter in the skirt. Finish out the length with a wide flounce with a three-inch hem at the bottom, and a ruffle at the top edge gathered by a cord. Trim the coat-sleeve with a ruffle or with cambric edging. Be careful that the shoulder seams are not very long. The trimming at the top of the sleeves makes the shoulders appear broad enough. Long shoulder seams are uncomfortable and unfashionable. Wear a colored belt and large ribbon bow at the throat. If your neck is short and fair cut the dress very low in the neck, and wear a black velvet ribbon tied at the back with long ends or clasped with a locket in front. Caution your laundress against putting too much starch in your muslins.
Harper's Bazar, August 1, 1868

A nansook morning dress has an untrimmed round skirt of medium length, a compromise between short dresses and trains. The French waist, gathered into a belt, is tastefully trimmed with bretelles of inserted puffs, extending over the shoulders and narrowing toward the belt. Full coat-sleeve, with puffs on the wide cuff. Pink ribbon bow at the throat. Sash, with four loops and ends at the side. Pompadour slippers, with large pink rosettes.

Close-Fitting Lace Paletot.

This lace paletot is without sleeves, and is trimmed around the neck and armholes with two pleated rows of lace, which are arranged in the manner shown by the illustration. A belt of black silk and lace completes the paletot. This paletot may also be made of guipure net or figured tulle, or may be lined with colored silk.

SHORT MUSLIN DRESSES.

Instead of the ponderous style of long, flowing dresses for morning, short gored skirts and sacques are adopted. These are convenient, as they are suitable for breakfast and for morning promenades, exchanging the fancy slipper for a walking-boot, being the only alteration necessary. Muslins, lawns, linens, cambric, and Chambery are made in this way, trimmed with ruffles of the same. A short suit of buff Chambery, made by a tasteful modiste, was sold at $15. The sacque should not be full, but must have a cool, négligé appearance. The seams under the arms are all that is necessary to give it proper shape. The under-waist should be prettily trimmed, and belted with a ribbon belt the color of the skirt.

The Art of the Hoop: 1860 - 1869

HINTS ABOUT SLEEVES.

The two pieces of a coat-sleeve should not be cut together. Many ladies who make their own dresses spoil the sleeve by shaping the upper and under portion precisely alike. The upper part should be an inch and a half broader than the under piece. It should also be longer, and held next the sewer, that it may be slightly fulled into the under part as it is sewed. At the arm-hole the front should be a convex curve, while the under part is concave. The sleeve should not be straight, but rounded to fit smoothly on the arm when half bent, as that is the position most frequently assumed.

The sleeves of wash dresses are now shaped like the ordinary linen under-sleeve so much worn. Cut an ample coat-sleeve long enough to reach half-way between the elbow and wrist, and finish out the length with a deep, loose cuff. The cuff must be interlined to make it hold starch, and is fastened with two buttons on the outside seam, or closed to run the hand through.

Tastes differ about the length of trains. For your height we would advise sixty inches as the length of the back width. In the most graceful skirt pattern there are three widths slightly gored on each side, with a straight width in the back. Many modistes prefer, however, to gore only two side widths. Get the proper length of the front and back widths, and slope the others gradually. If your gros grain is heavy do not line the skirt. Work button-holes up the front of corsage, by all means. Make a panier sash, with four puffed-out loops and two broad short sides. Bind the sash, and do not line it. Trim the sides with pipings, and the ends with fringe. Put your pocket and opening in the skirt in the second side seam.

Paniers are decidedly in fashion. Some gored skirt patterns have a sloped seam in the back, but it is considered safest, and paniers require it, to make the back breadth full.

Harper's Bazar, August 8, 1868

Summer Toilettes.

Fig. 1. – Dress with high blouse waist of lilac mozambique. The skirt is cut in large scallops round the bottom, and trimmed with two narrow flounces of the same material. A lappet of lace insertion, underlaid with lilac ribbon, and bordered with a frill of mozambique, is set at the point of each scallop. The blouse waist, sleeves, and ends of the sash are trimmed in the same manner.

Fig. 2. – Walking suit of violet and white striped foulard. Both skirt and paletot are trimmed with violet and white silk gimp and narrow puff of white foulard. White Neapolitan hat trimmed with white ribbon and wild flowers.

Fig. 3. – Walking suit of light gray poplin trimmed with gray satin in the manner shown by the illustration. Skirt looped up in the Watteau style. Gray beret with gray feathers.

Fig. 4. – Walking suit of green and white figured organdy. Under-skirt of green batiste with three flounces. Skirt and paletot trimmed with green ribbon. Green silk sash. Italian straw hat trimmed with green ribbon and wild flowers.

Fig. 5. – Pink barége dress with high-necked basque-waist, with pleated trimming of the same material. Flowing sleeves. Sash with loops at the top and long ends, finished with bows, and trimmed like the dress.

Harper's Bazar, August 15, 1868

Vest Blouse.

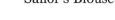

Sailor's Blouse.

Muslin Blouse with Chemise Russe.

← Chevalier Blouse.

Harper's Bazar, August 22, 1868

ANSWERS TO CORRESPONDENTS.

Trim your dress with tassel or cord fringe about three inches wide, with a heading of two narrow folds of silk or satin with piping in the centre. If you do not want an outside garment make a tight-fitting basque, but we advise a plain waist instead, with a fichu or a scarf-shaped mantle looped in the back with rosettes. You are safe, we think, in goring the front and side widths of your skirts. Our best modistes continue to gore all but the back widths. There is always a risk in making up handsome materials in an intermediate season.

Green and white are the most fashionable colors for evening dresses at present. Pale buff, French gray, and white for street and house. Skirts are still gored in front and at the sides, and are quite full in the back, being frequently looped up in paniers. The wide Spanish flounce is more fashionable than three narrow ones.

Harper's Bazar, August 29, 1868

CARRIAGE DRESS.

Carriage Dress of Gray Silk. – The sacque is made with large plaits in the back, and has a guipure hood; the sacque is much longer at the back than at the sides, where it is gathered up with large knots of ribbon.

It is very important, in making up new dresses, to remember that the three front widths only are gored, the other widths are all cut straight, and gathered at the waist, so as to give fullness at the back and sides. The short dresses, as well as the trained ones, are made in this way; and in order to be in the fashion the skirts must be very flat and plain in front, and very much puffed out at the back. Ruffles, pinked-out-ruches, pleated quillings, with the pleats reversed; fringe, gimp, and rows of brocaded braid, are all popular for short, as well as for long costumes. The latter are a good deal trimmed with lace and bows of ribbon. But the trimming, as well as the style of making a dress, is so varied that it can be left to the taste of wearer, only remembering that it must be full at the back and plain in front.

Morning jackets are still made of a loose shape, but for wearing out-of-dors [*sic*], they are made tight-fitting with basques. Moreover, the small over-garments with waistbands, which are now worn out-of-doors, resemble jackets much more than paletots; no dress bodice need be worn under these small, tight-fitting garments.

CORSAGE CAPRICE.

Corsage Caprice is of black silk, with a deep basque formed entirely of ornamental fringe. The sleeves and body are also trimmed with fringe, and the whole body has quite a Spanish look.

CORSAGE RIVERE.

Corsage Rivere of Black Silk, trimmed with gimp fringe and lace; with this body, as well as with the *Caprice*, a large crinoline puff is worn.

Amongst the novelties are some clear white muslin aprons, with lace insertions and edging, and a colored ribbon run through the band. Worn with delicate silks or muslin the effect is charming.

Peterson's Magazine, August 1868

Dresses are often looped up by means of a wide ribbon, which commences at the waistband and forms a large bow at a short distance from the bottom of the skirt; the skirt is raised and passed over the ribbon, and for walking *toilette* should be fastened to it by a few invisible stitches. This fashion is not unknown to our readers; they saw it last season in evening *toilettes*. Formerly evening *toilettes* had fashions and ornaments of their own; now there is no rule – all things are confused and mixed. What are looped-up dresses and draperies, rosettes, bows of ribbon, and ornaments, if not proper to evening dresses? But now all these things are seen as well in the street as in the drawing room, and at all hours of the day.

Fig. 4. – Evening-dress of white grenadine. The bottom of skirt is trimmed with a fluted ruffle put on in points; above these points are puffs also put on in points and divided by bands of lilac silk. Low corsage, trimmed with bretelles of silk edged with lace. Belt of lilac silk, from which sash ends fall at each side; these ends are trimmed with lace insertion and joined together by small rosettes.

Fig. 5. – Walking-dress of silver-gray silk. The edge of skirt is trimmed with three narrow ruffles bound with green silk. The polonaise is made tight-fitting, turned back at the throat with revere of green silk. The edge of skirt is trimmed with a row of black lace headed by a narrow green silk band; narrow green bands finished by a button extend up the front.

A Polonaise dress of purple gros-grains silk is buttoned slantways, both on the bodice and all down the skirt, with purple satin buttons; it is also bound with purple satin. The skirt is short and edged with fringe round the bottom. It is worn over a black silk underskirt not quite touching the ground. Tight sleeves, trimmed at the top and bottom with a strip of purple satin and fringe. Waistband of purple satin with scarf lapels at the back.

Fig. 10. – Alpaca bodice. This bodice is either white or pearl gray, and trimmed with festoons of satin, blue, mauve, or light Bismarck. A tress or plait of satin conceals the raw edge of these festooned trimmings. The sleeves are ornamented in the same manner. This model can also be made in foulard or cashmere, and the trimmings, although arranged in the same style, can be varied. Garibaldi bodices are trimmed this season with colors that contrast with that of the material of which they are made.

Small aprons are worn for morning *toilettes*; they are made of black or colored silk contrasting with the morning dress, or of fine thin muslin either ornamented with embroidery or ruffles; for young ladies the latter are pretty trimmed with bright ribbons.

Godey's Lady's Book, September 1868

Promenade Toilettes.

Fig. 1. – Dress with Watteau over-skirt of lilac poplin, trimmed with lilac satin pipings, rosettes of lilac ribbon, and lilac silk tassels.

Fig. 2. – India mull dress with double-skirt and fichu. The under-skirt is edged with a quilling of the same. The over-skirt is gathered in a large puff behind, and is furnished in front with two rounded lappets, also trimmed with quilling. The fichu is crossed in front and trimmed behind with a large bow of mull, as shown in the illustration; the ends are laid in two pleats. Swiss muslin petticoat, edged with needle-work insertion. Pink lace bonnet.

Fig. 3. – Dress with double skirt of light green silk barége. The under-skirt is trimmed in front with three pleated flounces of the same material, surmounted with bias folds of green satin; the upper-skirt is caught up on each side with rosettes of green ribbon, and is edged from the sides, where it falls over the under-skirt, with a pleated flounce. Two sash ends of green satin, trimmed with piping and fringe, are fastened on the shoulder with rosettes of green ribbon, and are crossed under the belt.

Fig. 4. – Under-skirt of pink foulard; overskirt with long casaque of pink Chambery gauze. The trimming consists of puffings and pleatings of the same material. Bonnet of white figured lace. White parasol with pink silk lining.

Directions for Looping up Dresses.

This new arrangement for looping up dresses is very simple and convenient. Sew three buttons on the skirt just below the belt, one behind and one at each side. Twenty-two inches below the belt behind, and sixteen inches below it at the sides, make loops which are worked of silk the color of the dress, and are buttoned over the buttons when the dress is looped up. The distance of the loops below the buttons depends on the length of the skirt. The illustrations show the skirt before it is looped up and the front and back after it has been looped.

The Art of the Hoop: 1860 - 1869

ANSWERS TO CORRESPONDENTS.

If you mean by paniers merely the *tournure* or bustle we refer you to the New York Fashion article of this Number. If you allude to the dress skirt, we warn you that you are attempting a difficult task, and one that is seldom well done by unpracticed hands. The simplest arrangement is to make the front width plainly gored, with three or, if you choose, four other widths also sloped, and from a quarter to three-eighths of a yard longer than the pattern of your upper skirt. Join these widths by a band, two inches wide, cut bias, and corded. The bands are the proper length of your skirt. The long widths are gathered into the bands, producing a puffed appearance. A lining of coarse net is sometimes used to stiffen the puffs. Strictly speaking this is the Watteau skirt, but it is called paniers here, and fashionably worn. The real panier puff is formed by a cord extending from the side-seams across the back widths.

The silk skirt worn beneath grenadine should be made separate, but cut similarly. It is simply a petticoat. The silk waist lining should be sewed in with the grenadine, as grenadine is not strong enough without lining to bear the stress on the arms. A trained skirt requires a different pattern from a short skirt as it is much fuller at the bottom. Ruffles of the same are used to trim grenadine. Yours may be prettily bound with purple. Ribbon for binding flounces is sold at sixty cents a piece of twelve yards. The Spanish flounce three-eighths or half a yard wide is much worn on trained skirts.

Modistes continue to gore the front and side widths of trained skirts. The back widths are full, and from sixty to seventy inches long. Use real thread lace to trim your black gros grain, with a heading of satin folds and piping. Lace is always valuable, and is more suitable for an indoor dress than fringe. You will observe in our plates that the corsages of plain silk dresses are very little trimmed. An epaulet and cuff on the sleeves is all sufficient. A thick cord of white and black silk will make a stylish heading to your lace if your do not object to using white.

Harper's Bazar, September 5, 1868

Violet and Lilac Silk [*Walking*] Dress. – This dress has a double skirt of violet and lilac silk, the under-skirt with a narrow [*word missing: flounce?*] and the upper with a wide flounce of the same material. The front of the upper skirt is shorter than the back, which is arranged en panier, as shown by the illustration, and trimmed with a violet silk bow.

Many ladies of fashion have abandoned sashes as common, wearing instead a narrow waistband fastened at the side with sharp pointed ends, the bow at the side being what is called a sword bow.

Light Brown Silk Dress. – This [*walking*] dress is made with two skirts, both of which are trimmed with a pleated flounce A separate piece also trimmed with a pleated flounce is added to the upper skirt, which is looped. At each side of this piece are arranged long and broad ends of the same material as the dress in the manner shown by the illustration.

Harper's Bazar, September 12, 1868

ANSWERS TO CORRESPONDENTS.

Four yards of single width material are necessary for a dressing-gown. Merino or solid colored cashmere is preferred to figured materials. The trimming is wide flat braid, or thick cord sewed on plainly or in waves. The lining should be of soft pliant stuff slightly wadded. The front is neatly quilted. The back is only tacked.

Folds are from one to three inches wide. Striped materials cut bias are fashionable as folds on plain goods. ... The satin stitch is done by a succession of stitches, always across the work, and lying close to but not over each other. French embroidery includes all the delicate and most expensive kinds worked in satin stitch, with overcast and the various open and fancy stitches.

Promenade Dresses.

Fig. 1. – Suit of bear's ear poplin. Under-skirt trimmed with three narrow flounces; short overskirt edged with wide black lace, and caught up in the back under a basque-ceinture formed of two rows of pleats. Close sleeves, with mousquetaire cuff of black lace. High corsage, pointed in the neck. Linen collar and cuffs. Small black lace toque, with lavender flowers.

Fig. 2. – Under-skirt of Mexican blue silk, trimmed with India galloon. High corsage and sleeves of the same material. Over-skirt of white foulard, with cashmere stripes, looped up very high with a puff of the same. Sash and bow of the same foulard. Corsage of white striped foulard, edged with a blue ruche, and open to the waist in the front and back. Magistrate collar.

Evening and Dinner Dresses.

Fig. 1. – White tulle evening dress for young lady. Under-skirt trimmed with a flounce and three bouillonnés. Over-skirt looped up on each side with clusters of roses. Abbé mantle, fastened with roses in the back alone, and loosely caught up on the arm, or can be left flowing.

Fig. 2. – Dinner dress of blue silk. Under-skirt plain and trained; over-skirt, edged with a ruche of black silk bound with orange, and caught up in the Watteau fashion, very full behind. The *engageante* which holds the folds is trimmed with a ruche of black silk, bound with orange, with large bows at the sides. The folds which depend from the neck are likewise trimmed with bows. High corsage and close sleeves.

Harper's Bazar, September 19, 1868

MORNING ROBES.

Cashmere robes de chambre are in bright, warm grounds, poppy-red, garnet, green, or black, with gay cashmere borders in which yellow predominates. The border extends around the skirt and up the front widths. The robe is worn flowing loosely from the shoulders, unconfined by a belt. Flowing sleeves are represented on the diagrams that accompany each pattern, with narrow borders for trimming. The price ranges from $15 to $24. Cashmeres sold by the yard at $1 75 have white or scarlet grounds with wide-spreading figures and palm leaves.

Harper's Bazar, September 26, 1868

Trimmings, and, in fact, even the style of making the dress, is left so much now to the individual taste, that only a few general rules can be laid down; after that one's own idea of the fitness of things must decide the rest. A letter from Paris says, though, that "some things are indispensable:" First, that there shall be abundance of crinoline, or bustle, or *panier*, or *tournure* (for the bunch at the back goes by a variety of names) just below the waist, but that there should be little or none at the lower half of the skirt.

Secondly, that there should be no trains worn in the streets, long skirts to be kept exclusively for indoor wear. That if a lady desires to wear a train when driving out during the day, the skirt should be so short in front that her feet are plainly visible. Therefore pretty boots are indispensable.

Thirdly. A medley of materials quite indescribable; the more flounces, ruches, bows, and *pompons*, the more the skirts are looped up in bunches, the better is the wearer's right to consider herself elegant and fashionable.

An easy way to loop up a long skirt, provided the skirt is not too full, is to have a piece of elastic, fastened inside the side breadths, about a quarter of a yard from the waist, with a hook attached to that on the one side, and an eye to that on the other. Just at the place where they are sewn the seam must be left unstitched for about an inch, so that when not used the pieces of elastic may be slipped inside the skirt; when, however, these are hooked together, they shorten the skirt sufficiently in front, and all the fullness at the back can be drawn through the loop so made *en paniers*.

WALKING DRESS.

Walking Dress of Blue Silk, trimmed with black silk braid; a row of black and blue fringe is placed near the bottom of the dress. The upper-skirt is made open in front, and is trimmed with fringe also. The sacque partially fits the figure at the back, and has long square, mantilla ends in front.

WALKING DRESS.

Walking Dress of Black and White Striped Poplin. – The under-skirt is trimmed with two ruffles; the upper-skirt is puffed very much at the back; the Lamballe cape has long ends which run below the waist, and are buttoned to the sides of the upper-skirt.

THE BAILLY PALETOT.

We give, this month, a new and elegant pattern for a fall paletot. It is called the "Bailly," and is made of black silk. It falls loose in front; the back is without any seem in the middle, but is cut longer than the rest of the paletot. The lower part is fastened by a passementerie ornament; lastly it is entirely trimmed with satin braid and Chantilly lace. This trimming simulates a pelerine in front. The sleeve is ample at the top, narrow at the bottom, with ornaments to match. We here give a diagram, by aid of which it may be cut out.

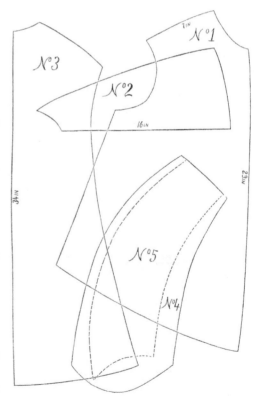

No. 1. Front.
No. 2. Side-Piece.
No. 3. Back.
No. 4 and 5. Under-Part of the Sleeve.

Peterson's Magazine,
September 1868

Persons soon get used to everything, even to eccentricities, and our present costumes appear natural, in spite of the resistance which they at first met with. It must be confessed, however, that it is often not the fashions which are ridiculous, but the manner in which they are interpreted.

Dresses for walking costume are all made with two skirts, the under skirt being plain gored, the upper one being cut gored only at the sides and front, the back breadths being left plain and gathered in French gathers. Some of these dresses are so full as to require six or more breadths in the back, this is not at all necessary, three breadths of ordinary width material makes a very nice fulness in the skirt.

Fig. 1. – Dress of Metternich green silk, trimmed with two narrow pinked-out flounces. Overskirt of black silk, open at the sides, and trimmed with wide thread lace. Plain corsage, with lapels of black silk; coat sleeve trimmed to correspond. Hair arranged in puffs, and ornamented with narrow green satin ribbon and small rosettes.

Fig. 2. – Dinner-dress of Havana brown silk, with an underskirt of a lighter shade. This is trimmed with puffs, each puff being divided by a button. A wide puff extends down each seam of the skirt; the upper skirt is trimmed with a ruffle. Plain corsage, and sash trimmed to correspond.

Fig. 3. – Walking-dress of purple silk poplin, made with two skirts. The upper one is scalloped and bound with satin, and looped up at one side by the sash that is fastened at the side. The lower skirt is likewise scalloped, and trimmed with fringe and satin bands. Two satin rosettes are placed on the lower skirt, in the space left by looping the upper skirt. Plain corsage, buttoned over to one side.

Fig. 4. – Evening-dress of white silk. The bottom of the skirt is trimmed with embroidered bands of pink silk, each band being finished by a tassel. The upper part of the skirt is trimmed to simulate an upper skirt, with bands of pink silk and narrow white lace. Low square corsage, trimmed with lapels of pink silk.

Fig. 5. – Walking-dress of stone-colored Irish poplin, with an underskirt of blue. The dress is scalloped around the bottom, and edged by a deep plaited flounce. It is looped up at the sides by sash ends, bound with satin, and the ends edged by a ruffle. Black velvet *paletôt*, buttoned over to one side, and trimmed with chenille fringe and satin trimming.

The double and triple skirts looped back *en paniers*, are better understood now, and it would be difficult to quote the variety of styles we meet on our fashionable promenades. The following deserves particular notice, however, on account of its beauty and originality: Imagine a round skirt of *foulard carmelite*, ornamented below with two plaited flounces, which are bordered at the top by a fold of silver-gray silk. The upper skirt, of silver-gray silk, is looped back at the sides by bunches of *carmelite*-colored ribbons. It is ornamented all round with a narrow fringe of the same shade, with a narrow fold at the top. The cassock of *carmelite foulard* fits tight to the waist, and is looped back *en paniers* where the upper skirt ends. A long knot behind marks the centre of these paniers, which are much puffed. The tight-fitting sleeves of the lower waist are made of silver-gray silk.

Fig. 6. – Costume of gray silk, consisting of a skirt *à paniers*, looped up over a turquoise blue petticoat, and of a fichu edged with blue frills. The fichu is crossed over the chest, then the ends descend the skirt and hold up the pannier, being joined at the back under a large bow. This illustration gives a very fair idea of what is called a pannier skirt; the front breadth is plain, the side ones are gored, and the back straight and full, being gathered to the waistband. Then the skirt is completed with a *bouffant*, or bustle, made of the same material, and lined with stiff muslin, and likewise gathered into the band; the bottom of the pannier is lastly confined by gathers, and fastened on the skirt. The bow which joins the two ends of the mantelet under the pannier is made separate, and sewn on one of the ends, the other being fastened to it by either buttons or hooks.

It is said it is the Princess of Metternich who has given the vogue to panniers; she, with many other ladies of fashion, very soon discarded the Empire dresses; the Empress herself was always partial to ample-flowing skirts. Thus, for once, good taste has had the better of fashion, and, from the scant, ungraceful robes of the First Empire, we are rapidly going back to the more becoming fashions of the reigns of Louis XVI. and Louis XV. Parisian dressmakers study historical costumes of that period, and think far more of copying than of inventing. With the Louis XV. costumes the pannier jupon is indispensable.

Materials of two colors, and toilets composed of two colors, have now become quite general. The former are not, strictly speaking, new. They were formerly called *shot*; they are now known by the name of *glacé*. When both the colors harmonize well together the effect is very pretty.

As for toilets of two materials and colors, they obtain great favor, and are most useful as a means of employing to advantage a somewhat worn or faded silk or poplin dress. It is easy to transform such a dress with a little arrangement and retrimming into an under dress, over which another is worn with a short or looped up skirt. The waist being of the same as over-dress, trimmed with the same color as underskirt. Two old dresses can be made to answer the purpose, a black and colored one.

We see a good many striped materials that are used more to complete a suit than to make a whole suit of; they are mostly used for underskirts. The material is cut on the cross, for the bottom of the skirt, so that the lines appear slanting; this is done in almost all materials.

Godey's Lady's Book, October 1868

Some French walking dresses just arrived have the tunic or upper skirt without a front width. The side widths are buttoned to the front seams of the under-skirt. This is a good plan as it gives the flat front so desirable with paniers. The simple trimming may be easily made at home by any expert needle-woman. The tunic is scalloped and bound with silk. Inside each scallop is a button the color of the binding, with a button-hole simulated beside it. Sleeves are close-fitting with a puff at the top, and sometimes a puff at the elbow.

Promenade, Dinner, and Carriage Dresses.

Fig. 1. – Promenade dress of foulard écru, with a deep flounce, bordered with a band of foulard of a darker shade, and surmounted by a double ruche. Low corsage with long sleeves. Mantelet with crossed ends, of the same material as the dress, edged with *bouffette* trimming of foulard of a darker shade, and with black guipure two inches wide. The sleeves are trimmed in the same manner. Black lace bonnet with pomegranate blossoms.

Fig. 2. – Dinner dress of bright blue silk with train. The trimming consists of a pleated flounce of the same material as the dress, a flounce of white silk gauze, and a pinked ruche of rose-colored silk. Three rows of this trimming encircle the skirt. Tunic like the dress, and trimmed in the same manner. The tunic is looped up on each side by a bow and ends of rose-colored fringed ribbon. Low-necked fichu like the dress edged with a rose-colored ruche. Coiffure of white tulle, composed of a pleated diadem and a veil, and trimmed with roses.

Fig. 3. – Carriage dress of reseda taffeta. Over-skirt of black silk grenadine edged with fringe, and caught up on each side by a large bow of black satin ribbon. Mantelet like the over-skirt. Silk bonnet of the same shade as the dress, and trimmed with grasses and wild flowers.

ANSWERS TO CORRESPONDENTS.

If you prefer silk for your walking suit get one of the frog greens, a dark garnet, or a blue and brown chameleon. Black silk is most serviceable, because it is always fashionable. The striped satin skirts worn beneath it this season make it very gay. In woolen goods get a changeable poplin or an all-wool serge. You will find full descriptions of the new dress goods in last week's Fashion Article. Make two skirts, the under one plainly gored, trimmed with a bias flounce; the upper skirt plain in front and caught up almost to the waist at the back and sides. Many upper skirts have no front width, being attached to the side seams of the under-skirt. If you like a sacque, make it short and almost tight fitting, with revere front and coat-sleeves, but scarf capes are newer, crossed under the belt in front, and looped in the back by rosettes.

Gore the skirt of your black alpaca suit similarly to those worn last winter, that is, with the front and two side widths gored flat, and the back width left full. Trim with a bias ruffle eight inches wide, or ten if you are tall. It is a matter of fancy whether the ruffle is gathered or pleated. If gathered one-third extra fullness is required. The polonaise is worn larger this season, reaching almost to the top of the ruffle on the skirt. It is almost tight, is fitted into the figure and worn with a belt, the skirt looped by four deep pleats on the hips, high up in the side seams. A newer polonaise has wide spreading puffs at the back but is too complicated for you to attempt to make without seeing it. A small cape like a bertha in front with pelerine ends, forming a sash behind, gives an air of style to the plainest polonaise. Trim this garment with two narrow bias ruffles on the skirt and sleeves.

In altering a full skirt the shape depends on the number of breadths you have. A sloped front width, three gored side widths, and a full width behind, is the popular style for trained dresses. Only two gored side widths are sometimes used, but they are as broad as the three widths when finished. Trim your wine-colored silk with satin or faille of the same shade, cut in bias strips five or six inches wide, caught in puffs at intervals by bands of velvet. Place this around the skirt, ten inches from the edge, and up each side of the front to the belt. A row of handsome fringe falls from beneath the satin around the skirt, but does not extend up the front. With the same trimming design a bertha on the waist, and deep cuffs on the sleeves. The bias velvet bands you mention will trim your poplin stylishly. Put pleated ruffles of double silk on each side of the band, sewn in with the velvet. The pleats all run the same way. The ruffle is an inch wide when completed. Make your merino house dress with short gored skirt, with one flounce, and a short jaunty jacket, rounding in front to disclose a white linen waist, tucked and embroidered. Striped cambric waists, with turned-over collars and wide cuffs, are worn for morning. Directions for making an alpaca suit will be found in answer to Maria Louise [*above*]. Large bows of ribbon four or five inches wide are used instead of a breast-pin on the collar. The ribbon is either striped, changeable, or a solid color, to match the trimming of the bonnet. It is a regular bow, or four or five loops, or merely a knot with ends.

The most exclusive ladies in New York attend the Jockey Club races, attired in short dresses, very jaunty and gay, or stylishly plain, as the fancy of the wearer may dictate.

Harper's Bazar, October 3, 1868

For several seasons large invoices of plaid goods have been thrown upon the market here, and merchants anxious to sell have declared plaids would prevail; but they were never seen except in the shop windows or on school-girls, and it became a problem to know what was done with the plaids. Again it is affirmed we are to be arrayed like Scotchmen; and as our Parisian sisters have conceived a fancy for northern fashions, it is probable we will have at least a short reign of this gay attire for demi-toilette. It can never be full dress. The modistes just returned from Paris report as among their importations Highland costumes for morning promenades and traveling, which we describe below. They are also using plaid poplins, silk, and velvet, as trimming, "but very carefully," say the modistes; "not broad bands of plaid, but narrow cords, piping, and binding."

A traveling costume of Parisian make is of large plaid, irregular, blue and green together. It has two skirts, a ten-inch flounce bias, and pleated on the lower skirt, three folds of the material piped with black silk on the upper skirt. Short full sacque with belt, caught up with rosettes at the sides and back. A scarf of the material, half a yard wide, is knotted on the right shoulder, and tied loosely under the left arm.

ANSWERS TO CORRESPONDENTS.

Gore your green poplin closely, the skirt just escaping the floor. Over this make a tunic, open in front, rounded and held up in a short panier puff behind, by gathering the edge under the trimming. Straps underneath hold the puff in position. Around the skirt put two flat quillings of white satin eight inches wide, the box-pleats nearly touching each other, and sewed flat at top and bottom. Narrower quill on the tunic. High corsage open to the belt, with white satin revers. Belt with fan-shaped rosette behind. No sash. Lace chemisette. Sleeves puffed to the elbow, and finished with a frill. White satin boots. Gilt boots are tawdry and theatrical. Make your opera wrap a burnous, trimmed with heavy chenille fringe.

The front and side widths have a pleat under the seams. Back widths are gauged. Brown satin braid half an inch wide, three rows, above corded fringe, will trim your dress stylishly. We have not seen a sleeveless jacket this season. Cloaks are longer. Black is the best color, as it suits any dress.

Harper's Bazar, October 10, 1868

Tirettes for looping up Skirts.

Fig. 1. – Skirt Looped up with Tirettes. Fig. 2. – Tirettes for Looping up Skirts.

The illustrations which we give herewith show an easy and simple manner of making tirettes, by means of which a trained dress may be looped up in a puff behind in the Watteau or Camargo style. Sew small brass rings on the back of the skirt in the manner shown by Fig. 2; the distance of these rings from the belt varies according to the length of the train of the dress. Through these rings run two silk cords of the color of the dress, sew one end of these cords fast inside the belt of the dress, and run the other end through a small button-hole between the front and side breadths of the skirt. Finish the ends on this side with a button covered with the material of the dress, which prevents them from slipping through.

When it is desired to loop up the dress draw the cord, thereby pulling the skirt in the manner shown by Fig. 2. In letting it down, pull the skirt slightly behind, whereupon it falls easily.

Carriage and Evening Toilettes.

Fig. 1. – Dress of violet taffeta, trimmed with two bouillonnés, encircled with three bias folds of violet satin. Short over-skirt of black silk gauze, bordered with a flounce of the same, and looped up at the sides by gauze rosettes. Gauze fichu like the over skirt and trimmed in the same manner.

Fig. 2. – Dress of light-blue faye, trimmed with white moss fringe arranged on the front *en tablier*, and round the bottom in irregular points. Low corsage trimmed with fringe arranged *en plastron*.

Fig. 3. – Dress of rose de Chine satin, glacé with white, with flounces of the same, arranged as a tunic, and rosaces of ribbon to match, looping up the skirt so as to form a large puff behind. Soutane corsage, with piece adjusted behind, and falling loose; this piece is edged with narrow bias folds of velvet of the same color as the dress. Close sleeves trimmed with similar folds and ribbon rosaces. Black lace bonnet, trimmed with green leaves and large China rose. Gloves to match the dress.

ANSWERS TO CORRESPONDENTS.

Square linen cuffs are worn inside the dress sleeve. They fit best when attached to an undersleeve. Make your black silk long, the front width and one each side of it gored, the others full, and looped in a panier puff by a sash. Pleated flounce with puffs at the top formed by reversing the pleats. Passementerie braid with tassels on each seam. Heart-shaped surplice corsage with lace chemisette.

Gray, garnet, and black are the fashionable colors for street dress. Changeable goods are newer than solid colors.

Drab is trimmed with garnet this season – brown with a darker brown and black.

Brocade silks do not require much trimming. Make the long gored skirt plain. A bertha of fringe or lace on the high corsage. Coat-sleeves. Make the white dress a baby waist, with puffed sleeves, and fichu trimmed with Valenciennes.

Morning and Reception Dresses.

Fig. 1. – Trained skirt of white alpaca, embroidered round the bottom with a wreath of blue braid, with sprays running up each breadth. Little Moldavian jacket, cut square at the bottom and heart-shaped in front, trimmed like the skirt and bordered with a ruche of blue ribbon. Chemise Russe of white muslin, with puffed sleeve; a narrow blue ribbon is run through the last puff and tied at the wrist. Dead gold medallion on a blue ribbon round the neck. Hair dressed in the Watteau style, combed up very high from the nape of the neck, and confined by a blue ribbon with rosette at the side. Blue satin slippers with silver buckles.

Fig. 2. – Dress of green taffeta, glacé with chestnut. Short skirt trimmed with three scalloped flounces, each of which is headed by a narrow pinked ruche. Large puff at the back, caught up very much on the sides. Flat, square tunic in front, connected with the puff by a broad hanging lappet at each side. The bottom of the puff and tunic is edged with a scalloped flounce, and the lappet is trimmed with a narrow pinked ruche. Plain corsage and close sleeve; a scalloped frill forms the epaulet and cuff, with a pinked ruche as the heading. Sash with broad ends, bordered with a scalloped frill. Swiss standing collar and cuffs. Saxony gloves. Bronze gaiters.

Harper's Bazar, October 17, 1868

Maria Theresa Dress.

To alter a skirt gored closely about the waist into the present full style you must substitute two full widths behind for the sloped widths worn a year ago. A more economical way of modernizing a gored skirt is to make a separate panier put on over the skirt, according to the directions given in the New York Fashions of this Number. The sample of striped poplin you send will make a stylish petticoat for a suit, with over-skirt and mantle of changeable poplin, scarlet and black, or, if this is too gay, solid black. You will find hints about over-skirts in this Number of the *Bazar*.

A stout lady should not wear a Garibaldi dress.

Make a gored slip of the merino, shaped by seams at the side. The fullness front and back forms a broad box-pleat like the Watteau fold. A wide sash of ribbon or of the merino embroidered confines it at the waist. There is no way of getting rid of the front seam in your dress. It is the buttons that are so objectionable. Remove them and place trimming over the seam.

Take four deep pleats about the hips on the side seams of your polonaise. Put a large button on each pleat. A sash of gros grain depends from the centre of the belt. It is composed of several loops or a very large bow. The ends must not be more than half a yard or three quarters in length.

Harper's Bazar, October 24, 1868

Some ladies wear their short dresses *too short*. Three inches, at furthest, is the proper length from the ground: even this, in many cases, is too much. What is wanted is to have the dress short enough not to touch the ground in any event, and two inches will generally effect this. Many young ladies, however, are tempted by the idea of showing off a pretty pair of boots, and so have their walking dresses made excessively short. Now there is not one girl out of five, even in America, who can stand the test of this free exposure of the foot and ankle. Even in those who can, the fashion has an air of being "fast." That, at least is our opinion.

The Art of the Hoop: 1860 - 1869

LOUIS XIV. TUNIC.

Louis XIV. Tunic of Lilac Silk, over a long skirt of the same color. The front has but little fullness, and is looped up at the side, where it meets the larger tunic at the back, which is made full, looped up, and finished with a ruche.

Flounces are very much in fashion, especially for full dress; and the low bodies are as frequently cut square as round. The becoming *Marie Antoinette* sleeve is also gaining in favor; it is made almost tight to the arm as low as the elbow, and is then finished with ruffles of lace; this is particularly becoming to a thin arm.

PANNIER PETTICOAT – BACK AND FRONT.

Skirt with Panniers – front view. – This skirt can be made in muslin, barege, or any light material. It consists of a short skirt bordered with a flounce; there is a *bouillonne* above the flounce, and a heading above the *bouillonne*. The *panier* is formed by a *bouffant*, which measures two yards and a half in width and twenty-four inches in length, the front being rounded. The top is gathered into the waistband; the front is sewn to a small *plastron*, which turns afterward to the back, and forms the crossed ends on the skirt. These ends, and likewise the small *plastron* in front, are edged with a narrow flounce. The bottom of the *panier* is then gathered and sewn to the edge of the band or strap that appears to hold it. Panniers are very frequently lined with stiff muslin, but this is useless with a washing material.

FRONT OF MANTELET – (SEE DIAGRAM.)
BACK OF MANTELET – (SEE DIAGRAM.)

In the front of the number, we give engravings of the front and back of a new style mantelet suitable for fall wear. We add here a diagram by which to cut it out. It will be seen that it consists of four pieces, which represent one half of the mantelet – the front, the back, the basque for the back, and the waistband.

The front and back are joined on the shoulders, the back is sewn into the top of the waistband, and the basque or *tablier* in then gathered and sewn to the bottom of the band like a skirt. There is no joining in the center either of the back or basque, therefore they must be cut double in the paper. The notch on the edge of the diagram, which represents the *tablier*, indicates where the gathering commences; the small piece that remains is left plain. The entire basque should be sewn into twelve inches of the band, and if it is gathered it presents the *bouffant* effect now so fashionable. The waistband fastens in front with a rosette of ribbon, a satin button forming the center; another is also added at the back. For a mantelet to fit a medium-sized figure, two yards and a quarter of silk will be

required, nine yards of lace, and eighteen yards of rouleau. If preferred, the *tablier* at the back may be open down the center, or it may be made square. The readiest plan is to cut the pattern out in muslin, and try it on before making up the silk, as it is impossible to give patterns that will suit individual figures.

The water-proof costumes are made thus: a petticoat bordered with a flat ruche, piped with black silk; the second skirt plain and looped up by bows of black ribbon; a short, loose paletot, trimmed with flat ruches. It should be as simple as possible, for it is a costume for rain – a costume without any pretension whatever.

Peterson's Magazine, October 1868

Fig. 1. – Dress of gray poplin, with one pinked out ruffle around the bottom. A narrow ruffle extends across the front breadth and up the sides. Black velvet coat with cape, and trimmed with satin and fringe.

Our Parisian modistes are trying hard to introduce short dresses for general wear, but there are as many ladies against as in favor of them. We think the short dress, for a time, will continue, as it has been, to be the street costume; what changes may be made, as the season advances, we cannot now predict. Double skirts are the prevailing mode; these are generally trimmed with one flounce of ten inches, or with three narrow ones; fringe is also extensively used for trimming the upper skirts. The upper skirt is looped up *en paniers* in the back, in an endless number of varieties. With these, the skirt with panier top is worn. They are not ungraceful when worn in moderation, but when worn with a gored dress, the effect is simply ridiculous. Many of our readers may think such a costume would not be worn by any person, but we can assure them there are many who make fashions appear still more ridiculous by partly following them.

Calico dresses, as all others, are now out with the back breadths full, the side and front breadths gored; they are left plain; the back ones gathered. The waist is made a loose sacque, trimmed with ruffles, and worn with a belt.

Fig. 3. – Dress composed of two skirts; the lower one of black silk trimmed with satin leaves; above this extends a row of fringe headed by a satin trimming. The upper skirt is of green silk, trimmed with a narrow ruffle, and looped up *en paniers*. Plain corsage trimmed with ruffles forming a cape. Hat of black velvet, trimmed with pink roses.

With a colored dress, a black, or the same shade as the trimming, can be worn; with a black dress, a colored one. One of black silk, trimmed with black guipure trimming, the front is precisely like a gored apron without a bib; the back is full, and very little shorter, caught in a single puff with curved sash ends gathered at the top under the rosette.

A house jacket, that is very convenient and becoming, is half tight, square in front with rounding backs open a trifle in the centre, and edged with a plaited ruffle. The short skirt of the jacket was laid in two plaits on the hip and centre seam; from the latter depended a sash, with plaits straight across the end, and ruffled, made in brown cashmere; the ruffles bound with gold-colored ribbon. This is a stylish and matronly breakfast jacket.

In sleeves, we see the coat sleeve with a large puff at the top. The Cavalier sleeve, with puffed heading, straight arm piece and broad-pointed flowing frill. A style of sleeve much admired now is in broad puffs from the shoulder to the wrist, round the arms, with flat bands of the same width between each puff, edged with two rows of narrow trimming.

Godey's Lady's Book, November 1868

ANSWERS TO CORRESPONDENTS.

Line your bombazine skirt. Face with stiff wigging sewed merely to the lining. Put one puff around the arm-hole of your coat-sleeve. The puff is bias, about a quarter of a yard wide before sewing on. Trim the waist with a quilling of crape beginning at the belt and extending over the shoulders like a bertha.

In order to be stylish, your dresses should have demi-trains, say from a foot to half a yard in length. Short evening dresses just escape the floor. The length you mention is neither short nor trained. Take one of your seven breadths and piece the three full back breadths. Gore the remaining three breadths. Make a black silk panier to conceal the joins, according to the directions given in Harper's Bazar, No. 52. It is inexpensive, requiring only a yard and a half of silk, with some fringe or lace for trimming. If you think the panier puff too dressy, let the material hang plainly from the belt, like an apron.

Harper's Bazar, November 7, 1868

ANSWERS TO CORRESPONDENTS.

Silk should be wadded, only woolen goods are lined with flannel.

If you are very short and fleshy the double skirt will not be becoming. A single skirt and baschlik is better for you. If you prefer two skirts, make the upper-skirt without a front width, buttoning to the under-skirt on the seams of the front. Trim with a pleated silk frill three inches wide, the pleats all running one way. The material of the dress makes a very nice trimming.

Cut your corsage heart-shaped and wear with a white chemisette. You can also make a kind of yoke of the same material, to be worn inside the dress when you do not wish to use a chemisette. Tapes at the corners tied under the arms will keep it in place. Trim with two bands of velvet, bias, an inch wide, edged with narrow crocheted passementerie. Put these around the heart-shaped opening, one band on the wrist, another slanting at the elbow. Belt and loops at the back are trimmed in the same way, and a pointed apron is outlined on the front width. Small tassels at the points. If you object to velvet, use ruches of the material or of silk. Cut your green plaid poplin just to escape the floor, scallop it, and bind with black silk, piped with green merino.

When you do not gore the skirt at all you must begin the gathers far forward, within about three inches of the front. The ends of the blouse pattern fall over the hips under the belt of the skirt. This is the *chemise Russe* fashion adopted by French modistes instead of sewing the body and skirt together.

Harper's Bazar, November 14, 1868

House Dresses.

Fig. 1. – Dress with double skirt of light gray poplin, trimmed in the manner shown by the illustration with piping of dark gray satin, satin buttons, and gray silk fringe.

Fig. 2. – Dress of dark blue serge, caught up behind in a panier puff, with a black silk sash and bow, in the manner shown by the illustration.

Fig. 3. – Short dress of gray foulard. The under-skirt is trimmed round the bottom with a narrow flounce of the same material surmounted by a bias fold of satin;

the upper skirt is formed into two puffs behind, and is trimmed with a flounce and bias satin folds. High corsage, closed with satin buttons.

Fig. 4. – Dress of black silk. Under-skirt, under-waist, and sleeves of striped satin. The trimming of the dress consists of black satin piping and silk fringe.

Fig. 5. – Dress of brown moire antique, with long peplum, trimmed with brown satin folds and buttons.

Under-skirts of walking dresses are quite narrow, measuring from three yards and a fourth to three and a half in width, and are frequently worn without crinoline.

Harper's Bazar, November 21, 1868

WALKING DRESS.

Walking Dress, with the under-skirt of dark crimson silk striped with black satin; the upper-skirt is of dark gray silk with black satin stripes; it is edged with a narrow bias ruffle of the same, and has a double *panier*. The sleeves are long and close, and the plain waist is covered by a small cape with a ruffle.

Next we give a very elegant walking dress. It is a single toilet of blue alpaca, trimmed with ruches of the same material. The dress has a skirt plain, and a second one slightly looped up at the back, and forming an apron in front. Small loose paletot, cut out into a square on either side. These alpaca dresses are pretty in all colors.

A third costume is a dress, with an under-skirt of pink glace silk, shot with white; the upper one, of white silk gauze, is trimmed with gathered flounces of the some material, with a heading fastened with a cross-strip of pink silk. Narrower flounces form braces upon the bodice; these braces are fastened upon the shoulders by pink bows. The same trimming simulates rounded basques upon the skirt. A pink waistband goes round the waist, and is tied at the back. The white skirt is slightly looped up at the back by a large pink bow, and the train of the silk skirt shows underneath. A dress of white muslin can be substituted for the gauze, and any other color used in place of the pink.

Here is a little toilet which one would think copied from a picture of the time of Louis XV. It is a dress of gray silk, with pleated flounces of the some material, and turquoise blue cross-strips. The first skirt is round; the second is looped up on one side with a blue bow. The bodice is fastened as a shawl in front, with blue cross-strips. There are pleated flounces, and cross-strips at the waist and sleeves. Small hat of blue silk, with a garland of field daisies. One daisy fastens the scarf in front.

SKIRT WITH PANNIERS.
Back View. Front View.

This pannier consists of a first skirt bordered with three narrow flounces, each four inches wide, with a similar space between. The skirt is plain in front and gathered to at the back, and is trimmed down the center of the front with a series of small bows. Lastly the bustle, or pannier, is made by cutting a sort of large, round basque out of stiff muslin, which serves for the lining. The pannier is of the same material as the skirt, and cut in the same as the lining, only longer and wider, so as to make it *bouffant*. It is gathered at the top and bottom, and then sewn on the lining. It is quite independent of the skirt, only sewn to it at the waist; it can therefore be raised up when the wearer sits down so as to prevent crushing it. Bows with ends of ribbon, ornament the back and center of the pannier. Those who do not wish yet to adopt the pannier content themselves with a short skirt and tunic to match, but the tunic is looped up high, and at several places, so as to make it full and prominent just below the waist.

The Art of the Hoop: 1860 - 1869

Panniers should be adapted to the size and style of the person who wears them. On short, stout figures they should be smaller than on slim, tall ones. The latter look best in this new fashion. The fault of American women is that they slavishly adopt the Parisian fashions, without any attempt at the fitness of things; whereas, the true way is to study the becoming, altering and modifying each new style in whatever manner is most suitable to the person who is to wear the dress.

NEW STYLE WALKING-DRESS.

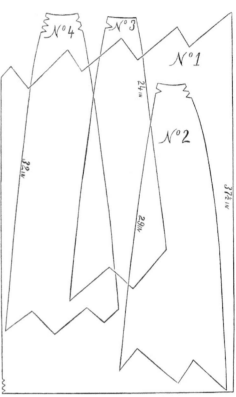

We give, this month, a new style walking dress, which is particularly suitable for fall and early winter wear. It consists (as will be seen from the diagram on the next page) of four pieces or breadths. The front breadth is the smallest, and has one notch at the top of it; the three breadths are notched, so as to join in regular succession. There is no join down the center of the skirt; therefore, that material must be cut double. There is no fullness except at the back breadth, and that must be gathered before sewing on to the waistband. The skirt is cut in vandykes at the edge, but should vandykes be objected to, the paper pattern may be so laid on the material, and the skirt cut straight at the edge; but whatever the form individual taste may dictate for the edge, the top of the breadths must be gored and cut according to the pattern, and the skirt mounted, to look plain in front, and gathered at the back.

We give here an engraving of a very pretty evening dress with a short skirt. It is of white muslin; round the bottom there is a deep gathered flounce, headed with a garland of roses; above this flounce, the dress is arranged in slight puffings, studded with roses. A piece added on to the bodice forms a short court-train and becomes a part of the second skirt, very short, and looped up on one side with a fastening of roses. The low bodice and the sleeves are also trimmed round with a garland of roses. A ruffling of white lace completes the sleeve. The waistband, of white ribbon, passes under the folds of muslin, forming a train at the back.

Peterson's Magazine, November 1868

Dresses open in front grow more and more into favor. It is thought they will be adopted for all *toilettes*, with the exception of winter walking dresses. There are several styles of open dress; they are cut either as a shawl, *à la Watteau*, or *à la Bretonne*. The dress opening as a shawl, describes a point at the bottom, and the bodice is frequently fastened at one side; at the opposite side there is a second row of buttons. The Watteau body opens squarely, and a muslin fichu is worn beneath. This fichu crosses whilst forming folds. The Bretonne bodice opens very low, and is rounded off at the sides; instead of terminating with a straight line as the Watteau, it finishes off with a curved line. It is the prettiest and most dressy of all the three different styles. Inside the Bretonne bodice either a bouillonne of muslin is arranged, or else a narrow plaiting of muslin edged with lace. It is cut too low to admit of lace only.

Fig. 1. – Suit of brown and black changeable poplin. The bottom of the skirt is edged with three narrow plaited ruffles. The polonaise is made partly tight fitting, and is drawn around the edge to form a puff in the back. The polonaise is edged with a ruffle, headed by a narrow-plaited quilling and two rows of silk braid. Brown velvet bonnet trimmed with flowers and lace.

Among the importations from Paris are Highland costumes for morning promenades and travelling, one of which we describe. A travelling costume of large plaid, irregular blue and green together. Made with two skirts; a ten inch flounce, bias, is plaited on the lower skirt; three folds of the material, piped with black silk, trims the upper skirt. Short full sacque, with belt caught up with rosettes at the sides and back. A scarf of the material half a yard wide is knotted on the right shoulder, and tied loosely under the left arm. These scarfs of gay plaids are also worn with black suits, tied as above. They are also using plaid silk, velvet, and poplin for trimming, but very moderately, not in bands, but narrow cords, piping, and binding.

Fig. 3. – Suit of bear's ear colored serge. The upper skirt is looped up in a new mode over an underskirt of the same, with a narrow flounce around the bottom. Sack of the same, trimmed with flat silk braid and anchors.

Fig. 4. – Travelling suit of waterproof cloth, of the new shade of gold-color and black mixed. The skirt is trimmed with two bias bands, bound with silk, from which small square pieces, also bound, are fastened. Long loose sacque, with hood at the back, and belted in at the waist. The skirt of this is looped up with buttons, and gives the appearance of an upper skirt to the dress. Bonnet of brown velvet, trimmed with satin and narrow brown lace.

Water-proof cloth can now be purchased in brown and black, yellow and brown, black and orange; this is an advantage, as it is so much used for suits, and it makes up much prettier than the kind formerly used. Serge and Scotch winsey for suits also; and lastly cloths of rich shades of color – garnet, mulberry, and olive green, with a surface like satin, which are imported expressly for winter suits for ladies, and, with appropriate trimmings and furs, form the ideal of a winter costume.

Poplins are in great demand this winter; we see an endless variety of styles and colors. The Irish poplins are the handsomest; they come in plain and changeable goods, and in white and all light shades for evening wear; these are as handsome as a very elegant silk, and much more economical, as, after they are soiled, they can be dyed for a street dress, and look equal to new, an advantage not obtained in a silk, which looks well after being dyed.

Fig. 30. – Dress of gray silk poplin, cut in scallops, and open at each seam, and fastened together by bands of the same bound and fastened with buttons. The underskirt, sleeves, and upper part of the waist are of blue.

Godey's Lady's Book, December 1868

ANSWERS TO CORRESPONDENTS.

As you are slight you can wear a loose polonaise belted in at the waist. Trim with a plaited frill of corded silk raveled at the edges about half an inch. Trim only on the cuffs and arm-holes. Belt of narrow folds of silk and a short sash with quilling at the ends.

You can easily make the tirettes yourself with some rings and cord purchased at any fancy store. Use chambery gauze, gilt or silver shot with a color over your silk. If this is not thick enough to hide the soil turn the silk dress. The gauze is from $1 25 to $2 75 a yard.

Your empress cloth will make a very nice suit, trimmed with bias silk bands and fringe, or merely scalloped and bound with silk. Make the upper skirt with five widths gored and looped high on the sides. A flounce on the petticoat. The bonnet matches the over-garment.

Colored paniers and tunics are worn over black dresses. A black silk panier looks well with any dress, either colored or black. A kind of peasant waist, made low and square, should be made of the material of the panier. Make a jockey basque or else a large fan-like bow to be worn at the back of your black silk, or add panier puffs in the way described in Bazar No. 52. Get a brown cloth or a gray poplin for your street suit.

Velvet waists are still worn. Handsome gros grain at $6 a yard is now preferred to moiré antique. Twelve yards make a trained dress.

Hooped skirts worn with trains measure about three yards around the bottom. Gored petticoats made with train, and flounced on all but the front width, are worn over the hoop skirt. Make your house sacque short and loose with revers front, coat-sleeve, and trimming of bias silk with several rows of machine stitching.

Harper's Bazar, December 5, 1868

Trains are reported to have been increased in length, but we have not seen a model worthy to be quoted that measured more than eighty inches from the waist to the floor. Three quarters of a yard added to the length of the figure is advised by the best modistes, who, we find, always avoid extremes.

Trains appear to have grown longer because they are worn over very small hoops, or without any. A skirt of hair-cloth gored and trained, with three deep flounces on all but the front width, is the fashionable substitute for a steel spring skirt. They are expensive at present, costing from $10 to $15, but could easily be made at home at much less cost.

The Louis XV. corsage, high and round, with long narrow opening in front for a chemisette, is in vogue for full dress dinner parties. The chemisette reaches almost to the belt, and is only about four inches wide. Sleeves to such dresses are nearly tight, with a Pompadour bow by way of epaulet, and a deep pleated ruffle at the elbow headed by ruches. The Maria Theresa style, with wide folded chemisette and half long sleeve flowing from the elbow, is familiar to our readers.

A gathered flounce from ten to twenty inches wide, with a heading of puffs and ruches, is the most prevalent mode of trimming trained skirts. Tablier designs of lace and ruches on the front width, with large butterfly bows at each end, are in vogue. The three full back widths are lined at the top with stiff muslin, and box-pleated, to form a panier. A sash from the belt supports the panier, and is knotted beneath it.

Few evening dresses are made without a panier or tunic, except for stout people, and then the trimming is made to simulate a tunic, and a short sash with several loops is added, to give a full tournure. Colored silk or satin panier skirts, with apron fronts and peasant waists, are worn over white silk, and are especially pretty with short dancing dresses. Sometimes they are worn with dresses of contrasting hue, such as fawn color with cerise, blue over salmon, and, in the Pompadour colors, pink with drab or blue. These are gay and striking, and people of more quiet taste prefer the dress and panier of two shades of the same color. This is a convenient way of concealing the soiled parts of dresses of last season, as they are usually most defaced on the front width and under the arms. A piece of chamois leather sewed in the armhole is the most efficient dress-protector.

Lace tunics, with a flounce to match, are more used than ever. A lace point is draped to form a reversed tunic by putting the centre in front, looping it with flowers at the side, and interlapping the ends high at the back. If lace can not be afforded, billowy pads of tulle, divided by satin pipings, form pretty over-skirts.

Sashes are fastened at the left side near the front when the skirt has a panier; otherwise they are placed behind to give a bulky tournure. Fan-shaped ornaments of pleated satin, bows with triple loops, and the fluted Renaissance bows, are in better style than sashes.

Harper's Bazar, December 19, 1868

[*Paris*] The most elegant toilettes are displayed at Compiègne. The ladies dress four times a day, and vie with each other in magnificence. The walking dresses are short and of comparative simplicity. The indoor dresses are trained. The evening dresses are naturally also trained and *decolletées*. There is dancing every evening.

ANSWERS TO CORRESPONDENTS.

Make a tight-fitting bodice, merely reaching to the belt in front, extending over the hips to form a pointed jocky basque behind like those seen on riding habits. Trim with lace, either thread or guipure, headed by a ruche of faille or a row of passementerie. If you have broad shoulders, design a Pompadour square with the trimming; if you are narrow, make bretelles. The coat-sleeves have a ruffle of lace at the elbow.

The goods you send is a species of poplin. Make a single skirt and polonaise. Line the polonaise with flannel, and add a cape also flannel lined. Trim with a pleated ruffle of the same six inches wide on the skirt, three inches on the polonaise.

Puffs around the sleeve at the arm-hole appear to shorten long arms. Puffed bretelles graduated give the appearance of breadth to a slight figure. A small cape, square in front and pointed behind like a hood, is also becoming. Bands of black satin piped with orange is the trimming for your dress.

Harper's Bazar, December 26, 1868

Modern crinolines are completed by a *tournure* of horse-hair, which gives the necessary support to the Louis XV. puff, formed by the skirts of almost all fashionable dresses. Or again the tournure forms *paniers* at the sides, for dresses quite in the Pompadour style.

WALKING DRESS.

Walking dress of the new striped silk; novel material of gray and dark blue; the upper skirt is of the same color and material as the lower, only of a finer stripe. It is looped up and trimmed down the front with a trimming formed of blue braid and large buttons.

The striped costumes, which were so pretty and so popular during the summer, have been replaced by a material composed of wool and silk, with satin stripes, green and black, blue and black, etc. One of the most convenient arrangements of the present season is the introduction of a black under-skirt, either of silk or cashmere; and an economic method of renewing the wardrobe is rendered very easy by the union of two dresses, always bearing in mind the following advice:

The dresses must not be of two different patterns; one material should be a simple color, and, if possible, a neutral tint, such as gray, black, or brown. This may indifferently form the upper or the under-skirt, according to taste. The mantelet may match either the petticoat or dress, as most convenient.

SENORITA JACKET.

ORIENTAL JACKET.

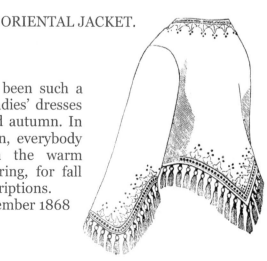

Never before has there been such a uniformity in the style of ladies' dresses as for the past summer and autumn. In Paris, from a duchess down, everybody wore striped cambrics in the warm weather, and are now wearing, for fall and winter, plaids of all descriptions.

Peterson's Magazine, December 1868

Hints About Dress-Making.

French dresses, when buttoned in front of the corsage, are no longer very high at the throat. The neck is disclosed as far down as the slope of the shoulders. Vandyked and scalloped bands are universally worn. They fit more neatly when cut bias, and should match the trimming in color. Another plan is to stitch a row of points on a narrow band. The points are formed by doubling small squares of silk, then folding toward the centre.

Under-skirts of imported costumes have a belt defined on the skirt, plain and smooth in front, but are gathered in the back with a drawing-string.

The best plan for finishing the edge of a skirt is to sew the material of the dress and facing together on the wrong side, making a broad seam, then turn over evenly, and press smoothly. The seam may be from a quarter of an inch to an inch wide, and if sewn without puckering, serves to make the edge of the skirt stand out firmly. The old practice of turning up the material of the dress on the facing is objectionable, as the skirt is apt to cut out at the edge. An excellent modiste advises us that skirt-braid for binding is no longer considered essential. The French, who finish their work in the most beautiful manner, doing almost every thing by hand, have entirely discarded braid. The material of the braid is so different from that of the dress that they will not shrink alike, and all worsted braids shrink slightly, even though dipped in scalding-water before they are used.

ANSWERS TO CORRESPONDENTS.

Slope the front width and one each side of it. Leave the others full and gather to a belt. It is now fashionable to gore muslin skirts to the knee and to finish out the length with a ruffle. If the puffs go around the arm small cords from one band to the other will hold them in place; if puffed to the elbow and ruffled the puffs are made secure over net or tarlatan. Middle aged ladies can wear white waists, but black lace or Brussels net is more becoming. Fichus are worn as a street garment.

Harper's Bazar, May 23, 1868

DRESS BODICES.

The shape of closed corsages is not materially altered from the styles given in the spring. French models are round waists of medium length with narrow belts. Points will be introduced later in the season for full dress. Shoulder seams are short and high, defining the outline of the shoulder – a fashion that makes the figure look square. To prevent this the corsage is cut very full at the bust by means of short darts placed near together. Some French dresses have three darts on each side to give the required fullness. The back is broad at the shoulders, has well-curved side-bodies, and is tapered down to measure only one-third of the length of the belt. The bodice is higher at the throat than the styles worn in warm weather. All imported dresses retain the half-inch standing band. If cut low at all it must be only in front, as dresses sloping at the sides and back are generally unbecoming. Buttons and button-holes are indispensable. Half a dozen hooks and eyes sewed on the belt and above it relieve the button-holes from the strain at the waist. A narrow facing of the dress material is sewed beside the buttons to prevent the white under-clothes showing through the button-holes.

The trimming begins at the belt, extending up the front near the buttons, forms a square in the back, and is brought down again to the belt. Pompadour squares and round berthas are designed on plain waists. Several rows of piping, with fringe on the last row, form a round collar.

OPEN WAISTS.

Open waists with chemisettes are very much worn. The Maria Theresa waist, square with an inside fichu of folds is suitable for handsome materials. It should always be accompanied with the open sleeve, tight to the elbow, and ruffled. The rolling collar, or revers, is a revival of an old fashion familiar to all. We commend this to ladies with narrow chests, as it gives the appearance of greater breadth. It is fashionable for demi-toilette, both for the house and street, with a chemisette of muslin or cambric. When used for more dressy attire a lace chemisette is necessary. The heart-shaped waist opens very low, and will not admit of lace alone. Young ladies with plump figures wear two narrow puffs of muslin edged with lace, or of net, extending up the front of the corsage and around the neck. The surplice or shawl waist has deep pleats on each shoulder falling in folds to the belt and crossed like a fichu. This is becoming to slender figures. The back is slightly fulled into a belt, or sloped over the hips, and held in place by a draw-string.

French modistes make all waists and skirts separate; a bad plan for any but slight persons, as it requires several thicknesses at the belt, making the waist large and clumsy.

LOW CORSAGES.

Evening corsages are very low and square and filled out to the proper height with tulle folds *à la Grecque*, and lace. When made entirely of the dress material they are not cut so indecorously low as were many dresses last season. Lace is to be the favorite garniture. Wedding toilettes this winter will be conspicuous for their elegant simplicity.

SLEEVES.

Coat-sleeves still prevail for street dresses, but with additional trimming. They are small at the wrist and trimmed to simulate a wide pointed cuff. A bias puff at the top gives the appearance of broad shoulders. A new idea is to add three or four inches to the length of the front half of the coat-sleeve and hold it slightly full from the elbow to the arm-hole. A broad pleated puff at the elbow is gaining favor. A pointed cap put on in box-pleats is a good style. There is greater variety in sleeves for house dress. The styles called Cavalier and Marie Antoinette are similar to the Maria Theresa sleeve. A French sleeve is half long, straight, and nearly tight. It is cut off square at the elbow, and the lower part of the arm is covered by a puffed under-sleeve.

TRAINED SKIRTS.

Trains are more moderate and graceful than the extreme styles worn of late. With the exception of the panier puff the general effect of the skirt is similar to those of last season, though made with fewer gores. To particularize, a trained skirt should measure from five yards to five and a half in width to prevent hooping. It should be flatly gored in front and at the sides, but very full and *bouffant* behind. The front width is gored closely. Stout figures require two gored side widths, slender persons only one. New skirts are not made with three side gores unless the material is so narrow as to compel it. A word of advice here; never piece gored breadths at the bottom. Design the shape and number of gores with reference to the width of the material. Two full widths are placed behind, and some French dresses have three full back widths. The front and the first gored widths are sewed to the belt without fullness. The back widths are gathered or arranged in small pleats all turned one way. A thick silk cord is used around the skirt instead of binding braid.

PANIERS AND TUNICS.

The panier puff is generally adopted on long dresses. It is very becoming to tall, slender forms, but requires to be worn with moderation by the short and stout. To form a panier puff a quarter or half a yard extra length is added to the top of the full back widths and gathered in to the side seams. The fullness extends a quarter or three-eighths of a yard below the belt. A drawing-string or a row of trimming is then extended across the back widths, drawing them in to fit closely over the crinoline. The full material then falls over the drawing-string and forms a puff. The sash is fastened-at the side seams under the belt, and tied in a large bow below the centre of the panier.

A closely-gored skirt may be modernized by the addition of a double panier puff. This consists of two lengthwise puffs attached to a belt. A band two inches wide and half a yard long extends down the back. Into this is gathered on each side a width of the material of the dress three-fourths of a yard long. The front is rounded at the lower corners and held slightly full beneath the trimming, which consists of folds and fringe or a ruffle. Bows or buttons on the band in the back. The puffs should be lined with thin crinoline or stiff muslin. This panier may be made of black silk, with a small square apron and bretelles, and worn over colored dresses that have become defaced.

Tunics are worn reversed, fastening behind like an apron. They are long in front, rounding to the belt in the back, disclosing a panier puff on the trained skirt. A good plan, designed for a lady too stout to wear a double skirt, is to simulate a tunic on the front and adjacent side widths, adding a crescent-shaped extra width at the second side seam, on which the trimming is extended up to the belt. On a heavy black silk the tunic is simulated with a pleated flounce of satin. This is an economical arrangement, and has all the effect of a full tunic.

Belts with fan-shaped bows are more worn than sashes. If a sash is preferred it must be double of the material of the dress, tied in a large bow with short fringed ends.

SHORT DRESSES.

Short dresses are adopted for breakfast, for the promenade, for church, for dancing, and on all occasions but those of great ceremony, such as bridal calls and wedding receptions.

Street suits are made with two skirts, or a polonaise with added fullness behind that produces the appearance of a double skirt. The lower skirt barely escapes the floor, is quite narrow, hanging almost straight from the waist, and seems to cling to the figure. It is worn over very small crinoline, without steels in front, like the "winged" skirts before-mentioned. The upper skirt has an apron front, with panier puffs behind made in the manner already described. If the upper skirt is looped at the sides and back instead of puffed do not be afraid of looping it too high. It is only necessary that the edges do not "hoop." Over this is a short loose basque confined by a belt. A round cape, caught up in the back and shoulders, completes the suit. The baschlik mantle is in great favor. This and other styles of wrapping have been made familiar to our readers by frequent descriptions of French suits. Mantles and basquines are lined with flannel or wadded to make them comfortable in cold weather. Flannel is preferred as it is most pliable. Cloth suits are sufficiently heavy for the coldest weather. Six yards and a half of double width cloth makes a suit. The trimming is bands of faille edged with satin. Thirteen yards of Empress cloth of stripes of two sizes, are sold for suits. A diagram shows the style in which it is to be made up. There is no trimming necessary. The price is $15. Modistes require from fifteen to twenty yards of material for a flounced suit.

MORNING DRESSES.

Morning dresses are worn loose and flowing from a round yoke like a collar. They are lined throughout with white mohair or alpaca, and are slightly wadded in front. The Watteau wrapper has a broad fold in the front and back. Trimming extends down the centre of the fold. Serge braid is a serviceable trimming for cashmere. Another wrapper is short at the sides to disclose a striped petticoat. Lavender and cherry is a pretty contrast for robes de chamber. Pale blue cashmere is trimmed with white serge braid.

Harper's Bazar, October 24, 1868

Servants' Dress.

The English journals are agitating the question as to whether by some means Bridget and Molly can not be persuaded to lay aside tawdry finery for a neat and becoming dress. One writer goes so far as to propose that the ladies shall form an association, pledging themselves to adopt, each family for itself, a uniform for their female servants, and to admit none into their service who refuse to wear it. The uniform is not to be old-fashioned or disfiguring, but merely neat, simple, and consequently becoming. The following ornaments are to be absolutely prohibited: Feathers, flowers, brooches, buckles or clasps, earrings lockets, neck-ribbons and velvets, kid gloves, parasols, sashes, jackets, Garibaldis, all trimming on dresses, crinoline, or steel of any kind. No dress to touch the ground. No pads or frisettes, no chignons, no hair-ribbons.

Morning dress: Lilac print, calico apron, linen collar. Afternoon dress: Some lighter print, muslin apron, linen collar and cuffs. Sundays: A neat alpaca dress, linen collar and cuffs, or a frill tacked into the neck of the dress, a black apron, a black shawl, a medium straw bonnet with ribbons and strings of the same color, a bow of the same inside, and a slight cap across the forehead, thread or cotton gloves, a small cotton or alpaca umbrella to keep off sun and rain. The winter Sunday dress: Linsey dress, shepherd's-plaid shawl, black straw bonnet. A plain brown or black turndown straw hat with a rosette of the same color, and fastened on with elastic, should be possessed by all servants for common use, and is indispensable for nurse-maids walking out with children. Should servants be in mourning, the same neat style must be observed – no bugles, or beads, or crape flowers allowed.

It is scarcely likely that any thing so sweeping will be achieved; but it is certain that if servants would follow these suggestions, at least in the kitchen, it would conduce to the comfort of themselves and their employers. However, as another writer sensibly remarks, the reaction in favor of a neat and simple style must come from above and not below. When ladies of position and fortune cease to lavish their thousands on millinery, the imitative race in the kitchen will no longer squander their wages after their example.

Harper's Bazar, March 14, 1868

The Grecian Bend

SARATOGA GRECIAN BEND. – 1868
Harper's Bazar, September 19, 1868

THE AGE OF INSANITY.

Would it be believed that any sane woman would adopt as a fashion the Grecian Bend – or, as it is more properly called, the Colic Stoop! Yet we find that it was attempted at Saratoga, that fashionable place of immorality. The position is that of a poodle dog, standing on his hind legs with his fore paws before him – his tail answering for the protuberance introduced into the dress. It is firmly believed by many that if Fashion should decree that her votaries should imitate the walk of the porcine order of four-footed animals, there would be many to follow the Fashion. It is said that the Grecian Bend was originated by a young lady who had spine disease. We once wrote about the "Grecian Wriggle" – the way that ladies contirive [sic] to get their dress over a gutter without touching it with their hands – but this is beautiful compared with the Grecian Bend. A Saratoga correspondent gives the following description: –

"In the first place, a toilet is affected, which of itself suffices to turn a woman in full dress into a caricature. The body and waist of the dress are remarkable in only one respect – the last is exceedingly tight, and the former rather loose at the top and exceeding low. It is below the waist that what is monstrous in the costume first attracts and then repels the eye of man. A hoop of moderate dimensions overspread with an underskirt or two, and a dress of whatever fabric, are worn. Underneath the rear of this hoop, just below the waist of the person designated, is bound a coil of wire from two to three inches in diameter, which 'throws out' and elevates the upper portion of the dress behind, and forms the foundation, so to speak, of an exterior protuberance called the *panier*. The *panier* is a bustle, more or less enormous, upon which, in successive folds or layers gathered up, or confined by a band encircling the dress from the stomach of the wearer around and beneath, an extra skirt, reaching just below the hips, hangs, or rather 'wobbles' to and fro. The dress has a train from four to six feet in length.

"The posture affected in order to set off this dress is called the 'Grecian Bend,' a contortion of the body which, as it is highly improper in itself, I find it difficult to describe with propriety. High-heeled shoes dispose the wearer to incline forward, and high-heeled gaiters are therefore adopted by the 'belle of the season.' She is thus the more readily enabled to elevate her hips unnaturally behind, enhancing the aspect

of the *panier*, to contract her stomach, and to form an S-like curvature of her upper shape by thrusting out her chest, drawing back her shoulders, and bending forward her head. So bent and deformed, the belle constrains her elbows against her sides; and, with horizontal forearms and little gloved hands dangling from limp wrists, tilts painfully along. The profile of such a figure, and its ungraceful gait, are irresistibly suggestive of a lame kangaroo. When it is whirled and tossed about in a dance by one of the fashionable jumping-jacks in black broadcloth, who are here so numerous, and so much alike that you can hardly tell one from another, the sight – what with the bobbing up and down of the woman's *panier* and the agile sidelong leaps of the jumping-jack across the floor – is too exasperatingly ridiculous for laughter."

To better illustrate our meaning, we annex a drawing cut in silhoutte [sic] from an actual dress as it and the wearer appeared at Saratoga. We confess to having blushed a little when we saw this engraving, but concluded if the ladies were not ashamed to wear it, we need not be to publish it.

Godey's Lady's Book, November 1868

1869

No. 1. – A Pretty Simple Dinner Toilet. – This dress is made of light-colored foulard; the first skirt is plain and train-shaped; the second skirt is of the same shade of foulard, with a pattern of black flowrets. It is looped up on either side with a large bow of ribbon with long lappets. There is a very small corselet with waistband, which has a deep point at the back. This corselet is worn with a bodice entirely made stripes of black lace insertion, with tight sleeves. The waistband is fastened above the bodice with a dahlia of glacé silk of the color of the dress.

No. 2. – A New Style of Ball Dress. – The dress is made of white gauze de Chambéry. The first skirt, plain at the top, is trimmed round the bottom with a gauze bouillonné headed by a black ribbon velvet, edged on both sides with white blonde. The second skirt, entirely bouillonné, is also of gauze de Chambéry, edged and separated at equal distances by a black velvet ribbon, bordered on both sides with white blonde. The bodice is low and cut square, the sleeves are gradually bouillonné from top to bottom.

The Boulevard skirt is without any seam; it is shaped to form a gored petticoat. The material is soft, light, and very thick; thus it prevents the outline of the crinoline from being seen, and at the same time its lightness is wonderful. It is made in various colors, trimmed with black braid, and bound with black. This petticoat is also manufactured with a printed border, embossed to imitate raised braiding, and the execution is so good as to deceive an experienced eye.

The most popular material, during the winter season, will probably be cloth. Olive-green is a ladylike looking shade, and trimmed with chinchilla, looks very distinguished.

The leading dressmakers are making cloth costumes in the following manner: The petticoat is ornamented with seven rows of worsted braid; the tunic, which is bordered with a cloth flounce, is likewise ornamented with seven rows of braid, and is looped up at the sides with agrafes of silk and worsted braid. A small mantelet is added to the costume; it is made of cloth, and trimmed with braid; the ends fall in front, and pockets ornament the ends. The muff is made of cloth to match the rest of the toilette; it is trimmed either with braid and large tassels or with two bands of fur.

Some trim these cloth costumes with fur in preference to braid, and replace the tunic with a Polonaise crossed in front, and looped up at the sides, the entire garment being bordered with a band of chinchilla fur. At the edge of the wide open sleeves, and likewise round the throat, there is also chinchilla; a band of fur is added round the centre of the muff.

The silks this season are extraordinarily rich and thick. For day wear the dead-looking silks, which have no gloss on them, are preferred, and all shades of maroon and claret are popular. The dresses made of these rich materials are but little trimmed – a fan-shaped basque and a handsome sash suffice. Still, if a very dressy toilette is required, a *panier,* trimmed with either a notched-out ruche or with lace, is added.

The make of outdoor costumes is simple. The celebrated Worth makes them consist only of a petticoat and a casaque, the casaque serving for skirt.

The short dress is worn in demi-toilette only, and for out-walking. The drawing-room dress displays as ample a train as ever.

The Régence costume consists of a satin skirt, and a dress and paletot of black or colored velvet. The mixture of blue and green is more fashionable than ever; it is seen in shot, striped, and checked materials; in velvet, satin, silk, and woollen tissues. The plaid satin looks remarkably well for a trimming.

The Lady's Friend, January 1869

Fig. I. – Walking-Dress of Deep Pink Cashmere. – The petticoat is trimmed around the bottom with festoons and bows of cashmere. The upper-skirt is of gray cashmere, looped up with bows of pink. Over the gray body is worn a tight-fitting body with a full basque of pink cashmere, and a deep cape with a pointed hood. Sash with wide ends of pink cashmere.

Fig. II. – Morning-Dress of White Alpaca, trimmed with a pleating of the same between rows of blue velvet. The under-sleeve is tight to the arm, with a loose, flowing sleeve.

Fig. III. – Evening-Dress of Light Green Silk, trimmed with white silk. The green flounce does not extend over the front breadth, but the white one does, and is trimmed with two ornaments in white and green silk, like the one which fastens back the side of the skirt. The body is low and square, and, like the Marie Antoinette sleeve, is richly trimmed with lace.

Fig. IV. – House Dress of Gray Dotted Silk: five pipings of cherry-colored satin trim the bottom; large buttons ornament the front; the pannier is held back by the sash: the ends of the bretelles, which trim the body, cross at the waist, and are trimmed with cherry-colored satin and fringe; small bows on the shoulders.

Fig. V. – Walking-Dress of Yellowish Fawn-Colored Merino. – The under-skirt has a very deep flounce plaited to near the bottom, and ornamented with dark marigold-colored bows of velvet. The elaborate upper-skirt is likewise ruffled and trimmed with marigold velvet ribbon and bows, very small cape, and loose sleeves over the long, tight ones.

WALKING-DRESS.

Walking-Costume of Blue Silk. – The underskirt is quite plain, and is striped diagonally with claret-colored velvet ribbon. The upper-skirt is short, very much puffed at the back, and trimmed with a deep plaited flounce; the front is cut in sharp points; the sleeves and body are ornamented like the lower-skirt.

WALKING-DRESS.

Walking-Dress of Dark-Blue Serge, trimmed with black gimp and fringe; the upper-skirt is cut in large points, and is short at the back. The body is made with a basquine lined with flannel, and over it is worn three capes to add to the warmth.

All evening dresses, and what may be termed *fete toilettes,* will be extremely costly this season, while all short morning costumes will be the reverse – as simple as it is possible to make them.

The *elegantes,* for example, are now rarely to be seen on foot, except in costumes made either of cloth or reps. The leaders of fashion wear costumes composed thus: A petticoat trimmed according to the taste of the wearer, either with one deep flounce, or with several narrow flounces, or with numerous rows of braid; the polonaise or redingote is made of the same material as the dress, is trimmed in accordance with the petticoat, and is looped up on the hips. This is all. The sleeves are very close fitting, and the polonaise is fastened straight down the front. A wide *grosgrain* waistband; and if the weather is cold, a small paletot to match, are added.

The Art of the Hoop: 1860 - 1869

Evening-Dress of Plain Muslin. – Very low, plain bodice, ornamented with a bouillon, through which a ribbon is run; large berthe of Spanish lace looped up into a drapery. Under the bodice there is a high chemisette, with small tucks ornamented with insertion. Sleeves of silk tulle. The skirt is looped up at the back, and trimmed with a lace flounce, headed with a narrow cross-strip of silk. Waistband of ribbon, covered with lace insertion, with lapels of embroidered muslin crossed with ribbon.

Persons who prefer very simple toilets, without bows or any looping up, more willingly wear an under-skirt just touching the ground, and a second skirt, shorter from twelve to sixteen inches, but not looped up.

Almost all dresses are made with double skirts, with a more or less pronounced *tournure*. Both skirts are not always of the same material; the under one is often striped, while the upper one is plain.

PANNIER OVER-SKIRT.

This costume is made of claret cashmere, and trimmed with frills of the same and satin piping to match. The paper pattern itself consists of three pieces, and represents one half the *panier* skirt (see diagram on next page.)

1. Half *tablier* Front.
2. One Rounded Side Breadth.
3. Half of Back Breadth.

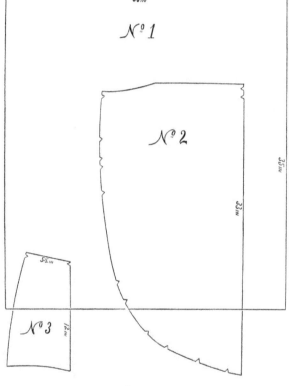

The *tablier* front is to be cut double, and without a seam down the center; a notch will be found on one side of it, and a corresponding notch on one side of the rounded side breadth, showing how these two pieces are to be joined together. The back breadth and side breath are joined by the corresponding two notches. Both sides of the *panier* are alike; when the back breadths are all joined, the edge of the rounded side breadth is to be laid in points from notch; there are in all five plaits – two at the top, then a space, and three below, and every plait is folded upward. The edge of the *panier* is then trimmed with a cross-cut band measuring one inch and a half, and a frill two inches and a half in width. Both band and frill are more effective when piped with satin. The skirt should be gathered at the back of the waist,

and a satin rosette added at the side where the first two plaits are arranged. A crinoline bustle should always be worn beneath this style of skirt. Should the *tablier* front be found unbecoming, we give an illustration (in our second figure) how the front breadth may be reduced, split up the center, and worn only at the sides.

To make the skirt, cut out a paper pattern from the diagram we give, enlarging it to the proper size. For this purpose we give the number of inches to which each piece should be enlarged.

Peterson's Magazine, January 1869

Even cloth costumes are looped up panier-fashion. We all wish to resemble the *grandes dames* of the Court of Louis XV.

Sashes are become of an enormous size; the lapels are sometimes as much as twenty inches wide, and the numerous loops of the very full bows are composed of ribbon not much narrower. The waistband is narrower, and the very large bow is always placed at the back.

SIDE, FRONT AND BACK OF AN EVENING DRESS.

Frank Leslie's Lady's Magazine, February 1869

Side, front and back of an evening dress. Train petticoat, of white silk, with four flounces of *point d'Angleterre*. The over-skirt, of rose-colored silk, opens in front and forms a long rounded train. It is finished by a single row of lace. The dress, of rose silk, fits closely in front. Here the short skirt forms one large scallop, and is gathered in beneath a narrow white lace. The back breadths are very long, and turned up to the top of the corsage, where they are quilled. A rouleau of silk and a fall of lace support the large puff of this Watteau corsage. Short full sleeves.

Short Costumes. – Fig. 1. Dress of an Algerian material, yellow with black satin stripes, bordered with a black satin flounce, headed with two crossbands of the same. Black satin over-skirt very *bouffant*, and looped up at the sides with yellow bows. It is edged all round with a flounce piped with yellow silk. Above the flounce there is a black *bouillonné* corded with yellow, and another down the centre of the over-skirt. Low black bodice, square both back and front, edged with a narrow flounce corded with yellow silk. High *guimpe* and sleeves of the Algerian material. Plain linen collar and cuffs, simply back-stitched.

Fig. 2. – The material is waterproof tartan cloth. The costume consists of a plain under-skirt cut so that the plaid is on the cross. Tunic to match, looped up with rosettes and buttons. Small *casaque* fitting the figure, straight in front and forming a wide plait at the back in the centre of the *basque*. Coat-shaped sleeves, trimmed with bands of the tartan cloth cut on the cross.

Some beautiful reversible sashes have been made; both sides being alike prevents the untidy appearance when the end turns, which cannot be always prevented. Those made of double satin ribbon, twenty inches wide, are very elegant.

A pretty and stylish walking costume. Also a new-shaped paletot trimmed with astracan or sealskin.

The mantle of walking dress is made of gray cloth, bound all round the edges with black velvet ribbon, and round the bottom with black silk fringe. Upon the seams of the back there are, besides the velvet border, small bows of velvet placed at regular distances. The round waistband is fastened under a velvet rosette. Small scalloped-out collar, bound with velvet; at the sides sash ends ornamented with black silk braiding, and trimmed with velvet and fringe. Tight sleeves embroidered at the wrist.

The Lady's Friend, February 1869

There is but one rule, for the street the dress must be short, looped up, or with two skirts, and being a full *tournure*; for evening wear, a long train; these may be modified in any way to suit the taste of the wearer. Modifications of various historical costumes are becoming popular for evening dresses. Satin is very much in favor for these dresses, as it looks so remarkably brilliant at night. The mixture of blue and green is adopted not only for plaid, but also for shot or striped tissues. They even speak of ball-dresses, which are to be of blue satin, covered with green tulle; this will look very soft, but will not be very becoming, however, one must possess a dazzlingly fair complexion to be able to wear this mixture of blue and green.

The Art of the Hoop: 1860 - 1869

WALKING DRESS.

Walking-Dress. – The under-skirt is made of blue and gray striped poplin; the upper-skirt is of gray poplin, with an apron front, and ornamented with blue ribbons.

WALKING DRESS.

Walking-Dress. – The under-skirt is of rich fawn-colored silk, with a deep plaited flounce; the second skirt is deep in front, slopes up at the back, and is trimmed with two puffings of silk, headed by pipings of satin; the under-dress is of brown velvet, cut in points, looped up with velvet bows, and trimmed with black lace.

For House-Dress there are many fashions; but these depend principally on the material. Woolen materials should be very simply trimmed, rather long, though less so than last year; a trimming down the front of buttons, and a band is sufficient. When the dress is of silk, nearly all are trimmed with a "Duchesse" flounce, headed with one or two rows of ribbon. The bodies should be trimmed to imitate a round square or pointed pelerine. There has been a talk of making them pointed, but there is no appearance that there will be any change in that respect; round waists are still the prevailing make.

Bows on the shoulders are common additions to house-dresses.

HOME DRESS.

House-Dress of Green and Blue Woolen Plaid. – This dress is buttoned down the front, and ornamented with bias bands of the material, edged with narrow black velvet.

Short dresses are deservedly more in favor than ever, the long skirts being reserved entirely for the house and visits of ceremony. The tournure is worn very large by some persons, but a more moderate-sized one is considered better by people of good taste. The materials and colors of the dress goods are innumerable; plain materials of all imaginable colors: stripes, plaids, and changeables, are all fashionable; and velvets, satins, silks, reps, poplins woolen plaids, and a thousand varieties of worsted goods are seen. No one material nor color can strictly be said to be the fashion.

Peterson's Magazine, February 1869

Nos. 4, 5 and 6. *Ball toilet*. ... Train slip of light blue silk. The deep flounce is of white tulle. A blue satin ribbon runs across the upper part, and terminates in a large bow, which lifts the skirt at the back. This flounce supports the puffed tulle skirt. The tulle upperskirt has a flounce of blonde lace, with a heading of blue satin ribbon. At the back it is lifted by a large satin rosette with long tabs edged with lace. Puffings of tulle and lace trim the corsage. Large loops of blue satin ribbon fall from the shoulders and waistbelt. Ribbons in the hair.

Balls require a special style of dress, made with a view to dancing – the object of the ball. It must neither be short nor long. The most approved of toilet for a ball is this: Dress-skirt coming just over the feet, without completely hiding them, however; second skirt looped up, or, which is still more fashionable, tunic skirt, train-shaped at the back, but raised into a large puff, so as not to prove cumbersome while the dancing is going on.

For dinner and reception toilets, and also for visits of ceremony, the demi-train is adopted.

The simplest and easiest way of gathering up the upper part of the back of the skirt into a puff is this: cut out a half circle of stiff muslin measuring about ten inches in its longest part, and lay it upon that part of the skirt which is to form the puff, on the wrong side of the material. Sew the muslin on as a lining, then place brass circles upon the outline of the puff at regular distances, and sew them on firmly; after this run two pieces of ribbon, one in one direction and one in the other, through all the rings, and place a button covered with the same material as the dress at the end of each ribbon; by drawing out these ribbons and tying them together, you at once form the puff; and by untying them you can undo it when you please.

But no puff gives up as it should do, unless it is worn over a proper crinoline.

Frank Leslie's Lady's Magazine, March 1869

No. 1. – Visiting Toilet. – The dress of amethyst violet gros-grain silk, upon which a gathered flounce, headed with a bouillon, with a bow on either side, simulates a double skirt, and a mantelet of gros-grain silk, trimmed with flounces. The upper part of this mantelet is crossed as a fichu upon the bosom with scalloped-out revers, bordered with satin; the front under the revers is gathered; the lower part forms a basquine with a flounce, headed with satin scallops.

No. 2. – In-door Toilet. – The train-shaped under-skirt is quite plain. The second skirt, puffed at the back, is trimmed with black velvet cross-strips simulating a third skirt, both skirts being edged round the bottom with a silk pleating. Plain high bodice, trimmed at the back with a pleating forming a basque. Black velvet buttons. Tight sleeves, trimmed round the arm-hole and wrist with a velvet cross-strip, headed by a little silk fluting.

Walking Dress with Watteau Paletôt. (front and back view). – Made of brown summer poplin, trimmed with ruffles of the same, and bias folds, edged with brown silk; paletôt fastens with silk buttons and loops of heavy silk cord.

No. 1. – Robe de Chambre of white cashmere, trimmed with ruffle of the same, and bias folds of cherry satin, worn over a striped skirt, black and cherry. Sash of cherry satin.

No. 2. – Walking Dress. – Petticoat of brown silk, with bias flounces. Cloth skirt of the same color, with points. Casaque of the same material, trimmed with Astrachan, or box-pleated satin ruches.

The Lady's Friend, March 1869

The Art of the Hoop: 1860 - 1869

We have also had engraved, and give above, two very pretty costumes, one a walking-dress, quite novel in style, which may be made of dark-blue cloth, poplin, or even a summer worsted material. The under-skirt is quite plain, just touching the ground, without any train. All the widths of the second skirt, with the exception of the front one, which is straight, are gored and fastened one to the other by buttons and button-holes; these buttons are of metal. Casaque, with a full basquine, forming a puff at the back. Basque falling loose in front, with buttons; high bodice, and small pelerine. Tight sleeves.

The other is a costume for the house. It is of shot glace silk, green and gray, with a trimming of pleated flounces of the same material, headed with cross-strips of green satin. This dress has three skirts trimmed in the same way: the first is train-shaped a little; the second, of the same shape, is draped at the sides; the third one forms a basquine, looped up into a puff at the back and open at the sides; it is ornamented with silk rosettes. Bodice gathered at the bottom, with a small pelerine, simulated by a fluting headed with a cross-strip; rosettes on the shoulders. Tight sleeves, with a fluting and rosettes at the wrists. Round waistband fastened with a rosette. Coiffure of green satin ribbon. Both of these costumes are of the newest and suited for spring.

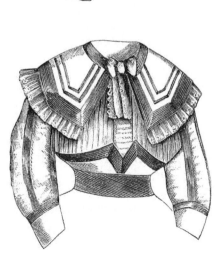

WALKING-DRESS.

Walking-Dress of Black Silk. – The lower-skirt is trimmed with two lilac ruffles; the upper-skirt is trimmed with one ruffle, and looped up with a large lilac bow; and the basque, which has a deep skirt, is looped up like the upper-skirt. Small, square cape, trimmed with a lilac ruffle, and lilac sash.

To keep our readers from falling into extravagancies, we will recommend them, for instance, to keep strict watch over their coiffures and tournures. ... The same reflection is equally applicable to all the varieties of aids to shape which have succeeded the defunct crinoline. That costumes and dresses must no longer fall straight as formerly is admitted; but between that point and the astounding extravagancies which we so frequently see, there is a limit which ought not to be passed; and real ladies will scrupulously avoid following the example of many of their sex, who, in their eagerness to be dressed in the very latest style, present the most grotesque appearance that can be imagined.

WALKING-DRESS.

Carriage-Dress. – The under-skirt is of green and white striped silk, with one deep bias flounce; the upper-skirt is of ordinary home length, trimmed with a plaiting of silk, and looped high up at the sides with a bow of silk. Large cape, trimmed with a deep ruffle of black lace and silk plaiting, and looped up in the back with a rosette.

BODY.

Peterson's Magazine, March 1869

The shape of dresses, certainly, differs very much from what it was last year. The fashion of wearing the skirt entirely plain, with all the widths gored, has been of short duration. Now the front width alone is slanted off from about half way be shut to the waist; all the other widths are cut straight, and gathered very fully at the top, so that even when the actual puff is not worn, the upper part of the dress is always sufficiently *bouffante*. The costume, such as it appears in its most *quiet* form, is composed of a skirt, not much longer than used to be the petticoat over which the dress was formerly looped up by means of *tirettes*, when it was inconveniently long. The casaque, formed of a tight bodice, and an ample skirt, looped up with bows or rosettes, answers a double purpose; it is at once an upper-dress and a tight-fitting paletot. For the summer this style of dress will be very pleasant to wear, as it will avoid the wearing of two bodices, and two pair of sleeves, one over the other.

No. 1. – *Visiting toilet* of violet-colored Irish poplin. Upon the round lower skirt a large tablier is simulated by a plaited flounce with a heading composed of a fold of satin; a similar trimming supports the full panier, and finishes the broad floating ends of the large bow. The close corsage buttons down the front, and is trimmed with a fold of satin. From beneath this falls a narrow plaiting of satin, which crosses the back; a puff and plaited satin compose the cuffs of the straight sleeves; satin waistband; linen collar and under-sleeves.

No. 2. – *Evening dress* of rose-colored silk. The long skirt is edged with a deep fall of white lace (*dentelle d'Anglelerre*). Butterfly-bows of satin lift it over a petticoat of the same. Lace trims the low corsage and short sleeves. The third skirt, which is of white muslin, is very short in front, and long at the back, where it is carried to the top of the corsage in order to form the Watteau folds. The large puff thus effected is supported by a fluted flounce of the same, ornamented with very large bows of rose-colored satin. Coiffure of long princess curls.

No. 3. – *Walking dress.* The round petticoat is of silk, striped black-and-gold. The two flounces, which have very little fullness, are of black silk; they are scalloped at each edge, and bound with gold-colored silk. Dress of black silk. This is fastened down the front by large black-and-gold buttons, and bordered with a heavy cord to match. Upon the close corsage eight bias bands of black, framed in gold, simulate a pelerine; three similar bands drape the skirt at each side; at the back it is lifted by a black-and-gold cord; bias bands and buttons trim the straight sleeves; black silk waistband, bordered with gold, and fastening beneath a double bow.

No. 4. – *Visiting toilet* of changeable green glace silk. The very deep flounce is scalloped and bordered with a small ruching and green silk fringe. A wide bouillonné of silk forms the heading. Each breadth of the upper skirt is gathered to form a large puff. Plain close corsage. Fringe heads the straight sleeves. Silk waistband, with four large bows, and long ends.

No. 5. – *Dress* of pearl-gray foulard. Four rouleaux of gray satin border the long skirt. Three rouleaux trim the short open tunic. Two others finish the revers of the open corsage, and simulate cuffs upon the straight sleeves. The silk waistband is framed in satin rouleaux, and fastens at the side beneath a large bow. Lace chemisette and under-sleeves.

No. 6. – *Half-mourning toilet* of Lyons gros-grains black silk. The very deep flounce of the lower skirt is surmounted by two rouleaux, of which the upper is the larger. Above this is a row of silk leaves, each framed in a small rouleau of the same. The train skirt of the over-dress opens in front. It is entirely bordered and trimmed with fluted flounces of the same material. These are divided near the upper edges by bias bands of silk. At each side a flounce is carried upon the skirt, which is draped beneath a large fan-shaped bow. The waistband fastens beneath a similar bow. Close corsage. A fluting of silk trims the straight sleeves.

Few paletots or mantles of any sort are made independently of the dress. Ladies no longer wear plain dress; they wear costumes. Each costume consists of three or four articles: skirt, dress, bodice, sash and mantle of some sort.

If some of my lady readers object that this is a very expensive style of dressing, I can only say that it is preferable to have a complete costume in any of the pretty, cheap materials so abundant now-a-days, than to have a dress even of the richest silk if it be out of fashion.

In these days of often-shifting fashions, I should advise all my sisters, both of Europe and America, to provide for each season a certain number of toilets, fresh and fashionable, as elegant as their means will permit, but limited in quantity, so as to renew them with each change of season. This is the great secret of the elegance of Parisian ladies. Even those whose fortune is not very large contrive to appear in toilets of great *fraicheur* – new, dainty, and coquettish – in the very newest style of fashion, because they purchase cheap silks and fancy materials, which look very well when gracefully cut out and nicely made up and trimmed. I do not mean to say that tissues, rich and beautiful in themselves, would not look better – of course they would; but I do mean that when economy is a thing to be studied, it is best to overlook the quality of the material, and to choose what will look fresh and pretty, even when it is not so durable as more expensive ones would be.

Dresses with draperies *à la Watteau* are still worn, but the puff, or *vertugadin*, is preferred, or the short Camargo skirt, looped up with bows of ribbon.

Jacket bodices are come into fashion again. The basque is always gathered or plaited at the back, if not all round. A waisband [sic] is worn over it.

Her majesty has not adopted the short costume, and therefore the train-shaped skirt continues to be the appendage of all full-dress toilets.

There is a new style of porte-jupe called the *porte-jupe Trianon*. It loops up the dress at the back, just as the young Marie Antoinette looped up her skirts when she acted the milkmaid's part at her mimic farm of Trianon. This porte-jupe consists of hooks, which are concealed under rosettes or bows of ribbon.

Flounces are also employed once more in trimming dresses, but they are rarely placed straight all round; they are arranged in fanciful outlines. Sometimes, indeed, they are put on in straight rows upon the front part of the dress, which is plain, but they are not continued all round the skirt. One flounce is frequently placed round the edge of the train only, and then continued on each side, gradually decreasing in size to the waist. It is the same with other trimmings, which often simulate a train-shaped tunic upon the dress.

Frank Leslie's Lady's Magazine, April 1869

Lady's Toilette. – Short dress of cigar-colored silk, flounced, with an ornamental heading. Tight-fitting paletot of heavy black silk, trimmed with a rich fringe.

Bodice ornamented with a braided *plastron*, which forms the front as well as the back, descending from the shoulders and tapering towards the waist. It fastens *en biais*, the braiding hiding the mode of fastening. The sleeves are also braided. Butterfly bows velvet at the waist and on the shoulders.

White satin dresses, trimmed with a decided color, such as ruby, emerald green, turquoise blue, &c., are very elegant. Tunics of black lace are worn over yellow, blue, rose, or bright green satin. For full visiting dress, black lace, or guipure, is also worn in flounces on velvet, satin, or faille dresses, and with a rich velvet mantle trimmed with lace, forms a very handsome toilet.

Dinner dresses are made in different styles; not unfrequently open, square or heart-shaped, as well as quite low. The skirts should be very long, or looped up with a scarf. Black is always becoming, and many charming toilets are made of it. For example, some dresses of rich black gros-grain are made with low bodies, and either covered with a lace tunic or with flounces of lace put on so as to form a kind of tunic, looped up on paniers by means of a violet, blue, red, or autumn-leaf colored satin scarf, bows of the same satin being placed on the black lace berthe.

We are asked if it is considered more stylish to have the dress, jacket and bonnet all of one shade. It certainly may be called more thoroughly Parisian than the richest toilet formed of a variety of colors.

The Lady's Friend, April 1869

WALKING-DRESS.

Walking Dress of Black Silk. – The under-skirt has three ruffles, the middle one of which is of blue silk; the upper-ruffle is headed by a roll of blue silk. The upper-skirt is edged by a plaiting of black silk, pinked, and put on with two rolls of blue, and is looped up at the back with three very large bows of blue silk without ends. The pointed cape is trimmed like the skirt, and has a row of blue bows down the back.

WALKING-DRESS.

Walking-Dress of Blue and Green Plaid Poplin. – The under-skirt is made with one deep bias flounce; the upper-skirt is made bias, is looped up slightly at the sides, and is trimmed with a rich fringe. The large cape is crossed in front, cut with deep-pointed ends, made sufficiently deep to loop up with a rosette at the back.

No change is seen as yet in the make of dresses; the *exaggerated* tournure and pannier are no longer seen; and the present fashion has at last settled down to a sensible short skirt over a very *small* crinoline, gradually looped up in all varieties of whims, by bows, rosettes, etc. We think the street-dress was never prettier than it is at the present. Prophecies come from Paris that the pannier will be discarded, but we have seen no evidence of it as yet.

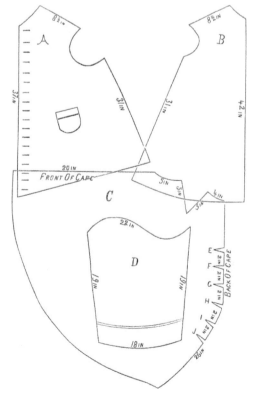

WATER-PROOF CLOAK.

We give this month an engraving (front and back) for a water-proof cloak, which will be found particularly useful in the wet weather of spring. We also give a diagram, on the next page, by aid of which the cloak may be cut out. It is in four pieces, viz:–

A. Half of Front.
B. Half of Back.
C. Half of Cape.
D. Whole of Sleeve.

The back of the cape is to be gathered up at E. F. G. H. I. J. When the cloak is made up, finish it by ornamenting it with rosettes of cloth, as seen in the engraving.

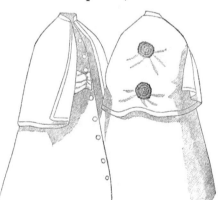

Water-proof cloth is often made into short dresses now.

One is made with a plaited flounce of the same round the skirt, bound with braid; there is but one skirt, and a kind of round cape of the same material as the dress, scarcely reaching to the waist, is worn with it.

Peterson's Magazine, April 1869

BACK, FRONT, AND SIDE OF A ROBE DE CHAMBRE

Morning Dress of Pearl-gray Leno. – The round skirt has three deep, box-plaited flounces. The upper one is headed by a band of rose silk, upon which are small rosettes of the same. Narrow bands of rose silk trim the close corsage, and outline a small, shaped collar and square bertha. A deep, rounded train, lined with rose-color, falls from beneath the lower band of the bertha. It is trimmed with three rose-colored bands. The sides are turned back and fastened down by rosettes. Double sleeves. The lower are straight and finished by three narrow bands. The others are square and hanging. The bands, rosettes and fringe, are all of rose-colored silk.

There is a great deal of variety in the fashions, although they are generally confined to one style, that in vogue about a century ago, during the last years of the reign of Louis XV. and the beginning of that of the unfortunate Louis XVI., whose beautiful young queen showed ever the most exquisite taste in the choice and ornamentation of her toilets.

The full tournure is become indispensable in all toilets. The walking dress, of the simplest description, consists of a skirt not quite touching the ground, trimmed with one or more flounces, and of a tight-fitting casaque, which at once answers the purpose of both a bodice and a looped-up second skirt. If this casaque is chosen of black silk it can be worn with any skirt or under-dress, and thus becomes quite as useful as the black silk paletot, which is now very much gone out of fashion.

Our lady readers are so numerous that they belong to all ranks and fortunes, so that there are, no doubt, some among them forced to study economy in their toilet, though still wishing to follow the fashions of the day.

To these I should certainly advise the choice for this summer of an upper-dress of black silk, as it will enable them to wear all their dresses of a former season not made exactly after the fashion of the present moment. Suppose you possess a dress made quite plain, with all the widths gored, and a very long train at the back. Cut it off at the top, leaving the fuller under part for the lower edge; make it of the length of modern skirts – not quite touching the ground – so as not to have to be looped up at all. With the part cut away at the top, make a fluting, as deep as the material will allow of, and put it on round the bottom of the skirt. If the bodice is still good, you may leave it as it is; if not, you can wear a white foulard or cambric bodice instead. Over the shortened dress you wear a black silk short tunic dress, which dispenses you from wearing a mantle of any kind out of doors.

The tunic dress must have a tight-fitting bodice and a very short skirt, open and rounded off, or looped up on either side, and raised at the back into a large puff. The usual trimming for an upper-dress of this style is a fluting of the same material, headed with a cross strip of silk or satin. This trimming simulates a pelerine, fichu, or low corselet upon the high bodice.

This model is generally preferred to all others when it is of a different material to the under-dress, but when the costume is complete of one material, there are other models also very fashionable.

But while simple dresses, meant for walking out on foot, are made with moderately short skirts, the elegant toilets of our *grandes dames* still appear with sweeping trains.

The last compromise we hear of between long skirts and short skirts is this: the dress is made with a first skirt just touching the ground, and second skirt, very short in front, and rounded like an apron, very long at the back, so long, indeed, that to attempt to walk with such an incumbrance is impossible, and that it must be looped up, or less carried on the arm. The latter method is adopted by a few of *la crême de la crême* in the Bois de Boulogne when they leave their carriages to take a turn in those wide avenues where a few sedan chairs are beginning to make their appearance, as if every fashion belonging to the ancient *régime* were now to be revived.

But, to return to trains. Wearing them upon the arm is no new fashion; it was much practiced in Paris by the *élite* of feminine elegance during the last years before the great French Revolution, and it may be seen in the fashion-albums of the time. The end of the enormously long train was gracefully thrown over the left arm, and this style of dress was entitled, *Robe queue du diable*. If the fashion comes in again, I don't see why this very original name should not be kept; but perhaps, as our ears have become more delicate, the name would prevent the dress from being worn; which indeed would be no bad thing, for it is as ridiculous as it is cumbersome and uncomfortable

Without going the length of having to carry one's dress upon the arm, one can have an elegant dress of glacé silk or *poult-de-soie*, made as above described, with two skirts – the upper one short and rounded in front, and train-shaped at the back.

Frank Leslie's Lady's Magazine, May 1869

Fig. 1 – This visiting toilet is made of colored poult-de-soie-violet, blue or green. The dress and tight-fitting casaque are trimmed with flutings and fan-shaped bows of the same material. A scarf with lappets ornamented in the same way is passed within a waistband of violet silk braid. Under-skirt of plain violet satin. Diadem fanchon of violet terry velvet, trimmed with white roses and a small curled violet feather; velvet strings edged with narrow black lace, and fastened in front by a cravat bow of violet satin; velvet bow with streaming ends falling at the back, and finished off with fringe.

Fig. 2 – A ball or grand dinner toilet. Dress of blue glacé silk, shot with white. Two skirts; the first one is very short and cut out into deep points. The trimming consists of blonde borders, headed with rouleaux of blue satin, and with bows of the same material as the skirt. The trimming follows the outline of the second skirt and forms large scallops at the bottom of the first. The dress is puffed out at the back, and plain in front. The low bodice is ornamented with a square berthe, edged with a satin rouleau and a lace border. Short puffed sleeves.

The round skirt, just escaping the ground, is still made with three gored breadths in front and three straightway at the back. They are left either without trimming or with a wide flounce, a much narrower flounce being put round the tunic. Instead of flounces, ruches, bias pieces or cords are used, the two former being composed of the material, the latter either of silk or satin of a suitable color.

The tunic camargo in lace may be considered the style of skirt which has met with the most decided success. It is worn with any dress, being caught up either at the back or sides by large bows of ribbon; and nothing is easier than to alter these bows to suit the underskirt worn with it.

For ordinary costume the chemise russe has in some measure replaced the corsage. Many are made open in front, some are of velvet trimmed with small satin bows, and frequently they have revers of velvet or satin; sometimes the revers and little bows are colored. Those of black velvet can be worn with any skirt; made of plaid foulard they have a pretty effect if worn with a black skirt.

The Lady's Friend, May 1869

The styles of trimming dresses are so various, that we can only refer our readers to our fashion-plate and wood-cuts for the newest patterns. All dresses will be worn very full at the back, but not too much puffed out. Trained skirts are as popular as ever for the house, and these are trimmed with ruffles, quillings, bands, and puffings to suit the fancy of the wearer. Some of the mohair walking-dresses are made with one skirt, with several small ruffles, and with a moderate length basque; this is very simple and pretty. A beautiful short walking-dress of check silk is made with five narrow bound ruffles on the bottom skirt; the upper-skirt and body are cut in one, like a deep basque, made full at the back and on the hips, and is trimmed with one ruffle. This basque reaches to the top ruffle of the lower-skirt, and is a good deal looped up with bows. This very stylish dress costs seventy-five dollars.

The Art of the Hoop: 1860 - 1869

WALKING-DRESS.

Walking-Dress for a Watering-Place. – The under-skirt is of pink and white striped silk, made quite plain; the upper-dress is of pearl-colored silk, open in front, and with a train finished with a ruffle; this train is made to loop up so as to form a pannier. The waist is plain with *revers*, and the cuffs formed of the striped silk.

WALKING-DRESS.

Walking-Dress of Gray Poplin. – The lower-skirt is trimmed with eight fluted ruffles. The upper-skirt has but one ruffle, and is looped carelessly up to the waist at the back. Black silk basque without sleeves, but with a large cape.

Scanty Skirts, or the Reverse. – Our Paris correspondent writes to us as follows, apropos of the prevailing fashions in skirts:– "On the other hand, another category of women have long indulged in unsightly scantiness of skirts, and, at the present time, a woman so dressed looks anything but respectable or genteel. A lady well-known in the fashionable world here, was not long since refused admittance to on hotel because her toilet bore too close a resemblance to an umbrella-case. 'We do not receive ladies unattended,' was the remark made, and when the new arrival had given her name and title, the ferocious hotel-keeper simply remarked, with many apologies, that he had been led into error by the scantiness of her skirts. But since the new season, ladies have run some risk of being unfavorably judged, if they presented themselves in too voluminous a toilet; the fact is that a lady should have just enough *tournure* not to resemble either a stem of asparagus or a shapeless bundle of clothes."

HOUSE-DRESS.

Morning-Dress of Violet Percale, figured down the front with black.

HOUSE-DRESS.

Back View of a Black and White Plaid Summer Poplin House-Dress. – The bias bands are bound with black velvet.

NEW STYLES FOR ... PANNIER SKIRTS.

We also give in this number new styles of making summer bodies, waists, capes, etc.; also a sample of making a plain, looped-up skirt at the back, with a double pannier, by drawing the skirt up to fall over the bottom.

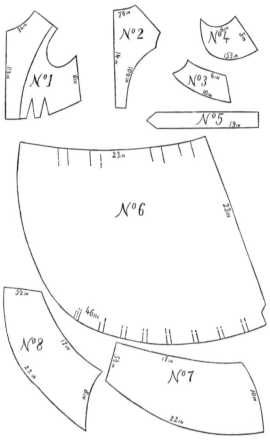

CASAQUE CARMAGO.

We give, this month, a drawing of a new style of walking-dress, called the Carmago Casaque; and also a diagram, by aid of which it can be cut out.

This Casaque is to be trimmed with a flounce on the bottom of the under-skirt of dress eight inches in depth, put on in single pleats two inches apart, headed by a band of the material bound on both sides. Arrange this under flounce to meet the skirt of the Casaque, as seen in the design. The flounce up the Casaque is graduated at the waist, beginning there with three inches in depth, and increasing to six inches at the back; three inches in depth for the collar and sleeves. The skirt of the Casaque is looped at the back with large bow and ends.

No. 1. Half of Front of Body.
No. 2. Half of Back.
No. 3. Half of Side-Piece of Back.
No. 4. Half of Collar.
No. 5. Half of Waist Belt.
No. 6. Half of Skirt of Casaque.
No. 7. Upper Half of Sleeve.
No. 8. Under Half of Sleeve.

This Casaque is especially suitable for spring and early summer. It has great style, and yet is not extravagant. The diagram, it will be seen, gives the size of each piece, and is arranged for a lady of medium height. From the diagram, cut a paper pattern.

Peterson's Magazine, May 1869

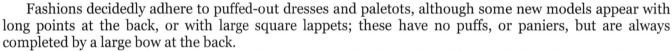

Fashions decidedly adhere to puffed-out dresses and paletots, although some new models appear with long points at the back, or with large square lappets; these have no puffs, or paniers, but are always completed by a large bow at the back.

The short costume is more in vogue than ever, now that the under-skirt is only just short enough not to touch the ground, thus rendering it unnecessary to loop it up in any way, and train-shaped skirts are exclusively reserved for evening parties, and for visits of ceremony.

The walking costumes are either composed of a skirt and a tunic-casaque, forming at once a second skirt and a bodice, or of a double-skirted dress and a mantelet. The latter are preferred for dresses of any thin material, such as grenadine, barege, *gaze de Chambery*, and so on. The bodice is made quite plain, to wear under the mantelet, trimmed with flutings or ruchings; but frequently a small pelerine or a bertha is made of the material to wear over it when the mantelet is removed.

BACK, FRONT AND SIDE OF A TOILET

Costume of Light Lemon-colored Silk. – Above the deep flounce upon the lower skirt is another of Chantilly lace. A bias band of silk divides this near the top. The skirt of the princess dress forms a rounded tablier, or apron, and is gathered up at each side beneath a large lace rosette. The sides are shaped; the back is rounded. A piped bias band of silk with a fall of lace compose the trimming. The lace only is continued around the tablier. The close corsage opens upon a plaited cambric chemisette, and is fastened by two large silk buttons. Narrow lace edges the deep collar. Extending half way up the front of each straight sleeve is a quilling of lace, headed by very small silk rouleaux. Waistband of the same fastens at the back beneath a large lace rosette.

Long dresses, being more particularly destined to very elegant toilets, are mostly made of glacé silk or *faille, poult-de-soie,* or *gaze de Chambery.*

The most tasteful are made with a very long train, very ample at the back and sides, but plain in front. They are trimmed round the bottom either with three narrow lace flounces, headed with a vandyked border of the material of the dress, edged with satin; or, again, with five or seven flounces of the material of the dress gathered and put on with a heading. The trimmings are placed all round the dress, or else they simulate the shape of a tunic, open in front, and come up to the waist on either side, while the bodice is trimmed with five or six rows of lace, forming a jabot. The greatest *nouveauté* of the season for dressy toilets is the bodice, open in front in the shape of a heart, with *revers à chale*, or else in the shape of a plastron [*sic?*], with sleeves *à la Marie Théràse*, not coming down further than the bend of the arm, and finished as with deep lace *engageante.*
Frank Leslie's Lady's Magazine, June 1869

Petticoats are no longer gored, but shaped in front only, where they lie flatly over the figure, and the fulness is given at the hips and back by gathers on a running band. They are trimmed with rows of work and puffs; a flounce edged with lace covers the hem.

Short Dress of Light Brown Summer Poplin, trimmed with flounces, surmounted by a puff. Tunic and cardinal cap trimmed with fringe and bows.

Morning dresses are made of pretty prints of brilliants, or of piqués; the style is varied, one of the prettiest being made with a looped-up puff trimmed with doubly fluted frills, and with a small cape or fichu trimmed to correspond. This style is very convenient for the country or seaside, a simple hat and silk necktie being all that is required in addition for a stroll on the beach, a walk in the grounds, or even a drive to the neighboring station. These dresses are also made with two skirts; the upper loops into the indispensable puff with lappets. This dress is most easily washed; we must think of this in selecting our summer dresses. Where the laundresses use washing powders, white dresses are preferable – embroidered piqué and marcella; the embroidery and braiding in black. The white brilliants, too, are very *distingué-looking;* they are trimmed with fine black braid, and made with puffs and the dear little cape or fichu, so becoming to a slight figure. Some of these are handsomely trimmed with thick embroidery work, and ribbons are placed beneath this, while Louis XIV. bows raise, *or* rather appear to raise, the camargo puff.

The present style is simply a development of dresses and jackets *en suite,* only instead of being in the old style of "suits" – that is, a short, square jacket and plain top and underskirts, all of on material and trimming, we now find the short square jacket almost discarded; the dress has two or three skirts, and the lower one often of a different color, the body is close fitting, forming together with the upper skirt a sort of tight-fitting casaque, which, in some toilets may be of black silk, but is more generally like the dress, and all these parts of the costume are most elaborately trimmed, so as thoroughly to harmonize together. We have the full floating or panier style of upper skirt, and over this are worn at the back large bows with floating ends of various forms, or fluted or fan-shaped tabs, these bows and ends forming part of the waistbelt. Every part of the dress is made to harmonize in the same way that was done in suits.

The full tournure at the back is generally adopted, and in-door dresses are made with flounces or flutings and ruches round the bottom, and a puffing at the top of the skirt. A trimming of flutings or ruches simulates either a fichu or pelerine or a low corselet upon the high bodice.

However much present fashions may be criticized for out-of-door toilets, one must confess they are very charming in a ball-room.

See this lovely white tulle dress, the first skirt entirely covered with small flounces, so delicately gathered they seem like flakes of new-fallen snow. Then the second skirt gracefully looped up with sprays of pale pink roses, and fastened on one side with a wide sash of blue satin. Or in a richer style, this beautiful dress of pale blue poult-de-soie, looped up en paniers, with flounces of point lace and sprays of exquisitely fresh white lilac. The same lovely blossoms are arranged as feathers in the hair, with one small bunch of blue forget-me-nots just above the forehead.
The Lady's Friend, June 1869

EVENING-DRESS.

Dinner-Dress of White Chambery Gauze. – The first skirt is made with a long train, and is covered at the top with a tunic *pouf*, edged with a *bouillonne*, and looped up at the sides. The low, square bodice terminates with a sash tied at the back; the sleeves are replaced by an epaulet formed with a double plaiting. Hair powdered and adorned with a satin bow.

Blue Silk Dress. – The skirt is covered with narrow pinked-out flounces, alternate pink and blue; it is covered with a blue tulle skirt; low bodice, trimmed with several narrow frills of pink and blue silk; sash tied with a large bow at the back. A wreath of pink roses in the hair.

Toilets of grenadine or Chantilly gauze are very becoming for young ladies. They should be trimmed with colored satin, either bias pieces of the material edged with small quilling, or light plisses or ruches made entirely of the satin.

Open skirts, forming a tablier, may be made in tulle or tarlatane. In this case, medium width flounces are placed round the lower-skirt, headed by a ruche or *bouillonne*, and the tunic, which is long, is opened at the sides of the front, and fastened by light wreaths of flowers ending in a bouquet.

WALKING-DRESSES.

Sea-Side Dress. – The under-skirt is of dark-blue summer poplin, trimmed with three rows of black silk quilling; the upper-dress is of gray poplin, trimmed with one row of black quilling and rosettes, and gathered up at the seams. This skirt is made so as to lengthen or shorten at the pleasure of the wearer. The body and sleeves are of gray poplin. Cape of blue poplin, with a small pointed hood. Chinese-shaped hat, trimmed with blue.

Sea-Side Dress of Crimson Cashmere. – The skirt is trimmed with a ruffle of cashmere put on loosely, a pleated ruffle of crimson silk and a puffing of cashmere; the body and sleeves are plain. The cloak is of gray and white striped summer cloth, is without sleeves, and forms an upper-skirt; it is deep back and front, and is looped up at the sides. It has a Capuchin hood of crimson cashmere, which may be worn over the head at pleasure.

All dresses for the street are short, that is, just escaping the ground, not exposing the ankle, as they are sometimes worn. Flounces are generally worn, a great many narrow ones, if there is but one skirt with a casaque or mantle, two or three narrow ones, or one or two broader ones, if two skirts are worn. The sacques, mantles and capes, worn with costumes, are of innumerable patterns, and they can be either of the same material as the dress, or black.

Peterson's Magazine, June 1869

CASAQUE OF BLACK DOTTED TULLE.

Casaque of black dotted tulle. It is close-fitting; there are no sleeves, and the broad fold at the back opens from the waist, in order to give place to the two large puffs. Lace and narrow rose-colored ribbons compose the trimming. The wide silk ceinture passes partly above the fold. Ribbon bows; that upon the skirt is very large, and the long ends pass beneath a lower puff.

Frank Leslie's Lady's Magazine, July 1869

Swiss Corsage. – In four pieces – front, back, side-piece and sleeve. Trimmed with a ruche, and worn with a white, pleated chemisette, or a colored one, uniform with the underskirt.

The ball dress preferred this season has a skirt but just touching the ground and trimmed with flounces, but there is a separate train added to it at the back, which is either left to trail upon the ground or looped up gracefully with bows of ribbon or sprays of flowers.

The bodice is always very low, both in front and at the back, while remaining rather high upon the shoulders, with a lace border, or sometimes merely a bunch of flowers, as an apology for a sleeve.

Ribbons and lace make evening dresses look very pretty this season. The lace is put on in flounces on the skirt, and round the edge of the train. The bows of ribbon must be tastefully arranged here and there.

It is especially in ball dress that the Louis XV. style is most closely adhered to. The paniers and trains, the lace trimmings and ribbons, might be copied from portraits one century old.

Corsage for Evening Companies. – Dress of sky-blue silk, the skirt trimmed with five tarlatan flounces, and the low, square-cut corsage finished with a tarlatan ruffle, edged with blue ribbon. Sleeves very short and bouffantes, also finished with a ruffle. Corsage fastened with blue buttons. Sky-blue sash, simply tied in a bow behind.

The Lady's Friend, July 1869

Fig. I. – Dinner-Dress of Lavender-Colored Grenadine over a silk slip of the same color; the skirt is quite plain, the body cut square, and the sleeves puffed at the elbow, where they are finished by a fall of lace. White cashmere mantelet, with a hood, embroidered in gold, and lined with gold-colored satin.

Fig. II. – Short Dinner-Dress of Canary-Colored Silk, trimmed with seven narrow flounces; over-dress of thin, white spotted muslin, looped up over the same. The sleeves are short, and waist low of the silk body, and long and high of the white body.

Fig. III. – Evening-Dress of Poppy-Colored Silk. – The skirt is quite plain. The camargo pannier is trimmed with a ruffle, headed by a ruche of the same material, and looped up by a large bow. At the waist is a large sash bow without ends. The low body is finished by a ruffle of the silk.

Fig. IV. – Dinner-Dress of White Mohair. – The front width is made *en tablier*, and trimmed with quillings of green silk; the deep flounce commences at each side of the front width and is headed by a quilling of green silk; the high waist, sleeves, and pannier are trimmed to correspond.

Fig. V. – Walking-Dress of Blue Changeable Silk. – The lower-skirt is trimmed with four deep puffs. The upper-skirt and body are in one; the body is worn open over a chemisette; the skirt made quite long, and open in front, over a kind of apron trimming, and ornamented with a puffing and narrow frill.

Cherusques, or wide fan-shaped trimmings of gauze or lace, recalling somewhat the Elizabethan frill, are often worn to complete the low bodies. Hitherto they have been merely worn as evening-dress, but it is said they will be fashionable with the spring toilet.

We find the dinner and evening-dresses are made, for example, opened in front, with a revers of very wide lace, the same lace forming the cherusque.

EVENING-DRESS.

Evening-Dress of White Chambery Gauze, with a pink satin stripe. The upper-skirt is rather long in front, and made in the Watteau style at the back, and both skirts are trimmed with black lace.

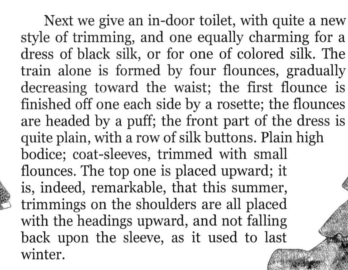

Next we give an in-door toilet, with quite a new style of trimming, and one equally charming for a dress of black silk, or for one of colored silk. The train alone is formed by four flounces, gradually decreasing toward the waist; the first flounce is finished off one each side by a rosette; the flounces are headed by a puff; the front part of the dress is quite plain, with a row of silk buttons. Plain high bodice; coat-sleeves, trimmed with small flounces. The top one is placed upward; it is, indeed, remarkable, that this summer, trimmings on the shoulders are all placed with the headings upward, and not falling back upon the sleeve, as it used to last winter.

Some variety is being introduced in walking-dresses; for the numerous forms of mantles, sacques, etc., of black silk, white muslin, grenadine, etc., which the French call *confections*, are somewhat replacing the *costumes*, which are the walking-dresses with sacque, skirts, waist, all made of one color and material. These *confections* will give a much greater variety to the dress; and for young ladies nothing can be prettier than fichus basques, mantles, etc., of white muslin, trimmed with knots of ribbon ruffles, or white grenadine over colored linings.

WALKING-DRESS.

Walking-Dress for a Young Lady. – The under-dress is of blue poplin, made quite plain with a high waist and long sleeves; the upper-dress of white-iron barege, has short sleeves, low, square waist, and is looped up by large blue rosettes; a piping of blue or deep white fringe finish the trimmings.

Fashion, after having made vain attempts to bring back the scant narrow toilets of the First Empire, attempts which good taste reproved, after having tried successively and simultaneously several other styles, is now completely devoted to the Louis XV. style, to the models of the time of the youth of Marie Antoinette, of graceful memory.

And so we see nothing but skirts and tunics looped up into puffs, gathered flounces, pinked-out ruches, and bows with large loops. All materials which can be draped well are fashionable; this is easy to understand with the puffs and loopings-up of modern toilets. Two ancient materials are come back to us, and have not even changed their names; they are *chaly* and *mousseline de laine*; chaly, a very soft woolen, material forms graceful folds; mousseline de laine, much lighter will be worn with under-skirts.

BASQUINE FOR A YOUNG MISS.

This is a Basquine, with a Pelerine Garrick, for a young Miss of twelve or fourteen years of age. In the design, we give a back and front view complete. The bottom of the basquine is finished with a flounce set on four inches in depth, cut bias and bound with black satin on the bottom. The pelerine is trimmed to simulate three capes, with a serpentine braid above a binding of black satin.

On this page we give a diagram by which to cut out the basquine.

A. Half of front of Basquine.
B. Half of Back of Basquine.
C. Side-Piece of Back.
D. Upper and Under Part of Sleeve.
E. Pelerine Garrick.

This is a very seasonable, as well as a very pretty, article of dress.

Peterson's Magazine, July 1869

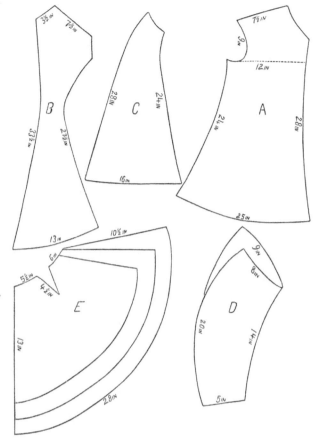

I will now describe the latest fashion of making up a rich silk dress:

A first skirt, of moderate length, is trimmed with three flounces. A second skirt is draped over it twice or three times with bows, rosettes or other ornaments. The bodice always fits better when it is cut out and made separately from the skirt, but it should have a sort of basque or wide border depending from the waist, which is to be placed *under* the skirt and under a separate waistband, finished off at the back by a number of large loops.

The dress made thus, with high bodice, double skirt and sash, is fit for wearing out walking. For the evening, for ceremonious visits, or grand receptions, a court train of the same color and material is added, and fastened at the back. For evening parties a low bodice is worn instead of the high.

Low bodices are extremely so – rather high upon the shoulders, they are cut down very deeply into a square shape both in front and at the back; so much so as to render it almost necessary to wear a lace border inside.

No. 1. – Dinner or ball-dress of pink silk. The bottom flounce, edged with a satin cross-strip, is headed by a bouillon and a flounce of pink gauze de Chambery. The whole skirt is trimmed with gauze bouillons, divided by satin cross-strips. The upper skirt is very short, and made of gauze, forming a vertugadin, looped up at the back, and trimmed with a flounce, edged with satin. Pink satin waistband. Low, square bodice, short sleeves, bordered with Valenciennes lace.

No. 2. – Walking toilet. Greene barège. The first skirt is trimmed with six small flounces, headed by a deep bouillon. The second skirt forms a puff at the back, and long basques in front, trimmed with a flounce and cross-strip of the same material. A bodice, open in front, trimmed with a flounce and lace. Sleeves puffed at the top, and terminated with six flounces.

No. 3. – Costume of grenadine. The round skirt has a deep flounce, headed by three puffings and a fluting of the same; the front of the high corsage is close-fitting; at the back are large double folds. This fullness is carried into the deep basque, which is ruffled, and gracefully draped, and lifted at each side by a fluted rosette of silk of a darker shade. The basque fronts are rather short. Silk ceinture with rosette. Muslin collar and undersleeves.

No. 4. – Walking-dress of summer silk. Pearl-gray, striped with blue. Close corsage and straight sleeves. Upon the round lower skirt are two wide bias bands of the same. The upper skirt forms a large puff. The little corselet is of black silk; the pointed basque falling at each side is edged with lace. Double bows of black ribbon are placed at the shoulders, and fasten the waistband; from this depend large loops with shaped floating ends, trimmed with lace and finished by large ribbon rosettes.

Frank Leslie's Lady's Magazine, August 1869

No. 1. – Seaside Costumes. – Composed of changeable silk and wool, green and gray. First skirt trimmed with narrow bias bands of green silk, and the second looped up with a bow.

No. 2. Short skirt striped red and black. Second skirt of black silk, looped up on each side. Corsage low and square, worn over a red corsage.

The tendency to a reaction from exaggeration and eccentricity, is taking place chiefly because a large number among French ladies of the best society, having an innate sense of true elegance, are determined no longer to follow implicitly the suggestions of professional artists.

The dress is fully gathered at the back, and when no puff is worn the sash bow is made very full, with a large number of *coque* loops, but no lappets or very short, wide ones.

The skirts are cut in square-shaped trains, and thus an awkwardness is avoided by those unaccustomed to these long sweeping dresses. Costumes of silk and crape are exceedingly useful, and are worn in every stage of mourning.

Dinner and Walking Toilets.

No. 1. Dinner Toilet. – Dress of black poult-de-soie, forming a puff at the back, lined with light silk forming large revers to the skirt. Blue silk underskirt, with garland of black embroidery. Bodice open, square in front, with a high Medici collarette of Brussels point lace. Short puffed sleeves, with a deep border of the same lace as the collarette.

No. 2. Walking-Dress. – Dress of gray twilled foulard. The first skirt is ornamented round the bottom with braid of the same tint placed lengthwise. The second skirt is trimmed like the first one. Bodice with a long round basque. Henry III sleeve.

No. 1. – The young lady's toilet is of beautiful foulard, finely striped, of two shades of blue; first dress trimmed with a flounce, headed with a marquise ruche; second dress, or rather tunic-casaque, tight-fitting, trimmed with a similar marquise ruche. Bows upon the bodice and on one side of the skirt. The whole of the same material. Plain sleeves, with a ruche at the wrists. The neck is cut rather low, with a sailor collar in embroidery and Valenciennes lace. Persian hat, blue like the dress, ornamented with a white feather and a black aigrette.

No. 2. Toilet for a Married Lady. – Dress of pearl-gray poult-de-soie; train trimmed with four flounces, of which two only come up, becoming gradually narrower towards the waist. The upper flounce is headed with a cross-strip stitched in scallops. Casaque in Louis XV. style, of black poult-de-soie, with a basque gathered at the back and turned back in front in large revers. This basque is trimmed all round with black lace; sash with large loops and lappets, edged with lace. Coat sleeves with revers, edged in the same way. Bonnet formed of a puff of blonde with feathers and an aigrette. Lappets of tulle and blonde, fastened in front with a flower.

The Lady's Friend, August 1869

The Art of the Hoop: 1860 - 1869

DINNER-DRESS, WITH BLACK SILK PANNIER.

Dinner-Dress of Green Silk. – The under-skirt is plain, but very long, and trimmed with a heavy black and green cord around the bottom. The upper-dress is of rich black silk, trimmed with fringe, looped at the sides with rosettes, and has no sleeves.

One of the prettiest new walking-dresses which we have seen had but one skirt, which was ruffled three fourths of the way up at the back, and all the way up the front breadth; the bodice was made tight-fitting, with a postillion-basque behind; this is jaunty for a nice figure, and newer than the looped up skirts.

WALKING-DRESS.

Walking-Dress of Black Silk, with the under-skirt and casaque trimmed with a rich plaiting of black silk.

PANNIER MANTILLA.

Among the novelties of the month is a Pannier Mantilla, an engraving of which we give above. It will be quite a fashionable article of dress; and it is so simple that any lady can make it for herself. It would be quite suitable for young ladies made in book muslin, with hemmed frills, edged with narrow thread lace and goffered. It may be made of the material of the dress, in black lace, or in the most useful of all materials, black silk. Of silk, twenty-four inches in width, four yards and a half would be needed, and sixteen yards of black satin rouleau.

On the next page we give a diagram from which it may be cut out.

No. 1. Front.
No. 2. Back.
No. 3. Half of Pannier.
No. 4. Half of Band.

The Pannier is to be pleated into the band. A more useful article of dress is not likely to appear this season, and will more than repay for the slight trouble of making it.

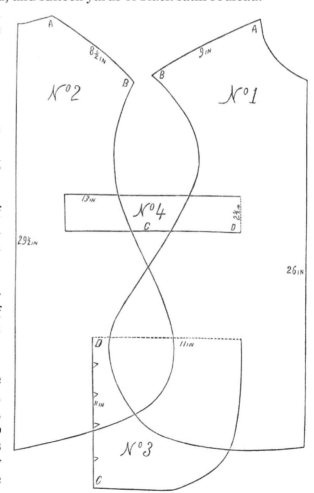

The Puff Reigns Supreme. – Puff upon the head, puff behind the back; skirts, dresses, casaques, bonnets, all must conform to the puff. The fashions of Louis XV., in fact have it all their own way.

Plain Bodices are trimmed in the shape of a berthe or fichu; often they are open in front, upon a fichu of pleated tulle or very fine muslin. This style of fichu is newer than a high chemisette.

The newest things about the present fashion are the *Confections*, as the French call them, that is paletots, basques, etc., etc., in black or colored silks, muslin, grenadine, etc., not made to match the dress, only to harmonize with it. We will not say that no more paletots are worn. It is too convenient a fashion, too necessary even, in the female toilet for them to be able to dispense with it. We will then say only that the paletot transforms itself this year into a tunic-casaque, forming at once a tight-fitting bodice and a second skirt. Whether this garment be called a casaque, or a second dress, it is no less true that it takes the place of a paletot, and that especially when made of black silk, it quite answers the same purposes. The tight-fitting casaque is worn either merely upon an under-skirt, to avoid putting on two tight bodices, one over the other, or else upon a dress with a plain bodice.

CARRIAGE-DRESS, WITH MANTILLA.

Carriage-Dress of Mauve and White Striped Silk. – The bretelle mantilla, or skeleton skirt, as it is sometimes called, is made of black silk. This garment has no sleeves.

The Watteau Casaque, with large draped folds at the back, falling loose from the neck, is also worn, but less, however than other models.

PANNIER DRESS.

Pannier Dress of Mauve-Colored Foulard. – One deep ruffle trims the bottom of the under-skirt. The edge of the upper-skirt, body, and sleeves are trimmed with narrower ruffles.

Peterson's Magazine, August 1869

To suit gored dresses to the present fashion, wear them as underskirts, for the upperskirts, even when no bouffant or puff is made at the back, are very fully gathered all round, except in front, and a scant dress cannot by any means be made to look fashionable this summer. But any silk skirt can be worn as underskirt with a short black silk dress, and the material taken off the upper part to shorten it, can be used to trim it with a flounce or fluting round the bottom.

1st figure in Tussore des Pyrenees, a new fancy material of a light shade of buff. The round skirt, without train, is trimmed with a flounce seven inches deep, headed with two narrow flounces, and a bouillon with a straight heading, pleated like the flounces. The tight-fitting casaque is looped up as a second skirt; it forms a double pleat in the middle of the back; in front it is rounded and fastened upon either side by a how. The round waistband is fastened by a similar fan-shaped bow at the back. The large pleat which loops up the casaque is fastened down under the waistband. The basque is edged round the bottom with a small fluting. The tight sleeves are trimmed at the wrists with a bouillon and two headings. Diadem bonnet of black tulle and blonde, with a border of field flowers in front; small rouleaux of red silk, and red bow at the back.

No. 2. A Young Lady's Toilet. – Dress of blue and white striped foulard, first skirt trimmed with two strips of the same material, put on crossway, second skirt looped up. Plain high bodice. Corselet with braces and basques of dark blue silk. Sash bow and long lappets at the back. The basques and sash lappets are trimmed with black guipure lace. There are bows on the shoulders, at the waist, and on the lappets. Bergerette hat of English straw, trimmed with blue ribbon, a bunch of blue cornflowers and meadow daisies, mixed with brilliant grasses.

For balls and concerts, white dresses of gauze or tarlatan are made with double skirts, wreathed with flowers. The bodices are trimmed with small berthes crossed in front like a small, low fichu.

Low silk dresses are also worn, looped up over striped silk skirts and trimmed with lace.

For married ladies, silk dresses are generally made with a first skirt just touching the ground, a tight-fitting bodice with a deep bouffant at the back, and a separate train fastened under the bouffant; this train can be taken up and draped, or else left to sweep the ground.

In other cases the dress consists of a skirt and a tunic casaque, forming the tight bodice and the full tunic skirt, open in front. The usual trimming is a deep fluting, with flounces for the underskirt; but sometimes this is replaced by a silk fringe.

Tunic and Corselet for Wearing over a High Dress.

This tunic will be found an exceedingly useful garment for wearing either over a morning or an afternoon toilet. It can be made in a variety of materials, but it looks best in black poult de soie, trimmed with a narrow quilling of black satin ribbon, and piped with black satin.

The pattern consists of five pieces, which represent one half of the entire tunic – half of front, half of back, three narrow gored breadths to form the tunic. The breadths are notched at the top, so that no difficulty will be found in joining the right ones together. The front breadth is the shortest, and has one notch at the top of it. Each breadth is corded, and the edge of both tunic and corselet is finished off with a quilling of satin ribbon. There is a waistband and sash, both made of poult de soie, and piped with satin; the latter forms five loops – two at the top and three below; these terminate with two sash ends, which are pointed like the breadth. There is a bow, made of similar materials, upon each shoulder. The plait in front of the corselet is marked on the paper with tiny holes. This tunic may be made in muslin, and trimmed with colored ribbon; in that case it would be better to cut all but the front breadths considerably longer than the paper pattern given, so that they might be gathered to look bunchy and full at the upper part. It also looks well in self-colored silk when the dress worn underneath is striped; the tunic should then be of the same color as the darker stripe. For imparting freshness to a light silk dress that has done duty for one season, this pattern will be found very useful.

[*This pattern could be ordered from the magazine.*]

The Lady's Friend, September 1869

Fig. I. – Walking-Dress of Sultan-Colored Silk. – The skirt is made with one deep flounce, pointed at the top and bottom, bound with black silk, and put on with a narrow bias band; a deep, full puff without trimming falls nearly to the top of the flounce at the back. The small mantilla, round at the back, with long, square ends in front, has a round hood, and is trimmed to correspond with the skirt.

Fig. II. – Evening-Dress of Canary-Colored Tarletan. – The skirt is trimmed with three ruffles; the bottom one extends all around the skirt; the other two finish the two full puffs at the back, and in the middle are fastened by two wide satin bows; a row of smaller bows trims the front of the dress. The effectiveness of this dress is very much increased by the white flowers, with black velvet leaves which ornament it. The hair is studded with white flowers and black leaves.

Fig. III. – Evening-Dress of Apricot-Colored Satin. – The lower-skirt has only a rich quilling of satin; the upper-skirt is very short, and is of blue satin, trimmed with ruffles and puffings of satin. There is a low, square, blue waist attached to the skirt, which comes just below the quilling of the apricot-colored waist.

Fig. IV. – House-Dress of Green Striped Silk. – The long skirt has one bias flounce of medium width; the low corsage is covered in front and at the back with a white muslin cape, trimmed with Valenciennes, and fastened on the shoulder by a bow of green ribbon. A similar bow ornaments the front. Broad ribbon sash at the back, and long close sleeves.

WALKING-DRESS.

Walking-Dress of Stone-Colored Poplin. – The under-skirt is made with two deep ruffles, not put on very full; the upper skirt and body are cut in one, forming a deep casaque, which opens in front, and is looped up in two places on each side, and trimmed with fringe.

WALKING-DRESS.

Walking-Dress of Violet-Colored Poplin. – The lower-skirt is trimmed with three deep flounces put on in full plaits. The upper-skirt and body (all in one) is of dark-gray poplin, trimmed with a plaiting like that on the lower-skirt.

It is evident that a more ample and flowing style of dress than that worn of late years, is now deemed indispensable to all who would lay any claim to elegance.

The dress, fully gathered at the back, must be more or less puffed out; nor is this unbecoming when not exaggerated; far from it, it sets off a slight figure to great advantage. When no puff is worn, the sash-bow is made very full, with a large number of *coque* loops, but no lappets, or very short, wide ones.

CHEMISE RUSSE.

The Chemise Russe is of white cashmere, trimmed with rows of blue velvet; red, green, violet, or black velvet may be employed in place of the blue, or black, violet, red, or blue cashmere may be used, as fancy dictates.

ISABEAU BODICE.

The Isabeau Bodice is of black or colored silk, cut low and square, and ornamented with a deep lace border, standing up like old-fashioned collarettes. Short sleeves, puffed, trimmed with two lace borders. Sash with wide lapels and bow of a new shape.

Suggestions for Stout Figures. – Stout persons complain of the fashions now in vogue. Double skirts, panniers, and bouffant sash, are not for them. Tight casaques disclose the figure too plainly, and shawls, gathered up over the arms, increase the appearance of the size. The best drapery for such ample figures is that which fit the shoulders closely, and hangs loosely below, such as short, loose sacques without sleeves for young ladies, baschliks and mantillas for those more advanced. Trained skirts give the appearance of less breadth. Short dresses are unbecoming, and should be worn to touch the floor. An upper-skirt may be outlined by a scant ruffle ten inches wide, on which two very narrow ruffles are placed. Folds and other flat trimmings should be used by large ladies. Low-throated dresses are becoming to short necks. A bonnet without a coronet or face-trimming is best suited to broad faces.

The Art of the Hoop: 1860 - 1869

PANNIER DRESS WITH CAMARGO SASH.

We give here a very pretty pattern for a Pannier dress, with what is known as one of the fashionable Camargo Sashes. On the next page, we give a diagram, by which it may be cut out: the size of each piece, it will be seen, is marked in inches on the diagram. Enlarge these diagrams, by taking a piece of old newspaper, and having thus made a full size paper pattern cut out the Pannier and then the Sash The diagram consists of two pieces.

No. 1. Half of Pannier.
No. 2. Half of Sash.

This is one of the prettiest styles that has come out from Paris, and is exceedingly easy to cut out and make up, and will amply repay for making it.

Peterson's Magazine, September 1869

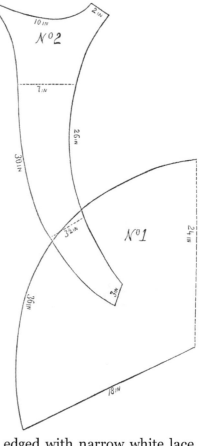

Crinolines are now almost invisible – I mean, of course, that they scarcely show at all under the dress. The tournure is worn *à volonté*, and pads are neither so general or as voluminous as they were.

No. 1. – A dress of pale buff-colored silk. The deep flounce of the round plain petticoat is brocaded with a small violet flower. The puffed heading is confined at intervals by straps of silk, bound with violet, and edged with narrow white lace. Rouleaux of violet silk border the flounce and the short, brocaded skirt; this is finished by a wider lace, and lifted by broader bands. The corsage is close-fitting, with straight sleeves and a puffed basque, all trimmed with lace and rouleaux. The plastron of the plain material is similarly trimmed; it has rows of violet silk buttons and silk revers. Ceinture to correspond with a large violet rosette. Linen collar and undersleeves.

No. 2. – Promenade costume of garnet-colored silk. The round, gored skirt has a deep, gathered flounce, divided near the top by a piping of black satin. The second skirt is also gored, bordered with two rows of piping, and edged by a very deep flounce of black lace. The corsage is plain and high; the straight sleeves have satin cuffs, trimmed with narrow lace. The casaque is of satin; it is open in front, and without sleeves; it is entirely edged with lace, and the skirt is lifted at the sides. Silk ceinture and satin rosette. Lace and pipings cross the broad band which lifts the second skirt. Linen collar and undersleeves.

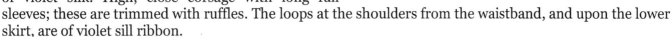

No. 3. – Toilet of silver-gray foulard. The long skirt has a box-plaited flounce of the same. The tunic skirt and rounded basques are simulated by flounces of violet silk. High, close corsage with long full sleeves; these are trimmed with ruffles. The loops at the shoulders from the waistband, and upon the lower skirt, are of violet sill ribbon.

No. 4. – Costume of light-blue silk. The full skirt has a deep flounce, headed by a bias band of white silk, edged with narrow white lace. The loop-bows and ends are of blue silk and lace. Louis XIII. casaque. The fronts are open, the sleeves straight, and the deep skirt puffed. The revers and bands are of white silk, edged with lace. White pipings border the large double bows. A gold buckle fastens the white ceinture. Jabot and undersleeves of *point d' Alençon*.

Frank Leslie's Lady's Magazine, October 1869

For walking-costume, the programme of fashion is almost invariable; underskirt elegantly trimmed, and tunic with puff and lappets. Very small and slightly gathered flounces, called *frizettes*, are now the most fashionable trimming for underskirts. Sometimes these frizettes are graduated in size, becoming smaller towards the top. In glace over plain silk they look very pretty.

Elegant little jackets of cloth or cashmere for wearing on cold evenings or days are trimmed with a contrasting colored velvet. Thus a gray jacket has blue, or violet, or brown collar, binding and trimming, or a white looks fresh and cool with a rich purple collar. Fastened with buttons of shaded pearl.

Ladies also wear loose jackets of white cloth of very fine texture, embroidered with a light pattern in chain stitch or point russe, with black or colored silk. This pattern is not put on all round, but only in the middle of the back, upon the fronts, sleeves and pockets.

Evening Bodice (*front view*).

Evening Bodice (*back view*).

Evening Bodice. – This bodice may be made of black or colored silk. It is cut low and square, and trimmed with lace to simulate a berthe in front and braces behind, which terminate in long sash lappets. Louis XIII. bows of satin ribbon are placed in front and at the waist behind.

Some new-fashioned Garibaldi bodices are made of white alpaca, with blue satin trimmings laid on to simulate a sailor's shirt. A wide piece of blue satin is put on at the neck, which is very open, just as sailors' shirts are; wide cuffs of blue satin, and three bands of blue in front, to imitate three folds, complete the trimming.

Tulle and Ribbon Bodice. – This engraving represents a low bodice, composed of net and ribbon, and will be found useful for wearing over a plain bodice, and thus giving variety to the toilet. It consists of satin ribbon covered with a fold of tulle, and edged round the top with rich blonde.

Trimmings are most fanciful this year. Light fabrics, even white muslin, are trimmed with black velvet, silk dresses with gauze flounces of the same color, dark material with pipings of the most brilliant tints.

The Lady's Friend, October 1869

EVENING-DRESS.

Evening-Dress of Pink Silk. – The skirt is trimmed with four flounces, one being of white lace. The overdress is a Watteau of white gauze, trimmed with white lace, and looped with pink ribbon bows.

DRESS FOR THE OPERA.

Evening-Dress of Blue and White Striped Satin. – The skirt is long and plain; the opera sacque is of fine white cashmere, trimmed with a heavy gold embroidery just above the gold and white fringe.

A New Style of Tunic has been introduced that can be worn indiscriminately, no matter whether the dress be high or low. The material of the tunic is China crepe; the front describes a round *tablier*, and at the back it forms a double *panier*, the whole being

The Art of the Hoop: 1860 - 1869

bordered with black velvet, and either fringe or guipure; a bodice is sewn to the tunic; it is low and square, and a wide band of black velvet replace, the *berthe*; short sleeves, edged with black velvet; black velvet sash, with a bow at the side, and a large velvet bow fastening up the *panier*.

The same style is made in white China *crepe*, with cross-cut bands of white *gros grain*, ornamented with gimp.

WALKING-DRESS.

Walking-Dress of Havana Brown Poplin. – The under-skirt is trimmed with four ruffles. The upper-dress is short, and trimmed with two shades of brown fringe; the part which forms the *panier* at the back is not trimmed, but it falls quite low on the under-skirt.

WALKING-DRESS.

Walking-Dress of Violet-Colored Poplin. – The under-skirt is trimmed with three ruffles edged with narrow, black guipure, and each ruffle is headed by a row of narrow velvet. The upper-skirt has one ruffle, and is caught up on the hips by a bow of black velvet; the sleeves are of violet silk, with bands of black velvet running around them. Black lace guipure cape, with square tabs back and front.

An old silk dress can be freshened up very nicely by putting ruffles plaitings, or flounces of clear white organdy, or Swiss muslin on it. If the wearer is very slim, this can be extended to the waist, or a thin, white muslin dress can be looped up over an old silk, if it is of a pretty bright color, to look very stylish.

AUTUMN JACKET.

We give, above, an engraving of a very desirable jacket for fall wear. The pattern consists of five pieces. Half of front and half of back, side-piece, half of *panier*, and upper part of sleeve, (the under part being marked on the paper.) There is a notch on the front to mark where the seam of the sleeves is placed. A plait is pricked on the front, so that the *casaque* falls to the figure. The *panier* is gathered at the top and sewn on to the back of the waist; the line where the pricked marks are should also be gathered. The sides of the *panier* are fulled in to the front at the upper part, both being caught or bunched up with bow and ends.

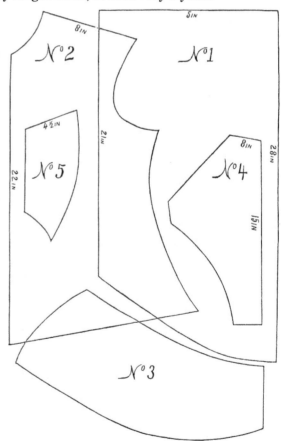

The sash is made of the same material as the rest of the mantle. Our model is of black silk, and trimmed with frills and satin rouleaux.

This jacket takes two yards and a quarter of a material that measures twenty-seven inches in width.

On the next page we give a diagram of the five pieces of which this jacket is composed.

Long Dresses are in great favor for the house, whilst the short ones retain an undiminished popularity for the street. The former are usually trimmed with ruffles, or one deep flounce, whilst the latter are also ruffled, ruched, and puffed up as at the back, as has been the fashion for some time. The gored dresses, which were so much worn two or three years ago, now look very antiquated in the present full, flowing style of costume; but they can be utilized by wearing them as under-skirts, for the upper-skirts, even when no bouffant or puff is made at the back, are very fully gathered all round, except in front, and a scant dress cannot by any means be made to look fashionable. But any silk skirt can be worn as under-skirt with a short, black silk dress, and the material taken off in the upper part to shorten it can be used to trim it with a flounce or fluting round the bottom.

Some new-fashioned Garibaldi bodices are made of white alpaca, with blue satin trimmings laid on to simulate a sailor's shirt. A wide piece of blue satin is put on at the neck, which is very open, just as sailors' shirts are; wide cuffs of blue satin, and three bands of blue in front, to imitate three folds, complete the trimming.

Peterson's Magazine, October 1869

The Louis XV style of fashions is rather going out; the puffs and paniers, at least, seem already to have lost much of the short-lived favor they enjoyed.

A more dressy style than the redingote, which is always considered demi-toilet, is the tunic dress, which has a first demi-train skirt, and a second one open in front, and forming the tunic; it is generally cut out in scallops or vandykes. A sash is worn with this style of dress, and the bodice is cut low and square in front, while the demi-wide sleeves do not come down further than the bend of the arm.

Frank Leslie's Lady's Magazine, November 1869

No. 1. – Costume of heavy lustreless black silk, trimmed with flounces of black satin. The underskirt has six flounces, reaching to the upperskirt, which is also edged with a flounce, put on with a heading and slightly deeper. The tunic similarly flounced falls in four large points. Casaque adjusted to the figure, a round basque in front and large point behind.

Fashions are betraying quite a masculine tendency. Our élégantes wear double-breasted jackets and redingotes, or riding-coats. These are looked upon as very stylish.

When the bodice is not cut square, it is generally made en redingote – that is, double-breasted and open with revers, like a gentleman's coat. This will be very fashionable for winter dresses of thick materials, and the revers of cashmere dresses will be of velvet.

The dress skirt is fully gathered at the back and sides, while the front part alone is gored off and put on plain to the waistband.

No. 1. Ball Toilet of White Tarlatan. – The skirt is ornamented round the bottom with a deep gathered flounce, put on with a heading, edged on each side with narrow lace. Under the heading of the flounce, a garland of roses is entwined round folds of tarlatan. The low bodice is completed at the back by wings of tarlatan slightly gathered, beginning from the shoulder and fastened to the waist by a bow of turquoise blue ribbon, mixed with a bunch of roses, buds and foliage. Bodice and wings are edged with lace.

No. 2. Dinner or Evening Dress. – It is made of maize and fire-color shot poult de soie.

The train-shaped skirt is looped up into a puff at the back. The bodice, very much curved in, very low both in front and at the back, is lengthened in front into long basques. It is trimmed all round with a fire-colored cross-strip, and round the bottom only with a handsome silk fringe. A bow of fire-colored ribbon is placed upon the left side of the bodice. Marie Antoinette sleeve, finished at the elbow, and trimmed with fire-colored cross-strips and bows; sleeves of white lace, coming up into a narrow border as far as the shoulders. Fichu of white gauze inside; black velvet with locket round the neck.

The Art of the Hoop: 1860 - 1869

Corsage a Revers.

There is but little change in the forms of dress bodies, and sleeves are still worn nearly tight-fitting.

For the Raphael bodice there are most becoming chemisettes of white tulle, arranged in pleats, within each of which is run a strip of blue ribbon. The chemisette is square at the top, with a double ruche of blonde, divided by narrow blue ribbon. The long sleeves are pleated in all their length, and with blue ribbons also.

The fashion of wearing low-necked dresses is general. A pretty chemisette becomes the necessary complement of the toilet.

The low, square bodice, with an elegant chemisette of muslin or tulle, is certainly a becoming style. Even cashmere dresses are made with these Raphael bodices.

Flounces will be very much worn to dress shirts, and narrow pipings will be much used as trimmings to these styles – very rich silks, or those of any new color, however, will often be made with long trains, and the skirts almost without trimming.

The Lady's Friend, November 1869

WALKING-DRESS.

Walking-Dress of Gray Poplin. – The under-skirt is plain, with a pointed trimming of black velvet; the waist and sleeves are also plain. The upper-dress is short in front and looped up very much at the back, where it is confined by a large rosette of black velvet. The wide falls at the side, which cover the sleeves, are trimmed like the skirt to correspond with the under-dress.

Light water-proof cloths in shot colors, such as violet and black, or brown and gold, are much in demand. Costumes in this material should be quite plain, with a simple hem at the bottom of the skirt, which is short, and raised behind. Paletot sacque, with revers of taffetas, and plaited sash of taffetas, or the material of the dress. A small crinoline, of the same material as the dress, will be found very serviceable to put on in wet weather, as it serves to sustain the skirt, and preserve the ankles from the damp.

WALKING-DRESS.

Walking-Dress of Cashmere of a Brownish-Yellow Tint – The under-dress in trimmed with a deep ruffle, which is ornamented by a wide band of dark brown velvet. The upper-skirt is also trimmed with a narrow ruffle, headed by a puffing, and ornamented with brown velvet; it is looped up at the back by two deep puffs of cashmere and three sash-ends of brown velvet trimmed with fringe. A small, square apron front, and brown velvet belt and bow.

Traveling-dresses are still made of Scotch plaid, serge, Chinese cloth, or drab beige. The skirts are often made of a deeper shade than the rest of the costume, and trimmed with fringe.

BLACK LACE OVERDRESS FOR EVENING

It is the combination of the pretty and simple of the more elaborate and rich garnitures that secures the right to the title of real elegance. The large *paniers* at the back are very ungraceful. One can get over the difficulty, though still remaining in the fashion, by wearing upon a single skirt a very wide sash, with a large bow with loops. This is elegant, and shows off a small waist. In all cases it must be well understood that the dress must be fully gathered at the back. We are very fond of the fullness and the flowing draperies of modern fashions; what we do not like is that thick, short puff, the too frequent appendage of the toilets of the day.

Peterson's Magazine, November 1869

For the evenings, toilets of white gros-grains silk, trimmed in colors are quite the success of the season. For instance, a dress of white gros-grains silk, with a train-shaped skirt, ornamented with three cross strips of green silk, vailed over with point lace. A tunic does not come down lower than half way; on the skirt it is ornamented with an embroidery pattern of small autumn leaves of different shades of green, tinted down to yellowish brown. The tunic is puffed out at the back with cross-strips of green silk covered with lace. The sash is of brown silk, with a fan-shaped bow, mixed with lace. The bodice has a bertha trimmed to correspond.

FRONT, BACK AND SIDE VIEWS OF A COSTUME

For evening and dinner parties silk dresses, with bodies cut square and entirely open in front, showing handsome lace chemisettes, which are sometimes high and sometimes half-low. The dress has generally a double skirt or tunic, and the sleeves are made in the Marie Antoinette style – loose and open at the elbow, with *engageantes* of real lace to match with the chemisette.

Frank Leslie's Lady's Magazine, December 1869

No. 1. – Dress of Figured Silk, with a flounce of the same. Upperskirt ruffled to match.

No. 2. – Brown Cashmere Dress. – the flounces bound with black velvet. Revers and cuffs, and belt of black velvet.

Very rich materials, or those of novel colors, are generally used for trains, and have a very small amount of trimming on them, as much trimming would rather detract from their quality of richness, or from their novelty of color.

Worth's black velvet casaques are very long, indeed, sufficiently so to dispense with the tunic, and are to be worn over silk petticoats, so that there can be great variety in the toilet, as the petticoat can be easily changed.

Black satin is very much used as a trimming for outdoor garments, sometimes in ruchings or narrow frillings, sometimes in plaits; other casaques are trimmed with lace; others again are trimmed with brilliant colored satin, so as to contrast strongly with the black velvet.

No. 1. High Corsage with Round Basque. – This is made of the same material as the dress and trimmed to match There is a pleat in the basque behind.

No. 2. All-Round Skirt. – As all-round skirts are now so universally worn, a pattern of one will be found useful to our subscribers. These skirts are now trimmed in various ways, the newest style being a flounce from twelve to sixteen inches in depth, according to the height of the wearer. If the flounce is plaited, the folds all fall in the same direction in the Russian style; if gathered, either a heading or a ruche is added to the flounce.

Our pattern consists of four pieces: – Half of front breadth, half of back breadth, and two side breadths. The order in which the pieces join will be known by the notches on the side of the paper, which must correspond. The front breadth has a single notch on the side on which it joins to the next breadth. The back breadth has three notches. The two front breadths are sewn plain to the waistband if the figure is slight, but they must be somewhat eased should the figure be stout. The remaining breadths are gathered. It has recently become fashionable to wear a train skirt over a short all-round one, and the style of the newest creation is given in the accompanying illustration. This train, which can be slipped on and off at pleasure, imparts a very dressy appearance to the toilet for either indoor or outdoor wear.

[*These patterns could be ordered from the magazine.*]
The Lady's Friend, December 1869

Dresses for the house have the body cut open, rather low, *but narrow* in front, and almost quite high at the back and on the shoulders. This is a beautiful style, we think; and with a black velvet ribbon, with a pendant locket, is becoming to almost all persons. The coat-sleeve, so long popular, is still much worn; but is frequently replaced now by a sleeve tight to the elbow, and which is trimmed with ruffles; for a pretty arm this is a desirable change, and much less stiff and more dressy than the coat-sleeve. When the latter is worn, it is finished at the hand by a deep cuff, which turns up and relieves the sleeve of its formal look.

SHORT HOUSE-DRESS.

House-Dress of Two Shades of Amber-Colored Silk. – The skirt has a deep bounce set on in large, flat box-pleats. The upper trimming is made of the lighter shade, and is itself trimmed with the darker. A double tunic. Waist cut square in the neck.

With regard to the make of dresses, only slight modifications have taken place. The short dress, or "costume," as it is called, is the only one ever seen on the street now, and for an ordinary house-dress it is a great deal worn. This style is much less elegant than the train-skirt, but certainly much more convenient; the train-dress is, however, universally worn of an evening, except by quite young ladies. It is most difficult to keep the short dress from looking vulgar and ridiculous, if the fashion is at all exaggerated; the habit of wearing very small hoops, (or none at all, as some do,) makes it somewhat risky to appear in the large panniers, which some persons exaggerate to a fearful degree. The well-dressed women will wear the underskirt, not to end at the top of her boots, but as long as she can, so that it does not touch the ground; she will have it moderately trimmed; and she will wear the upper-skirt rather long, and looped up so as to form moderate-sized puffs at the back, or on the hips. No respectable French woman looks like a top, as so many American women do now.

WALKING-COSTUMES.

Walking-Dress of Black Silk, with six straight ruffles on the skirt, edged with black velvet. The basque is a little loose. The skirt is rounded, and trimmed with a silk ruffle. The front and sleeves have revers of velvet. Small velvet hat.

Walking-Dress of Green and Blue Plaid Cashmere, made with a second skirt, and two capes, and trimmed with a bias fold of the same, and with worsted fringe.

Peterson's Magazine, December 1869

Manner of Making Dresses.

Bodices are of medium length, and round at the waist. Shoulder seams are short and high, defining the slope of the shoulders. The two darts in each front are short, but taken very deep, to make an easy tapering shape. Side seams are directly under the arm. Forms in the back are stitched on the outside, and are an inch apart at the belt. Open fronts with revers, shawl-shaped surplice with funess [*sic*] from the shoulders to the belt, square necks, and the broad sailor collar of the dress material are more worn than ever during the warm weather. The neck of a plain bodice is cut out very low and round if the wearer has a handsome neck, otherwise the high neck and ruche will be most becoming, and will not look old-fashioned.

A novel and stylish way of trimming bodices of silk dresses is to form a kind of ruff made by a bias flat band put on to define a berthe, and above this a standing band of the silk an inch and a half wide lined with satin of a contrasting color. This erect band is without fulness, except four shallow plaits at the turn of the shoulders. A fan bow disclosing the satin lining is at the front und the back.

Thin washing goods are made with the *chemise Russe* or blouse waist, without lining or belt, and detached from the skirt. A drawing-string is in the back, and the ends of the bodice pass under the belt of the skirt, which holds the fulness in position. Grenadine and Chambery gauze are made plain over a silk lining.

Skirts. – Trained skirts have a flat gored front width, two narrow side gores, and two full back breadths. The fulness is laid in plaits beneath the side seams. The back breadths are in French gathers. Five yards is the width of a moderate train to be worn over small crinoline. Two yards is an extreme length. Silks and poplins of light quality are lined throughout with paper muslin. Heavy silks are lined three quarters of a yard deep with stiff foundation or pliable hair-cloth, covered near the edge with alpaca the color of the dress. Skirts of French dresses are not bound with braid, but hemmed up an inch deep, the stitches taken only through the facing. Thin dresses are gored similarly, gathered at the top, and faced with the material of the dress.

Suggestions to Stout Figures. – Stout persons complain of the fashions now in vogue. Double skirts, paniers, and bouffant sashes are not for them. Tight casaques disclose the figure too plainly, and shawls gathered up over the arms increase the appearance of size. The best drapery for such ample figures is that which fits the shoulders closely, and hangs loosely below, such as short loose sacques without sleeves for young ladies, baschliks and mantillas for those more advanced. Trained skirts give the appearance of less breadth. Short dresses are unbecoming, and should be worn to touch the floor. An upper skirt may be outlined by a scant ruffle ten inches wide, on which two very narrow ruffles are placed. Folds and other flat trimmings should be used by large ladies. Low-throated dresses are becoming to short necks. A bonnet without a coronet or face-trimming is best suited to broad faces.

Travelling Dresses. – A useful garment for summer travellers is a gored sacque wrapper of brown linen, buttoned up the front, belted and worn over a handsome travelling suit to protect it from the dust. With the addition of a mantle, it would serve for short journeys in warm weather without an under dress. The durable pongees of mixed silk and linen remain the favorite material for handsome travelling dresses. They retain their bright gloss, do not shrink, and their smooth surface repels the dust. Young ladies select the pale brown and buff shades, or light gray, and trim with bright satin pipings. A handsome gray suit has the skirt trimmed with two flat plaited frills an eighth wide, bound below with black silk, corded with coral-colored satin. A flat black silk strip, with coral piping in the centre, heads each frill. Apron front overskirt with two broad puffs behind. Short basque with revers. The pale buff pongees are trimmed with dark brown findings, or else with bright plaids. Darker mixtures of black and gray are chosen by older ladies, and trimmed with fringe and flat bands piped with black silk.

The Lady's Friend, August 1869

Making Up a Rich Silk Dress

I will now describe the latest fashion of making up a rich silk dress:

A first skirt of moderate length is trimmed with three flounces. A second skirt is draped over it twice or three times with bows, rosettes, or other ornaments. The bodice always fits better when it is cut out and made separately from the skirt, but it should have a sort of basque or wide border depending from the waist, which is to be place *under* the skirt and under a separate waistband, finished off at the back by a number of large loops.

The dress made thus, with high bodice, double skirt and sash, is fit for wearing out walking. For the evening, for ceremonious visits, or grand receptions, a court train of the same color and material is added, and fastened at the back. For evening parties, a low bodice is worn instead of the high.

Low bodices are extremely so – rather high upon the shoulders, they are down very deeply into a square shape both in front and at the back; so much so as to render it almost necessary to wear a lace border inside.

Although puffed dresses are certainly fashionable, the puff should not be exaggerated in order to be graceful, and a second draped skirt always looks better, to my taste, than one arranged into a regular round puff. Indeed, our *grandes dames* seem to have understood this, and most of the elegant toilets, I notice, are rather *draped* than puffed out.

Frank Leslie's Lady's Magazine, August 1869

Economy in the Toilet

Our lady readers are so numerous that they belong to all ranks and fortunes, so that there are no doubt some them forced to study economy in their toilet, though still wishing to follow the fashions of the day.

To these I should certainly advise the choice for this summer of an upper dress of black silk, as it will enable them to wear all their dresses of a former season not made exactly after the fashion of the present moment. Suppose you possess a dress made quite plain, with all the widths gored, and a very long train at the back. Cut it off at the top, leaving the fuller under part for the lower edge; make it of the length of modern skirts – not quite touching the ground – so as not to have to be looped up at all. With the part cut away at the top, make a fluting, as deep as the material will allow of, and put it on round the bottom of the skirt. If the bodice is still good, you may leave it as it is; if not, you can wear a white foulard or cambric bodice instead. Over the shortened dress you wear a black silk short tunic dress, which dispenses you from wearing a mantle of any kind out of doors.

Frank Leslie's Lady's Magazine, May 1869

The Grecian Bend.

This Parisian eccentricity of deportment, which the fashionables of Saratoga were so quick to adopt that they were accused of originating it, appears in its best aspect in our Fashion Plate this month. *It may serve as a warning.* The most graceful lady is liable to fall into these stooping ways if she will wear her heels excessively high. The extreme of this fashion we have not thought worth while to illustrate, as it would serve no purpose but to astonish our readers. A cut of boots and shoes lately put forth by a cotemporary, were so like hoofs that we seriously took them for caricatures meant to be laughed at. As we have before remarked, the heel should be level with the front of the boot. If it is higher, the most serious faults in standing and walking are inevitable and quickly apparent.

In our Eastern cities, this "Grecian Bend" has been so mercilessly satirized – the caricatures so industriously circulated and so universally laughed at, that we do not think the ladies here are in any danger of deliberately copying it. Its race was about run with the Saratoga season. The few exquisites in fashion whom we now see here and there affecting it, are stared at as monstrosities, and probably do not feel comfortable in their singularity. This panier fashion is eyed very doubtfully by the majority of gentlemen; and we advise the ladies to take it with all possible moderation, lest they offend those whom they wish to please.

The Lady's Friend, January 1869

Clothing and Fabric – Cleaning, Repair, and Care

*I do **not** recommend that you use any of these recipes or techniques. In fact, in most cases I recommend against using them. Some are poisonous, others are caustic. Many are downright dangerous. I've included them just to show how women dealt with clothing care challenges during this period.*

1860

To Remove Grease Spots From Crimson Damask Without Changing the Color. – Upon a deal table lay a piece of woolen cloth or baize, upon which lay smoothly the part stained, with the right side downward. Having spread a piece of brown paper on the top, apply a flat iron just hot enough to scorch the paper. About six or eight seconds is usually long enough for the purpose; after which, rub the stained part with a piece of cap paper, very briskly, and the marks will be found to have gone away.
Arthur's Home Magazine, January 1860

Superior Washing Soap. – Dissolve one pound of soda and half a pound of hot lime in one gallon of boiling water; next dissolve one pound of sliced, hard soap, in two quarts boiling water; when cool mix them together. This forms a compound for washing linen, &c., superior to any of the washing fluids and patent soaps in use. When "washing day" comes round, make a strong suds of this soap, and boil the clothes, previously soaked, for half an hour. Take them out, drain them well, pour boiling water on them, when they will be found to be clean; nothing more being required than to rinse them well, to free them from the remains of the suds.
How to Whiten Linen. – Stains occasioned by fruit, iron rust, and other similar causes, may be removed by applying to the parts injured, a weak solution of the chloride of lime – the cloth having been previously well washed – or of soda, oxali acid, salts of lemon, in warm water; the parts subjected to this operation should be subsequently well rinsed in soft, clear warm water, without soap, and be immediately dried in the sun.
Peterson's Magazine, April 1860

To Impress Patterns of Embroidery on Linen. – The black sheets, (which may be bought separately,) belonging to a Manifold Writer, is an effective agent in transferring patterns. Place on the linen such a black sheet, on that the pattern to be transferred; then trace with a knitting needle or other blunt point over the pattern, and every line will be faithfully reproduced on the linen.
Arthur's Home Magazine, June 1860

FRENCH'S CONICAL WASHING MACHINE.
With this most simple, compact, durable, portable, efficient and economical machine, one woman can easily and perfectly do the washing of an ordinary family before breakfast!
This is the only machine that will wash all kinds of clothes perfectly without injury. It has been tested in the laundry of French's Hotel, and in numerous private families, and elsewhere, with all other washing machines making any pretensions to novelty, and has, in every instance, performed its work in less than half the time required by any other, and much more thoroughly and satisfactorily.
By all the ordinary methods of cleaning fine fabrics, such as laces, &c., the greatest care is required; while, with this machine, the most delicate materials can be washed, without the possibility of being damaged, a most conclusive recommendation to all those housekeepers who know the difficulty of getting clothes washed without tearing! It will wash a single handkerchief, collar, lace sleeve, six shirts, or all of these articles together, without the necessity of soaking or boiling.
These results are produced by the constant reaction of the suds, and not by friction of rubbing surfaces. It is admirably adapted for introduction into homes with stationary tubs, as it may be inclosed and connected with the waste and water pipes, and will make an important feature in houses with all the modern improvements.
Frank Leslie's Monthly, July 1860

Mode of Employing Soda in Washing. – Into a gallon of water put a handful of soda, and three-quarters of a pound of soap; boil them together until the soap is dissolved, and then pour out the liquor for use. This mode of preparing this detergent for washing will be found far preferable to the usual mode of putting the soda into the water, or of adding, as is usual, a lump to the water in the boiler, in consequence of which so many iron moulds are produced in many kinds of clothes. In the washing of blankets, this mode of proceeding will be found admirable, and render them beautifully white.

Receipt for Washing Muslin or Printed Dresses. – Boil soap and make starch according to your number of dresses. With soft cold water make up a lather in two tubs. Wash one dress first in one, then in the other, and put into a tub of clean hard water, where it may be till your other dresses are washed. When well rinsed, put a good handful of salt with the starch in the last water, and hang to dry in the shade.
Peterson's Magazine, July 1860

We desire to whisper into the ear of our lady friends a valuable secret affecting Blue Monday. Ladies are aware, as well as mankind in general, that about one-third of the entire time of every household is devoted to the mysteries of the laundry, much to the discomfort of all concerned, causing deformed and blistered hands and other personal and petty annoyances, aggregating into a very grievous burthen. The newly-invented Conical Washing Machine (and here comes in our secret) is the little but potent magician whom the good fairies have sent to dispel the gloom and the weariness, the blistered hands, and the sloppy horrors of " Blue Monday." This is a true benefaction for woman, and its inventors and proprietors are the right kind of "ladies' men," substantially kind and thoughtfully considerate. God bless them! They have brought the strong arm of machinery, moulded with a cunning skill, into the battlefield of washing-day, and the ugly array of dirty linen which has oppressed the daughters of freedom so long, has at last found its Magenta and Solferino in French's Conical Washing Machine.
Frank Leslie's Monthly, September 1860

For the benefit of the mistresses whose help still remain prejudiced against that very useful and labor saving article the Washing Machine, we venture to make an observation or two regarding it. One common error of the servants is not to have the water which is used sufficiently hot. In ordinary washing it must necessarily be cool enough to allow of the hands being put in it. There is no need for this when the washing machine is employed; and the water must be *boiling*, if the clothes are to be clean. Then, soap is not employed with sufficient liberality; and a little soda seems also indispensable. It is truly a labor and clothes saving machine; and in either of these items it saves ten times the cost of the additional soap: to say nothing of the wear of temper, and the family discomfort which, under the old régime, were the indispensable accompaniments of washing day at home.
Frank Leslie's Monthly, October 1860

To Clean Gold Lace. – Gold lace is easily cleaned and restored to its original brightness by rubbing it with a soft brush dipped in troche-alum burnt, sifted to a very fine powder. ...
A Method of Reviving Old Black Lace. – I have often dipped some of mine into cold tea, or a little beer; when ironed out after this it looks nearly like new.
Peterson's Magazine, October 1860

To Clean Silk. – Dresses cleaned by the following method have not the appearance of being cleaned: – Quarter of a pound of honey; quarter of a pound of soft soap; two wine glasses of gin; three gills of boiling water. Mix and let stand until blood-warm. Spread the silk on a clean table, with a cloth under it – there must be no gathers. Dip a nail-brush into the mixture, and rub the silk well, especially where there are stains, or the most dirt or spots, and with a sponge wet the whole breadth generally, and rub gently. Then rinse the silk in cold, soft water; hang it up to drain, and iron it damp. The quantity stated is for a plain dress.
Washing. – A little pipe-clay dissolved in the water employed in washing linen, cleans the dirtiest linen thoroughly, with about one-half the labor, and saving full one-half of soap. The clothes will be improved in color equally as if they were bleached.
Washing Prints. – To wash prints, delaines, and lawns, which will fade by using soap, make a starch water similar for starching prints; wash in two waters without any soap; rinse in clear water. If there is green in the fabric, add a little alum to the starch water.
Arthur's Home Magazine, November 1860

To Clean Silk. – Dresses cleaned by the following method have not the appearance of being cleaned: – Quarter of a pound of honey; quarter of a pound of soft soap; two wine-glasses of gin; three gills of boiling water. Mix and let stand until blood-warm. Spread the silk on a clean table with a cloth under it – there must be no gathers. Dip a nail-brush into the mixture and rub the silk well, especially where there are stains, or the most dirt or spots, and with a sponge wet the whole breadth generally, and rub gently. Then rinse the silk in cold, soft water; hang it up to drain; and iron it damp. The quantity stated is for a plain dress.
Peterson's Magazine, December 1860

1861

If you are troubled to get soft water for washing, fill a tub or barrel half full of wood ashes, and fill it up with water, so that you may have lye whenever you want it. A gallon of strong lye, put into a great kettle of hard water, will make it as soft as rain water. Some people use pearlash, or potash; but this costs something, and is very apt to injure the texture of the cloth.

To Dye Silk Black. – Impregnate the material with a solution of acetate of iron, and then boil in a decoction of madder and logwood.

Godey's Lady's Book, January 1861

[When washing a craped neck-tie, use] two lumps of sugar dissolved in half a pint of hot water, and let remain till cold; ... If the work is at all soiled, wash it with white curd soap and water; then rinse it perfectly, and squeeze in a cloth very dry; after that dip it in the sugar and water, squeeze it slightly, and lay it out on a doubled sheet to dry; afterwards take off the calico, sew it up, and add the tassels. The washing and rinsing in sugar and water will always give it the appearance of being new.

Washing. – A little pipe-clay dissolved in the water employed in washing linen, cleans the dirtiest linen thoroughly, with about one-half the labor, and saving full one-half of soap. The clothes will be improved in color equally as if they were bleached.

To Clean Silk. – Dresses cleaned by the following method have not the appearance of being cleaned: – Quarter of a pound of honey; quarter of a pound of soft soap; two wineglasses of gin; three gills of boiling water. Mix and let stand until blood-warm. Spread the silk on a clean table, with a cloth under it – there must be no gathers. Dip a nail-brush into the mixture and rub the silk well, especially where there are stains, or the most dirt or spots, and with a sponge wet the whole breadth generally, and rub gently. Then rinse the silk in cold soft water; hang it up to drain; and iron it damp. The quantity stated is for a plain dress.

To Wash China Crape Scarfs – If the fabric be good, these articles of dress can be washed as frequently as may be required, and no diminution of their beauty will be discoverable, even when the various shades of green have been employed among other colors in the patterns. In cleaning them, make a strong lather of boiling water; suffer it to cool; when cold, or nearly so, wash the scarf quickly and thoroughly; dip it immediately in cold hard water in which a little salt has been thrown (to preserve the colors); rinse, squeeze, and hang it out to dry in the open air; pin it at its extreme edge to the line, so that it may not in any part be folded together; the more rapidly it dries the clearer it will be. *Godey's Lady's Book*, February 1861

To Prevent Children's Clothes Taking Fire. – So many lamentable accidents, with loss of life, occurring from fire, we remind our readers that, for the preservation of children from that calamity, their clothes, after washing, should be rinsed in water, in which a small quantity of saltpetre (nitre) has been dissolved. This improves the appearance, and renders linen and cotton garments proof against blaze. The same plan should be adopted with window and bed curtains.

Stains Of Wine, Fruit, &c. – Rub the part on each side with yellow soap. Then lay on a mixture of starch in cold water, very thick; rub it well in, and expose the linen to the sun and air till the stain comes out. If not removed in three or four days, rub that off, and renew the process. When dry, it may be sprinkled with a little water.

Godey's Lady's Book, April 1861

Clear Starching. – Collars, undersleeves or handkerchiefs, of very fine muslin or lace, will not bear much squeezing or rubbing when washed. They can be made perfectly white and clean without either, by the following process: Rinse them carefully through clear water, then soap them well with white soap; place flat in a dish or saucer, and cover with water; place them in the sun. Let them remain two or three days, changing the water frequently, and turning them. Once every day take them out, rinse carefully, soap and place in fresh water. The operation is a tedious and rather troublesome one, but the finest embroidery or lace comes out perfectly white, and is not worn at all, where in common washing it would be very apt to tear. When they are white, rinse and starch in the usual way.

Arthur's Home Magazine, May 1861

Washing Lace. – The following method of washing lace, lace collars, or crochet collars, not only makes them look well, but saves much of the wear and tear of other washing: Cover a glass bottle with calico or linen, and then tack the lace or collar smoothly upon it; rub it with soap, and cover it with calico. Boil it for twenty minutes in soft water; let it all dry together, and the lace will be found ready for use. A long piece of lace must be wound round and round the bottle, the edge of each round a little above the last, and a few stitches to keep it firm at the beginning and end will be found sufficient, but a collar will require more tacking to keep it in its place.

The Use of Silk. – Silk is an agreeable and healthy material. Used in dress, it retains the electricity of our bodies; in the drapery rooms and furniture covers. It reflects the sunbeams, giving them a quicker brilliancy, and it heightens colors with a charming light. It possesses a cheerfulness of which the dull surfaces of wool and linen are destitute. It promotes cleanliness, and will not readily imbibe dirt. Its continually growing use by man, accordingly, is beneficial in many ways.

Godey's Lady's Book, May 1861

To Remove Grease from Cloth. – Take soft soap and fuller's-earth, of each half a pound, beat them well together in a mortar, and form into cakes. The spot, first moistened with water, is rubbed with a cake and allowed to dry, when it is well rubbed with a little warm water, and afterwards rinsed or rubbed off clean.

To Give Shirt Collars a Glass-like Look. – To one tablespoonful of starch put one of cold water; beat very smooth, and add another tablespoonful of water. Then pour on boiling water until it becomes the consistency required. Add a little melted *white* gum (about the size of a pea before melted), and a few shreds of white wax. This will give the articles a clear, glassy appearance.

Godey's Lady's Book, June 1861

To Remove Stains from the Hands. – Damp the hands first in water, then rub them with tartaric acid, or salt of lemons, as you would with soap; rinse them and rub them dry. Tartaric acid, or salt of lemons, will quickly remove stains from white muslin or linens. Put less than half a teaspoonful of the salt or acid into a tablespoonful of water; wet the stain with it, and lay it in the sun for an hour; wet it once or twice with cold water during the time. If this does not quite remove it, repeat the acid water, and lay it in the sun.

To Clean Leather. – Mix well together one pound of yellow ochre and a dessertspoonful of sweet oil. Then take one pound of pipeclay and a quarter of a pound of starch. Mix with boiling water, and when cold lay it on the leather. When dry, rub and brush it well.

Silks. – No silks look well after washing, however carefully it be done, and this method should therefore never be resorted to but from absolute necessity. It is recommended to sponge faded silks with warm water and soap, then to rub them with a dry cloth on a flat board, after which to iron them on the inside with a smoothing iron. Sponging with spirits will also improve old black silks. The ironing may be done on the right side, with thin paper spread over them to prevent glazing.

Godey's Lady's Book, July 1861

To Restore Faded Parasols. – Sponge the faded silk with warm water and soap; then, rub them with a dry cloth; afterwards iron them on inside with a smoothing iron. If the silk be old, it may be improved by soaking with spirits, in which case, the ironing should be done on the right side, thin paper being spread over to prevent glazing.

Arthur's Home Magazine, August 1861

How to Do up Shirt Bosoms. – Take two ounces of fine gum arabic powder – put it in a pitcher, and pour on a pint or more boiling water, according to the degree of strength you desire – and then having covered it, let it stand all night – in the morning pour it carefully from the dregs into a clean bottle, cork it, and keep it for use. A tablespoonful of gum water stirred in a pint of starch, made in the usual manner, will give to lawn, either white or printed, a look of newness when nothing else can restore them, after being washed.

Care of Linen. – One of the most important departments in the management of a household is that which embraces a care of linen. Accordingly, when this is well dried and put away in the wardrobe, the next part of our duty is to secure it from the effects of damp and the inroads of insects. These intruders are often destructive, but they may be prevented from doing injury by a judicious mixture of aromatic shrubs and flowers, cut up and sewn in silken bags, and the drawers and shelves interspersed by them. Rosemary, lavender, thyme, cedar shavings, roses, powdered sassafras, cassia, lignea, mixed with a few drops of otto of roses or other strong perfume, may be agreeably adopted for this purpose in all cases. It will be found that the linen, as well as all other washable articles, will be economized by being examined, and where necessary, carefully repaired previous to their admission to the laundry. The articles ought also to be numbered and arranged after washing, so as to have their regular turn in domestic use. Another saving will be found in purchasing soap in large quantities, cutting it in pieces of about a pound weight each, and keeping it in a place of moderate temperature. As linen is sometimes scorched in the getting up without actually being burned through, the effect may be removed by the following means: –

To Remove Scorching from Linen. – Add to a quart of vinegar the juice of half a dozen large onions, about an ounce of soap rasped down, a quarter of a pound of fuller's earth, one ounce of lime, and one ounce of pearlash or any other strong alkali. Boil the whole until it is pretty thick, and lay some of it on the scorched part, suffering it to dry. It will be found that on repeating the process for one or two washings, the mark will be completely removed without any additional damage to the linen; provided its texture is not absolutely injured as well as discolored.

Godey's Lady's Book, August 1861

To Take Grease out of Colored Silk. – Take French chalk, finely scraped, and put it on the grease spot, holding it near the fire, or over a warm iron reversed. This will cause the grease to melt, the French chalk will absorb it, and it may then be brushed or rubbed off.

To Clean Silks. – Dresses cleaned by the following method have not the appearance of being cleaned: Quarter of a pound of honey, quarter of a pound of soft soap, two wineglasses of gin, three gills of boiling water. Mix, and let stand until blood warm. Spread the silk on a clean table, with a cloth under it – there must be no gathers. Dip a nail-brush into the mixture, and rub the silk well, especially where there are stains, or the most dirt or spots, and with a sponge wet the whole breadth generally, and rub gently. Then rinse the silk in cold soft water; hang it up to drain, and iron it damp. The quantity stated is for a plain dress.

Wash Your Own Laces. – The difficulty of getting laces washed right, especially out of a great city, is very great.

Every lady, therefore, should know how to wash her own thread lace. If any fair lady is ignorant of this art, we can teach her in a very few words. Let her first rip off the lace, carefully pick out the loose bits of thread, and roll the lace very smoothly and securely round a clean black bottle previously covered with old white linen, sewed tightly on. Tack each end of the lace with a needle and thread to keep it smooth, and be careful in wrapping not to crumble or fold in any of the scollops or pearlings. After it is on the bottle, take some of the best sweet oil, and with a clean sponge wet the lace thoroughly to the inmost fold. Have ready, in a wash kettle, a strong lather of clear water and white Castile soap. Fill the bottle with cold water to prevent its bursting; cork it well and stand the neck secured well to the ears or handle of the kettle, to prevent its knocking about or breaking while over the fire. Let it boil in the suds for an hour or more, till the lace is clean and white all through. Drain off the suds and dry it in the sun; when dry remove the lace from the bottle, and roll it round a wide ribbon-block, or lay it in long folds; place it within a sheet of smooth white paper, and press it in a large book for a few days.
Godey's Lady's Book, November 1861

Blue Dresses. – The beautiful ultramarine blue print (cotton) is fixed by an ingenious process, that may be thus briefly described. The blue is mixed with white of egg, which, in its raw state, is perfectly soluble in water; it is then put into the steam-chest in the usual way, when the white of egg is, so to speak, boiled, and being then insoluble in water, the color is fixed. The most beautiful goods, exhibiting the greatest variety of design and colors, are obtained by this process of printing with steam colors.

Substitutes for Soap. – As an article of domestic economy, *fuller's earth* might be employed in the cleansing and scouring of anything *woollen*, being an excellent substitute for soap, of which great quantities are consumed, that might be saved in house cleaning. The sawdust of fir and pine trees contains a very large proportion of resinous and saponaceous matter; so that it has been usually employed by the country people of Norway and Sweden instead of soap in washing coarse linen.
Godey's Lady's Book, December 1861

A French chymist has just discovered a mode of rendering muslin, lace, and all kinds of light stuffs, incombustible. He makes no secret of the means. It is merely necessary to mix the starch used in making them up, with half its own weight of carbonate of lime, commonly called "Spanish white," or "Spanish chalk." The muslin, or other fabric, is then ironed as usual, the chalk thus used making no perceptible difference in its appearance; neither does it injure the substance of the article, nor take from its whiteness.
The Ladies' Companion, December 1861

1862

Remove Stains from Mourning Dresses. – Boil a good handful of fig-leaves in two quarts of water till reduced to a pint. Bombazine, crape, cloth, etc., need only be rubbed with a sponge dipped in this liquor, and the effect will be instantly produced.
Peterson's Magazine, February 1862

To Test Mauve and Solferino Colors. – These colors are *sometimes* very fleeting. Obtain if possible a small piece of the material which you wish to purchase, soak it in vinegar, and then leave it to dry. If the color has flown, it will not have been genuine; if it remain unchanged, you will be assured of its continuing durable to the end of its wear.

To Restore Violet Ribbon. – Strong soda-water – that is to say, water with rather a large proportion of soda mixed in it – will often restore violet ribbon, and it might have the same effect with blue. The ribbon should be dipped in the water, then taken out, and immediately ironed with rather a hot iron.
Peterson's Magazine, March 1862

To Extract Grease from Cloth. – Take off the grease with the nail, or, if that cannot be done, have a hot iron with some thick brown paper; lay the paper on the part where the grease is, then put the iron upon the spot; if the grease comes through the paper, put on another piece, till it does not soil the paper. If not all out wrap a little piece of cloth or flannel round the finger; dip it into spirits of wine, and rub the grease spot.

To Preserve Furs. – When laying up muffs and tippets for the summer, if a tallow candle be placed on or near them, all danger of caterpillars will be obviated.
Peterson's Magazine, April 1862

To Prevent Muslins, Linen, and Cotton articles from Taking Fire suddenly, – Rinse them in alum water, made pretty strong with the alum. The article then, if applied to a lighted candle or a flame, will only smoulder like woolen substances – not break instantly into a flame, and so destroy the wearer. As much as possible, in winter, articles of dress liable to flame should be avoided, and woolen textures substituted.

To take Ink Spots out of Linen and Calico. – Cut a lemon in half, and press the stained part close over one half of the lemon, until it is wet with the juice. Then place on it a hot iron, and the spots will soon disappear.
Peterson's Magazine, May 1862

Flannel. – Flannel should be worn, in summer and winter, during the day, but should be taken off at night. In summer it allows the perspiration to pass off without condensing upon the skin, and prevents the evil effects of the rapid changes of temperature, to which we are liable in our changeable climate, when out of doors. In winter, as a non-conductor of heat, it is a protection against cold. At night the flannel jacket or Jersey should be exposed to a free current of air and allowed to thoroughly dry; it should never be put in a heap of clothes by the bedside. Flannel is usually only worn over the chest and abdomen.

Protection against Moths. – The best security against the depredation of moths is to place the muff, boa, cuffs, etc., in a glazed-holland bag, and tie them closely up. Supposing them to be entirely free from the moth when thus enclosed, no harm can happen to them, as these winged destroyers cannot enter to lay their eggs. The moths that fly about in the dark do not destroy cloth of any kind.

Permanent Ink for Marking Linen. – Take of lunar caustic (now called nitrate of silver), one drachm; weak solution of tincture of galls, two drachms. The cloth must be wetted first with the following liquid, viz: salt of tartar, one ounce; water, one ounce and a half; and it must be made perfectly dry before it is written upon.

Peterson's Magazine, June 1862

To Prevent Muslins, and Linen, and Cotton articles from Taking Fire suddenly. – Rinse them in alum water, made pretty strong with the alum. The article then, if applied to a lighted candle or a flame, will only smoulder like woollen substances – not break instantly into a flame, and so destroy the wearer. As much as possible, in winter, articles of dress liable to flame should be avoided, and woollen textures substituted.

Godey's Lady's Book, July 1862

To Clean While Kid Gloves. – Stretch them on a board and rub the soiled spots with cream of tartar, or magnesia. Let them rest an hour. Take a mixture of alum and fuller's earth in powder, and rub it all over the gloves with a clean brush, and let them rest an hour or two. Then sweep it all off, and go over with a flannel dipped in a mixture of bran and finely-powdered whiting. Let them rest another hour. Brush off the powder and you will find them clean.

To Remove Grease Spots. – Magnesia will effectually remove grease spots from silk on rubbing it in well; and after standing awhile, apply a piece of soft brown paper to the wrong side, on which press a warm iron, gently; and what grease is not absorbed by the paper can be removed by washing the spot carefully with warm water.

To make Washing Fluid. – Add one pound of unslacked lime to three gallon of soft, boiling water. Let it settle and pour off. Then add three pounds of washing soda, and mix with the lime water. When dissolved, use a large wineglassful to each pailful of water. Add one gill of soft soap to a pailful of water.

To take Mildew out of Linen. – Take soap and rub it well; then scrape some fine chalk, and rub that also into the linen; lay it on the grass; as it dries, wet it a little, and will come out at once.

To Extract Stains from Silk. – Essence of lemon, one part; spirits of turpentine, five parts; mix, and apply to the spot by means of a linen rag.

Peterson's Magazine, July 1862

Glossing Linen. – Inquiry is frequently made respecting the mode of putting a gloss on linen collars and shirt-bosoms like that on new linen. This gloss, or enamel, as it is sometimes called, is produced mainly by friction with a warm iron, and may be put on linen by almost any person. The linen to be glazed receives as much strong starch as it is possible to charge it with, then it is dried. To each pound of starch a piece of sperm, paraffine, or white wax, about the size of a walnut, is usually added. When ready to be ironed, the linen is laid upon the table and moistened very slightly on the surface with a clean wet cloth. It is then ironed in the usual way with a flatiron, and is ready for the glossing operation. For this purpose a peculiar heavy flatiron, rounded at the bottom, and polished as bright as a mirror, is used. It is pressed firmly upon the linen, and rubbed with much force, and this frictional action puts on the gloss. "Elbow grease" is the principal secret connected with the art of glossing linen.

Sewing on Black Cloth. – To remedy the difficulty which persons with defective eyes experience when sewing on black cloth at night, pin or baste a strip of white paper on the seam of black cloth to be operated upon; then sew through the paper and cloth, and when the seam is completed, the paper may be torn off.

White Soap. – Take a pound box (a sheet-iron, not a tin one) of the Concentrated Lye, knock off the lid carefully, and throw box and contents into one gallon of boiling water. Next morning add two gallons more, and when the whole is boiling, throw into it four and a half pounds of clean fat; boil gently for two hours and ten minutes, then sprinkle into it a half pint of salt, and boil for thirty-five minutes longer; add a half gallon of hot water, and boil again for ten minutes; then pour it into a wet tub or box. The next morning cut the soap into cakes with a twine.

The quality of the soap will be improved by the addition of a quarter of a pound of powdered borax.

The soap should be allowed to harden before using; turn over the cakes and expose them to the air to promote the drying.

Self-tucking Attachment for sewing-machines. – A practical and very useful improvement, and important to those who possess a sewing-machine.

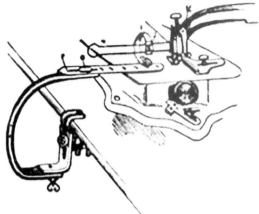

Tucking new forms so important a part of the labor that is performed on a sewing-machine, that a simple yet efficient aid to this rather tedious process is more than ever required. This aid is secured in this 'ztucking" attachment, which performs the work of folding and creasing a second tuck while stitching the first, thus greatly facilitating the operation, besides accomplishing it much more accurately.

All persons who have done much tucking on any machine know that the labor of measuring and folding is much more difficult, and takes much more time, than that of merely stitching. All this is saved by this tucking attachment, which is invaluable in families or dress-making establishments, where there is tucking to be done. The Tucker is very simple and easy of adjustment, and never gets out of order. It does not retard, but rather facilitates, the regular operation of the machine, so that experienced hands say it works more rapidly, and with greater ease. Our own experience in using it has been so entirely satisfactory, that we can recommend it with pleasure to those who are so fortunate as to possess a good sewing-machine. In fact, once tried, it becomes indispensable as a sewing machine itself.

They are retailed at $5 each. Mme. Demorest, 473 Broadway, has the exclusive agency them, but we suppose they can be ordered through any of the agents for the various sewing-machines. When ordering, it is necessary to state on what machine they are to be used.
Godey's Lady's Book, August 1862

To Take the Stains out of Black Cloth. – Boil a large handful of fig-leaves in two quarts of water until reduced to a pint; squeeze the leaves quite dry, and put the liquor into a bottle for use. The article should be rubbed with a sponge dipped in the liquor. The word "poison" should be written on the bottle, to prevent accident.
Peterson's Magazine, September 1862

Rain spots may be removed from cloth by carefully sponging the article all over with cold water, and hanging to dry in a cool place.

To Remove Coffee Stains. – Mix the yolk of an egg with a little milk-warm water, and use it as soap on the stain. For stains which have been on the material some time add a few drops of spirits of wine to the egg and water.
Godey's Lady's Book, November 1862

Rain Spots may be removed from cloth by carefully sponging the article all over with cold water, and hanging it to dry in a cool place. *Or:*– You may get rain spots, or nearly anything else, out of cloth, by rubbing it with benzine.
Peterson's Magazine, November 1862

To Clean Whole Silk or Satin Dresses. – The safest way to dry-clean a silk or satin dress of any color is to take the body off the skirt, and clean each part separately. If the dress is a valuable one, take off the sleeves also. When they are cleaned, remake them; all the French workmen do it.

Have two clean earthen vessels that will hold two gallons each, and put half a gallon of camphine in each; have a smooth board, six feet long and three feet wide, suitable brushes, and four or five clean sheets. Be very particular about the sheets being dry and clean. Your sheeting board is not to be encumbered with all your sheets on it; have only one on it. Begin by cleaning the body first. Put the body in the first liquor of camphine, then lift it on to the board, brush the inside well, and then the outside. When this has been done, put it back in the first liquor of camphine, then in the second, and let it drain over the second a minute; spread a sheet on the board, lay the dress on it, and directly begin and rub it dry with the clean Indian cotton cloths. While rubbing it, keep it smooth and shape it, so as that, when dry and cleaned, it will look as if it had not been wetted. Take the sleeves next. Clean them in the same manner as the body. The skirt comes next, one after another, and it is to be cleaned exactly in the same manner as the body and the sleeves, by passing it through the two camphine liquors, brushing, and sheeting it up dry before leaving it. Dispatch is the life and soul of this work, as the camphine is of such a drying nature that it requires great expedition in the cleaning. When the dress is done, it must be hung up for some hours in an airy room. The smell of the camphine will come off in a few hours in every hot stove room. The best method is to clean the camphine work in the afternoon and hang it in the stove room all night to lake the smell off. Any silk or satin dress can be cleaned whole by this method, but it is safer to take the skirt off the body, which most cleaners do that intend not to be beat.

To Clean Ladies' Dresses etc., from Paint. – We can confidently recommend the use of Benzine Collas or benzol to remove the paint marks; the only objection to it is, that a somewhat disagreeable smell remains; but a few hours exposure to the open air soon causes this to disappear.

To Raise the pile of velvet, hold it over a basin of boiling water, the wrong side of the velvet being next the water. To clean a silk dress, make the following mixture: Two ounces of curd soap shredded finely, two ounces of salts of tartar, two gallons of water. Boil these ingredients together, and then add another two gallons of water. Wash the dress in the mixture, rinse in cold water, and iron as soon as possible.
Godey's Lady's Book, December 1862

1863

How to Remove Mildew from Linen. – First of all take some soap (any common sort will do), and rub it well into the linen, then scrape some chalk very fine, and rub that in also; lay the linen on the grass, and as it dries wet it again; twice or thrice doing will remove the mildew stains. Another way is to mix soft soap with powdered starch, with half the quantity of salt, and the juice of a lemon. Lay this mixture on with a brush, and let the linen lay out on the grass for a few frosty nights, and the stains will disappear. All linen will turn yellow if kept long unused, locked up in a linen press, excluded from air and light; so the best way that we have found of restoring it to its color, is to expose it to the open air in nice dry weather. Exposure to the light and continual airings will be found the best way of preserving its whiteness.
Peterson's Magazine, June 1863

To Wash Black Lace. – Carefully sponge the lace with gin, or if preferred, with green tea, and wind it round and round a bottle to dry, as if touched with an iron it would become glossy and have a flattened appearance. Some fill the bottle with warm water, which causes the lace to dry more quickly. It must on no account be placed near the fire as it would lose its color, and have a rusty appearance.

To Remove Grease from Silk. – Take a lump of magnesia, and rub it wet over the spot; let it dry, then brush the powder off, and the spot will disappear; or, take a visiting card, separate it, and rub the spot with the soft internal part, and it will disappear without taking the gloss off the silk.
Peterson's Magazine, August 1863

For rendering muslins uninflammable, they should be passed through starch made with water in which sulphate of ammonia has been dissolved, in the proportion of two ounces of the former to a pint of the latter. This mixture has not the slightest influence on the colours of the muslin, and is perfectly efficacious.
The What-Not, October 1863

1864

Washing Fluid. – The following is a good and economical washing fluid: – Dissolve one pound of soda in one quart of hot water, and add to it four quarts of lime-water; when this settles pour off the clear. Next dissolve three ounces of borax in one quart of boiling water, and add to it the five quarts of clear water. When cold dissolve in it. two or three ounces of pulverized carbonate ammonia. Put it in bottles, and keep it tightly corked. Use half a pint, or less, to about five gallons of water; put it, with some soap, into the tub of clothes the night before washing-day, or a short time before boiling the clothes. Many who are in the habit of using washing fluids do not appear to be aware of their nature and specific objects. They are intended to provide a slight excess of alkali to combine with the grease and dirt on the clothes. They should be sparingly used at best, and wholly discarded in washing laces and fine linens. Good soap-suds of sufficient strength make the best washing fluid for fine white textile fabrics. The chloride of soda makes an excellent fluid for whitening linen that has become yellow in color, and as a washing fluid inferior to none. The use of strong caustic alkalies imparts a yellowish tinge to fine linens and tends to injure them, and therefore should be used (if at all) with much caution.
The Lady's Friend, February 1864

To Clean Black Veils. – Pass them through a warm liquor of bullock's gall and water; rinse in cold water; then take a small piece of glue, pour boiling water on it, and pass the veil through it; clap it, and frame to dry. Instead of framing, it may be fastened with drawing-pins closely fixed upon a very clean paste, or drawing-board.

To Restore the Color of black Kid Boots. – Take a small quantity of good black ink, mix it with the white of an egg, and apply it to the boots with a soft sponge.
Peterson's Magazine, February 1864

To Remove Ink-Stains. – When fresh done and wet, hasten to provide some cold water, an empty cup and a spoon. Pour a little of the water on the stain, not having touched it previously with anything. The water, of course, dilutes the ink and and lessens the mark; then ladle it up into the empty cup. Continue pouring the clean water on the stain and ladling it up, until there is not the slightest mark left. No matter how great the quantity of ink spilt, patience and perseverance will remove every indication of it. To remove a dry ink-stain, dip the part stained into hot milk, and

gently rub it; repeat until no sign is left. This is an unfailing remedy.
Peterson's Magazine, March 1864

To Detect Lime-bleached Linen. – Lime has such an injurious effect on linen and calicoes, and is so much used for bleaching purposes, that the following simple test may be applied with advantage before purchasing any large quantity: Put a sample of the linen into a glass, and pour upon it a little good vinegar; if there is lime, its presence will be detected by the vinegar effervescing.
The What-Not, March 1864

To Clean a White Ostrich Feather. – A lather should be made with luke-warm water and white curd soap; the feather must then be shaken in the lather for some time, occasionally passing it between the fingers, until, from the state of the water, the principal part of the dirt appears to have been removed. A second lather must then be used, but not containing quite so much soap. After well rinsing the feather in this, it must be gently pressed with a soft, clean handkerchief, and then waved backward and forward before the fire, but at a little distance from it, until quite dry. A very small quantity of soda and a slight coloring of *blue* should be added to the water before the lather is made.
To Smoothe a Rumpled black Silk Dress, etc. – A little rock ammonia (bought at the chemist's) and a piece of common soda put into a bottle, and about half a pint of boiling water poured on to dissolve them; then, when cold, sponge the silk with the liquid on the right side, and iron it on the wrong. This receipt wonderfully improves anything black, and is quite good for cloth, though, of course, that must not be ironed.
Peterson's Magazine, April 1864

Cleaning Carpets. – To one pail of warm water, add one pint of ox-gall; dip a soaped flannel into the mixture, and well rub the surface of the carpet, piece by piece, rinsing it as you proceed with clean cold water, taking care not to make the carpet too wet, and finishing off by rubbing with a dry coarse cloth. The carpet, of course, must be well beaten before it is operated upon. This process is simple and surprisingly effective in renovating the colors. The only drawback is the effluvium given off by the gall; but this is soon remedied by exposure to the air, or by opening the windows if the carpet be laid down.
Peterson's Magazine, May 1864

Oil Stains in Silk and Other Fabrics. – Benzine *collas* is most effectual, not only for silk, but in any other material whatever. It can be procured from any chemist. By simply covering both sides of the greased silk with magnesia, and allowing it to remain for a few hours, the oil is absorbed by the powder. Should the first application be insufficient, it may be repeated, and even rubbed in with the hand. Should the silk be Tussah or Indian silk, it will wash.
Oil Stains can also be entirely removed from silks and all dress materials, also leather, paper, etc., by applying pipe-clay, powdered and moistened with water to the consistency of thick cream, laid on the stain and left to dry some hours, then lightly scraped or rubbed off with a knife or flannel, so as not to injure the surface. If the pipe-clay dries off quite light in color, all oil has been removed; if it comes off dark-looking, then more should be laid on, as grease still remains to be removed. Pipe-clay will not injure the most delicate tints of silk or paper.
To Clean Black Lace. – Scald some bran with boiling water, and dip the lace up and down in the bran and water when warm, and when clean, squeeze the water off and shake out the bran. Lay it out, and pull out the edges, etc. Iron it between linen on a blanket, so that the iron does not glaze it. Or if the lace is dipped in cold milk, and ironed in the same way, it will be found to clean it equally well.
To Sponge a Black Silk Dress. – Sponge the black silk lightly, on both sides, with a perfectly clean sponge dipped in spirits of wine, then, with a moderately warm iron, smooth the silk over on one side, not the side that will form the outside when remade. If the selvedges are too tight to allow the silk to become smooth, they will require snipping at intervals.
Peterson's Magazine, July 1864

To Clean Ribbons. – Take one tablespoonful of brandy, one of soft-soap, and one of molasses. Mix thoroughly together; place the ribbon upon a smooth board, and apply the mixture with a soft brush; after which rinse in cold water, then roll up in a cloth until nearly dry; iron with a flat-iron, not too hot.
Peterson's Magazine, November 1864

To Stain Leather Gloves. – Those pleasing hues of yellow, brown, or tan color, are readily imparted to leather gloves by this simple process: – Steep saffron in soft, boiling water for twelve hours; then, having sewed up the tops of the gloves, to prevent the dye from staining the inside, wet them over with a sponge dipped into the liquid. The quantity of saffron, as well us of water, depends on how much dye may be wanted, and their relative proportions on the depth of color required. A common teacup will contain quite sufficient in quantity for a single pair of gloves.
Wrinkled Silk. – To make silk which has been wrinkled and "tumbled," appear exactly like new: – Sponge it on the surface with a weak solution of gum-arabic or white glue, and iron it on the wrong side.
Peterson's Magazine, December 1864

RESPECTING CLOTHING &c.

(1.) *Putting away Woolens.*

The following method of putting away all the woolen and worsted articles of the house, will be found an infallible preservative against moths: and the cost is nothing in comparison to the security it affords of finding the things in good order when opened for use on the return of cold weather. Procure, at a distiller's or elsewhere, a tight, empty hogshead, that has held whiskey. Have it well cleaned, (without washing) and see that it is quite dry. Let it be placed in some part of the house that is little used in summer, and where it can be shut up dark.

After the carpets have been taken up, and well shaken and beaten, and the grease-spots all removed, (see 4) let them be folded and packed, closely down in the cask. Put in also the blankets, having first washed all that were not clean; also, the woolen table-covers. If you have worsted or cloth curtains and cushions, pack them likewise, after they have been freed from dust. Also, flannels, merinoes, cloaks, coats, furs, and, in short, everything that is liable to be attracted by the moths. Fold and pack them closely, making all the articles fit advantageously into the space, and so disposing them that each may find a place in the hogshead. The furs had best be sewed up in linen before they are put in. If well packed, one hogshead will generally hold all the woolen articles belonging to a house of modern size, and a moderate sized family. Then nail on the head of the cask, and let the whole remain undisturbed till the warm weather is over. While the house is shut up, and the family out of town, in the summer, you may safely leave your woolens put away in this manner.

Choose a clear dry day for unpacking them in the autumn; and when open, expose them to the air till the odor of the whiskey has gone off. If they are put away clean, and free from dust, it will be found that the whiskey atmosphere has brightened their colors. As soon as the things are all out of it, nail up the cask again, and keep it for next season.

Where camphor cannot be conveniently procured, furs, flannels, &c., may be kept through the summer by sewing them up in linen, and interspersing properly among them bits of fresh sassafras bark, or shavings of red cedar. But there is nothing so certain to preserve them from moths as an old whiskey cask. Never keep hair trunks. They always produce moths.

(2.) *French method of washing Silk Cravats, Scarfs, Shawls, &c.*

Make a mixture in a large flat dish, of the following articles:— A large tablespoonful of soft soap or of hard brown soap, shaved fine, (white soap will not do); a small teaspoonful of strained honey, and a pint of spirits of wine; have ready a large brush, (a clothes brush, for instance); make perfectly clean. Lay the silk on a board or on an ironing-table, stretching it evenly, and securing it in its place with weights on its edges. Then dip the brush into the mixture, and with it go all over the silk lengthwise of the texture, beginning at the part least seen when worn, and trying a little at a time, till you have ascertained the effect. If you find that the liquid changes the color of the silk, weaken it by adding more spirits of wine.

Having gone carefully over the whole of the article, dip it up and down in a bucket of clean water; but do not squeeze or wring it. Repeat this through another clear water, and then through a third. Afterwards spread it on a line to dry, but without any squeezing or wringing. Let it dry slowly. While still damp, take it down, pull it and stretch it even, then roll and fold it up, and let it rest a few minutes. Have irons ready, and iron the silk, taking care that the iron be not so hot as to change the color.

The above quantity of the washing mixture is sufficient for about half a dozen silk handkerchiefs, one shawl, or two scarfs, if they are not too long. If there be fringe on the scarfs, it is best to take it off and replace it with new; or else to gather the ends of the scarfs and finish them with a lapell or ball. Brocaded silks cannot be washed in this way.

Gentlemen's silk or chaly cravats may be made to look very well washed in this manner. Ribbons, also, if they are thick and rich. Indeed, whatever is washed by this process, must be of very good quality. A foul or dyed silk dress may be washed this way, provided it is first taken apart; silk aprons also. We have seen articles washed by this process, and can assure our readers it is a good one. This is also a good method of washing blond, using a soft sponge instead of a brush. When dry, lay the blond in long folds within a large sheet of white paper, and press it for a few days in a large book, but do not iron it.

In putting away ribbons or silk, wrap or fold them in coarse brown paper, which, as it contains a portion of tar or turpentine, will preserve the color of the article, and prevent white silk from turning yellow. The chloride of lime used in manufacturing white paper renders it improper to keep silks in, as it frequently causes them to spot or to change color.

(3.) *To make a soiled Coat look as good as new.*

First clean the coat of grease and dirt (see No. 4,) then take one gallon of a strong decoction of logwood made by boiling logwood [*word missing*] in water. Strain this liquid, and when cool, add two ounces of gum arabic in powder, which should be kept in well stopped bottles for use. Then go gently over the coat with a sponge wet in the above liquid diluted to suit the color, and hang it in the shade to dry. After which brush the nap smooth, and it will look as good as new. The liquid will suit all brown or dark colors if properly diluted, of which it is easy to judge.

(4.) *To extract Oil or Spermaceti from a Carpet or other Woolen.*

If oil has been spilt on a carpet, that part of the carpet must be loosened up, and the floor beneath it well scrubbed with warm soap and water, and fuller's earth; otherwise the grease will continue yet to come through. You may extract some of the oil by washing that part of the carpet with cold water and a cloth. Then spread over it a thin coating of scraped Wilmington clay, which should be renewed every two or three hours. If you have no Wilmington clay, take common magnesia.

To remove spots of spermaceti, scrape off as much as you can with a knife, then lay on a thin, soft, white paper upon the spots, and press it with a warm iron. By repeating this you may draw out the spermaceti. Afterwards rub the cloth where the spots have been, with some very soft brownish paper.

Wilmington clay, which may be had in small round balls, is excellent for removing grease spots however large. Scrape down a sufficient quantity, and rub on the spot, letting it rest an hour or more then brush it off, and continue to repeat the process. The genuine Wilmington clay, pure and unmixed, is far superior to any other grease ball sold by the druggists.

(5.) To extract Grease Spots.

Grease of the very worst kind, (whale oil, for instance,) may be extracted even from silks, ribbons, and other delicate articles, by means of camphine oil. As this oil is the better for being fresh, get but little at a time. Pour some camphine into a cup, and dip lightly with a clean, soft, white rag. With this rub the grease spot. Then take a fresh rag dipped in the camphine, and continue rubbing till the grease is extracted, which will be very soon. The color of the article will be uninjured. To remove the turpentine odor of the camphine, rub the place with Cologne water or strong spirits of wine, and expose it to the open air. Repeat this process if any odor remains after the first.

(6.) To take Mildew out of Linen.

Take soap and rub it well; then scrape some fine chalk, and rub that also in the linen; lay it on the grass; as it dries, wet it a little, and it will soon come out.

(7.) To take Paint off of Cloths.

Rub with spirits of turpentine or spirits of wine, either will answer if the paint if but just on. But if it is allowed to harden, nothing will remove it but spirits of turpentine rubbed on with perseverance. Use a soft sponge or a soft rag.

(8.) To clean White Kid Gloves.

Stretch them on a board, and rub the soiled spots with cream of tartar or magnesia. Let them rest an hour, then take a mixture of alum and fuller's earth in powder, and rub it all over the gloves with a clean brush, and let them rest again for an hour or two. Then sweep it all off, and go over with a flannel dipped in a mixture of bran and finely powdered whiting. Let them rest another hour; brush off the powder, and you will find them clean.

(9.) To wash Colored Kid or Hoskin Gloves.

Have, on a table, a clean towel, folded three or four times, a saucer of new milk, and a piece of brown soap. Spread a glove smoothly on the folded towel, dip into the milk a piece of clean flannel, rub it on the soap until you get enough, and then commence rubbing the glove, beginning at the wrist, and rubbing lengthwise to the ends of the fingers, the glove being held firmly in the left hand. When done, spread them out to dry gradually. When nearly dry, pull them out the cross way of the leather, and when quite dry, stretch them on your hand.

(10.) To clean White Leather Gloves.

White leather gloves may be cleaned to look very well, by putting on one at a time, and going over them thoroughly with a shaving brush and lather. Then wipe them off with a clean handkerchief or sponge, and dry them on the hands by the fire, or in the sun.

(11.) To preserve Furs from Moths.

Wrap up a few cloves or pepper ears with them when you put them away for any length of time.

(12.) To extract Durable Ink.

Rub the ink stain with a little sal-ammonia moistened with water.

(13.) To remove Stains from Cotton and Linen.

Put a small quantity of brimstone into an iron vessel, and drop in a live coal of fire; having first wet the stained spot with water, lay the cloth over the vessel, so as to let the fumes have full access to the stained spot, and it will soon disappear, or become loose os [*sic*: so] as to wash out.

(43) Washing and Bleaching Liquid.

Take 1/4 lb. unslacked lime and pour upon it 6 qts. boiling water, stir it all up, and when it has stood long enough to entirely settle strain off the clean water and dissolve in this water, by boiling 3 lbs. sal soda.

For washing – to every pail full of water add for boiling, 1/2 pint of the liquid. The clothes must be put in soak the night before washing, taking care to rub all the dirt spots with soap; then boil them with the liquid 35 minutes. They are then to be drawn and put into a tub, and clear boiling water poured over them; then rub them out rinse them well and they and they are fit for drying.

<u>How to Do It</u>, 1864

1865

To Remove Mildew from White Clothes. – Having well washed the part with soap and water, lay upon it, while it is yet wet, a thick plaster of finely-scraped chalk, expose it to the air, and as the chalk becomes dry, wet it again and again, until the spots are quite removed, which will most likely to be on the second if not the first day. A grass plot in the shade is the best situation for bleaching.
Peterson's Magazine, January 1865

To Bleach Straw Hats, etc. – Straw hats and bonnets are bleached by putting them, previously washed, in pure water, into a box with burning sulphur; the fumes which arise unite with the water on the bonnets, and the sulphurous acid thus formed bleaches them.
Peterson's Magazine, April 1865

If Your Clothes Take Fire. – How to act, when the clothes take fire, is what everybody ought to know. Three persons out of four rush up to the victim, and begin to paw with their hands without any definite aim. This is wrong. It is also useless to tell the sufferer to do this or that, or call for water. In fact, it is generally best to say not a word, but to seize a blanket from a bed, or a cloak, or any woolen fabric; if none is at hand, take any woolen material, and hold the corners as far apart as you can; stretch them out higher than your head, and, running boldly to the person, make a motion of clasping in the arms about the shoulders. This instantly smothers the fire, and saves the face. The next instant throw the unfortunate person on the floor. This is an additional safety to face and breath, and any remnant of flame can be put out more leisurely. The next instant, immerse the burnt part in cold water, and all pain will cease with the rapidity of lightning. Next, get some common flour, remove from the water, and cover the burnt parts with an inch thickness of flour, if possible; put the patient to bed, and do all that is possible to soothe until a physician arrives. Let the flour remain until it falls off itself, when a beautiful new skin will be found. Unless the burns are deep, no other application is needed. The dry flour for burns is the most admirable remedy ever proposed, and the information ought to be imparted to all. The principle of its action is that, like the water, it causes instant and perfect relief from pain, by totally excluding the air from the injured parts. Spanish whiting and cold water, of a mushy consistency, are preferred by some. Dredge on the flour until no more will stick, and cover with cotton batting.
To Remove Mildew from Linen. – This can be done by mixing with soft-soap, a little powdered starch, half the quantity of salt, and the juice of a lemon, and applying it the mildew stain with a paint-brush on both sides of the linen. The stained article should then be left out on the grass day and night until the spot be removed.
To Extract Grease from Silk. – Scrape French chalk, put it on the grease-spot, and hold it near the fire, or over a warm iron, or water-plate filled with boiling water. The grease will melt and the French chalk absorb it. Brush or rub it off; repeat, if necessary.
Peterson's Magazine, May 1865

How to Prepare Starch for Use. – Take a quart basin and put into it a tablespoonful of the best starch, which, with a clean wooden spoon kept for the purpose, gradually moisten and rub down with a quarter of a pint of cold spring water, adding only a tablespoonful at a time. When in a perfectly smooth state, and about the consistence of cream, gradually stir into it a pint of boiling water. Then pour the mixture into a clean glazed pipkin, kept for the purpose, and stir over a gentle fire till it boils, adding a lump of sugar which prevents the starch from sticking to the hot iron. While in a boiling state, take a piece of wax-candle and turn it round two or three times; this gives a smooth and glossy surface to the linen after it has been ironed. Then strain the starch, thus prepared, through a piece of coarse muslin into a basin, cover it over with a plate, to prevent a skin forming on the top, and then before it is quite cold it ready for use.
To Wash a Muslin Dress. – Make a good lather, and wash the muslin in *cold* water – never putting it into warm water even to rinse it. If the muslin is green, add a wineglassful of vinegar to the water in which it is rinsed; if lilac, the same quantity of ammonia. For black and white muslins, use a small quantity of sugar of lead.
To Clean Silk. – Quarter of a pound of soft-soap, one ounce of honey, one pint of gin. Put on with a flannel, or nailbrush, and afterward brushed with cold water, then dipped in cold water five or six times, and hung out to drain, then ironed (*wet* on the wrong side) with a hot iron.
To Extract Grease from Silk. – Wet the part with eau-de-cologne, and gently rub the silk upon itself, between the hands. When dry, the grease will disappear. This will, also, remove recent paint and the grease from a wax candle.
To Perfume Linen. – Rose-leaves dried in the shade, cloves beat to a powder, mace scraped. Mix them together, and put the composition into bags.
To Wash Flannels. – Wash them in warm water, rather above luke-warm, in which the soap has been boiled or dissolved, and not to rub the soap upon the woolen. Rinse them thoroughly in water rather hotter than that in which have been washed; this removes the soap from the material instead of allowing it to remain and get hard, as does if the last water is not decidedly hotter than the first. This plan will also be found to succeed perfectly with or Berlin wool; but then I generally wring the different articles or skeins by twisting them up in a linen cloth, so as to avoid straining the wool, and do not dry them too quickly. But the important point is certainly getting them thoroughly free from the soap, which would otherwise thicken and stiffen in the fine pores of the wool.
To Bleach a Straw Bonnet. – First scrub the bonnet well with a brush dipped in clean water. After this, put into it

box a saucer containing burning sulphur; it must remain there a short time, and as soon as it is removed, the bonnet must be placed in the box and well covered up, so that the sulphuric atmosphere may whiten it.

Peterson's Magazine, August 1865

To Remove Stains from Silk. – Stains produced by vinegar, lemon-juice, oil of vitrol, or other sharp corrosives, may often be removed from silks by mixing a little pearlash with soap lather, and passing the silk through them. Spirits of hartshorn will also often restore the color.

To Remove Lime Spots. – Lime spots on woolen clothes may be completely removed by strong vinegar. The vinegar effectually neutralizes the lime, but does not generally affect the color of the cloth. Dark cloth, the color of which has been completely destroyed in spots six inches square, has thus had its original color perfectly restored.

To Make Calicoes Wash Well. – Infuse three gills of salt in four quarts of boiling water, and put the calicoes in while hot, and leave them till cold; in this way the colors are rendered permanent, and will not fade by subsequent washing. So says a lady who has frequently made the experiment herself. Nothing can be cheaper or quicker done.

To Remove Spots of Wax from Velvet. – Apply toasted bread, very hot, to the part spotted. This will answer for any color except crimson. It is better to lay the velvet on the toast.

Frank Leslie's Lady's Magazine, September 1865

To Clean Silk. – One pint and a fifth of gin or whiskey, four ounces of soft-soap, and six ounces of honey: to be well mixed in an open dish. Lay the silk on a clean deal table, and rub it well on both sides with a sponge dipped in the above mixture. Have ready two pails filled with cold, soft water, and rinse the breadths separately, first in one bucket and then in the other, and put them in the open air upon a towel-horse to drain (a shady, cool place is best.) When the silk is nearly dry, iron it on the wrong side. It will be of little use to turn a silk dress without first removing all grease-spots, as any marks very speedily work through.

To Clean Gloves. – Spread them out smooth on a clean board; rub the dirtiest places with cream of tartar or with magnesia, and let them remain an hour or more. Mix powdered alum and Fuller's earth, rub the mixture all over the gloves with a little brush (a tooth-brush, or such like,) and again leave them for a time. Brush off the mixture and rub the gloves with flannel dipped in bran and finely powdered whitening. After again letting them lie an or two brush off this powder, and the gloves will be clean.

To Wash New Flannel. – Cut the soap small, and boil it in a little water. Have two tubs with water as hot as the hands can bear, previously blue the water well to keep the color of the flannel, and put some of the boiled soap into one tub to make a lather; then wash the flannel without squeezing it. Put it into the other tub, and wring it in a large towel. Shake it then out, and, after drying it, smooth with a cool iron.

To Wash Merino Stockings. – The same method should be pursued as for flannels, and all woolen and cotton goods. Boil the soap to make a lather, wash them in this warm, and rinse in a second lather, (if white, mix a little blue.) Never rinse in plain water, or use cold lather, and never rub the soap upon the merino or flannel; the one shrinks, the other thickens and spoils the wool.

To Dye Gloves the Color of Limerick Gloves. – With soft water make a strong or weak (according to taste) infusion of saffron; sew up the opening of the gloves, and brush them over with the dye.

Peterson's Magazine, October 1865

Washing Preparation. – Put one pound of saltpetre into a gallon of water, and keep it in a corked jug; two tablespoonfuls for a pint of soup. Soak, wash, and boil as usual. This bleaches the clothes beautifully, without injuring the fabric.

Peterson's Magazine, December 1865

1866

To Wash Flannel. – First wash it in two waters, not very warm, and without soap. Take out the flannel from the water and rub a little soap upon it; put it into a pan, and pour upon it a sufficient quantity of boiling water to cover it entirely. Let it remain in this for ten minutes or a quarter of an hour, then rub it as usual, using a little more soap, if required, so as to make a very slight lather, adding a small quantity of blue. After this rinse and take out the flannel, wring it, shake it well, and dry it in the open air.

To Renovate Black Silk. – Rub the silk all over on the right side with a solution of ammonia and water, (two teaspoonfuls of powdered ammonia to quarter of a pint of warm water,) and smooth it on the wrong side with a moderately hot iron, and the silk will regain a bright black appearance.

To Perfume Clothes. – Cloves in course powder, one ounce; cassia, one ounce; lavender flowers, one ounce; lemon-peel, one ounce. Mix and put them into little bags, and place them where the clothes are kept, or wrap the clothes round them. They will keep off insects.

Peterson's Magazine, January 1866

To Restore the Pile of Velvet, stretch the velvet out tightly, and remove all dust from the surface with a clean brush; afterward, well clean it with a piece of black flannel, slightly moistened with Florence oil. Then lay a wet cloth over a hot iron, and place it under the velvet, allowing the steam to pass through it; at the same time brushing the pile of the velvet till restored as required. Should any fluff remain on the surface of the velvet, remove it by brushing with a handful of crape.

Grease-Stains in Silk. – A sure and safe way to remove grease-stains from silks, is to rub the spot quickly with brown paper; the friction will soon draw out the grease. Or: Lay the silk upon a table with an ironing-blanket under it, the right side of the silk downward: put a piece of brown paper on the top, and apply a flat-iron just hot enough to scorch the paper. I have found this receipt more efficacious than any scouring-drops ever compounded.

Tincture to Destroy Moths. – One ounce of gum camphor, and one ounce of powdered shell of red pepper, are macerated in eight ounces of strong alcohol for seven days, and then strained. With this tincture the furs or cloths are sprinkled over, and rolled up in sheets. This remedy is used in Russia under the name of "Chinese tincture for moths," and is found very effective.

A bit of glue, dissolved in skim-milk and water, will restore old crape.

Soft soap should be kept in a dry place in the cellar, and not used until three months old.

Peterson's Magazine, April 1866

To Wash Doeskin Gloves. – Wash them in water of blood-heat, wring as dry as possible, and let them hang in the house, away from heat, until two-thirds dry; then stretch until soft. Wash leather, used for cleaning glass or silver, may be washed as above; also buckskin mittens, shirts, etc.

To Cleanse White or Fawn-Colored Feathers – Dissolve fine soap in boiling water; add a lump of soda, strain the suds and cool a little; when you can bear the heat of the water, pass the feathers through it, squeezing them gently, and passing them through the hand; repeat the process with weak suds, without soda; rinse them in cold water, and strike them on the left hand until nearly dry; then take a small blunt-edged knife, and draw each fibre over the edge, curling it as you please; if desired flat, it may then be pressed between be leaves of a large book. Black feathers are cleansed with gall water, and dried as above.

Godey's Lady's Book, May 1866

Clean Kid Gloves. – Make a strong lather with curd soap and warm water, in which steep a small piece of new flannel. Place the glove on a flat, clean, and unyielding surface – such as the bottom of a dish, and having thoroughly soaped the flannel (when squeezed from the lather), rub the kid till all dirt be removed, cleaning and resoaping the flannel from time to time. Care must be taken to omit no part of the glove, by turning the fingers, etc. The gloves must be dried in the sun, or before a moderate fire, and will present the appearance of old parchment. When quite dry, they must be gradually "pulled out," and will look new.

The Advantages of Borax. – The washerwomen of Holland and Belgium, who get up their linen so beautifully white, use refined borax as washing powder, instead of soda, in the proportion of one large handful of borax powder to about ten gallons of boiling water. They thus save in soap nearly half. All the washing establishments adopt the same mode. For laces, cambrics, etc., an extra quantity of the powder is used, and for crinolines (requiring to be made stiff), a strong solution is necessary. Borax being a neutral salt, does not in the slightest degree injure the texture of the linen. Its effect is to soften the hardest water, and therefore it should be kept on every toilet table.

Godey's Lady's Book, July 1866

Improvement in Starching. – Take two ounces of white gum-arabic powder, put it into a pitcher, and pour on it a pint or more of boiling water, (according to the degree of strength required,) and then, having covered it, let it stand all night. The next day pour it carefully from the dregs into a clean bottle, cork it, and keep it for use. A tablespoonful of this gum-water, stirred into a pint of starch that has been made in the usual manner, will give lawns (either white, black, or printed,) it look of newness when nothing else can restore them after washing. It is also good, much diluted, for thin white muslin and bobbinet.

To Bleach a Straw Bonnet. – First scrub the bonnet well with yellow soap and a brush dipped in clean water; after this, put into a box a saucer containing burning sulphur; it must remain there a short time, and as soon as it is removed, the bonnet must be placed in the box and well covered up, so that the sulphuric atmosphere may whiten it; next dissolve a little oxalic acid in boiling water. Wash all over the bonnet with a small paint-brush; put it into a pail of cold water, and let it remain half an hour; then hang it out to dry; it must afterward be stiffened with gelatine, dried again, and then pressed into shape.

Furs. – Furs may be preserved from moths and insects by placing a little colcynth pulp, (bitter apples,) or spices – as cloves, pimento, etc., – wrapped in muslin among them; or they may be washed in a very weak solution of corrosive sublimate in warm water, ten or fifteen grains to the pint, and afterward carefully dried. Furs, as well as every other species of clothing, should be kept in a clean, dry place.

To Wash a Muslin Dress. – Make a good lather, and wash the muslin in cold water – never putting it into warm water, even to rinse it. If the muslin is green, add a wineglassful of vinegar to the water in which it is rinsed; if lilac, the same quantity of ammonia. For black and white muslins, use a small quantity of sugar of lead.

To Clean Silk (Black or Colored.) – Mix spirits of wine with water, sponge on the right side, and iron on the wrong; it will look new again.

Peterson's Magazine, August 1866

RULES FOR WASHING.

Except woollens and colored clothes, all other kinds should be put to soak over night, the very dirty parts having soap rubbed on them. If you use a washing-fluid, it is usually mixed in the soaking water; if you use no wash mixture, the next morning wring out the clothes, and proceed to wash them carefully through two warm waters; then boil them in clean water rather briskly, but not longer than half an hour. Wash them out of the boil, rinse through two waters. The last rinse water should have a delicate tinge of blue, likewise a small quantity of starch for all cottons or linens; reserve those you wish stiffer for the last and mix more starch in the water. Shirt bosoms and collars, skirts, in short anything you wish very stiff, should be dipped while dry. Swiss and other thin muslins and laces are dipped in starch while dry, and then clapped with the hands until in a right condition to iron. Calicoes, brilliants, and lawns of white grounds, are washed like any other white material, omitting boiling, until the yellow tinge they acquire makes it absolutely necessary. Unbleached cottons and linens follow the white clothes through the same waters, but must in no case be boiled with them, as they continually discharge a portion of their color, and so discolor the white clothes. Calicoes, colored lawns, and colored cottons, and linens generally are washed through two suds and two rinsing waters, starch being used in the last, as all clothes look better and keep clean longer if a little stiffened. Many calicoes will spot if soap is rubbed on them; they should be washed in a lather simply. A spoonful of ox gall to a gallon of water will set the colors of almost any goods soaked in it previous to washing. A teacup of lye in a bucket of water will improve the color of black goods. Nankeen should lay in the lye awhile before being washed; the lye sets the color. A strong clean tea of common hay will preserve the color of those French linens so much used in summer by both sexes. Vinegar in the rinsing water for pink or green calicoes, will brighten them. Pearlash answers the same end for purple and blue. Flannels should be washed through two suds and one rinsing water; each water should be as hot as the hand can bear, unless you wish to thicken the flannel. Flannels washed in lukewarm water will soon become like fulled cloth. Colored and white flannels must be washed separately, and by no means after cotton or linen, as the lint from these goods adheres to the flannel. There should be a little blue in the rinsing water for white flannel. Allow your flannels to freeze after washing in winter.

Godey's Lady's Book, September 1866

How to Prepare Starch for Use. – Take a quart basin, and put into it a tablespoonful of the best starch, which, with a clean, wooden spoon kept for the purpose, gradually moisten and rub down with a quarter of a pint of cold spring-water, adding only a tablespoonful at a time. When in a perfectly smooth state, and about the consistency of cream, gradually stir into it a pint of boiling water; then pour the mixture into a clean, glazed pipkin, kept for the purpose, and stir it over a gentle fire till it boils, adding a lump of sugar, which prevents the starch from sticking to the hot iron. While in a boiling state, take a piece of wax-candle, and turn it round two or three times; this gives a smooth and glossy surface to the linen after it has been ironed. Then strain the starch thus prepared through a piece of coarse muslin into a basin, cover it over with a plate, to prevent a skin forming on the top, and then before it is quite cold, it is ready for use.

Peterson's Magazine, October 1866

To Renew Black Tissue Veils. – Dip them in thin glue water; shake them gently until nearly dry; spread black silk or cambric on the ironing blanket, and press with a moderate iron.

To Bleach White Silks or Flannel. – Wash the articles clean, rinse in suds, and smoke with brimstone while wet; the silk must be brushed or washed with a sponge; if rubbed, it will never press smoothly; expose the goods to the air, and the odor will soon pass off.

Godey's Lady's Book, November 1866

To Clean Ribbons. – A tablespoonful of brandy, one ditto of soft-soap, and one of honey, and the white of an egg mixed well together; dip the ribbon into water, lay it on a board, and scrub with the mixture, using a soft brush; rinse in cold water, fold in a cloth, and iron when half dry.

Peterson's Magazine, November 1866

To Clean White Ostrich Feathers. – Four ounces of white soap, cut small, dissolved in four pints of water, rather hot, in a large basin; make the solution into a lather. Introduce the feathers, and rub well with the hands for five or six minutes. After this soaping, wash in clean water, as hot as the hand can bear. Shake until dry.

To Take Ink out of Linen. – Dip the spotted part in pure melted tallow; then wash out the tallow and the ink will come out with it.

Godey's Lady's Book, December 1866

To Wash Flannels. – Wash them in warm water, rather above luke-warm, in which the soap has been boiled or dissolved, and not to rub the soap upon the woolen. Rinse them thoroughly in water rather hotter than that in which they have been washed; this removes the soap from the material, instead of allowing it to remain and get hard, as it does if the last water is not decidedly hotter than the first. This plan will also be found to succeed perfectly with fleecy or Berlin wool; but then we generally wring the different articles or skeins by twisting them up in a linen cloth, so as to avoid straining the wool, and do not dry them too quickly. But the important point is certainly getting them thoroughly free from the soap, which would otherwise thicken and stiffen in the fine pores of the wool.

To Clean Black Lace. – Take the lace, and wipe off the dust carefully with a cambric handkerchief. Then pin it out upon a board, inserting a pin in each projecting point of the lace. Sponge it all over with table-beer, and do not remove the pins till it is perfectly dry. It will look quite fresh and new.

Wrinkled Silk. – To make silk, which has been wrinkled and "tumbled," appear exactly like new. Sponge it on the surface with a weak solution of gum-arabic or white glue, and iron it on the wrong side.

Peterson's Magazine, December 1866

1867

To Clean Kid Gloves. – Make a strong lather with curd-soap and warm water, in which steep a small piece of new flannel. Place the gloves on a flat, clean, and unyielding surface – such as the bottom of a dish – and having thoroughly soaped the flannel, (when squeezed from the lather,) rub the kid till all dirt be removed, cleaning and resoaping the flannel from time to time. Care must be taken to omit no part of the glove, by turning the fingers, etc. Blow the gloves out with your mouth or a pair of bellows. Dry them gradually in the sun, or before a gentle fire. When quite dry, pulling them well out will restore them to their proper color.

Gum-Arabic Starch. – Get two ounces of line white gum-arabic, and pound it to powder. Next put it into a pitcher, and pour on it a pint or more of boiling water, (according to the degree of strength you desire,) and then, having covered it, let it set all night. In the morning pour it carefully from the dregs into a clean bottle, cork it, and keep it for use. A tablespoonful of gum-water stirred into a pint of starch, that has been made in the usual manner, will give to lawns (either white or printed) a look of newness to which nothing else can restore them after washing. It is also good, much diluted, for thin white muslin and bobbinet.

To Remove Mildew from Linen. – To every four ounces of chloride of lime add two quarts of boiling water, and when it has dissolved, six quarts of cold water. Steep the linen in the mixture for twelve hours, and the mildew will disappear.

To Remove Ironmould. – Rub the mark with tartaric acid, and wash afterward in pearlash and soap.

To Keep away Moth. – Put the end of a tallow-candle in some part of the drawer, and the moths will keep away.

To Preserve Furs. – Wrap some cloves or peppercorns with them and keep in a dry place.

To Restore Linen that has long been Stained. – Rub the stains on each side with wet brown soap. Mix some starch to a thick paste with cold water, and spread it over the soaped places. Then expose the linen to the sun and air; and if the stains have not disappeared in three or four days, rub off the mixture, and repeat the process with fresh soap and starch. Afterward dry it, wet it with cold water, and put it in the wash.

Peterson's Magazine, February 1867

To Wash a White Lace Veil. – Put the veil into a strong lather of white soap and very clear water, and let it simmer slowly for a quarter of an hour. Take it out and squeeze it well, but be sure not to rub it. Rinse it in two cold waters, with a drop or two of liquid blue in the last. Have ready some very clear weak gum-Arabic water, or some thin starch or rice water. Pass the veil through it, and clear it by clapping. Then stretch it out even, and pin it to dry on a linen cloth, making the edge as straight as possible, opening out all the scallops, and fastening each with pins. When dry, lay a piece of thin muslin smoothly over it, and iron it on the wrong side.

Godey's Lady's Book and Magazine, March 1867

To Clean Kd [*sic: kid*] Gloves. – Have some new milk in one saucer and a piece of common yellow soap in another, and a clean cloth or towel folded three or four times. On the cloth lay out the glove about to be cleaned quite smoothly. Dip a piece of flannel in the milk, and then rub off a good quantity of the soap on to the wetted flannel, and rub the glove downwards towards the fingers, holding it firmly with the left hand. Continue this process until the glove, if white, looks yellow but clear; if colored; till it looks dark. Lay it to dry, and when pulled out it will look quite new.

Arthur's Home Magazine, June 1867

Hard Soap. – Pour four gallons of boiling water on six pounds of sal soda, and three pounds of unslaked lime; stir and let stand overnight. Pour off carefully, and add six pounds of perfectly clean fat or grease, and boil two hours, stirring most of the time. If it does not seem thick enough, put another pailful of water on the settlings; stir well; when settled, drain off carefully, and add to the mixture as required. Try it occasionally by putting a little to cool. When it is ready to remove from the fire stir in a handful of salt. Have ready a tub in which cold water has been standing to prevent sticking; put the soap into it and let it stand till solid, then cut into strips. Or pour the soap into moulds for cakes. This will make about forty pounds of soap at a cost of two cents per pound.

Godey's Lady's Book and Magazine, July 1867

Ink-Stains. – Ink may be taken from Morocco by rubbing it with a flannel and soap, not very wet and then polishing it up with a dry, soft cloth or flannel.

Arthur's Home Magazine, August 1867

To Keep Silk. – Silk articles should not be kept folded in white paper, as the chloride of lime used in bleaching the paper will probably impair the color of the silk. Brown or blue paper is better; the yellowish, smooth India paper is best of all. Silks intended for dress should not be kept long in the house before they are made up, as lying in the folds will have a tendency to impair its durability by causing it to cut or split, particularly if the silk has been thickened by gum. Thread lace veils are very easily cut. But dresses of velvet should not be laid by with any weight above them: if the nap of a thin velvet is laid down, it is not possible to raise it up again. Hard silk should never be wrinkled, because the thread is easily broken in the crease, and it never can be rectified. The way to take the wrinkles out of silk scarfs and handkerchiefs is to moisten the surface evenly with a sponge and some weak glue, and then pin the silk with some toilet pins on a mattress or feather bed, taking pains to draw out the silk as tight as possible. When dry, the wrinkles will have disappeared. The reason of this is obvious to every person. Some silk articles should be moistened with weak glue or gum-water, and the wrinkles ironed out by a hot flat-iron on the wrong side.

Walnut Stains. – Walnut stains on the fingers are usually removed with a little sherry. In general, walnut stains are removable by lemon juice. For stains in linen it would be well to try salts of lemons.

Godey's Lady's Book and Magazine, August 1867

Cheap Way to Clean Straw Hats. – Pounded sulphur, cold water, one brush. Make a paste of pounded sulphur and cold water; wet the hat or bonnet, and cover it with the paste till you do not see the straw. Rub hard. Hang the hat up to dry. When dry, brush the sulphur off with a brush till the straw gets beautifully white. This method is easier than the sulphur bleaching-box, and can be done very quickly. I recommend it, for I have tried it many times.

A good way of cleaning oil-cloth is to sponge it well with skim milk, as it brightens it and preserves the color.

To clean cloth from claret stains put it in boiling milk as soon as possible after the claret is spilt. The part of the cloth which is stained must not be put in water before is dipped in the milk, or the stain will not come out.

Godey's Lady's Book and Magazine, September 1867

To Wash White Lace. – The following receipt for washing white lace is generally found more successful than any other. Cover a glass bottle with white flannel, then wind the lace round it, tack it to the flannel on both sides, and cover the whole with a piece of flannel or linen, which sew firmly round it. Then steep the bottle overnight in an ewer, with soap and cold water. Next morning wash it with hot water and soap, the soap being rubbed on the outer covering. Then steep it again for some hours in cold water, and afterward dry it in the air or near the fire. Remove the outer covering, and the lace is ready, no ironing being required. If the lace is very dirty, of course, it must be washed it great deal.

To Take Mildew from Clothes. – Mix soft-soap with powdered starch, half as much salt, and the juice of a lemon; lay it on the part with a brush; let it lay on the grass, day and night, till the stain comes out. Iron-moulds may be removed by the salt of lemons. Many stains may be removed by dipping the linen in sour buttermilk, and then drying it in a hot sun; wash it in cold water; repeat this three or four times. Stains, caused by acids, may be removed by tying some pearlash up in the stained part; scrape some soap in cold, soft water, and boil the linen till the stain is gone.

To Wash New Flannel. – Cut the soap small, and boil it in a little water. Have two tubs with water as hot as the hands can bear, previously blue the water well, to keep the color of the flannel, and put some of the boiled soap into one tub to make a lather; then wash the flannel without squeezing it. Put it into the other tub, and wring it in large towel. Shake it then out, and, after drying it, smooth it with a cool iron.

To Wash Merino Stockings. – The same method should be pursued as for flannels, and all woolen and cotton goods. Boil the soap to make a lather, wash them in this warm, and rinse in a second lather, (if white, mix a little blue.) Never rinse in plain water, or use cold lather; and never rub the soap upon the merino or flannel; the one shrinks, the other thickens and spoils the wool.

Peterson's Magazine, October 1867

To Remove Wine Stains. – Rub the part on each side with yellow soap, lay on a mixture of starch and cold water, very thick, and having rubbed it well in, expose the linen to the sun and air until the stains disappear. If the first attempt should not be successful, repeat the process.

Starching Cuffs and Collars. – After washing and rinsing them, let them dry as if for ironing. Having made some starch a little thicker than cream, put them in, wring them out again, let them dry before the fire until they are fit for ironing, roll them in a cloth, and iron. To give them a good gloss, take the end of a wax candle and stir it through the starch when quite hot, and do not let the iron be too hot. A little salt put into the starch when hot will prevent the iron from sticking, and some soap rubbed on it before using will answer the same purpose.

To Prevent Prints from Fading. – The dress should be washed in lather, and not by applying the soap in the usual way direct upon the muslin. Make a lather by boiling soap and water together; let it stand until it is sufficiently cool for use, and previously to putting the dress into it throw in a handful of salt; rinse the dress without wringing it in clear, cold water into which a little salt has been thrown; remove it and rinse it in a fresh supply of clear water and salt. Then wring the dress in a cloth and hang it to dry immediately, spreading as open as possible, so as to prevent one part lying over another. Should there be any white in the pattern, mix a little blue in the water.

Godey's Lady's Book and Magazine, November 1867

1868

To Remove Wax Stains from Cloth. – Lay over the stains two thicknesses of blotting-paper, and apply for a moment the pressure of a moderately hot iron. The stains will be instantaneously and entirely removed.

Waterproofing the Soles of Shoes or Boots. – This simple and effectual remedy is nothing more than a little beeswax and mutton suet, warmed in a pan, until in a liquid state; then tub some of it lightly over the edges of the sole where the stitches are, which will repel the wet, and not in the least prevent the blacking from having the usual effect.

HINTS ABOUT HEALTH.

The Mother to be Cared for. – No farmer's wife who is a mother out to be allowed to do the washing for the family; it is perilous to any woman who has not a vigorous constitution. The farmer, if too poor to afford help for that purpose, had better exchange a day's work himself. There are several dangers to be avoided while at the tub – it requires a person to stand for hours at a time; this is a strain upon the young wife or mother, which is especially perilous; besides, the evaporation of heat from the arms, by being in warm water and then raised in the air alternately, so rapidly cools the system that inflammation of the lungs is a very possible result; then, the labor of washing excites perspiration and induces fatigue; in this condition the body is so susceptible to taking cold that a few moments' rest in a chair, or exposure to a very slight draft of air, is quite enough to cause a chill, with results painful or even dangerous, according to the particular condition of the system at the time. No man has a right to risk his wife's health in this way.
Godey's Lady's Book, January 1868

To Clean Gloves. – Spread them out smooth on a clean board; rub the dirtiest places with cream of tartar or with magnesia, and let them remain an hour or more. Mix powdered alum and fuller's earth, rub the mixture all over the gloves with a little brush, (a tooth-brush, or such like,) and again leave them for a time. Brush off the mixture, and rub the gloves with flannel dipped in bran and finely-powdered whitening. After again letting them lie an hour or two, brush off the powder, and the gloves will be clean.
Peterson's Magazine, March 1868

To Extract Ink from Colored Articles. – Drop tallow on the stains, and then soak and rub the same with boiling milk. Effectual.

Another Mode. – Gather the leaves of the wood sorrel, dry them in the sun, powder them, and sprinkle the powder thickly on ink stains on colored prints, etc. Pour boiling water upon the sorrel, and after lying a short time the stain will disappear.
Godey's Lady's Book, April 1868

To Secure Muslin Dresses from being inflammable is a very easy matter, and it is greatly to be regretted that the process is not better understood. Either of three substances – phosphate of ammonia, tungstate of soda, or sulphate of ammonia – can be mixed in starch, and, at the cost of two cents a dress, deaths from burned garments can be rendered impossible. Articles of apparel, subjected to those agents, can, if they burn at all, only smoulder; and in no case can they blaze up in the sudden and terrible manner in which so many fatal accidents have occurred to the fair wearers of crinoline. Any druggist can supply the articles.
Peterson's Magazine, April 1868

To Wash Doeskin Gloves. – Wash them in water of blood-heat, wring as dry as possible, and let them hang in the house, away from heat, until two-thirds dry; then stretch until soft. Wash-leather used for cleaning glass or silver may be washed as above; also buckskin, mittens, shirts, etc.

To Wash White Alpaca and Mohair Garibaldis. – Boiled white soap and lukewarm water must be used (hot water will make the material yellow at once), and after the alpaca has been washed in this, and the soap thoroughly removed by rinsing in cold water, it must pass through water with a very little blue in it, and afterwards ironed while damp with a handkerchief or linen cloth over it.

To Dye Black. – Rusty nails, or any rusty iron, boiled in vinegar with a small bit of copperas, makes a good black.
Godey's Lady's Book, May 1868

Garments are often seriously injured by iron rust. The following process is said effectually to remove stains of iron rust from linen or cotton: Wash the cloth through one suds and rinse. When wet, rub ripe tomato juice on the spots. Expose it in the sunshine until nearly dry, and wash in another suds.
Harper's Bazar, May 16, 1868

To Wash White Lace. – The following receipt for washing white lace is generally found more successful than any other. Cover a glass bottle with white flannel, then wind the lace round it, tack it to the flannel on both sides, and cover the whole with a piece of flannel or linen, which sew firmly round it. Then steep the bottle overnight in a ewer, with soap and cold water. Next morning wash it with hot water and soap, the soap being rubbed on the outer covering. Then steep it again for some hours in cold water, and afterward dry it in the air or near the fire. Remove the outer covering, and the lace is ready, no ironing being required. If the lace is very dirty, of course, it must be washed great deal.

To Take Mildew from Clothes. – Mix soft-soap with powdered starch, half as much salt, and the juice of a lemon; lay it on the part with a brush; let it lay on the grass day and night, till the stain comes out. Iron-moulds may be removed by the salt of lemons. Many stains may be removed by dipping the linen in sour buttermilk, and then drying it in a hot sun; wash it in cold water; repeat this three or four times. Stains caused by acids may be removed by tying some pearl-ash up in the stained part; scrape some soap in cold, soft water, and boil the linen till the stain is gone.

To Wash Flannel. – Cut the soap small, and boil it in a little water. Have two tubs with water as hot as the hands can bear; previously blue the water well to keep the color of the flannel, and put some of the boiled soap into one tub to make a lather; then wash the flannel without squeezing it. Put it into the other tub, and wring it in a large towel. Shake it then out, and, after drying it, smooth it with a cool iron.

To Wash Merino Stockings. – The same method should be pursued as for flannels, and all woolen and cotton goods. Boil the soap to make a lather, wash them in this warm, and rinse in a second lather (if white, mix a little blue.) Never rinse in plain water, or use cold lather; and never rub the soap upon the merino or flannel; the one shrinks, the other thickens and spoils the wool.

Peterson's Magazine, May 1868

[Ad] GENUINE IMPROVED COMMON SENSE FAMILY SEWING MACHINE. This machine will stitch, hem, fell, tuck, quilt, cord, bind, braid, and embroider in a most superior manner. Price only $18. Fully warranted for five years. We will pay $1000 for any machine that will sew a stronger, more beautiful, or more elastic seam than ours. It makes the "Elastic Lock Stitch." Every second stitch can be cut, and still the cloth can not be pulled apart without tearing it.

Harper's Bazar, June 27, 1868

Borax is used in many large washing establishments as a washing-powder, instead of soda. It does not in the slightest degree injure the texture of the linen. Its effect is to soften the hardest water, and therefore is a pleasant and useful addition to water for bathing. It is also recommended as excellent for cleansing the hair and the teeth.

Harper's Bazar, July 4, 1868

The dressing of calicoes is a dangerous trap in which many of our readers have often been caught, and will be again. Goods are offered them of the most promising appearance, with a silky gloss, clear print, and brilliant colors, but, alas! of the stuff that dreams are made of; a little wearing, a little washing, and only a flimsy rag remains. All the low-priced cotton prints are highly stiffened by means of strong solutions of gum-arabic and starch. These substances, being soluble in water, carry off the color and leave the thread bare. This is easily proved. Take a piece of calico, ascertain its exact weight, lay it in water for an hour or two, wring it dry, and weigh it again; one-fifth of the whole weight will be gone, and the colors will be either blurred together or entirely washed off.

Harper's Bazar, July 25, 1868

Ostrich Feathers. – Dissolve some fine white soap in boiling soft water, and add a small piece of pearl-ash. When the water is just cool enough for the hand to bear it, pass the feathers through it several times, squeezing them gently with the hand. Repeat the same process with a weaker solution of soap, and then rinse the feathers in cold water, beating them across the hand to get rid of the water. When they are nearly dry, draw each fibre over the edge of a small blunt knife, turning it round in the direction you wish the curl to take. If the feather is to be flat, place it between the leaves of a book, to press it.

Godey's Lady's Book, August 1868

The best authorities say it is impossible to clean real blonde lace.

Harper's Bazar, August 22, 1868

How to Clear Soapsuds. – It is well known that a little alum dissolved is very effective in clearing muddy water; but a short time since some alum was applied in a manner which, from its novelty and its valuable results, is worthy of notice. In a place where water was scarce, a little alum was dissolved in hot water, and thrown into a tub of thick soapsuds. In a short time the soap curdled, and, accompanied by the muddy particles, sank to the bottom, leaving the water above perfectly clear, pure, and devoid of smell. This water was found very useful for washing clothing in again, when poured off the sediment. A similar result was attained in a quick manner by filling a boiler with soapsuds, placing it on a fire, and throwing a bit of alum into it. When the suds boiled, the scum went over, and left the water clear, soft, and as useful for washing clothes as it had originally been.

To Clean Riding Gloves. – Doeskin gloves may be cleaned by rubbing them thoroughly in dry fuller's earth and alum, spreading them out on a flat surface or stretching them on a wooden hand while this is being done. Removing this mixture – which should be finely powdered – with a brush, some dry bran and whiting should be sprinkled over them, and afterwards the gloves should be thoroughly dusted with a soft brush. Or rub them with pipe-clay made into a paste with beer, after having been washed in lukewarm water and bran tea, and put on the wooden hands. They must dry by degrees, and when about half dry they should be well smoothed by rubbing, and then drawn into shape. When dry they may be brushed and ironed with a paper over them. The iron must not be very hot.

To Remove Oil Stains. – Take three ounces of spirits of turpentine, and one ounce of essence of lemon; mix well, and apply it as you would any other scouring drops. It will take out all the grease.

To Restore Linen that has long been Stained. – Rub the stains on each side with wet brown soap. Mix some starch to a thick paste with cold water, and spread it over the soaped places. Then expose the linen to the sun and air; and, if the stains have not disappeared in three or four days, rub off the mixture, and repeat the process with fresh soap and starch. Afterward dry it, wet it well with cold water, and put it in the wash.

Extinguishing Burning Clothes.

There are few accidents more terrible than the setting fire to the loose vestments worn by women. Instantly the lower part of a dress is ignited the flames rush upwards with great velocity, and the whole of the garments are involved in the conflagration. Even if almost immediately extinguished, so large a portion of the skin is scorched that death often ensues from the shock to the system, though perhaps the actual injury does not appear to be severe. It is needless to say how largely the number of deaths by burning has been increased by the fashion of wearing crinoline, because if it could be demonstrated to a moral certainty that one woman out of every fifty who followed the fashion of the day, whatever that might happen to be, was doomed to the most painful of deaths, it would still be followed, each one believing that the fatal result would not happen to herself, but to some less careful sister. Nevertheless, we may express our pleasure, at least, in this department of our journal, that the fashion of wearing iron hoops – one which is to our old-fashioned notions alike inelegant, inconvenient, indecent, and dangerous – is almost a thing of the past; for not only was it, from the distension of the dress, the cause of many more burnings than would have otherwise occurred, but it in almost all cases prevented the extinction of the flames until fatal injury had been inflicted.

Godey's Lady's Book, September 1868

To Clean Gold Embroidery. – Gold and silver embroidery may be cleaned with spirits of wine, diluted or not, rubbed on with a small piece of flannel.

Godey's Lady's Book, October 1868

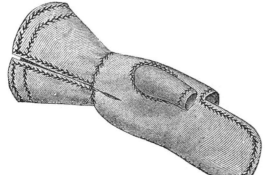

Ironing Glove. – Under Part.
Ironing Glove. – Upper Part.
Ironing Mat.

This mat will be found very convenient in ironing to rub off the starch which collects on the iron from damp starched clothing. It is made of twine, and consists of single strips worked in point de reprise and joined by a kind of cross stitch. The outer edge is ornamented with a threefold row of picots crocheted of twine.

Harper's Bazar, October 10, 1868

To Clean Kid Gloves. – A subscriber asks for a good receipt for this purpose. The most available is to have ready a little new milk in one saucer and a piece of brown soap in another, and a clean cloth or towel, folded three or four times. On the cloth spread out the glove smooth and neat. Take a piece of flannel, dip it in the milk, then rub off a good quantity of soap to the wetted flannel, and commence to rub the glove toward the fingers, holding it firmly with the left hand. Continue this process until the glove, if white, looks of a dingy yellow, though clean; if colored, till it looks dark and spoiled. Lay it to dry, and the operator will soon be gratified to see that the old gloves look nearly new. They will be soft glossy smooth and elastic.

Peterson's Magazine, October 1868

To Remove Grease from Silks. – Powdered French chalk is very useful to remove grease from silk. If the powder is applied quickly after the grease has fallen upon the silk, the latter will be speedily absorbed; the powder may shortly afterwards be dusted off, when the spots will be found to be entirely obliterated.

A sure remedy for fleas, no humbug, is *Pennyroyal*. This scattered under the carpet, between the bedding during the day, and worn in small packages about the person or persons where fleas abound, will completely relieve the sufferers. Nine years' trial enables me to recommend the use of the above named article. Mrs. J.

Godey's Lady's Book, November 1868

Ladies living in cities usually consign their valuable furs to a reliable furrier during the summer months. For the benefit of those who take care of their own furs we give some advice gathered from the highest authorities. Do not wear your furs late in the spring. On the first advent of warm weather beat each piece separately, whipping it with small rods in order to cleanse thoroughly; then wrap with paper, and place in a paper-box made as air-tight as possible and kept in a dry closet. During the whole summer this process should be repeated once in three or four weeks, according to the heat of the season, in order to keep the hair smooth and straight, and to prevent the accumulation of animalculæ. This is the only positive preventive. Camphor and cedar trunks are excellent for preserving furs, but even these are only partial mediums, requiring that the furs be aired during the season.
Harper's Bazar, November 7, 1868

Among new importations of Russian leather goods is a useful and pretty sewing-apron, to preserve the dress when using a sewing-machine. It is admirably shaped like a gored apron, has a bib and pockets, and is pinked at the edges and stitched with white silk. It is in the pale leather, russet color, black and blue. It is a novelty, and therefore expensive, costing $15.
Harper's Bazar, November 28, 1868

How to Produce a Fine Gloss. – Take two ounces of fine white gum arabic powder – put it into a pitcher, and pour on it a pint of boiling water (according to the degree of strength you desire), and then having covered it, let it set all night. In the morning pour it carefully from the drugs into a clean bottle, cork it, and keep it for use. A tablespoonful of gum water, stirred into a pint of starch that has been made in the usual manner, will give to lawns (either white or printed) a look of newness, when nothing else can restore them after washing. It is also good (much diluted) for thin white muslin and bobinet.

To Clean White Satin and Flowered Silks. – Mix sifted stale bread-crumbs with powder blue, and rub it thoroughly all over, then shake it well, and dust it well with clean soft cloths. Afterwards, where there are any gold or silver flowers, take a piece of crimson ingrain velvet, and rub the flowers with it, which will restore them to their original lustre.

In looking over the October number of your magazine, I perceive a desire expressed to find something that will effectually remove mildew from linen, etc. I can with confidence, from my own experience and that of friends, recommend the use of *Javelle Water*, which can be procured at most of the druggists, who will direct as to the proportionate quantity to be used *with water* in *safety*. Carefully done, no fabric can be injured. It should be immersed in it, laid on the grass immediately, and sprinkled with a weakened solution until the spots disappear. I have a formula for preparing *Javelle Water*, but few would like to go to the trouble of preparing it when it can be procured at the apothecary's. The formula is in the "Dispensatory" at every druggist's, I presume.

To take Mildew out of Linen. – Tomato and salt, applied two or three times and hung in the sun.
Godey's Lady's Book, December 1868

1869

To Take out Tea and Wine-stains. – A glass of white wine, or a cup of tea, upset over a dress, would completely spoil it if allowed to dry on. When an accident happens, immediately get some clean towels, and rub the dress till perfectly dry, and in most cases there will be no stain left. If the tea is very strong, sponge with a little cold water first. Port-wine, or claret-stains are seldom got entirely out, but the stain may be lessened by sponging with cold water before the rubbing.
Frank Leslie's Lady's Magazine, January 1869

To Save Wet Gloves. – If gloves are wet by rain or perspiration, wring them in a towel, and stretch the leather until quite dry; if dried before this can be done, wet them again, and stretch until dry.

To Wash Doeskin Gloves. – Wash them in water of blood-heat, wring as dry as possible, and let them hang in the house, away from heat until two-thirds dry; then stretch until soft. Wash leather, used for cleaning glass or silver, may be washed as above; also buckskin mittens, shirts, etc.

To Wash A White Alpaca Dress. – There is no difficulty in washing a white alpaca dress. It should be treated as flannel. Lather it well in lukewarm water and soap, wring it out of suds, dry it in the air, mangle it damp, and iron it on the wrong side. The trimmings must be removed, and the gathers unpicked.
The Lady's Friend, January 1869

Starching Shirts and Collars. – Allow one teaspoonful of good starch to each shirt and collar; take just enough cold water to wet the starch; mash it free of lumps, add a little more, and stir it well; add, for each shirt, a piece of sperm or white wax, as large as a dry pea, and a quarter of a spoonful of clean salt to three of starch; pour on boiling water, slowly stirring all the time; let it boil hard fifteen minutes without scorching; skim and strain it while hot; this can be done only by dipping the strainer in cold water, while the starch is in the bag, and squeezing it immediately before it becomes hot. It is impossible to give a rule for the quantity of water to the spoonful of starch, as there is such a diversity of taste in regard to the stiffness of bosoms and collars. Wet the bosoms and collars in hot water, wring them very dry, and starch while wet; rub them well, that the starch may penetrate, and wring them in a dry towel, to remove all the starch left on the outside; spread them out evenly, rub them down with a dry cloth and roll them tightly; let them lay two or three hours, and then iron them.

Directions for Washing Tatting – Get a common stone bottle (a quart porter bottle will do), sew a piece of thin flannel evenly all over it; wrap the tatting on, carefully tacking each row as flatly as possible to the flannel. Sew a piece of tarlatan (or very thin muslin) over it, leaving the tarlatan long enough to tie firmly both at the bottom and top of the bottle. Sink the bottle in a large basin of cold water, and soak it all night. Cut up a piece of white soap, put it in a large stew-pan of water with the bottle, and stew for six hours; if the tatting does not look quite clean, rub the bottle a little with the hand and more soap, and stew it again; rinse well in clean, cold water, and put the bottle in the sun or near the fire to dry, when the tatting can be untacked and taken off. If it has been tacked on well, and in its proper form, it will be just like new tatting. This is also an excellent recipe for washing valuable lace. The flannel can be left on the bottle for future use.
The Lady's Friend, May 1869

To Wash and Pink Silk Stockings. – Wash the stockings in soap and water, and rinse them well in clean water. Now make a rinse-water, containing the juice of half a lemon, in which wash off the color from a pink saucer till it gives the color desired; finally dry and iron them between flannel. The iron must not be very hot, otherwise the color will fade.
Frank Leslie's Lady's Magazine, May 1869

To Take out Marking-ink. – Before sending to the wash, touch with a solution of cyanide of potassium till the stain disappears. N.B. – Oxalic acid and cyanide of potassium are poisons. Careless persons should not be allowed to use them. They should not be used by one whose skin is cut or cracked.

To Take Grease out of Woolens. – If there is any thickness of grease, such as drops from a lighted candle, it should scraped off the surface. This can be most effectually done when the grease has become cold. To take out the remainder, made a common poker red-hot, and hold the heated end over greasy the greasy spots, about one and a half inches from the material, moving the poker a little backward and forward to prevent scorching. If the material is fine, such as French merino, it is better to place a piece of blotting-paper over the spots, to prevent the hot poker from scorching or taking the color out; but for thick things, such as table-covers, blotting-paper is not necessary.
Frank Leslie's Lady's Magazine, June 1869

Washing Muslin Dresses. – An English lady thus gives her experience: – "So many inquiries have been made of late as to the best means of preserving the bright colors of muslin dresses when washed, that I think it right to give the benefit of my experience. I have had black and white, blue and yellow, and green dresses, washed to look equal to new, by simply soaking each dress for twelve hours in a gallon of cold water, in which one pennyworth of sugar of lead has been dissolved. The dress is then wrung out and dried by the fire, before it is sent to the laundress, who has directions to wash it in a cold lather of soap and water, and not to put it in any soda or any other substance, and particularly not to rub any soap into or on the dress; also to dry it in-doors, as exposure to the air or sun would decidedly fade the color. Thus treated, my dresses wash again and again, without losing either their clearness or brilliancy of tint. The sugar of lead being poisonous, I always make a point of seeing that my maid's hands are perfectly free from any scratch or cut before I allow her to squeeze the dress out of the soaking water, and I have never known her experience any bad result from the process."
The Lady's Friend, June 1869

Glossy Starch. – Take two ounces of white gum arabic powder, put into a pitcher, and pour on it a pint of boiling water, according to the degree of strength you desire, and then, having covered it, let it stand all night. In the morning pour it we fully from the dregs into a clean bottle – keep it for use. A tablespoonful of gum water stirred into a pint of starch that has been made in the usual manner will give lawns, either black or printed, a look of newness, when nothing else can restore them after washing. It is also good much diluted for thin white muslin and bobbinet.

To Make Calico Transparent and Waterproof. – Take six pints of pale linseed oil, two ounces of sugar of lead, and eight ounces of white resin; the sugar of lead must be ground with a small quantity of it, and added to the remainder; the resin should be incorporated with the oil by means of a gentle beat. The composition may then be laid on calico, or any other such material, by means of a brush.
Frank Leslie's Lady's Magazine, July 1869

Removing Claret Stains. – Wine stains of any description can be removed effectually from linen by merely holding them for a few minutes in boiling milk. This must be done before the linen is washed, as afterwards it is of no use.

How they Wash. – In the way of getting up linen and other dainty fabrics, there are none who can beat the Dutch. In their own country they use no machines – borax is the magic word. This article, refined, is liberally employed as a powder in place of soda, in the proportion of a large handful to about ten gallons of boiling water – cambrics and laces requiring a somewhat stronger solution. In addition to other advantages, a saving of one half the soap is thus secured.

Wrinkled Silk. – To make silk which has been wrinkled and "tumbled" appear exactly like new, sponge it on the surface with a weak solution of gum arabic or white glue, and iron it on the wrong side.

Ammonia, or strong black tea, cold, is a good thing to clean black silk.
The Lady's Friend, July 1869

IRONING WITHOUT FLATIRONS.
Not long since I read a notice of a machine to iron without heat. As I have not seen it, I cannot speak of its merits; but the following method which I have practised for a couple of years past, will save many hours of sweltering toil. Fold coarse towels, sheets and tablecloths in the same shape you want them after being ironed; pass them through the wringer as tight as possible; unfold and hang to dry where the wind does not blow very hard. They will need little or no ironing.

Stains in Muslin. – The following receipt is for taking out the stain of fruit, red wine, ink or mildew from white articles: An ounce of sal-ammoniac (or hartshorn), and an ounce of salt of tartar, well mixed; put them into a pint of soft water and bottle it or use, keeping it very tightly corked. Pour a little of this liquid into a saucer, and wash in it those parts of a white article that have been stained. When the stains have been removed by this process, wash the article in the usual manner.
The Lady's Friend, September 1869

Reviver for Black Cloth. – 1. Boil in two pints of water down to one, two ounces each of Aleppo galls, in powder, and of logwood, one ounce of gum arabic, then add one of sulphate of iron. This may be evaporated to a powder. – 2. Galls, eight ounces; logwood, green vitriol, iron filings, sumach, of each one ounce; vinegar, two pints. – 3. Take two pints of vinegar, and infuse in it one ounce each of iron filings or sulphate of iron, of copperas, and of ground logwood, with three ounces of bruised galls. – 4. Galls, a quarter of a pound; logwood, half a pound; copperas, two ounces; boil for two hours in quart and a half-pint of water, until it is reduced to a state that about one and a half pint will drain from it.
Frank Leslie's Lady's Magazine, October 1869

French Method of Washing Colored Muslins, &c. – Prepare some rather warm (not hot) lather, made with soft water and the best yellow soap; wash the dresses one at a time, i.e., don't soak them. As soon as the first lather looks soiled, squeeze the dress from it, which at once wash again in a fresh lather. When thoroughly clean, rinse in pure cold water; lastly, in water slightly blued; squeeze (not wring) the water completely from the dress, and hang it in a shaded place to dry; if wet weather, dry it off quickly by the fire. The best prints will fade if hung in the sunshine. When dry, starch in nearly cold starch. Iron on the wrong side. Muslins should have small portions of gum and isinglass dissolved in the starch, which gives them a clear, new look. Colored dresses treated thus will look well for years.
The Lady's Friend, October 1869

To Make Linen White. – The washerwomen of Holland and Belgium, who get up their linen so beautifully white, use refined borax as a washing-powder instead of soda, in the proportion of a large handful of borax-powder to about ten gallons of boiling water; and they save in soap nearly half. For laces, cambrics, etc., an extra quantity of this powder is used. Borax being a neutral salt, does not in the slightest degree injure the texture of the linen; it softens the hardest water, and, therefore, it should be kept on every toilet-table. It is advantageously used for cleansing the hair, and is an excellent dentifrice.

[*ad – wash wringer*]

THE NOVELTY,
IS THE ONLY WRINGER THAT HAS THE
PATENT FLANGE GOG-WHEELS
On both ends of the Rolls.

Peterson's Magazine, October 1869

To Make Linen White. – The washerwomen of Holland and Belgium, who get up their linen so beautifully white, use refined borax as a washing-powder instead of soda, in the proportion of a large handful of borax-powder to about ten gallons of boiling water; and they save in soap nearly half. For laces, cambrics, etc., an extra quantity of the powder is used. Borax being a neutral salt, does not in the slightest degree injure the texture of the linen; it softens the hardest water, and, therefore, it should be kept on toilet-table. It is advantageously used for cleansing the hair, and is an excellent dentifrice.

Grease-Spots. – Mix powdered French chalk with lavender-water to the thickness of mustard. Put it on the stain, and rub it gently with the finger or palm of the hand. Put a sheet of clean blotting-paper and brown paper over it, and smooth it with a warm iron. When dry, the chalk must be removed, and the silk gently dusted with a white handkerchief. If a faint mark still remains, a second application of French chalk and lavender-water will generally remove it. If wax has fallen thickly on the silk, it will be better to remove it first very carefully with a penknife.

To Clean Feathers. – Dissolve four ounces of white soap, cut small, in four pounds of water, moderately hot, in a basin, and make the solution into a lather by beating it with a small rod; then introduce the feathers, and rub them well with the hands for five minutes. They are next to be washed in clean water, as hot as the hand can bear it.
Peterson's Magazine, October 1869

Removing Claret Stains. – Wine stains of any description can be removed effectually from linen by merely holding them for a few minutes in boiling milk. This must be done before the linen is washed, as afterward it is of no use.
Frank Leslie's Lady's Magazine, November 1869

HOUSEKEEPER'S HINTS.

A Few Words About Washing. – The linen for a Monday's wash should be collected on Saturday evening, and sorted and put to soak in cold water, according to various kinds. The body linen should be put into one tub, the bed and table linen in another, and the fine things separately. Plain collars, cuffs, and wristbands, should be strung through the button-holes on a piece of bobbin long enough to enable the articles to be easily divided for rubbing, starching, etc. By soaking dirty clothes in cold water, the stains are loosened, and the error of washing in too hot water is obviated.

All washing is better done by suds than by rubbing on soap; only the very soiled places require soap rubbing.

The best way to get good suds is to shred into an earthenware jar yellow soap cut into very fine shavings, and to pour boiling water to the quantity required. One pound of soap is plenty for one gallon of water. Add to this quantity half a pound of best Scotch soda, and set the jar covered on a stove or at the back of the kitchen range, till the soap is quite dissolved. If this be done on Saturday evening, the soap will be a smooth liquid fit to use on Monday morning.

The body linen is the first batch that requires "tubbing." If hand labor is used, every portion of the garment should be rubbed over, and afterward rinsed through clean suds. The things are then fit for the copper. The water in the copper should be cold when the clothes are put in, and should contain (if of moderately large size) about five ounces of soda and a pint and a half of soap-jelly of the above proportions. To prevent burning, the linen requires stirring about occasionally. It is also a good plan, to avoid burning, to have a piece of coarse basket-work laid at the bottom of the copper. Ten minutes after the water has come boiling heat is long enough for the clothes to remain in the copper. They should then be taken out and thrown into the rinsing trough. The whiteness of linen depends fully as much upon good rinsing as upon hard rubbing. If it can be managed, the rinsing should be accomplished by setting the trough under a tap of running water. After rinsing, blueing is the next process. The best stone blue tied up in a bag of very stout flannel of several thicknesses is most suitable for plain linen. Only one article should be blued at a time, or, if small, as many as the washer can hold in her hand. If the clothes are allowed to drop to the bottom of the trough, the particles of blue are liable to settle in the folds of the linen and make streamy marks, very difficult to get out.

Bed and table linen do not usually require more than one tubbing with suds. If much soiled, the labor will, of course, be greater. The things should afterward be submitted to the same treatment as the body linen.

Woolens do not require soaking previous to washing. It is bad economy to wash such articles in suds used for other purposes. All flannels require special care; no soda should be used for them, nor soap rubbed on. If so, the flannels will surely turn yellow and shrink. The soap-jelly should be prepared as described, with the addition of a packet of Manby's washing crystal-powder instead of soda. Water for washing flannels should only be lukewarm, and woolens should never be rinsed in clear water, neither must they be wrung, but only squeezed from the suds.

In getting up dimity and *piques,* the failure is not generally in the washing, but in starching. A good-sized panful of starch should be used, in which three or four inches of composite or other candle has been melted whilst hot. The articles should be thoroughly squeezed from the starch and folded whilst wet between folds of old sheeting or table linen. They should then be passed beneath the rollers of a mangle, or through a wringing-machine. All lumps of starch are thus removed. Dimity requires no other finishing, except that when it is half dried on the lines it should be taken down and shaken, and pulled into the ribs formed in the stuff. Afterward it may be left on the lines till perfectly dry.

Piques should be ironed as lightly as possible, and the iron ought never to come into contact with the outside surface of the *pique.* An old cambric handkerchief is the best thing to use under the iron.

The above observation applies to plain linen collars and cuffs. They need to be ironed, with a fine piece of muslin or cambric between, till dry enough to take the glaze from the iron. There is a little art also in folding plain collars to make them set well round the neck. In ironing collars the laundress should, when they are nearly finished, hold one end erect between the thumb and finger of the left hand, whilst she swiftly passes the iron backward and forward with the right till the collar seems disposed to curl. The collar should then be turned over the band in its right position, and worked by the fingers of the laundress till it may lie rolled evenly round a small roller. Shirt collars should never be put aside flat. The above is the only plan to make them settle without crease round the neck.

Fine laces require nice management. The following will be found an excellent plan for getting up old point and similar lace. Cover a wine-bottle with a piece of fine flannel, which must be stitched smoothly over the bottle; then tack one edge of the lace with fine cotton round the bottle, and afterward the other edge, preserving the proper width of the lace as carefully as possible. When all the lace has been secured, cover the bottle with a fine piece of flannel, and begin to wash the lace by gently squeezing and rubbing the surface with clean suds made of soap-jelly. When the

...ce is thoroughly clean, rinse freely, by setting the bottle in a pan of cold water under a flowing tap. For starching, make the starch the thickness of an invalid's arrow-root; melt a small quantity of fine white wax and a little loaf-sugar in the starch. Plunge the bottle a few times into the starch, pressing the lace with the hands, and immediately afterward dip the bottle into cold water; then set the lace to dry in the sun, or keep filling the bottle with hot water till the lace is dried by evaporation; when nearly dry all through, remove the lace and put it out in some place where it will not be disturbed till perfectly dry.

Clear-starchers, having proceeded thus far, raise the pattern of the lace by rubbing ivory punches, rounded at the point, into the pattern of the lace. But many ladies will not allow their old lace to be thus treated, owing to the undue wear entailed. Besides, new lace does not wear this appearance when it leaves the pillow; and why should it be embossed afterward?

When the washing of large pieces of lace, such as shawls and mantles, is concerned, "popping" in the open air must be resorted to in order to give an appearance of lightness after starching. By popping the lace through the hands till nearly dry, all the gluey nature of the starch is removed. The lace should afterward be pinned out to dry in the shape it is required to assume. Before putting laces aside for any time, every particle of starch and soap should be rinsed out.

Muslins, if elaborately painted and of very fine quality, are fitter subjects for a dyer to clean than for a laundress to wash. Many of the colors now in vogue, frail as they may be in the hands of a washerwoman, are easily fixed by the mordants in use by dyers. No general rule can be given for washing such muslins successfully at home, each class of color requiring a different treatment. Chloride of lime is the laundress' favorite chemical. She sees no reason why it should not clean all things equally well. And so it does – removing the color as well as the dirt. Black and white mixtures, and black braid on white, require salt to be put freely in the rinsing water, and also in the starch. The things should not be removed from the salt and water till the lines are ready to receive them. Means should also be taken to keep the folds apart while drying, or they will stream in chocolate-colored stains.

Peterson's Magazine, November 1869

Mildew from Linen. – 1. Wet the spotted part with a solution of chloride of lime, or chlorine water, and the stain will immediately disappear; then wash out at once in warm water. – 2. Mix some soft-soap with powdered starch, half as much salt, and the juice of a lemon; lay it on the spotted part with a brush; then let the garment lie on the grass day and night till the comes out.

Frank Leslie's Lady's Magazine, December 1869

Peterson's Magazine, November 1869

Bibliography

Arthur's Lady's Home Magazine. January – December, 1860. Philadelphia, PA
Arthur's Lady's Home Magazine. January – December, 1861. Philadelphia, PA
Arthur's Lady's Home Magazine. January – December, 1867. Philadelphia, PA
A Complete Practical Guide to the Art of Dancing, Thomas Hillgrove. New York, NY: Dick & Fitzgerald, 1864
The Englishwoman's Domestic Magazine. January – December, 1866. London, England
Le Follet, Journal du Grand Monde. October – December, 1863. London, England
Le Follet, Journal du Grand Monde. June – December, 1864. London, England
Le Follet, Journal du Grand Monde. January – December, 1865. London, England
Frank Leslie's Lady's Magazine. July – December, 1865. New York, NY
Frank Leslie's Lady's Magazine. January – December, 1869. New York, NY
Frank Leslie's Monthly Magazine. July – December, 1860. New York, NY
The Galaxy. August 1868. New York, NY
Godey's Lady's Book and Magazine. January – December, 1861. Philadelphia, PA
Godey's Lady's Book and Magazine. January – December, 1867. Philadelphia, PA
Godey's Lady's Book and Magazine. January – December, 1868. Philadelphia, PA
Harper's Bazar, A Repository of Fashion, Pleasure, and Instruction. November – December, 1867. New York, NY
Harper's Bazar, A Repository of Fashion, Pleasure, and Instruction. January – December, 1868. New York, NY
Harper's New Monthly Magazine. January – May, 1860. New York, NY
Harper's New Monthly Magazine, January – November, 1861. New York, NY
Hints on Self-Help: A Book for Young Women. Jessie Boucherett. London: S. W. Partridge, 1863
How to Do It: Or, Directions for Knowing and Doing Everything Needful. John H. Tingley. New York, NY: John H. Tingley, 1864
The Ladies' Companion. July – December, 1861. London, England.
The Ladies' Companion. October – December, 1862. London, England.
The Lady's Friend, January – December, 1869. Philadelphia, PA
The London and Paris Ladies' Magazine of Fashion, January – December, 1861. London, England
Once a Week. September 15, 1866. London, England
Peterson's Magazine, January – December, 1860. Philadelphia, PA
Peterson's Magazine, January – December, 1862. Philadelphia, PA
Peterson's Magazine, January – December, 1863. Philadelphia, PA
Peterson's Magazine, January – December, 1864. Philadelphia, PA
Peterson's Magazine, January – December, 1865. Philadelphia, PA
Peterson's Magazine. January – December, 1866. Philadelphia, PA
Peterson's Magazine. January – December, 1867. Philadelphia, PA
Peterson's Magazine. January – December, 1868. Philadelphia, PA
Peterson's Magazine, January – December, 1869. Philadelphia, PA
Photographs of Paris Life. Chroniqueuse. London: William Tinsley, 1861
The What-Not; or Ladies' Handy-Book. January – December, 1863. London, England
The What-Not; or Ladies' Handy-Book. January – June, 1864. London, England

About the Author

I adore nineteenth-century fashion magazines. I love Victorian-era fashion and dressmaking books even more.

Learning to sew in the loose-fitting fashions of the later twentieth century gave me no hint of the intricacies of structured clothing, or of the amazing things women were willing to put themselves through to trim their gorgeous dresses. This jeans and sweat-shirt girl quickly learned to appreciate the techniques those seamstresses employed. After many years of collecting, I wanted to share their original writings with other historical-dress enthusiasts.

I'm the owner (and sole employee) of The Mantua-Maker, quality historical sewing patterns for the modern sewing artist, established in 1993. I fell in love with costuming when my boyfriend took me to BayCon's Masquerade in 1986, and I've been making historical and fantastic clothing ever since.

My designs have won awards at World Con, Costume Con, WesterCon, and BayCon.

Please have a look at my previous books. All are available on Amazon.

Elephant's Breath & London Smoke:
Historical Color Names, Definitions and Uses in Fashion, Fabric and Art

Fabric à la Romantic Regency:
A Glossary of Fabrics from Original Sources 1795 – 1836

Victorian Bathing and Bathing Suits:
The Culture of the Two-Piece Bathing Dress from 1837 – 1901

The Art of Fashion: 1850 - 1859
Fashion, Sewing, and Clothes Care Advice

The Art of the Mantua-Maker: 1870 - 1879
Fashion, Sewing, and Clothes Care Advice

You can see more of my work at www.mantua-maker.com.

CPSIA information can be obtained
at www.ICGtesting.com
Printed in the USA
BVHW010214040222
628063BV00016B/163